GW00579921

4 1 0521820 2

THE LION

— AND —

THE ROSE

THE LION
— AND —
THE ROSE

THE 1/5TH BATTALION OF THE KING'S OWN
ROYAL LANCASTER REGIMENT
1914-1919

KEVIN SHANNON

FONTHILL

This book is dedicated to the memory of those men who served in the 5th

(later the 1/5th) Battalion of the King's Own (Royal Lancaster)

Regiment during the Great War.

Fonthill Media Language Policy

Fonthill Media publishes in the international English language market. One language edition is published worldwide. As there are minor differences in spelling and presentation, especially with regard to American English and British English, a policy is necessary to define which form of English to use. The Fonthill Policy is to use the form of English native to the author. Kevin Shannon was born and educated in Liverpool; therefore British English has been adopted in this publication.

Fonthill Media Limited
Fonthill Media LLC
www.fonthillmedia.com
office@fonthillmedia.com

First published in the United Kingdom and the United States of America 2017

British Library Cataloguing in Publication Data:
A catalogue record for this book is available from the British Library

Copyright © Kevin Shannon 2017

ISBN 978-1-78155-555-2

The right of Kevin Shannon to be identified as the author of this work has been asserted by him in accordance with the Copyright, Designs and Patents Act 1988.

All rights reserved. No part of this publication may be reproduced, stored in a retrieval system or transmitted in any form or by any means, electronic, mechanical, photocopying, recording or otherwise, without prior permission in writing from Fonthill Media Limited

Typeset in 9pt on 13pt DejaVu Serif
Printed and bound in England

Foreword

This project began some six years ago as a simple quest to learn more about a grandfather who served with the 1/4th King's Own during the Great War. As I delved deeper, it became clear to me that there were so many stories that deserved a wider audience—that further works were the only way to tell these. This volume on the 1/5th King's Own is the second part. In Vol. 1, I explained how the actions of the 1/4th fitted into the greater strategic picture, but as the 1/5th were with them from January 1916 onwards, I have not repeated this—though the backgrounds to their earlier actions are described. Similarly, I have not repeated details of the formation, recruitment, and training of the TF. The 1/5th was just one battalion, and if I have ignored the parts played by others units, this is purely because of the limitations of time and space—not because their actions were any less worthy.

There were significant numbers of men transferred into the Battalion after the Armistice, though I have been able to identify most of these and have eliminated them from my 'Roll' in the appendices. The ranks given in the narrative are the ranks held at the time the event took place, whereas the ranks in the appendices are those held when the individual left the Battalion, or when the war ended. Any promotions that took place between the end of the war and discharge have not been applied. It is inevitable that I have made some errors with these, and for that I apologise in advance.

The numbers men held were 'Battalion' and not 'Army' numbers—these were only introduced post-war. Numbers in the TF ran from 1 to 9999, but it became clear that this was inadequate, and in March 1917, TF men were given a new six-figure number. Soldiers posted 'missing' were rarely declared 'dead' until the passage of approximately a year, so many men missing in mid-1916 were allocated six-figure numbers, even if it was later decided that they had been killed at the time. Regular soldiers continued to hold four-figure numbers, and from the beginning of the war, men who joined 'Service' battalions, or were later conscripted, had five-figure numbers, even if posted to a TF battalion. The numbers given in narrative and appendices are the later numbers if these were allocated. Inevitably, some men have the same name, so as to differentiate these in the narrative, I have used the Army practice of giving their last three numbers in brackets; for example, William Smith (059).

One of the problems with war histories is that they tend to break war up into a series of 'events', jumping from one major confrontation to the next, as if absolutely nothing happened in between these acts of significance. As less than half the fatalities in the Battalion occurred in 'set-piece' battles, this would be an omission too far. War diaries reinforce this interpretation, as they are very much an outline of the day's events—much of the detail had already been sent up to brigade or division in myriad returns concerning just about everything a battalion did, used, or saw. I have used these and many other sources to fill in these gaps and tell the story of the Battalion and the men who served in it for the entire period of the war.

War diaries introduce another complication, in that for most (but not all) of the time, they documented events and casualties for a period part way through one day to the same time the following day—the actual time depending on the time of year. For example, an event at 11 a.m. on the 4th of a month may actually be entered into the diary under the 5th. This process was not universal—occasionally battalion, brigade, or divisional diaries recorded their events for the calendar day and very rarely was the battalion's diary actually in synchronisation with the divisional diary. This can lead to discrepancies between the date a casualty was recorded in a war diary, a service record, or by the Commonwealth War Graves Commission. Fortunately, other sources all help to establish the actual date something occurred. At times there are some serious discrepancies between the dates reported in other sources and the dates in the Battalion's war diary, which was often written up at a much later date. Wherever possible, the dates used in the narrative are those that can be confirmed by additional sources—where there are doubts, I have mentioned this in the narrative or endnotes.

Understanding the actions of the Battalion is greatly improved by walking the actual ground, but as most readers are unlikely to be able to do this, I have given the coordinates of positions, which can be entered as 'Placemarks' on Google Earth. These coordinates have been written as degrees, minutes, and seconds, as this format is also that most frequently used in a car's Satnav, but is easily converted in Google Earth to other formats if preferred. A combination of this and Google 'Street-View' add a dimension that a paper map cannot bring. Where these coordinates are based on map references given at the time, they are as accurate as the original map references—though coordinates based on trench maps themselves will be accurate to within 10 yards. If the coordinate is of a trench, then this is either a central position along its length or a part relevant to the narrative. I have also included sketch maps for many of the Battalion's positions, and these will be available on the Lion and Rose Facebook page (@LionandtheRose). A printout of these will help the reader follow the action. These are only roughly to scale and are drawn using information gleaned from a combination of often-conflicting evidence from original trench maps, sketch maps in official, divisional, and regimental diaries and histories, modern maps, aerial photographs, and written narrative. These sketch maps do show the relationship of various positions to each other. What maps do not easily show are fields of fire, and having walked the ground, I have used a 'soldier's eye' to comment on these when appropriate. One change I have made is to the order in which a sequence is described. The British Army always list from right to left, but as most civilians are used to the opposite, I have narrated from left to right.

Acknowledgements

This book would not have been possible without the help and patience of my wife, Glynis, whose assistance with research, photography, and proofreading was crucial to its completion. I would also like to thank the staff at Lancaster Library and the National Archives for their great help in locating various primary sources and original publications. These include Peter Donnelly and the King's Own Museum, for their kind permission to use photographs from their collection; Liverpool Record Office, for their great help in locating various primary sources and their kind permission to use some as illustrations in this book; John Banning, for the photograph of Charles Banning; David Fuller, for the photo of the three Whitehead brothers; Donna Broadbent, for the picture of Jack Cowell; Phil Wild, for the photograph of Ernest Porter; Kate Mears and the Deighton family, for the photographs of Capt. John Deighton; and Ian Birnie, for the photograph of Hugh Butterworth. This work would also have been much more difficult without the knowledge and expertise of the many contributors from the Great War Forum, who answered those obscure queries, enabling me to add that extra detail into my narratives. Special thanks to Trevor Henshaw, whose knowledge and expertise about RFC losses in the First World War is truly encyclopaedic and who has been invaluable in identifying those airmen witnessed by the men on the ground. Acknowledgements too must go to Chris Baker, for his excellent website—The Long, Long Trail—that ought to be the first port of call for any new researcher of the First World War. Finally, many thanks are due to Jay Slater, Joshua Greenland, and all the staff at Fonthill Media, without whom this book would not have been possible.

CONTENTS

Glossary and Abbreviations

4.2 and 5.9: German 105-mm and 120-mm Howitzers. The Imperial designations were used to describe both gun and round

Accid.: accidentally

AOC: Army Ordnance Corps

APC: Army Pay Corps

ASC: Army Service Corps

B Team: see Second Line

Beds: Bedfordshire Regiment

Bn: Battalion

CCS: Casualty Clearing Station

CdG: French Croix de Guerre

CdVM: Romanian Croix de Virtue Militara

Cheshires: Cheshire Regiment

CLLE: Charger Loading Lee-Enfield

Comm.: commissioned

Coy: Company

CRA: Commander Royal Artillery

CRE: Commander Royal Engineers

CSgt: Colour Sergeant

CT: communication trench

CWGC: Commonwealth War Graves Commission

D: died

DCLI: Duke of Cornwall's Light Infantry

DCM: Distinguished Conduct Medal

Deliberate attack: a pre-planned and coordinated use of firepower and manoeuvre to carry out an attack

DG: Dragoon Guards

Div TC: Divisional Tunnelling Company

DLOY: Duke of Lancasters Own Yeomanry

DOW: died of wounds

DSO: Distinguished Service Order

Effective fire: enemy fire that begins to cause casualties amongst one's own troops.

E. Kent: East Kent Regiment

E. Lancs: East Lancashire Regiment

E. Surreys: East Surrey Regiment

FGCM: Field General Court Martial

GCM: General Court Martial

Gds: Guards

Glasshouse, the: British Army military prison

Glosters: Gloucestershire Regiment

GRU: Grave Retrieval Unit

GS wagon: general service wagon

H: Only saw home service with the battalion

HE: high explosive

IBD: Infantry Base Depot, or the 'Bull Ring'

ICT: Inflammation of the Connective Tissue, or Internal Cruciate Tear

IR: Infantry Regiment (German)

Jct: junction

K.: Killed

KAR: King's African Rifles

KIA: killed in action

KLR: King's Liverpool Regiment

KORL: King's Own Royal Lancaster Regiment

KRRC or KRR: King's Royal Rifle Corps

KSLI: King's Shropshire Light Infantry

LC: Labour Corps

Leics: Leicestershire Regiment

LF: Lancashire Fusiliers

Lincs: Lincolnshire Regiment

LNL or LN: Loyal North Lancashire Regiment

MC: Military Cross

MCR: Manchester Regiment

MGC: Machine Gun Corps

MiD: Mentioned in Dispatches.

MFP: Military Foot Police

MM: Military Medal

MO: Medical Officer

Monmouths: Monmouthshire regiment

MSM: Meritorious Services Medal

N. Staffs: North Staffordshire Regiment

O Group: Meeting of officers

OH: Official History of the Great War. 109 volumes based on official sources.

OP: Observation Post

OR: other rank

OBL: Old British Line

OBLI: Oxford and Buckinghamshire Light Infantry

RA: Royal Artillery

RAMC: Royal Army Medical Corps

RDC: Royal Defence Corps

RE: Royal Engineers

RFA: Royal Field Artillery

RFC: Royal Flying Corps

R. Fus: Royal Fusiliers

Rgt: Regiment

RIR: Reserve Infantry Regiment (German)

RN: Royal Navy

RR: Reserve Regiment (German)

RSAF Enfield: Royal Small Arms Factory in Enfield

R. Warks: Royal Warwickshire Regiment

RWF: Royal Welsh Fusiliers (they didn't become 'Welch' till 1920)

Rwy: railway

Second Line: a proportion of the battalion kept back from the front line as a nucleus to reconstitute the battalion. Also known as the B Team

S. Lancs: South Lancashire Regiment

Sherwoods: Sherwood Foresters

SMLE: Short Magazine Lee-Enfield

Soldiers Died: Soldiers Died in the Great War volumes.

SWB: Silver War Badge

TMB: Trench Mortar Battery

Tr: trench

VC: Victoria Cross

WR: Duke of Wellingtons (West Riding) Regiment

W. Surreys: West Surrey Regiment

WIA: wounded in action

Yeo.: Yeomanry

Yorks and Lancs: Yorkshire and Lancashire Regiment

August 1914–14 February 1915: 'Your Country Needs You'

In 1914, the 5th Battalion, King's Own (Royal Lancaster) Regiment comprised of eight companies with a headquarters in Lancaster. 'A', 'B', 'C', and 'D' Companies were based at Lancaster, 'A' also having a drill station in Galgate; 'E' was at Morecambe and 'F' at Carnforth, with drill stations at Arnside, Silverdale, and Caton; 'G' was at Fleetwood, with drill stations at Poulton, Garstang, and Blackpool; and 'H' was also in Fleetwood and had drill stations at Preesall and Thornton. Issues concerning 'Pals' Battalions in the First World War and the tragic consequences on their local recruitment areas after heavy losses are well-known, and though technically the 5th was not a 'Service' or 'Pals' battalion, similar issues arose as men in the TF needed to live locally to their nearest drill hall. Consequently, men came from geographically concise areas. Even local papers consistently referred to the 5th as the 'Pals', differentiating them from Service Battalions whom they referred to as 'Kitchener Battalions'.

Many of the 5th worked together and many were related, with brothers, cousins, in-laws, uncles, fathers, and sons all serving in the same place at the same time. These close relationships helped sustain them in times of need, but also increased the horror and tragedy of war, not only at home, but also on the battlefield.

Recruits to the TF infantry were expected to be at least seventeen years old and no older than thirty-five; they also had to be at least 5 feet 2 inches in height, with a sliding scale of acceptable chest measurement depending on age and weight (Oddly enough, the minimum heights for the Army Postal Service TF were greater). A lad of fourteen could enlist as a bugler or a drummer in both TF and Regulars, providing the consent of a parent or guardian had been obtained, but service overseas would be at the discretion of the Colonel and it was expected that these lads would be kept as much as possible out of harm's way. The number of fourteen to seventeen year olds was limited, and in the case of infantry, the normal establishment was sixteen—though a discretionary maximum of one extra per company was allowed to bring this to twenty-four. The total establishment of a TF infantry battalion was set at 1,009 all ranks, twenty-nine of whom were officers, including the regular officer attached to the battalion as adjutant.

With service permissible from fourteen, it was uncommon for a recruit to lie about his age before the outbreak of the war, though some, such as Matthew Farrell, clearly did. However, after war began, underage enlistment became endemic; young men, sure that it would be 'over by Christmas', desperately tried to get involved. No proof of age was required, and recruiting sergeants would take a likely looking lad's word for it if he said he was nineteen. No statistics exist to say just how many underage soldiers fought with the 1/5th in their first two years of deployment, though it is fair to say that numbers must have been considerable as twelve soldiers aged seventeen or younger were killed or died from wounds. There was clearly no official policy of condoning underage recruitment as surviving records illustrate that numbers had their military careers cut short and were sent home immediately after the Army found out that they were underage, those in the training system below military age similarly dispensed with. It was not just the young who were guilty; considerable numbers of older men subtracted years in order to be accepted—some were in their late forties when they enlisted. Compulsory registrations under the Military Service Act of January 1916 mostly put an end to fraudulent enlistment.

Every man and officer in their first year of enlistment was expected to attend for a minimum of forty days, twenty of which must have been carried out before the Recruits Musketry Course and the fortnight's annual camp (held every August). For subsequent years, the requirement was a minimum of ten days prior to annual camp, the camp itself, and the annual musketry course. The TF was seen as a Home Defence force and the Army was fully aware that their training could not be nearly as thorough as the Regulars. The expectation was that by the time they were needed, they could be brought up to the same standard as their Regular counterparts, the men of the National Reserve being used to replace casualties in Regular units.[1]

To begin with, recruits were taught basic drill and the care and presentation of uniforms. The lessons of the Boer War were still fresh in the minds of the military, and physical fitness and musketry were very high on the agenda. TF infantry spent as much time as possible on the range, and all soldiers, including cooks and clerks, were expected to pass the same stringent annual marksmanship test as the Regulars. Expectations in 1914 may come as a shock to today's generation of soldiers—who almost never engage targets beyond 300 metres with a rifle—but the Field Service Regulations of 1909 described ranges of up to 600 yards as 'close', 600 to 1,400 yards as 'effective', and between 1,400 yards and 2,000 yards as 'long'. The rifle used by the 5th in 1914 was the Charger Loading Lee Enfield (CLLE). The SMLE introduced to regular units in 1907 had not then filtered down to the TF. In the early years of war, rifles were in such short supply that many new recruits never even held an Enfield until they got to France, having carried out their basic training with the Arisaka rifle, of which 150,000 were purchased from the Japanese in late 1914. Recruits joining the 5th were luckier, as photographic evidence shows that in 1915, recruits had the CLLE.

Physical training was covered by regular sessions of callisthenic exercises, cross-country runs, football, rugby, but most of all by frequent route marches. The Army of 1914 marched almost everywhere, transport by rail or bus being extremely rare unless long distances needed to be covered and marches of 10 to 15 miles were routine. Falling out of the line of march without permission was judged as a heinous crime by both officers and senior NCOs, who believed it reflected badly upon the unit. Even today, the '10-Mile Bash', part of the Annual Fitness Test for all soldiers, has to be covered in less than two hours.

The 980 men of a peacetime battalion were not all riflemen as there were a number of other vital roles to fulfil. Each battalion was armed with two Maxim machine guns, requiring one sergeant, one corporal, twelve men, and two drivers. A further twenty-eight drivers were required for the battalion's transport and horses. Each battalion was allowed eighteen horses for various purposes; two general service wagons and a machine-gun transport. Specialist sergeants were needed as farrier, battalion cook, pioneer, saddler, shoemaker, armourer, and quartermaster sergeant. In May 1915, they were lucky enough to have the services of a former Birmingham gunsmith, S/Sgt Arthur Davis of the AOC as armourer-sergeant. A further fourteen men from the Regulars were attached as drivers and medics, but when war was declared, these returned to their parent units and the posts were filled internally. Once a battalion was on a war footing, two GS wagons were clearly insufficient and more transport was acquired as a matter of urgency. The war diary for 14 February 1915 lists a total of seventy-two animals, comprising fourteen 'riding' horses and fifty-eight draught and pack animals, all to be loaded onto the SS *Manchester Importer* along with six GS wagons; eleven limbered wagons; two machine-gun carts; one medical cart; two water carts; and one cart for the Officers' Mess.[2] The requirements of this extra transport also drew on the manpower available to fighting companies, with Transport and Stores requiring around 100 men.

The Advance Party for their seventh annual camp at Kirkby Lonsdale left Lancaster on Thursday 30 July, but even as they were establishing camp for the rest of the battalion, expected on Sunday, many of the necessary stores and equipment were ordered back to the Ordnance Depot. When the Main Party marched through the heavy rain from the station to the camp, they discovered tents were in short supply and had to sleep nine to a tent. There was only one blanket per man, no groundsheets, and a severe shortage of cooking utensils—these items having already been returned. Rumours of impending war had been circulating from the moment they gathered and the lack of equipment served to strengthen these. Shortly afterwards, Col. G. L. Hibbert DSO, Brigade-Commander of the West Lancashire Division, warned not to make arrangements for a long stay, as the troop trains had been detained in readiness at Kirkby Lonsdale and further orders were expected returning troops to their peace stations. These arrived shortly before midnight and the Battalion departed for Lancaster early Monday morning. Once detachments reached their various headquarters, men were dismissed home with a warning that mobilisation may be imminent. The mobilisation telegram reached Lancaster late on 4 August, giving orders to assemble next morning and travel up to Barrow to guard this important munitions centre.

The first fatality happened that very day. Pte James Hall, a nineteen-year-old farm labourer from Pilling, received his Mobilisation Notice in the morning's post. An hour later, he went into the shippon, where his father saw him trying to clean his rifle barrel with a piece of string—the cleaning rod being broken. His father went to try to find him a better alternative to the string, and upon hearing a shot ten minutes later, rushed back to find his son slumped dead against the cattle trough. Medical examination determined that the muzzle of the rifle had been inside Hall's mouth when the rifle had been fired. The deceased had shown no obvious signs of worry about his impending mobilisation and left no suicide note, but Mr N. Holden's (the coroner) summing-up left no doubt as to his opinion:

> The deceased had evidently taken his own life at a time when he was perfectly sane. At such times when soldiers are called up to serve their King and Country, it was the act of a coward to go and take his own life.[3]

He instructed the jury that, in light of the father's evidence that the deceased was sane, they had no alternative but to deliver a verdict of suicide—which they then did. While there seems little doubt that it was suicide, the sentiments expressed by the coroner as to him being 'perfectly sane' and that his suicide was an act of cowardice are much at variance to how we would perceive this tragedy today. James Hall went unrecorded by CWGC, but as he had received his mobilisation orders, he was undoubtedly a casualty of the war. Regrettably, he was only the first of six men to die before the Battalion deployed overseas.

On the afternoon of 5 August, the Battalion marched from the drill hall to Lancaster Parish Church, led by CO Lt-Col. Lord Richard Cavendish, where they met the Lord Mayor, Mr Noel Briggs, and a formal congregation of councillors and aldermen. Once everyone was seated inside the church, the Colour Party, carrying the King's and Regimental Colours, formed up at the entrance to the King's Own Chapel. It was a moment steeped in history, the faded Colours of the First Royal Lancashire Militia from the Crimean War and the Boer War Colours of the Militia hanging limply from the dusty beams overhead. Coloured light from the large stained glass window commemorating those fallen in South Africa played on the faces of the Colour Party as the congregation sang 'O God our Help in Ages Past'. The Colours, which would remain in the church until the end of the war, were handed to the vicar, the Rev. J. U. N. Bardsley and his clergy, who placed them either side of the altar.[4]

One notable absentee was the Quartermaster, Lt Albert Hodgkinson—a headmaster from Morecambe. His men were busy loading a train with all the equipment for the move to their wartime station, but he had left early that morning to organise billets in Barrow. The Battalion made the short march from church to station, and at 4.50 p.m. departed for Barrow, the bridge outside the station packed with cheering onlookers.[5] The Battalion was tasked to guard warships in the docks and patrol the roads leading to Barrow; however, their stay was brief, for a week later they returned to Lancaster and were billeted in the empty and quite dilapidated Wagon Works in Caton Road.

The declaration of war led to great upheaval in the normally well-ordered lives of 1914 Lancashire. Using their powers under the 1871 Regulation of Forces Act, the

Government took over the railways and immediately stopped all 'excursion' trains—stranding a number of Lancastrians who had been enjoying their summer holidays. The first air raid scare happened as early as 5 August, when alarms sounded in Barrow and Lancaster. Newspapers reported panic-buying from grocers' around the town, resulting in price rises for flour and other such items—the price of sugar doubled in just two days.[6] Throughout the country, there were spy scares—fed in part by a government announcement on 5 August reporting the arrest of twenty-one foreign spies in one day (though only nine of these were actually spies)—the total 'padded out' with innocent foreign citizens.[7] A Bill prohibiting the movement of 'enemy aliens' from, to, and within the United Kingdom without a special permit was hurriedly pushed through Parliament, coming into force on 10 August.

A number of German nationals almost immediately fell victim to this new law. Wilhelm Mertensen and Herman Schletten—two German crewmembers on the SS *Chloris*, arriving at Glasson Dock with a cargo of Russian timber, were immediately arrested. The pair unsurprisingly insisted that they had not known that there was a war on as it had been declared while they were at sea. Both were detained awaiting deportation. Another unfortunate was sixty-two-year-old Emille Dexter, resident in Britain for forty-two years. He was married to an Englishwoman, lived and worked as a cabinetmaker in Dublin, and was visiting his wife's family in Lancashire when war was declared. He was arrested attempting to board a ship home to Dublin where he had presumed he needed to register as an alien. Unusually, at a time when hysteria frequently outweighed rationality, he was discharged from court and ordered to register immediately upon arrival in Ireland.

Throughout the land, walkers, bird watchers, and anyone with a camera or binoculars became the object of instant mistrust—particularly if seen by any of the Boy Scout movement, who had been urged to report suspicious persons. Two British-born brothers of German extraction, Leo and Aloysious Beers, both professional violinists, were reported by Sea Scout John Perry for taking photographs of Tynemouth Castle.[8] They were remanded in custody—though they must have been released soon after as both served in the DCLI and their brother Joseph was killed with KOYLI. Laws were passed banning foreigners from owning carrier pigeons; two men, Max Nagel and Charles King (both from London) were charged with possessing sixty-five birds. The pair claimed these were show birds and unable to fly any distance, and King also protested vehemently that he was Dutch and not German. Both were remanded in custody, and their pigeons, along with thousands of other birds seized, were destroyed.[9]

On 14 August, a mere two days after the Battalion had returned to Lancaster, they were on the move again, this time to Didcot in Oxfordshire to guard a stretch of the GWR between Reading and Swindon. Once again, the departure of the Battalion in two special trains took on a carnival atmosphere, the platforms crowded with families and friends. Vendors did a brisk trade in fizzy drinks, chocolate, and toffee, and some of the men wore mascots fastened to their uniforms—one waving a teddy bear wrapped in a small Tricolour and Union Jack. The first train arrived at 9 p.m. and the Battalion bivouacked for the night as no billets had been arranged. By 9 a.m., four companies were sent west towards Swindon and three eastwards—each company distributed along the length of their section of line. 'D' remained at Didcot station, along with Battalion and Brigade HQ.

Even though the locals embraced the Battalion with open arms, this was a problematical situation for the Battalion; training was almost impossible to organise—and with the Battalion spread along 53 miles of track, ration supply presented complications. Initially, the Battalion was given exclusive use of a motor train to transport rations to each company HQ, conveniently placed at stations, though after three days, rations were conveyed by normal scheduled services. From these stations, supplies were distributed to the outposts and one cart per company was assigned for this. As soldiers since the dawn of time have done, men improvised and 'acquired' various items to make their lives that little bit more comfortable. Any stray cats and dogs in the vicinity found their lives improved immeasurably when men adopted them as pets. The QM's staff, finding a stray, grey tabby kitten in the meat store one day, named it 'Didcot', fitted it with a collar and an ID disc similar to the men's, and added it to the ration strength.

Maintenance of discipline was also challenging with the Battalion so scattered, and it says a lot about the quality of these men that so few seem to have ended up on disciplinary charges. One who did was L/Cpl Robert Baird, a stone dresser from Lancaster. On 9 September, he appeared before the CO accused of being drunk (off duty) and urinating against the outside wall of his billet. The thirty-six-year-old, who had served since 1898 in the Volunteers and TF, marched out of the CO's office a private.

In the coming weeks, numbers of men would be discharged due to sickness and injury. Many of these, such as thirty-seven-year-old Pte George Myers from Blackpool, were older than the average recruit and found the life taxing. There was, however, only one mortality due to illness before the Battalion deployed to France and that was Morecambe resident, nineteen-year-old Pte Harold Snowden on 19 October. The close proximity of men and trains had potential for tragedy, and on 29 August Pte Albert Gordon, who was guarding the bridge at Faringdon, became the first to die. A month later, twenty-five-year-old Pte John Huartson was hit and killed by an express at Twyford. The married father of a young child was on sentry duty on the bridge and was discovered some 100 yards down the line. In light of his terrible injuries, it was judged that his death was instantaneous. The inquest gave a verdict of 'accidental death' and the body was returned by train to Lancaster for burial. For John's older brother—thirty-nine-year-old Richard, Richard's brother-in-law, seventeen-year-old Pte James Nash, and another brother Tom—the accident must have been deeply shocking. For two of them, the clock was also counting down.

The next day, another two were killed. Pte Ernest Halton, a twenty-six-year-old, and Pte James Walton, a twenty-two-year-old, both from Calder Vale, were killed while on patrol near the level crossing at Steventon. CWGC and 'Soldiers Died' give the date of death as 4 October, but this cannot be correct as the Lancaster paper reporting their deaths was published on 3 October. That article reports the accident as happening late on 30 September.[10] It is believed that the two men crossed to the other line to avoid the 'Up' milk train—unfortunately, they went straight into the path of the 'Down' express. Mercifully, there were no more accidental deaths during their remaining time in England. Considering that sentries' rifles were loaded and men were under orders to challenge anyone approaching their posts between dawn and dusk—shooting anyone who did not immediately obey their orders—it is a miracle there were no tragic shootings of innocent civilians or of other soldiers.

Since mobilisation, repeated appeals were made for volunteers, and hundreds of men from Lancaster, Morecambe, Fleetwood, Blackpool, and surrounding areas responded. Volunteers were given a medical examination, and if passed fit, would then be attested. As doctors were only paid for men accepted, rather than men examined, some highly suspect decisions were made, and in some towns, there was palpably wholesale dishonesty by the medical profession, who passed men fit with disabilities obvious to any nonprofessional. Mostly, the doctors in Lancaster seem to have been honest and surviving records evince no examples of glaringly obvious fraud. One young man who did slip through was twenty-year-old Edward Bunce from Lancaster. When he took his medical on 1 February 1915, he must have managed to keep a mangled hand hidden from the doctor. Some five months before enlisting, his right hand had been run over by a tramcar and left permanently misshapen—his thumb rigid and sticking out at an angle. Not surprisingly, this was identified very quickly once he began training, as he was unable to hold a rifle and was medically discharged.

When it mobilised, the Battalion had been in the rare position of being up to strength, but it was clear to the CO that some men were unlikely to cope with the rigours of field service. Volunteer numbers were such that the 5th was able to begin forming a reserve battalion on 15 August, and at 7.30 p.m. on 7 September, 200 of the best recruits from this marched to the station singing 'It's a Long Way to Tipperary' and were dispatched to join the 5th at Didcot to continue their training.[11] Many of the 'Two Hundred' were from the professions, and it was not unusual for a platoon to contain architects, bankers, teachers, solicitors, and, in the case of Scotsman Rowland McGowan, a dental surgeon among its ranks. It must not be assumed that these men, used to sedentary occupations, would find the physical hardships a problem as virtually all were members of some of Lancaster's best sporting clubs. Three were former captains of the Vale of Lune Rugby Club, another was the secretary of the Lancaster Cricket Club, and almost to a man, the eligible members of the John O' Gaunt Rowing Club had volunteered.[12] This new draft allowed Lt-Col. Cavendish to weed out the least fit and still field a full-strength battalion.

On 11 November, the railway guard was taken over by reservists and the Battalion left for Sevenoaks, the new recruits all successfully integrated. West Lancashire Division was concentrated around Sevenoaks and Tonbridge as part of London's defence, but few of the other battalions were as well off for men. As early as the end of November, it became clear that the division was unlikely to deploy as a 'stand-alone' and would be broken up, its component units going to other divisions. Surprisingly, considering the issue of National Security, local papers at this time were reporting that the 10th Lancashire Battery, RFA, had been refitted with new guns ready for overseas deployment and that 5th King's Own was soon to follow suit.[13] The men were billeted with local inhabitants and, on the whole, looked after as if they had been their hosts' own sons.

Now they were all together again, the Battalion was able to concentrate on training. Two of the lasting myths of the First World War are that trench warfare was some sort of surprise and that men, burdened with heavy loads, lined up shoulder to shoulder with each other and walked slowly forwards into the attack. The latter had not been the case for decades and trench warfare was nothing new either—though the duration of static warfare in trench systems was not something that had been forecast. In January 1915, infantry battalions were reorganised from eight into four companies. Each company consisted of four platoons—which in most battalions were numbered 1–4 for 'A' Company; 5–8 for 'B', etc. The platoon was divided into four sections, usually between eight to twelve men, though there were many variations on these numbers depending on the manpower and stage of the war. Each section was led by an NCO, with the platoon commanded by an officer and a sergeant. Initially, all men were riflemen and prior to the issue of the Mills bomb, grenades were only issued to specially trained men, each company later forming a 'dedicated' bombing squad of approximately twenty men led by a junior officer and a sergeant.

Two basic formations were used when advancing. The first was 'artillery formation', with men well-spaced apart in single file. Once engaged from the front, men moved into 'extended order', (line abreast), which gave more protection from MG fire to their front. Hostile fire from the front when in artillery formation, or from the side when in extended order, was known as 'enfilading fire' and was far more deadly—a single burst could bring down an entire section. Once engaged, they advanced in alternate sections—those not moving providing covering fire for the others. The heavier the enemy fire, the shorter the rushes between cover. When close enough to their objective, men would charge as quickly as possible, with the idea being to deliver the maximum number of men in the shortest achievable time to overwhelm the adversary. Whenever practicable, attacks would begin from as close to the enemy as possible, but in certain cases, this was not feasible and it was these attacks that occasioned the greatest casualties. Throughout the war, it was artillery that was the nemesis of the infantryman, the majority of casualties resulting from it. Small arms fire accounted for approximately one-third of casualties and poison gas for less than 2 per cent of all those killed.

Trench warfare had been in the infantry training manual for years and photographs from 1914 show the 5th Battalion digging practice trenches at Sevenoaks. Trench design developed greatly during the war, and local conditions also dictated the type used. In areas with a high water table, it was not possible to dig down far as the trench would fill with water. In such places, a shallow excavation was made and sandbag walls, known as breastworks, were constructed. These needed to slope at a proper angle to avoid collapse and a minimum thickness of forty-inches was necessary to stop a bullet— consequently, the width at the bottom of the wall was much greater. Breastworks were far more vulnerable to shell fire than a trench cut into the ground and a direct hit with an HE shell could destroy a section, often crushing defenders under sandbags. Apart from rotting, heavy rain also caused the sandbags to settle—of particular concern to taller men who may find themselves exposed in a place where they had been adequately protected days before. Early trenches also significantly lacked in two areas of design— that of drainage and effective top cover. While the small dugouts built into the side of the trenches provided some protection from shrapnel, a nearby hit by HE could collapse the entire structure, crushing or suffocating all inside.

It was not all work, and as Christmas approached, the locals threw themselves into making the men's Christmas as happy as possible. No leave was granted, though there were two exceptions. Twenty-eight-year-old Capt. William Fawcett was due to get married in Lancaster on 23 December—his best man was twenty-three-year-old ironmonger's apprentice Pte Fred Eltoft from 'B' Company. While this may initially appear to transgress the rigid rank, social, and class structures of the era, Fred Eltoft (one of the Two Hundred) was the son of a distinguished veterinary surgeon, a friend and fellow member of Lancaster Rowing Club, and the bride was his sister. The respite, however, was only brief, and both men had to be back on Christmas Eve. Capt. and Mrs Fawcett caught the 3.40 p.m. train to London for their brief honeymoon.[14] Regrettably for Mrs Evelina Fawcett, tragedy would hit their family in less than five months.

Several men wrote to the Lancaster papers describing their Christmas in Sevenoaks.

> A Lancastrian at Sevenoaks says, 'The people gave us a great time this Christmas and I think that there are very few who were not merry. If they didn't it was their own fault. The people have treated us with every kindness.' One of the Pals writes, 'We spent the early part of Christmas Day very quietly, but in the evening things improved wonderfully, as most of us were invited to the residences of the well-to-do people of Sevenoaks, according to the accommodation at their disposal. Nine of my company had dinner at Bishop's Court, the residence of the Bishop of Rochester (Dr Harmer), who with his wife and daughters and their private guests did everything to make us enjoy ourselves as much as possible, and succeeded admirably. Both the Bishop and his wife were extremely kind and, he told us that to him it was the most unique experience he had ever had. I can assure you we all regretted it when the time came to leave'.[15]

One man's festive period ended in tragedy when terrible news reached Cpl James Carney on New Year's Day. At 4 p.m. on New Year's Eve, his four-year-old daughter, Margaret, burned to death at home in Lancaster—the youngster's flannelette nightgown igniting after she had wandered upstairs and into a room where there was an unguarded fire.[16]

Towards the end of January 1915, the Battalion received orders to prepare for overseas, though the CO was given no indication as to where. New wagons were issued to replace those requisitioned in August, and men received webbing pouches to replace their bandoleers and replacement uniforms. An issue was made of Mk VII ammunition to replace the round-nosed Mk VI, and presumably new rifles were also issued—though no record remains to confirm this. The CLLE needed alterations to both rear sight and magazine to accurately fire and feed the Mk VII round; factories such as RSAF Enfield were working flat out to adapt them. In February 1915, this factory reworked nearly 28,000 rifles for issue to troops deploying abroad. It is reasonable to presume that a 'one-for-one' exchange was made of their old CLLEs for modified ones. There were a few instances of units deploying with unmodified CLLEs, but this generated much adverse comment in their war diaries, and as no such mention is made by the 1/5th, it is presumed that they were unaffected. In the early hours of a very wet Sunday morning on February 14, the Battalion boarded two trains bound for Southampton.

15 February 1915–3 April 1915: In a World of Strangers

Coordinates for Positions Named in this Chapter

Burnt Farm	50°45′50.60″N	Trench 10A	50°45′39.00″N
	02°51′26.30″E		2°52′9.00″E
Dressing station	50°45′50.30″N	Trench 8A	50°45′33.80″N
	2°50′40.30″E		2°52′12.70″E
Souvenir Farm	50°45′32.30″N	Trench 9	50°45′34.50″N
	2°51′27.70″E		2°52′9.50″E
St Quentin Cabaret	50°45′28.40″N		
	2°51′21.80″E		

The majority embarked on the SS *Manchester Importer*, with the remainder on the SS *Oxonian*, arriving at Le Havre at 10 a.m. on 15 February. Unloading took considerable time, and it was not until 2.30 p.m. that they began the 2-mile march up the hill to their bivouac at Sanvic. Despite the rain, cheering crowds of locals, buoying men's spirits considerably, lined their route. This lapsed somewhat over the night and following day, spent in leaky tents on an exposed hillside, constant rain and a bitterly cold wind chilling everyone to the bone. In the early hours of the 17th, most of the Battalion left for the station in Le Havre, leaving Capt. Fawcett and two platoons of 'A' Company behind to clear up the camp, with orders to follow on later that day.

An interpreter, Pierre Lemunier, joined the Battalion, considerably easing the task facing the billeting officer. Soaked to the skin after their march down to the station, the men were far from impressed when they learned that their transport consisted of cattle wagons that, according to the signage on their sides, were suitable for forty men or eight horses. The weather remained very cold and freezing wind pierced the slots in the wagon sides—ideal conditions for hypothermia. It was so cold that twenty-five-year-old Sgt James Kirkby commented that men were afraid to sleep in case they froze to death.[1] Even after some straw was acquired to sit on, this was far from opulent. Misery on this interminable twenty-six-hour journey was compounded by a lack of decent food. At one wayside station, it had been arranged that a party of eleven would disembark to collect rations deposited there. However, due to a monumental foul-up by the railway staff, as soon as the men left the platform to collect the food, the train was flagged away, stranding them. Subsisting only on a diet of bully beef and biscuit, the remaining journey was not a happy time.

The Battalion reached Bavinchove at 7.45 a.m. on the 18th and marched 6 miles to Winnezeele, where they were billeted in barns. One Morecambe man wrote:

> No one has any idea how hard it is marching with full pack after being in a cramped position for a long time and having very little to eat. Most of the battalion were billeted in barns, not unoccupied, as rats were frequent visitors and one person I know lost part of his underclothing through these hungry animals.[2]

A brave rat indeed. Another wrote: 'I was considerably startled when a rat jumped on my face as I lay asleep'.[3] Capt. Fawcett caught up with them at 8 p.m., however, it was very late that night when the ration party eventually arrived, having cadged a lift on a train full of artillerymen. The Battalion was now part of 83 Brigade, 28 Division.

After morning inspection, men were set to improving sanitary arrangements in their billeting area, where a multitude of new latrines required digging and facilities for washing and cooking constructing. Once this was concluded, the Battalion set off at 2 p.m. on a 7-mile march. Until 27 February, the pattern remained consistent, with route marches interspersed with practice in the various infantry formations and trench digging (day and night). The weather remained bitterly cold and the route march on 24 February was memorable for the blizzard conditions throughout the journey. The men, wearing iron-nailed boots, found these long marches on French roads quite difficult: 'The roads round here are awfully bad, especially the cobbled ones as they are so poorly laid'.[4] On the 27th, the Battalion returned from a 5-mile march shortly before midday and was told to be ready to move to Bailleul. A warning order to move always brought about intense activity as a vast amount of kit had to be assembled, cleaned, then packed onto the transport; billets also needed to be cleansed. At 3.45 p.m., when the order came cancelling the move, there must have been considerable cursing at all the wasted effort.

On 28 February, a barn occupied by two platoons of 'D' Company caught fire, an incident one Morecambe soldier described:

> Last Sunday was most exciting as one of the barns was burnt to the ground in half-an-hour. There was no fire brigade in the village so the men were soon busy carrying water in buckets. A fairly good amount of equipment, rifles and ammunition was lost, but luckily all the men were got out. Had the fire been at night, more serious might have been the consequences.[5]

Despite this, the Battalion still made an 8-mile route march, beginning late afternoon; after dark, they rehearsed occupying and relieving practice trenches. Early the next day, a Court of Enquiry into the causes of the fire concluded that the source of ignition had come from outside and had not been the responsibility of anyone from the Battalion. This was the last day at Winnezeele as the next morning, at 9.15. a.m., the Battalion departed in London buses for Bailleul, 11 miles away, where three companies were billeted in the school and one in the lunatic asylum.

No. 83 Brigade were temporarily attached to 5 Division and the Battalion was absorbed into 14 Brigade, who gave them a brief introduction into trench warfare. Initially, it was just officers and NCOs, but on 6 March, all of 'A' Company went to Wulverghem in the Dranoutre sector to experience their first twenty-four hours in the line.

In the 'C' sub-sector at Wulverghem were Trench 8A and Trench 9, which together were manned by a single company—Trench 10A was longer and required a complete company. Another company was in 'support' at Souvenir Farm, the remaining fighting company in 'reserve', at either Burnt Farm or Watermill Farm; HQ was in St. Quentin Cabaret.

The trenches here were breastworks and in very poor condition owing to recent bad weather. Many parts lacked trench-boards—often referred to as 'duckboards'— though strictly speaking, a duckboard was wider and used to make walkways outside of the trenches. There was little or no revetment and the sides of the trenches continually subsided—the battle to maintain them an uphill struggle. Negligible shelter existed and it was fortunate that their stay in a section of trench before relief was kept short.

The Battalion suffered its first casualty at 1.30 p.m. on the 7th, when Pte John Liver from 'A' Company was hit in his left shoulder by shrapnel—the ball narrowly missing the artery as it exited through his back. He got off quite lightly as the shell also blew in the parapet of the trench, cut his hat into strips, and his greatcoat had no less than ten holes in it. Due to the lack of CTs (communication trenches), Liver had to lie in the slush of his trench until it was dark enough to evacuate him. The married man from Lancaster was sent back to England for treatment and did not serve with the Battalion again, returning to France with 2/5th King's Own in February 1917. The company suffered another casualty the next day, when L/Cpl William Gudgeon was wounded.

At 1.45 p.m. on 7 March, 'B' Company departed for trench fatigues to Nieuwkerke, and in the evening, 'C' Company left to relieve 'A'. Seventeen-year-old Pte Maurice Robinson from 'A' Company wrote to his father, a former NCO of the King's Own, then a clerk at Bowerham Barracks:

We entered the trenches on Saturday night. Before we got so very far we were fired upon by the Maxims, which they had trained on the field we had to cross. I dropped pretty quickly. When I got up I was covered with mud. We got a bit further on, and then I found myself up to my knees in mud. We then got into the trenches and we had nicely settled down when 'Ping, ping!' The Germans started but nothing happened until three o' clock in the afternoon, when we began shelling their position. They started to dart about, and we had to fire at them. That just suited me to the ground.[6]

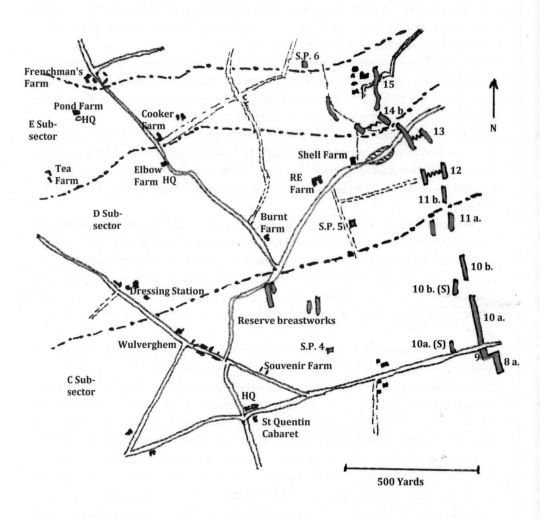

500 Yards

📛   Strongpoint

- - · Sub-sector boundary

▮   Breastworks

HQ   Sub-sector HQ

DRANOUTRE SECTOR

By 6.30 p.m. on 8 March, 'D' Company, having left their billets in St Jan Cappel earlier that afternoon, relieved 'A' in the trenches at Wulverghem. One soldier from 'D' wrote:

We marched for the trenches about 5.30 p.m., so that we arrived when it was dark and we had about a mile to go to our trenches within range of the Germans. It was at this point of our expedition that we felt most likely to get a bullet through us. We were alright so far, until one of the flares was sent up by which the Germans had seemingly spied us. Then the bullets began to whizz past. One chap, third from me, felt as though he had been hit somewhere and next morning, on looking in his valise, he found a bullet in a pair of socks. It had gone in through the bottom of his valise, through his hold-all, a singlet, ration tin and succumbed in his socks! It seemingly had struck his valise when he was lying down. We weren't long in stretching ourselves in the mud when the bullets started to fly. One could not pretend to lie down this time—that game of pretending is past now. At last we got into our trenches without any further excitement from bullet, an odd one of course going whizzing past. The main thing after that was to keep from stepping off the road into a Jack Johnson hole. As the road is an artificial one made of branches, and it being pretty dark, one was apt to stray unless you kept the chap in front in view. The holes made by the German shells were pretty big, and some full of water. One that had been recently made right in the roadway we had to walk through, and you had to sort of feel the depth as you couldn't see it. A good few chaps plunged into the holes. I think they would have preferred a bath at home. If you didn't keep to the artificial roadway in some places you would get layered, as it has been trodden on so much and the rain has increased the plastic state of the ground.

   The main thing when we got into the trenches was to keep a look-out, and keep one's head as low as much as possible. The flares were going up every five seconds or so and lit up the immediate ground around it. The trench that we were in was in the firing line, and there was a reserve trench behind, but we had no communicating trenches. Nothing very exciting happened through the night. The artillery didn't even start. Of course there was intermittent rifle fire. Through the day several of our aeroplanes went over the German lines and were fired on. The shells bursting round the first aeroplane were worth seeing. There would be a dozen shells fired at it, but the shelling was without effect in any of the cases, though there were some near shaves. Our guns started to shell the German trenches and one of them sent its shells right over our heads. You could hear them whistling through the air and follow their course until they got to the trenches, and then- bang! The Germans simply thought this too much of a good thing, so they started shelling ours, but without any casualties. Last night (March 9th) we got safely out of the trenches again, and marched back to our billet this morning. I don't think I mentioned before that we have goat-skin coats. They are useful to us in the trenches, and it is pretty cold, especially if you had been up to the knees in water in a ditch or shell hole.[7]

Not all the companies were as fortunate. On 8 March, 'C' Company lost nineteen-year-old Pte William Walls, the first to be killed in action. His platoon sergeant, Harry Gill, writing to his own mother, who also lived in Morecambe, described the day:

We had a taste of both German rifle fire and artillery fire. Their rifle fire is not up to much but their artillery don't half give you what for. Their shells make a terrible hole when they explode and throw stones and mud up in the air. We came out on Saturday night and went in with the whole company on Sunday night until Monday night. We passed through some small villages in Belgium on our way to the firing line, and it is a very sorrowful sight to see. The square has some big holes in the road where the German shells have dropped, and quite a lot of houses are completely demolished by German artillery. We also saw a hospital which the Germans had shelled on Friday morning, and it was a complete wreck and several wounded English soldiers were killed. The Belgium people have to leave the town during the day while the place is being shelled, and they return after dark to sleep. I think they are all leaving now, because the Germans seem determined to completely destroy the place. Most of the Belgians in the place were removing all their furniture out of their homes this morning (Tuesday).

We have also had the bad luck to lose one of the Morecambe boys yesterday (Monday). This was William Walls, son of Mr Walls, the sugar boiler, of Queen Street. The poor lad was shot by a German sniper about 7 on Monday morning, and he was buried about two miles from the firing line in Belgium. He was in my section and I stopped behind to see him buried. The grave was dug in an orchard adjoining a farm house, and the burial service was read over the grave in only the light of a small electric torch, and a very weird service it was. We came back from the trenches covered all over with mud, and it is a sight to see the fields that ought to be getting prepared for sowing grain, trampled into a mudpool by the troops passing to and from the firing line. The Germans are quite a tricky sort of people and at night are continually sniping, throwing up flare lights to see what we are doing. Yesterday while we were in the trenches, our artillery shelled the German trenches and they did some good work. The Germans then shelled us with shrapnel, but they did not hit our trench once, though they came as near as ten yards from the trench.[8]

William Walls lost his young life because his curiosity to look over the parapet was greater than his sense of self-preservation—the brief exposure as he raised his head to peer over was all the opportunity the sniper needed. Tragically, he would not be the last.

The demeanour of the regular troops giving the Battalion their induction was a great help in settling the men to life at the Front. One soldier wrote:

The night was one continuous clatter of bullets over our trenches and our lads were working all the time filling sandbags and repairing the damage done to the trenches. During the day two shells dropped within twenty-five yards of our trench. They simply made the earth tremble when they dropped. Although I felt nervy over these things the composure of our regular soldiers gave me very great confidence. They were singing and cleaning their rifles during the time the shells were dropping, and treated the matter with utter contempt. Could the people of England see these lads undergoing the hardships and risks of life in the trenches they could not help but admire them. I talked to nearly all of them and heard no one grumble all the time I was with them.[9]

The mutilation of towns, villages, and land disturbed many of the men, and outrage regarding this was a regular feature of early letters—though it did not take long before the sight was so common that they became inured to it. One man declared:

It is an awful sight to see the villages close to the firing line. The houses are all blown up by shell fire. Churches are not respected either. One certain village that we passed through the church was blown to atoms, and hardly a tombstone in the churchyard was standing. Another village that we passed through when we were coming back from the trenches for the first time, I counted no fewer than twelve carts with furniture on of people who were leaving the place, as it was shelled so much. Some of the people were taking a few things on a barrow, and others were carrying a few things in baskets. When you see sights like those it makes you realise how fortunate the English people are in England. The roads here are awfully cut up with the transport and the troops. I have often heard France called sunny France, but I think it can well be named muddy France now.[10]

In a letter to a friend in Lancaster, Sgt Thomas Gill light-heartedly commented that 'it is also wonderful to see our airmen—quite a common thing to see them here. No half-crowns to see one now! All for nothing, only to keep ducking'. His tone darkens towards the end of the letter: '...to see the towns and villages in Belgium that have been wrecked by shells is awful. Scientific murder is the name for the greatest war in history'.[11] Thomas Gill was not to know just how prophetic these words were.

Not everyone from a company moved up when it was their turn at the Front. The CQMS and Company Stores personnel remained behind with Transport, making the nightly trek forwards after dark, burdened with rations and other necessaries for the trenches. With this being a training period, each company's stay at the Front was kept brief and the nightly ration-run dodging shellfire was much reduced from what would normally be expected during a tour in the trenches. One CQMS found this experience strange:

The night the boys marched off I felt like a leper—I dare not go near them. I stood in the dark watching them flit past like a phantom army. When the last file passed such a feeling of desolation came over me as I have not experienced before. Had I not been English I believe I should have shed tears. But being of a buoyant nature I did a wiser thing- I went to sleep, and the morning's duties gave me little opportunity of suffering from *ennui*. I am in a world of strangers, but I have made many friends. Many Canadians are here as well as Indians. The latter seem rather distressed with the trying weather. But when the sun asserts itself, I anticipate a great change in them.

The Ghurkhas look everything that has been said of them. I saw two of them charge a flock of goats and they were having a fearful time.[12]

The Battalion, advised by their more experienced counterparts in 2/King's Own, used the ubiquitous sandbag for more than its originally intended use. Rations were divided into six-man-per-day allocations and placed into a sandbag. These, tied in pairs, were slung across the back of a horse or mule, or packed into a limber. Other trench stores, such as wood, barbed wire, coal or coke, ammunition, and water were loaded into GS wagons and the convoy would ferry these to a dump as close to the trenches as the transport could safely manage. Once deposited, men from the forward company, or working parties from others, would lug it all forward. Winter naturally amplified the problems of supply, not just because of more difficult ground conditions, but also because far more fuel was needed to prevent men becoming hypothermic. Possibly the most important ration item when climate and events conspired to make life miserable was the issue of rum. The distribution of the tot was strictly monitored and could only take place under the supervision of an officer, and although issue was at the CO's discretion, not many commanding officers were blinkered enough to ban it.

The weather continued to be poor, with frequent snow—men also contending with deep mud and slush. The stench in this sector was frequently commented upon; the origin being the very shallow burials of French casualties close to the trenches, and in some cases actually in them, a situation that was poor for health and morale. One soldier from 2/King's Own reported:

We were over the knees in mud and water. The first thing I saw was a pair of shoes, soles up in the mud. Being badly in want of a pair I took hold of one of them only to find that it was on the foot of a soldier. After pulling we brought to the surface the body of a Frenchman, whom we had to cover up with the mud. We had several to bury like that. It was a gruesome experience.[13]

The weather did nothing for men's health and numbers reported sick with various pulmonary disorders. For thirty-two-year-old Sgt John Arkwright, a married man from Lancaster, bronchitis became pleurisy. Eventually, he was diagnosed with general debility and DAH (Disorderly Action of the Heart); he was evacuated home and medically discharged in April 1916. The close proximity of men also amplified the spread of infectious and contagious diseases, and one that particularly worried MOs was cerebrospinal meningitis—known as 'spotted fever'. Approximately three out of every four sufferers died and it also had the potential for epidemic, so as soon as a case was diagnosed, his close companions were quarantined. On 10 March, the wife of thirty-two-year-old L/Cpl Thomas Hartley received a telegram informing her that her husband was dangerously ill with this. The next day, the father of four from 'C' Company died, his wife being informed by another telegram two days later.

'C' Company's misfortunes continued on the evening of 12 March, when they took over the trenches from 'D' and Pte Albert Mogg from Morecambe was killed. The seventeen-year-old gave his age upon enlistment as twenty-three, his father enlisting in the Welsh Fusiliers at the same time. His father, who had already been wounded twice, was home on leave when the letter bearing the bad news arrived. German artillery fire was particularly savage the following day, mainly in response to the attack at Neuve Chappelle, 12 miles to their south and intended to spoil any preparations for a similar assault in that sector.

The 2IC Major John Bates, at HQ with the stretcher-bearers, wrote home to a friend about 'C' Company's day:

> We were not in the thick of it, but if it was any worse than our little stretch it must have been hell. The guns began to shell thousands of rounds an hour. They can pitch them straight and marvellously accurate, to just a few yards. Right in the thick of it, orders came down the trenches, 'All stretcher-bearers out'. They were not under rifle fire but the shelling was awful.

At 12.45 p.m., father of four young children Pte Hugh Rourke from Lancaster was hit, dying fifteen minutes later without regaining consciousness. Another man was also wounded, though his name is no longer on record. Maj. Bates was full of admiration for the courage of the responding stretcher-bearers:

> Three Morecambe lads went- Waddington, [Frank Waddington] Greenwood and Cotton. [Cyril Cotton] Brear [Frank Brear] was also out but not with this particular party. Their job was to go down to the dressing station; go back and back again for more, under the hottest shellfire that could be brought to bear upon them. Pluck is not the word for it. How they came through it can only be put down to God's good will. They were out for hours and did splendid work. Stanley saw it all. [His son, Lt Stanley Bates] He was in the trench (firing line) immediately behind them. He told me of it and expressed the opinion that if these chaps did not get the DCM it was not worth having. I was proud of the lads. I have seen one of them several times since, but all he will say that he 'was jolly frightened when he set off, but he got used to it'. Stanley also had a rough time. He was shelled for twelve solid hours. To make things more unpleasant our own guns went short and plugged a dozen shells on top of his sandbags before he could stop them by telephone. He lost one man [Hugh Rourke] and another wounded. A couple of feet more would have wiped them all out. They are only lads, but men in pluck. I was talking to their company officer [Capt. Eaves] and he told me they had no fear.[14]

It is not entirely clear from Maj. Bates' account if these two casualties were caused by 'friendly fire', though it reads as if they were. Sadly, British artillery fire dropping short onto British troops was a common problem—more due to worn guns shooting inconsistently, poorly made ammunition, or breakdowns in communication between guns and infantry than by incompetent gunnery. Particular poignancy was added to the death of Hugh Rourke as it was also his thirty-sixth birthday, just three days after his wife's. Mrs Rourke learned the news when she opened her mail on 17 March. The first letter was from Capt. Frederick Eaves, sending sympathy from himself and Lt-Col. Cavendish; the next letter was a birthday card to her from her husband, in which he had penned a few lines wishing her a happy birthday, adding that he hoped to be spared through the war and be able to say 'Hurrah for Old England'.[15]

The wounded collected by the stretcher-bearers included casualties from the regiment holding the adjoining length of trench. Twenty-one-year-old Pte Frank Brear received the MM for his courage and Cyril Cotton, a MiD. For the others, apart from praise from the CO and approbation of their peers (such as Pte George Bell, who wrote home expressing his admiration for their deeds), no official recognition was forthcoming. Bravery awards, particularly in the early years of the war, were frequently turned down at higher levels, purely because the limited 'quota' for the month had been exceeded—a situation that affected officers and men alike. It must also be remembered that the only awards that could be awarded posthumously were a MiD and VC—if the deed was below the considered standard for a VC and the soldier was killed in the act then no medal could be awarded. This did not change until 1974.

Once safely back in billets, one of 'C' Company's signallers wrote to a pal in Morecambe:

We are just about getting used to farm and country life. The barn is our combined dining, sitting and bedroom. We are only about three miles from the German position here. Our big guns are going nearly all day and part of the night, but we don't let the noise disturb our peaceful slumbers. We have had a turn in the firing line, and I know what it is like to be under shellfire. I am a signaller and we are now busy learning the Morse code. We have lost two of our boys up to the present—both Morecambe lads. We shall soon have forgotten what a bed and a bath are like. All the days are alike here. Last Sunday I was having an exciting time from 3 till 4. The Germans were shelling us, and I thought of you enjoying the same time in the P.S.A [the P.S.A., or 'Pleasant Sunday Afternoon' Brotherhood, was a Non-Conformist association for Christian men].[16]

'A' Company suffered one wounded on 13 March. Twenty-year-old Pte George Squirrell was waiting for their relief by 'B' Company and decided to scrape the mud off his boots. As he lifted one foot up onto the fire step, a shell exploded overhead, a jagged splinter hitting him in the knee. As he was being carried out of the firing line by L/Cpl Storey, the NCO stumbled and both sprawled face-down in the mud—a fortunate accident as another shell exploded nearby, peppering the area where they would have been standing with shrapnel. Squirrel was evacuated to England for treatment, and after his partial recovery, transferred to the Labour Corps.[17] His younger brother, John, also in 'A' Company, was soon to leave the Battalion in equally unhappy circumstances. This day was also the last day in office for RQMS Joseph Woodcock, who was invalided home sick, C/Sgt Tom Wolfenden becoming RQMS.

As fatalities rose, the QM's memoirs no longer recorded the names of individual men killed. Three tragedies occurred on 15 March, although one took place about as far away from the front line as it was possible to get. While Lancaster soldier Pte Thomas Goulding was in the trenches, his thirty-two-year-old wife, Agnes, heavily pregnant with their eighth child, died at home. The inquest determined that death was due to heart failure, brought about by a swollen liver.[18] Since mobilisation, it had been a long time away from their families and their loved ones would have been constantly in men's thoughts— especially in the miserable conditions they were currently existing in. The news of his wife's death must have been extremely distressing, exacerbated by the knowledge that his seven children now had neither mother nor father to comfort them. One thing that can be assured was that his mates in his section and platoon would have closed ranks around him to help him through it. Goulding was granted compassionate leave from 2 May to arrange for the care of his children. 'D' Company, operating Trench 10A, lost twenty-six-year-old Pte Seth Bond from Fleetwood. Terribly wounded, he died that night *en route* to the CCS. Also killed was another Fleetwood man, nineteen-year-old Pte Geoffrey Hayes.

On 16 March, 'B' Company suffered their first casualty when Pte John 'Jack' Ghorst was hit in the arm by a machine-gun bullet. His brother, Harry, also in 'B' Company, wrote to their mother the next day:

> I suppose you will be sorry to hear that Jack has been wounded in the arm. He'll not see the war again. You can expect him home again in about a fortnight. He'll be a long time before he is better. His arm is broken. I helped to carry him to be dressed. He is quite cheerful. It is rather a dangerous place where we are stopping today. We have just been relieved from the trenches after having been in three days, and we are in a barn. Two or three shells have been quite close to. I'd sooner be in the trenches. We are hoping to be moved tonight for a few days' rest. I hope you will keep sending me an ounce or two of twist. The tobacco we get here is rotten. Don't be alarmed about Jack, and don't get bothering about me. I'll be all right.[19]

Unfortunately, Harry Ghorst was quite wrong with two of these assumptions.

On 17 March, as they left the trenches for their billets, 'B' Company soldier twenty-four-year-old Pte Herbert Carradice (known to friends as 'Lewthwaite') was wounded in the leg by shrapnel. He is a good example of how close the family ties were within the Regiment as his brother (George), two brothers-in-law (Christopher Townson and Percy Smith), and a nephew (Lawrence Tetley) all served in the Battalion, and his older brother William was with 1/King's Own. For Lewthwaite, there would soon be terrible news. There were seven father-son combinations in the Battalion and all bred tragedy.

Twenty-six-year-old Pte William Grove from Fleetwood was also seriously wounded as he carried rations to Capt. William Carter in 'D' Company's reserve position at Burnt Farm. The projectile entered an eye and carried away part of his skull. Amazingly, he survived the injury, but was medically discharged in November. Ration delivery was particularly dangerous as enemy artillery, knowing that this was a regular activity, had the routes into the firing line accurately registered and would fire speculative barrages throughout the night. In a letter to his father, Pte Albert Richardson from the Transport section explained that even though he had only made one trip up delivering rations, fresh shell craters along their route made the journey difficult. He also reported how his pal in the same section, Pte Adam Billington from Pilling, got a bullet straight through his hat when he made the journey, but had only laughed about it.[20]

On 18 March, 'D' Company had another man wounded while in support. Twenty-four-year-old Pte John Entwistle was hit in the left leg by shrapnel and evacuated home. On 20 March, Pte George Hillman, from 9 Platoon, took advantage of some 'down time' as they were in reserve and wrote to his father, a builder in Morecambe. His letter attacked the 'knuts' who had not enlisted, and was forwarded to the local paper by his father. Knuts, or 'nuts' were idle and blasé young men for whom everything was 'just too much trouble', epitomised by Basil Hallam's popular music hall character Gilbert the Filbert:

It is terribly hard weather here, snow and sharp winds. We feel it most at night; no such thing as bedtime, it is all roughing it here, and we have not had our clothes off since we left England! Every British soldier out here deserves a small fortune. I am not saying this because I am here, but if I had my way I would make some of those 'knuts' in Morecambe come out here and have a try of it; and then they would not say that we were fools for coming out. It would be a bad thing for England if we all felt the same.[21]

Pte Charles Williams from Lancaster also wrote home:

I am well, but a bit tired. We are in the trenches at present; today is out fifth day, and we don't expect to be relieved until Tuesday night, so I do not think we are doing badly for Territorials. This is the third time I have been in the trenches, so I am getting quite used to it by now. We are in—but what part I dare not say. This morning I went for a walk to the end of the trench, and in one field close to a farm there were seven cows and a pig dead. All the farms are in ruins that are in range of artillery fire. The Germans respect nothing. Fine churches and houses are blown to atoms with their fire. It is no unusual sight to see a monster German shell laid in the road which has not exploded. They are a cunning lot of chaps we have in front of us. Yesterday (Sunday) they were trying to draw our fire with dummy men that they kept sticking up in their trenches. They were not successful as we had no desire to be sniped.[22]

'C' Company had two men wounded on 21 March: L/Cpl James Mackereth's wound was inconsequential and he was soon back; Pte William Parr was evacuated home and after recovery was discharged as his term of enlistment was over. He re-enlisted in April 1916, although not into the infantry, volunteering instead for the Ordnance Corps. Unsurprisingly, cold, wet conditions led to trench foot and twenty-two-year-old Pte George Morley from Carnforth was evacuated home with it. He was transferred to the RE upon his recovery and killed in action in February 1918. Trench foot happened when feet that had been cold and wet for days on end swelled (boots restricted blood supply); eventually, if left untreated, gangrene set in, with amputation the only solution. Doctors soon realised the cause and the incidence of trench foot was much diminished in subsequent winters when proper precautions were taken. Trenches became better drained, gum-boots were issued, platoon officers inspected the feet of their men on a daily basis, both in and out of the line, and men rubbed their feet with whale oil—a vile-smelling, but effective preventative.

The night of 21–22 March was a busy one for 'B' Company, who spent six hours during a blinding snowstorm out in front of the parapets of Trenches 8 and 9A, trying to build up an earth bank in front of the sandbag wall—only clambering back to their own side of the sandbags as dawn approached. Throughout the night, the enemy sent up flare after flare and the rattle of small arms fire was incessant. Pte Joseph Bateson from Lancaster was hit in the wrist and evacuated home—the injury proving serious enough to prevent further military service and he was medically discharged in November—no doubt to the relief of his wife, whose sister had recently lost her husband in the war. Another casualty was Pte William Wood, also evacuated home and transferred to the Labour Corps as no longer 'infantry fit'.

Movement along these trenches was fraught with danger as in places it was open to German observation, and enemy snipers maintained a vigil on these vulnerable spots. Twenty-year-old Pte Watkin Rundle from Lancaster volunteered to carry rations to men in the next section of trench and was shot through the shoulder and lung by a sniper as he crossed the exposed traverse. His pals braved a similar fate to crawl over and drag him back behind cover, patching his wound as best as they could. Watkin's pal, Pte Edmund 'Teddy' Hannam, the Honorary Secretary and Treasurer of Lancaster Cricket Club before enlistment, heard the shot and went to the end of the trench to see what had happened to his pal. He too was hit, the round striking him in the abdomen. Teddy's pals pulled him back into cover and patched the entry and exit wounds. Both men lay in the trench until it was dark enough to evacuate them safely. Teddy wrote from hospital in Manchester to Procter, a friend in Lancaster:

After I was hit I lay in the trench until about 8 p.m. I was pretty comfortable, excepting for cold feet. The other fellows looked after me first rate. I had about a mile to go on the stretcher to headquarters. Dr George didn't do anything as I was well bandaged. I went from there in a motor ambulance to D__ [Dranoutre], where the RAMC doctor attended to us. Shaking up on those rotten roads was pretty bad. From there we went to Bailleul and lay up till 9 a.m., when we were taken to the train and lay on the seats of a first class corridor. We left and got to Le Tréport, via Boulogne in the early hours of the morning. We expected to leave any day, but actually stayed till Easter Sunday. I was quite alright there. Leaving at 9 a.m., we got to Havre about 10.30 p.m. The French trains are fearfully slow, and stop at thousands of places. I came across on the *Oxfordshire* and it was very comfortable. It was all fitted up with beds and I couldn't feel any motion at all. We got to Southampton about 9 a.m. and left at 1.15 p.m. The trains were fitted up with beds, top and bottom, running lengthways, and we could sit up and look out of the window. I enjoyed the journey first rate. Whenever we stopped people gave us fruit, cigarettes, etc. We got to Manchester at 8 p.m.[23]

Remarkably, Hannam survived this wound. He was transferred to the RE after he left hospital, commissioned with them in 1917, and survived the war. Rundle's journey mirrored that of his pal until their arrival in England, when he went to a Glasgow hospital. He too recovered from his wound, was posted to 2/5th King's Own, and went to France with them in 1917, rising to sergeant by the end of the war.

Stretcher-bearers remained behind when their company went forward, staying near the dressing station, waiting for the call to deal with casualties. One of 'B' Company's bearers carried his friend and fellow violinist, Rundle, out of the line:

Our company up to now has been singularly free from many casualties, so that I have not had much to do. 'C' Company, the Morecambe lot have got it worst so far, and their stretcher-bearers have had some trying cases. But there will be lots to do for all of us when the big advance we have heard so much about takes place. Already three bullets have whizzed within an inch of me, apart from the usual stray shots that are the lot of all those who have to walk about amongst and behind the trenches. After a time we get quite used to bullets and never stop or duck when the German star shells go up and light up the scene. Most soldiers become temporary fatalists—'if you are going to be hit, you will be hit and you can't bother to dodge each bullet that comes, especially when you are carrying a man on a stretcher'. This is the usual attitude. In one case it took our bearers five hours to get a man to the dressing station. The Germans had spotted them, and got a Maxim on a corner of a trench round which they had to go, and they were on the ground for twenty minutes without moving. We get some exciting times, but on the whole our men are a lively and cheerful crush—the stretcher-bearers I mean. I am getting used to the life here and am enjoying myself. Certainly it is strange working at night, but as long as I can get enough to eat, and occasionally something to read I can last as long as you please.[24]

Another man also had to be carried out:

Towards night it came on very cold, and we have no blankets or bear skins, only our overcoats and oilsheet. I was seized with the cold and could not move a muscle. They sent for the stretcher-bearers and they came. Geo. Slinger and another comrade very bravely volunteered to carry me out. They had to do it in the dark and under fire. It was a two-mile walk to the dressing station. After a rough journey I arrived safe and was left under the good care of Dr George.[25]

After relief by 3/Monmouths on the night of 22 March and a long and exhausting trek, their 3 a.m. arrival at billets was a great relief. Less welcome was the demand for 500 men from 'A', 'B', and 'C' Company on the morning of 25 March to dig a new trench line near Wulverghem—a working party that lasted until 1.30 a.m. on the 26th. At 5.30 p.m. on 27 March, they marched out of their billets, bound for the trenches near Wulverghem again, arriving at 8 p.m. 'A' Company occupied 8 and 9A; 'D' Company in 10A; 'B' in support at Souvenir Farm; and 'C' in reserve at Watermill Farm.

'A' Company had their first casualty as they moved up, when Pte John Ismay was hit in the stomach. Orphaned at a very early age, he was fostered by Mrs Cooper, the mother of Pte John Pye (296). Their uncle, John Pye (785) was a sergeant in 'C' Company at the time, though reverted to Pte at his own request shortly afterwards. Pye (296) wrote to his mother about the man he considered his brother: 'I saw him before they took him to hospital and he said he would get all right again. He told me to write to you and send you his love. He will be coming over to England shortly'.[26] Sadly, that was not to be the case and he died on 30 March. The matron at the hospital penned a few lines to Mrs Cooper:

> We did all in our power to save him but it was to no avail. God called him to his rest. He was in hospital three hours after he received his wound, and so was treated in good time. He will be buried in our small cemetery tomorrow. May God comfort you.[27]

For poor Mrs Cooper, worse was to follow.

The next fatality, on 29 March, was 'A' Company's Pte Charles Stirzaker, a popular twenty-five-year-old from Lancaster. As was far from uncommon, his family heard about their son's death in letters from his friends and officers before the official notification letter reached them from the Infantry Records Office in Preston. George Mawson and John Cooke, Stirzaker's pals from 'A' Company, both wrote, as did his platoon officer, Lt Frank Bingham, and company commander, Capt. Ernest Atkinson. Officialdom's delay in contacting his kin was neither inefficiency nor an uncaring attitude by Records— official notification had to pass through a number of hands before it reached them, a process that took time. They also tended to get overwhelmed, particularly when a big action was under way. On just one day in 1917, Preston had to send notifications of over 4,000 casualties from 55 Division alone—no doubt also having to convey the news of dead and wounded from other divisions, who also came under Preston, one of only twelve offices dealing with infantry battalions from seventy-five divisions.

The two companies in reserve and support were kept busy while their comrades operated the Front. Three platoons from 'C' were attached to the RE for three days— digging CTs and building defensive wire entanglements. 'B' had to provide a platoon to guard Point T10a, the remainder engaged in general trench maintenance and carrying parties. Over the 29th and 30th, a number of casualties ensued. On 29 March, Pte William Jackson from 'B' Company was wounded. The diary records a total of three wounded on the 29th and another two on the 30th, however, division recorded this as one on the 29th and four on 30 March. Slight inconsistencies like this abound, and men who became casualties late at night usually (but not always) appear on the paperwork for the following day. Two of these were from 'D'—Pte Harold Matthews, who returned to the Battalion after his recovery and Pte Adam Bailey, who was later transferred to the Tank Corps. 'C' Company's Pte Thomas Robinson was hit in the calf by a bullet as he helped the RE to erect barbed wire, but the injury to thirty-four-year-old Pte James Madden from 'A' is unusual.[28] His service record notes him as being 'wounded in action', but the injury he was treated for was a bayonet wound to the left leg.[29] Had this been an accidental injury, it would have been noted as such, but there is no record of any patrol activity. The most seriously wounded was also from 'A' Company; Pte Thomas Jones's injuries led to his death at Bailleul on 7 April. On 31 March, the Battalion was relieved by 3/Monmouths and left for Ravetsbergh and onto Boeschepe at 3 p.m. on 3 April for rest.

Their first month in the trenches had been very unpleasant as far as conditions went, but the casualty list was quite a gentle introduction to the horrors of industrial warfare. Eighteen NCOs and men had been wounded, one man died from disease, and another seven were killed in action or died from wounds. However, it is doubtful if anyone in the Battalion foresaw what was about to happen to them over the next five weeks.

4 April 1915–30 April 1915: Scientific Murder

Coordinates for Positions Named in this Chapter

Cemetery, Polygon Wood	50°51′25.00″N 2°59′22.20″E	Polygon Wood L-trench	50°50′55.90″N 2°59′34.90″E
Crossroads N of St Jean	50°52′25.30″N 2°53′54.20″E	Polygon Wood R-trench	50°50′56.50″N 2°59′12.70″E

The Battalion remained at Boeschepe until 8.30 a.m. on 9 April, then returned to 28 Division at Ypres. Their arrival coincided with a barrage of shrapnel from enemy artillery, though providentially men and animals reached cover without loss. Much of the city still lay more or less intact, though the eastern edge, Cloth Hall, and cathedral had been devastated earlier. Civilians still occupied the town, but wisely remained in their cellars during artillery exchanges. The next day, ten of the officers went forward to inspect the trenches the Battalion would shortly be occupying, and one unlucky company was put straight onto fatigues, another taking their place the following day.

Cpl Robert Davies from Lancaster penned a letter to his old headmaster at Bowerham School, Mr G. R. Roberts:

We have enjoyed ten days rest since our last sojourn in the trenches, and ten days of actual bliss they were, although we were billeted in dirty barns which had sheltered many a thousand troops before we occupied them. Rest when out of the trenches is only a relative term, as generally three parades a day have to be gone through. Personally, I have worked rather hard during 'rest' as witness a sample day.

5 p.m. up, dress and wash so as to be ready to draw rations for breakfast for my section. Breakfast over, it is time for physical drill, and I have to be responsible to the officer in command of my platoon that my section is out ready and correctly dressed. Then for drill. This altogether takes until 8.30 a.m. From this until 10 a.m. we are busy cleaning rifles,

etc., because at that hour rifles are examined before company drills are commenced. This parade is from 10 a.m. until 1 p.m., with another parade looming in the near future, i.e. from 3 to 5 p.m. After dinner (1 p.m.) I have to check each man's ammunition to ensure that he has 120 rounds plus fifty on a bandolier. If any shortage, I report to the platoon sergeant and go with him to draw the rounds deficient. After 5 p.m., tea being over, there are multifarious duties awaiting one's time, such as written reports on the day's work etc. I finish generally about 5.30 p.m. after about 13 ½ hours work. Not bad eh![1]

At 8.30 p.m. on 12 April, the Battalion moved off to relieve the Monmouths at Polygon Wood, one company leaving every fifteen minutes. For one platoon, there had been changes; Boer War veteran L/Sgt James Rumley had incurred the wrath of authority and marched up to the line as a private soldier once more. Unfortunately, relief was not completed until 2.45 a.m. as the Monmouths' guide got them lost and two men were wounded on the journey. One was thirty-year-old Pte Frank Bradley from Lancaster, who wrote to his mother from No. 8 General Hospital in Rouen. She passed this information along to the local paper:

He was seated on the ground, resting, along with the others, on the way to the trenches when he was wounded in the thick part of the left leg. Bullets were flying in all directions and he was kept in a dugout in a wood for twenty hours before removal to hospital, where he says, he is being looked after 'champion' and doing well. Of course he adds, 'I am for the firing line again when I get better, and I wouldn't like to come home and think my mates were all at war. I am game to the finish.'[2]

Polygon Wood had until very recently been French-held. Lt-Col. Cavendish was unimpressed, as he commented in his diary:

It was very interesting seeing French trenches for the first time. They are different from ours- the traverses badly built, badly drained, and in many places the parapet not nearly thick enough. The Germans are active opposite. The lines are about 200 yards apart at their widest and gradually converge until they almost touch.[3]

This extension to the British line had been requested by Gen. Joffre, the French commander. The Official History (OH) describes these positions as being isolated groups of shallow fire and support trenches, with sandbag walls so thin that they were not bullet-proof; they also lacked a parados, had little or no sanitation, and had few CTs— those that did link fire and support trenches were only around 2 feet deep.[4] There was also concern about the dugouts, which were little better than shelter from the weather and provided sparse protection from hostile artillery. The French had relied upon their 75-mm guns to make these trenches defensible. The British with their limited artillery and ammunition supply did not have this option.

'D' Company held reserve and 'A' support. 'C' manned the left trench and 'B' the right. The CO's concerns about the parapets were confirmed next day.

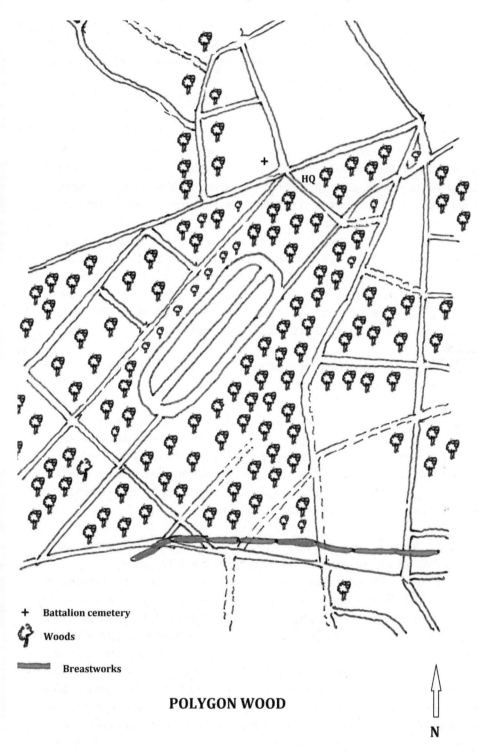

+   Battalion cemetery

Woods

Breastworks

POLYGON WOOD

N

Enemy trench mortars targeted the front line for much of 13 April, the Battalion, lacking any form of retaliation—British trench mortars virtually non-existent at this time—suffered almost as many casualties on that day as in the whole of the previous month. One of the first to be wounded, when a trench mortar round exploded adjacent to him, was Pte Sydney Walker. A former classmate, Pte Joseph Mashiter, wrote to their old teacher:

> Sorry that I have to convey to you the sad news that one of our Caton boys was seriously wounded on the 13th—Syd Walker. He was hit in the head at 7.30 in the morning, and had to stay in the trench until night before we could remove him. He suffered much pain but stuck it like a hero, being very patient. You will be surprised to hear that there were only ten yards between our trench and the Germans, so we were able to talk to them quite comfortably, as there was one German who could talk English well, and there were many exciting passages exchanged. But of course we had to be careful not to show ourselves, as they had, too. I had a very narrow escape as we were going into the trenches. A bullet passed into my valise (that is our bag which we carry on our back for our necessaries), through a package of salt and into a tin box of cigarettes. That is what I call a close shave. I am keeping the box as a souvenir.[5]

The proximity of the Germans led to some amusing interactions. One man, writing home during his next rest period, avowed:

> We have been in the worst trenches—'Hell's Gate'—and a right name for it! The German trench is only ten yards away, and they threw a parsnip over with a piece of paper tied to it saying, 'Our rifles sing a song of hate to you'. We sent it back and told them, 'We fight like Englishmen. How would you like a half-hour with the bayonets?' but they were having none. They say we are 'mad Lancaster devils', for they know what our first and second battalions gave them to go on with.[6]

On another day, it was potatoes instead of parsnips and the Lancastrians in that end of the trench retaliated with the massed mouth organ playing of 'Tipperary'.[7]

Even a near miss could cause significant damage, and twenty-five-year-old Pte Robert Higginson was badly bruised and had the wind knocked out of him when he was buried under a pile of sandbags blasted from the parapet. Mid-morning, five Carnforth men from 'C' Company finished repairing one section and were standing together, when a mortar round landed inside the trench next to them. Twenty-one-year-old L/Cpl John (Jack) Harper took the brunt of the blast and was killed instantly—his body undoubtedly partially shielding the others. Nineteen-year-old Pte Frank Iniff was wounded in both legs and Pte Myles Mason in his back—both men's wounds necessitating evacuation home. Twenty-four-year-old Pte Henry Burrows' head wound was minor and he spent time in a base hospital in Rouen. The last of the five casualties was Pte Robert Forrester—admitted with concussion and a minor head wound to the same hospital.

Although happy with his medical care, his letter home was less than enthusiastic about Polygon Wood:

> We are doing champion. The trenches we are in are the worst in the whole line. Capt. Eaves was about done in when so many of us were getting wounded. We had thirteen wounded in our platoon in half-an-hour.[8]

Forrester was wrong about these being the worst trenches in the whole line—they would discover these on the Frezenberg Ridge in May.

The other man killed on 13 April was seventeen-year-old Pte Joseph Nash from Lancaster, shot through the head. The news first reached Lancaster when the licensee of the Athenaeum Hotel, thirty-year-old Pte Herbert Hunter, wrote to his wife the next day (Herbert Hunter rose to sergeant, was commissioned in October 1917, and killed in action with the 1/4th in April 1918). Another pal, twenty-four-year-old Pte Francis Gardner, wrote home about his pal's death:

> One of the chaps who was killed was my chum, and he was only five yards off me when it happened. Poor Joe, only two minutes before he was shot he said, 'Allemande! Good if he doesn't shoot me.' He was hit immediately after and died without saying another word. He was a good pal and I shall miss him. Two days afterwards a shell dropped in the trench and killed three more. I helped carry them down to Headquarters.[9]

This was not the last time that standing near to Francis Gardner would turn out to be perilous.

Shelling continued throughout 13 April, and around 5 p.m., twenty-one-year-old Pte Edward Gardner was hit in the leg. The wound warranted evacuation home, but at least his wait in the trenches for the cloak of darkness to protect his evacuation was shorter than for many. For twenty-four-year-old Pte Richard Hothersall from Marsh, what seemed a minor wound, proved deadly. A shrapnel ball hit him in the left thumb while he was holding his rifle in the 'aiming position', travelled up inside the length of his arm, and penetrated his chest. With just an entry wound to the thumb, the medics treating him in the trench could not have realised how serious the wound was—even if they had, there was no way to evacuate him before dark. He died at the field hospital from a wound that would probably even prove fatal today.

Even under the shroud of darkness, evacuation was still fraught with danger. With so many casualties, Capt. Eaves asked for volunteer stretcher-bearers and Pte Thomas Helm from Lancaster stepped forward immediately. As he helped to carry Frank Iniff's stretcher, he was hit in the back by a bullet that penetrated his liver. The three uninjured stretcher-bearers carried out a piece of rapid triage and, much to his surprise, Iniff once again found himself lying upon the ground—his place on the stretcher taken by Helm, who was evacuated to a London hospital where the bullet was eventually extracted. Luckily for Iniff, two stretcher-bearers on their way back to the trenches stopped, and between them carried him to the dressing station. Helm received a medical discharge.

Around 6 p.m., former Lancaster schoolmaster Pte Harold Chapman was guiding the Brigade-Major through the trenches when a bullet ripped through the sandbags and struck him in the left arm near the shoulder. A field dressing was applied in the company-commander's dugout, and with the help of a pal, Pte William Pinch, Chapman made his own way back to HQ. *En route*, they met a stretcher party from 2/Kings who were lost and guided them to their own dressing station before continuing. When they arrived, the ambulance had already left, so, after Dr George dressed his wound properly, Chapman spent the night in the Guides' dugout. The next morning, he was passed down the medical chain until he reached a hospital with X-ray equipment, where the bullet was extracted.

There was no respite on 14 April. As men assembled for the routine dawn stand-to, there was a 'crack' and twenty-two-year-old machine-gunner Pte Christopher Whiteside from Lancaster fell dead, shot through the head by a sniper. The news reached home quickly as both his younger brother, Joseph, and platoon sergeant Thomas Gill wrote. It was not Gill's only letter that day—his earlier description of the war as 'scientific murder' coming to pass. Less than an hour later, as sixteen-year-old Pte Matthew Farrell from the MG section helped the stretcher-bearers lift Whiteside's body, the sniper claimed his second victim. Farrell was another to lie about his age on enlistment, but got away with the deception as he was 6 feet tall and built strongly. His height was probably his undoing, as the distraction of moving his friend's body was enough for him to forget to bend low in those badly built trenches. A few days after his death, a number of letters dropped through his mother's letterbox—the one in Matthew's handwriting eagerly opened first. Dated the 13th, it ended: 'Don't bother about me. I will look after myself. I shall see that they go over my head ... but I hope I will have the good luck to see this job over'.[10]

The second letter was from Pte Daniel Winder, who was courting Ellen, Matthew's sister (they married in 1916):

> It's bad news I'm sending you. Matt was killed today (Wednesday.) He was not in any pain, death being instantaneous. Chris Whiteside was killed about half-an-hour before, in the same place. I feel broken-hearted about it.[11]

Farrell had not quite been the youngest to go to France with the Battalion—that honour went to Pte Ronald Oswald born in May 1899, who later transferred to the RWF.

The previous day's bombardment had highlighted the weaknesses of these French-built trenches. Apart from the thin walls, the portions dug into the ground had no revetment and continually collapsed inwards. Few of the materials requested by the CO turned up—he had ordered 3,000 sandbags, but only received 650—and no wood for revetment had arrived. In the late afternoon, an 'A' Company working party was in the woods cutting timber for the repairs, while others built more dugouts. Either seen or heard by the enemy, they were on the receiving end of nine rounds of shrapnel in a matter of minutes, causing numerous casualties—just one shell accounting for ten.

One of those killed was nineteen-year-old Pte John 'Jack' Churchouse from Lancaster, stepson of CQMS Thomas Byrne. Capt. Atkinson immediately sent a runner to find the CQMS, who was on his way forward with the company's rations. Byrne did not want his wife to hear about their son's death by letter and got his pal, Armourer-Sergeant John Lamb, to write to his wife—a friend of Mrs Byrne—asking her to break the news gently. Giving this letter a day's start, he then wrote his own letter:

I little thought when I wrote to you last Wednesday that I would next have to let you know that our dear son had been killed. I was informed when we were half-way on the road with their rations, and they asked if I would like to go and see him. I went to where he had been laid, but he had been buried when I got there. They laid him peacefully away. The Colonel and other officers came and asked me to express their great sorrow and sympathy with you in the great blow. I was informed that his end was peaceful. He would not be conscious as he was killed instantaneously.[12]

Also killed was twenty-six-year-old father of two Pte Tom Clarke from Lancaster. Twenty-five-year-old Pte William Smith from Lancaster was very badly wounded in the head; he died on the 16th at a CCS in Hazebrouck. Twenty-three-year-old Pte Oswald Towers succumbed to his wounds the next day. Pte Gilbert Shaw's wounds to hand, arm, and shoulder resulted in transfer to the Labour Corps, no longer fit enough for the infantry. Pte Charles Skeats' arm wound was treated in England, but he would return; Pte Ernest Graham's wound above the knee was less serious, and after a few days in hospital, he was back on duty. One of the blasts buried twenty-two-year-old Pte George Pearcy, but twenty-three-year-old Pte George Auty dug him out—something his rescuer would need doing for himself in less than a month. George Pearcy was physically uninjured, but led away to the dressing station, deeply shocked. Though Pte Frederick Cottam's head wound put him in hospital, he was able to write to his wife:

I have been wounded, but it is not very serious—just a crack on the head with shrapnel. It happened about four o'clock in the afternoon. There was about a hundred of us digging, when all at once a shell burst right amongst us, and then they came rapidly for about five minutes and finished just as suddenly. I did not get hit till the last shot.[13]

Pte William Owen was wounded in the bombardment, and although evacuated home for treatment, he later returned to the Battalion. He wrote to a friend in Lancaster about the ordeal:

...well, we had been working for a couple of hours, when we got a shock, and then seven more followed. Oh it was terrible and we might all have been wiped out. I dropped flat on the ground every time one came. This presence of mind, for which I thank God for, saved my life, because I was talking to one chap before the crisis, and when I looked round again I found him with his brains blown out. Poor lad! I thank God that I did not share the same fate as some of my comrades, who have died honourably for their country. Our greatest sympathy must go out to their parents. I'm getting on grand. I see they put my photo in the *Guardian*. I was surprised when I saw it, also that of my chum, Drummer C. Brodie who is in the same ward as me.[14]

Twenty-year-old Pte Charles Brodie (7) was wounded in the knee—the married father of three very young children never served in the infantry again. However, both his brother, Joseph, and father, Charles (010), were still with 'A' Company and far from safe.

Another man wrote home on the 17th about his close escape during this barrage:

We have got shifted again and it's a terrible shop. We had a lot of casualties the first day. It was an experience of what hell is and I don't want another. As we were going to some trenches we had to go through a wood which was literally swarming with dead horses, and the smell was awful. We had just got into the centre of the wood when the Germans started shelling it. Well we had to take any cover we could get, and I tumbled over a dead horse. Its ribs went in, but I laid where I was, till another shell banged the top of a tree, and it caught me fair on the 'thinking box', and I made my way out of the wood after the nerve-testing experience with a champion heart. Our company had just had a severe blow, twenty-two casualties. I helped the stretcher-bearers tonight when they brought in a young lad who was shot through the head and killed. War is simply hell let loose. There have been over fifty killed and wounded in less than twenty-four hours [he should be forgiven for this exaggeration, as the week's total would be far greater]. You feel it when your mates go down.[15]

The final death of that day demonstrates perfectly the drawbacks caused for next-of-kin by a postal system that operated more quickly than official casualty notification. This could be a good thing—as in the example of Jack Churchouse—however, with twenty-year-old Pte Thomas Robinson, this was anything but the case. His mother first heard about her son's death from a journalist, who had asked her to confirm it. Confirmation from another, kindlier source came when his older brother, Robert, a corporal in the Battalion (known as 'Herbert' to the family), wrote to his father explaining how he had first heard the news:

I did not know whether it was right or not, so I got permission from the platoon officer to go to the Headquarters when it was dark, and I came across the medical orderly who was a great friend of Tom's. He said that they had buried him earlier in the night. They buried him with all his things except the ring which my dear mother gave him, which I shall get later and send home. Tom died instantaneously, and it did not disfigure him.[16]

Tom Robinson was struck in the right side by a large shell splinter while he was carrying a despatch, and his brother was undoubtedly accurate in describing death as instantaneous. It was not just the speed of unofficial notification that caused problems, the accuracy sometimes left much to be desired. Local papers twice reported Pte George Coulton from Beetham dead and once as seriously wounded; fortunately, all three reports were unfounded, but it must have been an agonising time for his wife.

On 15 April, 'A' Company were brought forward from support and fed into the left of the line to strengthen the depleted 'C' Company. In turn, 'D' Company was pulled forward from reserve and placed as support in the communications trench immediately behind the left of the line, although it was 'B' Company's turn to be targeted that day, as artillery fire was concentrated on the right. Although no one was killed, some discovered that the protection of their dugouts was mostly illusory. Although the diary only lists five men wounded, records indicate the actual figure was eight. Pte Frank Bower and his pal, Pte Andrew Jackson, were sheltering in their dugout when shells burst above—two very close to the dugout. Believing they were safe, the pair elected to stay put, but the next shell landed directly on top of the dugout and breached the roof. Bower suffered serious cuts and bruising to hands and arms; Jackson suffered a serious leg wound. Their decision was probably correct—it was more dangerous outside. Another wounded while sheltering in his dugout was twenty-eight-year-old Pte Albert Dixon from Lancaster. He was not seriously injured and returned after a couple of weeks. Bruised and shaken after being partially buried, eighteen-year-old Pte William Crarey was treated at the dressing station, but soon returned to duty. Twenty-four-year-old Pte John Parkinson, who was in the trenches rather than a dugout, was hit by shrapnel in the ankle and evacuated home. Artillery fire continued into the night, wounding two men. Cpl Charles Heys from Galgate had an eardrum burst by a shell exploding directly above him, a minor head injury, and the rifle he was holding smashed to pieces—a remarkable escape. The other, Pte Frank Brooks from Morecambe, was buried by sandbags in the remains of his trench and suffered abdominal crush injuries. These persisted and he was transferred to the Labour Corps and awarded a small pension following the war.

Friday brought their fourth consecutive day of bombardment—the casualty list increasing as 'B' Company bore the brunt. At 9 a.m., hearing the sounds of an incoming mortar rounds, a number of men dived for cover in the dugouts. Twenty-four-year-old Pte Reginald Simpson, twenty-year-old Pte Reginald Blackhurst, and twenty-three-year-old Pte Fred Eltoft all made for the same dugout. With space for only one on the right-hand side, Simpson dived in there—Blackhurst and Eltoft taking the left. The mortar round landed square on top of the left-hand dugout with catastrophic results. Blackhurst, who had pinned a 'lucky' horseshoe to his clothing when he left Lancaster Station in 1914, was killed outright. Eltoft was terribly injured, but remained conscious for a while before he passed away. His brother-in-law and friend, Capt. Fawcett, must have had some appallingly difficult letters to write. Pte Hubert Lilley was wounded by the same shell:

> I got two nasty shrapnel wounds in the small of the back, but I am pleased to say that I am going on well, but I'm afraid my back will be very weak for a long time owing to the shock. Reggie Blackhurst and Freddie Eltoft, two of my chums of the Two Hundred, were killed by the same bomb. I feel awfully sorry for the Blackhursts as Reg was their idol.[17]

Lilley was evacuated home and spent his eighteenth birthday in England. Just 10 yards from where the shell landed, thirty-six-year-old stretcher-bearer Pte John Livesey, a father of six from Lancaster, was flattened by the blast and evacuated that evening with shell-shock. A gentle soul and pre-war member of St John's Ambulance, the scenes of carnage among his friends were just too much for him. His condition did not improve and he was given a permanent medical discharge and pension for 'total incapacity' just under a year later.[18]

A third man from the dugout, Pte John Ogden, was also killed. In a letter to his parents in Lancaster on 18 April, Pte Harry Read mourned the loss of Blackhurst and Eltoft:

> [They were] two of the best pals. I have had my usual luck. Three fellows were killed in the dugout that I was in. Out of our section we only have four men left, including myself, so you can tell how heavily hit our lot has been. If people in England knew what it was to go through a period of shelling, and if they saw all the lives sacrificed, they would stop striking, as working men have been doing, for a paltry sum of money. Last night after we had been relieved, there was a perfect bombardment of the enemy's lines by our heavy artillery, and this morning news has come through that the place had been taken [the attack on Hill 60 by 13 Brigade]. Thank heaven that we were not in the attack. It must have been sheer murder. Even the sound of the firing was enough to drive anyone silly. Half of our men have shattered nerves. I have had two rifles blown to bits in the trenches, and the only touch I have got is a bruise with a piece of shrapnel on the knee. I feel sure we will never suffer as badly again in the trenches. This has been an exceptional case. The war is not far from finishing.[19]

Read could not have been more wrong.

One of the two fatalities on 17 April was most unlucky. Twenty-three-year-old Pte Thomas Hesketh from Fleetwood was trying to find his way forwards from HQ to the reserve trenches when he lost his direction and wandered into the firing line—a bullet hitting him in the chest. Although *Soldiers Died* lists him as 'died of wounds', a letter from his brother states he was killed instantly.[20] At 2.15 a.m., Pte Herbert Teasdale and nineteen-year-old Pte Frank Holding, from Lancaster, were standing in the trench, chatting quietly to each other, when a bullet hit Holding in the head, killing him immediately (Holding's brother, Richard, was posted to the Battalion in September 1917 and killed just two months later). The snipers facing them were extremely skilled: 'B' Company's Pte James Redhead asked his wife to post him a mask, and when it arrived, the twenty-three-year-old placed it on top of the parapet that night—it got a bullet straight through the centre within seconds. Two men were wounded that day—Pte Frank Cantrill was one, his luck finally running out after two previous close shaves—he had been right next to Albert Mogg when the latter was killed and also had three bullets pass right between his legs when he was moving into the trenches one night. Cantrill returned to the Battalion and rose to sergeant. The other casualty was Pte John Hodgson (035) from Lancaster. Upon his recovery, he was posted to the 2/5th and killed in October 1917.

No one was unhappy when 3/Monmouths relieved them later that night, the Battalion reaching their billets in Ypres at 2.15 a.m. on 18 April. The diary gives the casualties for this brief stay in the trenches as twelve killed and forty-six wounded. What they did not count in these figures were men who were treated and then returned for duty. With these included, the total wounded rises to fifty-four and the total dead, including 'died of wounds', to fifteen. The MO was also concerned that of the three shellshock cases, two were so severe that they may be permanently afflicted.[21]

Twelve of the dead were buried to the north of Polygon Wood, in a little cemetery initiated by the Guards, who buried eighteen of their men there (interred elsewhere were Richard Hothersall, William Smith, and Oswald Towers). Although a sketch map delineating individual graves was drawn up, none of this dozen have known graves today. This cemetery was well away from later trenches or wire defences, but even so, it was possibly obliterated by shell fire in 1917, destroying the 4½-foot-deep burials. Grave retrieval units cleared this area in 1920, and an examination of all 177 pages of *Burial Return Forms* for the nearby Butts Cemetery indicate that only one British soldier, of unknown name and regiment, was from this grid reference. Perchance, their graves remain there undiscovered. Maj. Bates wrote home to a friend about the burials:

We could not get them down from the trenches till dusk. We bury them about 9 o'clock. Poor lads! It makes my heart ache. On Wednesday night (14th) we buried five, on Thursday (15th) two, and tonight (16th) there were three more. The Colonel (Lord Richard Cavendish) takes the service and I accompany him. Apart from the Pioneers who make the graves and the stretcher-bearers, we are alone. It was a sad affair, noisy through the booming of heavy guns and rifles cracking all round. We soon forget it all, but however horrible is this war, we realise we are fighting for posterity, and we pray it will soon be over. They are a lot of gallant fellows. You have no idea, nor can you picture the life we are leading. Still we are bright and feel equal to anything that may crop up. We have four days' rest. I must get on with my work. The Colonel and myself share the same rabbit hole. We are lying in water, but making ourselves comfortable.[22]

Killed in Action, or Died from Wounds, 12–17 April 1915

Pte Reginald Blackhurst	2073	KIA: 16/4	Pte Richard Hothersall	1255	DOW: 17/4
Pte John Churchouse	1003	KIA: 14/4	Pte Joseph Nash	2154	KIA: 13/4
Pte Tom Knight Clarke	2740	KIA: 14/4	Pte John Ogden	1921	KIA: 16/4
Pte Fred Eltoft	2104	KIA: 16/4	Pte Thomas Robinson	1308	KIA: 14/4
Pte Matthew Farrell	1440	KIA: 14/4	Pte William Henry Smith	2524	DOW: 16/4
L/Cpl John Hirst Harper	999	KIA: 13/4	Pte Oswald Towers	1244	DOW: 15/4
Pte Thomas Hesketh	1978	KIA: 17/4	Pte Christopher Whiteside	2810	KIA: 14/4
Pte Frank Holding	2117	KIA: 17/4			

Known to have been Wounded, 12–17 April 1915

Pte Charles Austin	240399	WIA: 13/4	Pte George William Keen	1950	WIA: 13/4
L/Cpl John Alfred Bindloss	240199	WIA: 16/4	L/Cpl Robert William Kendall	240202	WIA: 15/4
Pte Frank Bradley	1857	WIA: 12/4	Pte Hubert Lilley	2141	WIA: 16/4
Pte Frank Bower	240488	WIA: 15/4	Pte John Livesey	2308	WIA: 16/4
Pte Charles Brodie	7	WIA: 14/4	L/Cpl Myles Mason	2393	WIA: 13/4
Pte Frank Brooks	2839	WIA: 15/4	Pte Jack Newboult	240528	WIA: 16/4
Pte Henry Johnson Burrows	240370	WIA: 13/4	Pte James Nicholson	1143	WIA: 14/4
Pte Frank Cantrill	240903	WIA: 17/4	Pte William Owen	240270	WIA: 14/4
Pte Harold Chapman	240473	WIA: 13/4	Pte John Parkinson	1976	WIA: 15/4
Pte Fred Cookson	1095	WIA: 13/4	Pte Herbert Parkinson	1837	WIA: 16/4
Pte Frederick Cottam	240545	WIA: 14/4	Pte George Pearcy	240575	WIA: 14/4
Pte William Crarey	3061	WIA: 15/4	Pte Albert E. Porter	240982	WIA: 14/4
Sgt Thomas William Denwood	240297	WIA: 13/4	Pte William Raine	1279	WIA: 14/4
Pte Albert Dixon	1881	WIA: 15/4	Pte Herbert Rickerby	265831	WIA: 16/4
Pte John Duckworth	240174	WIA: 13/4	L/Cpl Thomas Sanderson	1260	WIA: 13/4
Pte Thomas Edmondson	2852	WIA: 16/4	Pte Gilbert Shaw	2520	WIA: 14/4
Pte Robert H. Forrester	1510	WIA: 13/4	Pte Charles Skeats	240656	WIA: 14/4
L/Cpl Edward Gardner	1232	WIA: 13/4	L/Cpl Albert Edward Smallshaw	240191	WIA: 14/4
Pte Ernest Graham	240855	WIA: 14/4	Pte William Smith	3077	WIA: 13/4
Pte Richard Hargreaves	1930	WIA: 14/4	L/Cpl Walter Tedcastle	240144	WIA: 13/4
Pte William Thomas Harrison	240510	WIA: 14/4	Pte John Leonard Twigg	1620	WIA: 16/4
Pte Thomas Helm	2131	WIA: 13/4	Pte Sydney Walker	1523	WIA: 13/4
Cpl Charles Heys	240051	WIA: 15/4	Pte John Cochrane Watson	240291	WIA: 13/4
Pte John Hodgson	240035	WIA: 17/4	Pte John Cooper West	2174	WIA: 16/4
Pte John Hoggarth	1093	WIA: 13/4	Pte Thomas Wilkinson	240316	WIA: 14/4
Pte Frank Iniff	240221	WIA: 13/4	Pte George Wolfendale	1766	WIA: 16/4
Pte Andrew Jackson	2959	WIA: 15/4			

Their billets at the Asylum in Ypres were far from secure, and as shelling intensified, it was decided late on the night of 20 April to withdraw the Battalion to bivouacs in a field outside St Jean. One man was wounded, although L/Cpl Ralph Haslam's injury was minor and he returned the next day. The Battalion were just told to dig into the banks and hedgerows to hide and shelter the men—a task easier said than done as they had been ordered to leave all the picks and shovels behind at Polygon Wood. One soldier described the apocalyptical scene as they filed out of the city:

> The destruction of life and property in the town was appalling—men, women, children, soldiers, horses, and practically every living thing blown to bits and houses, hotels and churches blown to fragments. The exits from the town were crowded

with horror-stricken refugees. The Germans had no mercy, shell following shell in rapid succession- big thumping naval 17-inch shells, 'Jack Johnsons,' 'coal boxes,' 18-pounders, whiz-bangs and shrapnel.[23]

Another observed as they moved to their new position: 'We could see in front of us buildings blazing, church, cattle, men, women and children blown to bits'.[24]

During the night, the Battalion was ordered to move nearer to St Jean, and at 4 a.m. on 22 April, orders were received to move again to a crossroads to the north of St Jean and dig in. There was heavy shelling during the day, although few casualties. Nevertheless, some had very close escapes, as twenty-eight-year-old Pte Richard Irving described in a letter home:

> Time after time shells missed us all, the gases made most of our eyes smart, and nearly sent us to sleep. Lt Kirk was in the same dugout, and while he was having a rest, after being up all night, I went behind a hedge. Some earth thrown up by the shells caught me in the leg, and when I got back the officer had moved the position of his legs during his rest. Where his legs had been there was sticking in the earth a piece of shrapnel the size of a finger. He was lucky![25]

The Battalion was not the actual focus of German artillery—merely on the periphery of the bombardment of Ypres and the key roads leading in and out of the old city. Transport and stores had remained behind in Ypres and were not ordered out until later on the 22nd. The shelling was much reduced and the QM began to ferry the stores out, but just as the last batch was leaving around 5 p.m., an intense bombardment fell on all the roads leading in and out of the city—fortunately, without casualties to transport.

Initial indications of a major attack came shortly afterwards, when two greenish-yellow clouds were observed moving along the ground either side of the Langemarck road, behind which, it was judged by the crackle of rifle fire, the enemy was advancing. Soon afterwards, French infantrymen, artillery, steadily increasing crowds of refugees all began to flee over the canal bridges to the north of Ypres. Their left flank completely open, Canadian 3 Brigade fought a desperate holding action and succeeded in halting the enemy, but it was evident to commanders that the Canadians were in danger of being enveloped. As soon as he saw the crowds of refugees, Lt-Col. Stephenson of 3/Middlesex took it upon his own initiative to move his battalion from their billets to the crossroads where the 1/5th had dug in, and shortly after, 2/Buffs were ordered to join them. No. 1/York and Lancaster, in reserve to the west of Ypres, was also dispatched. At 12.30 a.m. on 23 April, these battalions were assigned to the Canadian Division, who immediately placed them under Col. Geddes of the Buffs—subsequently referred to as 'Geddes Detachment'.[26]

At 4.15 p.m. on 23 April, the following order from Geddes was received by Lt-Col. Cavendish:

Following has been sent to East Yorks and Yorks and Lancs, begins—The 13th Brigade crosses by the pontoon bridge at 3 a.m. and advances to the attack at 3.45 p.m. with the middle on the Pilckem-Ypres road. First objective Pilckem. OC East Yorks will send an officer at once to report to General O'Gowan [Brig.-Gen. R. Wanless O'Gowan] at pontoon bridge C.19c. East Yorks and Yorks and Lancs will cooperate in this attack east of the Pilckem-Ypres road, East Yorks on left of that road and maintaining touch with 13 Brigade. Yorks and Lancs will move on the right of the East Yorks. Two battalions of the 27 Division will cooperate in the attack on the right of the Yorks and Lancs. Buffs and 3/Middlesex will hold their present line. 5th Kings Own Royal Lancaster, less one company, will follow the attack in Reserve moving with its left on the Pilckem-Ypres road. Each battalion will move on a front of 500 yards. HQ will remain for the present at Wieltje, where reports should be sent. Colonel Geddes. 3.35 p.m.[27]

Thirty minutes later, the Battalion advanced, with Maj. Bates' 'C' Company in the vanguard, followed by Capt. Atkinson's 'A' Company and Capt. Sharpe's 'B' Company. An attack towards an entrenched enemy over a mile of ground (sloping gently upwards and devoid of all cover) was perilous enough, but the Battalion had no fire support, and in the clear light of the spring afternoon, every man was plainly visible in the sights of the enemy's weapons. Critically, the Germans were not just to their front, and they were able to pour enfilading fire from both flanks. Much of this came from a spur of the Mauser Ridge south-east of Boesinghe (modern-day Boezinge), erroneously believed to be occupied by the French. Although the Germans had used chlorine gas deployed from cylinders for their main attack, the gas shells fired by artillery against this attack contained lachrymatory (tear) gas.

As may be imagined, the instant the attackers broke cover, a storm of rifle, MG, and artillery fire scourged their ranks. British observers were astounded by the courage of men who stood up in broad daylight under such fire from a hidden enemy.[28] Soon after the outset, the Battalion encountered a deep ditch—causing some delay—and men were ordered to go to ground while this was sorted. For 600 yards, the only cover was a few isolated manure heaps—an illusory safety, hardly bullet resistant, and far from offering protection, actually drew fire. By the end of the day, each heap had a pile of dead or wounded behind it. Shortly afterwards, the attack continued, and around 7 p.m., the Battalion reached their objective—finding a mixed group of soldiers from about fifteen regiments and very few officers. The East Yorks had virtually ceased to exist, and with further advance impossible, the Battalion was ordered to dig in. As soon as it was dark, Cavendish collected as many of his battalion together as possible and arranged an entrenchment line. He and Maj. Bates then made their way to Wieltje, where they eventually found Geddes in a cellar. Geddes ordered the Battalion to remain where it was. Later they were ordered to pull back another couple hundred yards and dig a new line—a task carried out by 'A' Company, with a platoon from 'D' sent up to assist. The remainder of the Battalion was pulled back to their start line of that afternoon.

Some, such as Pte James 'Cliff' Mawson, became casualties before they had even left their trench. Shrapnel struck the twenty-one-year-old stretcher-bearer from Hest Bank as he sheltered from the bombardment; he died from his wounds the following day (his father, architect Thomas H. Mawson, was the driving force behind the building of the Westfield 'Lancaster Memorial Village', catering for disabled ex-servicemen, and opened by Sir Douglas Haig in 1924). For those who took part in this attack, the experience was life-changing. In 'C' Company's leading platoon was twenty-year-old L/Cpl Edward Mason from Caton—wounded in the chest—who wrote home from hospital in Rouen:

> I wonder how they are going on, for they were fighting when I left the battlefield- fighting like heroes. I never thought our battalion would go into a charge, but every man went for it and we saw plenty fall before we joined in the charge.... This is a great change from the trenches [hospital]. It seems strange not to hear the guns and rifles going, and it was a bit before I could get the noise out of my ears. The big guns were shelling us out of our position, but we soon dug ourselves in along the roadside. Our eyes were nearly burned out by the nasty fumes, and you would have thought we were crying, but we put up with it nearly all day till we made our charge. We saw a lot of troops coming along and thought they were our relief, as we had had nothing to eat for twenty-four hours, but the Capt. called out 'Fix bayonets, and charge'. 'C' Company led the way, with our platoon first in. I felt rather frightened but off we went. With full packs on our backs and blankets in, it was awful trying to run. I threw mine off and put it in front of my head every stop we made. I said, 'you can have a do at this before you hit me in the head.' I didn't half go when we got the word to advance in short rushes. Every step we made we lay flat as flukes, but we never knew the minute a shell would come to burst on top of us. They were putting an awful lot out of action. I was lucky not to get a bit of shell over my head, for they burst in front and behind us all the way along. I shall never forget 23 April, for I saw a sight I never wish to see again—farms on fire, the town behind us on fire, and the place where we were billeted in ruins. We were lucky to get out of it.[29]

Also from 'C' Company was L/Cpl Thomas Huartson from Lancaster—writing to his wife from hospital:

> I'm glad to say it's only slight to what some got. I got one in the jaw and Willie got one in the hand [nineteen-year-old Pte William Docherty from 'A' Company was his wife's brother]. Willie saw me and ran to me and bandaged me up. Then he had not gone many more yards before he was wounded in the hand. I think we were lucky to get out with such wounds. We are both in the same hospital in Boulogne. The battalion have fairly got cut up. It brought tears to my eyes when I lay and saw them dropping. Talk about a battlefield. It was one. They were lying dead all over the shop.[30]

Huartson was also worried about his brother, Richard, from 'A' Company, whom he feared had 'got knocked over as [he] didn't know where he was'. He was right to be concerned as, mortally wounded by a shot to the chest, the thirty-nine-year-old Private was carried from the field by Christopher Cooper and John Howson. The bullet that killed him struck his rifle first, splitting the barrel as it passed through to pierce his chest. Richard was the second of the three Huartson brothers to die. Sadly for the family, there would be further tragedy before the war ended.

'C' Company's L/Cpl Thomas Brayshaw—a twenty-eight-year-old married man—was hit in the thigh and fell immediately. Two of his Morecambe pals, Pte Herbert Thacker and Pte George Downham, ignored the heavy fire sweeping the field and ran to help him. As they reached him, Brayshaw lifted his arm and a round passed straight through it, hitting Downham in the forehead. Both men were medically discharged. Downham died in October 1918, thirty months after his discharge, but his inclusion on the CWGC database means that his death was service-related. Pte Herbert Eccles from Burton was shot in the foot:

> We reached a spot about forty yards from the German trench, which we easily took. We then took matters somewhat easily, and while lying on a ditch bank I felt a sting in my left foot, and called to a Canadian who was digging himself in that I had got a bullet through my foot. He replied, 'You had better tumble in on top of me or you will get one through your head.' I accepted his offer, and in about five minutes after he received a bullet through his hand. After lying for three hours to await darkness we set out for the dressing station. With the help of the Canadian and my rifle I got along fairly well. First aid was rendered to us, after which we were sent a mile behind the firing line. The Germans shelled the dressing station, out of which we had to clear as well as we could. The Red Cross assisted as many as possible out of the building, but two or three men were unavoidably left behind.[31]

Eccles recovered and rejoined the Battalion.

Thirty-five-year-old Pte George Gill from Scotforth wrote to his wife about his experience in 'C' Company's attack:

> I have got wounded by a piece of shell in my left arm, between the muscle and the elbow. I have been under the X-ray and will be sent to England. We got orders to charge with fixed bayonets through the open fields. It was like going to our doom, for we were under rifle fire, machine gun fire, and shell fire. It was nothing but murder. Hell can be no worse than this was, for men were dropping in scores. We took the trench but lost a great lot of lives. God only knows how they have gone on. I lost everything on the battlefield but my rifle, but could not use it being wounded. I made my way as best I could to the dressing station. Dr George and Dick Clarkson [Pte Richard Clarkson (238)] saw to my arm, and then I had to walk two miles to another dressing station and wait for the buses to take us away to the hospital, which is just like Morecambe. Don't be downhearted.[32]

Gill did not return to the Battalion, he was transferred to the RFC, and later the Labour Corps. It was an anxious time for the family of nineteen-year-old Pte Robert Burrow from

Warton, who was being treated in No. 8 Stationary Hospital at Wimereux after being hit in the head—his skull fractured. Frequently, this sort of wound ended with the death, but Burrow survived a number of operations, though the injuries resulted in his discharge.

Sometimes families were just notified that their husband or son were missing. Twenty-two-year-old Pte Thomas Kew from Lancaster, a driver with 'C' Company, was officially missing—but others passed news of his fate to his family from the Battalion. He was known to have been helping 'A' Company's Pte Thomas Bigland, also from the MG transport. Transport Officer Lt Harold Bell wrote to thirty-year-old Bigland's wife:

> I regret to have to inform you that your husband was killed on 24 April while carrying out his duties. He was in charge of the machine gun section, which was being sent up to the battalion. After some severe shelling his body was found by the master tailor of the Canadian regiment, who buried him and reported the circumstances to us at the first opportunity. The report did not state the exact position of the burial, but it is somewhere near the village of St. Jean, which is just outside Ypres. I need not say how sorry I am to give you such a report and please accept my deepest sympathy in your sad loss. I must say that your husband carried out his duties in a most efficient manner, and he had served his country equally to those in the firing line. The enclosed book of psalms was the only thing in his possession which was handed over to me.[33]

Known to be behind the lines, there was no possibility of Kew being wounded and a prisoner, so his parents had to accept the worst. Family members in the Battalion often relayed updates on the wounded to England. When 'A' Company's Pte Leonard Monks (229) visited his wounded platoon leader, Lt Thomas Owtram, in hospital, he discovered his brother, twenty-one-year-old Pte Thomas Monks, and cousin, Pte James Newby, in another of the wards. Both had been wounded charging with 'C' Company. Thomas Monks' bullet wounds to shoulder and chest led to his discharge in 1916. James Newby, less seriously injured, returned to the Battalion a couple of days later; he was discharged as time-expired in early 1916 and conscripted back into the Battalion later that year.

'A' Company, following on behind 'C', took just as much fire. Twenty-three-year-old Pte Joseph Cragg was hit in the chest by a bullet. His pal, L/Cpl William Bell, wrote to Cragg's mother:

> He was closely attached to me and always by me when in action. He was next to me when he was killed on the 23rd when we were making an attack. It may cheer you a bit when I tell you he had no pain. He got hit through the lungs and just said, 'Oh, Billy,' and then passed away. We buried him the next night at the place where he fell.[34]

William Bell earned the MM for his courage at Ypres.

Twenty-one-year-old Pte George Beckett was also buried by friends. Pte Thomas Goulding identified the body and was present with three other men, the CO and Capt.

Eaves when he was interred. Beckett's sister was looking after Goulding's children until he could return home to make more permanent arrangements for them. Fifty-one year-old L/Cpl Charles Brodie (010) saw the second of his sons wounded when Joseph was hit. In such an action it was inevitable that so many of the casualties were connected by family and friendship ties and two of the three Corless brothers in the Battalion were wounded. Neither Albert nor Richard returned; Albert receiving a medical discharge because of his injuries. The third brother, Pte Robert Corless, was uninjured—this time.

In a letter to a former pupil, who had written asking what battle was like, schoolmaster twenty-five-year-old Cpl Wilfred Brash replied.

We crept stealthily along the roadside under the cover of the hedge side and a little hillock that screened us from the enemy. Now the bullets began to 'ping' and the shells hurtled and screamed through the air. But this was as nothing to what was to follow. It was merely the foretaste. All at once we filed out into the open. Where was the enemy? No need to ask, for hell was let loose to our right. 'Down' came the order, followed by every NCO's whistle, and every man fell prone in an orderly line at five paces distance. Then the enemy's Maxims and rifles spat, and their artillery thundered with redoubled fury. Bullets fell like hails and shells tore up the ground in all directions, whilst shrapnel ripped the air above our heads. The whistles are blown again, and once more we are rushing onward through that awful inferno. Down again and forward once more! Would we never reach our goal? But what were those gleaming on the ridge top? Hurrah! German helmets! Forward, boys! What a mad rush that final spurt was. We ran, almost knocking each other down, shouting, yelling and gesticulating, and the excitement was so great that for one or two minutes we never noticed that the enemy had turned tail and was fleeing for their lives. But our blood was up, and we had just commenced to go in pursuit when the order was given to retire. And so we turned about and walked back to our original positions.[35]

Among 'A' Company's dead, soon after the advance began, was twenty-two-year-old Pte Douglas Wright from Lancaster—shot through the eye. A golfer of some local renown before the war, he was 6 feet and 3½ inches (one of the tallest men in the Battalion) and very popular. His best friend, Pte Harry (known as Gilbert) Towers, was alongside him when Wright was hit—shortly after, it was his turn. His account illustrates the evacuation process:

Douglas Wright was hit early on and I was wounded about ten minutes after. I had just jumped a brook, and threw myself down with my feet in the water, when a piece of shrapnel struck me in the back of the leg. It was about 6 p.m. I called out. 'I'm hit.' Someone shouted, 'Lie still.' The order came to advance. Corporal Jackson, who was then beside me said, 'Wait till we have got away and then try to get back.' I waited a few minutes. The bullets were like a shower of hail. I made it back across a field and came across the platoon of ours following on. Two chaps put me a bandage on, and took me back to a dressing station, and from there to a village about two miles away. There we got a van [ambulance] and went across country to another station, and stayed to 8.30 Saturday morning. They started shelling us. We got out only in time; a shell landed right into the barn killing some of the fellows. From there we walked through [Ypres]. They were still bombarding it. We walked to a village further away, and then by van to another place, where we had tea and then trained to Hazebrouck, a base hospital. We arrived at midnight on Saturday, and left Sunday at 3 p.m. by train for Boulogne, arriving at 11.30 p.m. I was in hospital all night, and was moved next day to a camp outside the town and slept there until 5 a.m. We went on Tuesday, 27 April by van to the harbour, and by boat to Le Havre, reaching there at midnight. I went all round the boat looking on the beds for someone I knew. I found no one. I went up into the saloon. A chap was playing the piano, and I was just making myself comfortable, when a voice said, 'Are you King's Own?' I replied, 'Yes.' He said, 'There's a chap over there you will know.' It proved to be Billy Pinch. I was thankful to come across some I knew, and had a long talk. I found that Dick Irving had a finger hit before the attack. Pinch had been nearly through to the last but he has a bullet in his left arm. Harry Wright of Morecambe had one of his legs broken. Harry Cross was all right up to Friday. It was fearful.[36]

'A' Company stretcher-bearer twenty-year-old Pte William Jones was hit in both legs and the back by shrapnel before he had even begun his work:

I was lying on a bank side and was watching a chap shoot horses that had been hurt with shrapnel, when all of a sudden a 'coal-box' burst five yards from me. It wounded three—two stretcher-bearers and a chap out of the line. It broke one chap's leg, and hit the other in the calf.... This war is nothing else but sheer murder.[37]

Stretcher-bearer Edward 'Douglas' Alston was also badly wounded; he was hit in both knees, his thigh, calf, and the back of his neck. Having just turned sixteen, he was evacuated home and medically discharged. Another stretcher-bearer wounded was twenty-two-year-old Pte George Sandall from Lancaster: '[I] got a bullet through my left thigh. They hit me when I was not looking, but it's a lot better than I thought it would be'.[38] It was over a year before he returned. The next time he risked his life to help his comrades, the outcome would be worse.

Intense fire and lack of cover made attempts to reach most of the wounded during daylight suicidal; for similar reasons, there was no possibility of any resupply, so men had to make do with whatever they had with them. Some of the wounded, particularly those hit early in the charge, chose not to stay where they were until dark and began to crawl back. One who made it was Pte Richard Rogerson from Lancaster. Shot through the left arm, he crawled back for 250 yards until he reached safety. Thirst was a problem for all, and later that evening, 'C' Company's Pte Joseph Mashiter put some of his pre-war skills to good use. Miraculously, a cow had escaped the hail of fire, and in the early evening, it had wandered close to where the Battalion were dug in. The young soldier expertly milked the beast and passed the very welcome liquid to the nearby wounded. One of the stretcher-bearers, Pte George Mawson, ended up tending his uncle, Sgt Henry Tennant, hit in the leg. Tennant, a widower with one child, was medically discharged in August 1916.

Even darkness offered little protection for anyone assisting the wounded back. Pte William Thompson (326), a machine-gunner from 'B' Company, was helping to carry one of his wounded pals when a nearby shell burst sent a 2-inch-long splinter into his side, just missing a kidney. He eventually recovered and was transferred to the KLR. For some, even their successful evacuation from the battlefield did not help. Thirty-three-year-old father of two Pte Thomas Towers shot in the head, and he died three days later at the CCS. Cpl Brash helped search for the wounded after dark:

> In three hours' time from the first advance to attack, everything had quietened down except for some desultory artillery fire, the Germans as usual attempting to shell our dressing stations and field hospitals. Then the full moon rose and cast its ghostly light upon the battlefield. And what a scene! Scores, nay hundreds of dead and dying lying with their faces ghastly-white turned to the moon with their fixed and glassy eyes staring into eternity: the tranquillity of the night disturbed by the moans of the dying and wounded or by the eerie call of some bird of prey seeking a repast. Rifles, bayonets, packs, hats, and other things lying about the field in wild disorder. Parties of stretcher-bearers out on their errands of mercy carrying their sad burdens to a dressing station or to a last resting place beneath the soil of Belgium.

The censoring officer actually appended this letter with the words: 'Some description! And not exaggerated either. Those days were Hell!'[39]

The third wave of the attack was by 'B' Company. Two Cathcart brothers (George and James) charged side by side. Just over half way across, James looked round, but failed to spot his nineteen-year-old sibling. James wrote home to their worried parents:

> He was by my side for over half the way, and then we discovered that he was not about. His last words to me were, 'Jim, throw your valise off,' which I did immediately. There are a good number who have got lost and gone to other regiments, and I hope that George is one of them. I still have hopes of him returning to us. George, I and Fred Monks were all together in the advance.[40]

George was officially posted as 'missing', although a ray of hope arrived when his parents received a letter in early June from someone who had thought he had seen him being taken prisoner. This proved to be incorrect; their son had indeed been killed during the attack. Their sole-surviving son, seventeen-year-old James, was, however, far from safe. It was possibly tougher being in the third wave than it was in the first as the men would be passing all the casualties from those that had gone before them. One man described this:

Men lay dead, dying, bleeding to death in scores. We dropped in the open fields to take cover, and they were being shot down like mowing grass. I was very lucky. I had a bullet through my valise and one through my trenching tool. Then shells started bursting about ten yards in front. Lots of my pals were blown to bits. Legs flew all over. One poor fellow—a Canadian—had his head clean blown from his shoulders. The Germans mowed us down like corn. It brings tears to my eyes when I think of it. We kept going, falling over one another till dark. Then we had to return back to our old place, and glad I was to get there.... The sights were—well I can't explain: but I shall never get it out of my eyes if I live to be a thousand. Wagons, cattle, horses, pigs, human beings, motor cars, bicycles, dogs and soldiers blown to bits all along the roads. Big holes you could bury fifty men in all over the place.[41]

Some from 'B' Company had very close escapes, such as the battalion cook Pte George Hopson. He had the peak blown off his cap, a bullet ran the length of his sleeve, splitting the material, but missing his flesh, and after the action, he found a piece of shrapnel in his trousers.[42] Pte Isaiah Lightfoot considered himself lucky to be alive after he was shot through the nose, and to make matters worse, it was also his twenty-third birthday. Just days after his twenty-first, Pte Victor Keyworth was less fortunate; a bullet hit him in the mouth, killing him instantly. For Mrs Needham, there was bad news concerning her husband and son, who both suffered head wounds. Her husband, forty-year-old Sgt Frank Needham, returned to the Battalion in November, but her son, Pte Joseph Needham, was transferred to the Labour Corps upon his recovery. If this was not bad enough, her brother, L/Cpl John Simpson, was also wounded. His wound was not serious, but when his time expired in May 1916, he enlisted in the Labour Corps. Pte Frank Stamp's arm wound brought about his eventual discharge in January 1917, but his wife's visit to his hospital bed in Manchester must have been a joyful experience as it was also his first sight of their nine-week-old baby girl. Not everyone in the company shot in the arm survived. A friend had seen twenty-four-year-old Pte Reginald Stamper hit in the arm by a bullet, but when the roll was called that night, the private was missing. He was eventually listed as 'died of wounds', but the details of his fate were never known. 'B' Company lost one of their most experienced NCOs when L/Sgt Charles Shaw was hit. His parents received a telegram from No. 2 General Hospital in Le Havre warning them that their son was dangerously ill after having a leg amputated. Fortunately, the thirty-six-year-old widower survived, receiving a medical discharge in May 1916.

For one of 'B' Company's wounded, nineteen-year-old town hall clerk Pte Thomas Blakeley, the future held something that he could never have imagined as he lay in hospital. After his recovery, he served as a corporal at Loos, and in 1916, he was commissioned—far from unusual in this highly educated battalion. He was awarded the MC later that year—again far from unusual. Uniquely among officers and men from all three TF battalions of the King's Own, he had a feature of the Western Front named after him in 1917.

One of 'A' Company's pioneers did not want to be left out of the attack and charged armed only with his spade. Thirty-seven-year-old Pte Richard Stevenson, a well-known 'character' from Lancaster, originally enlisted in the 'Volunteers' in 1896. Had he reached the enemy lines, the spade could have proved itself a formidable weapon, but he was shot through the right hand before he got that far—a wound that led to medical discharge. Another who probably should not have been there was thirty-nine-year-old father of five Pte Thomas Slater, the battalion cook. He too attacked with his pals, his fall and death from his wounds a couple of hours afterwards subsequently testified by them. The impact of his loss was magnified many-fold by the death of his youngest child the day before he was killed—the child's body was still in the house when his wife received the news of his death.[43] The mother of nineteen-year-old Pte William Theobald found out about her son's death quite accidentally. She had just received a cheery letter from him and was standing talking to her neighbour about it when the neighbour remarked that she had just received a letter from her son, also with the Battalion, but had not opened it yet. She then unsealed the envelope and read the letter, which contained the news about William's death. Official confirmation arrived four days later.[44]

Twenty-one-year-old 'B' Company soldier Pte William Wareing (938) wrote to his old headmaster about his wounding:

> We made a charge on Friday night at the place where the Germans took some ground of ours from the French, but we got it back all right. I had an awful experience when I got shot and had to crawl nearly a mile for safety. The shells were bursting all over.

His letter home contained more detail:

> The Germans were firing their awful shells that nearly poison you with the smell. I got the poisonous gas in my eyes and it made them run for two days.... It was murder. We were walking over the dead men and you could hear chaps moaning. Our battalion nearly got wiped out. We have lost a lot of men killed and wounded. I can tell you I'm lucky. I can walk about a bit, but I can't sit down yet. It's only a flesh wound.[45]

One platoon from 'D' Company, led by company commander Capt. William Carter, was ordered forward after dark to help the survivors dig in. As they advanced, he was shot through the head and killed. His body and personal effects were recovered, the former being buried at a farm near Potijze. Casualties among officers were severe as the MO Lt George described in a letter written on the 26th to a friend back in Lancaster:

> We are just done up for want of sleep, and cannot get our letters through, but the men are wonderfully good and have stuck to their terrible time wonderfully well. Lt Briggs was slightly wounded but is quite okay and only requiring dressing. The same with Capt. Sharpe, who is also all right, but very tired and weary. We are all alike. I have had some narrow escapes. A big 'Jack Johnson' fell just behind the house, fortunately

in the field, otherwise we should not be here. Also, three shells came through the roof of our barn. We shall probably not be able to write now. I have none of my kit with me, and have not had a wash for over a week. I have not had my boots off for ten days. What we would all give for a wash! We have not had three hours sleep for nearly a week, and are just about done. We shall never forget out first experience of a battlefield for as long as we live. We are all years older, but quite cheery, and looking for a rest. Capt. Carter was shot through the head, Kirk through the chest, and he may be dead now. 'Boy' Coupland was seriously injured too. 'Mery' Evans through the wrist, and Tommy Owtram twice in the leg and side, but neither serious.[46]

Lt William 'Noel' Briggs—the only son of the Mayor of Lancaster—was wounded a further three times before the war ended. Twenty-year-old Lt Henry Coupland from Lancaster died from his wounds on 24 April. Lt Edward Lloyd-Evans from Lancaster recovered from the wound in his wrist, but time was running out for the twenty-one-year-old. Thirty-one-year-old Lt Gerald Kirk had joined as a private when war was declared and had been rapidly promoted. Carried to the dressing station by Pte Cyril Whiteside and others from his platoon, he died the next day. This was only the first of three occasions Lt Owtram was wounded—his actions in volunteering to carry out the dangerous reconnaissance prior to the attack and continuing to lead his platoon, despite receiving two wounds, earned him the MC.[47]

Not mentioned by Lt George was 2Lt Frank Huntington, another commissioned from the ranks:

I have been sent over to Blighty, as Tommy Atkins would say. I was wounded at Ypres on the second day of the battle. It is not very serious. I was burned on the face—with severe conjunctivitis. However my eyesight is now all right, though groggy. It was those poisonous bombs that did the trick, two of which burst within a yard of me. I got all the fumes, but nothing else, so I consider myself very, very lucky to come through.[48]

A number of men were affected by the gas, though for most, the effects only lasted a few hours or days. Lachrymatory gas, though harmful in concentrated doses, was far less lethal than chlorine. However, its effectiveness was magnified because the men had no gas protection whatsoever. Like Lt Huntington, twenty-two-year-old Pte Richard Charnley from Galgate was evacuated home, all power of speech lost due to its effect on his throat. He was medically discharged in 1916.

There is an issue with the reported dates for 'D' Company's casualties, with the exception of Capt. Carter—virtually all of whom are listed for 26 April. That day's actions do not support this, particularly as the diary reports: 'Left for Potize [*sic*.] at 3 a.m. arriving without further casualties'.[49] Totals given in the Battalion's diary for casualties in the attack of the 23rd are considerably higher than were recorded for that day's casualty list. However, if 'D' Company's figures from the list of the 26th are added to the 23rd, this tallies with the diary's total and makes more sense. The four surviving service records for 'D' Company casualties give the 26th as the date of wounding, but this would be taken from the casualty list, and was not necessarily the actual day they were wounded. Although I have left the date of death for L/Cpl John Walmsley and Pte John Woods as the 26th in the table later in this chapter, I consider some time after sunset on the 23rd much more probable. However, I have changed the dates listed for those wounded to the 23rd. Omitted from the totals in the diary are those wounded who remained at duty and those suffering from the effects of gas. Where this information is known from other sources, I have included these men in the table. It is quite understandable that 'D' Company's casualty returns were tardy since they had lost their company commander, and their casualties were probably all from the platoon detached to support 'A' Company.

This had hardly been a textbook example of attack. In his diary, Lt-Col. Cavendish complained:

> No details were given to us, and of course we had not the slightest knowledge of the ground or the position of the German trenches. This applied also to the regiment we were supporting. The whole thing was very badly planned or rather there was no plan at all. None of the battalions [six battalions had been hurriedly pulled from their rest positions to take part] had the slightest idea what they were going to do, none of them had been near the place before, and not a single officer had the slightest idea of the proper direction. The attack changed direction twice and finally fizzled out in a ditch about five or six hundred yards from the German position.[50]

By this time, the attacking battalions had virtually ceased to exist as a fighting force. Two of these battalions had also been from 83 Brigade—2/East Yorks lost 394 killed, wounded, and missing, and 1/Yorks and Lancs, 447.[51]

The Battalion began to consolidate their defences and though they were heavily shelled on 24 April, casualties were light, and, much to the relief of the men who had been without food since they left Ypres, the QM managed to get rations forward at midday. Even though St Jean was also heavily shelled, Transport escaped without casualties. During the night, men scoured the battlefield for wounded and attempted to bury as many of the dead as possible. The Canadians had withdrawn from their positions forward of the Battalion, and although some French infantry had arrived, the line was quite lightly held. Cavendish was concerned that any German attack would roll right through them, especially as he had no communications with any other units and no way of calling in fire support. At 2.30 a.m. on 25 April, a message arrived telling them that there was to be a big attack against the German positions to their right and that the Battalion needed to be ready to go in to support this. Apart from this message, the only communication received all day from Geddes was that he had been shelled out of his HQ in Wieltje and had retreated to St Jean. In the afternoon, the Battalion was shelled for about three hours at a rate of fire of two or three rounds a minute. Despite enemy artillery judging the range just right, only five men were wounded. Regrettably, one of these, Pte Albert Aspden of 'D' Company, died just after reaching the dressing station. Other wounded were less critical: twenty-seven-year-old L/Cpl William Marsden of 'A' Company received shrapnel wounds to chest and leg; twenty-four-year-old Pte Joseph Caton from 'A' Company was hit in the left thigh by shrapnel and evacuated home; and Pte Thomas Porter from 'D' Company was wounded. The fifth casualty is unknown, as he appears on a different day's list.

At 3 a.m. on 26 April, the Battalion left the line for Potijze without further loss. Respite was short as, on the 27th, they were ordered forward to support a counter-attack against Mauser Ridge. Their advance was met by heavy artillery fire and a single shell killed twelve and wounded five. Once in position, they dug in and remained there, still under sporadic shellfire for the rest of that night. Another man was killed and a further fifteen wounded, the youngest fatality being sixteen-year-old Pte Harry Grice from Scotforth. Seventeen-year-old Pte Tom Bolton from Caton, one of the five killed by the single shell, was not much older, having added two years to his age upon enlistment. His friend Pte Tom Fairclough witnessed his death:

> You will be more sorry to hear of young Tom Bolton's death. I was within twenty yards of where he was killed and saw him fall. He was killed by a high explosive shell and his death must have been instantaneous. These few lines you must make the most of, for when I come home I shall tell you nothing of this great battle, for tongue can't tell and people won't believe, and if I get home safe I want to forget this wicked and bloody war.[52]

The same shell killed twenty-year-old Pte Jack Halliwell from Skerton, specific details of the results of it upon him were rather surprisingly passed to the newspapers by his pal, Pte Joseph Guy.[53] Another killed by this shell was twenty-three-year-old Pte Fred Glover from Scotforth; he had two brothers in the Battalion (Walter and Charles), both of whom saw him hit. He died soon afterwards and Walter passed the bad news home. Thirty-nine-year-old Pte John Knowles subtracted four years from his age when he joined to serve alongside his stepson, Pte Anthony Atkinson. Knowles was killed instantly by this shell, his stepson wounded in the back, although luckily not seriously. The oldest killed was forty-three-year-old Pte John Pye (785), the tidings passed home by his nephew, Pte John Pye (296), who had now lost both his uncle and step-brother in less than a month. However, for his mother, Mrs Cooper, these deaths were not the end of her woes.

When this shell killed Pte John Prince, just a day after his twenty-first birthday, his younger brother, Edward (Teddy), was too distraught to write home. Instead, Capt. Gerald Sharpe wrote to their parents:

> We were all lying down ready to advance, and suffering from a terrible artillery fire. Your two sons were together, and with them the rest of their platoon, when a huge shell dropped into the midst of them, killing and wounding a great many. Your younger son I

am glad to say escaped absolutely untouched, while poor John was killed. I am glad to say however that he did not suffer any pain, but was killed instantly. We are all grieved at losing so many gallant fellows, and especially your son, who always did his duty well and died a soldier's death. We buried them all side by side and Capt. Deed made a cross and put all their names on.[54]

It emerged that Teddy was underage for overseas deployment and he was immediately returned to England, though not discharged. He later went to France with the 8th Battalion and was killed in action with them almost two years to the day after his brother died. With so many of the men related to one another in these early years, tragedy was becoming almost routine. Pte Patrick Naylon watched thirty-six-year-old Pte James Ward, his wife's brother, killed by this shell; he wrote to his wife:

I saw it with my own eyes. He had his breast blown away. Harry Winder was another one. When I saw Ward killed I thought I should have gone mad, for I was only talking to him ten minutes before, but I kept my head and pulled through all right.[55]

Thirty-seven-year-old Pte Henry Winder had survived the Boer War without a scratch, but his luck ran out that day. He had two brothers in the Battalion (Thomas and John) and two brothers-in-law (Isaac Phillipson and John Crossley), but it was his nephew, twenty-five-year-old Pte John Rowe, who witnessed his death. Winder left behind five children, all under the age of eleven. Tragedy was to hit this family twice more before the end. One of those wounded by this shell, twenty-eight-year-old Pte Leonard Thompson, clung onto life for two days before succumbing to his wounds at Boulogne.

Near John Prince was twenty-three-year-old L/Cpl James Redhead. He was knocked out by the blast, remained unconscious for four days, and was evacuated to a hospital in Amphill. Some of the wounded had miraculous escapes, like twenty-two-year-old Pte James Smith, who wrote to his aunt:

There were about twelve of us taking cover behind a hedge when they were throwing gas shells at us, when one dropped right in the middle of us. I was lifted over a hedge about fifty yards, where I was picked up three hours after with a lump torn out of the shoulder and arm. What became of the other fellows I don't know. They must have been blown to bits. I had nearly half a man around me. I have a good souvenir. You know the watch I took to Sevenoaks. I had it in my left breast pocket. It saved my life. It stopped a large piece of shrapnel from going through. The doctor told me it saved me. I have it here in bits. I have a lot of pain, as it is a nasty wound.[56]

The wound spelled the end of James Smith's Army days and he was discharged in August 1916. Pte Reg Simpson, who had had such fortune when their dugout was hit eleven days earlier, was not so blessed this time; he was struck in the thigh by a large shell splinter and also had five smaller pieces pierce his leg. Although this was a 'Blighty' wound, he returned to the Battalion later that year. L/Cpl Richard Taylor, wounded on the 27th, was behind the firing line repairing a broken signal cable in a dugout when a shrapnel ball came through the doorway and struck him just below the knee. He later returned, rising to sergeant before the war's end.

'B' Company's position was absolutely untenable—a curtain of shellfire falling among them and to their front—and they were ordered to move to a nearby field one platoon at a time. While Capt. Sharpe guided platoons to their new position, Boer War veteran thirty-three-year-old Sgt Alfred Price volunteered to take charge of the remaining men. Despite the continuing bombardment, he remained cool and unflustered, his courage having a considerable calming effect on the men. In March 1916, he was awarded the DCM for this and his later service as temporary CSM.

The Battalion remained in the same positions on 28 April, and although shelling was heavy, the Battalion lost only one killed and another wounded. According to the OH, the Geddes Detachment units were ordered back to their own brigades after dark on the 27th; however, the brigade diary records these only returning under their command on 29 April.[57, 58] Geddes himself was killed early on the 28th, when a shell hit the room he was waiting inside to collect a replacement for a map he had lost. On 29 April, the Battalion was pulled back for a well-earned rest to huts just outside Vlamertinghe. Even as they retired, they suffered another casualty when twenty-seven-year-old L/Cpl Richard Rigby was caught by gas on the march back and evacuated home—the effects serious enough for him to receive a discharge just over a year later, suffering from gastritis brought about by it.

Once they were safe in their billets, Maj. Bates wrote to a friend back in Lancaster:

The past fifteen days have been most strenuous and I have appeared to have lived years during that time. We have seen a lot of fighting and while our good God has spared me and my lad for a little while, he has called to Himself many of my dear comrades. I thank Him many times daily for His mercy not only to me, but to the dear ones I have left behind. We have constantly been under heavy shellfire for the past fifteen days, and on two of these we did heavy fighting ourselves. Our lads behaved with splendid heroism.

Lancaster in future years will look with pride on the bravery of their sons. I cannot tell you now what the General [Lt-Gen. H. C. O. Plumer] told me this morning, but it made my breast swell with pride for our gallant lads. We lost many, over sixty the week before last, and well over 200 on Friday last, in less than two hours. It was awful. Nothing but my faith in my Maker could have made me go on. Shell, machine gun and rifle fire mowed our lads down like ripe corn. Still their comrades went on, not a shirker amongst them. On! On!! On!!! Death facing them at every step. What brave fellows they were.

It may not be my good fortune to come back to tell all I saw them do, but this I can say: although we were only in Reserve we reached the goal before many battalions who were in the firing line, and went right through them.

I pray to God that I may never see such an awful sight again. My heart is sad and aches for those dear ones left behind. To the everlasting shame of the Germans who used asphyxiating powder against us, we fought them at long odds. Its awful stuff, gets into your eyes and chokes you. Nothing but grit and sheer determination can stand against it: to stop means being suffocated. There is nothing for it but going on, but at what a cost.

To see God's handiwork blown to atoms before your eyes! Yes, at your very side, it is a shock that few can face without a falling heart. However we have put these things behind us, and look to the future. We can mourn for them later. Poor Lt Coupland, my son Stanley's mate! He went down early, shot through the stomach. He was such a fine lad. I loved the little fellow—the most conscientious chap and one of the hardest workers I have ever met. His men adored him. He fell leading them like the little hero he was. I can feel for his parents knowing what it would be if I had lost my own: but he was a fine, good-living lad, brave as the young hero he was. Although he has been taken from them, when time has healed the wound of parting with their loved one, they will look back at his memory with pride, knowing he was a good lad and gave his all for his country.

We lost a big squad on Tuesday last. A big shell dropped into the middle of them, killing twelve and wounding several others. Such is war, may God punish the responsible criminal who caused this awful bloodshed.... Things are supposed to have eased off a bit. We may now have a little rest. Trench life will be a picnic after this last outing.[59]

At fifty years old, Maj. John Bates was really too old for a field officer and his health was noticeably deteriorating. He was admitted to hospital shortly after he wrote this letter, and he was then sent home for treatment on 6 May, his days with the Battalion over. Sadly, while still in hospital in England, he would be told the worst possible news.

The Battalion lost fifty-two killed and 169 wounded in this six-day period and that did not include those sick or gassed. At this stage of the war, those suffering from the effects of gas were counted as 'sick' in official figures (later on, gas casualties were categorised separately), but throughout this book, unless stated at the time, gas casualties are counted as 'wounded in action'. When the returns noted in the brigade diary are taken into account, another seventeen casualties due to enemy action can be added—almost certainly those whose injury was gas related, giving a total of 236 of all ranks.[60] Many of the wounded would not return to the Battalion—either being posted or transferred elsewhere after recovery, medically discharged, or home-posted due to medical downgrading. One such case was CSM George Nelson, who was posted to the depot after leaving hospital. He died in June 1918.

Killed or Died of Wounds 23–29 April

Pte Edward Adams	2069	KIA: 23/4	Pte Thomas Kew	1913	KIA: 24/4
Pte Albert Aspden	1940	DOW: 25/5	Pte Victor Keyworth	1653	KIA: 23/4
Pte John Bagot	1153	KIA: 27/4	2Lt Gerald Kirk		DOW: 24/4
Pte George Edward Balderstone	1386	KIA: 23/4	Pte John Knowles	3087	KIA: 27/4
Pte Ernest Beck	384	DOW: 27/4	Pte John Lawrence	541	KIA: 27/4
Pte George Beckett	1363	KIA: 23/4	Pte Vernon Lennon	1908	KIA: 23/4
Pte Thomas Bigland	1887	KIA: 24/4	Pte Sidney George Lynes	2142	DOW: 25/4
Pte Tom Bolton	3058	KIA: 27/4	Pte James Radcliffe Mawson	2152	DOW: 24/4
Pte Alfred Bostock	2266	KIA: 27/4	Pte Arthur Parkinson	2321	KIA: 23/4
L/Cpl William Henry Bratherton	1732	KIA: 27/4	Pte John Thomas Prince	1674	KIA: 27/4
L/Cpl Thomas Burrow	1512	KIA: 23/4	Pte John Pye	785	KIA: 27/4
Pte Edward Butler	2651	KIA: 28/4	L/Sgt William James Frederick Ray	134	DOW: 5/11
Capt. William Arthur Rowe Carter		KIA: 23/4	Pte Peter Rimmer	2248	KIA: 23/4
Pte George Cathcart	2093	KIA: 23/4	Pte James Simpson	1515	KIA: 23/4
Lt Henry Coupland		DOW: 24/4	Pte Thomas Slater	568	KIA: 23/4
Pte Joseph Cragg	1767	KIA: 23/4	Pte Reginald Stamper***	240628	DOW: 23/4
Sgt John Hinde Gardner	454	KIA: 27/4	Sgt Walter W. Standen	144	KIA: 23/4
Pte Fred Glover	1297	KIA: 27/4	Pte William Henry Theobald	1324	KIA: 23/4
Pte Anthony Gradwell	300	DOW: 27/4	Pte Leonard Thompson	2056	DOW: 29/4
Pte Harry Grice	1675	KIA: 27/4	Pte Thomas Towers	2215	DOW: 26/4
Pte Jack Halliwell	1373	KIA: 27/4	Pte Henry Ernest Waite	1381	KIA: 23/4
Pte Thomas Herdson Hine	2034	KIA: 27/4	L/Cpl John Walmsley****	1486	KIA: 26/4
Pte Richard Huartson	2197	KIA: 23/4	Pte James Ward	2342	KIA: 27/4
Pte Henry Huyton	2384	KIA: 23/4	Pte George Wilkinson	2635	KIA: 27/4
Pte John Johnson*	1687	KIA: 23/4	Pte Henry Winder	2546	KIA: 27/4
Pte John Septimus Johnston	1505	KIA: 23/4	Pte John Woods****	2173	KIA: 26/4
Pte Arthur Jones**	1483	DOW: 8/9	Pte Douglas Campbell Wright	2037	KIA: 23/4

* *Soldiers Died* and the CWGC record John Johnson as KIA on 2 June; however, he appears on the casualty list for the 23 April and comrades wrote to his family about his death at this time.

** Arthur Jones' fatal wounding happened on 26 April.

*** There was obviously much doubt as to the fate of Reginald Stamper; despite eventually being listed DOW on 23 April, he was initially recoded as 'missing'. Usually, if nothing was heard within a year, a man was then declared 'dead'. He is unique among men missing at this time as he was given a six-figure number, allocated in March 1917.

**** Almost certainly killed on 23 April.

Known to have been Wounded 23–29 April

Pte James Henry Akrigg	240671	WIA: 27/4
Pte Edward Alston	2028	WIA: 23/4
Pte R. Anderton	877	WIA: 23/4
Pte George Anderson Atkinson	241159	WIA: 24/4
Pte Anthony William Atkinson	1303	WIA: 27/4
Pte Albert Bamber	1191	WIA: 23/4
Pte Robert W. Bamber	1357	WIA: 23/4
L/Cpl Isaac Bennett	240226	WIA: 23/4
Pte Alan Bennett	240204	WIA: 23/4
Pte Henry Dawson Blades	240842	WIA: 23/4
Pte Thomas Stapleton Blakeley	2452	WIA: 23/4
Pte William Bowker	1848	WIA: 23/4
Pte Alfred Bowker	240161	WIA: 23/4
Pte John Bowman	3046	WIA: 23/4
Pte Harold William Bransden	240563	WIA: 23/4
A/Cpl Thomas William Brayshaw	1033	WIA: 23/4
Lt William Noel Briggs		WIA: 23/4
Pte Joseph Brodie	1205	WIA: 23/4
Pte John William Brown	1338	WIA: 27/4
Pte William F. Bunter	2227	WIA: 23/4
Pte Robert. Burrow	3285	WIA: 24/4
Pte Frederick Calderbank	1415	WIA: 28/4
Pte Michael Carradus	1044	WIA: 23/4
L/Cpl Sidney Cartmell	240500	WIA: 24/4
Pte Fred Cartmell	1998	WIA: 23/4
Pte Harold Cartmell	1562	WIA: 23/4
Pte Joseph Caton	240064	WIA: 25/4
Pte Richard Ogden Charnley	958	WIA: 23/4
L/Cpl William Stephen Clarkson	1288	WIA: 23/4
L/Cpl Herbert Collinson	2084	WIA: 23/4
L/Cpl Samuel Cooper	240546	WIA: 23/4
Pte Albert Edward Corless	2188	WIA: 23/4
Pte Richard Corless	2083	WIA: 23/4
Pte William Henry Cornthwaite	240257	WIA: 23/4
Pte Thomas Cornthwaite	240991	WIA: 27/4
Pte John Crahan	1544	WIA: 23/4
Pte John Dainty	243449	WIA: 23/4
Pte James Dillon	1799	WIA: 23/4
Pte Charles William Dixon	645	WIA: 23/4
Pte William Liver	2146	WIA: 23/4
Pte John Lofthouse*	240868	WIA: 23/4
Lt Edward Meredyd Lloyd-Evans		WIA: 23/4
Pte Benjamin Charles Love	2202	WIA: 24/4
Pte Edward Makinson	240258	WIA: 23/4
L/Cpl William Marsden	1442	WIA: 25/5
Pte Edward Mason	1055	WIA: 23/4
Pte Thomas McCormack	486	WIA: 24/4
Pte John McGreevy	1958	WIA: 23/4
Pte Thomas Miller Monks	2205	WIA: 23/4
Pte James Muckalt	1733	WIA: 23/4
Pte Edward Nash	240551	WIA: 23/4
Sgt Frank Needham	820	WIA: 23/4
Pte Joseph Needham	240121	WIA: 23/4
Sgt George Edward Nelson	240012	WIA: 23/4
Pte James Walter Newby	34211	WIA: 24/4
Pte Charles Arthur Oldham	1393	WIA: 23/4
Pte William Henry Osborne	1379	WIA: 23/4
Lt Thomas Cary Owtram		WIA: 23/4
Pte Walter Painter	2320	WIA: 24/4
A/Cpl Bruce Parker	2246	WIA: 23/4
Pte Thomas Parker	240200	WIA: 27/4
Pte John Patterson	1993	WIA: 24/4
Pte George Pearcy	240575	WIA: 23/4
Pte James Edward Peel	1790	WIA: 23/4
Pte Joseph Peel	2185	WIA: 23/4
L/Cpl William Pinch	240471	WIA: 23/4
Pte Thomas Porter	240561	WIA: 25/5
Cpl Charles William Povell	1078	WIA: 23/4
L/Cpl Harry Rawes	2918	WIA: 23/4
Pte Robert Redfearn	1665	WIA: 23/4
Pte James Redhead	1214	WIA: 27/4
Pte Edison Riding	240352	WIA: 23/4
L/Cpl Richard Rigby	2009	WIA: 29/4
Pte Edward Rigg	240625	WIA: 23/4
Pte Edward R. Rimmer	242508	WIA: 23/4
Pte Ambrose Robinson	240817	WIA: 23/4
Pte Maurice James Robinson	1707	WIA: 23/4
Pte Richard Rogerson	1423	WIA: 23/4

Pte John Wilson Dixon	1365	WIA: 24/4	Pte Thomas Roocroft	1749	WIA: 23/4
Pte Harry Dixon	240791	WIA: 25/5	Pte Reginald Llewellyn Ruddock	1821	WIA: 24/4
L/Cpl William Docherty	240197	WIA: 23/4	Pte George Stanley Sandall	868	WIA: 23/4
			Pte Robert Sanderson	240247	WIA: 26/4
Pte William Henry Doran	1945	WIA: 23/4	Capt. Gerald Whittaker Sharpe		WIA: 23/4
Pte George Douch	2225	WIA: 24/4	L/Sgt Charles Edward Shaw	887	WIA: 23/4
Pte Thomas Downey	2184	WIA: 27/4	Pte Francis Henry Shaw	1769	WIA: 23/4
Pte George Downham	2239	WIA: 23/4	Pte Joseph Shuttleworth	240052	WIA: 23/4
Pte Herbert Eccles	240639	WIA: 23/4	Capt. Charles Vernon M. Simpson		WIA: 23/4
Pte George Edmondson	240143	WIA: 23/4	L/Cpl John Simpson	1556	WIA: 23/4
Pte William Elkin	240910	WIA: 23/4	Sgt William Edward Simpson	265238	WIA: 24/4
L/Sgt Thomas Ellison	432	WIA: 24/4	Pte Reginald Simpson	240534	WIA: 27/4
Cpl M. England	1563	WIA: 23/4	L/Cpl George Lewis Skinner	1478	WIA: 23/4
Pte Harry Ferguson	240130	WIA: 27/4	Cpl Charles Smalley	240657	WIA: 27/4
Pte George Frederick Fleming	1508	WIA: 23/4	Pte Percy W. Smith	1789	WIA: 23/4
Pte William Gardner	240439	WIA: 23/4	Pte William Smith	265376	WIA: 23/4
Pte William Gardner	240479	WIA: 23/4	Pte James Robert Smith	1783	WIA: 27/4
Pte George H. Gill	2122	WIA: 23/4	Pte George Spencer	240451	WIA: 24/4
Pte James Connor Gill	240511	WIA: 24/4	Pte Frank Stamp	1729	WIA: 23/4
Pte Percy Stobart Greenwood	240920	WIA: 23/4	Pte Bernard Stephenson	240453	WIA: 23/4
Pte Joseph Gregg	240799	WIA: 27/4	Pte Richard Stevenson	581	WIA: 23/4
Pte Robert Gudgeon	1361	WIA: 23/4	Pte James Taylor	1740	WIA: 23/4
Pte William Croft Hall	240089	WIA: 23/4	L/Cpl Richard Taylor	240325	WIA: 27/4
Pte James Edward Hardy	1432	WIA: 23/4	Pte Herbert Teasdale	240540	WIA: 23/4
Pte John William Hargreaves	240324	WIA: 27/4	Cpl Henry Tennant	464	WIA: 23/4
Pte John Harney	240423	WIA: 23/4	Pte William Thompson	1326	WIA: 24/4
Pte John Harrison	3020	WIA: 23/4	Pte James Marsh Thornton	2426	WIA: 23/4
L/Cpl Ralph Haslam	1008	WIA: 27/4	Cpl John Henderson Thwaites	2181	WIA: 23/4
Pte Thomas Hayhurst	242505	WIA: 23/4	L/Sgt Leonard Raymond Titchener	1474	WIA: 23/4
Cpl Robert Hetherington	240125	WIA: 23/4	Pte Harry Gilbert Towers	240543	WIA: 23/4
Pte Samuel Higginson	240193	WIA: 23/4	Sgt Joseph Edward Towers	348	WIA: 23/4
Pte John Hinde	240330	WIA: 23/4	Pte John George Townson	240070	WIA: 23/4
Pte John Hodgkinson	1959	WIA: 27/4	A/Cpl Bertrand James Vince	2177	WIA: 24/4
Pte William Hodgson	1588	WIA: 23/4	Pte Robert Wadsworth	240468	WIA: 27/4
Pte Harold Hodgson	3031	WIA: 27/4	Pte Robert Walker	2051	WIA: 23/4
Pte Thomas C. Holland	3050	WIA: 23/4	Pte William H. Wareing	938	WIA: 23/4
L/Sgt Harold Holmes	753	WIA: 23/4	Pte William Whalley	240021	WIA: 27/4
L/Cpl John Hooley	219	WIA: 23/4	Pte Richard Whiteside	240553	WIA: 23/4
Pte Robert Howson	240158	WIA: 23/4	Pte Robert Whiteside	2436	WIA: 23/4
L/Cpl Thomas Huartson	240365	WIA: 23/4	Pte Clarence Whiteside	1392	WIA: 24/4
Pte William James Hughes	240013	WIA: 23/4	Pte William James Wilkinson	243459	WIA: 23/4
2Lt Frank Derwent Huntington		WIA: 23/4	Pte Thomas Willacy**	1606	WIA: 24/4

L/Cpl Richard Irving	2044	WIA: 23/4	Pte Richard Wilson	1247	WIA: 23/4
Pte John C. Johnstone	265532	WIA: 23/4	Pte Jack Woodhouse	1622	WIA: 27/4
Pte William David Jones	240611	WIA: 23/4	Pte William Woolcock	1812	WIA: 23/4
L/Cpl Joseph Leack	240175	WIA: 23/4	L/Cpl Wilfred Worby	240327	WIA: 23/4
Pte Isaiah Lightfoot	241073	WIA: 23/4	Pte Harry Harold Wright	240467	WIA: 23/4

* Reported in newspapers as wounded on 4 May. As his injury was a bayonet wound to the right hand, this was probably an error, especially as the description of the circumstances fits that of the action for 23 April.

** Apart from gunshot wounds (bullet or shrapnel), Willacy was suffering from the effects of gas. It was the latter that led to his death from pneumonia in England in 1916.

1 May 1915–14 May 1915: The Frezenberg Ridge

Their time in billets was a tonic for the exhausted battalion, who rejoiced in the warm sunshine and played a series of rugby matches against anyone who would take them on. On Sunday 2 May, their match against the East Yorks, whom they beat 9–8, was accompanied by German shells hitting the road a mere 200 yards from the pitch— though play continued uninterrupted. The previous night, the CO had received a message forewarning that they were to return to Polygon Wood on Tuesday, information actually welcomed as the Wood was now deemed a 'quiet' area. Regrettably, it was not to be; shortly after the rugby match ended, new orders arrived to move to trenches on the Frezenberg Ridge later that night. Immediately upon Lord Richard receiving this, he despatched a party from 'C' Company to reconnoitre these positions. Capt. Eaves, A/ CSM George Barrow, and L/Cpl Harry Cross left for Frezenberg, Eaves on horseback, the NCOs on bicycles. George Barrow described their experience:

> There were officers and non-coms of other battalions on the same job. Whilst we were there the Germans started to attack. The first thing we saw was a green cloud, which burst all along the line, and clung to the earth like a mist. Then their artillery burst out. We set out to rejoin our battalion and made along the road to a small village where we had left our bicycles. The road was shelled from both sides. Imagine our dismay when we found that someone had taken L/Cpl Cross' cycle and left one with a big cut in the outer cover and punctured. We started to mend it and while doing so, shells kept falling around us. One knocked a tree down close to us. We saw some awful sights on the road as we made our way back to the battalion. We had some narrow escapes. One shell passed just in front of Capt. Eaves and made his horse shy, but we all managed to get back safely after a very exciting afternoon.[1]

With the loss of ground taken from the French during the first gas attack, the situation in the Salient was difficult for the British, their left flank open to attack; Sir John French was determined to withdraw the line back to a more defensible position. Due to French protests, this planned withdrawal was postponed twice (29 and 30 April) as Sir John had promised Foch that he would await the results of his counterattacks before actually withdrawing. When these failed, the withdrawal went ahead, beginning on 1 May and ending on the 3rd.[2] While making sound strategic sense, the plan was flawed in that units were not pulling back to previously prepared positions and British lines on the Mousetrap and Frezenberg Ridges were horribly exposed as both were on forward slopes.

The march to the Frezenberg Ridge on the night of 2 May was long; the Battalion had to divert around Ypres, which was under heavy bombardment. Even with this diversion, much shellfire still fell around them and two men were wounded. L/Cpl Joseph Smith, who just a fortnight earlier had received a graze across the top of his scalp by a bullet, was hit in the foot by shrapnel and evacuated home. Thirty-six-year-old Pte John Topham, a father of five from Lancaster, was thankful that the shrapnel bullet that struck him in the thigh had much of its velocity spent when it passed through the contents of his greatcoat pocket. He was also evacuated home, discharged from hospital in the second week of May and given a week's leave before returning. Once they reached their new trenches, the CO was horrified, and he confided in his diary:

> We are not in the same trenches, but in a second line, about two miles behind, close to the Ypres–Zonnebeke road. They are quite new, very narrow and only half finished; communications trenches very bad. I do not know why we are here. It looks commonly like a general retirement. I don't like this spot at all.[3]

He was right to be concerned. The trenches were just narrow ditches, 1½ feet deep in water in places, with neither breastworks nor wire to their front, no telephone communications to the rear, few shovels, and no Engineers' supplies available to improve matters. The trench line crossed the Ypres–Zonnebeke road at approximately 50°52'8.00"N 2°57'24.00"E, running in a north-westerly to south-easterly direction. Due to their orientation relevant to German positions, the enemy could bring enfilading fire to bear along much of the length of these trenches. Unknown to Lt-Col. Cavendish— or if he did know, he left no record of it—the enemy had occupied a number of houses, giving them a view along the length of much of his line and were using these to spot the fall of their artillery. The CO of 2/King's Own, Lt-Col. Martin, sent a number of messages to the artillery on 7 May asking for these to be targeted by British Howitzers, but nothing was done.[4]

As soon as they reached the line, 'A' and 'D' occupied the fire trenches and immediately began work with the meagre resources available. 'B' and 'C' took over the dugouts to the rear. Shelling began at 6 a.m. on 3 May, and soon afterwards, 'C' Company was ordered to depart to support 1 Rifle Brigade at 50°52'56.70"N 2°58'13.40"E, just over a mile to the north-west of Zonnebeke. It was not possible to make this journey without coming under enemy observation, and as they advanced along the left of the Zonnebeke–Langemarck road, they were heavily shelled and held up for some time. Eaves sent a runner back informing Lt-Col. Cavendish, who then contacted Brigade, who ordered

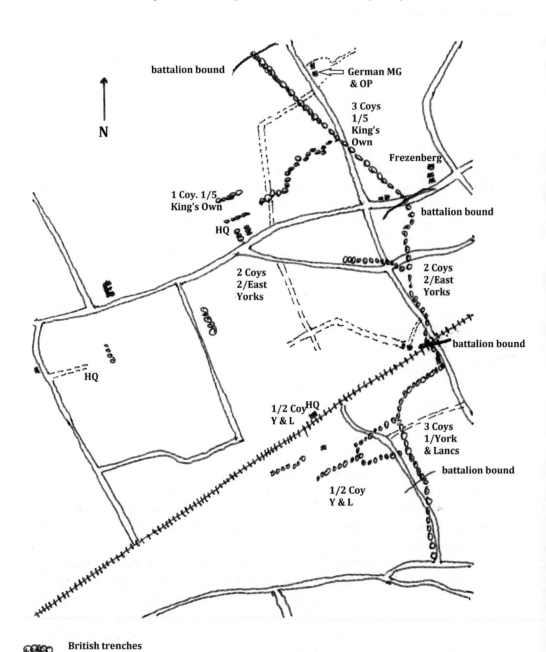

The Frezenberg Ridge
4 May 1915

that 'C' should continue. At 4 p.m., 'B' was detached, and along with elements of East Yorks and Yorks and Lancs, headed off to join 'C' Company, this detachment advancing to the right of the road. The composite force proceeded along either side of the road until they were close to the trenches, where they lay down awaiting dark. However, instead of moving up to the trench line, both companies were ordered to return as the line was to be pulled back as part of the final stage of withdrawal.

Casualty lists report two fatalities from 'C' Company that day, but as one was known to have been killed while he treated the wounds of another man—whose wounding is noted for 5 May—these dates must be treated with caution, especially as the CO's diary reports at least two killed and seven wounded for 'C' Company, possibly more.[5] Twenty-four-year-old Pte Rupert Radcliffe was hit in the thigh by shrapnel, and it was as he was being bandaged by his platoon-sergeant that a shell landed next to him, killing twenty-five-year-old Sgt James Kirkby from Carnforth, who was struck in the neck by a large shell splinter.[6] Also killed from 'C' was Pte William Wright (928). It is likely that another 'C' Company fatality that day was twenty-year-old Pte Roland Cariss from Scotforth. Although CWGC reports his death as being on 4 May, Eaves' letter of condolence to his father states it was the 3rd.[7] The letter to the family from his cousin, Charles Galloway, also supports this date:

> Almost as soon as we started the Germans saw us and opened a heavy fire with shrapnel on us. We got the order to scatter, and Roland and I got separated, and it was not until night that I heard the awful news. I at once went to the officer to see if by any chance any mistake had been made, but it was only too true. Poor old chap! He died a painless death, the piece of shrapnel entering his brain.[8]

A further twenty-one men from 'C' Company appear on the casualty list for 4 May, and at least six of these, if not the majority, must actually be from the 3rd, only two of whom can definitely be discounted for that date. One of the men likely to have been wounded on the 3rd was Sgt Richard Kirkby, James Kirkby's brother, who received a minor shrapnel wound to the head.

Two 'C' Company privates from Morecambe were posted missing from this detachment. Herbert Thacker and John 'Jack' Worden were in an advanced position, and when the rest retired, someone neglected to tell them. On the morning of the 4th, when the enemy discovered the British had withdrawn, they immediately occupied the former British line in force and these two found themselves alone against the might of the Kaiser's army. Quite sensibly, both surrendered and ended up in the POW camp in Sennelager. Worden recorded:

> I am going on all right and enjoying the best of health. Indeed, I am having a good time, and I hope that you are not worrying, for I shall be home as soon as peace is declared. There is one thing however, don't forget to send me a parcel of foodstuffs every week. The weather is lovely out here and we are right out in the country.

Thacker wrote:

> I am still in the land of the living, and am doing all right. I don't however hardly know
> what day it is; I only know that we are treated right; so don't worry. Jack is well.
> Remember me to all. Try to let me know how George Downham is.[9]

The climate in Sennelager may be 'lovely' in June, but the pair, who were used to
temperate Morecambe, would be in for a bit of a shock during winter. In June 1915,
it was doubtful if anyone believed the war would drag on until November 1918, and
as time passed, conditions became much harder for prisoners. Interestingly, Herbert
Thacker was given a medical discharge because of wounds (not injuries or sickness) on
31 December 1917, so he must have been part of a POW exchange for badly wounded
prisoners. How and when he was wounded is unknown, but he and George Downham
may have been reunited as the latter lived until October 1918.

The two companies in the Frezenberg trenches did not escape scot-free on 3 May, and
as 'D' entered the trench, a shell burst among them, killing five and wounding thirteen.
When men moved anywhere within range of enemy artillery, they kept well-spaced
apart; however, on entering any trench system, it was inevitable that bunching occurred
and it was most unfortunate that the shell hit at that time. Three of the dead had been
particularly close friends; thirty-two-year-old Pte James Fairclough, thirty-one-year-old
Pte Frederick Lowe, and twenty-six-year-old Pte Harry Angus had worked together at
Waring & Gillows. They had enlisted together, ate, slept, and worked together, and now
became comrades in death. Lowe left behind a wife and child, and Fairclough's wife had
only given birth to their first child nine weeks earlier—a child he never saw. Twenty-
year-old Pte John Wilson (182) and twenty-seven-year-old Pte Edward Winder—the
other two killed by this shell—also worked for Waring & Gillows. One of the wounded,
twenty-year-old Pte Edmund Alderson from Lancaster, was hit in the small of the back
and side by shrapnel and given the shrapnel balls as a souvenir by the surgeon. When
he was home on sick leave, he had one set as a brooch in a golden pin mounting as a
present for his mother.[10] Pte Roger Brown was buried by the shell, but quickly dug out
unharmed. Fate was not to be denied as shortly afterwards, he was wounded in the
knee by shrapnel, an injury that brought about his medical discharge in December. 'D'
Company bore the brunt of the Frezenberg casualties on 3 May, the only 'A' Company
casualty (twenty-five-year-old Pte Joseph Thwaites) was very badly wounded in both
legs by shrapnel. These wounds proved fatal and he died on 12 May at the Canadian
hospital in Le Tréport.

Once the two detached companies rejoined in the early hours of 4 May, 'B' occupied
the dugouts to the rear, the other three, the fire trenches. Shortly after dawn, the
enemy realising that there had been a general withdrawal, moved forward *en masse*
and occupied positions 800 yards from the Battalion's line. British artillery failed to fire
a single round into the Germans, the only hindrance to their advance coming from the
rifles of the Battalion. Encouraged by this lack of opposition, the enemy brought their

artillery closer and began a fourteen-hour bombardment of the Battalion. What made this barrage all the deadlier was that many of the Maxims and shrapnel-firing guns were able to enfilade the meagre trench line. One 'D' Company soldier from Skerton described the day:

> The Germans started advancing with artillery and machine guns to cover them. Their artillery is marvellous, but if our artillery had been going it would have wiped out the Germans. As it was we had to do it with our rifles, and believe me we got a bit of revenge [for the shell that hit the company the previous day]. We wiped a few of them out. They advanced in small groups, and we could not miss them. Our rifles got so hot we could not hold them. We burnt our fingers when we were lowering our sights. Seven of us in our traverse got a box full of ammunition off (2,500 rounds), so you can guess how busy we were.[11]

The Battalion lost heavily. Sixteen were killed immediately, six of the wounded later died, and a further ninety-nine were wounded. Eighteen-year-old Pte Herbert Carey wrote to his father from his hospital bed in Liverpool:

> We were under shot and shell fire and that murderous gas, which I escaped, but I received a bullet wound in the wrist on Tuesday night. On Monday and Tuesday the Germans were shelling us, and we were holding some new trenches which were not half finished. Our chaps retired from the old trenches too soon, as they thought the others were ready for them.... When we reached the new trenches (which had just been started on) it was raining hard and nearly daylight. We had to stick it, so we set to and began digging the trenches. We had not been at it long when we saw the Germans advancing over a hill about 600 yards away. We opened fire on them and gave them it hot. We held them there all day against heavy shell fire. I got buried twice, but soon got out unhurt. About noon there were eight of us left in our trench, but we still kept the Germans back.[12]

The youngest fatality was seventeen-year-old Pte James Cathcart, much to the palpable distress of his parents—he and his elder brother (killed on 23 April) had been the only sons. Cathcart was asleep in the trench late that night when a shell burst overhead. His pal, seventeen-year-old Pte Frederick Monks, wounded by the same shell, described the incident in a letter home:

> No doubt you will be surprised to hear that I am wounded—a slight wound to the head, caused by shrapnel. It is a mere scratch and I am now in hospital with some others. Jim (Cathcart) got a nasty blow on the head, which I think killed him. He was asleep; he never spoke, and never stirred an inch. The best of it is he never suffered any pain.[13]

Many of the wounded never served with the Battalion again, being transferred to other units or medically discharged because of their injuries. One such was twenty-five-year-old Pte Thomas Fox. From his hospital bed in Sandgate, Fox penned—with difficulty—a letter to his old headmaster:

> I got very badly wounded on 4 May at Ypres by a shrapnel shell bursting in the trench. Still, I was lucky, three men being killed out of five of us. I've lost half of my right hand, the first finger and thumb remaining intact, whilst I have a stump of the second finger. This is my first attempt at writing. I got a piece of shrapnel through my side, making a very troublesome wound, and necessitating an operation. It will be some time before I am able to get home.[14]

Even by July, Fox was still suffering nerve pain from fingers that no longer existed and his medical discharge was not until August 1917. He was transferred to the RDC after he had left hospital as an in-patient, where his duties would be commensurate to his disability. The Army did not discharge men in wartime while their treatment was still continuing—not because they were trying to hold onto men, but because, as soldiers, the wounded would receive full pay and have better access to medical facilities than they would as civilians.

Sometimes, the trauma of operations was fatal. Twenty-one-year-old Pte Alfred English had a leg amputated on 20 May in England and died just after midnight on 21 May, never regaining consciousness after his operation. Sadly, his parents, summoned by telegram when the seriousness of his condition was recognised, arrived too late. Another who died after amputation was a thirty-three-year-old married man from Lancaster, Pte John Howson. His badly mangled left arm was amputated at the shoulder on 9 May, and he gradually slipped away and died on the 22nd.

The men in the front line could clearly see the enemy massing for attack, but lack of communication to the rear meant direct fire support was impossible. Twenty-year-old Pte William Gibson from Fleetwood was given the task of delivering a written 'fire mission' to the Artillery-Officer:

> We were in the tightest corner imaginable, having been under continual bombardment, and our trench had been blown to pieces. Dead and wounded were lying all over the place. The Germans advanced and got to within thirty or forty yards of us all along the line. I had a good time and put several out of action. You could not miss hitting them. It had to be done. Just afterwards, a letter was passed down from man to man. I was the last man in our trench. The message had to be delivered to an artillery officer. I delivered the message, which was, 'Enemy concentrating behind farmhouse in great numbers.' The usual message would have been to telephone from our trench right back to the artillery, but our wires were broken and that was why the message had to be so transmitted. I had only to cross an open space of forty–fifty yards to get to another trench, but although I was crawling on my stomach all the time the Germans sighted me. Having got three wounds I got permission to try to find a dressing station. So I started off again. I should think I crept about a mile towards safety when I just lifted

my body up and the Germans hit me again. After that I lay in a 'Jack Johnson' hole. I felt so weak that I gave myself up to die. How long I lay there I cannot remember, but I knew that all the time shrapnel was bursting overhead. This was to stop any reinforcements coming to help our troops. Suddenly a sense of strange strength came over me. I got up and ran over fields and ditches. I was lost, but on I went until I came to a road. Something told me in which direction to move, so off I went again, shrapnel falling in every direction. At last I got out of the danger zone and came to an empty house. I say empty, but the furniture was still there, even dirty coffee mugs had been left on the table. I sat down for a short time and then recommenced my journey until I came to some cross-roads. I went down one and could hear English voices. This sounded the sweetest music I had ever heard. At last a doctor came up, examined the wounds and inserted morphia: then I slept peacefully. I was later conveyed to the other side of Ypres, and the road along which I was being driven was swept by shrapnel. I eventually arrived at Boulogne, where I stopped one night, then sailed for England, landed at Dover and removed to Oxford. I will never forget how one man died in my arms. About eight o'clock four wounded men left our trench to make for the dressing trench. Only one got about fifty yards when he fell, so I went out after him to give him a drink of water and to take him behind some cover. I had just raised his head and given him a drink when the poor fellow got another bullet in the heart.[15]

What Gibson did not mention was that this man took half an hour to die and that he remained with him, exposed to enemy fire, until the man expired. He was medically discharged in August 1916 and awarded a very well-deserved DCM. Others too got the DCM, one of whom was L/Cpl William Lynch. He also braved fire to deliver a number of messages to the rear and attended to wounded men lying in the open. After this, he worked a machine gun single-handed after all the crew had become casualties. Sadly, he was wounded the next day, but would return. Cpl Eric Bennett went out numerous times to repair breaks in the telephone wire and even delivered some messages by hand, despite the heavy and close-range fire from machine guns and rifles. He was awarded the DCM, and was yet another who did not come through these few days unscathed—one of many casualties of 8 May.

The MG Section, always a priority target, suffered badly. Sgt Joseph Hall from Silverdale was seriously wounded—hit in knee, shoulder, chest, and both hands. Nineteen-year-old Pte Edward Hoggarth from Lancaster was killed—the same shell wounding nineteen-year-old Pte George Hutton in the left leg and both hands. CWGC have Hoggarth's death as 3 May, but other sources, including the letter of condolence to his parents from the replacement MG-Officer Lt George Milnes, all give 4 May as the date. Hutton had already experienced a number of close escapes; one day, a tin of tobacco in his pack, which he was carrying for a comrade, was shot to bits—on another, he had his water bottle blown off his belt. His luck ran out on the Tuesday as he should not even have been on duty at that gun. The man whose task it was fell into one of the ditches and got soaked through, so Sgt Hall sent him to the rear to get dry clothes, replacing him with Hutton. Hutton's wounds were serious and there was concern that he may not survive them, though he did eventually pull through and was medically discharged.[16] Pte Joseph Peel later corresponded with his wife about this:

> It was a pitiful sight to see. One of our team (Maxim) was killed and a sergeant and four men wounded. We were sent to help the Fleetwood team and some of them are injured. Our gun was put out of action early in the morning, and I was just missed by a miracle. Later on a piece of shrapnel dropped on my boot, cut it, went through my sock and just grazed my foot. We dare not show our faces for fear of having our heads blown off.[17]

MG-Officer 2Lt William Wolfendale, with the Battalion for just seven weeks and only twenty-years-old, behaved with great courage. He held his position for twenty-four hours, despite having his clothing and equipment riddled with bullet holes—the gun twice put out of action by enemy fire. Each time, he repaired it and single-handedly kept it firing until a shell landed on the parapet directly in front of it, destroying the weapon and burying him. Fortunately, he was missed by some of his brother officers, who went searching for him and dug him out just in time. Initially, it was thought that he was suffering from the effects of gas, but once in hospital in Boulogne, severe concussion was diagnosed. He returned home for treatment, and after two months in hospital, he went to 3/5th King's Own at Blackpool as a Machine-Gun Instructor, the MC a reward for his bravery and determination.[18]

Three brothers were wounded on 4 May—two by the same bullet. The round that struck Pte Burgoyne Hall in the leg passed straight through and hit his brother, James, in the knee. They and the third brother, Gilbert, all went home for treatment. Pte Joseph Mashiter, whose milking skills had been so useful on 23 April, was shot in the knee and, after dark, helped from the field by his brother, Charles. When a father of three, thirty-year-old Pte Henry Milne from Lancaster, was wounded in the thigh, he risked all to reach the dressing station:

> A German shell came amongst six of us, blowing the trench down. It killed one and injured the others, I being one of the wounded. There were some awful sights I can tell you. I had a pound's worth of stuff in my bag and it was all blown to bits. The Germans bombarded our trenches with shrapnel, 'Jack Johnsons', and gas bombs. When I got hit I and another chap made a bolt for it, but the Germans put a Maxim gun onto us. They hit the other chap, but I got away, and crawled a quarter of a mile with my wound. I got it dressed under awful shell fire. I had to lay there ten hours before I could be shifted.[19]

Thirty-four-year-old Pte James Rumley, a prominent Lancaster footballer and Boer War veteran, also risked crawling back in daylight after he had received a wound to the thigh. He too made it, but the damage was severe enough to end both his footballing days and his military career.

The Halls were not the only family members hit by the same projectile. New York-born forty-six-year-old Lancaster motor agent Sgt Mortimer Thomas and his son—also called Mortimer, but known as 'Tim'—were seriously wounded by the same shell and evacuated home. Mortimer senior quietly 'lost' ten years from his age when he enlisted and his serious wounds to right arm and leg proved too much—he died from these on 9 June. Tim was still in hospital and was too poorly to attend the funeral in Lancaster, but the coffin was borne by six members of the Battalion who were home after being wounded and many of his comrades who were on convalescent leave also attended.[20] Tim recovered, but was medically discharged in April 1916.

Yet another wounded on his birthday was thirty-nine-year-old Pte James Wilson, a father of three from Skerton. Though the minor wound to his left arm was not the sort of present he had been hoping for, it is easy to presume that his time in hospital, with clean sheets and some rest, was much more the thing. Seventeen-year-old Pte Jack Woodhouse from Morecambe had an unbelievable escape from what should have been a fatal wound. A shell splinter entered his head just in front of his left ear, passed clean through, and exited the right side of his head. Had it deviated just a fraction, it would have caused devastating and disfiguring injuries, or death. As it was, he was released from hospital in Southend just three weeks later.[21] Another seventeen-year-old was not so fortunate. Pte Ernest Wright from Lancaster was hit in the right thigh by shrapnel, just six days before his eighteenth birthday, and after four operations, was medically discharged in September 1916.

Sometimes a casualty's kin were unknown to anyone in the Battalion, and the official notice was the first the family received. When a shell killed twenty-one-year-old Pte George Shuttleworth (078) from Morecambe, officialdom made a dreadful mistake. Infantry Records in Preston sent notification to the mother of Pte George Shuttleworth (737) from Lancaster. His distraught mother was mystified as to how her son could be killed by the Germans—she thought he was safely with 2/5 King's Own in Sevenoaks. Fortunately, a telegram from her son soon reassured her and a convoluted series of correspondence between Battalion and Records tried to find the underlying cause of the error—the Battalion insistent that it was Shuttleworth (737) who was dead. An investigation carried out by the War Office determined the blunder had transpired when their numbers had become transposed in Battalion records prior to deployment to France—though the individual soldiers continued to use their proper numbers. Thankfully, this sort of heart-breaking mistake happened rarely.

It was not just those in the firing line who suffered on 4 May. Signallers spent much of their time in dugouts, but whenever there were problems, they left this relative safety to investigate the fault. All too frequently, this was when it was most dangerous to be out in the open—as nineteen-year-old L/Cpl Charles Lund discovered. He and Sgt Herbert Eaton were two of those responsible for maintaining communications, and the telephone wire they had managed to lay was repeatedly broken by shellfire. Four times they went out to repair it, but on the fifth, Lund was hit in the leg by shrapnel. Although he was recommended for a medal, none was awarded. Once safely back in billets on 6 May, signaller Cpl Tom Fairclough described that day in a letter to his sister:

H__ [possibly Herbert Eaton] and myself were on the telephone wires, but the shells cut them and we had to go out and mend them, crawling on our stomachs and shells and bullets flying all over. But we got back safely, and in a few minutes they were broken again, so we had another attempt, and the same thing happened again. So we went again under cover of darkness and mended between forty and fifty breaks, so you can imagine what it was like…. Three of our signallers [out of six] are wounded, and out of action. One young chap was hit in the head and his instrument blown to pieces, so you can imagine what it was like. One was hit while he was mending wires and I believe he has been recommended for some decoration or other. I went from our trenches and brought the broken instrument to our trench, and fixed the batteries in our instrument, as ours were very weak. I can tell you it was a case of life or death, but we don't think about it until after we have done it.[22]

Fairclough wrote his next letter from hospital.

As darkness fell, artillery fire directed onto the foremost trenches dwindled and the range lengthened to pound the rear. On the night of 4 May near Verlorenhoek, shellfire fell around men from Transport as they brought the rations forward. 'B' Company CQMS Albert Wilson wrote to the parents of Pte Richard Yare:

About 10.30 p.m. a shell exploded nearer than usual and 'Dick' was wounded in the chest and toe with shrapnel. After being hit he helped with one of the other men who was wounded at the same time. He was then sent to the dressing station and then sent to base. 'Dick' is a grand lad, and cares nothing for German shells. He has no fear of any kind, and he was about the bravest chap I have met for a very long time.[23]

Another injured by this shell was Pte Robert Silverwood from Quernmore—hit in the left arm and leg. Thirty-year-old Cpl Edwin Lidford was awarded the DCM for his courage during this incident. As shells continued to fall around him, he disengaged a number of wounded horses from the transport, ignoring the peril to his own life as he worked single-handed. Many of the drivers had sought cover, unnerved by the shock and violent concussion of bursting shells, the cries of the wounded, and the screams of injured horses. Lidford's coolness under fire steadied the others and they rallied round to help clear the carnage and continue the delivery. CQMS Albert Wilson was also recognised for his courage and awarded the MM. In all, three horses were killed and five drivers and storemen wounded. One seriously wounded man, who may have been one of these casualties, was thirty-seven-year-old father of four L/Cpl Joseph Newton from Lancaster. Though the newspaper report of his death from wounds on 7 May gives the 6th as his date of wounding, it is more likely that he was wounded in this incident.[24] CQMS Byrne was given a MiD for getting the rations through under fire, although his citation mistakenly gives 4 June as the date.[25] One inexplicable casualty from 4 May is that of twenty-two-year-old Pte Richard Butler (served as Stanley Butler) from Fleetwood. His service record notes him as being 'wounded and missing' on 4 May, and he is recorded as dying from wounds and buried by the Germans at Frezenberg on 19 May.[26] How he managed to be captured on 4 May is an enigma, especially as he was in 'D' Company, and not from one of the two companies detached a day earlier.

As dawn broke, enemy artillery again targeted the men in the fire trenches. Nineteen-year-old Pte Harold Airey had two narrow escapes within minutes as showers of earth from bursting shells covered the men sheltering in the trench; Airey pulled his equipment off and placed it on the earth bank immediately behind him, and seconds later, a shell splinter smashed the belt buckle and cut his belt. Before he could react, another shell landed directly in the parapet in front of him, but it failed to explode. Two days later, he was just as blessed when another piece of shrapnel struck his pack, smashing a tin containing tea and sugar, while a second ball lodged in his valise. One item in his kit that escaped damage was the 'lucky' rosary given to him by the lady who owned the house where he had been billeted—alas, when he returned through this village, the house had taken a direct hit from a heavy shell and only a pile of rubble remained.

The following day, seventeen-year-old Pte Louis Warwick wrote to his mother about the early morning bombardment:

> Up to the present I am well, but we have had a hot time in the trenches.... The danger is worse, however getting in and out, for we have to cross some land called 'The Death Plain', (It sounds a bit unhealthy.) To tell the truth I am tired of it all, and the sooner peace is declared the better. The other day we were just tackling breakfast when the Germans sent a shell tearing into our trench. It exploded near to me, wounding three of my mates and throwing me over with my nose in the frying pan. Needless to say the breakfast was lost. Reuben Bartholomew was wounded in the arm by shrapnel, but it was not severe enough to get him a passage home.[27]

When he wrote this letter, this brave teenager had less than two days of his young life left.

The 'birthday curse' struck again when thirty-one-year-old Pte Thomas Roocroft was hit in the back of the leg by shrapnel following a shell burst on his dugout. He was, however, more fortunate than his three comrades, who were all buried by the explosion. Twenty-one-year-old Pte Joseph Auty probably thought that Wednesday could not have been any worse than Tuesday—he was wrong. He had received a minor wound on Tuesday, but had stayed in the line. He was hit again on Wednesday, and wounded in the back and both feet by shrapnel, remaining in the trenches until after dark when he could be evacuated. Some of the wounded tried to reach the dressing station in daylight—with disastrous consequences—as Sgt Alfred Clowes described in a letter home to a friend in Lancaster, written on the 7th:

> Poor Lt Gardner! I do feel sorry about him. He was wounded in the trenches and tried to get to the headquarters dressing station and when about ten yards from the road I

saw him shot dead. I saw about half a dozen done the same way. Poor David Owen! He was killed about fifteen yards behind me. He was shot in both legs with shrapnel, and had them dressed in the trench. He said, 'Algy, [*sic.*] where is the dressing station?' I said, 'You stick here until night,' and implored him to stay, but he said, 'No, I will try and get there.' Then they put a Maxim on him and he was killed instantly. We buried him alongside Sgt R. Wallbank, who was killed while firing at the enemy by one of their snipers.[28]

Thirty-three-year-old 2Lt Robert Gardner had enlisted as a private and was commissioned just before deployment. Twenty-one-year-old Pte David Owen's brother, William, also served with the Battalion and their father was a CSM with the 2/5th.

Just after Owen was killed, twenty-year-old Pte Charles Hewitson was hit while on top of the parapet and fell outside the trench. Thirty-four-year-old Pte Henry Brewer, a tough ex-Regular, climbed out of the trench and, using his own body to shield Hewitson against a hail of small arms fire, gradually worked his way back towards the dressing station. This act of selfless bravery was witnessed by Capt. Atkinson, who recommended Brewer for a DCM, and although it was not awarded, the MM was. Sadly, Hewitson was posted to and killed with the 8/King's Own in September 1917. One of the wounded, who wisely decided to remain in cover, was twenty-four-year-old machine-gunner Pte John Smith (058) from Lancaster. He had shrapnel wounds to right ankle, left thigh, and left shoulder. Although he had to lie in the trench for ten hours until it was dark enough to evacuate him, he survived and was discharged in April 1916. Every single one of the sixteen stretcher-bearers became a casualty over these two days.

After dark on 4 May, a new batch of junior officers arrived; by dawn, three had been wounded. Second Lieutenant Edgar Carr was evacuated to a London hospital, but he died on 18 May. Also sent home for treatment were thirty-one-year-old Lt Ralph Bustard from Liverpool and forty-two-year-old Lt Spencer Barrow, a Lancaster architect. Another of the subalterns, Lt Charles Saer, was also wounded. Sgt John Gilchrist, injured in the head by shrapnel, wrote home from his hospital train:

We are a train load of wounded. Indeed my throat is also affected by the damnable fumes the German devils used. They will stick at nothing and must for the sake of humanity be brought to their knees. There is a huge casualty list. Lt Barrow got his arm injured six hours after he joined us in the firing line. He will be no use as a fighter again. My rotten luck is nothing compared to his. I don't know where I am going, but I long for a good night's rest; I have only had one since I landed in France.... We want more and more men, and more guns and ammunition, and less of the deliberate unconcern of the British public. Everyone must give more attention to this anxious war. Perhaps you think that I have got wound up, but I am all right. Lots of things have improved lately, but the Germans are strong and active and mean business, though they are swine. I believe our depleted battalion is due for the firing line on Thursday night; their position will be a dangerous one I believe.[29]

John Gilchrist's prediction was out by one day, but remarkably prophetic. Lt Barrow persuaded surgeons not to amputate his arm. By early November, he had partial feeling back into the limb and was looking forward to being allowed home for Christmas. This was not to be; the first time he was allowed out of his London hospital, he caught a chill, suffered a relapse, and septicaemia set in. He died on 16 November. Another of the wounded to die many months after his initial wounding was eighteen-year-old Pte John Toulmin from Morecambe. His severe leg wound continued to cause problems and he died from these on 22 May 1916, aged only nineteen. Before antibiotics, the onset of infection into a wound frequently led to amputation, although if infection spread beyond the limb there was no cure.

Joseph Auty had not been the only soldier who elected to fight on after being wounded. Thirty-eight-year-old A/Cpl Richard Mansfield (born Richard Jervis), a veteran of the Boer War with twenty-years-service with Regulars and TF, also made that choice. On 6 May, forty-seven-year-old Pte William Wilson wrote to his wife, a neighbour of the Mansfields:

> I am sorry to send you some more sad tidings and give you another sad task of breaking the news. Dick Mansfield was killed yesterday. He was slightly wounded on Tuesday 4 May, and after being dressed by the stretcher-bearers, [Pte Thomas Masters—wounded on 5 May] refused to come out of the trench, saying it was not much, and as we were rather short of non-com officers, he would stay with his men, and did so until yesterday, when a shell burst over him. A large piece struck him at the back of the head and killed him instantly. He was buried in the evening by Private G. Thompson of Skerton, and another man, close to where he fell. It was hard lines for him, as he was going to be made sergeant as soon as we came out of the trenches.[30]

The CWGC have 4 May for the date of death for Mansfield, but other sources give 5 May as the actual date. Another to soldier-on was nineteen-year-old Pte William Metcalf from 'B' Company. He received minor wounds to his head and back, and just four days later, he was hit again in the head. This time the wound was more serious and he was evacuated to Chatham for treatment. After his recovery, he transferred to the KLR and subsequently the RE as a telegraphist.

Forty-two year old father of five Pte James Jackson, a highly experienced soldier with fifteen years' service in the Volunteers and TF, was slightly wounded in the trench and was waiting to have his wounds dressed when another shell killed him outright. His brother, Richard, a sergeant (also in 'A' Company), would by the end of the day find himself A/CSM. 'A' Company's hugely experienced CSM, forty-seven-year-old William Ralph—over thirty years' service with the Colours—was wounded in the leg and evacuated home, though he must have been relieved that his seventeen-year-old son, also William and a private in the Battalion, had got through okay. Numbers of wounded perished in the trenches, either from being hit again, or from lack of medical treatment—the fire being too heavy to evacuate them. However, for twenty-five-year-old Pte Thomas Bamber, his serious abdomen wound had probably been beyond any medical treatment. Whenever possible, men gave a dead comrade a decent burial and many took the time to write to relatives to let them know this. Nineteen-year-old Pte Alfred Lockley, something of a local celebrity for saving the life of a drowning seven-year-old in a spate-swollen River Lune, was buried by John Ridding and Leonard Harrison, with Capt. Atkinson reading the service. All three wrote to Lockley's mother sending their condolences. During the course of the war, two out of these three would have comrades do the same for them.

Wednesday brought no improvement when it came to maintaining communications. As soon as a wire was repaired, shellfire caused another break. Consequently, the Battalion had to rely on runners to deliver important messages. At 11.15 a.m., Pte William Huntriss volunteered to take a vital despatch from Capt. Atkinson to HQ. Despite the heavy fire, he made it through and as dusk fell, underwent the perilous journey back. He was awarded the MM for his courage.[31] Sometimes messages were reported to have been conveyed in bizarre ways; a local paper related that, late on Wednesday night, Mrs Lupton had distinctly heard her son thrice cry out, 'Mother!'[32] Whatever the veracity of this, the worst possible news for this distraught mother came on 9 May when she was told of the death of her son, twenty-one-year-old Pte Fred Lupton.

At 6 p.m. on 5 May, the Battalion was instructed that 2/King's Own would be relieving them that night and they were to return to the huts near Vlamertinghe. Relief was completed by 11 p.m. to everyone's relief. Constant bombardment and numerous casualties had left many very shaken by their experience, and Lt-Col. Cavendish believed that his men, already exhausted when they went into the trenches, would not have been able to sustain another day in that position—which in his opinion was 'absolutely untenable'.[33] It is possible, reading Lord Richard's diary, to see that he too was beginning to feel the strain. He was a conscientious and well-respected CO, who asked nothing he was not prepared to do himself—and his men obviously recognised and appreciated this. If he could be accused of one weakness, it was probably his love of the Battalion he had built. To see it cut to pieces in front of him, knowing as he did every man who served in it, and in many cases their families too, was obviously beginning to bear heavily on him. During the charge of 23 April, the CO had been up there with them and when the attack stalled, he had gone from one wounded man to another, issuing his supply of opium tabloids to ease their pain—putting their welfare above his own personal safety. Casualties had been severe, and although trench strength on 7 May was down to 398, over 100 of these reported sick that morning; according to Lt George, every single one was genuinely ill. What the Battalion needed now was rest and reinforcement. Unfortunately, what they got was the opposite.

On 6 May, 2/King's Own were shelled, but with nothing like the intensity the 1/5th had endured over the previous days.[34] For the 1/5th this was to be their only day of rest as after dark, many were needed to carry trench stores to the 2nd Battalion, a working party CSM George Barrow mentioned in a letter home:

We had just finished at dawn and got back to our dugouts. In a ruined house I found some cushions and a blanket, also a little oil lamp for cooking with. I was in luck's way and soon had some breakfast and lay down to sleep. I was soon awakened, told to get the company out and before long we were in a reserve trench.[35]

A good sleep was one of the scarcest commodities on the Western Front.

On 7 May, the Battalion was ordered to dugouts to the south of Brigade HQ in St Jean, and at 1 a.m. on the 8th, they were moved to a line of trenches running at right angles to the Ypres–Zonnebeke road, opposite Potijze Chateau. On arrival, they found these were already occupied by a mix of many regiments. Though the front line trenches did not get much shellfire during the night, the rear areas came in for a considerable pasting. 'A' Company marched off immediately upon the order's arrival at 1 a.m., and 'B' were awaiting their turn to leave. One man—impressed by the bravery of thirty-five-year-old Pte Christopher Cooper and Pte Thompson—sent a description of what happened to the local press in the hope that these two would get some recognition:[36]

'B' Company were at tea when a Jack Johnson came bursting amongst 'B' Company and buried about twenty of them. There was a fearful cry for help, and many of the men near were stunned by the concussion. L/Cpl Cooper (then a private) got hit in the back with a lump of earth, and another lump knocked his head, but when he pulled himself together he saw two fellows struggling to get free of the debris. He ran away, though shrapnel was sweeping the field, and released the two chaps. He saw the sole of a boot and knew another man was buried. In hot haste he liberated the man, whose mouth was full of slutch, and Dr George said that if he had remained a minute longer he would have suffocated. This comrade proved to be Pte Reuben Sumner [290] of 16 Graham St, Lancaster. L/Cpl Cooper sat down to have a rest, but there was a shout that more men were buried and they turned out to be Sgt Bert Threlfall, [Robert Threlfall] and Pte Ghorst, Bolton-le-Sands, [Harry Ghorst] both of whom were afterwards killed. A man named Kilbride [Pte Joseph Kilbride] was next found to be wounded, and he was carried away under fire by L/Cpl Cooper and Pte Thompson, who said that while they had so many rounds of ammunition and rifles, they would never leave a wounded comrade. They carried Kilbride a short distance amid a hot fire and did not expect to come through it, but had a marvellous escape. Cooper asked Thompson to carry the equipment and he would carry Kilbride on his back. They struggled on thinking that every moment might be their last, through shells bursting around them, but they managed to reach a farm with the wounded man, when an officer sent for a man to help them carry a stretcher. Pte Thompson immediately volunteered. Dr George asked Cooper if he could wheel Kilbride if he got a hand-cart. He managed to reach another Belgium farm yard, and then swooned over with exhaustion after his own injury. Dr George ordered him three days' rest, but the same night he returned to the trenches. The men's comrades expressed the hope that their bravery would be recognised.

The pair also pulled John Pye (296) out from under the earth, though for him it was too late and after Cooper had cleared the soil out of the casualty's mouth, he just managed to whisper, 'Goodbye, Lads, I'm done.' In previous months, Pye had passed the sad news home of the death of his step-brother and uncle and now someone would be contacting his mother. Among the dead was seventeen-year-old Louis Warwick, his last letter still *en route*. Another was twenty-three-year-old Pte Samuel Higginson. He and his brother, twenty-one year-old Henry—still at home with the 2/5th—were orphans. For Henry, the death of his brother must have been devastating. Twenty-year-old Pte George Lambert's leg was broken in three places when he was crushed in the debris, but he was luckier than his friend, twenty-one-year-old Pte John Wilcock (298). Fighting on the same ground his great-grandfather had fought over in 1815, Wilcock had been buried on both the 4th and 5th and each time his mates dug him free. This time he was beyond help—crushed and suffocated by the great weight of soil. Cpl Reuben Butler, who was treated for bruising and a minor head wound when a piece of the shell struck him, wrote to Wilcock's mother. She was confused by the news, as she had just read her son's letter about twice being buried and rescued, and clung to hope that there had been a mistake. Sadly there had not.[37] One of those dug free was nineteen-year-old postman Pte Stephen Cook, who wrote to his father in Caton:

> I was blown up in the air two or three yards and then buried. It felt as if every bone in my body had been knocked loose. I think I went mad for about half an hour. I did not know where I was going or what I was doing. You know the wash house yard of the last house we were in? Well you could nearly put it in the hole made by the shell.[38]

For 2/King's Own, intermittent shelling had continued throughout the day and the night was fairly quiet—little heralding what was to come. At 7 a.m. on 8 May, the enemy directed a heavy, accurate, and close-range bombardment against their fire trenches, blowing them in. This was followed by a massed infantry attack seizing the forward trenches. At 10 a.m., 2/King's Own managed to halt the advance 200 yards short of the support dugouts, but at a terrible cost—including the death of Lt-Col. Martin. On each flank, the enemy could be seen advancing westwards and it became obvious that 2/King's Own were in danger of being surrounded and cut off. At 11.35 a.m., the order reached the survivors to retire to Potijze—one officer and forty men returned. Casualties for 2/King's Own on 8 May were 914 officers and men killed, wounded, or missing—one of the highest casualty rates for any infantry battalion on a single day.

At 8.10 a.m. on 8 May, the 1/5th was ordered forward to occupy the GHQ Line as support and then, around 3 p.m., were ordered to advance and retake the trenches on Frezenberg Ridge. The Battalion, their numbers boosted to 550 by the addition of the remnants of 3/Monmouths and 2/King's Own, soon reached their starting point. Tired as they were, the men of the Battalion were keen to get stuck in and take back those dreadful trenches. Some of the 1/5th were ex-Regulars from 2/King's Own and others had brothers with them. Almost everyone had been classmates with at least one from the shattered battalion. This was personal and all were keen to avenge these losses.

The distance across open ground was about 1½ miles, and initially, they advanced in artillery formation—the big guns targeting them almost from the start. After only half a mile, very heavy rifle and machine-gun fire began to sweep their ranks and their advance became a series of rushes. Twenty-five-year-old Pte Robert Higginson set off at full sprint and turned his ankle, falling into a shell hole. His pal, twenty-four-year-old dental surgeon Pte Rowland McGowan, bandaged him and continued the advance. CSM George Barrow and twenty-year-old L/Cpl Allan Ripper were nearby L/Cpl William Morris from Caton, when a whizz-bang landed near Morris—the former secretary of the John O'Gaunt Rowing Club—badly wounding him in the thigh. The extremely popular and very talented Ripper ran to help his friend. Tragically, another shell screamed in and exploded next to Ripper, killing him instantly, shrapnel wounding CSM Barrow in the knee. Capt. Eaves wrote to Ripper's father, headmaster of the Lancaster School of Art:

> I cannot find words adequate enough to express to you my intense admiration for your son's personal character and bravery. He knew no fear, was my own specially selected Company guide, and was a great favourite with all his comrades. In your great sorrow, in which I humbly share, it will be some small consolation to know that he died instantly and suffered no pain, and that he has cheerfully made the supreme sacrifice in order to save you and yours from the appalling horrors of this cruel war. I personally feel a deep sense of loss and it grieves me bitterly to have to convey to you the sad news. So many of Lancaster's brave heroes have been laid to rest here on the field where they fell, that it is impossible for me to express my sympathy to all sorrowing relatives, but I was so deeply personally attached to your son that I felt it might be some slight consolation to you to have him Company officer's tribute.

Another friend of Ripper's, L/Cpl Edmund Simpson, wounded in the arm by shrapnel, wrote from his hospital bed in Beckenham:

> He died more than the ordinary soldier's death, because he had the opportunity of going back to a place out of danger with those who had paraded sick. He thought however, that he was not bad enough and if he went, it would savour of cowardice. His pluck cost him his life.[39]

Morris's evacuation was far from uneventful. His thigh wound was caused by the fuse cap of the 77-mm shell, weighing over 6 oz. After ploughing through his leg, it ended up lodged in his butter tin, also leaving its impression upon his tobacco pouch. Sickened by the sight of Ripper's death, Morris crawled painfully back. After covering considerable distance, he was spotted by other Caton men, who went to his assistance and helped him to the rear. As he was placed into an ambulance, German artillery began to shell them— one round hitting the ambulance, killing the driver and destroying the vehicle.

In a letter to his mother, Sgt Edmund Williams from 'B' Company described the advance and a later, unsuccessful night-time charge:

As we were resting the order came to get ready to advance, so off we went, our overcoats and packs, and we advanced in daylight against the shells. It was murder. We kept going the best we could, and we got to the firing line with thirteen of our company left to man a trench. Where the others had gone I don't know.

I found three of our men in Jack Johnson holes. I took them back, and we had been in the trench for about half an hour when the officer shouted, 'Get ready for the charge.' So we got over the parapet, little knowing that the enemy were only twenty yards off in our front. Well we crept up, and the officer gave 'the charge'. The enemy sent star shells up, fired at us as fast as they could, and shouted out in excited tones. Out of sixteen that went up, three came back. I don't know how I missed being hit, because I got fast in the wire entanglements three times, and that is where a lot of our fellows were riddled. I could see the enemy getting over the parapet, and I thought I would surely be captured. I pulled the stripes off my arm while I was trying to free myself from the wire. I got safely through and the three of us manned the trench in the best way we could. I spread the few out and made them go up and down the trench and fire here and there to make the enemy think the trench was full. It worked successfully, but what a time we had. They were Prussian Guards that were facing us. They would get up to their full extent, walk towards us and shout, 'Eh, you mad Lancaster devils, come over here and show us what you are going to do now.' Then they would whistle loudly and wave their spades at us. They also had the cheek to shout, 'Don't fire at us: we are your own men.' So I looked over again and there they were dressed in khaki. As soon as I got my hat up I got a bullet right through it. I was buried three times with the shells, but I missed getting hit each time.[40]

One man captured during this attack was Pte Edward Carter. Badly wounded he died in a German casualty clearing station on 19 May—his death such a shock to his mother— she died shortly after receiving the news.

When thirty-one-year-old Pte Ezekiel Goth, a former under-keeper at Hornby Castle, was shot in the leg about 8 p.m., two of his pals, one of whom was Pte Thomas Hodgson, 'brought him down under a perfect hail of lead to safety'.[41] Hodgson had some very close escapes that day. A piece of shrapnel took a piece out of one thumb and another went through his cap, burning his scalp as it did so. The young soldier considered none of these injuries worth counting as wounds. It was very difficult for soldiers when they were split from their pals. Hodgson, Goth. and Edmund 'Irvine' Alderson had been inseparable—all three from Hornby. Alderson had been the first to go, wounded on 3 May, and when Goth parted from Hodgson, he became very emotional. The trio would never serve together again, Goth transferring to the MFP. Only two would ever see Hornby again. Hodgson earned the MM for his courage during that week. Some soldiers carried their wounded comrades a considerable distance. Pte Hugh Butterworth, from the Pioneer Section, carried eighteen-year-old Pte Ernest Scriven over a mile through heavy shellfire—he actually offered to carry him the full 3 miles to the dressing station.[42] Scriven was shot in the shin and evacuated home to England, and was unfortunate enough to need an appendectomy while recovering from the wound. He never returned to the Battalion, transferring to the Labour Corps and eventually receiving a medical discharge.

Just 250 yards beyond where the small arms fire began, the CO was hit in the leg by shrapnel, wisely remaining where he lay until dusk. Caught by shrapnel from the same shell was father of five Cpl Joseph Storer. Neither served with the Battalion again. Despite determined opposition, the attackers got to within 300 yards of the enemy, then hurriedly dug in—impetus lost in the face of the heavy fire. Many casualties came from enfilading fire from a Maxim in a house on the north side of the Ypres–Zonnebeke road. The cost to the Battalion had been heavy, the survivors exhausted, but they still held their advanced positions. When Capt. James Bainbridge fell at the head of his company, shot through the right thigh, twenty-year-old Pte Richard Veevers came to the rescue. With complete disregard for his own safety, he slung Bainbridge across his shoulders and carried him out of the storm of machine gun and shellfire striking all around them. He then delivered his officer safely to the dressing station—an action that earned him the DCM. Another who risked his life to save his officer, was twenty-two-year-old Pte Samuel Palin. When Lt Alfred Seward was wounded in the right hip, Palin carried him to safety, but was severely wounded in the face in the process. Palin too was awarded a DCM, but never returned to the Battalion, being transferred to the Labour Corps and eventual medical discharge.[43]

After dark, many wounded made their own way to the rear, or were assisted by others from the Battalion. Robert Higginson was helped back to the dressing station by Pte William Yare (both were later commissioned) and passed along the medical chain to No. 3 General Hospital at Le Tréport. Here, he was asked to give blood to help save a badly wounded Canadian, whose leg was to be amputated (Pte Frederick Charles Perkins, 1/ Canadian Infantry). Sadly, the operation failed to save the young soldier's life and he died on 15 June. It was found that Higginson needed an operation for a varicose vein and he was sent home for this. Another of the wounded, later commissioned into the King's Own, was twenty-eight-year-old Pte Albert Ellwood. A talented artist and superb soldier, he went to the 1/4th, earned the MC as a captain at Gillemont Farm in 1917, and was killed on 14 April 1918 at Givenchy-lès-la-Bassée.

The intensity of fire often meant that wounded men in the open were hit again, such as thirty-two-year-old Cpl Robert Baines, who received no less than five shrapnel wounds: two behind the ear, two in the face, and one in the leg. His wounds ended a run of 'close escapes', having twice had bullets through his hat (both on the same day) and a shrapnel ball through his greatcoat sleeve. He did not return to the Battalion during wartime, transferring to the MFP, but did re-enlist with them post-war. Pte Walter Glover, who had written home just a week earlier to inform his parents of the death of his brother, Fred, was badly wounded. A shell buried him in a trench, wounding him in the chest and crushing his back. He was dug out just in time and helped to the rear by a Pte Richmond of 2/King's Own, who wrote to Walter's parents, reassuring them that Walter was going to be okay. Tragically for the family, another son, John, was killed with the Royal Scots Fusiliers in September. With the CO wounded and Maj. Bates sick in hospital in England, command passed (briefly) to Capt. Sharpe, and Capt. Bingham took over Sharpe's company. Signaller L/Cpl Tom Fairclough was guiding Capt. Bingham to his new company's position when shrapnel from an exploding shell caught the young NCO in the hip—leaving the captain unscathed. Fairclough returned to the Battalion after his recovery, but for some of the wounded, their injuries were too severe. Shrapnel to spine and foot paralysed twenty-two-year-old Cpl Frank Jackson, and twenty-one-year-old L/Cpl John Dodgson was wounded in the head. Both died on 10 May.

Twenty-year-old Pte Richard Lamb described how he was wounded in the attack when he wrote to the mother of his pal, twenty-year-old Pte Robert Cunliffe, who was posted 'missing':

> We had to go across a mile of open country and the Germans could see us quite plain. Our fellows were dropping, some wounded and some who had made the supreme sacrifice, but still the King's Own kept on. 'Always forward!' was our motto. We never run away. Me and Bob were still together behind some cover. We had about eighty yards to go, but it was swept by machine gun and rifle fire. Bob said to an officer and me, 'Come on Dick, we will make a dash for it.' I had just set off when I was shot through just below the ankle, and it came out of the bottom of my foot. That dropped me (unconscious). On looking round a bit later, I could not see Bob. I expect he got there all right. I sincerely hope so.[44]

Cunliffe was eventually declared 'killed in action' and is commemorated on the Menin Gate.

There was little let-up the next day, and among the first to be wounded was Boer War veteran Sgt Alfred Price. A shrapnel ball struck him in the forehead, but he 'stuck it out', as he considered the wound a minor problem and was unwilling to abandon his men. As dark fell, he was ordered to the rear to get it treated and evacuated to one of the base hospitals. As he commented in a letter to his parents, 'it was a treat to have a night in bed after so many weeks in the trenches'.[45] The Battalion's positions were more a series of enhanced shell holes than a proper defensive line. Few supplies had come up during the night and there was a limit to how far these trenches could be improved with just their entrenching tools and the few men remaining. The front line had earlier been augmented by the men from Transport, leaving just ten men to look after sixty horses and bring up all the stores and rations for the night—ammunition and water taking precedence.

The 'birthday curse' still seemed to operating at full effectiveness, and although John Squirrell's nineteenth birthday had seen him survive uninjured—even getting his birthday parcel from home—he was hit by a shrapnel ball in the shoulder as they left the line the next day. He was taken to the dressing station dugout, but just as he reached it, another shell landed very close by, wounding him above the right eye and causing crush injuries to his back and chest. Squirrell was evacuated to an Aberdeen hospital and never rejoined the Battalion, transferring to KOYLI upon his recovery. Pte Thomas Winder was wounded in the leg by shrapnel on the day before his twenty-third birthday—though the wound was not serious. His older brother, Henry, had been killed on 27 April, and if this was not distressing enough for his family, the youngest of the three brothers, John, was also wounded on 9 May. Eighteen-year-old Pte John Winder was actually wounded twice in a week. The first on 4 May was minor, and after it had been dressed, he returned to duty. It was a different matter on 9 May, when shrapnel wounded him in side, chest, and eye—the latter wound in particular proving very painful—though he did recover and was transferred to the MGC. A/CSM Richard Jackson, whose brother, James, had been killed on 5 May, was badly wounded by shrapnel—hit in arms, back, and a leg. The widowed father of four from Lancaster spent a considerable time in hospital before his discharge, with a pension, to munitions work in April 1917.[46] For the Brayshaw family, there would be more bad news following on from the wounding of Thomas on 23 April. Twenty-three year old Cpl Cecil Brayshaw was initially posted as missing, although a newspaper in November 1915 reported him a prisoner—having been wounded in the liver.[47] This information was, however, incorrect, and he is listed as 'killed in action' for 9 May.

This day also saw the death of two of the youngest. Seventeen-year-old Pte David Nelson from Low Bentham was hit near the heart by a shrapnel ball and died soon afterwards at the dressing station. He was the first from his home village to be killed. The other was 'C' Company officer, seventeen-year-old Lt Stanley Bates, the youngest full lieutenant in the Army. Despite his youth, Lt Bates was a popular officer. Sgt Edmund Williams described his death:

> Major Bates' son died in my arms. We had nothing to eat or drink for two days, so Lt Bates said he could spare us a bit of bread, and while he was handing it round the corner he was shot in the neck, and dropped into my arms. He only lived about two minutes.[48]

Heysham's first fatality of the war was twenty-one-year-old Pte William Osborne. The only surviving son of the family, he died from his wounds at the dressing station. Today he lies next to David Nelson at Klein-Vierstraat War Cemetery, their bodies moved there after the war when their small burial ground was cleared.

One of the most seriously wounded was nineteen-year-old Pte John (Jack) Cowell, his spinal cord severed by a bullet. Despite everything the hospital could do, his condition deteriorated and he got progressively weaker, became comatose on Saturday 15 May, and died early Sunday morning. The matron wrote to his parents:

> He was such a dear boy and so plucky. We are very sorry for you. I'm sure your loss is very great. He sent his love to you when he knew I was writing, and said you had not to worry. We did everything possible for him, but it was in vain.[49]

Signaller Pte Charles Galloway had spent the last few days attached to the brigade staff and had been required to take messages to and from the front line during daylight on a number of occasions—fortunately without injury. On the night of the 9th, he guided the brigade-major forward:

> Whilst I was going up to the firing line last night as orderly to the Brigade-Major, and only about 200 yards from the fire trench I heard a nightingale singing, the first I have heard. It seemed strange to listen to it, and then to look around and see dead men and horses and ruined buildings and shells flying about. It would be glorious out here if there wasn't a war on. The weather is fine and warm, but the smell of dead horses is enough to poison you wherever you go. It is lively where I am now. Every few minutes shrapnel keeps bursting right over the dugout and then we have to duck.[50]

All of 83 Brigade were relieved at 3 a.m. on 10 May, the Battalion bivouacking near Poperinghe. The casualties had been so grievous that the entire brigade now occupied accommodation for a single battalion. No. 83 Brigade had suffered 4,507 casualties between 23 April and 8 May.[51] In fact, so few infantry remained that all six battalions were combined into one composite battalion under Lt-Col. Worsley-Gough of 3/ Monmouths.

As dark fell, the exhausted survivors moved forwards again to dig shelters in the GHQ Line near Potijze. German artillery still targeted the rear, and a number of casualties ensued—though none fatal. Twenty-three-year-old Pte George Auty, whose brother Joseph had been wounded five days earlier, was buried by a shell. He was dug out by his comrades, with a shrapnel wound to the thumb, but was badly shell-shocked by the experience and evacuated home. His condition did not improve and he was medically discharged in August 1916. Twenty-seven-year-old Pte Harry Blair received a scalp wound from shrapnel, but was soon back with the Battalion. Sgt George Gill, badly affected by gas, was admitted to hospital and later transferred to the Labour Corps. Twenty-seven-year-old Pte John Winder was another affected by the gas, but he returned to the MG Section—eventually to the MGC, when all gunners were transferred. A further ten were admitted to hospital on 10 May, though records do not survive to state if these were due to illness or gas. None returned to the Battalion, being either transferred to other units or remaining on home posting and two died during the war—forty-two-year-old Capt. William Parsons, from pneumonia in October 1918 and Sgt Stephen Rydeard killed in action with the MGC in March 1918. Thirty-two year-old Pte Peter Thompson was admitted to hospital on 17 May, suffering from the effects of gas. His condition developed into pleurisy, which in turn led to a heart condition. He was discharged as medically unfit just under a year later and died in January 1917.

On 11 May, the composite battalion moved to the GHQ Lines, but was relieved by 1 Cavalry Division at 11 p.m. and returned to their huts near Vlamertinghe. Another man was admitted to hospital suffering from gas and general debility that day. Twenty-two-year-old Cpl Henry Riley from Fleetwood was evacuated home and discharged as time-expired on 17 November. The period of engagement for many of the Battalion ended before the onset of Conscription in 1916, and although some of these were later conscripted, many were not—either below the required standards of age or fitness or in jobs that were valuable to the war effort. Twenty-two-year-old Pte John Hill, wounded in the leg by shrapnel on 11 May while manning the GHQ Line, was another, his discharge in January 1916. Three men—Pte Richard Bullen from Poulton-le-Fylde, twenty-year-old, Pte John Cardwell from Blackpool, and twenty-one-year-old Pte Richard Snape from Fleetwood—died from their wounds on the 11th, though the actual date of their wounding is not known. All three died in different casualty stations.

Some 150 reinforcements from 2/5th King's Own arrived on the evening of the 10th, but these were not integrated until the Battalion was out of the line. The entire battalion was accommodated in a single hut and one small barn—the reinforcements bivouacked in the field next to them. The fighting strength of the Battalion—minus these reinforcements—was 210 officers and men. Three months earlier, it had been nearly 1,000. On 13 May, the Battalion was ordered to 'stand to', but this was cancelled soon afterwards and next day they were taken by bus to Steenvoorde, where they then marched to Ryveld for a very well-earned period of rest and reorganisation. In these nine days on the Frezenberg Ridge, the Battalion lost eighty officers and men killed and 257 wounded.

Killed or Died from Wounds 2–11 May 1915

Pte James Atkinson Airey	2446	KIA: 4/5	L/Sgt James Sargison Kirkby	376	KIA: 3/5
Pte Richard Alston	3044	KIA: 4/5	Pte Alfred Lockley	1224	KIA: 5/5
Pte Edmund Ambler	1471	KIA: 9/5	Pte Frederick Henry Lowe	2134	KIA: 3/5
Pte Harry Angus	2067	KIA: 3/5	Pte Fred Lupton	1353	KIA: 5/5
Pte Thomas J. Ashcroft	2554	DOW: 2/6	Pte Richard Mansfield	1604	KIA: 8/5
Pte John Ashton	2555	KIA: 9/5	A/Cpl Richard Eli Mansfield*	1222	KIA: 4/5
Pte Jonathon Assitt	1781	KIA: 6/5	Pte Peter McGreevy	1059	KIA: 5/5
Pte Samuel Bailey	1503	KIA: 8/5	Pte James McTigue	1032	KIA: 4/5
Pte Thomas Bamber	3014	KIA: 5/5	Pte Arthur Henry Millard	2597	DOW: 6/5
Lt Spencer Ellwood Barrow		DOW: 16/11	Pte George Moss	1014	KIA: 5/5
Lt Stanley Knight Bates		KIA: 9/5	Pte David Nelson	2395	DOW: 9/5
Cpl Harry Bowen	1518	KIA: 4/5	L/Cpl Joseph Newton	1771	DOW: 7/5
Cpl Cecil Brayshaw	740	KIA: 9/5	Pte William Henry Osborne	1379	DOW: 9/5
Pte Richard Bullen	1699	DOW: 11/5	Pte David Owen	934	KIA: 5/5
Pte Richard Stanley Butler	2653	DOW: 19/5	L/Cpl Charles Porter	1193	KIA: 8/5
Pte John Campbell	2012	KIA: 9/5	Pte John Richard Pye	1296	KIA: 8/5
Pte John William Cardwell	1599	DOW: 11/5	L/Cpl Allan Gilbert Ripper	2159	KIA: 8/5
Pte Roland Cariss	2097	KIA: 3/5	Pte Richard Roskell	2616	DOW: 7/5

Lt Edgar Joseph Augustin Carr		DOW: 18/5	Pte Hall Sheard Salthouse	1995	KIA: 4/5
L/Cpl James William Carter	907	KIA: 4/5	Pte Sheard Salthouse	1990	KIA: 5/5
Pte Edward Carter	1370	DOW: 19/5	Pte George Shuttleworth	3078	KIA: 4/5
Pte James Cathcart	2091	KIA: 4/5	Pte John Simpson	2210	KIA: 4/5
Pte Thomas Charnley	2566	KIA: 4/5	Pte Richard Rawlinson Snape	1036	DOW: 11/5
Pte William Conway	1803	KIA: 4/5	Pte Joseph Sparks	2016	KIA: 8/5
Pte Thomas Cottam	1975	KIA: 6/5	Pte William Stoddart	1429	KIA: 8/5
Pte John William Cowell	1401	DOW: 16/5	Pte James Stones	2021	KIA: 4/5
Pte James Cross	1678	KIA: 4/5	Pte William Strickland	2709	KIA: 8/5
Pte Robert Cunliffe	2467	KIA: 9/5	L/Cpl Thomas Tester	1966	KIA: 5/5
Pte Joseph Livingstone Dixon	3414	KIA: 4/5	Pte Lawrence Tetley	1682	KIA: 5/5
L/Cpl John Dodgson	1009	DOW: 10/5	L/Cpl Mortimer Thomas	2217	DOW: 9/6
Pte Alfred Ernest Clifford English	2105	DOW: 21/5	Pte James Marsh Thornton	2426	KIA: 8/5
Pte James Pearson Fairclough	2190	KIA: 3/5	Pte Joseph Thwaites	2803	DOW: 12/5
2Lt Robert Gardner		KIA: 5/5	Pte John Toulmin**	1654	DOW: 1916
Pte Samuel Higginson	240193	KIA: 8/5	Sgt Richard Wallbank	93	KIA: 4/5
Pte Edward Hoggarth	2118	KIA: 3/5	Pte Louis Warwick	1621	KIA: 8/5
Pte John Robert Howson	2194	DOW: 22/5	Pte Thomas H. Weedon	2632	DOW: 15/5
WO II Henry Irving	1221	KIA: 8/5	Pte John Wilcock	1298	KIA: 8/5
Pte James Newby Jackson	267	KIA: 5/5	Pte John Wilson	2182	KIA: 3/5
Cpl Frank Jackson	1280	DOW: 10/5	Pte Edward Winder	2213	KIA: 3/5
Pte Edward Kehoe	1576	KIA: 5/5	Pte William Thomas Wright	1928	KIA: 3/5

* Born Richard Jervis. Although CWGC have his date of death as the 4th, it is probable he was actually killed on the 5th.

** Toulmin's fatal wounding was on 5 May 1915. He died 22 May 1916.

Known to have been Wounded 2-11 May 1915

Sgt George Zacceus Abbott	240234	WIA: 4/5	Pte Thomas William Lawrence	243464	WIA: 4/5
Pte Edmund Irving Alderson	2066	WIA: 3/5	Pte Robert Ronson Leytham	34399	WIA: 4/5
Pte Alban Anderson	1424	WIA: 8/5	Pte W. Long	2680	WIA: 8/5
Pte William Angus	240127	WIA: 5/5	Pte Joseph Lucas	682	WIA: 4/5
Pte Richard Anyon	265763	WIA: 3/5	L/Cpl Charles Haley Lund	240115	WIA: 4/5
L/Cpl Stanley Ashton	1986	WIA: 9/5	L/Cpl William Lynch	240168	WIA: 5/5
Pte James Atkinson	1668	WIA: 4/5	Pte Robert S. Lyttle	2682	WIA: 4/5
Pte Joseph Auty	240235	WIA: 4/5	Pte James A. Mabbs	2245	HOS: 10/5
Pte George William Auty	977	WIA: 10/5	Pte Robert Leadbetter Martin	240438	WIA: 3/5
Capt. James Bainbridge		WIA: 8/5	Pte Walter Martin	579	WIA: 4/5
Pte George Baines	1755	WIA: 5/5	Pte John Martin	1844	HOS: 10/5

Cpl Robert Henry Walker Baines	331	WIA: 8/5	Pte Joseph Wren Mashiter	240389	WIA: 4/5
Pte Robert Samuel Baird	2072	WIA: 4/5	Pte Charles Mashiter	2059	HOS: 10/5
Pte George William Bamber	1480	WIA: 5/5	Pte James Mason	240306	WIA: 3/5
A/CSM George Walter Barrow	240011	WIA: 8/5	Pte Thomas Masters	2902	WIA: 4/5
Pte Reuben Bartholomew	240890	WIA: 5/5	L/Cpl Edmund Mayor	1648	WIA: 9/5
Pte Walter Beckett	240024	WIA: 8/5	Pte Thomas McNulty	240618	WIA: 9/5
L/Cpl William Bell	242410	WIA: 5/5	Pte William Thomas Metcalf*	1645	WIA: 4/5
Pte Harry Bell	1629	WIA: 8/5	Pte Joseph William Miller	1871	WIA: 4/5
Cpl Eric Latham Bennett	2071	WIA: 8/5	Pte Henry Milne	240062	WIA: 4/5
A/WO II Charles Berkins	330	WIA: 8/5	L/Cpl Walter Minns	1433	WIA: 4/5
Pte James Albert Bettany	240029	WIA: 5/5	Pte George Cyril Mitchell	1956	WIA: 4/5
Cpl Walter Betton	2235	WIA: 8/5	Pte Frederick Victor Monks	240529	WIA: 4/5
Pte Charles Bibby	240566	WIA: 8/5	Pte William Alfred Morris	2166	WIA: 8/5
Pte Frederick Anthony Bird	1839	WIA: 4/5	Pte William Mosey	240872	WIA: 8/5
Pte Joseph Alfred Birkett	1514	WIA: 9/5	Pte Patrick Naylon	240376	WIA: 8/5
Pte Harry Thompson Blair	240079	WIA: 10/5	Pte James Newsham	240712	WIA: 9/5
Pte Richard William Bleasdale	240156	WIA: 8/5	Pte Thomas Newsham	2020	WIA: 4/5
L/Cpl Harold Blondel	240421	WIA: 4/5	Pte Richard Nicholson	1763	WIA: 9/5
Pte Robert James Borrowdale	240487	WIA: 8/5	Pte Robert Nightingale	240071	WIA: 4/5
L/Cpl John Bostock	265756	WIA: 8/5	Pte J. Nolan	2689	WIA: 5/5
Pte Thomas Bradshaw	1980	WIA: 4/5	Pte John Oglethorpe	240183	WIA: 9/5
Pte Roger Brown	2065	WIA: 3/5	Pte Albert Onyett	1195	WIA: 9/5
Pte Albert E. Brown	875	WIA: 4/5	Pte Samuel Edward Palin	966	WIA: 8/5
Lt Ralph Bustard		WIA: 5/5	Capt. William Josiah Parsons		HOS: 10/5
Cpl Reuben Butler	240140	WIA: 8/5	Pte Joseph Peel	2185	WIA: 8/5
Pte Frederick James Cambray	240367	WIA: 4/5	Pte Richard Porter	1545	WIA: 8/5
Pte Herbert Carey	240591	WIA: 4/5	Sgt Alfred Price	32	WIA: 9/5
Pte Michael Carney	1889	WIA: 4/5	Pte Frank Knowle Pullen	240078	WIA: 5/5
Lt-Col. Lord Richard F. Cavendish		WIA: 8/5	Pte Rupert Francis Radcliffe	1828	WIA: 3/5
Pte Harold Chisholme	240019	WIA: 9/5	CSM William Ralph	240001	WIA: 5/5
Pte James Churchouse	240099	WIA: 8/5	Pte John Rawcliffe	240408	WIA: 4/5
Pte Richard Clarkson	240185	WIA: 4/5	Pte William Redman	1688	WIA: 4/5
Pte Isaac Routledge Clements	1362	WIA: 4/5	Pte Robert Relph	240301	WIA: 4/5
Sgt Alfred Clowes	1753	WIA: 8/5	Pte P. Richardson	1660	WIA: 8/5
Pte Lawrence Cottam	1552	WIA: 8/5	Pte William Henry Richardson	240762	WIA: 8/5
Pte George Coulthurst	2006	WIA: 8/5	Cpl Henry Riley	1165	WIA: 11/5
L/Cpl Robert Cowell	1121	WIA: 9/5	Pte Christopher Robinson	240943	WIA: 4/5
Pte William Crarey	3061	WIA: 9/5			
Pte Joseph Crook	2363	WIA: 4/5	Pte J. Robinson	2???	WIA: 8/5
L/Cpl Harry Cross	2092	WIA: 4/5	Cpl Robert Robinson	242411	WIA: 8/5
Pte John Dempsey	240443	WIA: 4/5	2Lt Andrew Rome		WIA: 8/5
Pte J. G. Dickenson	2098	WIA: 5/5	Pte Thomas Roocroft	1749	WIA: 5/5

Pte J. W. Dickinson	2657	WIA: 4/5	Lt William Edward Roper		WIA: 8/5
L/Cpl Thomas Didsbury	1960	WIA: 4/5	Pte James Boyd Rumley	917	WIA: 4/5
Sgt Edwin Dilworth	240100	WIA: 4/5	Pte William Rutter	1489	WIA: 8/5
Pte Harry Dixon	240791	WIA: 4/5	2Lt Charles Saer		WIA: 5/5
Pte Thomas Dixon	3151	WIA: 4/5	Pte Ernest Scriven	1509	WIA: 8/5
L/Cpl Henry Dolan	2100	WIA: 5/5	Sgt John Edward Seed	240145	HOS: 8/5
Pte Rennard Double	240740	WIA: 4/5	Lt Alfred Shrigley Seward		WIA: 8/5
Pte Orlando Henry Ducksbury	240674	WIA: 4/5	Pte John James Shaw	240068	WIA: 9/5
Pte John Duckworth	240174	WIA: 5/5	Cpl Leonard Shepherd	240178	WIA: 4/5
Pte Frederick Eastwood	240154	WIA: 8/5	Pte Harry Shuttleworth	2057	WIA: 5/5
Pte James Egerton	1982	WIA: 4/5	Pte Robert Silverwood	240336	WIA: 4/5
Pte Albert Ellwood	240565	WIA: 4/5	L/Cpl Edmund Richard Simpson	2157	WIA: 8/5
Pte Frank William Ensor	240095	WIA: 4/5	Pte Arthur Singleton	240821	WIA: 4/5
Pte Tom Fairclough	240503	WIA: 8/5	Sgt Fred Singleton	1108	WIA: 8/5
Pte John Fellows	1850	WIA: 9/5	Pte William Singleton	2049	WIA: 5/5
Pte Thomas Frederick Fitzgerald	243126	WIA: 4/5	Pte Percy Brown Skeoch	240767	WIA: 5/5
Pte Thomas Fox	2102	WIA: 4/5	Pte George Edward Smallshaw	240876	WIA: 4/5
Pte John James Fraser	240166	WIA: 4/5	L/Cpl Joseph Smith	1155	WIA: 2/5
Pte Henry Alexander Funk	240569	WIA: 8/5	Pte J. W. Smith	3000	WIA: 5/5
Pte James E. Gallagher	763	WIA: 4/5	Pte John Wilfred Smith	2058	WIA: 5/5
Pte Henry Gardner	240176	WIA: 4/5	CSM Matthew Smith	240047	WIA: 9/5
Pte James Gardner	2241	WIA: 9/5	Sgt George R. Snowden	185	WIA: 5/5
Pte Rowland Garstang	1551	WIA: 8/5	Pte John Speight	1814	WIA: 4/5
Pte Moses Geddes	240271	WIA: 5/5	Pte John Squirrell	1639	WIA: 9/5
Pte Harry Ghorst	2479	WIA: 8/5	Pte Arthur Sterland	2040	WIA: 4/5
Pte William Gibson	2577	WIA: 4/5	Pte William Stirzaker	240454	WIA: 8/5
Sgt John James Gilchrist	2036	WIA: 5/5	Cpl Joseph Storer	1538	WIA: 8/5
Sgt Thomas Foster Gill	1778	WIA: 10/5	Pte Bert Strickland	35154	WIA: 9/5
Pte Walter Glover	240180	WIA: 8/5	Pte Reuben Sumner	290	WIA: 8/5
Pte Harry Goodwin	201581	WIA: 4/5	Pte Albert Sweeney	51920	WIA: 5/5
Pte John Edward Goodwin	240506	WIA: 4/5	Pte Elvery Verdon Sykes	240384	WIA: 9/5
Pte Ezekiel Goth	2121	WIA: 8/5	Pte Herbert Norman Thacker	240578	POW: 4/5
Pte Ernest Graham	240855	WIA: 8/5	Pte Mortimer Cecil Thomas	3518	WIA: 4/5
Sgt George Arthur Grayson	51119	WIA: 4/5	Pte George Thornton	2714	WIA: 5/5
L/Cpl George Gudgeon	1927	WIA: 5/5	Pte Thomas Thorpe	244	WIA: 4/5
Pte John Gudgeon	240066	WIA: 9/5	Sgt Robert Threlfall	2176	WIA: 8/5
Pte John Newman Hall	240210	WIA: 3/5	2Lt John Hardman Todd		WIA: 8/5
Pte Burgoyne Hall	2192	WIA: 4/5	Pte John Topham	240322	WIA: 2/5
Pte Gilbert Hall	2193	WIA: 4/5	Pte Richard Troughton	240880	WIA: 4/5
Pte James Hall	240507	WIA: 4/5	Cpl James Vincent Turner	2013	WIA: 9/5
Sgt Joseph William Hall	757	WIA: 4/5	Pte Robert Tyson	22	WIA: 4/5
Cpl Frederick Hames	240441	WIA: 4/5	Pte Harry Verden	1587	WIA: 5/5

Pte Lewis Hamilton	240233	WIA: 8/5	Pte Arthur Wadeson	240881	WIA: 8/5
Pte William Hardy	240153	WIA: 8/5	A/Cpl Thomas Walton	1102	WIA: 5/5
Pte Frederick Hargreaves	240571	WIA: 5/5	Pte Edward Walton	240094	WIA: 9/5
Pte Albert Edward Harrison	2875	WIA: 4/5	Pte John Waterhouse	24	WIA: 4/5
L/Cpl Thurston Haslam	240448	WIA: 4/5	Pte John Cochrane Watson	240291	WIA: 4/5
Pte Edgar Hayton	2877	WIA: 8/5	Pte Paul Webster	240385	HOS: 8/5
Pte Edward Albert Helme	240572	WIA: 4/5	Pte Herbert Spencer West	240883	WIA: 5/5
Pte James Helme	240407	WIA: 8/5	L/Cpl Joseph Western	240404	WIA: 4/5
Pte Edward Herd	240694	WIA: 5/5	Pte Anthony Whalley	1351	WIA: 5/5
Pte Charles Hewitson	240856	WIA: 5/5	Pte Robert Whinray	240953	WIA: 3/5
Pte Herbert Hill	265772	WIA: 9/5	Pte Robert Whiteside	2436	WIA: 4/5
Pte John Smith Hill	1167	WIA: 11/5	Cpl John Wilding	595	WIA: 8/5
Pte George Hillman	2380	HOS: 10/5	Pte Joseph Wilkinson	1146	WIA: 5/5
Pte John Hodgson	1162	WIA: 5/5	Sgt Frederick William Wilkinson	51179	WIA: 8/5
L/Cpl William Hogarth	1290	WIA: 4/5	Sgt Thomas John Williams	240041	WIA: 4/5
Pte John Hoggarth	1093	WIA: 5/5	Pte James Wilson	1420	WIA:4/5
Pte George Holden	240412	WIA: 4/5	Pte William Wilson	68	WIA: 8/5
Pte William Hollinghurst	2758	WIA: 9/5	Pte Albert Wilson	1636	WIA: 9/5
Pte Richard Holmes	240077	WIA: 3/5	Pte John Winder	1447	WIA: 9/5
Pte Charles Holmes	501	WIA: 4/5	Pte Robert Winder	979	WIA: 4/5
Cpl James Hopwood	240250	WIA: 4/5	Pte Thomas Winder	437	WIA: 9/5
Cpl Joe Hopwood	241505	WIA: 4/5	Pte Ernest Winder	2216	WIA: 9/5
Pte William Huggonson	1343	WIA: 4/5	Pte John Winder	240357	WIA: 10/5
Pte Harry Hull	241007	WIA: 8/5	Sgt Albert Witham	1479	WIA: 4/5
Pte George Hayward Hutton	2763	WIA: 4/5	2Lt William Atkinson Wolfendale		WIA: 4/5
Pte John I'Anson	431	WIA: 5/5	Pte Albert Edward Woodburn	2347	WIA: 4/5
A/CSM Richard Newby Jackson	240151	WIA: 9/5	Pte Jack Woodhouse	1622	WIA: 4/5
Pte Thomas Jackson	1152	WIA: 4/5	Pte Lancelot Burton Wooff	1435	WIA: 4/5
L/Cpl Richard Jameson	1287	HOS: 10/5	Pte John Edgar Worden	240580	POW: 4/5
Pte John Jenkinson	240702	WIA: 4/5	Pte James Henry Wren	2592	HOS: 10/5
Pte Joseph Kilbride	240865	WIA: 8/5	Pte Ernest Wright	1637	WIA: 4/5
L/Cpl Richard Kirby	220	WIA: 4/5	Cpl Thomas Wright	240214	WIA: 8/5
Sgt Richard Henry Kirkby	240026	WIA: 4/5	Pte Richard Yare	240335	WIA: 4/5
Pte Richard Lamb	240707	WIA: 8/5	Pte George Yates	2178	WIA: 8/5
Pte George Lambert	1641	WIA: 8/5	Capt. James McLaren Young		HOS: 10/5

* Wounded again on 8 May and evacuated home.

15 May 1915–22 October 1915: Kemmel

Coordinates for Positions Named in this Chapter

Big Willie	50°29′53.80″N 2°46′47.50″E	Trench H1	50°47′3.70″N 2°51′42.40″E
Border Lane	50°29′34.40″N 2°46′29.50″E	Trench H2	50°47′4.40″N 2°51′48.00″E
Central Keep	50°29′39.40″N 2°45′51.10″E	Trench H3	50°47′5.90″N 2°51′52.80″E
CT off Hulluch Alley	50°29′44.40″N 2°46′46.10″E	Trench H5	50°47′6.10″N 2°51′38.70″E
Hohenzollern Redoubt	50°29′58.50″N 2°46′30.10″E	Trench K1a	50°47′25.10″N 2°51′35.90″E
New Sap	50°47′1.50″N 2°51′45.10″E	Trench K1b	50°47′26.10″N 2°51′42.70″E
O Camp	50°51′59.00″N, 2°47′13.70″E	Trench K2	50°47′26.00″N 2°51′46.90″E
Sanctuary Wood	50°50′7.70″N 2°57′3.60″E	Trench K2a	50°47′29.20″N 2°51′50.50″E
South Face Trench	50°30′1.40″N 2°46′51.20″E	Trench K2b	50°47′32.80″N 2°51′48.80″E
SP11	50°47′15.60″N 2°51′38.40″E	Trench K3	50°47′38.40″N 2°51′34.60″E
SP12	50°47′13.00″N 2°51′18.30″E	Trench L4	50°47′43.80″N 2°51′53.10″E
SP13	50°47′22.00″N 2°51′31.20″E	Trench L5	50°47′47.20″N 2°51′53.60″E

Spurn Head Sap	50°29'40.80"N	Trench L6	50°47'40.00"N
	2°47'0.30"E		2°51'42.80"E
Trench G4	50°46'58.60"N	Trench L7	50°47'48.20"N
	2°51'43.20"E		2°51'50.80"E
Trench G4a	50°46'52.60"N		
	2°51'42.30"E		

The Battalion remained at Ryveld until the afternoon of 21 May. Apart from the first day, which was spent resting, their time was spent reorganising, re-equipping, and training the replacements. In the afternoon of Sunday 16 May, the temporary brigade commander, Lt-Col. Marden (CO of 1/Welch), inspected the Battalion and was very critical of the turnout, until he was told what they had just been through and then expressed his apologies. Three days later, brigade command passed to Brig.-Gen. H. S. L. Ravenshaw C.M.G. On the same day, records show that Pte John Turner was killed in action. As the entire brigade were far behind the lines at this time, the only plausible explanation is that he was attached to the divisional staff at the time. On the 21st, the Battalion joined the rest of the brigade at Winnezeele, where they were inspected by Sir John French, who thanked them for their defence at Ypres. That afternoon, the Battalion marched off to bivouacs in woods near Vlamertinghe, a location that later became 'O' Camp.

In the early evening, Captains Eaves, Bingham, and Harriss left to reconnoitre the Battalion's next positions in Sanctuary Wood. As they began their return, around 2.30 a.m., forty-year-old Frank Bingham was killed instantaneously by a single shot from behind. William Harriss was just two paces in front of him and caught Bingham as he fell. The death of the popular father of three was a shock throughout the Battalion and back home in Lancaster. A former Derbyshire county cricketer and, despite his age, still a formidable rugby player, Capt. Bingham was a Lancaster GP, but had elected to serve as a fighting officer with the battalion he had joined pre-war. In December 1915, a bronze memorial tablet was unveiled in the Royal Lancaster Infirmary.

The Battalion occupied trenches in the southern part of Sanctuary Wood at 4.50 p.m. on 22 May, Transport locating to a field near the Asylum in Ypres and the Second Line and Stores to a field east of Vlamertinghe. Unusually, this sector could be approached in daylight as the routes in were hidden from hostile observers. In the war diary, 23 May is described as a quiet day, although that evening, shrapnel wounded forty-four-year-old Pte John Cameron in the right hand as he brought the rations forward, and twenty-seven-year-old Pte Alfred Gay in the right cheek.

This quiet interlude did not last, and the next day, the enemy carried out an attack supported by gas shells against the Cavalry Division to the Battalion's left. Although the enemy enjoyed initial success, they were driven back by a counterattack through Zouave Wood by two reserve companies of the Yorks and Lancs.[1] Fortunately, little of the gas reached the Battalion's positions as their only protection were goggles and cloth pads—

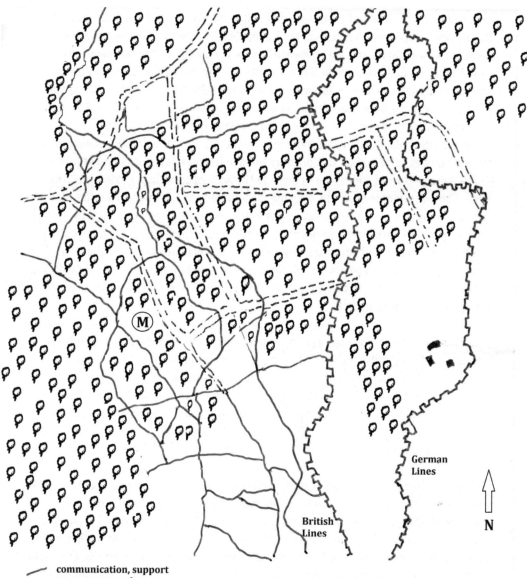

Sanctuary Wood
(the Sector occupied by battalion May 1915)

German
Lines

British
Lines

N

— communication, support
  or reserve trenches

(M) site of modern museum

♀ woodland

track

fighting trench

pre-soaked in a solution of bicarbonate of soda and tied around the face. Despite the Brigade diary reporting that none of the brigade's front line trenches were targeted, the Battalion's own diary states that between 2.30 p.m. and 3 p.m., the Battalion's trenches were heavily shelled, resulting in three casualties.[2, 3] Sgt Edmund Williams, with shrapnel wounds to his left arm, and twenty-nine-year-old Pte Robert Edmondson, wounded in the left shoulder, were both evacuated home. Twenty-one-year-old Pte Richard Simmons, from Fleetwood, died from his wounds at the dressing station.

The Battalion also lost another man that day. At 11 a.m., Hest Bank accountant Pte Dennett Davies—the last of 'D' Company to have been at Sevenoaks and still be with the Battalion—carried a message to Brigade HQ accompanied by a guide from 2/King's Own. The twenty-nine-year-old, recently recommended for commissioning, did not return that evening and word reached the Battalion that he had been 'slightly gassed' near Brigade HQ and taken to hospital. Sadly, this turned out to be incorrect as 1/ Gordons discovered his body to the rear of their trenches, the message still in his tunic. They buried him near to where he fell. He had been killed by shellfire and his guide was also missing. The letter to Davies' parents from Capt. Eaves illustrates that the strain was beginning to take its toll:

> My grief at the loss of so good a comrade and friend is little less than yours. It is heart-breaking day after day to see our brave comrades 'going west,' and one cannot help but look upon our small and daily decreasing unit with feelings of the deepest emotion. Life is so terrible and so uncertain out here that one never knows from hour to hour when one's own call may come, and I can only hope that if it is decreed that mine shall come I may face it with the same devotion and bravery that your son and our many hero comrades have done.[4]

Hostile artillery targeted their front trenches at 3 a.m. on 25 May and continued for seven hours. The only casualty was twenty-four-year-old Pte Samuel Milner—hit below the knee by shrapnel. The damage was severe and his leg was amputated at Boulogne, where to his surprise he was visited by his own GP (in France to visit his brother Lt Spencer Barrow, wounded with the Battalion on 5 May, and a patient in the same hospital). Milner was evacuated to London, where his first visitor on 4 June was his sister, a matron in a neighbouring hospital. Both visitors reported that the patient was doing well and believed he would soon be fit to travel home, so it was a great shock when he had a sudden relapse and died on 6 June.[5]

The Battalion was relieved by 1/KOYLI on the evening of 25 May and moved back to support in the GHQ Line (the preserved trenches of the Sanctuary Wood Museum occupy part of the central sector of the 1915 GHQ Line). At least one man appreciated their new location, as Pte John Fairclough described in a letter to his brother near Caton:

> The trenches we are in are good ones, about four feet in the ground and sandbags, so we are as safe as houses.... You can see some fine sights there when they are shelling

aeroplanes. It is grand to watch them. I have seen five brought down, and last week some of the fellows got one with their rifles, and the airman dropped just behind our trench, but he was dead enough, for he was full of bullet holes. The Germans have been up to their old game—using gas; but they got most of it themselves, for when they were firing it the wind changed and blew it back into their own trenches, and you should have heard them shout. We had a good laugh at that.[6]

After the casualties suffered, the dreadful sights of dead civilians, and the destruction of their property, the belief that German artillery deliberately targeted dressing stations (just as their snipers and machine-gunners deliberately targeted stretcher-bearers) with the use of poison gas had considerably hardened men's attitudes towards the enemy.

Just before they moved up to the line, forty-six-year-old father of three L/Cpl Ernest Harlowe wrote to a friend in Lancaster, in what was be his last letter:

Arrogant cowards [the enemy]. You cannot call them brave. They only exhibit any idea of bravery when they are about twenty to one and sheltered behind their trenches or under cover of their artillery. Had they had the pluck of a mouse on 5 May, not a man of the 5th King's Own would ever have seen Lancaster again, unless they had condescended to have taken us prisoners of war. They are big strapping fellows, many of them exceeding 6 ft, but as soldiers—bah! They are not equal to some of the rag and bone chaps in Lancaster.[7]

Support was shelled heavily all day on 26 May and overnight into the 27th. A number of men were wounded on the 26th, two of them stretcher-bearers. One was Cyril Cotton, the other was twenty-three-year-old stretcher-bearer Pte George Yates, who was talking to RSM Richard Snelson when a shell burst immediately overhead. The RSM was untouched, but Yates received a Blighty wound to his left shoulder. His comrade, George Mawson, took him to the dressing station. While on convalescent leave, Yates married the sister of his pal, Pte John Hargreaves—one of the wounded from 27 April. Both men rejoined the Battalion, but only one would survive the war. Others wounded on the 26th were Pte Will Eastwood from Blackpool and Sgt Walter Harrison.

Worse followed in the early hours of 27 May. Thirty-seven-year-old L/Cpl William Preston was in one of 'B' Company's dugouts, chatting to the other NCOs, before he went on duty. The last thing A/CSM Albert Dawes said to him was a warning to take care in the trenches as the enemy had been sending over shells intermittently. He had hardly left the dugout when one scored a direct hit on it. Preston hurried back to find a scene of utter carnage. Dawes and three others were dead. Sgt Robert Threlfall, who had been buried alive earlier that month, was one. The twenty-three-year-old had been awaiting his return to the UK for commissioning. Also killed were Cpl Albert Sandham and L/Cpl Ernest Harlowe. Dreadfully injured—though still alive when they pulled him out—L/Cpl Rowland McGowan died shortly after reaching the dressing station. All five were buried together, and Preston placed a cross over the grave, inscribed 'Till we meet again, Bill'. The last of the occupants from the dugout was former postman Pte Stephen Cook. He too reached the dressing station alive, but died on 29 May.

There were also casualties among those nearby. Standing just outside was Pte George Atkinson from Lancaster. Although his clothes were torn to ribbons by the blast, he did not suffer so much as a scratch. He was, however, admitted to hospital suffering from the effects of the toxic fumes from the explosion—possibly from entering the dugout to attend the casualties. Keen amateur footballer Pte Horace Frost had both hips shattered by shrapnel and was evacuated home. He was medically discharged in August 1916, although records show that this was for sickness rather than his wounds. L/Cpl John Gardner received shrapnel wounds to the head and the twenty-seven-year-old was also treated for rheumatism at the Canadian Hospital in France (although his records do not survive, his later battalion number suggests that he was discharged as 'time-expired' in early 1916, and then conscripted back into the Battalion some time in 1918). Severely shocked and with an injury to his knee when he was sent flying by the blast, thirty-two-year-old Pte Tom Norbury was admitted to hospital. The last of the wounded that night was twenty-six-year-old Pte Harry Hull from Poulton-Le-Fylde. Although he received a shrapnel wound to the face, it was inconsequential and he was back two days later.

Thankfully, enemy artillery was less active over the following days, but casualties still mounted as men spent their nights strengthening the GHQ Line. On 28 May, twenty-three-year-old Pte Albert Fleming had a very close escape when a shrapnel ball pierced the right breast pocket of his tunic, travelled down his sleeve, and wounded him in the right wrist. The wound was not serious and he returned a few days later. The records of the other casualty for that day, Cpl Benson Boyd, provoke more questions than they answer. Both his pension record and the *Casualty Return* give the date of wounding as 28 May, with him being evacuated home on 2 June—never returning to a theatre of war.[8] Records indicate he was one of the draft assimilated on 11 May. His pension record describes his wound as a 'bayonet wound of left middle finger at Ypres.', though also notes 'limping owing to wound on left leg.' The wound to his leg could easily be explained as being caused by shellfire, but the bayonet wound is a mystery. The Battalion were some way behind the front line at this time, did not enter No Man's Land, and a bayonet wound caused accidentally would not be described as 'wounded in action' in his records.

On 29 May, the ration party were returning from their supply run when shrapnel badly wounded Pte John Crossley twice in a leg and the back. He was evacuated home, but the thirty-three-year-old father of two died in a Glasgow hospital on 1 July. The war was a bleak one for his young widow as one brother, Pte Henry Winder, was killed with the Battalion on 27 April and both her other brothers wounded a week later. Enemy artillery remained fairly inactive during the day, and there were no more casualties until the night of Monday 31 May, when GHQ Line was bombarded by a mixture of HE, shrapnel, and gas. Seven casualties were from a single shell that exploded inside a trench—the men working in the open next to them completely unharmed. Twenty-two-year-old Pte Peter Husband, from 'A' Company's MG Section, one of the draft from the

11th, died from his wounds at the dressing station. The young man from Lancaster had twice been rejected when he had tried to enlist, only succeeding at his third attempt.[9] Another from the same draft, Pte John Douglas, received wounds to shoulder and skull, and although these were not serious, his return to duty was delayed until early September as he caught German measles at the convalescent camp at Wimereux. L/Cpl Harold Gradwell's leg wound required treatment in England, and once recovered, he was posted to the 1/4th. Another to make the long trip home was Pte Frederick Jenkinson from Garstang—admitted to a London hospital with six shrapnel wounds. Pte Harry Parkinson's wounds were not serious, although the shrapnel ball that struck him between forehead and left eye could easily have been fatal. He was back with his pals on 25 July. The final two casualties were Privates Arthur Simpson and Thomas Woodhouse. It was a clear night, which led to one of the more unusual reports in an infantry war diary, when the passage of a Zeppelin was noted due north of the Battalion's positions, heading west. This was probably *L.Z. 38*, which bombed north-east London, killing seven and wounding thirty-five civilians.

Although three men were wounded, 1 June was another quiet day. Both L/Cpl William Lynch and newly appointed Cpl Edwin Lidford suffered only minor wounds. Twenty-one-year-old Pte Thomas Dunn was wounded in the neck by a shell fragment, but returned. At 2 p.m. on 2 June, enemy artillery began to shell the Battalion's trenches, heavy fire continuing until 6.15 p.m. Four were killed and ten wounded; as luck would have it, one shell that burst in a dugout accounted for three of the dead and five of the wounded. Two killed by this shell were Pte Joseph Dalton and Pte James Lee, both resident in Fleetwood. The third was twenty-two-year-old Pte Harry Ghorst, who had carried his wounded brother to safety in March. His injuries were severe and he died shortly afterwards. Among the other casualties were two brothers, Charles and seventeen-year-old John Hodgson (241), both victims of the same shell. Twenty-one-year-old Charles, terribly injured—both legs broken and multiple shrapnel wounds—died soon after reaching the dressing station. His brother, John, with crippling wounds to right arm and a leg, was evacuated to Warrington Hospital where the leg was amputated.

Casualties from 2 June 1915

Pte Harry Birchall	1592	WIA: 2/6	Pte John Robert Hodgson	240241	WIA: 2/6
Pte Joseph Dalton*	481	KIA: 2/6	Pte Richard Hornby	240305	WIA: 2/6
Pte James Duggan	1685	WIA: 2/6	Pte James Linsley Lee*	2591	KIA: 2/6
L/Cpl John Estill	1151	WIA: 2/6	Pte L. Maloney	1961	WIA: 2/6
Pte James Gardner	241012	WIA: 2/6	Pte Thomas Nisbett	1041	WIA: 2/6
Pte Harry Ghorst	2479	DOW: 2/6	L/Sgt Walter Philips	240814	WIA: 2/6
Pte Charles Walter Hodgson	1228	DOW: 2/6	Pte Joseph Townley	240951	WIA: 2/6

*Both James Lee and Joseph Dalton are recorded as being killed on 3 June by CWGC. It is clear from other sources that their deaths were in the evening of 2 June.

Relieved by the Royal Fusiliers, the Battalion marched to huts near Ouderdom, 8 miles to the west. The next day, another punishing march of 15 miles was made to billets at Ryveld, the exhausted men near to collapse by the time they arrived six hours later. They remained in huts here until 15 June, and then moved to others at Zevecoton adjacent to 2/King's Own, remaining until 20 June. This period was spent training and absorbing replacements into the Battalion structure. Although seventy of the sick and wounded rejoined and fifty-four replacements from the 2/5th arrived, the Battalion was much under-strength. The newcomers were fresh to trench warfare, so needed to learn the skills of wiring, constructing, and maintaining defences and the knowledge to fight and survive at the Front. The replacements from 11 May were not that much more experienced and their education took up much of this period. For some, their interlude out of the line was be far less relaxing than it was for their pals, when they fell afoul of the disciplinary system. The attractions of the local estaminets were obviously too much for twenty-seven-year-old Pte Albert Hodson. On 12 June, he was up before the CO for being absent from Roll Call the previous night and drunk. He was fined 2s 6d (about two and a half a day's pay) and given a ferocious twenty-eight days' field punishment—sending a clear message to anyone else considering flouting the rules about alcohol. For Pte George Cowell, this would see the end of his short time at the front. The twenty-two-year-old had only reached the Battalion on 11 May, but was sent home on 17 June and medically discharged for chronic asthma. Also home in a Glasgow hospital, being treated for the effects of gas, was Cpl Frederick Lambert, gassed sometime between the 3 and 11 June. Another change was a new MO: Lt George, a great favourite of the men and pre-war GP for many, was posted to a base hospital, and on 11 June, his place was taken by twenty-eight-year-old Capt. John Deighton RAMC—who soon became just as well-liked.

On 11 June, Lt Briggs was put in charge of the new 'Grenadier Platoon', and he and his selected men departed to division for training in this new skill. Grenades at this time were highly dangerous in the hands of the untrained—and, in reality, not much safer for the experienced. Initially, the device in favour was a homemade bomb using an old jam tin, ammonal, and scrap metal—ignited by a fuse that had to be lit. Around this time, the Béthune or Battye Bomb was also making an appearance; although it was slightly more reliable, it also needed a fuse lit by either a match or, more usually, a Nobel fuse igniter crimped onto the end of the Bickford safety fuse. This just needed to be twisted to initiate. Possibly the grenade that caused the most concern to anyone nearby to someone armed with it was the No. 1 Grenade. This was contact-detonated and accidental detonation was responsible for numerous tragedies during training and in the field. The brigade was being equipped with the Hales rifle grenade around this time, another contact-detonated device, though no evidence survives to indicate that this filtered its way through to the Battalion at this stage. On 10 June, however,

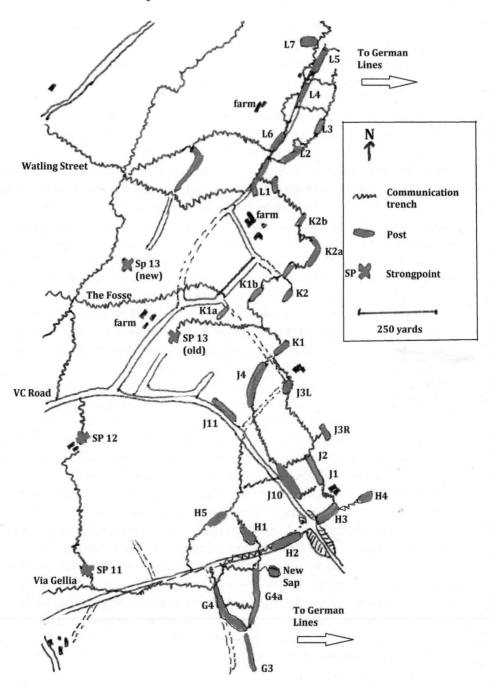

KEMMEL

an accidental explosion of one in their billets killed one man and wounded ten from 1/KOYLI.[10]

On 20 June, the Battalion moved to bivouacs near Locre (officially Loker), the next two days occupied with training and the nights with working parties to the trenches. Reinforcements had been far too few, and with the Battalion's trench strength under 400, Brigade decided to use the Battalion as general labour and detach companies to strengthen other battalions. Consequently, on 23 June, a very despondent 'D' Company went off with 1/KOYLI to man Trenches H1 and H2 in the right sector of the Kemmel trenches. The next day, 'C' Company went to Trench H5 with 2/East Yorks. Being attached to 'strangers' was always an unhappy duty and there was obvious concern among all ranks that they would be disbanded or amalgamated (as happened to 3/Monmouths). Apart from moving into huts near La Clytte, there was little change to the pattern of training and fatigues. The only casualty towards the end of June was a training accident when L/Cpl J. Smith was accidentally wounded. On 30 June, 'D' were relieved by 'A', and five days later, 'B' and 'D' became the two detached companies in H1, H2, and H5. The first man to be killed in the Kemmel sector was Pte Edward Callow from Dalton, the twenty-year-old from 'D' Company on a working party at the time.

Although there were no fatalities, a number of men were wounded. Appearing on two *Casualty Reports*, their injuries occurring between 1 and 6 July. Pte Thomas Higgins, Pte Tom Smith, and L/Cpl William Wood all appear on the first list. On the second was L/Cpl William Raine, who was transferred to the East Yorks upon his recovery, and Pte Clifford Roscoe from Morecambe, wounded in the wrist by shrapnel. He was another lost to the Battalion upon his recovery as he was commissioned in the Loyals, ending the war as a captain, before migrating to Canada. Pte John Wilson (176) from Carnforth was wounded in the left shoulder; another from this list, and known to be wounded on the 5th, was Pte Edward Nicholls from Lancaster, hit in the right knee.

Far from the flush of youth was a fifty-five-year-old cobbler Pte Charles Bennett. The father of eight, an ex-regular from 2/King's Own, had enlisted in the Battalion in 1908. Old soldiers could either be a boon or a menace—the worst drunken troublemakers, whose mere presence made life difficult for young soldiers and NCOs alike. The best of the 'breed', like Bennett, were a tremendous benefit, steady under pressure, extremely knowledgeable, and a fine example to the youngsters. The 1/5th had very few of the former and a good supply of the latter, a surprising number of whom were teetotallers. Sadly, the harsh conditions worked against their advancing age and very few were still in service by the end of 1916. On 8 July, Charles Bennett was promoted three levels and became the new Shoemaker-Sergeant—a post he held until May 1916, when he was discharged 'time-expired'.

On 12 July, 'A' and 'C' returned to the line, occupying some of the trenches in the centre sector. The firing line was not continuous and comprised of a number of fighting trenches, mostly connected by CT, though in some parts gaps existed in the line—passage between these sections only possible from the rear. Behind the front line, a series of strongpoints added backbone to the defences and both companies helped man two of these, SP12 and SP13. One welcome issue was the smoke helmet, a vast improvement over a cloth pad. Sgt John Green and Pte Arthur Goodman were evacuated to hospital with shellshock on 16–17 July—both would later be medically discharged. Pte Henry Wilkinson was admitted to hospital for deafness and he too was discharged two months later for DAH brought about by shellshock. Twenty-three-year-old Pte Leonard Monks, a father of one from Lancaster, was hit in both legs by shrapnel on 17 July while out on a listening patrol in No Man's Land. He was brought back to friendly lines by Sgt William Bell, who crawled all the way on his hands and knees, with the injured man on his back.[11] Monks was medically discharged the following April. Since arriving at Kemmel, the OC Maj. Edward Cadman had been lobbying Brigade for permission to deploy the Battalion to the front as a unit and permission was finally given to occupy the 'L' Trenches, K2b and K3 of the left sector. To achieve this, the Battalion had to strip Transport of every man they could spare. The Transport Officer Lt Harold Bell was given command of a fighting trench—the QM doubling up to also oversee Transport. Even so, they were unable to man the entire sector and detachments from 1/KOYLI and 1/Yorks and Lancs occupied K1a, K1b, K2, and K2a.

On 21 July, the Battalion moved up—'A', 'B', and 'C' to the forward trenches, 'D', minus forty men who were boosting the numbers of the other three companies, at Battalion HQ at York House. The Vickers teams set up in L5, L6, and L7. The front was fortunately quiet, and each night, 'D' carried the stores and rations forward. Brigade believed the 'unusual quietness' of the enemy was because he was concentrating on extending his wire in No Man's Land and behind his front line, and also draining his trenches.[12] The Battalion was now acknowledged as 'experienced', and on 24 July, the officers and two platoons from 6/Dorset and 7/Yorkshire Regiments (both 'New Army') were sent to them for instruction in trench warfare. They got a warm welcome, as the enemy shelled L4 and L5 vigorously. Apart from one man from 1/KOYLI who was wounded in K2a, twenty-three-year-old Pte John Wilcock (474) was wounded in the side by shrapnel. The wound was not serious and the former Lancaster teacher returned to the Battalion after his recovery. The next day was quieter, with only light shelling against the left trenches, though there was increased enemy air activity and after dark a reconnaissance patrol discovered the enemy working on his wire.

In the early hours of 26 July, a working party suffered a single casualty when twenty-seven-year-old Pte Charles Tyson was hit by what was probably random small arms fire. Capt. William Deed informed his parents:

Your son was shot in the early morning, about 12.30 a.m. on Monday 26 July, in the region of the abdomen. As you are no doubt aware a wound of that nature is almost always fatal. Your son was working in front of the trench with a party who were repairing the barbed wire entanglement. As I was walking along some distance off inspecting what had been done, I heard a disturbance, and found your son on the ground. We carried him into the trench, and he was immediately attended to by the stretcher-bearers. I gave him some morphia, and he was carried down to the dressing station where the medical officer took charge of him. He sank, and died after a few hours. He was buried last night in the soldiers' cemetery near the headquarters close to Kemmel. I need hardly assure you that everything possible was done for him.[13]

More casualties ensued when the trenches were shelled, and twenty-six-year-old L/Sgt James Anyon hit in both knees by shrapnel—a Blighty wound. He was discharged as 'time-expired' the following January, and as a ships' carpenter, he probably found employment in the munitions industry. Also wounded was twenty-year-old Pte Harry Hargreaves, hit in a hand and both legs. The young soldier—with the Battalion for just over a month—was comforted as he lay on the stretcher by his brother-in-law, CQMS Albert Wilson, who then wrote to reassure the family that Harry would be okay. Despite this reassurance, these injuries brought him a medical discharge in June 1916. There was one fatality from the shellfire: twenty-four-year-old Pte Patrick Murphy from the Yorkshire Regiment.

The Battalion continued to improve their trenches and patrol after dark on 27 July, with no casualties and. However, on the 28th, enemy artillery again targeted the trenches and casualties resulted—though none fatal. Of the eight recorded, five were from the 'learners' attached from the New Army. The luckiest escape was probably that of Pte Richard Bleasdale, who was slightly wounded in the head by a sniper's bullet. Eighteen-year-old Pte Edwin Murray was also wounded, though his injuries were due to shrapnel and he soon returned after a spell at base hospital (his service record gives his date of wounding as 31 July, but this is unlikely and the probable date—based on information in other sources—was 28 July). At least two men are known to have been evacuated after suffering from the effects of gas around this date. Pte Harry Parkinson had only been back with the Battalion for three days after treatment for his wound of 31 May, when he was caught without his smoke helmet on:

> I was almost blinded and my body became swollen something awful. I could not see anything. I am pleased to say the swelling has gone down, but it has settled in the back and legs. The only thing to do this was German gas.[14]

Parkinson was evacuated home and discharged as a result of trench nephritis in April 1917—dying from resultant kidney failure on 27 December 1920. From his description of his symptoms, it seems probable that he was already suffering from undiagnosed trench nephritis (symptoms of which include swollen face and legs), and the gas was the cause of his hospitalisation and subsequent nephritis diagnosis. The other man known to be gassed around this date was Pte Joseph Dawson from Carnforth, who was also evacuated home and then transferred to the Labour Corps.

As a result of carelessness, another man ended up in hospital on 28 July. Pte Frederick Clayton managed to shoot off the tip of one finger with his own rifle. After cleaning it, he was told that there was too much oil on the weapon, and when wiping this off, he managed to catch the trigger while his other hand was resting over the muzzle.

His punishment is not recorded, but it is probable that he got at least twenty-eight days' field punishment—though if there was the slightest suspicion that the injury was deliberate, then six months detention was the norm. Weapon handling concentrated more on shooting the enemy, rather than not shooting each other, and by modern standards, it left a great deal to be desired, leading to numerous negligent shootings, some fatal. There was only supposed to be a round in the chamber if the soldier was on sentry duty or had been ordered to 'make ready', and the safety catch had to be applied at all times—whatever the 'condition' of the rifle. To be fair, the Battalion had fewer accidental shootings than the 1/4th, who suffered five dead and more than a dozen wounded from poor weapon handling.

During the night of 28–29 July, a patrol in No Man's Land discovered the enemy building a gun emplacement in front of their parapet, and after bearings were taken to plot the position, they passed this information back to Brigade. Although no one from the Battalion was killed or wounded, thirty-five-year-old Pte Andrew Toole from 1/Yorks and Lancs was killed late on the 28th. For forty-four-year-old RSM Snelson, the last day with the Battalion was 29 July. This distinguished NCO had spent most of his adult life serving the Colours, but his health suffered from the rigours of active service and he was posted home to the Reserve Battalion and commissioned as a captain with them in January 1916. Thirty-nine-year-old George Brown, also with the Colours since the age of fourteen, was appointed RSM, but as he was still in England, CQMS Byrne acted as temporary RSM. Other new appointments included thirty-four-year-old wheelwright Edward Remington appointed Pioneer-Sergeant on 5 August.

By 11.15 p.m. on 30 July, the Battalion was relieved by 1/KOYLI and marched to bivouacs at Scherpenberg. Despite most positions being targeted by shrapnel, the only casualties in that final day in trenches were again from 1/Yorks and Lancs, who had three men wounded. Shelter in the bivouacs was provided by using two hop poles tied into an 'A-frame' at each end, the ridge pole another hop pole, and the weatherproofing coming from an army blanket. Hardly waterproof, nor secure in winds, but preferred by the men over billets in barns and other buildings, as these were generally lousy or flea-ridden. Back in England, 2 August was a Bank Holiday, as one man wryly commented in a letter home comparing his 'Bank Holiday' with those from previous years:

> ...and like those at home, we suffered from the weather. Instead of exchanging 'glad eyes' and chaff with the girls on the promenade at Morecambe, we were exchanging bullets and 'whizz-bangs' with the enemy, not half so pleasant, but more exciting.[15]

Their time at Scherpenberg was hardly 'rest' as large fatigue parties were required to work on the support lines and carry rations and other supplies during the night. Training took place during the day, though it has to be said that their time at Scherpenberg was not all hard work. On Sunday 1 August and Bank Holiday Monday, afternoons and evenings were set aside for sporting competitions. This idea came from CQMS Tom Byrne and Sgt William Bell, who approached Maj. Cadman about an inter-unit sports contest, followed by a battalion cricket tournament. Maj. Cadman was enthusiastic and promised to provide prizes for winners. The wrestling competition had plenty of contestants, but was eventually won by Pte Harrison (probably Leonard Harrison) from 'D' Company in a closely fought bout against Pte Sanderson of 'B' Company. In the final of the keenly contested tug-of-war, 'C' Company beat Transport, and Pte Wright from 'D' Company beat machine-gunner Pte Joseph Peel in the boxing competition. A special prize for boxing skill was awarded to Pte Warwick from 'D' Company, who was narrowly defeated on points by a much heavier man. Pte Ludlow, a former semi-professional boxer from the Yorks and Lancs, won the 'Open' boxing competition. The relay race saw victory to 15 Platoon, with Transport second, and 10 Platoon third. The sack race caused much amusement, although it was the spectacular tumbles rather than the skill of the winners that made for such good entertainment. It was won by L/Cpl Henry Gorst, with Pte Baker second—both from 'B' Company. Another highly popular match was the 'cock fight' in which a pair of men took on all comers (also in pairs). The winners from 'B' Company being Pte Lewis Brookfield, partnered by Pte Pedder (probably William).[16]

Brigade obviously believed that with their limited numbers, the Battalion could not sustain manning an entire sector, so once again companies were parcelled out to reinforce whoever needed them. On 3 August, 'B' and 'D' were attached to 1/Yorks and Lancs in the right sector until 10 August, and they provided the garrisons for H2, H3, and H5. The MG teams manned H3 and SP12—the latter positions also each containing six signallers and six stretcher-bearers from HQ. The next day, the rest of the Battalion moved to Locre, where later that afternoon, they were given a demonstration of the West Spring gun. This Heath-Robinson affair, powered by steel springs was Britain's answer to the lethally effective German trench mortars. An obvious advantage of the weapon was the lack of muzzle flash or loud bang to give away the location of the weapon, giving the intended target no warning to take cover before the bomb landed. There were, however, serious drawbacks as the West had a nasty habit of removing the fingers of its operators—including those of its inventor when he first demonstrated the weapon. Neither was the small bomb, little bigger than a grenade, of much use compared to the panoply of mortars available to the enemy. Eventually, the British caught up, but for considerable time, the only reply to trench mortars was to target them with a barrage of Howitzer shells—a tit-for-tat policy that contributed towards making mortar men as unpopular with their own side as they were with the opposition.

In the trenches, Pte Fred Jeffery and Pte Robert Dobson were both wounded, the latter only slightly. Pte John Bleasdale was also wounded in the head by a sniper, the twenty-three-year-old fortunate as the round just creased his scalp. Unfortunately, he was not so blessed the next time and was killed while attached to the Rifle Brigade a year later. Though all three appear on the *Casualty Return* for the 5th, Bleasdale is known to have been hit on the 4th. On 6 August, twenty-one-year-old Pte Edward Colgan was wounded in the wrist and back by shrapnel, his parents learning about the injuries to their only son in a letter from his best pal, Pte Hugh 'Pat' Butterworth, the 'sanitary man' from 'B' Company. Just two days later, Capt. Deed wrote to Butterworth's parents:

I have some bad news for you and your wife. Early this afternoon this trench was being shelled, about 1.45 p.m. Your son was hit by a piece of shrapnel in the jaw and neck, and died almost immediately. He did not, I think, suffer at all. He was unconscious and sank in a few minutes. His property will be collected and forwarded by the usual channel. I believe this makes the third son you have lost in this war, and I assure you that our sympathy is with you in this your new loss.[17]

Hugh Butterworth, an intelligent and smart soldier, unfailingly cheerful and always ready to help his comrades, had been a very well-liked man in 'B' Company—as testified by his many comrades who sent their condolences to his distraught parents. His father never got over the shock of this loss and died within a year. Tragically, a fourth son died in 1917. Hugh Butterworth's mother, Agnes, was one of four women chosen to unveil Lancaster's War Memorial in 1924—the four selected were seen as those whose losses had been particularly hard.

The men either side of Butterworth were not even scratched. Killed in the same exchange of fire, but with 'D' Company in the left-hand trenches, was twenty-one-year-old Sgt William Smith, slain when a shell burst immediately above his head. Amazingly, the men either side of him were also completely unhurt. Pte John West caught his second slight wound of the war when a small shell splinter cut his hand while he was at the back of the traverse. He returned after treatment a couple of days later. Both these shells blew the parapet in, but the only other man to be injured was Skerton soldier twenty-six-year-old L/Cpl Jack Smith from 'B' Company, who was looking through a periscope at the time and received cuts to his arm from broken glass. The casualties appear in the Battalion's diary under 9 August, although other sources, including the Brigade diary show that this occurred between 1.30 p.m. and 2.30 p.m. on the 8th.[18] In the evening of 10 August, 'A' and 'C' relieved the two companies in the trenches, the Yorks and Lancs rotating with 2/King's Own. No doubt L/Cpl Christopher Cooper from 'B' Company was relieved to be safely out of the trenches as, apart from the thunderstorms, which had made the trenches very wet and muddy, a sniper's bullet came very close to killing him, just nicking his ear as it passed.

On 11 August, the men not in the front line moved to bivouacs in a field at 50°47′53.90″N 2°46′16.70″E near Scherpenberg, with Transport in another field half a mile to their south-east. Despite being on the ranges all day and carrying parties overnight, the evening of Friday 13th was set aside for the long-awaited cricket final between the Officers' Mess team and the combined 'B' and 'D' Company team. This was a match deemed of sufficient local interest for a long and detailed report describing each player's performance, occupying several columns in the Lancaster newspapers:

> Unfortunately, the rain which had rendered the pitch, which had been carefully prepared by Sgt Lyson [*sic*] and party, very muddy and slippery, and rain fell during the first evening's play. The OC, (Major Cadman) formed up his eleven and marched them to the field of play in smart style, much to the amusement of the men. Lt Cadman

(brother of the OC) and Pte 'Bratty' Holmes, a former Vale of Lune player were the umpires.[19]

No man by the name of Lyson served in any battalion of the King's Own, and it is suspected that this actually referred to Sgt Sampson Tyson. Lt Christopher Cadman from the Yorkshire Dragoons had deployed overseas three weeks earlier. The match was very much dominated by the 'Company' team from the outset. They batted first and ended up 119 against the 'Officers', who were 54 all out. The second innings on Saturday evening was also watched by 'A' and 'C' Companies, who had returned from the trenches the previous night. Even though the pitch was much better, the result was similar, with 'Company' winning by 92 runs against their opponent's 62.

'B' and 'D' Company Team

Pte Airey		Pte Herbert Hunter	240548
Pte Clarke*		Pte Edward Osman	240304
Pte John Fairclough	1524	Sgt Stephen Rydeard	1964
Pte Joseph Hartley	2133	CSM Matthew Smith	240047
Pte Hesketh		Pte John Timms	2050
Cpl Charles Heys	240051		

The Officers' Mess Team

Pte Frank Ashworth	240888	Cpl George Farr	2221
Lt Harold Bell		Capt. William Fawcett**	
CQMS Thomas Byrne	240007	Pte J. Glynn**	1491
Maj. Edward Cadman		Capt. William Harriss	
Cpl Robert Davies	240505	Lt Eversley Mansfield	
Capt. William Robert Wheeler Deed		2Lt Joseph Allan Parkinson	
Capt. John Deighton RAMC			

* Probably 240848 Pte John Clark.
** Both substituted for Maj. Cadman when he was otherwise occupied by official business.

Of the twenty-one players who can be positively identified, only five remained with the Battalion in November 1918.

The respite was only brief, and at midnight on 15 August, 'A' and 'C' returned to the trenches to relieve the two companies of 6/Leicester Regiment under tuition from 2/

King's Own. The enemy facing them was known to be the 18th Regiment of the 2nd Bavarian Division; a discovery made the previous day by the Intelligence-Officer of 2/King's Own, when he got into a conversation with the enemy and persuaded them to throw over three newspapers for him—from which the information was obtained.[20] The first casualty was on the following afternoon, when a sniper shot Pte George Keen through the head. The twenty-five-year-old had been a talented artist, the best shot in the company, an only son, and a partner in his Father's Silverdale plumbing business. Even exposure during the hours of darkness could be dangerous—despite there being little moon—as a German eight-man working party discovered that night, when a sniper from 1/KOYLI in K2 killed six out the eight.[21] In H3 with the MG team, newly promoted Sgt John Wright was wounded in the arm by shrapnel. This capable twenty-five-year-old NCO was evacuated home for treatment, his arm fractured, though he returned. In common with all the machine-gunners, he was transferred to the MGC, but remained with 166 MG Company. He was awarded the MM on the Somme and killed in September 1917.

While 'B' and 'D' were on the ranges at Scherpenberg, Capt. Harriss and Lieutenants Mansfield and Parkinson went to reconnoitre trenches in the right sector during the afternoon. These two companies moved there and were joined by 'A' and 'C' by 11.50 p.m. on 17 August: Lt Parkinson and fifty men garrisoned G4a; Capt. Deed and thirty-nine men in G4; Lt Stanley Sunnucks and fifty-seven men in H1; one officer and sixty-seven men in H2; one officer and fifty-three men in H3; Capt. Harriss and seventy-three men in New Sap; and Lt Mansfield and forty-three men in SP11. Twenty-five men were also detached to 1/Yorks and Lancs in H5. With a trench strength of just 414 officers and men, it was perhaps fortunate that the sector was only about 600 metres in length and there was little enemy activity. The situation was undoubtedly worse for the officers as regulations stated that each section of trench should have one on duty at all times. Sleep was going to be at a premium. There was plenty of work to be done by the men too. CTs were deepened, wire defences enhanced, sections of parapet repaired where they had been damaged by whizz-bangs, and most of the trenches needed drainage improvements.

In the early hours of 18 August, listening patrols slipped out into No Man's Land and lay up in shell holes, alert for any signs of enemy movement. In the still night, sound travelled far and the patrols could clearly hear the enemy filling sandbags and carrying out pretty much the same sort of maintenance that the battalion was doing. A party of Germans heard cutting wire in front of Petit Bois were driven off by rapid fire from rifles, and one listening patrol reported the enemy carrying baulks of timber and throwing earth over the parapet opposite New Sap. One alarming observation was the sound of digging from below the right flank of H3. This was immediately reported to the Mining-Officer, the aptly named Lt Alfred Pick, who arrived post-haste at 1.45 a.m., with two trained 'listeners' from the Tunnelling Company's sap in J3. He finished at 3.15 a.m., declaring that he heard nothing and no immediate danger threatened. Brigade was, however, satisfied that mining operations had begun as this not the first

Details of G4 and G4a at Kemmel

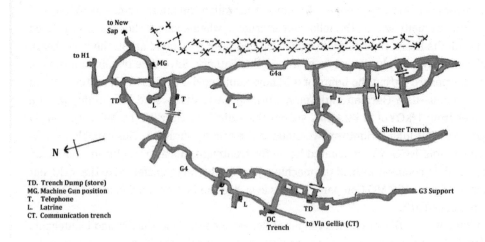

TD. Trench Dump (store)
MG. Machine Gun position
T.   Telephone
L.   Latrine
CT. Communication trench

time that the listening posts in No Man's Land had picked up the sound of tunnelling and timber to shore up these tunnels had been seen earlier. The patrols had also managed to locate an enemy MG position at 50°47′3.40″N 2°52′9.30″E that was causing trouble for men moving along VC Road (now Oosthoekstraat). The coordinates were passed to the Howitzers who made short work of this post. Although this is noted in the Battalion's diary for the 19th, the Brigade diary reports it happening between 5.30 a.m. and 11 a.m. of 18 August.

The first casualty of this tour was eighteen-year-old Pte Louis Holloway, wounded during the morning of the 18th. The next casualties—during the night of 19–20 August—were actually from an 'own-goal'. Pte John Roscow from 'A' Company managed to accidentally shoot both himself and his pal, nineteen-year-old Pte James Groves, with a pistol. The wound to Groves' right arm was treated in the hospital at Bailleul and he returned to the Battalion on 30 September. He was fortunate as the .455 Webley bullet was not inconsequential and must have missed the bone. As for Roscow, he too returned to the Battalion. The record of his punishment does not survive, but after hospital treatment, he would have been given a FGCM and sentenced to detention. The enemy had either repaired or replaced the MG reported on the 18th as it was in action again on the night of 19 August, firing bursts at varying intervals, and although the artillery was informed, they took no further action. The only casualty on 21 August was thirty-nine-year-old Cpl Patrick McConville, an Irishman resident in Fleetwood. A shrapnel ball grazed his scalp, but after having it dressed, he returned to duty.

On 22 August, the Battalion suffered another two casualties. Nineteen-year-old Pte John Berry was wounded and later posted to 7/King's Own, being killed with them in December 1917. The other casualty was fatal. At 5.05 p.m., nineteen-year-old Pte

Harold Dowthwaite from Caton was chatting quietly to his pal, Pte Charles Williams, when he was shot through the head by a sniper. The ground is quite undulating here and the right-angle turn in the lines at H3 meant that although a soldier may be covered from any shot from straight ahead, if he forgot to crouch low a cleverly positioned sniper in the slightly higher ground of the enemy lines, could often get an enfilading shot along one of the traverses at the range of a mere 250 metres. L/Cpl Tom Fairclough, also from Caton, was given permission to attend Dowthwaite's funeral at the little cemetery at Kemmel Chateau. This was their last day of this tour and they were relieved by 3/Monmouths at 10.30 p.m. These five days in the trenches had been quite quiet—though this is not the same as restful. Apart from the obvious physical graft involved repairing, enhancing the defences and patrolling, the Battalion had also been practising their skills in calling in fire support. These tests were at the behest of 28 Division, who ordered all three brigades to simulate this at least once every tour and began upon a signal sent at 2 p.m. by Brig.-Gen. Ravenshaw.[22] The star performer was New Sap under Capt. Harriss, who successfully completed his fire mission in twenty seconds. H1, H2, and H3, acting as a single position, took forty seconds and G4a sixty seconds. The ammunition returns for these five days also questions the dictionary definition of 'quiet', as 10,390 rounds of .303 were expended, though much of this was probably by the two MGs in H3 and the two in New Sap: G4a fired 3,740 rounds; New Sap, 3,510; and H1-3, 3,140 rounds.[23] The vast majority of this was directed against German working parties at night.

The Battalion remained at Scherpenberg until the evening of 28 August when they relieved 3/Monmouths in the Right Sector. The time out of the line was, as usual, spent training and providing large fatigue parties of up to 300 men to work on the defences or carry supplies to the front. Although there were no casualties during these activities, for two men from the Battalion, there was some considerable change—though for very different reasons. L/Cpl Henry Dolan was commissioned into the Regiment on the 24th, and two days later, seventeen-year-old Pte John Pattinson went home—a mere three months after joining them in France. Even though he had enlisted in February 1914, he had fibbed about his age, adding a year—and this had been discovered. He was not discharged, but posted to Oswestry and thereafter, a series of minor disciplinary charges—though with a high 'nuisance-factor'—triggered transfer to a succession of infantry units at home, before he ended his service in the Labour Corps.

There had been much more activity in the trenches while the Battalion were at Scherpenberg. Enemy presence in front of their trenches had increased and their artillery had been more vigorous. At 8.15 p.m., a mine was exploded to the front of J3, and although this caused no damage or casualties, it was followed up by a trench mortar and rifle grenade bombardment that did, and the trench garrison was reduced as a precaution. A British listening party subsequently occupied the crater on the night of 26 August. Unusually, the Germans sent a working party out at 2 p.m. on the 27th to try to repair damage to their wire caused by British artillery. Even though they had camouflaged themselves by fastening grass to their uniforms, they were spotted by British sentries and driven off by rifle fire, suffering a number of casualties. With heavy and constant sounds of lorry traffic coming from the enemy's rear, intensified activity in the trenches and around Petit Bois, an increased rate of fire from German artillery, and a stiff wind blowing from the east, favouring the use of gas, there was obvious concern that the enemy was planning an attack and British artillery stepped up their bombardment of the German rear. After dark in the British trenches, a machine gun was sited away from its normal emplacement to fire into Petit Bois, and selected trenches were ordered to direct regular rifle fire against the areas the enemy working parties had been seen in on previous nights. A 'rifle battery' of six guns was also deployed against the same target.

By 10.10 p.m. on 28 August, relief was successfully completed and the Battalion manned the Right Sector, with HQ in the Stables at Kemmel Chateau. On the previous tour, the day-to-day organisation of HQ had been solely up to Tom Byrne—still acting RSM. His workload was slightly reduced this time as 2Lt Reginald Phipp was now in overall charge of running HQ—though as a 'new officer', it is presumed that the RSM still ended up doing much of the actual organising. Ten new junior officers had arrived a few days earlier and these were immediately put to work. The deployment was pretty much the same as on their last tour—although officers and men were rotated to different trenches to improve their sector knowledge. The Battalion provided thirty men for three MG positions in SP11 under the command of Lt Mansfield, with 2Lt William Harrold to assist him. 'B' Company manned G4 (Lt Sunnucks and 2Lt Hubert Boys-Stones with thirty-six men) and G4a (Lt Kenneth Ogle and 2Lt Reginald Cattell with fifty men) and 'D' Company manned New Sap (Capt. Harriss, 2Lt David Knox, and 2Lt Herbert Bedford with sixty-four men). 'A' and 'C' Companies shared the 'H' Trenches, with Lt Parkinson and 2Lt Cuthbert Monks in H1 with forty men, and Capt. Fawcett and 2Lt John Gardiner in H2 with forty men. H3 was commanded by Capt. Briggs, assisted by 2Lt George Lloyd and another forty men. Twenty-five men were attached to 2/King's Own in H5 and any surplus men remained at Kemmel Chateau under the command of 2Lt Phipp.

One of their first actions was to send patrols into No Man's Land to check enemy defences. These got right up to their wire, which they reported was in particularly good condition. Enemy wire began about 20 yards from the front of their trench line and consisted of low entanglements fastened to wooden stakes 6 feet apart, each about 3½ feet high and six rows deep. In between the long stakes were shorter ones, with wire connecting the high and low posts, making an impenetrable obstacle. Most hostile patrol activity was just to the north in the centre sector and the Battalion was able to continue work on its own defences without interruption. Between 1.30 a.m. and 2.30 a.m. on 31 August, the enemy shelled New Sap (now officially titled H1a) and, though the damage was trivial, Pte Leonard Dixon was wounded—shrapnel breaking the radius of his left forearm. Sadly, he was lost to the Battalion as he was transferred to the RWF. The following day, thirty-four-year-old L/Cpl Isaac Winder was slightly wounded in the hand, and on 2 September, twenty-year-old Pte Robert Lamb was wounded in the head—though not seriously. It was not just at the Right Sector where the Germans were strengthening their defences; the other two sectors reported the same, although one patrol from 1/KOYLI in the Left Sector had a less than agreeable experience when they slipped into a disused trench halfway between L3 and the enemy line only to find it crammed with bodies in an advanced state of decomposition.

The Battalion was due to be relieved on 3 September, but as the Monmouths had departed the brigade, there was no available battalion to take over. Instead, the sector was split and 1/Yorks and Lancs took over part, leaving 'A' and 'C' Companies still in the trenches. For the men out of the line, there was little rest when they returned to Scherpenberg. In the early hours of 4 September, a carrying party of twenty was sent back to the front line and another 100 were set-to strengthening the subsidiary line. One of these, Pte William Angus from 'B' Company, received his second wound of the war when he was hit in the leg by a bullet. When not on working parties, men trained, focusing on bombing tactics.

At 6 a.m. on 6 September, a number of HE rounds landed behind H5 and H2 was hit by six whizz-bangs, though damage was slight. During the afternoon, Scherpenberg itself was shelled, although the only casualty from the Battalion that day was Pte Charles Pollard from Fleetwood. The forty-three-year-old lost his left eye from shrapnel, and as so often happens when one eye has received a penetrating injury, the vision in his other eye deteriorated too. He was invalided out a year later and died from TB in April 1920. Thirty-four-year-old Pte William Petty from Morecambe also ended up in hospital, his hearing damaged by repeated explosions, triggering medical discharge in January. The new RSM, George Brown arrived and Tom Byrne became RQMS. Four men from the Battalion were also given their commissions back in England: L/Cpl William Huntington went to 1/4th King's Own; Sgt John Gilchrist returned to the Battalion as a subaltern; the third, commissioned into King's Own and subsequently 166 MGC, was Pte Thomas Dixon; and the fourth, Sgt Leonard Titchener, returned to the Battalion, but departed again to join the RFC in August 1916. Sadly, he was killed on 3 December 1917 flying a F.E.2B with Sub-Lt H. K. Johnstone as his observer. There was a collision on take-off with the similar aircraft of 2Lt F. A. Biner and Air-Mechanic 1st Class W. D. Clement—all four airmen perished.

Although ground warfare had at times degenerated into barbarism, there was clearly still some of the chivalric attitude remaining among those fighting in the air. At 3.15 p.m. on 8 September, a German aircraft dropped a smoke bomb just to the north of Siege Farm, followed by a message to the rear of Sandbag Villa containing news about two British aviators recently shot down. At 9.40 p.m., 195 officers and men from 'B' and 'D' relieved the other two companies in G4, G4a, H1, New Sap, and SP11 in the Right Sector, the other part now garrisoned by 2/King's Own. For those out of the line, the training and fatigues continued as it had for the other half of the Battalion, with working parties of over 100 men most nights.

The right sector continued to be quiet. Most enemy activity took place against the 'J', 'K', and 'L' trenches, and on 10 September, when 2/King's Own rotated with 1/KOYLI, the only item of note in the Brigade diary was 'Germans wearing blue hats with a white cross in front were seen'.[24] They were probably from one of the Landsturm regiments as most had a cross that was either silver-coloured or of brass on their caps. The companies rotated on 15 September, and apart from 4.30 p.m. on 18 September, when the enemy dropped six 77-mm shells between G4 and G4a, their section of the front was remarkably quiet—most artillery action being directed elsewhere. At 10 p.m. on 20 September, 'D' Company was relieved by the Nova Scotia Rifles, leaving only 'B' Company and the four MG sections in the front line. The MG sections were in turn relieved at 1.10 a.m. on 22 September and 'B' Company at 8.45 p.m.—the sector handed over to 5 Canadian Brigade by 8.50 p.m.

Beginning at 9 a.m. on 23 September, the entire brigade marched off to Outtersteene, via Locre and Bailleul. The month had been a very quiet one as far as casualties were concerned, but there is a newspaper report of Pte Alexander Cooper being wounded on 25 September and treated at No. 1 Convalescent Hospital in Boulogne.[25] Although the Battalion was out of the line, the nineteen-year-old from Lancaster was a despatch rider, so the actual date could be correct; however, no casualties are shown for this date in the Brigade *Casualty Return* and the single entry for 'wounded' on 23 September is more likely to have been his. The month up to 23 September had been one of low casualties for the entire brigade, with twelve ORs killed, sixty-three wounded, two officers wounded, and one missing. This was set to change on 28–30 September when the brigade deployed in the Battle of Loos. Fortunately for the Battalion, they were on the periphery of this action.

Whenever troops were due to move there was a great deal to organise. *Movement Order No. 13* for 23 September illustrates well the forethought that went into this.[26] With an entire brigade on the march, it was essential to coordinate the movements of the five infantry battalions, Brigade HQ, Field Ambulance, Artillery, RE, and all the assorted arms that went to make up the brigade, to minimise congestion on the roads. The Battalion's breakfast was arranged for 6.30 a.m., with all utensils cleaned and returned to the cookhouse by 7 a.m. All Officers' kit, Mess kit, Orderly Room boxes, QM Stores, and cookers were to be loaded and ready to leave by 7.30 a.m. The Battalion paraded, ready to move at 8 a.m. The 1/5th were the penultimate unit to depart from Locre church—84 Field Ambulance just ten minutes behind them at 9.50 a.m. Not everyone marched together as 2Lt Boys-Stones, Cpl William Preston, and eight men from 'C' Company, were detailed to join the Brigade clearing-up party under Capt. Carew of the Royal Dublin Fusiliers—they did not leave Locre until 11 a.m.

The Brigade billeting parties, under Capt. Brazier of 1/KOYLI, left Locre church at 8 a.m. to arrange billets in Outtersteene. The QM was in charge of the Battalion's billeting party, comprising Privates Benson, Hesketh (as cyclist), Hartley ('B' Company storeman), William Herridge ('D' Company storeman), and Brockman (groom). Once these had located their billets, they moved back down the line of march until the group they were to guide arrived—then led them straight to their billets without 'check' to curtail bottlenecks. The Battalion marched in strict order, with HQ at the front, the four companies behind in alphabetical order, followed by the MG Section with their gun limbers and the Battalion's pack horses. Behind them were the 'tool limbers'; the 'small arms ammunition carts'; the 'water carts'; the 'travelling kitchens'; the 'Officers' Mess carts'; spare horses—which were to be led and not ridden; and then the men marching with the 'First Line Transport' under command of RQMS Byrne. At the rear was the MO and rear party—the latter consisting of 2Lt Monks and one NCO from each company—their duty to bring up the rear, collecting any of their own stragglers. Behind them, a Brigade Rear Party consisting of 2Lt Lloyd, Sgt William Bell and seven men from 'A' Company was detailed to march behind the Field Ambulance, collecting stragglers from all units.

The Battalion was warned that the Corps Commander, Gen. Sir Charles Fergusson would be watching them march through Bailleul (he was very complimentary). All men carried their complete equipment on the march, there being insufficient transport space to take their kit—this is when the bandsmen really 'lucked-out'. Regular halts were made whenever men marched (usually ten minutes out of every hour), and when halted, pack horses were placed with their heads facing the middle of the road—reducing the chance of mayhem occurring. Possibly remembering their billet fire in February, orders were given that no smoking or striking of matches whatsoever was to take place in any barn used as a billet, unless specifically ordered to do so by the Adjutant, and that anyone transgressing this would be immediately arrested. The lead elements of the brigade were established at Outtersteene at noon.

At 6 p.m. on 25 September, the Battalion was warned to prepare for a sudden move by either bus or a route march. Two-and-a-half hours later, another message arrived apprising them that any move would be unlikely before daybreak. The reason for the 'flap' was the British offensive further south at Loos, with 28 Division ordered south to join 1 Corps under Lt-Gen. Gough. One who missed this flurry of activity was the QM; he was sick and admitted to hospital that day. His duties were temporarily taken over by Lt Lloyd-Evans, who had returned a few hours earlier. At 3.15 a.m. on 26 September, the Battalion received their orders and at 5 a.m. set off to Robecq, where there was a planned dinner halt. At 2 p.m., the march continued towards Béthune, but shortly after 3 p.m., the brigade was ordered back to Robecq where billets were found for the night. At noon on the 27th, they were loaded into buses and taken to Noyelles-lès-Vermelles (the dairy erroneously records this as Foyelles). No billeting was available and a night of torrential rain was spent in a ploughed field, bereft of any shelter whatsoever. Five officers wounded at Ypres returned that day, and Messrs Huntington, Owtram, Hinton, Seward, and Roper must have wondered what they were coming back to. No. 83 Brigade was not deployed as an entity, and 1/Yorks and Lancs were attached to 85 Brigade; 2/East Yorks to 7 Division. No. 1/5th King's Own remained with 83 Brigade and were ordered to man the reserve trenches around Noyelles in case of hostile bombardment—300 men were immediately despatched on a fatigue party carrying rations and other stores up to 85 Brigade. Those not on fatigues spent another night in the same field—same weather too. At 10.30 a.m. on 29 September, the Battalion was 'stood-to' in the ploughed field. They were still there at 6.15 p.m., when they were ordered into the reserve trenches just over a mile to the east of Vermelles. The Battalion was commanded to carry a large amount of bombs up with them and the relief of 22 Brigade was completed by 1.30 a.m. on 30 September.

No. 2/East Yorks was already in the left of the front line—holding what had been part of the old German first and second lines—with 2/King's Own in the centre and 1/Yorks and Lancs to the right (1/KOYLI was still attached to 85 Brigade). The enemy had not been idle after losing this ground and a number of limited counterattacks had been attempted—sniping, artillery, and trench mortar fire was constant. The Battalion manned Border Lane in the OBL, and at 11.30 p.m., they received orders to deepen Spurn Head Sap—just to the rear of the East Yorks. These trenches were little better than the ploughed field and in many ways considerably worse. There was no shelter and men were up to their knees in mud and water, but what compounded the experience were the large numbers of British and German dead lying in the open after the succession of attacks and counterattacks.

A number of the Battalion were wounded that day. Twenty-one-year-old Pte George Ratcliffe from Lancaster was one; another was nineteen-year-old Pte Thomas Hargreaves from Knott End, hit in the right hand. Privates George Stephenson and Harry Simpson were also wounded, although details of their injuries have not survived. These last two days of September cost the brigade 349 officers and men killed, wounded, or missing.[27] Enemy counterattacks continued throughout 30 September, and for much of this time, the 1/5th was standing-to in their trench, ready to be sent anywhere needing immediate reinforcement. In 84 Brigade's sector, around noon, 2/Northumberland Fusiliers lost several bays of South Face Trench, and despite repeated counterattacks by their bombers, they were unable to regain the ground. By 5.45 p.m. things quietened down and the Battalion was relieved at 11.20 p.m. by 1/5th King's, marching to billets at Annequin. Lt-Col. Cadman returned to England sick, and his position was taken by Capt. Eaves, who had just returned from England and was rapidly promoted to Lt-Col. His predecessor never returned to the Battalion, being appointed as CO of 10/Cheshires and was killed with them in May 1918. By 5.20 a.m. on 2 October, the entire brigade was relieved by 6 Brigade and was in Annequin. However, the Battalion's rest was to be extremely short.

At 7.10 p.m., the Battalion was ordered to march via Vermelles and Barts to Central Keep to come under orders of 84 Brigade.[28] Upon arrival, 350 men were immediately tasked for fatigues, bomb, ammunition, water, and ration carrying details. The Battalion suffered a number of casualties on the night of 2–3 October while thus involved. The only fatality was Pte Alfred Griffiths of 'C' Company, though another four were injured. L/Cpl John Downham was wounded in the back when a round from a trench mortar landed near him. He was evacuated home and later transferred to the South Lancs. Twenty-four-year-old Pte James Holmes was hit in the head and hand and evacuated to a Manchester hospital, where he was overjoyed to be visited by his wife, whom he had married while home on leave the previous December. The other two casualties were Pte Henry Edwards from Carnforth and Charles Holmes (929) from Lancaster. By 4 a.m. on

3 October, the carrying parties returned and the Battalion gathered in Central Keep, in touch with the Grenadier Guards in Hulluch Alley.

Men were warned they would be taking part in an attack planned for the early morning; however, fog brought about its postponement—much to the relief of everyone when they later saw what they would have faced. The fog cleared to reveal a stretch of about 400 yards devoid of cover, the approaches bristling with German machine guns. Had they attacked, it is fair to surmise that they would once again have suffered terribly—especially considering what happened when the attack went ahead on 4 October. As their numbers were still only about 600, despite Capt. Eaves bringing a draft of 103 men with him on 1 October, another disaster may have spelled the end of the Battalion. Later that morning, the Battalion lost one of their most experienced NCOs, when Sgt Alfred Price DCM was wounded in the shoulder by shrapnel and evacuated home. He never returned, his term of service expiring the following March. Constant artillery fire fell all along the sector on 3 October. Parties of bombers from both sides made repeated probing attacks—the enemy trying to regain his lost trenches—the British equally keen to advance further. With so much activity, it is a small miracle that the only casualty from the Battalion was Pte John Entwistle. The twenty-four-year-old was evacuated home with a shrapnel wound to the head. Although he recovered, he was posted to the 8/King's Own and killed with them in September 1917—a mere three months after joining them.

At 9 p.m. on 2 October, 83 Brigade were told that they would relieve 84 Brigade in the line on the night of 3–4 October. At 5.30 a.m. on 3 October, 2/King's Own left for Central Keep, but less than two hours later, received orders diverting them to positions in Lancashire Trench and Sussex Trench. Late on 3 October, 83 Brigade were in their new positions and at midnight a CO's conference was held to go over details for the proposed attack early the next morning. That night, 1/5 King's Own were once again in Border Lane, thankfully not part of this rescheduled attack.

The assault against the Hohenzollern Redoubt was due to begin at 4.45 a.m. Only a half-hour bombardment by heavy artillery was scheduled, beginning at 4.15 a.m., and then lifting to the German rear areas. No. 2/East Yorks cleared the parapet at 4.20 a.m. and crawled forward 40 yards to their jumping-off positions, coming under heavy rifle and MG fire immediately upon leaving their trenches. They reported that the only bombardment from British guns was actually landing among themselves. The leading companies advanced about 60 yards, only to be met by heavy shrapnel and small arms fire, very few getting to within 80 yards of the German defences before they too were shot down. No. 1/KOYLI met a similar fate. When Capt. Law, OC of their second wave, reached the first wave, he found that already over half had become casualties. Combining both waves, they advanced into heavy fire, only about twenty remaining by the time they were halfway to German lines. Although small parties from this combined force tried to push on, it was hopeless. In the first four days of October, the Brigade suffered 426 officers and men killed, wounded, or missing.

Although they did not take part in the actual assault, the 1/5th were still utilised. At 3.30 p.m. on 4 October, they were ordered that once it was dark, they were to deepen the CT that ran from Hulluch Alley to Big Willie, and then garrison it so that they could continue the work through the day. During the night of 5–6 October, the Brigade was relieved by 2nd Guards Brigade and proceeded to billets, the Battalion arriving in Annequin at 5.30 a.m., and on to Censé de la Vallée at 7 p.m. on the 6th. They remained there training until the afternoon of 15 October, when they moved to billets at the Ferme du Roi near Bethune. They left for Le Préol in the morning of 17 October, and officers went to reconnoitre the trenches at Cuinchy, where the brigade was to relieve 22 Brigade of 7 Division.

The next day, the four MG teams proceeded independently to the trenches, one with 1/KOYLI and the other three with 2/King's Own. For the rest of the Battalion, it was training and working parties, with six officers and 300 men needed for one detail on the night of 19 October. Though the diary makes no mention of casualties around this period, one man, L/Cpl Harold Iddon, appears on a casualty list and the balance of probabilities is that he was wounded on this detail. On 21 October, the Battalion moved back to the billets in Censé de la Vallée, but a mere six hours later, they were moved to billets along the L'Eclème-Robecq road.

The entire division was on the move, and although some officers and men were detailed for divisional entraining duties on 21 October, the Battalion was not going with them. The 28th Division was off to Salonika, and although initially it had been planned that the Battalion would remain with them, there was a last-minute change of mind and the 1/5th was transferred to 2 Brigade of 1st Division. On 22 October, they left for their new assignment.

23 October 1915–7 January 1916: Business as Usual

Coordinates for Positions Named in this Chapter

Philosophe Billets	50°28′20.50″N 2°44′36.90″E	Victoria Station	50°28′13.40″N 2°45′9.90″E
Posen Station	50°28′40.10″N 2°47′24.80″E	Lone Tree	50°28′36.90″N 2°47′3.00″E
Posen Alley	50°28′9.90″N 2°48′37.90″E	Le Rutoire Alley (HQ)	50°29′10.10″N 2°47′23.50″E
Vendin Alley	50°28′33.30″N 2°48′26.50″E	Le Rutoire Fm.	50°28′56.00″N 2°45′55.10″E
Battalion Cemetery	50°28′55.60″N 2°44′18.70″E	Corons du Rutoire Keep	50°28′40.40″N 2°45′1.90″E
Gun Alley	50°28′1.50″N 2°47′49.90″E	Ninth Avenue (HQ)	50°28′58.60″N 2°47′30.80″E
North Loos Avenue	50°28′22.70″″N 2°47′14.40″E	Hulluch Road	50°29′9.00″N 2°47′35.30″E
65 Metre Point	50°28′0.80″N 2°46′45.40″E	Vermelles Rwy. Crossing	50°29′20.50″N 2°45′15.90″E
Lens Road Redoubt	50°27′42.60″N 2°46′19.00″E	Devon Lane	50°29′19.90″N 2°47′56.20″E
Fort Glatz	50°27′40.40″N 2°47′12.00″E	Hay Alley	50°28′54.10″N 2°48′21.10″E

The Battalion marched the 4 miles to their new billets in Ecquedecques where they trained until 13 November. Perhaps one of the greater changes was in the 'warranted' ranks. RSM Brown was put onto light duties on 9 November and shortly afterwards posted home. The RSM's health was poor, but it is clear from his service record that he and Lt-Col. Eaves did not enjoy the sort of relationship a CO and RSM need to run an efficient battalion. It was no easy matter to remove an RSM, and before it was authorised, Eaves needed permission from Brigade Commander, Divisional Commander and Gen. Rawlinson, commanding IV Corps. Twenty-seven-year-old CSM George Barrow, who had been with the Battalion since its inception, became RSM. Sadly, RSM Brown died from a heart condition in May 1917.

During this period of rest, four men were transferred to the ASC and others discharged as their period of engagement had finished—among them L/Cpl Rowland Cornall, L/Cpl Stanley Ashton, and Pte James Smith. Others, such as Pte John Barrow from Lancaster, went home sick. He was discharged and died in February 1919 from an illness related to his military service. Thirty-three-year-old Pte Tom Norbury from Lancaster returned home, suffering from rheumatism and was discharged in 1917. Another was thirty-year-old Pte Frederick Warbrick, suffering from conjunctivitis; he was transferred to the South Lancs and then the RE, but discharged with trachoma in August 1918. He obviously recovered as he re-enlisted in the King's Own in 1920. The last man known to have returned home was L/Cpl Isaac Winder, although the reasons for his posting are not recorded and he was discharged as time-expired in January 1916. The Battalion's manning levels received a small boost when eight men returned from base hospitals, though it is likely that the number lost exceeded the number gained as November was always a time when more fell ill. One who did end up in No. 11 Stationary Hospital in Rouen for a couple of weeks was Sgt Reuben Butler, who sprained his knee playing football.

Early on the morning of 13 November, the Battalion entrained at Lillers, bound for Nœux-les-Mines. From there, they marched to Mazingarbe, arriving at 9 a.m. As dusk fell, they relieved 19/London in the front line 'B' Sector, just west of the village of Hulluch. Owing to the heavy rain, these trenches were in dreadful condition—in many places flooded to a depth of 2 feet. The 14th was a quiet day, and men worked flat-out repairing and renewing damaged parapets and trying to shovel mud out of the trenches. With the approach of winter, these were ideal conditions for trench foot and at least one man, twenty-one-year-old Pte James Bilsborough, was sent home with trench foot—he did not return until the following April. Pte James Groves, who had recovered from his accidental wounding, was also hospitalised on 20 November for 'frostbite'—though this was almost certainly trench foot as it was often recorded as such in the early years. Considering the weather, the front trenches could have been worse, but there was no support line in this sector and no dugouts available to shelter troops from weather or shellfire.[2] Consequently, Brigade determined to make each battalion's stay as short as possible before they rotated out. Although there was virtually no rifle fire, a certain amount of shelling resulted in casualties for the Brigade, with three men killed and eleven wounded on 14 November.[3] The 1/5th lost one man, nineteen-year-old Pte Harold Cross from Lancaster. In the afternoon, he and his pal, Pte Francis Gardner, were next to each other in one of the trenches when a shell exploded just behind their trench. The nineteen-year-old was killed instantly and Gardner—who so far had escaped scot-free when others near to him were killed—was wounded in the left arm by shrapnel. The other casualty was Pte James Hardy, his second wound of the war. He returned to the Battalion, was promoted to sergeant in the MG section, and transferred to the MGC. However, he was later commissioned in the MGC and returned to the Battalion as a lieutenant.

Although unwounded, Cpl Christopher Cooper had another close brush with death, describing the events to his wife:

> This is a terrible place we are in. I have been buried twice and the last time I thought my number was up. I was covered with slutch from head to foot and on top of that were about twenty bags of sand. They had a job to dig me out, but I'm thankful to say apart from the shock I'm all right. The officers were very kind to me.[4]

For his wife, bringing up their three children alone and mourning the death of their baby earlier that year, this news must have been nerve-wracking. He was transferred to the RE in 1917 and suffered a serious fracture of the tibia that July. Returning to the front in June 1918, he was evacuated home with shellshock in September, returning to France for the first three months of 1919. He was discharged with a 20 per cent pension until April 1921 for the injury to his leg and shellshock—an amount further reduced when his ten-year-old daughter died in 1920.

Divisional Commander Lt-Gen. Sir Arthur Holland visited the trenches on 15 November to check on the conditions for himself. The divisional diary describes both 'A' and 'B' Sectors as 'atrocious', adding that 'the recent heavy rain seems to have washed away entire trenches and a great deal of work will have to be done before the line is fit to live in'.[5] The heavy rain had now ceased and the lift in cloud base had the added advantage that it allowed British aircraft to patrol above the sector— considerably reducing German artillery fire. Consequently, 2 Brigade only had two men wounded all day, one of whom was Pte John Lofthouse, wounded in the afternoon. The Battalion was relieved by 1/Loyals on the night of 17 November and returned to their billets in Mazingarbe. It was only a brief respite, with the 18th taken up with making good their kit, inspections, and a lecture on trench foot. At 4.30 p.m., the Battalion moved forward again to take over the support trenches in 'B' Sector, relieving 2/Royal Sussex.

There were still considerable quantities of salvageable weapons, ammunition, and equipment lying around after the battles of late September, and on 20 November, many men were involved in collecting this and dumping it at Posen Station. The rest were cleaning and repairing trenches, endeavouring to make them fit for purpose. Later that day, twenty-year-old Pte Frederick Barrow and twenty-one-year-old Pte Harry Birchall (both from Blackpool) were killed by shellfire. During the early hours of 21 November, Sgt Frank Needham was wounded yet again; an ex-Regular and veteran of South Africa, he had only rejoined three days earlier after recovering from his previous head wound. Once again, he was evacuated home for treatment, remaining on a home posting after leaving hospital. In February 1918, he was admitted to hospital for the removal of a large 'foreign body' from just beneath the skin. Although reluctant to be operated upon, he eventually relented and a rifle bullet was removed from his neck. On leaving hospital in March, he was transferred to the Labour Corps.[6]

In the evening of 22 November, the Battalion moved to the front line, although some had been up there the previous night. Twenty-seven-year-old L/Cpl William Livesey was one of the men detailed to work under the Brigade Wiring Officer Lt Boundy. Taking advantage of thick fog, they erected some 250 yards of *chevaux de frise* to the immediate front of the British trenches—less than 100 yards from the enemy and under constant MG fire the whole time (*chevaux de frise* are free-standing obstacles, consisting of two posts lashed into an 'X' shape, joined by a longer centre post to other 'X'-shaped constructions and liberally festooned with wire. Knife-rest wire is similar, but with just two 'X' shapes). William Livesey went out again the following night on another wiring party, his coolness impressing his superiors who recommended him for a MiD.[7] Some shelling of the Battalion's trench line occurred on 23 November, in retaliation for British shelling of Hulluch and the enemy trenches opposite the Battalion. No casualties stemmed from this, but the parapet was damaged in a few places and Posen Alley and Vendin Alley were both hit. On 24 November, the Battalion returned to the support line again, when 2/Welsh relieved them. Three men were wounded on 24–25 November, one of whom remained at duty. The others, Privates Albert Caton and John Rowe, both ended up in hospital—the former medically discharged because of his arm wound. The Battalion was relieved on 26 November and moved to billets in Nœux-les-Mines until the afternoon of 2 December, and despite the town being shelled on 30 November, these were the last casualties of the month.

At 6 p.m. on 2 December, the Battalion took over the 'A' Sector support trenches from 1/9th King's. Twenty-seven-year-old Pte Mark Greenwood was killed by shellfire as they moved along the short CT linking 10th Avenue to Posen Alley (50°28′25.40″N 2°47′16.20″E), but he was the only casualty. His body was taken to the rear and buried at the small cemetery (now a housing estate) just behind the Corons du Rutoire (*corons* are workers' houses); after the war, he was moved to Dud Corner Cemetery. The new (to 2 Brigade) trenches were the cause of some dissatisfaction, the Brigade diary commenting that 'they [were] very bad trenches, the soil [was] a crumbly form of chalk … and will not stand'.[8] Three companies remained in support, and 'C' joined 1/Loyals in the front line. Despite intermittent shelling, there were no more casualties, and as dusk fell on 4 December, the Battalion moved forward to relieve the Loyals.

Conditions were appalling, with Posen Alley thigh-deep in cold mud—ideal conditions for trench foot. One sufferer, twenty-year-old Pte Stanley Lee, needed a month's treatment in a Sheffield hospital and did not return to the Battalion until the following September. HQ was established in Gun Alley, and as numbers were too few to hold the entire length of their sub-sector, a company from 2/KRRC reinforced them. The weather did not help, and after several days of rain, the front line trenches were also knee-deep in water and mud. This was exacerbated by the enemy, whose artillery blew in part of 'C' Company's trench on 5 December, wounding Pte William Bamber. British artillery did retaliate, but the results were disappointing and described as 'not very effective— as the shooting was inaccurate and many rounds blind [did not explode]'.[9] The artillery exchanges lessened on 6 December, allowing the Battalion to repair most of the previous day's damage, but on 7 December, the fire intensified, wounding Pte Richard Casson of 'D' Company. It must have been very difficult to evacuate the twenty-six-year-old as the continued rain had rendered most CTs virtually impassable. William Bamber and Richard Casson both appear on the same casualty list, and although the actual date of their wounding is not recorded, the probability is that it was on the dates given above. At dusk on 8 December, the Battalion was relieved by 2/KRRC and returned to their billets in Philosophe. Today, Philosophe itself has been swallowed by Mazingarbe and these billets have been obliterated, the rows of parallel streets just a series of mounds in a grassy field. They are, however, easily accessible to the battlefield tourist, sherds of pottery and tile protruding from the chalky soil—a poignant reminder that these were once homes.

After dusk on 10 December, the Battalion returned to the 'A' Sector support trenches to relieve 1/Loyals, though this time in the right sub-sector (A1 Support). HQ was in the northern part of Loos itself; 'A' and 'C' were in Gun Alley, but had to provide a guard for North Loos Avenue; 'B' was divided between the keep at 65 Metre Point and Lens Road Redoubt; and 'D' were in the front line with the Loyals. One advantage of this sub-sector was that geography favoured the ration parties. Due to the lie of the land, Transport was able to ferry rations by mule almost up to Battalion HQ via the RE dump at Fort Glatz, saving considerable toil. In the other parts of the brigade front, rations were brought up on the light railway from Victoria Station, 600 yards to the south-east of Philosophe and delivered at Posen Station, where they were met by fatigue parties from each battalion. Though this method appears to save considerable effort, it was not quite so clear-cut. The wagons on the light railway were not pulled by a locomotive, but relied upon the sweat and muscle of 120 men from the various Transport sections, each of whom had to provide one NCO and twenty-four men on a nightly basis to push these up to Posen Station. Water was taken forward by the Battalion's own water carts, meeting the carrying parties at Lone Tree, 500 yards to the west of Posen Station.

The enemy shelled the area around HQ intermittently throughout the day on 11 December, and during his rest period, CSM Barrow sat in his shelter penning this surreal description of billet life to a friend in Lancaster:

We are doing our last four days in the trenches and then we have six days out. We started with six days in the trenches, two out, four in, then six out. The place we went to for our two days rest was just behind the trenches. It was a mining village with long parallel streets [Philosophe]. The cottages had been very decent once, having fancy coloured tiles, and being lighted with electricity. But when we saw it there wasn't a house untouched by shell fire. Almost every house had its windows and roofs battered in, and several had collapsed altogether. But what surprised us most was that although the place had been shelled every day, the biggest part of the people lived there and would not move. Children and women were knocking about unconscious of the danger. The house where I was billeted had the front and windows boarded up. A shell had burst near the window once and blown it all in, as well as perforating the walls and doors with bits of shell. Still the people lived in it and slept in the cellar. They gave another sergeant and myself a bed to sleep on which had a spring mattress. We had been in the trenches for six days without a wash or shave, and the trenches were up to the knees in mud and water; so you can guess how we slept when we stripped and got into bed. The next night we looked around the place, and right across was an estaminet or pub. They sold Bass' beer and stout from England. There was a large shell hole in the roof; through this the rain poured, covering the floor. The place was full of muddy soldiers, all keeping clear of the hole in the roof. Some were singing music hall ditties, and others were reciting their close escapes the last time they were in the trenches. From the doorstep you could see the whole of the firing line lighted up with the star shells, hear the rifles popping and the shells bursting. Just at the other end of the street were several of our batteries and these were constantly banging. Every bang shook more from some of the ruins. A little further on is a little shop where 'Tommy' buys bread or pork chops or eggs. Then 'whiz,' and a shell bursts over one of the houses. The women look scared, wondering where the next one will come, and as things quieten down, they calmly go on with their work. 'Business as usual' is different in many of these villages to what people in England ever dream of. The boys should make good soldiers in the future, because they are broken in to shell fire.[10]

That same afternoon, Philosophe was shelled heavily and the Battalion billeted there suffered twelve wounded.[11] This little village was a target of no mean value, not only was it a billeting area and artillery battery position, but it was also the location for the brigade headquarters for whoever held 'B' Sector.

Enemy artillery and aircraft activity increased markedly on 12 December, though all the damage was to the firing line and support remained intact. This situation continued the next day, shrapnel wounding nineteen-year-old Pte Thomas Rowland in the wrist. Although he recovered, he was transferred to the Middlesex Regiment after leaving hospital in England. Lt-Gen. Holland, still concerned about the conditions in the trenches, visited each sector every couple of days. When he saw the deterioration in 'B' Sector on 11 December, he ordered 3 Brigade to put an additional battalion into the line to reinforce improvement work. He was happier with 'A' Sector when he toured there on the morning of 14 December, finding considerable progress—much of this accomplished by the Battalion. Despite Gun Alley and nearby CTs being heavily shelled during the afternoon, there were no casualties and the Battalion was relieved by 1 Brigade later that night, moving to billets in Mazingarbe.

Their primary task, especially after time in such poor trenches, was to clean equipment and men. Normally, the first day out of the line was also set aside for rest; however, one officer and fifty men were detailed for a large brigade-wide fatigue party digging Le Rutoire Alley, a CT from Vermelles, to the ruined farmstead Le Rutoire. This particular fatigue was obliged for the next three days, much to the irritation of Brigade, who considered it disrupted training. The Battalion also furnished two NCOs and six men to help garrison Nœux Keep East and Corons du Rutoire Keep. Mazingarbe was shelled by 4.2-inch Howitzers in the afternoon of 16 December, and although no men were injured, one scored a direct hit on one of the buildings used for stabling—killing two Transport horses and two of the officers' mounts. 'Peggy', the only animal to survive, was unsurprisingly markedly nervous after this whenever she heard the sound of shellfire. On 17 December, when not on working parties cleaning the streets of mud, men were involved in company training, though all would have sought cover when the village was again shelled for half an hour from 1.15 p.m. No soldiers were injured, but a shell that landed near the QM Stores killed a woman from the village and mortally wounded her young son.

On 20 December at 3.45 p.m. the Battalion left to relieve 1/9th King's in the B1 Sector—the last man from each company disappearing wraith-like into the misty late afternoon, before the next company followed on five minutes later. HQ set up in Ninth Avenue, central to the sector, next to a CT leading forward. Apart from the tendency to become knee-deep in mud, this sector was unpleasant as it was situated just to the south of where the lines took a right-angle turn to the west—making it easier for hostile artillery to drop shrapnel and HE directly into them. Overnight, the Battalion had more wiring parties out, and once again, L/Cpl William Livesey excelled. Although, on average, No Man's Land was about 200 yards wide, his detail were given a difficult stretch—just 60 yards in front of the enemy—which he successfully completed without loss. His work impressed Lt-Gen. Holland, who personally complimented him, and he was put forward for another MiD. However, when it was realised that he had been similarly recommended a month earlier, this was upgraded to the MM.[12] On 21 December, Hulluch Road was heavily shelled, though no casualties reported. Patrols in No Man's Land during the night heard the sounds of hammering on wood and iron coming from the enemy line, and although the Germans put out a number of their own patrols that night, these were dispersed by rifle fire.

On 22 December, enemy 6-inch Howitzers tried to enfilade the trenches, firing from the direction of Cité St Elie. Though this caused no British casualties, they managed to land two shells in their own front line—no doubt eliciting some fairly abrupt comments from their infantry. That night they were relieved by 1/Loyals and returned to Philosophe for just two days. No mention is made in the diary of any casualties on 23 December, and though it is recorded that the railway crossing in Vermelles was shelled, the QM reported no casualties ensued from it.[13] Sgt James Hopwood and Pte Stanley Warwick are both listed as wounded 23 December, but this was probably while on their way back from the trenches the previous night and only recorded in Warwick's service record the following day, which notes he was wounded in the back by shrapnel and treated in England for the injury.[14] After recovering, the nineteen-year-old was transferred to the Monmouths and killed with them in April 1918.

In the late afternoon of Christmas Eve, the Battalion returned to the B2 Support trenches. Two officers and 100 men were already there, detailed earlier for a working party to clean, repair, and clear up this area. HQ was situated in a dugout just off Le Rutoire Alley. The Battalion held the 800 yards of Support Line from Devon Lane on the left, to Hay Alley on the right. There was no unofficial Christmas truce, as in 1914, but arrangements for Christmas on the other side of No Man's Land obviously did not please everyone as a deserter from the 5/Bavarian Light Artillery came over at 5.45 a.m. Christmas Day itself was quiet with little activity from hostile artillery on the Battalion's trenches—though their near neighbours 1/Loyals were less lucky, having Pte Thomas Rimmer killed and five men wounded.

A Divisional Order had been sent out that as many men as possible were to be rested on Christmas Day and working parties kept to an absolute minimum. Brig.-Gen. Henry Thuillier, OC 2 Brigade, visited every trench held by the Brigade and personally wished each man a Merry Christmas. Independently, Lt-Gen. Holland walked the entire length of the division's front line and then back along the whole of the reserve line, inspecting the condition of the trenches and talking to the men. Holland was still hugely concerned about the effects these poor trenches were having on the health and welfare of his men. Only three days prior to this, he had chaired a conference at Divisional HQ for his brigadiers and the CRE to discuss ways to improve trenches with more effective drainage, revetments to reduce the constant maintenance, and trench boards to help keep men's feet dry.

Reductions to working parties, or lack of artillery fire, did not last, and on 27 December, the Battalion worked on a reserve support trench, Tenth Avenue—a parallel trench 100 yards to the west of Ninth Avenue—repairing shelters, laying trench boards, and scooping mud out. The new forward Support trench was also widened and revetted. As for hostile artillery, there was considerable activity directed against Hulluch Road and Le Rutoire Farm between 11 a.m. and noon, though without loss to the Battalion. Work on Tenth Avenue's shelters continued next day, men putting in no less than 766 man-hours. As dark fell, the Battalion moved up to take over the front line from 1/Northants.

The next day, two platoons of 7/Royal Irish Rifles were attached for their introduction to trench warfare. The increase in manpower was opportune—despite these newcomers being unused to trench warfare—as the trench-strength of the entire Battalion had fallen to just 200 officers and men. Lt Lloyd-Evans was put in command of the combined 'A' and 'B' Companies (sixty and thirty men respectively) and Capt. Harriss, of 'C' and 'D' Companies, with forty men in each. The remaining twenty men were with Battalion HQ. The battle to stay one step ahead of the weather continued and eighteen new sump pits were dug in the trenches and existing ones unclogged. Additionally, in the early hours of 30 December, small reconnaissance patrols sallied forth into No Man's Land. One led by Cpl Herbert Dobson, returned with valuable information about the enemy's wire, reporting the enemy hammering stakes in for new wire. The twenty-year-old NCO, who as a teenager had been the first Queen's Scout in Lancaster, was personally congratulated by Lt-Gen. Holland and given a 'Green Card of Merit' to send home. He was also awarded the MM for his night's work, though sadly did not live long enough to actually receive his medal.[15] Holland was a great believer in personally congratulating his ordinary soldiers when they had performed well, a leadership touch appreciated by the men.

Toil on the trenches continued, with over 200 trench boards laid on the 30th and more sump pits cleared. There had also been some damage to the parapets from enemy artillery and this too was mended. Shortly after 4 p.m., the enemy exploded two mines—later known as Hairpin Crater—under positions occupied by 142 (6th London) Brigade of 47 Division, just to the north of 1 Division's sector. The blast, resulting in considerable casualties, was accompanied by an outbreak of heavy small arms and artillery fire both to the north and against the Battalion's positions, HQ and the support line.[16] The Battalion went to immediate stand-to, men lining the firing steps to return fire. The only casualty was Cpl Edwin Lidford DCM, who was badly wounded in the left leg as he brought the rations forward—a great loss to the Battalion as he was transferred to the Labour Corps upon leaving hospital. Holland, concerned that the mine detonation might herald an enemy offensive, put 1 Brigade on immediate standby until around 7 p.m., when it became clear that no such attack was under way. On 31 December, the Battalion expended much energy on repairing the trenches damaged the previous day, though thankfully activity from hostile artillery was much reduced—a day summed up by Brigade: 'Nothing of interest to report: Thus ends another year of the War'.[17]

At 3 p.m. on 1 January, 1 Brigade relieved 2 Brigade and after 10/Glosters took their place in the line, the Battalion moved to billets in Mazingarbe. The next day was spent cleaning up and resting—though not everyone was lucky enough to have the complete day off—as one officer and fifty men were detailed to shovel mud off the roads of Philosophe that evening. On the 3rd, after kit inspection, most men were either training or on fatigues, though Philosophe was shelled at 1 p.m. When they returned to billets, parcels from home had arrived and men eagerly opened them. Many folks in the Battalion's 'home area' sent parcels to 'their battalion', these home luxuries making life just that bit more bearable. L/Cpl Robert Davies, another former teacher from Bowerham School, wrote thanking some Lancastrians for their parcel:

We have just returned from a tour of duty in the trenches and on arrival at our billets I found your parcel of mittens and scarves waiting for me. As the weather here is so changeable—rain, sleet and frost in quick succession—you can appreciate that your gift will be greatly prized, and in the name of the rest of the battalion I beg to thank you and Mrs Yates for your kindly and seasonable gift. Your gift of cigarettes, though they left Lancaster a considerable time ago, is not yet to hand. I daresay the parcel is held up by the Military Forwarding Officer at Southampton, who keeps parcels back until he has a full consignment for any one battalion. I daresay they will come to hand in a day or so and when they come I will drop you a line to that effect.

You would smile I think, in common with other Lancaster people, if you saw our battalion come out after a tour in the trenches during wet weather. You can hardly tell where mud ends and uniforms begin. The billets we occupy are empty houses in a much-shelled mining village, part of which is still inhabited. It is shelled about every other day, and on the arrival of the first shell, the people rush to the cellars, where they remain during the time of the shelling. The shelling over, they pop up again and go about their daily duties as if nothing at all had happened. It is strange what people can accustom themselves to, is it not? We are looking forward in a fortnight or so to a decent rest—a month by all accounts, and you can be certain that we will make the most of it.... I handed over the parcel to the Quartermaster for distribution, as he knows best who need the most. Give my kind regards to all mutual friends in Lancaster. Tell them I am longing for the time when I shall have the pleasure of seeing them again.[18]

Robert Davies probably got to meet his old friends sooner than he thought as shortly after this letter was written, he was sent home for treatment for a heart condition. He served the remainder of the war in England, receiving a medical discharge in December 1918. It must have been strange for some of the ex-teachers within the Battalion as they were represented in just about every non-commissioned rank and in commissioned ranks up to captain. The equality of their relationship in the staffroom could not have continued in the Army, some even finding themselves commanded by ex-pupils.

Men were hugely appreciative of these gifts from the Home Front, but at times, some civilians back in England were the object of withering contempt. Long hours, low pay, dreadful conditions, a lack of replacements leading to more work for those left, what were seen as unnecessary casualties due to shortages of artillery ammunition all helped form these views. There was little love lost for munitions workers (seen as overpaid shirkers), but their greatest scorn was reserved for strikers, many feeling that they should be forcibly enlisted or even shot as traitors. The attitude of one doctor in South Westmoreland so enraged them that a group of NCOs and men sent a joint letter to their local paper:

While one of the wounded heroes of Ypres, belonging to the 5th Battalion Royal Lancaster Regiment, who was still attending the depot hospital at Lancaster for massaging purposes (and was allowed at periodical periods to visit his village home in South Westmoreland) he was one day confronted by the village doctor with these remarks: 'I see you are still at home. Don't you get any better?' And on the reply being in the negative he said, 'I think it is about time you were given something to do, for I think it is a shame to see such chaps as you walking about doing nothing, because all the time you are hanging round here we are having to pay for you.' Is this the sort of man for whom the British Tommy is sacrificing all for, even his life, don't you agree with us it is time such like men were out here at the business end of a rifle, under compulsory service? Do you think the inhabitants of a village would appreciate the unpatriotic character of such a man in their midst?[19]

On 4 January, a message was forwarded to Lt-Col. Eaves, notifying him that the Battalion was shortly to leave 2 Brigade. Although a surprise, this was not unwelcome as they were to rejoin the newly reconstituted 55 (West Lancs) Division. Hurried arrangements were made for the Advance Party to leave on 5 January, the rest of the Battalion following on the 7th.

8 January 1916–18 July 1916: Back to the Fold

Coordinates for Positions Named in this Chapter

Blaireville raid	50°13′32.10″N 2°42′58.90″E	R.34.b.65.75	50°13′51.10″N 2°43′20.00″E
Blamont Quarry	50°13′54.30″N 2°42′22.90″E	R.34.b.79.85	50°13′52.10″N 2°43′21.80″E
Blockhouse, the	50°13′15.50″N 2°41′47.00″E	R34.b.15.70	50°13′50.70″N 2°43′11.90″E
Boyau Couteau	50°13′33.60″N 2°42′24.20″E	Ransart road	50°13′16.30″N 2°40′57.60″E
Bretencourt	50°14′13.90″N 2°42′11.80″E	Sap head. R.24.c.7.2	50°14′28.20″N 2°44′28.00″E
Grouse Street	50°15′22.70″N 2°45′55.40″E	sap near G15	50°15′6.00″N 2°45′50.00″E
Le Hamel	50°14′8.10″N 2°41′28.30″E	Trench 133	50°12′42.20″N 2°40′15.50″E

It was not unknown for Regular divisions to treat TF units as 'second-class', purely because they were not Regulars, but as 55 Division was a TF division, none of its units would face this stigma. Brigade and divisional diaries give an impression that at times the 1/5th had been very much the 'poor relation' when it came to resources, especially replacements and that they had been seen more as additional resource for the Regulars rather than an 'equal'. Apart from the usual support units, 55 Division comprised of three infantry brigades—164, 165, and 166. The Battalion was allocated to 166 Brigade, alongside 1/10th King's Liverpool (Liverpool Scottish), 1/5th South Lancashire, and 1/5th Loyal North Lancashire Regiments—all of whom had already gained considerable fighting experience. The division was led by Maj.-Gen. Hugh Sandham Jeudwine CB, an Artillery officer, and commanding 166 Brigade was Brig.-Gen. Green-Wilkinson of the Rifle Brigade.

On 7 January, they marched off via Nœux-les-Mines to Béthune and boarded a train for Pont Remy, 4 miles to the south-east of Abbeville. Although they arrived at 7 p.m., there was still a 13-mile march to their billets at Fresnoy-Andainville. It was dark when the Battalion de-trained, but two guides from the Advance Party were waiting at the station. As usual, the companies departed first. Transport, which still had to be unloaded from the train and moved more slowly, followed later. The Battalion's guide, twenty-two-year-old Pte James Bettany, had only made one daylight journey to Fresnoy—a recipe for disaster. For several hours, all appeared well and during the routine hourly stop men chatted happily. As time and miles took their toll, men marched silently, just the sound of their nailed boots breaking the quiet of the night. Now, during halts, some exhausted men slept. Just after 1 a.m., the Battalion halted and the order was given to 'about-turn'. Steps were retraced a mile or two to the previous village, and a different road selected. Once more, after a couple of miles, the Battalion turned about and returned to the village—Bettany had clearly got them well and truly lost. Luckily, the adjutant Lt Milnes found their position using his map and compass and figured out which route should have been taken. Providentially, Transport also caught up and got the field cookers going to give the men a brew before the long march resumed—the Battalion reaching Fresnoy at 6 a.m. on 8 January. Poor Bettany received considerable 'stick' for his mistake and for years afterwards—long after he'd left the Battalion—the cry of 'Send for Bettany' was heard whenever a wrong turn was taken on the march (Bettany redeemed himself in July 1917).

Training began on 11 January, though many afternoons were put aside for sport and other recreations. Frequently, these involved physical training with a 'fun' element—such as the inter-company cross-country paper chase or the game of 'skirmishers.' Inter-platoon, inter-company, and inter-battalion football and athletics competitions also vied for time. On 10 January, a draft of forty-six men arrived, mostly from the 3/5th, though some were wounded or sick returning from hospital. This brought the strength of the Battalion up to twenty-eight officers and 554 men—still well below the 1,066 of eleven months earlier. The movement of men was in both directions as some, such as Privates Robert Hornby, Albert Onyett, John Douglas, and Thomas McCormack, returned to England for discharge, their time-expired (John Douglas died in July 1919, but as he is commemorated by CWGC, his death must be related to military service). Some men returned home sick, such as Pte Charles Galloway, who had an appendectomy and later transferred to the Middlesex Regiment. Cold, wet, and exposure had also resulted in some developing conditions making trench life a daily misery. Cpl Reg Simpson was only twenty-five, but his five leg wounds from April led to the onset of rheumatism. Another similarly affected was forty-four-year-old Pte John Cameron. Both were invalided home and though Simpson remained in the King's Own, he was only fit for Home Service. Cameron transferred to the Labour Corps. Some men simply transferred—such as Fleetwood fisherman Pte Francis Heafield. At forty-eight, he was far too old to be an infantryman and went to the MFP.

Not all the new replacements were the bargain they seemed either. Pte Henry Langstreth—whose older brother, John, had deployed in February 1915—managed to upset 'authority' a mere two weeks after his arrival. On 27 January, he was awarded seven days' field punishment for 'creating a disturbance in billets' and also fined 1s 8d for 'damaging by neglect Regimental property, i.e. rifle'. Not long afterwards, he was fined again, this time 2s for 'losing by neglect [his] drawers'.[1] On 19 March, he was sent to the base at Rouen to be shipped home for discharge. Young Henry had been economical with the truth regarding his real age, and his parents claimed him back. Neither parents nor older brother had made authorities aware he was underage when he had arrived to the Battalion in France, and I suspect that the youth had discovered soldiering was not the great adventure he had imagined—the realities of military discipline and a few weeks in the trenches generating a letter home asking to be rescued. Due to his youth, he was discharged rather than home-posted. The Western Front was no place for a sixteen-year-old. Langstreth was not the only 'Henry' on field punishment. 'D' Company cook Pte Henry Funk was given twenty-eight days on 5 January for 'neglect of duty' and was still serving his punishment when he was joined by Langstreth.[2] He later became a cook for the Officers' Mess.

Jeudwine had very firm ideas about what he wanted from his Division, and a six-page memoranda concerning training, dated 7 January 1916, details his initial thoughts.[3] He considered:

> Too great stress cannot be laid on the necessity of developing the moral and soldierly spirit of all ranks. [He dictated that the object of training should be,] to develop the confidence of all ranks in themselves, their weapons, their comrades, and their commanders, and to imbue each officer and man with the determination to dominate the enemy, and cause him all the damage and loss possible, whether fighting him in the open or in the trenches.

As a new division, there was much to be done to make sure that it could operate smoothly as a 'self-reliant fighting force'. Jeudwine indicated that until he gained more experience of their specific needs, his training syllabus was generalised, but once he had more information as to what these were, he would concentrate upon those. His memoranda detailed common elements he desired the division to train towards, giving commanders free rein as to how they achieved the spirit of his instructions. Jeudwine considered that units just out of the trenches needed to put extensive effort into smartening their equipment, uniforms, and general demeanour and thus ordered that each day should include time in close-order drill, and a march-past of a senior officer at the close of this. To the civilian, drill may appear to be an outmoded and pointless waste of time, but this view fails to recognise why it was (and is) practised in the first place. Drill gives a body of men cohesion and pride in their appearance and boosts self-confidence. It aids the maintenance of physical fitness, but above all, drill teaches men to follow orders instantly and without hesitation, and it is this level of discipline that helps men win and survive in combat—war being an environment where hesitation is often fatal. Fitness was also important and each battalion had to carry out at least one route march of a minimum of 6 miles in the first two weeks, and after this, one of no less than eight miles every fortnight—when a battalion would be accompanied by their transport with all equipment properly packed.

Jeudwine instructed that every officer and man in the division learned to prepare and throw both the No. 1 and Mills grenade, and that 'not less than eight men, and preferably one section in each platoon, are to be thoroughly trained grenadiers'. This latter group studied more complex tactics and the use of rifle grenades. He established a Divisional Trench Mortar School to train infantry in light mortars and Brigade Machine-Gun Schools. The division had not yet received the Lewis, but when they did, a school for this would also be founded. Brigade Bombing Schools were set up to train officers and NCOs to act as bombing instructors in their own battalions. The CRE inaugurated an Engineering School to train officers and NCOs in field engineering. Each battalion established its own Sniping Section of at least eight snipers under an officer—this in addition to any 'Company Snipers'. Jeudwine exhorted that training of snipers and observers must make use of the latest equipment and techniques.

A common misconception is that the role of an infantryman is so simple that any idiot can do it. While there may be an element of truth to this, a good infantryman took months of focused training and practice. Recruits joining a battalion from basic training were little better than cannon fodder, and it took considerably longer to turn them into effective soldiers. An analysis of the Battalion shows that an astounding 61 per cent of all men who became casualties did so within their first three months at the front. After this, the odds dropped considerably. One of the reasons for the high casualty rate of newcomers was that men needed to learn when to keep their heads down, but also fundamental was the ability of a trained and practised infantry section to use its skills to minimise casualties.

Jeudwine's training syllabus emphasised the need for musketry and bayonet training. The former is an obvious skill—it is always a good idea to actually hit what one is shooting at—but the latter was a controversial issue (and still is). Partly, the criticisms of bayonet drill came from the emphasis placed upon it in basic training—especially in the early months. The ascendency of the bayonet in basic training was in part due to lack of instructors, equipment, and knowledge; the bayonet is a cheap and 'easy' thing to teach, and unlike musketry, something that could be taught using a wooden rifle. Detractors of the bayonet fail to understand just how effective this weapon is for fostering aggression, something all soldiers need—after all, a soldiers' job is to kill people; infantrymen do this close up and face to face—not something that comes naturally to most people in civilised societies.

Jeudwine initially focused on ten areas of infantry training. Rightly, he was keen that his division kept the initiative, and to do so required fighting patrols, bombing raids, reconnaissance patrols, and the effective use of rifle grenades and sniperscopes. Methods of attacking trenches and in particular the indispensable skills of consolidating gains, protection of flanks, and the building of blocks in captured trenches needed repeated practice and refinement. Infantry needed to practice working with friendly artillery and acquire the skills of advancing under hostile fire. The attack and defence of villages required specialised techniques, as did training in reconnaissance and of scouts. Infantrymen required the techniques of engineers when it came to the construction of wire entanglements, revetments, loopholes, the construction of trenches, and the repair of blown-in trenches. The use of machine guns for indirect fire and map reading skills for all ranks were instilled. Every one of these aptitudes needed to be ingrained so men could perform them without having to think—by day or night. In January 1916, the idea that an attack may lead to a breakthrough and end trench warfare was still thought possible, so the division also trained for open warfare, just in case.

All ranks were given a comprehensive series of lectures by specialists. Included were 'the cooperation of infantry and artillery'; 'marking out of work from a dimension sketch'; the 'extension of working parties'; 'commencement of digging work laid out and wiring'; 'collection of information and its transmission to higher authority'; 'duties and responsibilities of officers, NCOs and men in the trenches'; 'the study of men's comfort, daily inspections of feet and protection against inclement weather'; 'first aid and hygiene'; 'gas and use of smoke helmets'; and, finally, 'morale, discipline and brave deeds'. Jeudwine ardently believed that when a man performed particularly well, news of his deeds was passed around the division as an example to others; even if the act did not result in an official award, the man should have a certificate to send home to proud families.

Schools for junior officers were established at brigade and division, where officers were not just given intensive instruction in the skills they needed as platoon-commanders, but also how to operate at higher levels. This education was carried over to men too—an initiative that paid off when some battalions ended up with NCOs acting as company-commanders during battle. One of Jeudwine's great strengths was his readiness to listen to men of any rank. The 55th Division later brought in a formal policy, of all platoon, company, and battalion commanders producing detailed reports of any set-piece operations they had been involved in—along with their recommendations for how things could be improved upon. Should the platoon-commander become a casualty, the report would be written by the senior surviving NCO or man in the platoon, and if the platoon split to carry out separate tasks, the NCO or man in charge of this sub-section would also complete a report. It is possible to follow the track of these documents through the military hierarchy as company and battalion commanders initialled them as they passed through their hands and many of these original documents have Jeudwine's hand-written notes and comments in the margins. Significant points would be distributed to all units, with recommendations for action. It is interesting to note that problems highlighted in one attack rarely reoccur—indicating that lessons were learned. In addition to the written reports, the general frequently visited men involved in any significant raid or action, and talked informally to them about it—one of his aides making notes in the background. The mythology of the Great War would not countenance a general talking informally to ordinary soldiers about how to improve his attack plans—yet the records of 55 Division demonstrate that this is just what did happen. It would be surprising if this was unique to 55 Division, but as records are so fragmentary, scant evidence remains.

As training intensified, exercises expanded, with brigade schemes with all arms, not just infantry and thence increasing in scale until the entire division trained as a whole. These not only gave individual units experience of operating as part of a larger formation, but also gave brigade and divisional staff much needed practice. From 4 February, the division marched in stages towards their new sector. At noon on 9 February, they came under the orders of VII Corps and were told that, at 10.30 a.m. on 16 February, they would assume command of the Rivière sector, about 5 miles to the south-west of Arras—then held by the 88th French Territorial Division. The transition began earlier, with elements of 166 Brigade occupying the line on 12 February. This area of front was divided into three sectors and although sometimes referred to by the names of the area immediately behind them, it was also assigned letters, with 'F' Sector being the left, 'E' Sector the centre, and 'D' Sector the right. Sometimes these individual sectors were further subdivided into left and right sub-sectors. There must have been mixed feelings about the return to action, but Sgt George Dixon probably felt it was a time for some pay-back, as he had just received a letter from home informing him that his older brother, Farrell, had been killed with the West Riding Regiment.

Liverpool Scottish and the Loyals carried out a daylight relief in the front line at 3.15 p.m., and although the relief itself went smoothly, twelve German shells landed in Bellacourt as the troops passed through, killing two from Liverpool Scottish and four from the Loyals. One officer and sixteen men were wounded. Although the French took most of their trench stores with them, they agreed to leave their flare pistols behind to delay enemy discovery that the British had replaced them. At 3.45 a.m. on 13 February, the Battalion paraded and moved to take over support from the French 176th Brigade in the left sub-sector, with two companies at the Quarry at Blamont and two at Grosville—on what today is the Rue de Grosville in Le Hamel. Transport was 9 miles away at Saulty, meaning considerable time was taken up bringing supplies forward, though much of this movement—apart from on a few roads visible from enemy lines—could take place during daylight. There was little interference from German artillery over the next three days and men were fully occupied on fatigue parties, burying signal wire, draining trenches, and repairing damage to CTs caused by heavy rain.

After dark on 17 February, the Battalion relieved Liverpool Scottish in the centre sector (from Boyau Couteau to 50°14'5.30"N 2°43'43.70"E). After the mud and high water table of Loos, these trenches seemed a huge improvement and far better than the French trenches inherited at Polygon Wood. The chalk soil was better drained and the construction of trenches and dugouts far superior, and though the trenches all had French names, these gradually morphed into more familiar English ones. Although initial impressions were favourable, harsh weather would highlight some of the shortcomings of their design. French trenches had vertical sides, no revetment and little in the way of drainage. Heavy rain was followed on 22 February by freezing

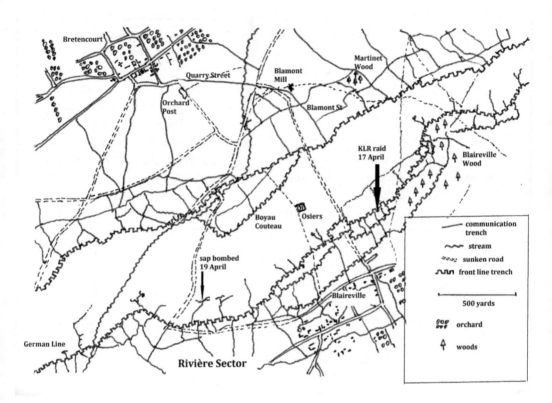

weather and heavy snow the day after. When this thawed, followed by more heavy rain, the chalky sides began to crumble away.

During the night of 20–21 February, a reconnaissance patrol got undetected to within fifty yards of an enemy sap and returned safely. Despite considerable activity by enemy snipers during the day, there were no casualties, and after dark on 23 February, the Battalion was relieved by Liverpool Scottish and returned to support—two companies in the Quarry, the other two in Bretencourt.[4] When the Battalion next deployed to the front, they had a very useful addition to their firepower. All the Vickers were pooled into Brigade Machine Gun Companies and battalions given the Lewis. Initially, the Battalion only received two, but by the end of the war, each platoon would have two. Using a forty-seven-round drum magazine, this weapon was portable and this—along with improvements to rifle grenade technology—enabled a complete rewriting of infantry tactics in 1917. Artillery activity remained at a low level, possibly as both sides were fully occupied just battling the weather. When an extremely heavy snowfall filled the trenches on 23 February, much shovelling was occasioned. The only casualty during this period was Pte Peter Renshall, hit by a spent shrapnel ball—the projectile just breaking the skin. The twenty-two-year-old Lancastrian would not be so lucky the next time.

The front remained quiet, and on the night of 26 February, the Battalion was relieved by 2/5th Lancashire Fusiliers and moved to Divisional Reserve at Bavincourt. For one man that was just the first stage in his journey. Sgt Thomas Coates' term of service had expired and he was on his way home. A good sergeant and talented amateur conjuror—whose skills had enlivened many a difficult time—he would be missed. Two days later, Pte Joseph Brodie began a similar journey, leaving his father, Charles, their last family member, in the Battalion. At fifty-two, Charles was clearly too old for front-line service, and in March, he was posted to the Divisional Sanitary Section. In April, he too returned home, graded physically unfit for service in a theatre of war. The Regiment continued to employ him on Home Duties, though tragically his wife died soon after his homecoming. During March, the Battalion continued to leach manpower whose period of engagement had expired. Pte Thomas Nisbett from Fleetwood and Pte John Nixon were both discharged in the second week of March. Shortly afterwards, Privates William Wilson and Peter Thompson, from Lancaster, and Albert Jenkinson, from Garstang, also left—Thompson's Battalion number of '11' illustrating just long he had served. Most of these found work in the munitions industry and were not recalled once conscription was introduced later that year—however, not all were so fortunate. Twenty-one-year-old Pte Hugh Haffey from Fleetwood was called up again and served with 2/5th King's Own in France. Just nineteen days before the war ended, he received multiple shrapnel wounds to hand, arm, and both thighs and was lucky to survive. L/Cpl Harry Hall left for home, a glowing character reference in his file, but was called up again on 11 August and went to France with 8/King's Own in April 1917. He was killed three weeks later. The Battalion also lost men from sickness—rates of which were always higher in difficult conditions. Twenty-one-year-old Pte Henry Battersby from Blackpool went home with a heart defect and was medically discharged in August. Despite the conditions, there are no surviving records for anyone suffering from trench foot at this time—no doubt in part due to the daily inspections and applications of whale oil—but also because all were now issued with Gum boots from the trench stores when they were in the line.

Time in reserve passed in the usual fashion, with a day of cleaning-up and resting, followed by training and fatigues. In the evening of 6 March, the Battalion relieved Liverpool Scottish in the Osiers Sector (left sub-sector of the right sector). Holding an area of line from 50°13′25.70″N 2°41′35.80″E to Boyau Couteau, aligned from left to right 'C', 'A', 'B', and 'D' Companies. To their left were the Liverpool Irish and to their right, one company of 1/5th South Lancs. Although there was still deep snow around, the thaw had begun and trenches were in poor condition, requiring every spare man to maintain them. On 9 March, the Battalion constructed a grenade store and also built a listening post in No Man's Land. They also sent two patrols out during the night, but the frosty ground meant that they were unable to approach right up to the enemy's wire. Patrols reported that the enemy were also busy working on their trenches. Later that night, snow began to fall again and continued through the next day. Enemy artillery fire resumed on 10 March, and although the Battalion suffered no casualties, 1/9th King's on the extreme left of the sector lost one man killed and another wounded by it. On 12 March, companies rotated so that each would get to know more of the line and maintenance continued on trenches and wire. On 13 March, enemy artillery was even more active and a tit-for-tat artillery duel ensued, with both sides targeting the opposition's rear.

Despite being in the front line, casualties were remarkably low, but this situation could not last. In the evening of 14 March, Capt. Lloyd-Evans visited HQ in Bretencourt. Around 10.45 p.m., he met the QM and Transport Officer, up delivering rations and chatted to them for a few minutes at the dressing station. He walked the couple of hundred yards with them to where they had left their horses in order to say farewell, and that was the last time he was seen alive. When he did not return to his company, a search party went out and his body discovered next morning. He had been shot through the left loin and was found roughly half way between the dressing station and where he had said goodbye to his two friends. The discovery was reported in the local papers:

> Colonel Eaves immediately went to examine him and found that he had been shot with a rifle bullet. The opinion of the Medical Officer was that he had died from shock. 'From the position of the blood where I found his steel helmet and handkerchief and on examination of the ground where he was picked up,' adds Colonel Eaves, 'I came to the conclusion that he fell immediately he was shot, and then got up and tried to reach the dressing station. The road he was on is periodically swept by indirect machine gun fire and no-one was likely to pass that way.'[5]

A sad and lonely death for the popular twenty-two-year-old and only son.

On 18 March, companies rotated and during the night of 19–20 March, a German working party was seen building a new trench near the Blockhouse. For the first time, the Lewis guns went into action, dispersing them. On 24 March, the companies rotated again—remaining in these positions until relieved by Liverpool Scottish on 30 March. 'C' and 'D' Companies immediately marched off to divisional reserve at Saulty, but 'A' and 'B' remained behind at Bellacourt. The next night, 'B' Company joined the rest of the Battalion, but 'A' Company was unlucky enough to remain where it was.

Divisional intelligence summaries for March substantiate Jeudwine's decision to set up specialist sniping sections. Sixty-four enemies were reported killed by the snipers; during the same period, the division lost sixteen dead from all causes. The enemy, who had plenty of their own snipers, displayed an astonishing naïveté at times. The intelligence summary for 8 March described one such incident:

> A German shot yesterday dropped a telescope in front of the parapet of sap head R.24.c.7.2. At 9.25 a.m. a man attempted to pick it up, he was fired at and withdrew. At 9.55 a.m. he made another attempt and was shot by our snipers; as he fell back into the trench the telescope again fell outside the parapet. At 10.05 a bald-headed man made a very cautious attempt to retrieve the article but was shot, the telescope remained outside.[6]

On 17 March, the intelligence summary reported:

Our snipers accounted for three Germans. They have considerably more difficulty finding live targets now and have to content themselves with periscopes, twelve of which were broken in the *Right Sector* in the last twenty-four hours.

This latter report was hardly surprising. To put German casualties from the division's snipers into perspective (with no more than twenty-four snipers in the line at any one time), enemy losses were the numerical equivalent of an entire British infantry battalion every fifteen months.

The Battalion (minus 'A' Company) remained at Saulty until 7 April. On 2 April, the bombers were involved in special training, though not everything went to plan when one grenade detonated prematurely, wounding Pte Thomas McNulty in the head—his second wound of the war. Time not spent on training was involved in fatigues. At this time, only two of their allocation of three RE Field Companies had been assigned to 55 division. In a letter to HQ VII Corps on 24 February, Jeudwine repeated a previous request for 1/1st West Lancs Field Company to be reassigned to him:

> ... This question was raised when the Division formed part of XIV Corps, and Lord Cavan, the then Corps Commander, gave me to understand that action was being taken and that it was only a matter of a week or two before this Field Company would be restored. Matters however do not seem to have advanced and it is possible that the situation is not fully understood.
>
> The only two Field Companies now with this Division have only just come out from home where their training was incomplete, and have no experience of active operations and no training, even at home, in trench warfare. The want of at least one Field Company with experience is most keenly felt.[7]

The problem was magnified because this had been a French sector and there was considerable work to do not just in the front line, but also in the rear, where the Divisional Medical Officer declared most of the accommodation unfit for human habitation; roads and water supplies were also considered inadequate. The Divisional Pioneer Battalion, 1/4th South Lancs had never been trained or equipped as a pioneer battalion, and GHQ even suggested that they return to work as an infantry battalion elsewhere and another pioneer battalion be posted in.

The result of this lack of specialised engineers was that infantry battalions were stretched to their limit supplying manpower on working parties. One man in the Battalion took matters into his own hands and consequently faced a FGCM on 2 April. Twenty-six-year-old Pte Lewis Brookfield had already been in trouble once, when he had forged his platoon-commander's signature on an envelope to avoid censorship on 17 January—resulting in twenty-one days field punishment. On 27 March, he incited his working party to refuse to obey orders and was charged by Sgt George Haywood. The FGCM awarded him another forty-two days field punishment. One good soldier, who did not join the Battalion when they returned to the line, was thirty-four-year-old Pte John

Dawson. On 30 March, he was hospitalised with influenza and sent home to recover. His MM—awarded for his courage at Ypres—was not *Gazetted* until December 1916, but by then he was with 12/King's Own, awaiting a posting back to France to the 1/4th.

After dark on 7 April, the Battalion relieved Liverpool Scottish in the Osiers Sector. The general situation remained quiet, with occasional flurries of activity—such as on 8 April, when the enemy fired eighteen whizz-bangs at the support trenches. Nightly patrols in No Man's Land found little or no evidence of the enemy working on his defences. On 10 April, the Battalion began to dig the straight stretches of the CTs leading forward from the bombers' posts. To distract enemy attention, a canvas screen was erected in another part of the line—drawing considerable fire. Companies rotated on 12 April, and the following day, a draft of twenty-three arrived from England, all trained Lewis gunners and a welcome addition as the Battalion now possessed eight guns. Among these was Pte William Ritchie, an apprentice designer from Lancaster and a talented young artist. Ritchie's records show that his stated age on enlistment was nineteen and a half. He had, however, been guilty of considerable exaggeration here as he had only just turned seventeen when he arrived at the Front. Once again, it was men arriving balanced by men leaving. Twenty-three-year-old Pte Harry Rainford went home to Garstang, time-expired. He was conscripted into the RFA four months later. Also sent home was thirty-three-year-old Pte James Light, whose hearing had been damaged, a condition that led to his medical discharge that August.

The first casualty of this tour was on 15 April, when L/Cpl Edward Waters moved up onto the firing step to avoid the men working on digging a sump in the trench floor. A German sniper grabbed the opportunity and put a round through the NCO's right shoulder, just missing his lung. Waters was treated in England, and after his recovery, he was transferred to the Monmouths and, later, the Pay Corps. Snipers continued to make life uncomfortable the following day, but scored no more hits—on the other hand, British snipers were not idle either:

> At 2 p.m. a sentry looked over the parapet at R34.b.15.70. wearing a blue cap with a white band. Shot by sniper (this man had been watched and waited for, for three days). At 3.30 p.m. man looked over the parapet at R.34.b.65.75. Round cap with white band. Shot by sniper. At 6.30 p.m. a gross elderly man got out of the trench at R.34.b.79.85. and ran cautiously back into the wood. Fire was opened on him and he jumped into the trench. The snipers of F Sector claim three hits.[8]

On 17 April, the companies rotated, and though German sniper activity had moderated somewhat, British snipers claimed another three hits.

Liverpool Irish, to the Battalion's immediate left, sent a raiding party of forty handpicked men against the enemy in the trenches opposite Blaireville during the night of 17–18 April, and as the lessons learned were to establish a divisional blueprint for future raids, it is worth examining in some detail. Those selected were pulled out of the line, billeted together, and carried out intensive training, with numerous rehearsals. The raiders were split into five groups—two Storming Parties, a Covering Party, a Parapet

Party, and a Wire Cutting Party. The Wire Cutting Party of two officers and two NCOs went out the night before to cut a partial gap through the wire. The night of the operation, a reconnaissance patrol went out at 9 p.m. to check that the enemy had not repaired their wire. It was bright moonlight and they could clearly see a German working party just 100 yards to their right, but remained unseen, returning at 11.30 p.m.

Once it clouded over around midnight, the main party advanced. One of the Covering Party marked the route from the gap back to friendly lines with white tape, and one of the two signallers with the Covering Party established communications by telephone. An earlier route-marking trial had found that paper blew away and chloride of lime made the men sneeze—hardly desirable. The Wire Cutting Party then advanced and completed the cut—one of the NCOs returning to fetch the main party and guide them through the gap. As the first man in the main party reached the gap in the wire, one of the signallers passed the code word 'slow' down the phone. This was the signal for artillery and MGs to begin a bombardment of the trenches to the north and south of their target. Once the Storming Parties passed through the gap, it was widened further to enable easier extraction.

The right and left Storming Parties each had nine men and an officer (most armed for close combat). Two men carried shields and a bayonet; another was armed with just a revolver; two bombers each carried six bombs (when these were expended, two bomb-carriers close behind them, with six Mills bombs, a smoke bomb, and an incendiary bomb apiece, would resupply them); another two men were armed with only a bayonet; and finally, two spare soldiers brought up the rear (one with revolver and wire cutters, the other with rifle and bayonet).

The Covering Party comprised one 'Tape Man', a telephone orderly, two signallers, and eleven riflemen. The Parapet Party encompassed eight men—two armed with revolvers and carrying ladders and six armed with rifles and spare bombs. The Storming Parties were the first to enter the trench, the officer of the left party shooting the sentry with his revolver. The second man from the right party immediately disabled any signal wires he found, while the two parties spread left and right along the trench, bombing dugouts. Upon the signal to end the raid—a long blast on a whistle, twice repeated—the parties returned to where the Parapet Party had placed the ladders for them (this party covering their extraction and the last to leave).

There was little enemy opposition, and although rifle fire and bombs were directed against them from dugouts, this was neutralised by bombs. Rifle grenades were also launched at them from the enemy support trenches, but without success. One man was struck in the chest by a piece of bomb, but saved by his shield, which was dented. As they left the enemy wire, the code word 'fast' instructed artillery to shorten their range to cover their escape. The euphoria from what seemed to have been a perfect raid was marred somewhat when it was realised that the officer in charge of the left Storming Party was missing. A search party returned, but found no trace. He had been seen on the parapet with the rest of his party, and it was presumed that he must have either returned to the trench for some reason or been hit and fallen back in. Thirty-year-old

Lt Edward Baxter was buried by the Germans behind their lines at the church in Boiry. He received the VC for his courage during the raid and his work on the two previous nights—his remarkable coolness when a primed and 'pin-less' bomb he was holding to cover the wire cutters slipped, and he quickly unscrewed the base plug, removed the detonator, and buried it in in the mud to muffle the crack.

Lessons learned went to every battalion in the division to aid their future planning. The wire cutters, of the large parrot-nosed type, handles padded with leather to prevent a 'click' when used, were found to be very effective, though the canvas gloves supplied with them had been ditched as they were too clumsy. The brown-painted wooden ladders, though light and strong, proved too short—the German trenches were 12 feet deep—but had they been needed, they would have made excellent emergency stretchers. Chewing gum was issued to everyone before the raid and was found invaluable for preventing coughing—especially among those with severe nicotine habits. Revolvers had also been found to be very handy—rifles less so as the trenches were very narrow. Every man had also carried a trench club, though no one actually had call to use it. Torches were deemed unnecessary as the moonlight reflected off the white chalk sides of the trenches. The raiders were of the opinion that a whistle was a poor signal as the enemy too used whistle signals—which had caused some confusion. Every man wore a balaclava, which aided both warmth and recognition, but the rubber thigh boots issued to the Covering Party were not satisfactory as they squeaked when men crawled over wet grass. The raiders killed at least seven of the enemy and gathered considerable intelligence about German defences. How effective they had really been would only be learned on 26 April.

On 18 April, Robert Higginson returned to the Battalion, though now a subaltern. It had been almost a year since he had been stretchered off and there were so few familiar faces, it must have seemed like a different battalion. With him were eighty-five men from the 3/5th—replacements that were gratefully received. In the early hours of 19 April, an offensive patrol under 2Lt Frank Huntington slipped into No Man's Land and stealthily moved 450 metres from their line up the slope to the sap at 50°13′15.00″N 2°42′4.90″E. When they reached their objective, they discovered that the wire to the front of the sap stretched right down to the road and was about 'four bays in depth' and a low entanglement.[9] To their left of the sap, the wire became plain wire and was only 'two bays in depth' and joined up with another sap 30 metres to the left. Still unobserved, the patrol approached right up to the edge of the wire on the left and threw eight bombs into the sap, before retiring to their own lines without sustaining a single casualty. Two nights later, a reconnaissance patrol near this sap heard a tinkling noise coming from the wire around it, indicating the enemy had placed alarms on the wire— usually just a stone in an old tin can strung from a strand of wire. During the night of a very wet 22 April, another bombing patrol slipped out into No Man's Land and fired eight rifle grenades into the same sap. At one part or another of the divisional front, similar raids became a nightly occurrence.

Companies rotated again on 23 April, and in the early hours of the following morning, a fighting patrol of twenty-six men and two officers under Capt. Owtram lay out in No

Man's Land for three hours, hoping to ambush an enemy patrol. Their luck was out as the Germans kept to their trenches. During the night of 24–25 April, the same patrol, though this time under 2Lt Anthony Hargreaves, lay out for three hours and thirty minutes—again without success, although they brought back information about more new enemy wire. That same day, a new piece of equipment was introduced that saved many lives. The issue of the Brodie helmet was now complete, and although initially unpopular because of the discomfort when wearing it—often leading to headaches—men soon got used to it and appreciated the protection it gave the head and neck. At 4.45 a.m. on 26 April, a German deserter from the 78th Landwehr crossed No Man's Land and surrendered to 'A' Company of the 1/6th KLR. From him it was learned that their raid earlier that month had killed fifty-seven of the defenders.

On 26–27 April, 2Lt Robert Holmes took a small reconnaissance patrol of ten men right up to the German wire, but retired under very heavy rifle fire. There was very little enemy patrol activity during April; in fact, two patrols were seen leaving their wire, then immediately returning. They were, however, deploying considerable manpower strengthening their lines of defence, particularly wire and dugouts, and also building new emplacements for observation and MGs—no doubt prompted by the constant raiding. One change that affected every battalion was an extension of the division's line to their right. At 6 a.m. of 30 April, 55 Division took over an extra 1,700 yards of front, up to and including Trench 133. The division still deployed seven battalions in the line at any one time, but rather than fielding two companies up and two further back, they now needed three companies in the firing line. April had been an astonishingly good month for the Battalion, with only one man wounded; although for one man, the month ended on a sour note. Twenty-six-year-old Pte Walter Lupton was in trouble once again. This patriotic Lancastrian served four years with the Battalion from 1908 to 1912, and despite being a widower with a four-year-old daughter, re-enlisted in November 1915. In late March, he was given five days' field punishment for neglecting to obey an order while on a fatigue party, but this time he was in more serious trouble. When Capt. Owtram did his rounds, he had discovered Lupton reading on sentry duty, and on 30 April, he was sentenced to twenty-eight days' field punishment. The charge sheet does not detail what he was reading, but it is easy to visualise him—newly arrived letter in hand—catching up on the news about his daughter, whom he must have been missing terribly.

On 1 May, the Battalion was relieved by Liverpool Scottish and went into brigade reserve at Bellacourt. Eighty men were required for divisional fatigues on 2 May, and one, twenty-year-old Pte Herbert Metcalfe, was wounded by shellfire—though he was back before too long (this was his father's birthday and definitely not the sort of present his father would have wished for). The next day, Liverpool Scottish took over and they moved back to divisional reserve at Gouy-en-Artois. The Battalion lost another twenty-year-old that day—this time to measles. Pte John Twigg from Blackpool was hospitalised, sent home for treatment, and posted to the 1/4th when he returned to France. In Britain today, most do not consider measles a potentially fatal disease, but this was far from true in the early twentieth century. When an epidemic hit 51 (Highland) Division in Bedford during the winter of 1914, it killed sixty-three men—10.8 per cent of all those infected.

On 9 May, twenty-one-year-old signaller Pte Richard Iveson was admitted to hospital, suffering from epilepsy. His brother, James, in the Royal Fusiliers at a nearby camp, only heard about Richard's hospitalisation in a letter from home, and initially believing his brother had been wounded, got permission to visit him at No. 28 general Hospital in Étaples.[10] Upon arrival, James found that Richard had just been transferred to Ipswich for treatment. Iveson was medically discharged in July. The Battalion remained in Gouy until 11 May and a number of men returned to England, time-expired. Sgt John Ridding, who as a private had helped bury Alf Lockley, was one. He was conscripted a few months later and killed in action as a private with 20/King's in August 1917. Fellow Sergeant John Richardson also left, but at forty-four, he was too old to be called up again, as was Cpl James Porter. Twenty-seven-year-old CSM Charles Berkins was not conscripted later—so must have found work in the munitions industry. The civilian skills of twenty-seven-year-old schoolmaster Pte James Sumner were found to be better employed elsewhere and he was attached to the 3rd Army Surveying Company, eventually transferring to the RE. It was not all on the debit side—one officer and fifty-two men arrived from England on 3 May.

In the evening of 11 May, the Battalion returned to the line. Earlier changes meant that the bounds of each sector had been adjusted slightly. Once again, they were in the left sub-sector of the right sector, but their right bound was now the Grosville–Ransart road. Three companies were placed in the firing line, a half company in reserve, and the other half company, boosted by an attached company from 1/5th Loyals—in support, in and near Bellacourt. The division had transferred to VI Corps, although this was purely an administrative change. The Battalion remained in the line until the night of 20 May, their time spent constructing bombproof shelters for sentries and Lewis guns, deepening CTs, and constructing dugouts. The only casualty was twenty-four-year-old Pte John Clark, wounded in the thigh by shrapnel on 18 May. He was evacuated home, posted to 1/King's Own upon his recovery, and killed with them in April 1917.

After relief by Liverpool Scottish during the night of 19 May, they moved into brigade reserve at Bellacourt. As always, most of the men were employed on fatigues and despite German artillery, the only casualties, as one man described in a letter home, were to their precious brews:

We had a lively time with the Germans yesterday; they started sending small shells,— what we call 'iron rations' over at tea time. Talk about dodging, we had to do plenty of that, but to make things worse, I lost the lid off my canteen and I had tea in it. Every time one of the shells came over we had to duck, and I had to put my drop of tea under me to try to keep the soil out. It was no good so I let the dirt settle and after it was over drank my tea. Some of the chaps got none at all. Today they started just the same, but we had got tea over so we did it on them. Thank God we all pulled through.[11]

On 27 May, the Battalion returned to the trenches they had recently vacated, Liverpool Scottish backing them up in reserve. To their left was 1/4th King's Own and to their right was 1/5th South Lancs. Although their trenches came in for attention by enemy artillery, the only casualty was stretcher-bearer Pte William Dawson, accidentally wounded by one of his pals. Gas alarms sounded throughout the division's area on 30 April. This turned out to be a false alarm, but must have gained the attention of Lt Mansfield, back after convalescence, and the seven fresh subalterns newly arrived from England—all on their way to Battalion HQ when the alarms sounded. Recently commissioned Thomas Blakeley and Richard Irving were among these and no doubt looked forward to meeting old friends. Second Lieutenants John Mackey, John Gardner, William Daniels, Frank Beckett, and R. Hall were all newcomers to the Battalion.

The beginning of June saw little change in the level of enemy aggression and things remained fairly quiet—there were still casualties though. On 3 June, one of the new draft from April, Pte John Robinson from Ulverston was accidentally stabbed in the side by another man's bayonet—something that happened all too easily in the confines of a trench. He was not badly injured and spent eleven days at the 1/3 West Lancs Field Ambulance. However, his guilty secret was about to be exposed. On enlistment in November 1914, he had stated his age was eighteen, something that his father who had enlisted with him had not challenged. He was in fact only just fourteen. His injury must have frightened his parents—his father had been medically discharged before deployment—and they informed the Army of his true age. Now, aged just sixteen, he was sent home and discharged. At 6.50 p.m. on 4 June, the Battalion was relieved by Liverpool Scottish and moved back to brigade reserve; three hours later, they were moved further back into divisional reserve at Gouy. The same day, official announcement was made of a number of awards gained at Ypres and Loos, and apart from the men mentioned earlier in the text, Lt-Col. Eaves was granted the DSO, the QM promoted to captain, and L/Cpl John Wright awarded the MM. One man who would be collecting his MM at home was Thomas Nisbett, who had been discharged in March. The Battalion also got a new 2IC on 2 June, when Maj. Rupert Anderson-Morshead was posted in from 1/Devonshires.

The Battalion remained in reserve until 12 June. Thanks to some sick and wounded returning and fresh drafts from England, numbers rose to 805 men and thirty-seven officers. This was not their 'fighting strength' as officers and men were required for other duties, such as Transport and Stores, or were on detachment to divisional and brigade posts—their actual trench strength being 700 men and thirty officers.

An incident back in England with a direct bearing on one of the Battalion was the strange case of nineteen-year-old Pte Henry Broe of 41st Provisional Battalion, a King's Own training unit at St Nicholas-at-Wade in Kent. On Sunday 11 June, he was shot dead by his best friend, Pte Thornborough. This was not, however, a tragic case of an accidental shooting. The pair had been drinking in one of the village pubs and when a shot was heard around 4 p.m., Sgt Septimus Gathercole ran to the upstairs room in the Sun Inn, where the two were billeted, to find Henry Broe dead on the floor—a bullet through his heart. Another witness, recruit Pte Norman Turner, told the inquest that he heard Thornborough, who sounded a little incoherent, say to Gathercole:

> I did it, Sir. He said "Shoot me, and I did it.' [A little later, Thornborough told the Sergeant,] 'I done it, Sir, but not on purpose. I wasn't myself. We both got drunk. We had four pints each at the Charles Dickens.' [Turner then handed the Sergeant a letter that was on Broe's bed,] 'Dear Father and Mother—just a few lines to let you know I am going to do it. It is the officers and billet folk that has done it, giving us punishment for nothing. So good-bye, everyone. From your loving son, Harry.[12]

Another witness, Pte Harold Ellershaw, stated he saw Broe writing this letter earlier. The coroner questioned a number of Broe's platoon and his company officers as to whether or not Broe had been disciplined for anything. All denied that he had not been in trouble, though Capt. Harriss did say that he placed the bar room of the Sun Inn out of bounds after complaints from the landlord about the behaviour of Broe and Thornborough—that he was going to call them into the Orderly Room on the Monday and give them a reprimand, but that was all. The jury was reluctant to agree that Thornborough had shot Broe deliberately as this would have meant that he was guilty of wilful murder and be hanged. The coroner, understanding of their plight, suggested that they could state that they did not think that there was sufficient evidence to say if Thornborough had fired the rifle deliberately, which after an hour's deliberation they did, allowing the coroner to bring about an 'open verdict'.[13]

The details of this sad case—played out in full in the local papers—must have been terrible for the family, and many from the Battalion knew those involved. For battalion-sniper twenty-five-year-old Pte Robert Dodgson, this was far more personal as he was married to Broe's sister, Annie, and the two men had enlisted together in October 1915. It is not hard to imagine that the news of his brother-in-law's death—arriving some days after it had happened—may have contributed to Robert Dodgson's fatal lapse of concentration on 16 June.

After dark on 12 June, the Battalion returned to their previous trenches, relieving Liverpool Scottish. There was still little aggression from the enemy and they settled into the routine of trench life. At 11 p.m. on 14 June, all watches were advanced one hour for British Summer Time, and on the 16th, stretcher-bearers were issued with full kit and rifles. Previously, they had been unarmed, but as they still got shot at, it was decided to arm them anyway. The first casualty for some time occurred on 16 June, and it was Robert Dodgson. When snipers moved into their positions, or used loopholes, they needed to employ considerable patience and cunning to avoid being spotted. The father of one was shot through the head by a German sniper and very seriously wounded. As might be expected, such a wound was mortal and he died on 21 June. Maj. Deed wrote the Battalion's letter of condolence as on 18 June, Lt-Col. Eaves was posted home to the War Office and Lt-Col. Charles Anderson of the North Staffs took command.

The 55th Division's locale was about to get considerably more active as orders were received from VI Corps on 13 June, directing that a series of 'demonstrations' were to be carried out against the enemy over a period of six days. These were to take the form of bombardments, wire cutting, and gas attacks, followed up by large-scale raids. The six days were termed U–Z and all planning was to be complete by 19 June, with U-Day the following day. This strategy aimed to divert German resources away from the planned main British attack on the Somme, a mere 8 miles to their south.

On 16 June, fatigue parties began to carry up 1,898 gas cylinders to the front line—a task that was not completed until 18 June. Jeudwine and his planners knew there was no realistic chance of any attack by a single division capturing and holding part of the enemy line. However, in 'F' Sector—on the extreme left of the division's front, where it joined 14 Division's sector—there was a length of 2,100 yards of enemy line that was vulnerable. Here, the enemy's main defences were on the reverse slope, but fourteen saps ran down the forward slope from 50°14′56.40″N 2°45′17.40″E on the left, to 50°14′17.80″N 2°44′10.90″E on the right. If these positions could be taken and held, the enemy would lose their direct close-range observation of 'F' Sector and allow the British to observe the Germans from a superior tactical position, facilitating future attacks. Jeudwine was unable to get additional men for his plan, so reduced his proposed attack to just over 1,000 yards. In the end, no large attack was sanctioned; instead, seven raids spread across the width of the division's front went ahead.

After dark on 20 June, the Battalion were relieved and moved into brigade reserve at Bellacourt—though one company remained behind in left-support for 1/5 Loyals in the right sub-sector south of Bellacourt. As might be expected with so much planned, everyone was on working parties. Artillery from both sides was considerably more active, and on 22 June, 2Lt Norman Gregory was wounded in the left ankle while leading a working party. U-Day began on 24 June and the division's artillery—mostly using 18-pounders and trench mortars—began to cut gaps in the wire accessing their chosen raiding points, while heavy artillery targeted German batteries.

On 25 June, a group of men on a working party at Wailly sheltered in a dugout prior to going on duty. Artist William Ritchie spent some of this time sketching three of his pals in the dugout, one of whom was nineteen-year-old Pte Herbert Beeley. Two hours later, Pte George Mason and nineteen-year-old Pte James Sturzaker left the dugout, followed seconds later by Ritchie. As they passed along the CT, a shrapnel shell burst directly above, killing the seventeen-year-old instantly—though leaving the other two unscathed. Beeley posted the sketch home, and it and condolences from some of Ritchie's comrades were published in the local newspaper.[14] For one NCO, former teacher Sgt James Ewan, this must have been particularly upsetting as Ritchie was an ex-pupil of his. He was buried near Capt. Lloyd-Evans in what is now Bellacourt Military Cemetery—the only two from the King's Own to rest there.

It was not just 55 Division's artillery that was busy—firing 54,570 rounds during these 'demonstrations'—as on 25 June, British artillery began pounding German positions all along the projected line of attack for 1 July. The planned raids went ahead at 5.35

p.m. on 28 June, although the Battalion did not take part in any of them. Results were mixed: Liverpool Scottish abandoned theirs when the wind carried the gas and smoke away from their target and, as such, attack was futile; and 1/4th Loyals got to within 15 yards of their target before concentrated rifle and MG fire pinned them down. Two of the three officers were killed, the other wounded. Out of fifty-six ORs, they lost nine killed, four missing, and eleven wounded—a high casualty rate. In complete contrast, 1/5th King's attacked with seventy-one, achieved all their objectives, and suffered only one man wounded. The 2/5th Lancashire Fusiliers were equally successful, though they suffered heavily, two out of their three officers missing, the other wounded; nineteen ORs wounded and sixteen missing—the highest casualty rate of any of the raiders. The 1/7th King's reached their sap-head, drove the enemy back, but were unable to gain entry—losing seven killed and fourteen wounded in the process. The 1/9th King's suffered very similar casualties, but were successful in taking their target—though one source of considerable annoyance was their inability to get at a number of Germans who retreated into a dugout. This had a stout door, and despite repeated efforts to break and blow their way in, resisted all attempts. Of the 400 officers and men making up the raiding parties, 136 were missing, killed, or wounded, a casualty rate of 34 per cent.[15]

It is clear from the pre-raid planning and post-mortem analysis that past lessons had been learned and that experience from these raids would be used in the future. Contrary to what most readers will have read in the past about the inability of British artillery to cut wire at this time, reports indicate that they were very successful here, with every planned cut achieved. Artillery also caused significant damage to enemy defences. The gas was less effective; apart from a couple the Fusiliers saw at the top of Blaireville Wood, no German gas casualties were found. It was concluded this was because the enemy had plenty of notice of an attack, due to the wire having been cut, and these gaps kept open by repeated bombardment by artillery and MGs fired on fixed-lines during the night. The gas cloud only moved about 3 mph, granting them some three minutes to don respirators. The Germans had sent up numerous red distress rockets and it was decided that to avoid future confusion with British signals, they were to use the 'Japanese daylight signals' next time, which burst with coloured smoke, dropping two white lights. The smoke screen was widely praised for helping cover both attack and withdrawal phases—though one group lost direction in it after donning their smoke helmets (the division later carried out considerable training in attack and navigation while wearing smoke helmets—and its replacement, the box respirator—particularly after this problem was again highlighted in August). Parties of RE accompanied the attackers and these were found to be of great value in destroying enemy installations. However, the biggest let-down was communications—failing in every case due to phone wires cut by enemy fire. This problem was never satisfactorily solved and would continue to be an Achilles' heel throughout the war. It was suggested that, in future, the first 20 to 30 yards of wire might be buried in No Man's Land prior to any attack, though there is no evidence that this was ever done. The casualty rate was thought considerable, but given the nature of the attacks—with long artillery preparation advertising a coming attack and the failure of the gas to do its intended job—this was not surprising. Jeudwine accepted that, in future, surprise was a key element, particularly during daylight. Had the smoke not been so effective, he believed that casualties would have been very much higher.[16]

Though the raids were over, 55 Division continued to bombard the enemy as part of the deception. On 30 June, the Battalion received another draft from England, this time just twenty-one men, bringing the total strength up to 852. As it was summer, the sick rate was low, but men were lost—such as talented violinist, nineteen-year-old Pte Samuel Wilson—admitted to hospital with rheumatic fever on 8 July and dying from pneumonia four days later. Another man died in the same hospital on 9 July, though there is no military record as to what disease killed Pte Will Eastwood. The MO, Capt. Deighton, also suffered a personal loss that week, when news came that his brother, Gerald, a captain in the Suffolks, had been killed on 3 July. Working parties were busy carrying stores and ammunition, building gun positions, and burying telephone wire—which needed to be at least 6 feet below the ground to protect it from HE. On 10 July—the day before the Battalion was due to go back into the line—six subalterns from 1/5th Royal Scots were attached to them: 2Lt's John Dobie, William Macfarlane, William Good, Francis Farquaharson, Lindsay Westwater, and William Robertson. Sadly, only two would survive to the end of the war and both those were wounded. It was a tough job being a junior officer in the infantry.

On 11 July, the Battalion returned to the line, relieving 2/5th Lancashire Fusiliers. On the 17th of the previous month, the division had extended its line yet again, this time on its left, taking over the left sub-sector of 'G' Sector from 14 Division. It was here (near Agny) that the Battalion was sent, their left bound at 50°15'33.40"N 2°46'38.80"E. Initially, this gave the division a frontage of just over 12,000 yards, needing seven full battalions to man the front line, but on 10–11 July and 12–13 July, a phased takeover of 'D' Sector and the western half of 'E' Sector by 46 Division reduced this to a more manageable span. The Battalion remained in front of Agny until 17 July, the enemy shelling their positions day and night and repeatedly firing rifle grenades into their trenches. The first casualty was twenty-year-old Pte Herbert Harley, when a round from a trench mortar killed him instantly while he was on sentry duty on 14 July. Twenty-one-year-old Pte Robert Roper was also wounded in the shoulder and leg by splinters.

The following day, Pte John Crahan died from his wounds, and on 27 July, twenty-two-year-old Pte John Bowman succumbed to his wounds in England. Though no record remains to show when the latter two were wounded, it was likely between 12 and 17 July, and in the case of John Crahan, no later than 15 July. Second Lieutenant George Shaw was wounded by shrapnel in the left thigh on 16 July, with another four men also joining the casualty list—though their names are no longer on record. Considering the amount of high explosive hurled at the Battalion during these five days, it is a testament to the quality of the dugouts that there were not more casualties. The rear areas and CTs also came in for considerable attention. Grouse Street was attacked with 77-mm and 5.9 on 17 July and blown in in three places. Grouse Street, a long CT leading from

Agny, ran just to the east of the old railway line to the approximate centre of the sector. The front line trenches of G13–G16 (the Battalion's right) were also targeted, with G14 and G15 badly damaged. British artillery retaliated regularly to these volleys with mixed results.

To divert German attention, further operations simulating a major attack were allotted to both 55 and 14 Division—the first beginning at 3 a.m. on 14 July. Artillery was ordered to cut wire and fire a pre-attack bombardment shortly before 'zero hour'. To achieve this, they were allocated 36,000 rounds of ammunition for the guns, 1,000 rounds of 2-inch mortar ammunition, and an unlimited supply of Stokes mortar ammunition. Between 3 a.m. and 4 a.m., the Battalion's Lewis guns were ordered to sweep the tops of the enemy parapets to make life uncomfortable for the enemy during their morning stand-to. A smoke screen was also scheduled— the responsibility of the Battalion and to their right, 1/5th South Lancs in 166 Brigade's 'G' Sector. In shell holes out in No Man's Land, a pair of men with smoke candles and phosphorus grenades—each with a relief— were positioned every 25 yards. Together, the two Battalions were issued with 8,288 smoke candles and 4,440 phosphorus grenades. Beginning five minutes before 'zero', each pair threw eight smoke candles in a fan-pattern forward of their position (repeated every three minutes until 'zero plus sixteen minutes', when three phosphorus bombs were thrown—this too repeated every four minutes until 'zero plus fifty-two minutes'). Initially, all went well, the enemy lining his parapet and opening rapid fire, but within minutes, the wind veered and blew all the smoke away to the north.

The Battalion was very active during the hours of darkness, and on the night of 14–15 July, they pushed a number of heavily armed patrols with Lewis guns into No Man's Land searching for enemy patrols to ambush—though none were found. Bombing patrols went forward to attack enemy saps, and the Battalion's bombers fired no less than sixty rifle grenades into the German trenches opposite G13–G15; another patrol successfully bombing the sap opposite G15. Another discovered a party of Germans cutting the grass behind their wire and drove them off with bombs. The Battalion's snipers also discovered a good position on 16 July, from which they claimed two hits. The Yorkshires relieved the Battalion in the early hours of 18 July, never to return here.

19 July 1916–1 October 1916: Chalk, Steel, and Mud

Coordinates for Positions Named in this Chapter

Arrow Head Copse	50°0'31.80"N 2°48'59.00"E	Maltz Horn Farm	50°0'4.40"N 2°48'55.40"E
Bivouacs 16 September	49°59'34.62"N 2°37'58.51"E	Pommier Redoubt	50°0'43.30"N 2°45'16.30"E
Briqueterie	50°0'5.66"N 2°47'28.06"E	RV-13 August	49°59'47.70"N 2°47'29.60"E
Carcaillot Farm	49°59'4.20"N 2°40'20.40"E	Rwy, east of Trones Wood	50°0'46.60"N 2°48'38.10"E
Cemetery, Briqueterie	49°59'53.00"N 2°47'37.40"E	Sand Pit bivouac	49°58'38.50"N 2°40'36.20"E
cemetery, Talus Boise	49°59'6.90"N 2°46'3.60"E	Talus Boise reserve	49°59'35.60"N 2°46'32.30"E
Citadel, the	49°58'31.80"N 2°43'2.60"E	Tea Support Trench	50°2'14.30"N 2°48'52.70"E
Cocoa Lane junction	50°1'52.40"N 2°48'57.50"E	Vivier Mill	49°58'59.42"N 2°38'50.64"E
Dublin/Casement Trench	49°59'52.70"N 2°47'20.45"E	Waterlot farm	50°1'13.50"N 2°48'47.67"E
Fricourt bivouacs 1	49°59'40.80"N 2°41'49.30"E	Wellington Redoubt	49°59'3.90"N 2°41'25.30"E
Fricourt bivouacs 2	49°59'0.20"N 2°35'41.99"E	York Trench	50°1'21.50"N 2°47'24.30"E
HQ-6 September	50°1'26.50"N 2°48'28.20"E		

The Battalion occupied billets at Sombrin, their strength 847 officers and men. Early on 20 July, they left for Bouquemaison, departing the next day for Boisbergues—leaving the sights and sounds of war further behind them as they entered unspoilt countryside. Prouville was reached on the morning of the 22nd. On 25 July, they travelled by train from Candás to Méricourt-l'Abbé and marched to bivouacs at Ville sur Ancre, though their allocated position was so boggy that it was impossible to find enough dry land for the bivouacs. Strength increased to 881 on 22 July, and the next day, a draft of eighty-seven men from the Cheshires, transferred *en masse* at Étaples, raised this to 968—the highest since April 1915. The QM later dubbed these the 'Unlucky Draft' and, indeed, it was a little over a week before the first was killed. By the end of the year, almost all had appeared on casualty lists.

As the division approached its final destination, command passed to XIII Corps of 4th Army. The signs of war were all around them on 27 July as they marched to bivouacs on the east-facing slope near Sand Pit. Empty 18-pounder ammunition boxes, piled high in the fields, made excellent building material for improvised bivouacs and men slept in these and some old artillery dugouts in the locality. On the following day, while the rest of the Battalion trained, Lt-Col. Anderson and the CO of the South Lancs went forward with the brigade-major to view the front line. On 30 July, the Battalion advanced some 1,200 metres to Wellington Redoubt, arriving at 11.15 a.m. Forty-five minutes later, they were welcomed by enemy aircraft attempting to bomb their camp—though luckily all the bombs fell wide. On 30 July, the division was informed they would be taking over a sector running from where the Guillemont railway emerged to the east of Trones Wood, southwards to where British and French lines adjoined near Maltz Horn Farm. At 5.30 a.m. on 1 August, the Battalion moved to reserve trenches at Talus Boise, Transport remaining near The Citadel.

In the evening of 1 August, a large working party, of ten officers and 378 men, was ordered to a road junction at 50°0'5.00"N 2°47'49.20"E, a couple of hundred metres to the east of the Briqueterie, their task to extend Hamilton Trench forward to the line on the eastern side of Trones Wood (50°0'34.00"N 2°48'35.20"E). Although the divisional diary reports that this was a quiet night and the construction of the advanced trenches went well, the returning working parties came under artillery fire and lost three killed and eleven wounded.[1, 2] The dead were twenty-five-year-old L/Cpl Neil Gregory, nineteen-year-old Pte Alfred Sanderson, and twenty-two year-old Pte Allen Woodhouse. The chaplain, Rev. Robert Gardner, wrote to Woodhouse's mother:

I have no doubt that you have already received the sad news of your son's death. While returning from work in the forward trenches, apparently a shell burst near his party and he was killed, while three others were wounded. The Sergt-Major tells me that his last thoughts were of you. He was buried this morning at 8.15 o'clock, in the little cemetery behind our lines. As there was no Wesleyan chaplain, [Woodhouse had been a Sunday school teacher at a Wesleyan chapel] I read the Church Burial Service over him. It will comfort you to know that on all sides you hear a splendid account of him. L/ Cpl Woodhouse, your younger son, was too late to be present. I had a long talk with him today and was able to take him to see his brother's grave.[3]

P woodland

+ battalion cemetery

--- road or track
(mostly sunken)

Guillemont
August 1916

His brother, L/Cpl William Woodhouse, was actually the older of the two at twenty-six. He remained unwounded for the entire war, though an injury to ligaments in his right knee in October brought about home posting and eventual transfer to the Labour Corps. The three were buried in the small divisional cemetery to the south of Talus Boise. When this cemetery was cleared in February 1920, all were reburied at Peronne Road Cemetery. The first of the 'Unlucky Draft' to perish—still listed as 6/Cheshire— was twenty-year-old Pte Charles Platt from Stockport. His head wound proved fatal and he was declared dead at the main dressing station. Another from this draft was possibly seriously wounded on 1 August; nineteen-year-old Pte James Hornbuckle died from his wounds at Abbeville on 4 August. Few of the casualty lists from this time survive, so the names of most of the wounded are not available, though one was twenty-five-year-old Cpl James Maguire, with shrapnel wounds to left arm and knee and buried by the explosion. He was evacuated home and saw no further active service.

At 4.30 a.m. on 2 August, Lt-Col. Anderson, accompanied by one officer from each company, reconnoitred the area to the front of Guillemont. The Battalion was to provide the fourth wave on 166 Brigade's flank of the attack against this forbidding enemy stronghold. What they saw cannot have filled them with confidence—British trenches were shallow, lacked sufficient space for the attacking forces, and were some distance from the enemy—whose defences at Guillemont were among the strongest on the Western Front.

Considerable effort was put into the planning of this attack and the consolidation of any gains—some of the ideas more practical than others. On 2 August, Brig.-Gen. Green-Wilkinson and his brigade-major attended a demonstration of a proposed ammunition resupply method for 166 TMB's Stokes mortars. The suggestion was to replace the fuse with a wooden plug and actually fire these into the area where they would be needed. Apart from the obvious drawback of injury to friendly forces, there was also a good chance that they would be damaged or lost and would certainly be scattered about the battlefield. Detonators and new projectile cartridges would need to be carried forwards anyway. The following day they watched 166 TMB practice this at the Briqueterie.[4] Common sense prevailed and the idea was dropped.

After dark, another large working party of six officers and 250 men, was sent to dig and consolidate an advanced trench at 50°0'17.10"N 2°48'43.40"E between Maltz Horn Farm and Trones Wood, 600 metres from enemy defences. While German artillery was fairly quiet during the day, it was the complete antithesis during the hours of darkness and a considerable weight of fire fell on rear areas and supply lines, the Citadel near Transport's position coming under fire. Just after dusk, 1/4th King's Own, holding the line forward of where the working party were to dig, became embroiled in a struggle to control an isolated trench to the right of Arrow Head Copse and roughly half way between opposing lines. The 1/4th were ultimately successful, but this action triggered a large-scale artillery duel lasting from 8.30 p.m. until midnight. Much of this landed around the working party, both on their way up and while they were working. The first casualty and only fatality was 2Lt Richard Irving. The former teacher was hit in the heart by a single shrapnel ball and died instantly. In a letter to Irving's mother, Capt. Harriss reported: 'The men who were with him at the time tell me that he did not speak after being hit, and the expression on his face when the body was brought back was one of perfect calm'.[5] The QM, writing to a mutual colleague back in Lancaster commented:

By the death of Lt Irving we have lost a fine soldier. You all know how quiet he was. He was just the same out here. Promotion did not spoil him, and his duty was all he thought of. Sgt Ewan [a former colleague of Irvine's] tells me he went into this particular action with some forebodings, but certainly with no fear.[6]

The Lancaster and District Teachers' Association posted a metal laurel wreath for the QM to fasten to the cross on Irvine's grave. Second Lieutenant John Mackey was also wounded, but of the twelve ORs, only Pte James Gardner is known. He was hit in the right leg by shrapnel on his way forward and ended up in the Australian Hospital at Rouen, returning to the Battalion in November.

On 3 August, it was the turn of Maj. Anderson-Morshead to reconnoitre the trenches opposite Guillemont, accompanied by another officer from each company. That night another large working party of five officers and 250 men set off to work on the same trenches as the previous night. There must have been considerable trepidation amongst them as German artillery fire had intensified—much of it directed against the front line and its immediate rear where the working party was heading for. Indeed, casualties were higher, particularly among 'A' and 'B' Company whose men were widely dispersed by the fire. Second Lieutenant William Good, one of the attached Royal Scots officers, was wounded. He returned to his parent unit and was killed with them in February 1918. Recently commissioned 2Lt Thomas Blakeley was also wounded, but remained on duty.

Twenty men were killed, or died from their wounds, and thirty-six were wounded. Two of the officers attached from the Royal Scots were commended for their leadership. Lt John Dobie and 2Lt Lindsay Westwater, helped by their NCOs, rallied the scattered men, organised the evacuation of the wounded, then took the survivors forward to complete their tasks.[7] The youngest killed was sixteen-year-old Pte Joseph Johnston from Workington. He added three years to his age when he enlisted and had only been with the Battalion eighteen days. His service record notes him as both 'killed in action' and 'died of wounds'. Another youngster to perish was seventeen-year-old Pte John Flood from Blackpool, who also declared his age as nineteen on enlistment. Pte Henry Higginson, whose brother, Samuel, was killed in May 1915, also lost his life. These three men have no known graves and are commemorated on the Thiepval Memorial. However, letters from CWGC, dated March 1920 in their service records, suggest that although their individual grave markers were lost, they are buried as 'unknowns' in Quarry Cemetery, Montauban.

The Battalion maintained a little cemetery to the south of the Briqueterie and these graves were relocated to Quarry Cemetery post-war. The dead from this barrage were the first to be buried here, and one of them, twenty-three-year-old Pte Ernest Dominick from Stockport— another of the 'Unlucky Draft'—was still badged as 6/Cheshire. In 1930, five bodies found at 50°0′21.10″N 2°48′41.20″E, along the route the working party travelled that night, were reburied in Serre No. 2 Cemetery. Three of these were men killed on this working party, another was an unknown soldier from the Battalion, but the last—an unknown member of the Cheshires—was buried in Plot 26, Row 'M', grave 5.[8] Eighteen-year-old Stockport soldier Pte Albert Walker is an extremely strong candidate for this burial. Sadly, it is impossible to deduce who the 'unknown' from the Battalion is, as it could be one of five. With over fifty casualties in just a few seconds, there was considerable confusion and disorganisation, and it was at times like this that good leadership transcended. At least 40 per cent of the group L/ Cpl Thomas Smith was with became casualties, and although he was wounded in the face, he calmly organised the treatment and evacuation of the wounded. Both the CO and brigadier recommended him for a MM, but he only received a MiD.[9] Another similarly acknowledged for his performance on both of these working parties was Sgt Robert Barton.

For some of the wounded, it was their second or even third time, such as thirty-five-year-old Pte George Wolfendale. His physical wound was minor, but he was badly shellshocked and later transferred to the ASC. For 'A' Company's Charles Bibby and 'B' Company's Moses Geddes, it was their second time. In May 1915, Geddes had been badly wounded in both thighs by shrapnel and this time it was his right leg that was hit—though not as seriously as before. Prior to evacuation, he asked a pal, Pte Thomas Mitchell from Blackpool, to write to his mum telling her not to worry. Days later, someone did the same favour for Mitchell. Stretcher-bearer Charles Bibby was hit in an arm and a leg, but managed to hobble to the dressing station unaided. He too asked a pal, Pte W. Carter, to write home to reassure his parents telling them that 'he hoped to get to the same hospital as he was before and [thought] himself lucky to get out of this lot'.[10] Both men survived the war, though Geddes's brother, Robert, with the 2/5th in England, died that December.

At 9.30 p.m. on 4 August, Capt. Owtram took out another working party, this time of three officers and 162 men, to dig CTs at 50°0′9.60″N 2°48′20.70″E. Although they were shelled, it was far less intense, and apart from 2Lt Frank Sutherland and three men—who all received very minor wounds and were able to continue once these were dressed—only Pte George Walker was seriously injured. He was evacuated to Warrington, where a shrapnel ball was removed from his left shoulder. Later in the war, he transferred to the RE. At 8 p.m. on 6 August, the Battalion filed out of their trenches and moved to bivouacs at the Citadel. Their short time in reserve had resulted in twenty-six deaths.

Killed or Died of Wounds on Working Parties 1–5 August 1916

Pte Alfred Cave	1808	DOW: 4/8	Pte Walter Robinson	4193	DOW: 4/8
Pte Ernest Horace Dominick*	4434	KIA: 3/8	Pte Thomas Roocroft	1749	KIA: 3/8
Pte John Flood	4028	KIA: 3/8	Pte Alfred Shaw Sanderson	4130	KIA: 1/8
L/Cpl Neil Gregory	1019	KIA: 1/8	Pte George Simpson	3791	KIA: 3/8
Pte Charles Gregory	3779	DOW: 11/8	Pte James South	3893	KIA: 3/8
Pte Joseph Eugene Hague	3915	DOW: 4/8	Pte James Stephenson	4107	KIA: 3/8
Pte Henry Higginson	3700	KIA: 3/8	Pte William Stewart	2794	DOW: 4/8
Pte James Hornbuckle*	4570	DOW: 4/8	Pte William Lyness Tyrell	1591	KIA: 3/8
2Lt Richard Irving		KIA: 2/8	Pte Albert Walker*	4282	KIA: 3/8
Pte Joseph Johnston	3553	DOW: 3/8	Pte John James Whittam	3702	DOW: 4/8
Pte John Law	2774	KIA: 3/8	Pte Thomas James Wilson	3575	KIA: 3/8
Pte William Birbeck Pedder	2786	DOW: 4/8	Pte Allen Woodhouse	4009	KIA: 1/8
Pte Charles Fred Platt*	4018	DOW: 1/8	Pte William Wright	4113	KIA: 3/8

*Still recorded as 6/Cheshires.

The Battalion had a quiet day on the 7th, but there was considerable activity throughout the divisional front as the final preparations for the attack on Guillemont progressed. The Battalion received an urgent signal, requiring them to send one company to the Briqueterie to relieve a company from 164 Brigade by 10 p.m., so at 8 p.m., Capt. Fawcett moved 'A' Company forward to occupy this position, each platoon spaced 200 yards apart. Sixteen unlucky men were delegated to carry boxes of .303 ammunition forward for the Vickers of 166 MGC, who were to occupy the same position—these to remain with 166 MGC as ammunition carriers in the event of the attack being successful and the guns advancing. The rest of the Battalion was placed on stand-by to move at very short notice—men allowed to only take their boots off when sleeping. 'A' Company was met by considerable artillery fire and although no casualties were suffered, two NCOs were buried by explosions and dug out unharmed.

The attack against Guillemont by 164 and 165 Brigades began at 4.20 a.m. on 8 August and was little short of disaster, with very high casualties and only minor gains on the right. The Battalion were warned that another attack would be made on the 9th and that they would be in reserve for this. The scope of this attack was considerably less than that of the previous day—the objective being to rescue the remnants of Liverpool Irish; however, it would still have to overcome the defences that had repelled a larger force just twenty-four hours earlier.[11] Six officers and fifty men were ordered to remain behind, and at 11.30 p.m., the Battalion left their bivouacs and marched via the Peronne road and Maricourt to an assembly point at Dublin and Casement Trenches.

It was a long and difficult march—the night pitch black—roads crowded with transport and troops. All around, vivid flashes and, every so often, the unbelievably violent concussion of a nearby explosion rent the darkness. At times like these, men clenched their teeth and hunched their shoulders—trying to withdraw upwards into their steel helmets—praying silently that the next one would not have their name on it. As they passed through Maricourt, the Battalion found their progress blocked by a column of French transport and stumbled along the muddy sides of the road to bypass it. At least five men were known to have been wounded before they reached the assembly point— the noise of approaching shells drowned by the rumbling of ironclad wagon wheels on *pavé*. Nineteen-year-old Pte Peter Barnes from Lancaster was wounded in a finger and both legs; twenty-two-year-old Pte William Fisher from Barrow received an abdominal wound; and thirty-eight-year-old Pte William Hornby from Fleetwood was wounded in the left arm. All three went back to England for treatment, but only Barnes returned. The other two, known to have been wounded before midnight, were twenty-two-year-old Pte John Gardner (921), hit below the right knee, and thirty-year-old Pte John Howard from Bowerham, with a shrapnel wound to his left thigh and a badly sprained ankle. Although officially recorded for 9 August, it seems probable that twenty-four-year-old Thomas Mattinson was actually killed on the 8th, if the time recorded in a letter by 2Lt Sutherland is correct; although, his attribution of the date must be mistaken as, apart from those who had remained behind later rejoining the Battalion—without casualties— the Battalion was static in their trenches on that date. Sutherland recorded:

About 10 p.m. on August 9th, we were making out way to the front lines under heavy shrapnel fire, when Pte Mattinson was hit in three places, head, chest and leg, death being instantaneous.[12]

In the early hours of 9 August—just as the Battalion reached the assembly point—the enemy fired an airburst phosphorus shell, which flung streamers of red fire out in all directions, igniting anything it touched. Unfortunately, a dump of Very lights was kindled and exploded in a display of pyrotechnical brilliance, exposing the entire Battalion to the view of enemy artillery observers, who almost immediately called down a barrage of 5.9 on them. Capt. Seward was wounded, one man killed, and several wounded. Reeling momentarily under the shock of the barrage, the Battalion hesitated, gathered itself, and moved onwards.

At 3.50 a.m., the last of the Battalion was placed in Dublin and Casement Trenches and the CO was able to brief his Company Commanders on the attack, planned to begin in a mere forty minutes. Just ten minutes after the attack began, the Battalion advanced to positions in the trenches vacated by the attackers. As they relocated, another barrage fell among them, wounding Capt. Briggs and 2Lt William Daniels. NCOs and men also suffered, Sgt Herbert Dobson being killed outright. His friend and platoon-commander, Robert Higginson, wrote to his parents:

The officers, NCOs and men of this company feel a great loss in his death, with all of whom he was so popular. He was my Platoon-Sergeant, a splendid one too, and to me it is a personal loss. Being in constant touch with him as a soldier I had grown to like him very much, and I appreciate, as others do, the splendid work he has done. It will be some consolation to you to know that his death was instantaneous, and occurred leading his men in an attack. Capt. Briggs and I laid him to rest at 7.30 p.m. on 9 August. Company Sergeant Major Barrow and Sgt Towers and B Company were present. Capt. Briggs read a few verses over his grave.[13]

Eight senior NCOs (only three of whom remained by Armistice Day) signed another letter of condolence. Poor Robert Higginson had now seen nearly all of his pals from their days at Didcot fall.

'A' and 'D' were able to squeeze into these trenches, but when 'B' and 'C' arrived, the latter now under the command of Capt. Owtram, they found these so overcrowded that they were forced to take cover in shell holes behind the position. This was clearly unsatisfactory, and when the CO reported the situation to brigade, the Battalion was ordered to position itself in trenches between the Briqueterie and Maltz Horn Farm— the very ones they had dug five days earlier. The attack on 9 August was no more successful than the previous day's—once again, uncut wire barred progress—and battalions suffered great losses for no gain.[14] The Battalion lost twelve men killed or dying from their wounds, and forty-seven officers and men wounded. Although some of the injured returned, others, such as twenty-nine-year-old Pte John Fellows, wounded in the back by shrapnel, were transferred.

Killed or Died of Wounds 8–9 August 1916

Pte Alban Anderson	1424	DOW: 10/8	Pte Thomas Hill	1617	KIA: 9/8
Pte Leonard Dabbs*	4545	KIA: 9/8	L/Cpl George Stanley Hine	3886	DOW: 9/8
Sgt Herbert B. Dobson MM	2746	KIA: 9/8	Pte John William Hornby	1390	KIA: 9/8
Pte William Henry Doran	1945	KIA: 9/8	Pte Thomas Rawes Mattinson**	4052	KIA: 9/8
Pte Joseph Etchells*	3972	KIA: 9/8	Pte Herbert Penrith	2403	KIA: 9/8
Pte Levi Garth Fernley	1425	KIA: 9/8	Pte Edward Sanderson	1572	KIA: 9/8

*Recorded as 6/Cheshire.
**Most likely killed around 10 p.m. on 8 August.

Although the support trenches in the sunken road to the east of the Briqueterie were on the receiving end of a heavy barrage two or three times during the course of the day, 10 August was comparatively calm. The Battalion's war diary notes three killed, four wounded, and one missing for this day, but CWWG records do not indicate any fatalities for the Battalion (or 6/Cheshires) on 10 August or subsequent days. The diary for August is typewritten, so it is possible that a mistake was made when this was later typed.[15] There were probably some wounded on 10 August—one newspaper report suggests at least three:

> While bandaging some of the *boys* who had been hit, he [twenty-eight-year-old Sgt Samuel Bates] received a bullet in the thigh, and is now undergoing treatment at Leeds Square Hospital, Manchester.[16]

Another article describes L/Cpl Thomas Bateson as being wounded in the right leg.[17] Although the papers attribute the above woundings to 11 and 12 August, events described in the Battalion's diary favour 10 August as the probable date. Another man likely to have been in the sunken road was Pte Henry Milne, admitted to hospital on 11 August, suffering from shellshock. He was discharged in May 1917 as a result, but volunteered for the Labour Corps in 1919. That night, the Battalion was relieved by 8/Queens and returned to near the Citadel, where four new officers were assigned to their companies (Lt Cuthbert Gaulter, 2Lt John Bainbridge, 2Lt Wilfred Baker, and 2Lt Arthur Shaw).

There was rest on 11 August, and the next day, the Battalion began to prepare for an attack to the south of Guillemont scheduled for 16 August—themselves and the Loyals in the vanguard. Two days were to be given over for the Battalion to train against similar trenches behind the lines, and preparations and the stockpiling and issue of equipment began. Rehearsals on Sunday 13 August went well and there was a spirit of optimism within the Battalion at a high chance of success. However, at 7 p.m., Church Parade was interrupted by a message ordering the Battalion back to the reserve trenches at Talus Boise. They would no longer be attacking on the 16th and working parties of 300 men were required for that night.

The first working party, under Capt. Fawcett, of five officers and 100 men, was to meet RE guides at the junction of the Maricourt–Briqueterie road and Dublin Trench, where they would be taken to deepen Duncan's Alley CT. 'B' Company, under Capt. Deed, with five officers and 100 men, was to report to the RE at Stanley Dump, where they would form a carrying party. 'C' Company, under Capt. Owtram, with four officers and 100 men, was to report to the brigade-major at Talus Boise, where they would be taken by a guide to where they would dig. These three parties had their numbers augmented by men from 'D' Company. In addition, thirty-six NCOs and men from the Bombers were to report to the RE at the junction of the Maricourt road and Casement Trench. The only company that actually achieved its objective was 'A', who lost one man wounded. The others reached their rendezvous, but no guides arrived. Considerable artillery fire fell around them as they advanced across the open, and 2Lt Macfarlane was wounded, though not seriously—refusing to allow his wound to be dressed until he had successfully led his party to their destination.[18] Deed and Owtram made every effort to find out their destination, but no one could enlighten them and no replacement guides could be found. Once dawn rose, both company commanders returned with their men, it later transpiring that their guides had become casualties.

On 14 August, the Battalion was warned that they might be relieved during the night, but that, despite this, working parties would still be required. The task given to the working detail that followed on the night of 14–15 August almost beggars belief. Labelled 'Z' Party and commanded by Maj. Anderson-Morshead, they were charged with digging assembly trenches for an attack on the 16th. 'Z' Party was divided into three groups. The first, a covering party of fifty men from 'B' Company, with rifles and two Lewis guns, was commanded by 2Lt Higginson, who was to reconnoitre the ground during the afternoon. The second group, from 'A' Company and led by Capt. Fawcett, with 2Lt Gaulter and seventy men, was armed with nothing more than picks and shovels (one pick for every three shovels). They were to dig a 4-foot-wide trench, 6 feet deep, and 270 yards in length, from 50°0′17.70″N 2°49′19.10″E to 50°0′10.80″N 2°49′12.80″E. The third group, gleaned from a combination of 'D', 'B', bombers, pioneers, and Regimental Police, amounted to 106 men and was led by Capt. Harriss, supported by 2Lts Macfarlane and Holmes. They were tasked with digging a similarly sized trench from 50°0′28.70″N 2°49′6.30″E to 50°0′25.70″N 2°49′17.30″E—and like the second party were armed to the teeth with shovels and picks.

The latter reference given above differs from that in the diary, which had been pencilled in at a later date and is almost certainly incorrect as it places much of this trench behind British lines. If, however, the same coordinates—but for the square to the right—are applied, then the trench is placed exactly where it was needed and described (maps from August 1916 are unbelievably contradictory—German positions on the sketch map in this chapter are based upon map references in divisional records and the combined indications of German positions from six different British maps and two German ones).

The Battalion's diary states that the distance varied between 50 yards and 100 yards from the enemy, but if the map references for these trenches and those given for German trenches in the divisional diary are correct, then Fawcett's trench was a mere 20 yards from the enemy in places and Harriss's trench not much better. Even on a dark night, this task was perilous; however, the night was clear and there was bright moonlight.

'Z' Party left Talus Boise at 7 p.m., and routed via Favière Wood and Maltz Horn Trench to meet the brigade-major opposite Guillemont. No casualties were sustained in the march—though they had to skirt a number of heavy barrages, particularly one targeting Death Valley. The Battalion was not the first to be given this job, but all previous attempts failed when those working parties withdrew after suffering heavy casualties. Brig-Gen. Green-Wilkinson had stressed to Harriss the importance of completing the task, stating that the honour of both brigade and division depended upon it being completed that night. Once the positions of the new trenches had been explained, Fawcett and Harriss—each accompanied by an NCO—crept forward into No Man's Land and marked the centreline for each trench with tape.

As these were some 400 yards apart at their centre points, the Covering Party split into two groups (each with a Lewis) and crawled forward to take up position between the enemy line and the marking tape—some within 15 yards of the German line. Almost as soon as the officers began to place the diggers, they were seen by the enemy, who opened up with rifles and machine guns. Twenty-seven-year-old Capt. Harriss had a particularly lucky escape when a bullet struck his entrenching tool, glanced off, and travelled through his haversack and tunic, scoring a long bruise and cut across his back. He ignored this injury and carried on. The men had been ordered to dig while in the kneeling position, but were still easy targets—though the deeper they dug, the more protection they gained. Conversely, the deeper they dug, the more serious the wound—head and chest shots more likely to be fatal. One man, shot in the head and killed instantly, was forty-one-year-old Pte Frederick Bird, a father of two from Morecambe. Sgt Henry Gorst and another Morecambe man buried him where he fell. One officer later wrote: 'The men behaved wonderfully well, and it was difficult making them keep down while digging'.[19] The men of the Covering Party were possibly at even greater risk, forward of the diggers, flare after flare illuminating them for German marksmen.

For five long hours, the men took everything the enemy could fire at them. Luckily, their proximity to the foe meant that artillery was not viable, but to remain steadfast under heavy, close-range small arms fire and unable to retaliate took a special breed of man. The Covering Party, under orders to reserve their fire unless the enemy advanced in mass, suffered many killed and wounded. Ghastly as it must have been for the ordinary men lying in the open, for their officers and NCOs, who were constantly moving from group to group to reassure and steady their men, it was worse; it was also terrible for the stretcher-bearers, exposed to the worst of the fire as they performed their selfless duties. RSM Barrow was in charge of the Covering Party protecting Capt. Fawcett, and he constantly crawled from position to position reassuring his men and organising the treatment and evacuation of wounded. At one point, his Lewis team—under effective fire—was about to move further back, but he steadied the gunners who then held until the withdrawal order was given. Although Lt-Col. Anderson recommended him for a DCM, it was downgraded to a MiD by brigade.[20]

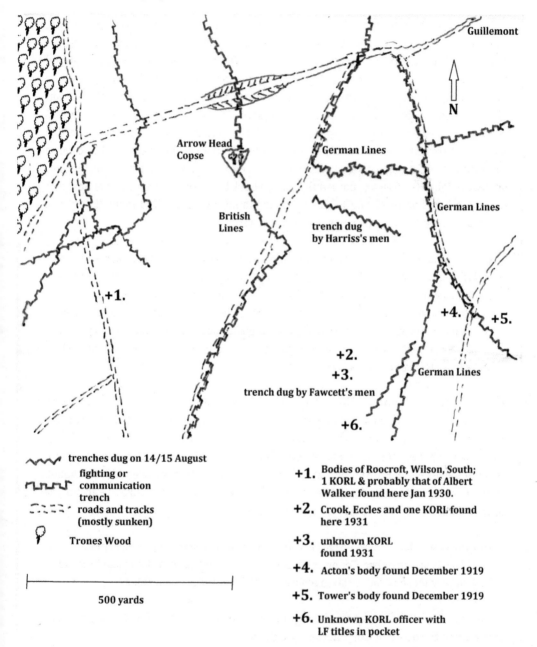

Detail of Guillemont Sector for Working Party 14/15 August 1916

One NCO singled out for praise by Capt. Harriss was Cpl Thomas Sanderson (030), who, like many of those recommended for an award that night, received nothing—though he would be luckier another time. Second Lieutenant Macfarlane also displayed great bravery, ignoring his own safety to tend the wounded under fire, which saw him awarded the MC for this and his courage earlier that month.[21] Second Lieutenant Thomas Blakeley, in charge of the line of diggers closest to the enemy, showed great courage and coolness supervising and steadying his men, for which he too was awarded the MC.[22] Stretcher-bearers suffered several losses. Twenty-four-year-old Pte George Yates from 'D' Company was shot and killed while carrying a wounded man. His brother-in-law, Pte John Hargreaves, passed the tidings back to his sister in a letter the next day, informing her that Yates had been shot near the left eye and killed immediately. Cpl George Bell, the NCO in charge of the bearers, wrote:

> He had gained the respect and esteem of all by his quiet cheerfulness and the knowledge that he gave his life nobly in the execution of his arduous duties should be a great comfort to you. The circumstances of his death were such as to make us proud to call him comrade for he was succouring a wounded officer, when an enemy bullet struck him in the head, his death being instantaneous and painless [there is no record of any officer being wounded]. He was laid to rest close to where he so gallantly fell and a cross will mark his grave.[23]

The MO, Capt. Deighton, wrote that Yates had been shot in the neck, but he may have confused him with another stretcher-bearer casualty. Pte John Hall and another bearer were bandaging a wounded man when they were caught by a burst of fire, Hall being hit in the thigh, the other in the neck and killed outright. Hall was treated in a Glasgow hospital for his wound.[24] Another stretcher-bearer known to have been killed—though he died shortly after reaching the dressing station—was twenty-three-year-old Pte George Sandall. Capt. Deed wrote to his mother:

> He died most gallantly while helping to carry in a wounded comrade under heavy fire from near the enemy's front line. For his conduct I have submitted his name for recognition and hope he may, though dead, be given some award that his relatives may value.[25]

Some wounded were killed before they could be evacuated. Pte Daniel Till wrote to his father about the death of Cpl Jonathan 'Jack' Acton:

> Alec Armistead [Pte Alfred Armistead] was running around getting the wounded in, and Jack shouted, 'Alec, I'm hit.' Alec went to him, but before he reached him, he was hit twice again, and had four wounds altogether and died.[26]

Twenty-seven-year-old Jack Acton was the last of his family, his wife and baby having died two years earlier.

Despite the best efforts of the bearers to get the wounded to the MO as quickly as possible, severe wounds were sometimes beyond all medical aid, six of the wounded later died. Pte James Threlfall held on longer than most, succumbing to his abdominal wound four days later. His last act before he slipped into unconsciousness, was to ask the nurse to write to his wife telling her he was 'going on well'.[27] It is also possible that Pte Leonard Johnson from Stockport was one of that night's casualties—though he may have been wounded earlier. Like the majority of the 'Unlucky Draft', he was still recorded as 6/Cheshires, as although some had been processed in the days leading up to this working party, most had not. Johnson died as a result of wounds to shoulder and lung on 27 August. Nineteen-year-old Cpl Frederick Monks was initially reported wounded and missing, though this was quickly changed to 'killed in action'—his death coming only four days after the death of his father. For men waiting for family or friends to return safely, the night must have seemed everlasting. For some, it was bad news and Sgt William Fleming had the heart-breaking task of writing home to his mother about the death of his younger brother George, one of the pioneers with Capt. Harriss. The twenty-one-year-old died shortly after reaching the dressing station.

One of the last men to be killed was thirty-one-year-old Sgt Joseph Towers of 'B' Company. He was shot through the heart as the parties withdrew at 3 a.m., their tasks completed. The first of the many letters of condolence to reach his widow was from her brother, Pte Robert Wadsworth, who wrote as soon as they returned to their bivouacs. Particularly badly affected by the death of the last of his old pals was 2Lt Higginson, who learned of it when the Covering Party withdrew to meet up with the diggers. Higginson returned alone to where Fawcett's men had been digging, telling RSM Barrow that he was going to bury Towers. He was never seen again. Initially posted as missing, the Battalion scoured the dressing stations the next day in the hope that he had been wounded, but to no avail. It was nearly a year before his wife—whom he had only recently wed—had his death confirmed.

After Guillemont was later taken, any bodies found were collected into groups close to where they had fallen and buried. Towers was buried at 50°0′18.90″N 2°49′29.20″E and rediscovered by a GRU in December 1919. He was reinterred in Guillemont Road Cemetery—one of only four 'killed in action' that night to have a marked grave. Found at the same time was Jack Acton's body. The other two— located in 1931, 100 yards to the rear of Capt. Fawcett's trench—were Joseph Crook and Thomas Eccles, both of whom are buried in Serre Road No. 2. The body of an unknown officer from the King's Own was discovered in 1919 at 50°0′15.30″N 2°49′22.60″E and buried in Guillemont Road, Plot XV, Row 'K', Grave 8.[28] The position of this body suggests that it is likely to belong to one of the three missing officers from 8/King's Own, killed in their attack against Guillemont; it is only remotely possible that this was Robert Higginson.

In 1931, a common grave containing three bodies was discovered at 50°0′12.42″N 2°49′11.83″E—one of whom was wearing officer's boots and belonged to the King's

Own.[29] While not proving beyond doubt that this was 2Lt Higginson, the location just to the rear of Fawcett's trench is significant and is not along the line of attack taken by 8/King's Own on the 16th. This officer had a pair of 7/Lancashire Fusiliers shoulder titles in his pocket, but I have been unable to discover any connections between the only four King's Own officers that could have been buried in the southern part of the battlefield and 7/LF. He was reinterred in Plot 34, Row 'N', Grave 8, in Serre Road No. 2. The three 8/King's Own officers missing in this general area between 16 and 20 August were Capt. George Sommerville, 2Lt Aubrey Patch and 2Lt Walter Sansom—though their attack was to the east of where the Battalion was working. The seven officers missing from 1/4th King's Own would have been considerably further north.

Casualties were profound for what was essentially a working party—the higher than usual proportion of dead to wounded emphasising the danger of their task. Even though the men had left the front line, they were not out of danger and as they marched back through Death Valley more casualties were sustained from shellfire, though none fatal. Twenty-five men were killed or died from wounds, and a further twenty-six were wounded. They arrived back at their bivouacs near Talus Boise at 6.30 a.m. Both CWGC and *Soldiers Died* record another two from the Battalion killed in action during this period: Pte William Howard for 16 August and Pte Joshua Airey for 18 August. Although both previously served in the 1/5th, it is certain that they were 8th Battalion when killed—especially as the letter of condolence to Airey's wife was written by the chaplain of 8/King's Own.[30]

Killed or Died from Wounds as a result of the Working Party 14–15 August 1916

Cpl Jonathan Richard Acton	3791	KIA: 15/8	Cpl Maurice Hodgson	2883	KIA: 15/8
Pte Albert Askew	3677	KIA: 15/8	Pte Ernest Jackson*	4482	KIA: 15/8
Pte James Charles Bilsborough	2560	KIA: 15/8	Pte Leonard Johnson****	4397	DOW: 27/8
L/Cpl Frederick Anthony Bird	1839	KIA: 15/8	Pte Walter Lupton	4008	KIA: 15/8
L/Cpl Robert Corless	1249	KIA: 15/8	Cpl Frederick Victor Monks	240529	KIA: 15/8
Pte Lawrence Cottam**	1552	DOW: 25/8	Pte Samuel Myerscough	3745	KIA: 15/8
Pte Joseph Crook***	2363	KIA: 15/8	Pte George Stanley Sandall	868	DOW: 15/8
Pte Douglas M. Dawson	242993	DOW: 15/8	Pte William Shepherd	4380	DOW: 16/8
Pte Thomas Cherry Eccles	3805	KIA: 15/8	Pte Thomas Stanley	3953	KIA: 15/8
Pte Thomas Edmondson	2852	DOW: 15/8	Pte James Henry Threlfall	2933	DOW: 19/8
Pte George Frederick Fleming	1508	DOW: 15/8	Sgt Joseph Edward Towers	348	KIA: 15/8
Pte Richard Clarkson Forrest	4124	KIA: 15/8	Pte George Yates	2178	KIA: 15/8
2Lt Robert Higginson		KIA: 15/8			

*6/Cheshires.

**Believed to have been wounded on 15 August, though possibly earlier.

***Soldiers Died lists as DOW, but service record and position of original burial clearly indicate KIA.

****6/Cheshires, believed to have been wounded on 15 August, although possibly earlier.

After a couple hours of sleep, the men from the working parties were woken, and after washing and shaving, they were paraded before Gen. Jeudwine at 11 a.m. He had come to thank them for their efforts of the previous night, and although no doubt appreciated, I suspect they would have preferred a longer sleep. At 2 p.m., the Battalion marched off in a torrential downpour to billets at Méaulte via Carcaillot Farm just to the east of Méaulte, where the brigade-commander reviewed them. On 16 August, they bathed in the Ancre, probably at Vivier Mill. That day, the division came under command of XIV Corps and prepared to make their own withdrawal. All of 166 Brigade were pulled out of the line for rest and on 19 August, the Battalion entrained at Dernancourt for Martaineville, then marched to Crépy, arriving at 5.20 a.m. on 20 August. The rest of the division followed, coming under the command of X Corps on 19 August, the entire division now billeted in the Abbeville area.

Almost a year earlier, the flow of volunteers for the army had dried to a trickle and conscription under the *Military Service Acts of 1916* was now underway, though it was clear that some compelled to register were less than keen to get involved. On 19 August, the *Lancaster Guardian* printed a list of seventy-one local men who had not reported for enlistment in June and early July; it published their names, ages, and addresses in the hope that a combination of peer pressure and a promise that any information helping authorities track them down would be treated anonymously may produce results.

One of the recent replacements took the opportunity to write home to his mum, with a rather unsubtle, though obviously successful ploy to tell his family where he was:

The life is very trying, especially in the trenches. I am more than thankful of the few days' rest. We are well behind the trenches and can hear the guns, but it is nothing like hearing them when you are in the trenches. Then the noise they make when they burst is terrific. We have gone though some experiences since we came here, and some of these experiences would be very interesting to you, but the authorities here are keen on what we say, our letters being censored by our officers. When in the trenches we generally sleep in dugouts; some of them are very elaborate, but unfortunately the trenches are infested with rats, and they are often in dugouts. Great black and brown rats, more like kittens than anything else. There are also insects of every kind under the sun, and to keep clear of them is some task. I have slept in all kinds of places and sometimes think that if photos could be taken that the people at home would not think they were real. I have slept under the stars with no covering at all, in old barns, and I have made a kind of kennel with all kinds of contrivances to get comfortable. I never thought I should be able to sleep on the ground, but when you are dead tired you can sleep on the fire-step, with the rats running over you. It is very hot during the day, but at night there is often a heavy dew, and then it gets very cold.

We don't undress; I have not had my clothes off since I left England. Water is a difficult matter here. It is scarce and hard to get, and in the trenches it has to be carried a considerable distance. We make our own tea in the trenches, cook bacon etc. we have a considerable quantity of tinned stuff. It gets monotonous having the same kind of food constantly, but taking the difficulties into consideration the men do very well. It is not of course Hotel Cecil fare; tinned bully-beef being the principal item on the menu.... I am not allowed to say where we are, or where we have been, but you will be interested to know that the ___ is the regiment which took Delville Wood [regiment's name removed by censor]. We have been given permission to mention this in our correspondence.... I have seen a few of the French villages, and one has only to see them to understand what the French have gone through. They are in a terrible state.[31]

The Battalion remained at Crépy until 29 August, and although it was not possible to give many men 'Home' leave, as many as possible were given 'Local' leave, with several parties of two officers and twenty-eight men going to the seaside for three days at a time—the weather cooperating for once, being warm and sunny. One man who was not able to enjoy any leave was twenty-seven-year-old Pte Harold Salthouse, a father of two from Lytham. On 25 August, he became seriously ill with dysentery and died on 15 September at hospital in Abbeville. The 55th Division came under command of XV Corps at noon on 30 August, but by then the Battalion was already heading back to the Somme.

Late on 29 August, they marched to Béhen; the next day, they were on to Pont Remy, entraining for Mericourt, arriving at 5.15 p.m. on 30 August. The men marched to bivouacs in a field (approximately 49°59′20.31″N 2°37′13.59″E) to the south-west of Albert, with nothing to shelter them from the pouring rain, apart from a number of sheaves of corn stacked in the field. Next day—the rain having finally stopped—the Battalion moved to tented bivouacs in a field at 49°59′32.60″N 2°40′19.60″E, a weak sun slowly drying their sodden uniforms. While they had been on the move, division had received warning of a German counterattack on the Corps' front and put 166 Brigade on stand-by to assist if necessary. Orders reached the Battalion that they should be ready to move at three hours' notice, but nothing came of it and they remained where they were for several days. Considering that just ten days had been spent on working parties, or in support trenches, August's 'butcher bill' had been exorbitant—sixty-three officers and men dead and 146 wounded.

Known to have been Wounded 1 to 15 August 1916

Pte Richard Atkinson	241129	WIA	Pte Thomas Holmes	240254	WIA
Cpl Charles Austin	240339	WIA	Pte William Hornby	33279	WIA: 8/8
Pte Peter Barnes	241514	WIA: 8/8	Pte John William Howard	241661	WIA: 8/8
Sgt Samuel Bates	1301	WIA: 12/8	Pte Matthew Hughes	240699	WIA
L/Cpl Thomas Smith Bateson	2683	WIA: 11/8	L/Cpl Robinson Hughes	241508	WIA
Pte Joseph Christopher Benson	240491	WIA	L/Cpl Walter Hull	240364	WIA
Pte James Albert Bettany	240029	WIA	L/Cpl William Johnson	241602	WIA
Pte Charles Bibby	240566	WIA: 3/8	Pte Wilfred Kernick	3750	WIA
2 Lt Thomas Stapleton Blakeley		WIA: 3/8	L/Sgt John Kewley	240803	WIA
Pte Henry Hodkinson Brewer	2080	WIA	L/Sgt Oscar King	241402	WIA
Captain William Noel Briggs		WIA: 9/8	Pte Thomas William Lawrence	243464	WIA
Pte James Burrow	3146	WIA	Pte James Lingard	241569	WIA: 15/8
Pte William Cartmell	241609	WIA	2Lt William Smith Macfarlane		WIA: 13/8
Pte John L. Clayton	4152	WIA	L/Cpl James Maguire	240092	WIA: 1/8
Pte Simeon Smith Coburn	241603	WIA	Pte George Mason	241638	WIA
Pte James Corless	241468	WIA	Sgt Henry Masters	240870	WIA
Pte Thomas Relton Cowell	241623	WIA	Pte John McDermott	242497	WIA
Pte Hubert Cumberbatch	241590	WIA	Pte Henry Milne	240062	WIA: 11/8
2 Lt William Ernest Daniels		WIA: 9/8	Pte Thomas A. Mitchell	240504	WIA
Pte James Dowker*	241561	WIA	Pte Thomas Parker	240200	WIA
Pte William H. Ellis	4145	WIA	Pte George Victor Pearson	241594	WIA: 15/8
Pte Harold Fell	241384	WIA	Sgt Walter Philips	240814	WIA
Pte John Fellows	1850	WIA: 9/8	A/Cpl William Pickthall	241036	WIA
Pte William George Fisher	200820	WIA: 8/8	Cpl George Quayle	2251	WIA
Pte John William Gardner	3921	WIA	Pte Robert Ralph	241075	WIA
Pte Thomas Briscoe Gardner	241277	WIA: 3/8	Pte John James Rawcliffe	241640	WIA
Pte Moses Geddes	240271	WIA: 3/8	Pte William Rossall	3420	WIA: 15/8
2 Lt William Knight Good		WIA: 3/8	Capt. Alfred Shrigley Seward		WIA: 9/8
L/Cpl Edward Goodall	240469	WIA	Pte James Shore	241120	WIA
Pte Vernal Gorst	241598	WIA	Pte Ernest Smith	241574	WIA
Pte Thomas Gregson	241253	WIA	L/Cpl Thomas Henry Birkett Smith	241071	WIA: 3/8
Pte James Hall	240507	WIA	L/Sgt Walter Tedcastle	240144	WIA
Pte John Newman Hall	240210	WIA: 15/8	Pte Peter Thompson	241518	WIA
Pte James Hannon	3580	WIA	Pte Thomas Topping	3992	WIA
Sgt Daniel Harris	240087	WIA	Pte Albert Townson	3428	WIA
Capt. William Harriss		WIA: 14/8	Pte William Vickers	241588	WIA
Pte Albert Edgar Hartley	241533	WIA: 15/8	Pte George William Walker	241516	WIA: 4/8
Pte Joseph Harvey	240091	WIA	Pte William Wareing	241576	WIA
Pte John Henderson	241645	WIA: 3/8	Pte Herbert Warwick	2630	WIA

Pte Reginald Thomas Hesketh	240994	WIA	Pte Anthony Whalley	1351	WIA
Pte Arthur Hibbert*	2431	WIA: 1/8	Pte George Wolfendale	1766	WIA: 3/8
Pte John Hine	241616	WIA	Cpl Thomas Wright	240162	WIA
Pte Thomas Hollingshead	3822	WIA			

*Possibly with 8/King's Own

At the beginning of the month, Maj. Atkinson returned with five new subalterns.[32] Second Lieutenant Wilf Brash, one of the 'Two Hundred', was no stranger—he had been a sergeant before commissioning. The other four were fresh to the Battalion, comprising John Beatson, Charles Appleyard, Frank Avison, and David Lewis. On 1 September, the Battalion was warned that they would be taking over trenches to the north of Delville Wood on 2 September; yet although officers and senior NCOs went up to recce these trenches at 3.30 a.m. the next day, and twenty runners were despatched to 72 Brigade HQ at Pommier Redoubt near Death Valley, the move was cancelled in the afternoon. Instead, at 6 p.m., the Battalion practised consolidating trenches on the low ridge to the north-west of Sand Pit. When they returned to bivouacs at 10.30 p.m., another three new officers were waiting to join them: 2Lt Lieutenant Frank Brooke was assigned to 'B' Company; 2Lt Joseph Goodman to 'A'; and 2Lt Gilbert Lord to 'D'. On 4 September, a draft of forty-nine men arrived from Oswestry, but it was decided to leave these behind for extra training when the Battalion relieved 72 Brigade the following day. Lt Dobie was appointed 'Divisional Reinforcements Officer' and detailed to remain behind to oversee the training of the replacements. Despite months of basic training and a week to ten days at an IBD, men new to the Western Front were still very much ignorant of the tasks expected of them and the skills needed to stay alive. Consequently, whenever possible, 55 Division gave new men approximately two weeks additional training before they were integrated into their new battalions.

The move to the trenches on 5 September was phased, with 'A' and 'C' moving up at 2.30 p.m., and 'B', 'D', and HQ at 5.15 p.m. The latter group met with guides at Pommier Redoubt—over 6 miles away—then following them forwards, platoons spaced 200 yards apart. Although the majority of men were in place by the early hours, due to the difficulty communicating by runner and poor conditions in the CTs, the relief was not officially completed until 7.30 a.m. on 6 September. Another impediment to the relief had been a German barrage on Delville Wood, causing one platoon to become lost. Realising this, Sgt George Haywood took the initiative to retrace his steps and searched the Wood until he found them, then guided them to their destination.[33]

'B' occupied the left of the front line and 'A' the right. The line ran from 50°2'6.00"N 2°48'31.30"E to the junction with Cocoa Lane on the right, and although this line crossed Flers Road near its left bound, this was the responsibility of another battalion. 'C' was in immediate support and 'D' was reserve in York Trench. HQ was in an old German dugout just to the south-west of Delville Wood. Communication and fighting trenches were in dreadful condition as a result of constant rain and heavy bombardment.

Although the reputation of the mud in the Ypres Salient has resonated down through the decades, soldiers at the time reckoned that the Somme was worse—the thick clays of the region both slippery underfoot and clinging—a most unpleasant combination. The Battalion immediately set to work building new fire-steps, revetting, draining, and constructing strongpoints to be later joined together to form a connected line. The trench they worked was subsequently designated King's Walk.

Apart from a quiet period between 5 a.m. and 8 a.m., hostile artillery constantly sought them out, a pattern repeated over a number of days. Most frequently targeted were the southern areas of Delville Wood and Waterlot Farm, with 4.2 shrapnel and occasional 5.9 HE—though smaller calibre shrapnel was liberally spread across the whole area. One part more or less unmolested was the front line, so battalion casualties were very light. Early on 6 September, an order for 'A', 'B', and 'C' to carry out a series of offensive patrols against Tea Support Trench—350 yards to the Battalion's front—was issued, though this action was dependent on 7 Division successfully carrying out an action to their right. As it happened, this was cancelled later that morning as all four battalions of 166 Brigade were to carry out their own attack instead. Lt Macfarlane took a handpicked reconnaissance patrol out that night, with orders to penetrate as far as possible along the Longueval-Flers road to locate the enemy. MacFarlane managed to infiltrate 550 yards forward of the Battalion's lines, but found no one manning the enemy front line. While he was out, a single German crossed in the other direction, surrendered himself to 'A' Company, and was escorted back to Brigade.

Hostile artillery again concentrated on the southern edge of Delville Wood and Waterlot Farm for most of 7 September—the lack of shell fire against the front line leading the Battalion to the conclusion that the enemy did not actually know where the British front line was.[34] 'C' Company suffered the worst from this shelling, with the area around Company HQ targeted by medium Howitzers for around four hours in the middle of the day, resulting in part of their trench line being destroyed and one man wounded. If German artillery was not bad enough, both 'B' and 'C', on the left of the Battalion's line, complained a number of times that they were taking casualties from British shrapnel firing short. Not surprisingly, this was a source of considerable vexation, especially when the batteries concerned denied that this could possibly be happening. The proposed attack by 166 Brigade was cancelled; instead, a series of strongpoints for a new front line were to be dug and manned by Liverpool Scottish—200 yards in advance of the current line. The Battalion were set-to improving their own trenches and working to rebuild a number of CTs. The work did not go smoothly, however, and commencement was considerably delayed when the RE officer (detailed to show the men where to site the strongpoints) became a casualty on his way forward. The junior officer charge of the party, 2Lt Hall, also had to be helped back out of the line with a badly sprained ankle and was subsequently posted to the 2/5th King's Own (apart from his initial arrival with the Battalion, 2Lt Hall is not recorded in any Divisional 'A & Q' Returns; the Regimental Archives in Lancaster have no record of him and there is no MIC for a 2Lt R. Hall from the King's Own).

German fire intensified on 8 September, particularly in the early afternoon, when South Street (where the road to the south of Delville Wood runs today) and HQ came under bombardment from 5.9 HE and 4.2 shrapnel. Unfortunately, once again it was not just enemy guns causing them problems. Earlier that morning, a 60-pounder Howitzer round had dropped short and exploded in 'B' Company's trench, killing one man and burying another two. CWGC records no one from the Battalion killed on 8 September—or a day either side—however, there are another two deaths from 6/Cheshire for 8 September. Twenty-year-old Pte Herbert Hoole was originally buried just behind 'B' Company's position at 50°1′55.70″N 2°48′47.10″E. The other from the 'Unlucky Draft' was twenty-one-year-old Pte Herbert Grundy. Although it is possible that he was one of those buried by the British shell, it is likely that he was killed in a different incident—the letter of condolence being written by 'C' Company's CSM Denwood.[35] There were obviously other casualties on 8 September, although not mentioned in the diary. The service record for twenty-one-year-old Pte Arthur Seddon shows that he was severely wounded and paralysed by a shell splinter in his back on 8 September.[36] He died from these wounds on 22 September in a London Hospital. In the early hours of 9 September, the Battalion, relieved by Liverpool Scottish, returned to Montauban.

The day was spent resting, and despite a number of lachrymatory shells fired into their general area, the day went without casualties. That night, two large working parties were required to continue to improve and strengthen King's Walk. Capt. Owtram took 100 men and a group of bombers from 'A' and 'C' to work there. Capt. Harriss brought another 100 men and a bombing squad from 'B' and 'D' to the old front line to connect this to the sector on the left and dig a CT forward to King's Walk. There were no casualties during the work, but as 'D' returned through Delville Wood in the early hours of 10 September, a shell landed among the men at the rear of the column, killing six outright and wounding another two (possibly three).

Casualties in Delville Wood, 10 September 1916

Pte Thomas Angus	240413	WIA: 10/9	Pte Edward Cliff Nicholls	240713	WIA: 10/9
Cpl William Green	1254	KIA: 10/9	Pte James Rose	4141	KIA: 10/9
Sgt William Eccles Holt	1963	KIA: 10/9	Pte William Leo Shepherd*	1485	DOW: 18/9
L/Cpl Edmund Mayor	1648	KIA: 10/9	Pte James Tattersall	3979	KIA: 10/9
Pte John McGreevy	1958	KIA: 10/9			

*Shepherd's date of wounding is unknown; however, the balance of probabilities are that he was a victim of this shell.

Only Edward Nicholls returned to the Battalion, Angus was posted to 2/King's Own in Salonika after his thigh wound had healed. Another wounded around this time was Pte Patrick Carr from Skerton (also wounded in the thigh), and although the actual date of his injury is no longer on record, it was within a couple of days of this incident.

One change was the transfer of all machine-gunners. These had been detached to 166 MGC for some time, but badged under their parent regiments. In August and September 1916, they were all rebadged to the MGC, although they remained with the division. Many of these became casualties later in the war, and where it is known that they were originally in the 1/5th, I have commented on this in the narrative. One gunner who received a medical discharge was twenty-year-old Pte Charles Skeoch from Fleetwood, whose brother, Percy, was an NCO in the Battalion. The circumstances of his injury were less traumatic than most as he injured his knee playing football. He was transferred to a home-based unit of the RE, but the injury persisted and he was medically discharged.

Although most managed a few hours' sleep after their overnight exertions, the morning of 10 September was a busy one for some. Men from 166 Brigade manned a runners' relay station between Montauban and Delville Wood. One of these was twenty-two-year-old Pte Edward Osman from Fleetwood, who had impressed Capt. Milnes more than once with his devotion to duty. That day, there was constant bombardment of the general area by German artillery, but the little valley where the relay station was situated came in for a particularly heavy gas attack. In the midst of this, an urgent message needed to be taken to the next relay station and Osman was detailed to carry it. Despite the fact that he needed to cross wide areas of open ground, shells falling all around him, he carried out this task without hesitation. Capt. Milnes recommended him for a DCM, but sadly it was downgraded to a MiD by Brig.-Gen. Green-Wilkinson.[37] At 6.30 p.m. the Battalion was relieved by 10/West Kent and moved to bivouacs west of Fricourt. On 11 September, they moved just over a mile to the south-west, to a mixed encampment of tents and huts, remaining there until 16 September. The time was spent reorganising and training, though sporting and leisure activities were not forgotten. One novelty was a night showing of *Battle of The Somme* in an outside cinema. The QM remarked that most men felt that for a home audience there were too many scenes of casualties—something they did not mention in their letters home.[38] This may seem at odds to some of the extracts from letters in earlier chapters, but attitudes had changed. People back in Britain were weary of long casualty lists and the Battalion was very different to the one that had gone to war—its men now sourced from a far more diverse population. Suffering and death were no longer newsworthy, and as the war progressed, local papers carried far less detail about individuals.

For the period of 2 to 16 September, there is a discrepancy between the names of men known to be from the Battalion and killed, and the numbers battalion submitted to division. Even with the two men from 6/Cheshires added, there is still one man unaccounted for. There is an outside chance that this may be 2907 Pte Henry Dobson, who is recorded as belonging to the 1/5th by CWGC. However, *Soldiers Died*, the *Medal Roll*, and *Wadham & Crossley* (1935) all assign him to the 1/4th, and he undoubtedly served with them.[39] His date of death of 10 September is no help as the 1/4th lost other men on that date. Neither is their casualty return to division as their combined total of dead and missing is five short of the number now known to be correct.[40] It is vaguely possible that he was posted or attached to 1/5th shortly before his death.

The main Amiens–Albert road ran past their camp, and it was clear from the volume of troops and supplies constantly passing towards the front that something big was afoot. It was not until 15 September, when the battle for Flers opened—with tanks used for the first time—that men knew what was happening. At 3 p.m. on 16 September, the Battalion moved 2 miles to bivouacs to the south-west of Albert. The weather was already considerably cooler and the bivouac area far less comfortable than the huts— the only shelter provided for the Battalion in this 'do-it-yourself' camp was just seventy tarpaulin sheets. To add insult to injury, German artillery shelled them for an hour from 5.30 p.m., though without result. They were not there long; at 1 p.m. on 17 September, the Battalion marched to a position to the east of Pommier Redoubt, near to Death Valley, to await further instructions. At 11.45 p.m., they were directed to relieve 8/ Queens in King's Walk, which was completed by 2.30 a.m. Men sheltered as best they could from the steady rain that fell all day, and at 4 p.m., further orders arrived to relieve 1/9th Kings in the left sector of the new front line, forward of Flers. The line ran from 50°3′18.40″N 2°49′25.60″E to 50°3′17.40″N 2°49′40.60″E, where half of 'C' Company held one strongpoint, then south to 50°3′8.00″N 2°49′35.10″E. The right of the line and the right-hand strongpoint was manned by 'A' Company and a group of bombers, with 'B' in between them. The other half of 'C' was in a detached strongpoint forward of the line at 50°3′19.80″N 2°49′26.40″E. The left flank—where their line met the New Zealanders—was left unmanned for the moment as that trench had been almost completely destroyed by shellfire, and 'C' Company's left strongpoint covered that stretch.

As the Battalion moved up at 7.30 p.m. to relieve the Kings, a shell landed at 50°2′40.20″N 2°49′39.50″E amid HQ personnel. Thirty-four-year-old Lt-Col. Charles Anderson, the only surviving son from his family, was killed outright, as was his orderly, Pte Edmund Alderson. The day after they received the notification of his death, his parents in Hornby received a letter from him, dated 16 September, in which he told them that he was delighted with the wristwatch he'd received from his sister as a twenty-first present a few weeks earlier.[41] Also killed was twenty-two-year-old stretcher-bearer Pte Frank Brear, the MO's orderly. The MO himself was severely wounded, carried back to the dressing station, then onto a CCS at Heilly. Sadly, Capt. John Deighton died on 19 September—a carved oak cross erected on his grave by the Battalion. Three men were also wounded by this shell, though one was able to return to duty after the wound was dressed. The only man who can be positively identified from these three is twenty-four-year-old Pte William Cardwell, hit in the arm and head and transferred to the Labour Corps after leaving hospital.

Capt. Milnes temporarily took command of the Battalion while Maj. Anderson-Morshead was summoned from Transport lines. There is one other fatality on record for 18 September, although the circumstances of twenty-year-old Pte James Hampson's death are not known. It is also possible that twenty-year-old Sgt Harold Airey was another casualty from this move to the front. After his evacuation home with shellshock, he wrote to his parents from his hospital ward in Southampton:

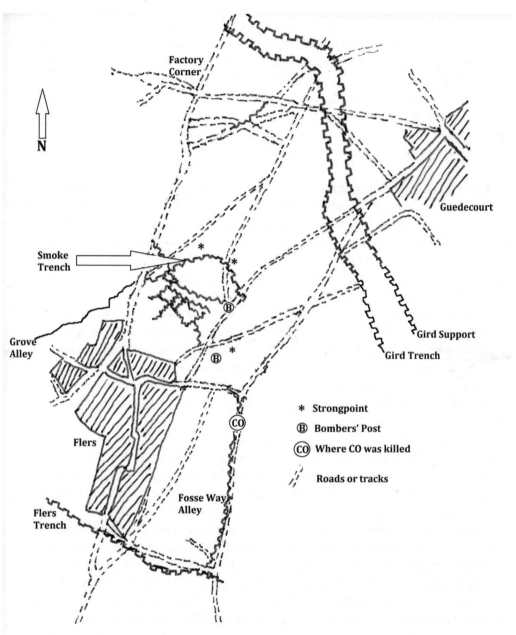

18 to 23 September 1916

I have arrived in England alright and am getting on well. I was put out on the Somme. I may tell you that I had the nearest escape to being killed that ever I had. I was buried completely by one of Fritz's heaviest, and when I managed to get out I was nearly stone deaf. We were in the open, so I crept into a shell hole and lay there for twenty-four hours. In that time, the deafness was partly gone, so I managed to get in touch with the battalion again. When we got relieved I was sent to the doctor and got my ears syringed. That is my experience on the Somme. I shall only be a week or so in hospital, and then I'll go on six weeks convalescence.[42]

Maj. Anderson-Morshead arrived at 11 a.m. on 19 September and took command. After dark, with heavy rain adding to the general unpleasantness, 'D' Company dug a new trench immediately behind the ruined one on the left flank; once completed, they manned it with half a company, permitting the other companies to spread out along the line. While this was transpiring, 'A' and 'B' constructed a series of strongpoints between those occupied by 'C' Company. The other half of 'D' started to dig a 120-yard-long CT forward from 50°3′16.40″N 2°49′25.90″E to the left strongpoint of 'C' Company, but had to adjourn when they came under artillery fire. The reference given in the diary for this trench is N.25.d.70.30; this is clearly wrong, being 350 yards to the right of the Battalion's right bound, but if changed to N.25.c.70.30, is just as described. 'C' Company were given the task of digging outwards from their two strongpoints to contact the New Zealanders on the left and 1/5th Loyals to their right, and inwards to join up with 'A' and 'B' Companies, though this latter task was ended prematurely by heavy enemy shell fire in response to an attack by the New Zealanders.

The Battalion suffered a number of wounded on the night of 19–20 September. Twenty-one-year-old Pte Ernest Wilson was buried by a shell, and although dug out, suffered a number of shrapnel wounds. He did not rejoin the Battalion, being medically discharged in November for epilepsy—that he had suffered from since 1913. Twenty-three-year-old stretcher-bearer Pte George Mawson was wounded while he was evacuating Ernest Wilson, though the flesh wound to his thigh was not too serious. He commented in a letter to his parents that he 'managed to get both [Wilson and himself] to the aid station with the help of some pals'.[43] Providentially for the wounded, the redoubtable Mawson returned. Three men were wounded on 20 September.[44] Another from the 'Unlucky Draft', Pte Harry Pownall from Stockport, was one—though by this time his transfer had been processed. On his recovery, he was posted to the 1/4th and killed with them a year later. Pte Herbert Pearson, whose brother, George, had been wounded in August, was another, though he returned to the Battalion. The third was nineteen-year-old Pte Thomas Liver, hit in the right leg and treated in one of the general hospitals in Rouen. He was posted to 8/King's Own when he left hospital and killed with them a year later.

On 20 September, a warning was passed to 55 Division that the French believed a German counterattack possible and all units were put on alert. The Battalion continued to work on the strongpoints that night, and once completed, it was named 'Smoke Trench' and deemed the main line of resistance. The old line (just behind it) became the support line and was renamed 'Flea Trench'. The same night, a reconnaissance patrol from the right-hand strongpoint crept forward and observed that the enemy—who were working near a knocked-out tank 250 yards to the front of the British line—had laid a line of white tape 400 yards to the front of the right strongpoint—a sure indicator of forthcoming attack. As maximum warning was always welcome, both 'A' and 'B' posted patrols of six men and an NCO into shell hole positions 200 yards forward of the strongpoint line—keeping them there throughout the next day. 'C' also positioned a four-man Lewis team and six riflemen near the tank, with orders to capture or kill any Germans who approached. In this heightened state of alert, artillery and MG barrages on both sides amplified greatly.

On the night of 21–22 September, work on improving the line continued right across 166 Brigade's frontage. Second Lieutenant Dobie and 100 men were detailed to work with the RE on a new trench to the right of the Ligny road—to be used as a jumping-off trench for 165 Brigade. This was to be 4½ feet deep, 3 feet wide, and about 140 yards in length, running from 50°3′19.44″N 2°49′21.72″E to 50°3′19.80″N 2°49′26.40″E. The rest of the brigade were to extend this trench further right across their front. Although it had finally stopped raining, the muddy conditions made digging difficult, with virtually every shovel load having to be scraped off. There was also much interference from enemy artillery, which shelled front and rear areas throughout the day. Around midnight, a shell landed inside one of the trenches, wounding Sgt George Campbell in the right arm and knee:

> I was hit about midnight on the 21st. We were caught in our line by a big shell. It landed clean amongst us and buried most of us. It was awful. I was glad to get out alive, as well as others. It must have killed some, but of this I'm not sure.[45]

Campbell was right to be concerned. Twenty-one-year-old Pte Harry Cragg was killed outright. James Ewan (now a CQMS), Sgt Charles Lamb, and Capt. Milnes all sent their condolences to his parents in Lancaster. He was buried near to where he fell. This was not the only letter Capt. Milnes and CQMS Ewan wrote that morning. Also killed was twenty-three-year-old Pte John Metcalfe—though initial notification undoubtedly came from his brother Herbert, who was also with the Battalion (he is erroneously commemorated by CWGC as 'Netcalfe'). Twenty-three-year-old Pte William Waterhouse from Glossop, yet another of the 'Unlucky Draft', also perished. The last of the four killed was twenty-one-year-old L/Cpl Alfred Gerrard, known as 'Harry' to his pals. When war had been declared, he was working as a clerk for Morecambe Council and had twice tried to enlist, each time failing the medical. However, he persisted and succeeded on his third attempt. Sgt Lamb was just one of those who wrote to his parents:

> Harry was killed on the night of the 21st whilst carrying out his duties. I can assure you he was a brave chap and was well respected by all who knew him, especially his section. We have missed him very much. I and two of his section buried him on the

spot where he fell. His personal belongings are being forwarded to you through the battalion. We received his parcels which were shared amongst his comrades.[46]

Gerrard had a postal order from his parents in his tunic pocket—the shell splinter that killed him cut right through it. The sharing out among comrades of the contents of parcels sent to a deceased soldier was normal practice, though this only applied to 'consumables', such as food and tobacco. Personal items were always returned to families. Though all four of these men are recorded by CWGC as being killed on 22 September, their death occurred at some time over the night of 21–22 September. Divisional records list them for 21 September—the only four ORs killed in the entire division.[47]

At least another four men were wounded. Twenty-eight-year-old Pte Thomas Bennett was hit in the arm—returning three weeks later. Also back in just over three weeks, after his hand wound healed, was L/Cpl Robert Searle. Twenty-one-year-old Pte Harold Jones—another hit in the hand—was less fortunate; he was evacuated home, transferred to the Labour Corps a year later, and shortly afterwards medically discharged. The most seriously wounded was nineteen-year-old Pte Harold Mawson. Although he was speedily evacuated to a base hospital in Étaples, he died from his head wound on 6 October. It is possible that Pte Robert Silverwood received his second wound of the war this night, though the exact date is no longer on record. He and Pte Robert Jackson from Lancaster are on the same casualty list as others known to have been wounded this day. It was not just the front line that suffered, the Flers–Longueval road also received considerable attention—so heavy that none of the ration parties were able to reach the ration dump. Sgt Haywood, unwilling to see the men go hungry, organised another party and led them to the dump by a circuitous route, bringing back the rations. For this and his work at Delville Wood earlier that month, he was awarded a MiD.[48] Promotion followed, and nine months later, he was commissioned into the KLR.

There was no let-up by either side's artillery during daytime of 22 September. That night, working parties began a second assembly trench fifty yards to the rear of the one completed the night before. On 23 September, the Battalion received notice that 1/9th King's would be relieving them that night, but before this, Capt. Owtram had one final task. As soon as it became dark enough to move out unobserved, he and a small party of men cautiously approached the knocked-out tank, which had provided cover for various enemy activities. With suitably placed explosives, he demolished the remains, leaving their front unobscured. By midnight, the Battalion was back in the bivouac area next to Pommier Redoubt, and although they were unaware, this was their last time in the front line of the Somme.

While the Battalion rested on 25 September, 165 Brigade attacked from the trenches dug by the Battalion. This was a great success, all objectives achieved with little loss—though casualties from shellfire for men of 164 and 165 Brigades in their captured trenches were greater than those lost in the attack itself. At 7 p.m. on 26 September, a working party of 100 men under 2Lt Westwater and 2 Lt Sutherland moved off to the

Flers–Longueval road, where they were guided to work on extending the light railway. This finished at 3 a.m. and they returned safely to bivouacs. Again on 27 September, another 100 men under 2Lt Robertson and 2 Lt Beatson set off at noon to work on the same railway. Throughout the day, intermittent shelling disturbed the work, men having to seek cover as shells dropped close to where they were labouring. Apart from these two working parties, their time in bivouacs had been quiet, with no artillery bothering them. Now some distance behind the lines, the QM described hillsides for miles around lit by the glow of thousands of candles in the soldiers' bivouacs. What had not been expected was that the enemy would bomb them at night, using these as an aiming mark. This nuisance became commonplace in the Salient. Fortunately, no one was hurt in the bombing, though there were casualties to some horses belonging to the Loyals.[49]

On 28 September, the Battalion was ordered to Ribemont. 'A' and 'B' drew the short straw and were billeted in barns—an unpopular option because of vermin—but the others were luckier and got huts. After twenty-four hours of non-stop rain, conditions improved at noon on 30 September when the Battalion entrained at Mericourt, arriving at Longpré-les-Corps-Saints at 8.30 p.m. The Battalion then began a long march via Pont Remy to Épagne to the south-east of Abbeville, arriving at their new billets at 2 p.m. Their time on the Somme left a feeling of dissatisfaction among officers and men.[50] They had worked hard and long (often in the appallingly difficult mud), and they had taken casualties, but had never had the chance to hit back, having instead to suffer the frustrations of being shot at with little chance to reply. Jeudwine obviously understood this as both he and Green-Wilkinson visited the Battalion more than once, thanking them for their labours under fire, losing no opportunity to stress that they thought the shovel just as important as the rifle.

2 October 1916–28 June 1917: Return to the Salient

Coordinates for Positions Named in this Chapter

'B' Camp	50°51′23.30″N 2°47′10.80″E	Kaiser Bill's Nose	50°52′6.80″N 2°55′41.50″E
Barrie Dump	50°51′41.10″N 2°47′59.10″E	'L' Camp	50°51′17.10″N 2°40′59.30″E
Beek Trench> West Lane	50°51′11.90″N 2°55′43.60″E	L2	50°52′32.56″N 2°51′9.08″E
Blakeley Crater	50°51′9.80″N 2°56′15.20″E	L4	50°51′7.90″N 2°51′45.40″E
Bliss Crater	50°51′12.90″N 2°56′9.50″E	L8	50°51′36.91″N 2°51′10.15″E
Burgomaster Farm	50°51′31.50″N 2°51′3.10″E	La Brique Post	50°52′0.50″N 2°53′48.00″E
C.21.2	50°52′41.60″N 2°54′26.40″E	Machine Gun Farm	50°51′16.80″N 2°52′6.41″E
C.22.1	50°52′22.50″N 2°54′49.90″E	Magazine, the	50°50′50.50″N 2°52′45.40″E
C/D Camp	50°52′5.90″N 2°47′12.20″E	Mill Cotts	50°51′47.30″N 2°55′23.90″E
Cambridge Road (Trench)	50°51′39.30″N 2°55′32.60″E	Mound, the	50°51′46.40″N 2°55′52.00″E
Canadian Trench	50°52′45.40″N 2°54′37.00″E	Outskirt Farm	50°51′45.50″N 2°53′23.70″E
Canal Bank	50°51′10.80″N 2°53′26.20″E	Pagoda Wood	50°51′50.60″N 2°54′56.40″E
Congreve Walk	50°51′56.60″N 2°54′31.80″E	Potijze Chateau	50°51′41.90″N 2°54′56.10″E

Cotter Crater	50°51′6.90″N 2°56′16.40″E	Prison, the	50°51′8.11″N 2°52′42.08″E
Crump Farm HQ	50°51′43.70″N 2°55′41.40″E	Prowse Farm	50°51′54.10″N 2°55′4.30″E
'D' Company dugout	50°52′3.20″N 2°55′33.40″E	Prowse Trench	50°51′46.80″N 2°55′5.30″E
Dragoon Farm	50°51′24.10″N 2°54′45.40″E	South Lane HQ	50°51′0.20″N 2°55′10.50″E
École, the	50°50′57.75″N 2°54′6.91″E	St James Trench	50°51′24.10″N 2°54′45.40″E
Elverdinghe Chateau	50°53′2.59″N 2°48′44.82″E	Stables, the	50°51′44.30″N 2°55′51.80″E
Goldfish Chateau	50°51′6.50″N 2°51′4.20″E	The Culvert	50°50′47.60″N 2°56′21.00″E
Half Moon Trench	50°51′22.00″N 2°54′47.20″E	Tower Post	50°52′25.20″N 2°54′16.80″E
Haymarket	50°51′37.30″N 2°55′27.80″E	Warwick Farm	50°51′55.80″N 2°55′34.30″E
Hedge Trench	50°50′58.80″N 2°54′51.20″E	West Lane front line	50°51′12.00″N 2°56′6.20″E
I.5.3.	50°51′30.20″N 2°55′56.10″E	Wilson Farm	50°52′6.50″N 2°53′35.20″E
I.5.9.	50°51′45.60″N 2°55′44.80″E	X4	50°51′44.70″N 2°55′7.50″E
James Crater	2°56′9.50″E 2°56′18.80″E	X5	50°51′48.90″N 2°55′3.60″E

On 2 October, the Battalion moved by train to Proven in Belgium, arriving at 4.15 p.m. They then marched the 4 miles to 'L' Camp, just over a mile to the west of Poperinghe, and on 4 October, travelled by train to Ypres where they were billeted in the Prison. For the very few still with the Battalion from its earliest days, this was a novel experience, as the railway had been so shell-damaged as to be unusable in 1915. Their area of Front was divided into two sectors (left and right) and ran from 50°52′18.40″N 2°54′43.50″E just to the west of Wieltje in the north, to 50°50′59.80″N 2°56′18.00″E some 150 yards south of No. 1 Crater. Each sector was split into left and a right sub-sectors giving four stretches of line—each manned by a single battalion. Although strongpoints, CTs, and enemy positions were given names, the front line in the Salient was labelled differently to those previously held. Short lengths of line were given a number based on their grid reference. For example, the left bound of the line was labelled C.28.10. This was because it was in 'Square C', 'Sub-square 28', and was the 10th section from the right within the square. The left sector was frequently referred to as the Potijze Sector and

the right as Railway Wood—though this was not universal, and to clarify matters, I will refer to each sub-sector by a named place central to it. Thus, the left sub-sector of the left sector becomes Wieltje; the right sub-sector as Warwick Farm; the left sub-sector of the right sector as Piccadilly; and the right sub-sector, Railway Wood.

The 166th Brigade were responsible for the left sector, and on 5 October, Lt-Col. Anderson-Morshead took company commanders forward to reconnoitre the Warwick Farm sub-sector. With an overall strength of 751 officers and men and a fighting strength of 648, the Battalion had approximately 100 men fewer than when they deployed to the Somme in July—and while this may not seem much, conditions and workload in the Salient would conspire to take a greater toll due to sickness. On 6 October, sixty men were required to work overnight on improving the drainage in the line, and the following night, a large working party went forward to Warwick Farm. Two officers and 100 men fixed U-frames in the front line; one officer and fifty men worked on The Strand, a long CT running forward from a junction with Prowse Trench to Warwick Farm itself; and another officer and thirty men worked on drainage. On 8 October, another similar-sized party continued this work. One new piece of equipment, which would prove invaluable over the coming year, was the small box respirator—a massive improvement over the smoke helmet. Prior to the working party, the men spent the day training on this new respirator.

Keeping a battalion healthy in the front line was always a struggle and a number of diseases ate away at manpower. When weather was bad and demands for labour high, men became worn out and less resistant to disease. Falling rolls due to sickness or battle casualties accelerated this process as manpower demands remained high, but there were less men to share the burden. One disease in particular that caused problems was scabies. It was not life-threatening, but on average, it hospitalised men for up to two weeks and was highly contagious. When twenty-three-year-old Pte Bernard Coyle was hospitalised with it, he was transferred to England for treatment when it became complicated by boils. He never returned to the Battalion, being transferred to 1/King's Own and killed with them in May 1917. Spread by a tiny mite, scabies lurked in dugouts and billets, and at one time or another, hospitalised 4.4 per cent of the Battalion. Divisional orders frequently carried instructions for its prevention, such as stripping canvas or sacking from bed frames and incinerating it, covering these instead with wire netting. All interior walls and roofs of lined dugouts and huts were lime-washed and men given every opportunity to bathe and have their clothes disinfected.[1]

It was not just scabies that concerned division. The spectre of dysentery had long-haunted armies in the field and massive amounts of excreta and manure conglomerated in divisional areas encouraged flies—disposal becoming a matter of priority. Regulations and practice concerning latrines was well-established and huge amounts of chloride of lime and creosol solution were issued; latrines inspected on a daily basis; and dire punishments meted out to anyone not using the proper facilities. The design of latrines was decreed to remove any gap between the hinged seat cover and the bucket below, preventing the ingress of flies. Units were ordered to collect all horse and mule dung

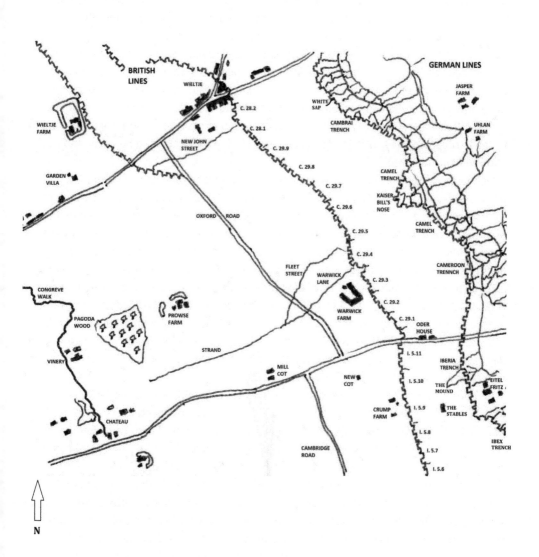

WIELTJE- LEFT SECTOR, RIGHT SUBSECTOR

into large centralised heaps—that were taken away and burned in designated areas on a daily basis for much of the year. In winter, it was collected into long rows, about 3 yards wide by 6 feet high, and buried—a fresh layer of soil being added after each addition of manure.[2] Considering the numbers of animals in a divisional area, this was no mean task, and transport officers were encouraged to induce local farmers to remove as much as possible for fertiliser. Every division appointed a sanitary officer, who in turn appointed a team of trained men, each responsible for a sub-area. These patrolled on a daily basis, reporting on any infractions, often leading to general warnings in divisional orders: 'Cases have recently been brought to notice of excreta being buried by units at their transport lines. This is to cease immediately. All excreta is to be burnt and not allowed to accumulate'.[3]

On 9 October, the Battalion was warned that they would be relieving 1/5th South Lancs on the night of 13–14 October; the following day, the CO met company commanders to discuss plans for a raid. Their target was to be a prominent position known as the Mound, projecting some 75 yards forward of the enemy's front line opposite Crump Farm. Their aims were to kill or capture any enemy present, secure identity of the enemy regiment, and capture a machine gun believed to be present in the sap head. Fifty men from 'A' Company, led by 2Lt Westwater and 2Lt Angus Dickson, would carry this out. A possible date of 15 October was selected and detailed plans for the raid passed to brigade for acceptance on 11 October. That day was spent marking out a full-scale mock-up of the Mound in a field to the north-east of the Prison, and the following day, practice trenches were dug and rehearsals begun. On the night of 12 October, 140 men took part in another large working party.

When the rest of the Battalion took over Warwick Farm sector in the late evening of 13 October, 'A' Company remained behind at the Prison, practising for the raid. With only three companies available, a company of 1/5th South Lancs remained in the reserve positions until after the raid. 'D' Company occupied the left (C.29.8 to Warwick Farm) and 'C' occupied the right of the front line (Warwick Farm to I.5.9), with 'B' in the support trenches. Two men were wounded overnight. The 14th remained quiet at the front, but there was considerable activity back at the Prison, with rehearsals in full swing. The raiders detonated a Bangalore torpedo to blow a gap in their practice wire— the first time anyone in the Battalion had used one. Evening rehearsals were watched by Jeudwine, who left satisfied that everything was ready for the night of the 15th. After Jeudwine's departure, 2Lt Westwater left for the front line, and at 9 p.m., he carried out a final reconnaissance of the Mound. Returning undetected, he reported that he had discovered an enemy listening post just to the south-east of the sap head—the very direction the raiders were planning to enter from.

Before Jeudwine's arrival, an incident in the afternoon had shocked everybody. Described in the diary as 'a most deplorable revolver accident', twenty-five-year-old Angus Dickson was killed. This phrasing suggests that the young officer was in no way responsible for his fate and that the negligence of a third party was to blame. Sadly, no details survive as to the circumstances of his tragic death as his records were later destroyed. Perhaps a hint may be found in divisional orders published shortly afterwards? These state:

> Many accidental wounds are due to the indiscriminate handling of loaded revolvers. It is difficult to issue an order defining when revolvers should, and should not be, unloaded. All ranks must use common sense in the matter, and officers must warn their servants not to clean their revolvers unless specially ordered to do so.[4]

Poor weapon handling has been mentioned earlier and was a problem that the division (and almost certainly the entire Army) never overcame. The following order was read out on a regular basis to every unit within the division, but accidents still happened:

> Before any attempt is made to clean a rifle, either outside or inside, the bolt will be first removed and then the magazine. After cleaning, the bolt will always be replaced and closed, springs eased, [trigger pressed to 'dry-fire' the rifle; though on the SMLE, if the trigger is held back when the bolt is pushed forward, this is not necessary] and safety-catch applied, before magazine is re-attached. Revolvers are not to be cleaned, either internally or externally, without first being unloaded.[5]

At 6 p.m. on 15 October, the raiders moved to Congreve Walk, where they collected their raid-specific equipment from the temporary dump. At 8.10 p.m., they left HQ and silently took up positions forward of their own wire. Each man wore a white armband to aid recognition and as pouches and other equipment were left behind, twenty rounds of .303 and two Mills bombs were carried in their pockets. All identifying badges, personal papers, and ID discs were removed before leaving billets and deposited with the company commander. They were divided into eight parties, each with their own tasks. A group of two NCOs and nine men were the first into No Man's Land. Two scouts from this party moved forward with a tape to 'Point A', about 50 yards south of the sap—80 yards from the enemy's front line. Pushing a wooden peg into the ground, they twisted tape around it, routed the tape to a point centre to the sap, and secured it to another peg. They were closely trailed by others with the electric detonating wire, which was also twisted around the pegs. Behind them, the rest of the group fetched the 13-foot-long torpedo and carefully slid it under the barbed wire, connecting it to the detonating wire. Once concluded, all eleven returned to 'Point A' to await the rest of the raiders, returning to their own lines when these arrived.

Two Lewis teams were placed in No Man's Land, each one with an NCO and two; the first team was located at 'Point A', and the second to the north of the Mound 50°51′49.90″N 2°55′50.30″E. Both teams were under orders not to fire unless there was an enemy counterattack, or if a patrol threatened the raiders. Also at 'Point A' was a stretcher-bearer—though he would only move forward if summoned. A further six bearers and four stretchers were in readiness close to I.5.9., the dressing station near HQ at Potijze Chateau on alert for casualties.

Undetected by the enemy listening post, the second party of one NCO and six men followed the tape, stopping a safe distance from the torpedo. This was detonated at 'zero hour' by a corporal from the RE in the advanced reporting centre, where Lt-Col. Anderson-Morshead, four runners, and two signallers with Fullerphones also waited. This was established in I.5.9 to relay information back to brigade as quickly as possible.

Immediately after the Bangalore blew, the 'Cutting Party' rushed to the breach in the wire—only to find that the wire was much thicker than believed. Although the torpedo had cut a clear path 18 feet long, the rest of the wire was only damaged. On the right, there was only about a yard of wire intact, but the left had nearly twice that depth. Aware timings were tight, with only ten minutes inside the sap allowed before the artillery barrage resumed to cover their retreat, they frantically began to cut the surviving strands with wire cutters. The enemy reacted very quickly and began throwing bombs almost immediately after the Bangalore detonated.

The 'Bayonet Party' of 2Lt Westwater and four men were directly behind, all five armed with a rifle and bayonet, an electric torch secured to their rifles to aid night shooting. These did their best to suppress enemy fire while the wire-cutting party attacked the wire. Westwater shot a German in the sap, but was almost immediately wounded by a grenade that landed to his right. Fragments struck him in the knee, elbow, and side, though his injuries were not life threatening and he was evacuated back to friendly lines. Behind Westwater's men, the left and right 'bombing parties'— each of one NCO and seven men—were also delayed launching their tasks by the uncut wire. The 'Right Party', led by Sgt Haywood, entered the sap and reached the junction with the main enemy trench, which they held until retirement was signalled. When he realised that the 'Left Party' had failed to cut through on their side, Haywood returned to his entry point and guided them in that way and they then bombed their way along the sap—all this time under a barrage of enemy bombs from the sap head and another nearby trench.[6] With timing critical because of the artillery and MG barrage, working to the clock rather than to events, the raiders withdrew before they were able to achieve success. For over ten minutes—after all raiders had been extracted—the enemy continued to bomb his own wire.

Apart from Westwater, four men were wounded and a further twenty suffered lacerations trying to infiltrate the wire. One of the most seriously injured, and not for the first time, was twenty-year-old L/Cpl Sidney Cartmell. With a face wound, two fingers blown off, and a compound fracture of the shinbone, he managed to crawl back under the enemy wire and reach sanctuary. The machine gun was not located; a British shell that landed in the Mound the previous night had caused a secondary explosion and the gun may have been repositioned in consequence. Once the raiders had returned, 'A' Company relieved the South Lancs in Congreve Walk.

A critique of the raid by the Corps Commander arrived at Battalion the following day. His first reproach concerned wire cutting, suggesting that a second Bangalore should have been immediately available and that alternatives had not been properly thought through. His second criticism concerned the timings, arguing that ten minutes inside the sap was far too short, and though both points had some validity, it would have needed a far larger raiding party and this raid had been deliberately planned to be a small and quick operation with limited objectives. Possibly his greatest criticism was for the time it took for information to travel from the advanced reporting centre to Brigade HQ, insisting 'information as to the result of the raid should be in this office within a very few minutes of the return of the raiders'.[7] Sometimes, it just was not possible to deliver when it came to communications. When phone wires were cut, the only way to get a message back was by runner and this was not a quick process. The enemy displayed considerable umbrage and immediately targeted the Battalion's front and rear areas with artillery, a state of affairs that continued for days.

There were other casualties that night. Another four men were wounded, and nineteen-year-old Pte John Davis from 'C' Company shot in the head while on sentry duty. He died an hour later without regaining consciousness. It was possibly a random shot, but there was considerable activity by German snipers both night and day. The 55th Division put much effort into their counter-sniping program, constructing hides for observation teams to locate their positions. Enemy snipers and artillery observers were top priority targets for the division's snipers, and by the end of the month, a number of enemy snipers had been eradicated—either by counter-sniping or by machine-gun and artillery fire called down on their observed positions. Divisional snipers accounted for thirty-one of the enemy in October, despite poor visibility preventing their activities on a number of days. Throughout the day on 16 October, mortar and 5.9 rounds fell around the Battalion's positions, and one man, thirty-five-year-old Pte John Tomlinson from Bolton, was killed in the afternoon and another wounded. That night, Capt. Harriss went on leave and 'D' Company was left in the hands of 2Lt Frank Beckett.

The 17th saw more heavy fire directed against the front line in retaliation for British heavy artillery doing likewise. Around noon, one trench mortar round landed directly on 'D' Company HQ's dugout, blowing it in. Twenty-six-year-old signaller, Pte Reuben Sumner (290)—buried once before in 1915—was killed outright. 'D' Company Signals-Sergeant Charles Lund was another casualty from this blast, wounded in the face and leg. Somewhat shaken by his premature burial, 2Lt Beckett was taken to the rear, command acceding to 2Lt James Punchard. Cpl Thomas Mountain from Fleetwood died from his wounds on 17 October, and though the date of his wounding is not known, his place of burial suggests that he was more likely one of the wounded from either 14 or 16 October, rather than from earlier that day.

The 18th began quietly enough, with just a few trench mortar rounds falling in the Battalion's area. Battalion snipers had been observing a position at 50°52'3.80"N 2°55'50.50"E, almost directly opposite from 'D' Company's HQ dugout, where there was a tree stump in the enemy front line. Although no shot had presented itself, they believed that the base of this stump had been modified and was now an observation post—a theory forwarded to Division. The quiet did not last, and at 9.50 p.m., a heavy bombardment of 5.9 and 77 mm fell across the front, causing considerable damage. Worst hit was 1/5th Loyals around Wieltje, Monmouth Trench, and New John Street—

just to the north of the Battalion—though 'D' Company on the fringes suffered, two men being wounded. As hostile machine guns kept up continuous fire during the duration of this bombardment, it was initially believed that they were preparing for a raid, though no enemy troops were observed to leave their front line. When the bombardment ended, around 10 p.m., the companies rotated, with 'A' and 'B' taking over the front line. That evening, another four new officers arrived from England, two of whom were 2Lt Ronald Macdonald and 2Lt Ronald Woodhouse. These two Ronalds would have markedly different military careers.

Further damage occurred during the day of 19 October when torrential rain initiated trench collapse, and that night, working parties from the South Lancs helped repair the destruction. Although artillery fire was much reduced due to poor visibility, another four wounded appear on the casualty return sent to Division for 18–19 October, though their names were not recorded. One was nineteen-year-old Pte James Lamb from Caton—hit in the right thigh and evacuated to No. 17 CCS at Lijssenthoek. His condition deteriorated rapidly and he died at 1.25 a.m. on 20 October. During the hours of darkness, both protagonists set to work repairing their lines. Patrols pushed out forward of the working parties reported the enemy hard at work in his front lines and wire, and much activity around the Mound—no doubt strengthening it against future raids. Although fighting patrols roamed close to enemy lines, not one German patrol was unearthed. The rain stopped by the morning of 20 October and visibility cleared. Although there was little enemy artillery, what there was seemed to be targeted against the Battalion, with 77-mm and 4.9 rounds hitting near HQ at Potijze Chateau and the left company in C.29.5. Trench mortars also targeted C.29.2 and C.29.7. Around noon, one struck 'B' Company HQ. No one was killed, but 2Lt Frank Brooke suffered crush injuries and 2Lt John Dobie a broken collarbone.

The morning of 21 October saw the first frost of the year, and although enemy artillery left the Battalion unmolested—apart from a few isolated 77-mm—three men were wounded. Numbers of enemy aircraft were active over the lines, one of which was attacked by a British fighter at 4.30 p.m. and fled back over his own lines at a very low altitude. The weather continued cold and clear on 22 October, and the Battalion suffered three wounded—presumably when Crump Farm on the right of the line was shelled by 77-mm. Enemy grenadiers in Kaiser Bill's Nose fired salvoes of rifle grenades into C.29.7 and C.29.8 between 1.30 p.m. and 3.30 p.m., but no casualties or damage followed.

The Battalion suffered one casualty on 23 October, when twenty-nine-year-old Pte George Royle, another of the 'Unlucky Draft', was wounded in the back by shrapnel. The day was generally quiet, and by 8.15 p.m., the Battalion was relieved by 1/4th King's Own and marched back to the Prison, then onwards by train to 'C' Camp to the north of Brandhoek (later renamed 'D' Camp). Time in camp was anything but a rest as large working parties were always required. At 7 a.m. on 24 October, three officers and 200 men from 'B', 'C', and 'D' Companies left to bury phone wire between Vlamertinghe and Brielen, returning around 1.30 p.m. The following day, another similar-sized party from 'A', 'C', and 'D' returned to continue this work. This pattern continued on the 27th,

28th, and 29th. While the Battalion suffered no casualties in these tasks, the work ate away at the fitness of the men and one was hospitalised on 26 October with trench foot. As this condition was now regarded as owing to negligence, the Divisional Casualty Return noted that this was 'due to not getting a fit in gum boots'.[8]

In the early years of the war, it was possible to have a rough idea of when a man was wounded by the publication date of the *casualty lists* in local newspapers—usually a week to ten days behind the actual event. However, by this time, these were neither comprehensive nor current. Lists published in late November 1916 record casualties from up to four weeks apart in the same list. The table below contains the names of men wounded sometime between 14 October and 13 November—only three of whom could be from November. The names of men appearing in the narrative have not been repeated here.

Pte Robert Airey	240280	WIA	Pte Robert Gudgeon	1361	WIA
Cpl William Arnold	241496	WIA	Pte Albert Halton*	241475	WIA
Cpl John Bakey	240043	WIA	Sgt Leonard Chase Harrison	240002	WIA
Pte Thomas Cragg	241366	WIA	Pte George Hirst	241393	WIA
Pte Robert Edmondson	240177	WIA	Pte Owen Hockey	241303	WIA
Pte Harry Ferguson	240130	WIA	Pte Matthew Hughes	240699	WIA
Pte John William Gardner	3291	DOW: 18/12	Pte Edison Riding	240352	WIA
Pte Joseph Gornall	240604	WIA	Pte Nathaniel Thornton	2531	WIA

*Albert Halton was posted to 1/King's Own upon his recovery and won the VC with them in October 1917. The King's Own Museum notes him as 'being wounded on the Somme in October 1916'. No one from the Battalion was wounded on the Somme in October 1916. Either he was a casualty from the third week of September and the casualty list is two months in arrears, or he was one of those wounded on the Salient in October 1916.

At 6.30 p.m. on 30 October, the Battalion returned to the Prison. Later that night, three officers and 100 men from 'A' and 'B' were tasked to work with the RE in Cambridge Road. The next evening, the Battalion relieved 1/4th Loyals in the same sub-sector of the front line they had occupied before. The relief went without casualties to either battalion, and their first day back in the trenches remained quiet. Although it had only been a few days since they were last in these trenches, there had been quite a lot of deterioration due to weather—the front line in particular was very wet. This was also the last full day that 2Lt Gaulter spent with the Battalion as his transfer to the RFC came through and he left for England to train as a pilot. The morning of 2 October seemed to herald a similarly quiet day, but this changed in the afternoon. Enemy artillery fired eight 10.5-cm and over forty 77-mm into Warwick Farm; and the line from C.29.5 to C.29.7 was targeted with 77-mm—the parapet blown in in four places, although fortunately without casualties. In addition to the usual trenches, an NCO and ten men from 'B' Company were sent to garrison Mill Cotts, 400 yards behind the front line. Though it may have been behind the front, this position's isolation from any CTs meant the garrison had to lay low during daylight hours, never seeing the sun while there.

There was less artillery directed at their positions on 3 November—enemy shells mainly falling either side of them. On 4 November, the Battalion were warned that 1/5th South Lancs would be relieving them that night. This battalion had a raid against the Mound planned for the following night, so British artillery was going to be carrying out a wire-cutting bombardment between 1 p.m. and 4 p.m. on the 4th. Consequently, 'C' and 'D' were pulled back from the front line, leaving just the 200-yard-long stretch in the centre between C.29.4 and C.29.3 manned. These two companies were placed in Haymarket CT for the duration, moving back into the line after the bombardment. The relief was completed by 8 p.m. and the Battalion marched back to Ypres, 'C' and 'D' returning to billets. 'A' and 'B', unfortunately, were selected for fatigue parties, marching straight through to Potijze for these before returning to Ypres. Three companies were billeted in the Prison, but 'C' were in dugouts in Canal Bank—far less satisfactory as these were damp and dirty. That night it was the turn of 'C' and 'D' to go off to Potijze for fatigues, though on 6 November, every man was required.

Transport experienced the wrong sort of bonfire on 5 November, when the transport sergeant's hut burned to the ground. Thankfully, no one was hurt, but Sgt Thomas Sanderson and Pte John Hallahan lost all their personal possessions. When many of the huts were built, the stoves had been wrongly sited by unskilled labour and the poor construction frequently led to fires. Throughout their time in the Salient, divisional orders contained frequent warnings about fire-safety:

> No stove or fireplace will be erected in any billet except in places selected and approved by an officer. The body of the stove is to be at least 18 inches from any wall made of wood or other inflammable material. The stove must always rest on bricks or sheet iron, and in the case of Canadian pattern stoves, the fire grate must be at least six inches from a wooden floor. No flue or stove pipe is to be within six inches of any woodwork throughout its full length. Flues are not to be allowed to project through, nor to be lighted near cob walls.[9]

Every hut had to have a sand bucket to extinguish fires and smoking or striking matches inside, or the lighting of open fires close to any building were banned. Any candle must be in an improvised candleholder—such as a tin full of earth or equivalent—and any lamps or candles placed near ceiling height must have a tin sheet affixed to the roof above it. Even as late as September 1917, inspections still discovered stove pipes touching wood where they passed through huts; stoves within 3 feet of walls; lack of fire buckets; and many stoves resting on wooden floors. Although no one was injured in the hut fire of 5 November, the Battalion would not be so lucky the next time.

By 9.20 p.m. on 8 November, the Battalion was back in the same sub-sector. 'B', bolstered by one of 'D' Company's Lewis teams, held the left of the line, and 'A', similarly reinforced, held the right. 'C', with a platoon from 'D', was in support in the Garden of Eden and the remainder of 'D' served as reserve in Congreve Walk. That night, men from 'A' were working on the wire in front of their right flank, when one was wounded by machine-gun fire, this section of the line then coming under fire from trench mortars. On 9 November—apart from few small shells—there was little hostile artillery. German aircraft were, however, much more active, and at various times, numbers of machines overflew the front line and Ypres. Overnight, trench mortars fell on the Strand and also between C.29.6 and C.29.3, though without damage or casualties. On 10 November, there was an early morning visit from enemy aircraft when one flew over at 8.30 a.m. and ineffectually dropped four bombs close to HQ and Haymarket. The 11th saw a number of 77-mm shells hit the line at C.29.6 and C.29.7, breaching the parapet in two places, wounding two, and killing twenty-year-old Pte Robert Seddon from Westhoughton. The Battalion was relieved by the South Lancs at 8 p.m. on 12 November, but only 'B' and 'C' returned straight to Ypres—the others held back for fatigues, although they did rejoin at midnight.

Although some men did get to rest on 13 November, most were on working parties—similarly the next day too. Though they were no longer in the front line, there was hardly anywhere in the Salient that was safe and Ypres certainly was not—about sixty 5.9 bursting around the railway and behind the Prison that afternoon. In the evening, a draft of eight officers arrived, one being Capt. Briggs, who had recovered from his wounding in August. The others, all new second lieutenants, were John Barton, Sidney Foxon, William Honey, Watlin Jones, Linden Keighley, John Stevenson, and Harold White. By 7 p.m. on 17 November, the Battalion had taken over some new positions. These were the 'L-Posts'—a series of strongpoints stretching in an arc between Ypres and Elverdinghe—garrisoned in case of a sudden enemy breakthrough: 'D' got L8; 'C' got L4, L2, and the Reserve Ration Store at L8; and HQ, 'A', and 'B' occupied billets in L6 at Elverdinghe Chateau. Although small working parties were required, most of the Battalion got a decent rest, interspersed with periods of training—particularly in bombing and the Lewis. On 22 November, 'B' took over L2 and L4, and 'A' relieved 'D', allowing these two companies rest and training. On 26 November, the Battalion marched to 'B' Camp north of Brandhoek. At 5 p.m. on 27 November, they moved by train back to Ypres, HQ and 'C' in the Prison; 'D' on the top floor of the Magazine; and 'B' on the bottom floor. 'A' Company found billets in the town. Although the Battalion was out of the line, some of their personnel attached to 166 TMB were very much involved. Under heavy fire, Cpl John Wilson dug out the Stokes rounds for his mortar, which had been buried by a near miss, receiving a MiD in recognition. One man lost to the Battalion was thirty-year-old Pte Harry Mellor. He had been wounded in the left thigh by shrapnel in September and returned after treatment, but on 2 December, was hospitalised with appendicitis. Posted to 8/King's Own on his return, he was again wounded in the thigh in September 1917 and medically discharged.

It was not until 8 p.m. on 2 December that the Battalion moved back up, occupying their usual positions. This time, 'D' were on the left of the front line, with 'C' to their right. 'A' was in Congreve Walk with one platoon in the Garden of Eden. 'B' manned X4 and X5 and one officer and twenty men were detached to Mill Cotts. Apart from some light shellfire against Warwick Farm in the afternoon, there was little enemy activity in the Battalion's sub-sector on the 3rd. Advantage was taken of this lull to carry out repairs on Haymarket during daylight hours—which did, however, hinder movement to and from the front line. Liverpool Scottish, to their left, identified a sniper's post to their front—the occupant making life difficult for their men. Rather than use one of their own snipers, they called artillery down onto his position resulting 'on a direct hit being obtained, sniper and his post disappeared'.[10] One change that 'C' Company noted was that, in response to repeated raids, the wire defences around the Mound had been noticeably thickened since their previous tour. The 4th was another comparatively quiet day, and though 'D' Company's trenches in C.29.7 and C.29.8 were targeted in the afternoon, the fire was ineffectual. Observers noted that overnight there had been changes to the Iberia Support trench, with what looked like a new machine-gun emplacement built at 50°51'48.10"N 2°56'1.00"E. A gun in this position would not only make life difficult for raiders against the Mound, but could also cause considerable inconvenience to anyone travelling up Haymarket and Duke Street as it enfiladed these approaches to the front line. There were increases in enemy artillery on 5 December, and Ypres was heavily shelled between 10 a.m. and noon. In the afternoon, 'D' Company was beleaguered again when Warwick Farm, C.29.4, and C.29.5 were hit by 77-mm— two men were wounded.

On 6 December, enemy artillery fired on the same area, this time rupturing the parapet at C.29.4 with a direct hit, though fortunately no one was hit and British artillery spent all day retaliating in kind. At intervals throughout the day, the bombers fired rifle grenades into the Mound—though a complete lack of response led to the conjecture that it was unoccupied during the day. This activity did not proceed to plan during the afternoon, when 'C' Company OC, Capt. Briggs, had a go. His grenade exploded prematurely, wounding him—the only casualty of the day. Fortunately, his wounds were minor, especially as he had only just returned after the last time, and he was back with the Battalion on 28 February. After dark, the artillery duels subsided, though there were occasional outbreaks, with both sides targeting working parties and supply runs. Visibility on 7 December was very poor, fog making it possible to walk right up to the front line in the open, and a very quiet day developed. By 7.30 p.m., the South Lancs relieved the Battalion, who returned to billets in Ypres. As expected, for many men, their time in billets was just long enough to dump their equipment before they re-tasked to working parties on the new trenches being constructed in Cambridge Road.

The Battalion remained in billets until the evening of 12 December, and when not employed on working parties—most days and evenings—the men trained. During this period, a single man was wounded on the night of 9–10 December. At 7.30 p.m. on the 12th, they relieved the South Lancs in their usual sub-sector, once again a casualty free changeover. This time, 'B' manned the left; 'A', the right; 'D' in X4 and X5; and 'C', Congreve Walk—with a platoon in the Garden of Eden. 'D' also provided an officer, a

Lewis team of three, two signallers, eight bombers, and thirteen riflemen for Mill Cotts. The Battalion had its first fatality for a month on 13 December, when twenty-nine-year-old Pte George Royle was killed—the father of three from Stockport another from the 'Unlucky Draft'. Two men were also injured, one of whom was Pte James Gardner (241), seriously wounded in the neck. A telegram from No. 2 CCS dated 14 December reported him dangerously ill, but he recovered and transferred to the Tank Corps. Unfortunately, the intelligence summary for that day is missing, so the circumstances surrounding these three casualties are unknown. There was some shelling of the front line trenches and immediate area and the divisional diary reported artillery fire directed around Garden Trench, close to the Garden of Eden. The other injured man was Lancaster father of one Pte Matthew Garth. He had just left his dugout to go on guard duty when he was hit through the neck and badly wounded. After recovering in an English hospital, he was transferred to the Labour Corps. Enemy artillery increased on 14 December, with over eighty shells landing in Ypres between 9 a.m. and 1 p.m. There were no casualties from the Battalion this day, though the dressing station was busy for other reasons, with the MO Lt William Cornwall leaving to join the Divisional Field Ambulance, his place taken temporarily by Capt. Albert Gunn. Enemy machine-gunners fired few rounds overnight, unlike the division's Vickers, which expended 14,250 rounds in barrage fire.

There was no let-up in hostile artillery fire on 15 December, though most of it was concentrated in other parts of the division's front. One man was wounded during this day, though name and circumstance are unknown. A patrol out at 8 p.m., observed an enemy working party at 50°52'5.60"N 2°55'47.60"E and immediately sent them scurrying with accurate Lewis fire. There was some puzzlement at division as to why there had been this increase in German artillery fire, unsure if was just down to an increase in their daily ammunition quota, or that their front line soldiers had been more vociferous in their complaints about increased British shelling and, consequently, demanded more retaliation. Whatever the reason, fire from both sides slackened considerably on 16 December—mainly because visibility was too poor for accurate observation of fall of shot. A number of reconnaissance patrols went out after dark all along 'A' Company's front and brought back detailed descriptions of the enemy's wire. One reported the sound of heavy coughing from a sap at 50°51'53.30"N 2°55'52.40", and while moving towards a row of shattered trees just to the north of this, were surprised to see a German jump up from these and run frantically towards his own lines. As he did so, a number of enemy flares went up and the patrol came under machine-gun fire from Cameroon Trench opposite Warwick Farm. They managed to extricate themselves and return to their own lines safely.

The 17th was another day of thick fog and zero visibility. Before sunrise, further harassment of the enemy with rifle grenades was carried out—once again, one malfunctioned, wounding 2 Lt Macdonald. Luckily for the Battalion, but very definitely not for the enemy, his injuries were minor. Two men were also slightly wounded, but all three returned to duty after their wounds were dressed—though it did give their brand-new MO, Capt. Francis Fletcher, something to do. This problem with the rifle grenades could not have filled their users with much confidence; however, reliability improved considerably and they proved invaluable in the soon-to-be-seen new infantry tactics. At this time, the division was so pushed for manpower that no men were available to come up and labour on the trenches, so work was performed by the trench garrisons themselves. There was sporadic shelling of the front line all along 'A' Company's frontage on 18 December, and twenty-three-year-old Pte Thomas Mitchell from Kendal was wounded. Although this was the first time he was actually wounded, he had already been twice buried by near misses, and when he returned to France in April, he was posted to 8/King's Own and killed with them in December 1917. The Battalion was relieved by 1/4th Loyals at 6.30 p.m. and marched back to Ypres, where they travelled by train to Vlamertinghe.

By 10.20 p.m., they were in billets in 'A' Camp. The Battalion remained there, training or providing manpower for working parties until 28 December, when they moved to billets in Ypres. Their third Christmas of the war was an improvement over their second—spent in the trenches at Loos—but still a time when families were missed more than ever. However, all were resolute to make the best of it and turkey (180 tins) and puddings were provided by the fund organised by the Mayoress of Lancaster (Capt. Briggs's mother) and other 'goodies' courtesy of the Manchester Guardian Christmas Fund. 'A' Camp had a large 'Church Army' hut, and that night, a concert was held with fifty-three acts on the programme. There was only one further casualty before the end of the year and that was 2Lt Henry Hart—either a victim of shellfire that fell around Ypres on either 30 December, or on 31 December while the men were watching a concert in the Magazine (he appears on the divisional casualty list for 31 December).[11] December had actually been a kind month for the Battalion, with one man killed, ten wounded, and three officers wounded.

The first day of the new year was dull and overcast, and men departed for the usual working parties. There was only one casualty from these—thirty two-year-old Pte Nicholas Newby from Lancaster. When he returned to France, he was posted to 2/5th King's Own. Badly wounded with them in October 1918, he died from septicaemia related to this in May 1919. By 6.35 p.m. on 2 January, the Battalion were back in their usual sub-sector: 'B' in the left front line; 'C' to the right; 'D' occupied Congreve Walk; while 'A' manned the two X-Posts and Mill Cotts. Although no concentrated fire was brought down on any single position, 'B' Company's line between C.29.7 and C.29.4 was hit by about forty 77-mm, though without casualties. After dark on 3 January, a patrol, sent out to examine the enemy front opposite these positions, found that there were fairly constant sweeps of machine-gun fire being directed across No Man's Land, hindering their approach to the enemy wire. They discovered an enemy working party labouring on the north face of Kaiser Bill's Nose and dispersed it with Lewis fire.

The 4th saw an increase in the severity of German artillery and the front line from Warwick Farm south to the Potijze Road; Haymarket, Strand, and Pagoda Wood next to HQ at Potijze Chateau, all receiving attention between 2 p.m. and 4 p.m. Despite constant enemy machine-gun fire—day and night—both front companies sent a number of night patrols out. These reported that the ground was very swampy and the enemy wire in good condition—up to 20 feet thick in places. One reconnaissance patrol reported a succession of flares fired from a sap at 50°52′2.70″N 2°55′52.50″E, and shortly afterwards, an enemy patrol of six men were seen to exit there.

There was less hostile shelling on 5 January—most of it directed behind the lines at Ypres—though Prowse Farm was lightly shelled. Once again, patrols went out into No Man's Land after dark, sheets of rain marring visibility. Just before 4.20 a.m. on 6 January, one 'D' Company patrol, consisting of 2Lt Foxon and three men, slipped out of their line at Crump Farm to take a close look at the wire around the Mound. They were within 50 yards of the position when Foxon spotted three Germans moving north across their front, close to their wire. Although not a fighting patrol, an opportunity too great to overlook presented itself, especially as the enemy appeared lost. Foxon and his men followed them, but the three suddenly changed direction and began to head straight towards the patrol. Signalling his men to lie flat, Foxon waited until the enemy were within 5 yards of himself and then jumped up ordering them in German to raise their hands, which they did. Three very frightened twenty-year-olds from 75 RIR were bundled back to the Battalion's lines, and despite them making a fearful din, continually shouting, 'Do not shoot, Comrade,' drew no fire from either side.[12] With poor visibility all day on 7 January, artillery of both sides was far less active, though Ypres was shelled with HE at seven-minute intervals throughout the afternoon and evening by a single 5.9 gun. The Battalion was relieved by the South Lancs at 7.30 p.m. and marched back to billets in Ypres. At some point during this day, one man was wounded.

On 8 January, beginning at 7.30 a.m., upsurging between 1.30 p.m. to 3.30 p.m., Ypres was very heavily shelled. Approximately 1,500 rounds struck, many landing close to the Magazine, Prison, and billets near the town square, men spending most of the day sheltering in cellars. Unfortunately, one shell hit a billet in the Magazine, wounding 2Lt Foxon, 2 Lt Stevenson, and five men. The two subalterns were not badly injured, but one of the men, twenty-year-old Pte George Evans from Ulverston, was very seriously wounded. With a compound fracture of the left thigh and seven wounds to his left hand, he was quickly evacuated along the medical chain to No. 10 CCS at Lijssenthoek. Sadly, the trauma proved too great and he died at 9 p.m. The names of the other four wounded are not recorded, though for some obscure reason, the divisional casualty return records the two officers and one man for 8 January and the other four for the 9th. It is likely that nineteen-year-old Pte Edward Carton from Dalton—who died from his wounds at Lijssenthoek on 10 January—may have been wounded then. He and Evans did their basic training together in England, so it is tempting to imagine them as pals placing themselves adjacent to each other in the billets. The 9th saw more shelling of Ypres, though of far less intensity than the previous day. These were the final casualties that month and the Battalion remained in reserve in Ypres until 13 January, when they travelled to 'C' Camp for rest. The next day, they marched to Poperinghe and travelled on by train to Bollezeele, all of 55 Division gradually relieved by 39 Division over a few days. Apart from rest, another thing the Battalion was thankful for was the arrival of 233 replacements between 10 and 17 January.

In the early hours of 14 January, a terrible fire occurred in one of the huts occupied by several senior NCOs. Due to an error, a tin of petrol had been stored in there—presumably next to the stove—this expanded, burst, and exploded after the vapour met the fire. As water was also supplied in old petrol tins, it is possible that someone believed that the tin held this and not fuel. One sleeping in there was twenty-eight-year-old Pte Richard Richardson, who wrote to his parents from his hospital bed in Boulogne:

> Excuse me for not writing sooner, but I met with an accident a few days ago. Our hut caught fire when six of us were in. I came out the best of the lot. I am not as badly burned as the others, only it has affected my eye. Tom Byrne and Matt Smith were badly burned about the face and hands, but I think we were lucky to get out alive. I think I will be all right in a few days. I have had everything burnt, all my kit, so if you can get me a razor I'll be glad, as I cannot shave myself in hospital.[13]

CSM Smith of 'B' Company and RQMS Byrne were both evacuated to Netley Hospital, Southampton. Postal-Sergeant Edward Cartmell was treated in London for burns to his wrists and forearms and badly bruised knees from falling to the floor after the explosion. The most seriously burned was RSM Barrow. He lay unconscious on the floor and was rescued by one of the Regimental Police, Pte Myles Newton—who braved the inferno to drag him out. George Barrow, blinded and with serious facial burns, was transferred to a base hospital in Boulogne on 17 January and visited by the CO the next day. He reported that, although the RSM was still in a serious condition, he was expected to pull through and was making satisfactory progress. Sadly, the father-of-one, who had been through so much with the Battalion, died in his sleep on 26 January. Newton was awarded the MSM for the rescue.

Fortunately, there were few working parties while the Battalion was at Bollezeele, and despite blizzard conditions on some days, they were able to concentrate on training. This was particularly important because of the high numbers of replacements the Battalion had received—many of these men tackling tasks, such as building a strongpoint in the face of the enemy—for the first time. As ever, inter-platoon, company, and battalion competitions were held to see who performed their military tasks the best, with everything from section attack to wiring competed for. Over several afternoons, football and cross-country competitions were held and morale-boosting activities, such as performances by the 'Divisional Pierrot Troupe' on 21 January, helped occupy the men in their down time. This all had to end sometime, and on 3 February, the Battalion moved to 'D' Camp, where 'A' and 'D' Company were billeted and Canal Bank where 'B' and 'C' were housed. One platoon from 'D' Company remained behind as one of them was diagnosed with spotted fever, so the rest were quarantined. One incomer to the Battalion was yet another familiar face. Edmund Simpson, Capt. Briggs' cousin and another of the 'Two Hundred', left the Battalion as a lance corporal after being wounded in the arm on the Frezenberg Ridge and now returned as a subaltern.

The weather was cold and frosty and working parties abounded. On 5 February, 'C' Company provided labour for the ASC, and on 6 February, 'B' Company did likewise. As the men returned to their billets in Canal Bank for dinner, a shell exploded directly over one group, killing Pte John Irving and wounding another four. The most serious of these was twenty-seven-year-old Pte Charles Glover, who died at Mendinghem on 11 February. Twenty-year-old Pte Robert Jackson was pierced by shrapnel in the chest, right arm, and left leg and evacuated home. The loan of one company per day to the ASC continued until 9 February, when the two companies in Canal Bank were relieved and joined the rest of the Battalion at 'D' Camp. In the evening of 14 February, the Battalion held a 'Reunion Concert' to mark of their second anniversary overseas and refreshments and entertainments were provided. It was business as usual the next day, and by 9 p.m., the Battalion was back in the Magazine and Prison.

On the evening of 16 February, the Battalion moved up to relieve the Black Watch in their usual trenches. 'B' manned the left of the line, 'C' the right, with 'D' in the X-Posts, and 'A' in Congreve Walk. This relief was not completed until 10.30 p.m. as the enemy shelled the road from Potijze to the front line very heavily with 77-mm and 4.2. The Battalion diary reports one officer and nine men wounded by this, and one of the Black Watch wounded. Unfortunately, the divisional casualty returns for this period show no casualties at all for the Battalion and no casualties for the entire division for the following day. However, the divisional returns do show eight men wounded on 20 February and 2Lt Linden Keighley on that week's return. Considering that this is a day the Battalion records as 'generally quiet [and] no outstanding feature happened during the day or night', it seems likely that the Battalion's casualty return was sent to division late, and thus Keighley appears on the return for the following week.[14] This still leaves one wounded man still to account for—this was possibly Pte Thomas Dainty. The twenty-year-old was attached to 166 MGC and, as such, appears on their return for the 16th. He was treated in Nottingham for a wound to his left hand, posted to 8/King's Own when he returned to France and killed with them in September 1918.

The thaw continued on 17 February, which began quietly enough. However, between 7 p.m. and 9.30 p.m., the Potijze–Verlorenhoek road was shelled from the ration dump right up to the front line—the enemy obviously targeting ration parties. Shortly after midnight, 'C' Company's trenches came in for a short, but heavy barrage lasting about twenty-five minutes. On 18 February, there was little artillery during the day, though a dozen heavy trench mortar rounds landed around 'B' Company's positions. No damage occurred, but two casualties are recorded, one of whom was twenty-seven-year-old Pte James Callon from St Helens. He was wounded by shrapnel in the chest, right shoulder, and foot and treated at No. 3 General Hospital in Boulogne, returning to the Battalion a month later. Once again, from 7 p.m. enemy artillery targeted the route from the ration dump, but failed to hit any of the carrying parties. This continued over the next three days until the Battalion was relieved in the evening of 21 February and returned to billets in the Prison. Unlike the previous occasion, this relief was completed without losses. They remained here until 23 February, then travelled by train to Proven. HQ, 'A',

'C', and a platoon from 'B' were found billets in Proven, while the remainder went to huts in 'K' Camp.

The next day, all those at Proven were sent to work on railway construction around Proven, returning to billets at 5 p.m. Sunday 25 February was declared a 'day of rest', and HQ moved to fresh billets in Proven—allowing the three platoons from 'B' to join the others. Monday morning saw a resumption of the railway work for all three Proven companies, while HQ drilled. 'D' did not escape as they were tasked to railway construction at Berques. This work continued until 1 March, though as it was well behind the lines, the work was during daylight hours, allowing men more sleep, and various entertainments were organised. One man wrote home about a concert held on the night of the 28th at 46 CCS:

> We are billeted in a very decent village a good few miles behind the lines. There are rumours that the Second Fifth are somewhere round here, but we can't get to know just where they are. If they are in our quarter of the globe they are not in a quiet place by any means [they were south-west of Armentieres]. The night before last we had a jolly fine concert. There were a few nurses there and one or two of them sang. It was the first time I have heard a lady sing since I was on leave. We expect to be in the trenches again very shortly, and who knows, we may find ourselves pushing the Boches back sooner than we expect. There's a cinema show round here tonight, but if I go I won't be able to finish this letter.[15]

Work on the railway continued on 1 March, though some men were diverted to begin work on a new aerodrome. While they were out of the line, the weather had begun to moderate and there were definite signs of spring in the air, with weak sunshine and mild temperatures making work slightly less unpleasant (until it became muddy). The thaw did have a downside though. In mid-February, Division ordered 'thaw precautions' to be observed. This meant that heavy wheeled traffic was banned from the roads on certain days and other arrangements needed to be made—changes having an adverse effect on Transport and their daily supply runs. The initial period for these precautions was extended and they were still in operation in early March. On 2 March, 'A' and 'C' were taken by train to Ypres, where they set to work improving the water supply. 'B' continued working on the new airfield. As if to make a lie of spring, 3 March began with light snowfall, but this soon ceased and the weather warmed up again.

The burden of command was handled in very different ways by different men. There are numerous instances of men refusing promotion, or NCOs reverting to the rank of private at their own request because they did not want to be separated from their old mates. The gulf between private and sergeant was wide, but not nearly as wide as that between officers and 'other ranks', and fraternisation between these ranks was absolutely frowned upon. On a one-to-one basis, this formality often vanished; indeed, many junior officers counted their servant as their friend, but whenever others were around, formality was imperative. Second Lieutenant Ronald Woodhouse broke this golden rule in a big way on 24 February, when he had more than just a few drinks with some of the sergeants. He appeared before a FGCM on 5 March, charged with 'drinking with and offering drinks to NCOs in Sergeants' Room'. He was dismissed from the service and almost immediately conscripted into the ASC as a driver (he survived the war, migrated to Canada, and became a vicar). It is somewhat disappointing that senior NCOs (who should have known better) allowed this breach to occur in the first place (although, knowing the natural cunning of the 'British SNCO', it may well have been a deliberate ploy to get rid of him). In contrast, the acting RSM, John Robinson, was lauded by a MiD on 8 March for his coolness and hard work under fire since the Battalion deployed in 1915 and for his excellent work as RSM after George Barrow's tragic accident.[16]

On the night of 5 March, 46 CCS hosted a concert and 'B' Company also provided a number of acts, which were very well-received. This was their last night on rest as they moved to billets in the École, just off the Menin Road outside Ypres. This new billet heralded a change in sector to Railway Wood, the right-sub-sector of the right sector. Here, the British trench line petered out in the south, the ground too marshy to support a trench line (the German line was continuous). Instead, a number of posts known as the Grouse Butts, and manned only at night, were all that prevented enemy incursions. In addition, patrols covered this ground throughout the hours of darkness. The line only picked up again on the Menin Road, at a position known as the Culvert, garrisoned by the neighbouring division—who also patrolled the marshy area north of the road. This sounds like a recipe for disaster, but apart from the adjutant of 1/4th King's Own, Capt. Robert Gardner, who was 'captured' in October 1916 and taken back for interrogation by a patrol from the neighbouring division, no friendly-fire incidents occurred with either of the King's Own battalions. After the episode with Capt. Gardner, the patrols nearest to the boundary frequently included either an officer of SNCO from the neighbouring battalion in a liaison role. The left bound of Railway Wood was where the trench line met the railway (now the N37), to the north of the Wood at 50°51'18.40"N 2°55'58.70"E.

Railway Wood was probably the 'hottest' stretch of the division's front, with opposing lines a mere 20 yards apart in places and almost constant mining activity, making life precarious for infantrymen above. A count on a trench map from April 1917 shows no fewer than twenty-seven craters in the sector. The first of these to be exploded in March was at 11.30 p.m. on the 1st, under German positions at 50°51'14.50"N 2°56'10.50"E and was British—later known as Buckley Crater. At 7.10 p.m. on 4 March, the enemy detonated one to the front of his line—only 25 yards to the east of British-held Crater No. 2a and of considerable concern. Immediately after it blew, British artillery began barrage fire, which unfortunately prevented 1/6th King's from immediately responding as it fell between them and their objective—some actually landed in Mud Lane, killing two men. By the time they reached the crater, the enemy had occupied and consolidated the lip nearest their position—beating off no less than three attacks by the King's over the next four hours. This crater was later named Cotter Crater.

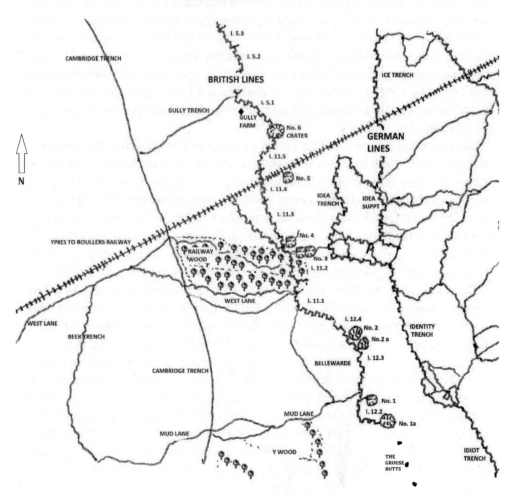

RAILWAY WOOD SECTOR

DECEMBER 1916

The Battalion relieved 1/6th King's in the front line in the evening of 7 March. 'D' held the left of the line from I.11.5 to where West Lane met the front line. 'B' supported them in Beek Trench, close to its junction with West Lane. 'A' Company, under Lt Horace Bennett, held the right from West Lane to Crater No. 2a. For half of 'A' Company, this was actually their very first time in the front line. In support of them was 'C', also in Beek Trench, close to its junction with Mud Lane and River Trench at 50°50'58.20"N 2°55'49.10"E. 'A' Company also provided men for the Grouse Butts and roving patrols, who toured the marshy area and outposts every three hours (the Battalion's diary gives I.8.2 as 'D' Company's left bound, but as this reference does not exist in this sector, it should be as mentioned earlier). Acknowledging the certainty of further mining, two consolidation parties under 2Lt Appleyard (in West Lane) and 2Lt Blakeley (in Mud Lane) were positioned close to the front line to take immediate advantage of any detonation. HQ was in South Lane, adjacent to the junction with the railway and a mere 250 yards forward from Hellfire Corner.

The relief was completed without hindrance and the Battalion settled down into the routine of learning their new home. One item of concern was a report from the OC of 177 Tunnelling Company about sounds of tamping from a German mine, leading him to surmise that an explosion was imminent under a point about 30 yards from the junction of the fire trench and Mud Lane. This must have been of serious trepidation to 'A' Company as it was right under their positions. The 8th was fairly quiet, and apart from a number of rifle grenades fired into the front line, little happened to disturb their day, which was dull and overcast—frequent snow showers reducing visibility considerably. It was exceptionally quiet on 9 March—suspiciously so according to the QM.[17] He was correct.

At 6.50 p.m., immediately after 'stand-down', Lt Bennett and 2Lt Macdonald went to examine a disused trench in the front line. They had hardly stepped off, when 25 yards away the ground heaved, rocked, and rose high in the air as a mine detonated. Although there were no casualties on the surface, it was another matter underground. This was probably a defensive mine aimed at destroying the RE's deep-mining activities, and twenty-four-year-old Sapper Sidney Firth (a married man from Leeds) was entombed by the explosion while working in Gallery 11N. He remains there still. Another two men were trapped in Gallery 11WG, but were subsequently rescued.[18] One minute later, British artillery—reacting to the sound of the explosion rather than an SOS from the Battalion—began a barrage on the previously arranged section of the German front line. Stokes and 2-inch mortars firing a 'cigar barrage' (shallow in depth, but across a wide front) between German positions and where the mine was believed to be. Unfortunately, the estimated position was over 100 metres from the actual seat of the explosion—both barrages falling in completely the wrong place.

Fortunately, the Battalion, concerned in case the enemy tried to rush Crater 2a from Cotter Crater, had placed a Lewis gun near 2a. Immediately after the dirt settled, L/Cpl Edward Nicholls opened up with this Lewis, catching the enemy as they climbed out of their trench to seize the crater. So effective was his fire (which enfiladed the enemy

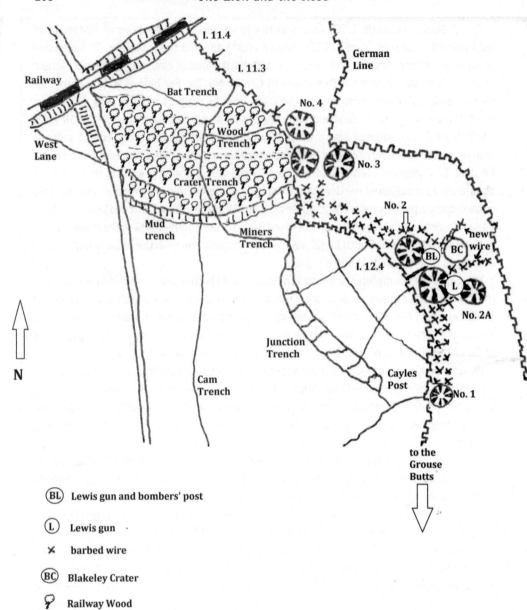

N

BL Lewis gun and bombers' post

L Lewis gun

✕ barbed wire

BC Blakeley Crater

🌳 Railway Wood

**BLAKELEY CRATER
9 MARCH 1917**

assault force) that he stopped them in their tracks. He continued to use his gun to great effect, only ceasing later that night when he was badly wounded—he earned the MM for his courage. The enemy tried to cover their assault with an intense bombardment of *Granatenwerfers*, a few heavy trench mortars, and a moderate barrage of 77-mm, which lasted for thirty minutes, targeting the front between Crater 1a and West Lane, as far back as Junction Trench. Luckily, most of the rounds landed just behind the front trenches and did not interfere much with the Battalion's operations to seize the crater.

Blakeley's consolidation party rushed from their position in Mud Lane as soon as they felt the blast, reaching their allotted position in No Man's Land six minutes later. They discovered to their dismay that the crater was nowhere to be seen—its position hidden from their view by Cotter Crater. The minute they left their lines, the enemy swept them with rifle and rifle grenade fire. One of the first to be hit was Blakeley, others from the consolidation party following in quick succession as they tried without success to locate the crater. Twenty-one-year-old Cpl Samuel Wilson was killed instantly by a rifle shot from Cotter Crater, the expression on his face still frozen into his habitual smile as his body was carried back.[19] Realising they were in the wrong place and could not actually reach the new crater from this direction, L/Sgt Thomas Huartson regrouped them and withdrew to friendly lines. Once back in the trenches, he hurriedly reorganised the survivors into groups of bombers, riflemen, wiring parties, and carrying parties, then took them further along to an exit point nearer the new crater, where he met Lt Bennett. By this time, Bennett had contacted the artillery and the barrage was now correctly targeted.

Immediately after the blast, 2Lt Macdonald returned to his fire trench and collected a motley bunch of bombers together from his own men. Leading them straight into No Man's Land, he established a bombing post to the west of the new crater at and directed their fire of No. 23 grenades onto Cotter Trench. Meanwhile, 2Lt John Beatson ordered L/Cpl Ashcroft's Lewis team forward to the near lip of the new crater, giving them a superb fire position. Crossfire from these two Lewis guns stopped every enemy attempt to advance and played a vital role in fire suppression. Twenty-seven-year-old Joseph Ashcroft from Stockport (Unlucky Draft) continued to man the Lewis despite the high rate of incoming fire, earning the MM for his courage and determination.[20]

With the reconstituted consolidation party ready at the junction of Mud Lane and the fire trench and now led by 2Lt Beatson, Bennett contacted the artillery to lift the barrage from the far lips of Craters 2 and 2a, allowing the consolidation party to exit. The new crater was 150 feet in diameter, and although it was very close to 2a, the lip was not broken by it. As soon as the barrage lifted, the various parties stormed forward, covered by the two Lewis guns and Macdonald's bombers. The enemy reacted vigorously to this and a furious exchange of fire ensued as both sides sought to gain fire supremacy—the consolidation party sandwiched in the middle as they worked. Beatson was wounded an hour later and once more Huartson, who was with the covering party, found himself in charge. Ten minutes after Beatson's wounding, 2Lt Foxon led a resupply party up to Macdonald's bombing post, each man loaded down with buckets of grenades. Unfortunately, he was hit on the way forward, becoming the third officer wounded in a little over an hour. Sgt John Kilbride took command of the carrying party, and despite the heavy rifle fire, which wounded a number of other NCOs, he led his men forward with the urgently needed ammunition. Without his determination, it is doubtful that Macdonald's bombers would have been able to hold off the enemy. Having distributed his supplies, Kilbride then took command of the left-hand wiring party, whose own NCOs had become casualties, completing the task under increasingly heavy rifle fire. These actions were recognised by the award of the MM.[21]

By necessity, two groups from the consolidation party worked nearer to enemy lines than others. The covering party were closest to the enemy and suffered numerous losses, including Huartson himself, who was wounded later on. Just to their rear, the right-hand wiring party of eight men commanded by Cpl Harold Lydiate strove to wire off the lip of the new crater about halfway along its right flank, then connect this to the existing British wire. Macdonald also ordered the construction of another bombing post at the junction between the new crater and 2a. Further back, other groups dug CTs joining the new crater to Crater 2, 2a, and the front line. The wiring party were pretty much sitting ducks while they worked—Lydiate was killed and three men wounded. L/Cpl Louis Dickinson, determined to finish the job, took command. Exposing himself constantly to enemy fire, he encouraged his men on until, by 9.50 p.m., both sides of the crater were wired and the wire extended to cover the two new bombing posts. Recommended for the DCM, this was downgraded to the MM by Division.[22] While they were working, enemy bombing parties twice attempted to annihilate the consolidators—each time thwarted by counteroffensives led by Macdonald—tireless in his efforts to protect the workers and constantly encouraging them on. For his courage and initiative, Macdonald was awarded the MC, the first of three he would earn in just thirteen months. Huartson's contribution was recognised with the DCM.[23] In an effort to help suppress enemy fire, Bennett sent an urgent message back for two additional Lewis guns to be brought forward, which was done.

Permission was gained from division to just consolidate the near lip of the crater, as any position on the far lip would actually have German positions in Cotter Crater to their rear—a decidedly unhealthy option. The crater was overlooked during daytime by the bombing post at the edge of No. 2 Crater and also by the firing line, so it was unnecessary to garrison it. Most of the Battalion's casualties came from small arms fire and *Granatenwerfers*—the high ratio of dead to wounded a consequence of the heavy sniping. One of those killed was thirty-five-year-old father of three Pte Robert Dawson. His body was found by his cousin, Pte William Dawson, who carried it back behind the lines. Other men also had bad news to pass home—among those who buried L/Cpl Stanley Lee was his brother, James. For some of the men, their first time in the lines was also their last. Father of three thirty-three-year-old Pte Edward Sighe had only joined the Battalion a month earlier. He died from his wounds at Poperinghe the next day. CSM Charles Lamb, assisted by Sgt Albert Smallshaw, had been of great help with the consolidation party after their officers had become casualties, but later that night, an exploding shell wounded him grievously, fracturing his skull. Sadly, the thirty-one-year-old died from his injures on 13 March.

Later that night, twenty-seven-year-old Intelligence Officer 2Lt Brash went out to inspect the new crater and was picked off by a sniper. The round hit him in the thigh and must have cut the femoral artery as he lost consciousness and died within minutes. His body was brought back and buried next to Lee and Wilson at Vlamertinghe. Around midnight, small arms and artillery fire petered out and the sector settled down. The cost of seizing this crater was high. Fourteen were killed or died from wounds, and a further seventeen were wounded. For some of the wounded, such as thirty-four-year-old Pte Robert Ralph (who lost his right eye), medical discharge would result. Command was delighted with the achievements of the Battalion and congratulations poured in from Division, Brigade, and Corps. On 14 March, permission was given to name the new feature Blakeley Crater in honour of Thomas Blakeley, a very rare honour.

Known Casualties at Blakeley Crater 9 March 1917

Cpl William Arnold	241496	WIA*	L/Cpl Stanley Lee	242511	KIA: 9/3
2Lt John Beatson		WIA	Pte John William Lunn	242713	KIA: 9/3
2Lt Thomas Stapleton Blakeley		WIA	L/Cpl Harold Lydiate	241488	KIA: 9/3
2Lt Wilfrid Brash		KIA: 9/3	Pte John Metcalfe	242450	KIA: 9/3
Pte Frederick Cooper	242659	KIA: 9/3	L/Cpl Edward Cliff Nicholls	240713	WIA
Pte Robert Dawson	240594	KIA: 9/3	Pte Robert Ralph	241075	WIA*
2Lt Sidney William Foxon		WIA	Pte Edward Sighe	243055	DOW: 10/3
Pte Edmund Hewitt	242635	KIA: 9/3	Sgt Cecil Smith	243085	KIA: 9/3
Pte Albert Hill	242573	KIA: 9/3	Pte Thomas Smith	242446	DOW: 10/3
Sgt Thomas Huartson	240365	WIA	Cpl Samuel Hadwen Wilson	240395	KIA: 9/3
WO2 Charles Lamb	241167	DOW: 13/3	Pte Walter Young	240422	WIA*

*Believed to be a casualty from this action.

Division carefully analysed the actions involving Cotter and Blakely Craters and drew up procedures for dealing with future events. The courage and determination of both battalions were praised, but it was believed that lives had been lost needlessly to gain just one small outpost on the edge of one crater (Macdonald's bombing post). In future—although consolidation parties would turn out as soon as they heard the explosion—they would not leave their trenches until the commander of the party was totally satisfied as to the location of the new crater. If the new crater had a lip that would allow the enemy to overlook British lines—or if it was immediately adjacent to British lines—then it was to be occupied immediately and consolidated to a pre-prepared plan. If, however, the enemy was found to already be in possession and could not be immediately dislodged with bomb and bayonet, then no further attacks were to be made until the position had been softened by artillery and trench mortars and a proper plan of attack prepared and rehearsed. The importance of thorough consolidation was emphasised, and it was stressed that work on this would continue night and day (if possible) until the new crater was fully integrated into the defences. Immediately following the detection of an explosion, the CO of the Battalion holding that sector was to immediately make his way forward to oversee operations; a staff officer was also despatched from Brigade to assist in the organisation and reporting.[24] Despite his already hectic workload, the OC of 177 Tunnelling Company, the talented and resourceful Maj. Edward M. F. Momber DSO MC, gave infantry officers a series of two-part lectures on crater consolidation. These were found to be very useful by those that attended (Maj. Momber died on 20 June 1917 from wounds received on the 18th).

Throughout 10 March—and despite the poor visibility that limited artillery exchanges—British trench mortars fired on Cotter Crater, giving the enemy no opportunity to mass there for a sally against Blakeley Crater. At 6.37 p.m. the fourth German mine of the month was detonated just south of the Menin Road, though this was just outside the Battalion's sector. Thirteen minutes later, another explosion was heard and felt when a camouflet was detonated between Crater1 and 1a. Camouflets were small charges designed to collapse the opposition's tunnels, and though no crater was formed above ground, the charge would have been enough to get the full attention of anyone in dugouts. These detonations were the cause of some grief and red faces; when new aerial photographs were taken following improved visibility the next day, three new mine craters were observed on and to the south of the Menin road. Enquiries were made—not unreasonably—as to how the enemy could explode three mines under British positions and nobody notice. These searching questions initiated by the Corps Commander were passed to down to Division, then Brigade, until finally they ended up in Capt. Milnes' hands. Each time the demands for answers were couched in terms of increasing outrage—Milnes, however, had an answer:

> A mine or camouflet was blown by the enemy. This was reported to me by the OC Right Company of the Battalion sector who said that no mine was apparent on his front. The Mining Officer informed me later that it was a camouflet blown by the enemy. No earth fell on our front. No new craters were observed next day.
>
> I received no special report from the NCO i/c of the *Grouse Butt* party on this subject, but he now states that he was visiting the posts at the time in company with the patrol officer of the Cambridgeshire Regiment on our right. Two explosions took place about the Menin Road and he thought he saw earth go up about six feet but none fell near him. He drew the attention of the officer to this and he (the officer) said it was not a mine. He did not report it to his company officer as the patrol officer said it was not a mine.
>
> I had no information to cause me to doubt the opinion expressed by the Mining Officer.[25]

The area where the mines were detonated was actually under the control of the Cambridgeshires, who manned the Culvert southwards. It can be presumed that when Milnes' report was digested by Corps and the information disseminated downwards, the patrol officer from the Cambridgeshires was summoned to a fairly uncomfortable interview with his CO (definitely no tea or biscuits).

Visibility on 11 March was considerably better and aircraft from both sides took advantage of this to update their aerial photographs. Around 11 a.m., two British Sopwith Strutters from 45 Squadron were attacked by three German fighters from Jasta 18 and shot down. One, crewed by Capt. the Hon. E. F. P. Lubbock MC. and Lt J. Thompson, crashed near the Ypres–Zonnebeke road, halfway between Ypres and Potijze. The other, crewed by 2Lt H. G. C. Bowden and 2Lt D. B. Stevenson, crashed in the moat at Ypres. All four airmen were killed.[26] At 12.30 p.m., another British observation aircraft was hit by anti-aircraft fire and force-landed in the main square of Ypres, both occupants shaken, but alive. Intelligence summaries commented on the extremely long range that one German anti-aircraft gun had—its shells actually bursting to the rear of Ypres.[27] British Ack-Ack was also active and succeeded in bringing down a German aircraft to the east of Zonnebeke.

Throughout the day, the enemy beset the Battalion's trenches with *Granatenwerfers*, particularly around Crater No. 2—also close to Junction Trench with heavy trench mortars, casualties ensuing. Thirty-five-year-old Pte Thomas Kirkman from Lytham was killed and nineteen-year-old Pte Harold Moody from Sheffield (only with the Battalion since late January) was wounded in the right thigh. He was treated in England for his wounds and allocated pre-deployment leave on 4 August, from which he promptly deserted—eventually surrendering himself on Christmas Eve 1919. He was sentenced to one year's imprisonment and then discharged, though happily, he was awarded his medals after having earned them the hard way. Another fatality was twenty-three-year-old Pte Peter Renshall, one of the few-remaining 'old guard' from 1912. His service record reports him killed on 12 March, but he was probably a casualty from the overnight *Granatenwerfer* attacks on 11–12 March. Similarly recorded was Pte Thomas Walling, with severe leg wounds. The twenty-six-year-old Lancastrian had his right leg amputated at Wimereux, but died from septicaemia on 22 March. Three men died from wounds at Lijssenthoek, and although the likelihood is that they were casualties from 11–12 March, it is possible that they were casualties from the consolidation of Blakeley Crater. Twenty-one-year-old Pte Frank Dutton perished from his wounds there on 13 March, but unfortunately, the recorded date of his wounding in his service record is water-damaged and illegible. Thirty-seven-year-old Pte Robert Waddington died on 14 March and forty-year-old Pte Ernest Boon on 18 March. The last of the known wounded from the *Granatenwerfers* was Pte John Sandham, although the thirty-one-year-old could not have been seriously injured as he was wounded again less than a week later.

The Battalion was relieved on the night of 12 March by 1/5th South Lancs, though it did not go smoothly. The Lewis team manning Blakeley Crater during the night became trapped in the mud inside the crater and it was an anxious three hours' work before they were safely extricated. Thankfully, the enemy remained unaware of their predicament and did not try to exploit it. Each company returned independently to the École once they were relieved. The Adjutant and MO remained behind until the Lewis team were rescued and did not arrive until 5.30 a.m. For most there was little rest, for as soon as they had dumped their equipment, they were tasked to carry barbed wire back up to the front line—possibly the most unpopular of all burdens. The 13th was devoted to cleaning, but working parties were still demanded. Despite heavy shelling around the Menin Gate on 15 March, those on the numerous working parties suffered no casualties. In the evening of 16 March, they relieved 1/4th King's Own in Canal Bank, and the next day, the Battalion went back to the line, this time to relieve 1/5th Loyals in the Cross Roads Farm Sector on the extreme left of the Division's flank.

The relief was completed without incident by midnight. 'B' were the left company (their left bound in C.21.2 and their HQ in Tower Post); 'C' were the right front company (their right bound at C.22.1); three platoons of 'D' were in left support, with the rest back at Wilson Farm; right support was 'A' Company; and HQ was in La Brique Post and the MO and dressing station at Outskirt Farm, 2,000 yards from the front line.

The 18th began quietly enough, with occasional shells falling in the rear area, but between 12.30 p.m. and 3 p.m., things warmed up considerably when over 300 shells were fired into Ypres; between 1 p.m. and 5 p.m., shells were fired on the Ypres-Vlamertinghe road. It was just the Battalion's misfortune that one of the sporadic shots in the morning caused three casualties, two of them fatal. Twenty-year-old Cpl John Price (later commissioned into the Battalion) wrote to the parents of twenty-one-year-old L/Cpl Robert Bowker, who was in the Orderly Room dugout when he was hit:

> He was sitting near the entrance of the dugout writing, when a small shrapnel shell burst outside. One of the bullets caught Bob in the right-hand side of the neck, severing the jugular vein. He jumped up and ran outside. When we got to him he was lying in the trench and quickly expired. He suffered no pain as far as I could see, and his face was calm when he passed away.[28]

Up until then, Bowker had not suffered so much as a scratch.

Also killed by this same shell was twenty-one-year-old Signals-Sergeant Charles Lund, who had been wounded twice previously. Badly injured, with severe shrapnel wounds to the left thigh, was Cpl Henry Bewes. The twenty-four-year-old eventually recovered and returned to duty. Overnight on 18–19 March, a reconnaissance patrol from 'B' Company went out to observe Dugouts 15 and 16 of Canadian Trench, facing the extreme left of the Battalion's bound; they managed to get to within 50 yards of the dugouts before a sentry challenged them. The patrol returned to friendly lines without loss. There was less enemy activity on 19 March, though Pte John Sandham was wounded for the second time in a week, returning to the Battalion some weeks later. Movement was spotted during daytime around Canadian Trench, and Brigade were anxious to know what was going on; therefore, on the night of 20–21 March, 'B'

Company sent out a small fighting patrol of one officer and eleven men to approach the dugouts again. The patrol ascertained that the six southernmost dugouts were manned, and although a sentry was spotted between the road and Dugout 1, there were no targets of interest and it was not worth exposing the patrol for one man, so they returned undetected.

Enemy artillery was considerably more vigorous on 21 March, no doubt due to the much clearer visibility, though mostly against the other sectors of the divisional front. The Battalion's rear areas were shelled, but no casualties resulted. Considerable traffic noise and movements were reported behind enemy lines overnight and some new aerial photographs analysed on the morning of 22 March showed three new craters behind enemy lines, all three on roads behind German support lines. Although divisional intelligence offered no immediate suggestion as to the purpose of these self-inflicted craters, with the approach of the 'campaigning season', they were probably an anti-tank obstacle for any forthcoming British offensive.

Despite signs that better weather was on the way, it snowed on 22 March. Even though the ground was white with fresh snow, the Battalion sent another patrol out to Canadian Dugouts. This time they found Dugouts 1 to 6 were occupied, the remainder empty. While there, a German patrol was observed, and they followed with the intention of ambushing it. However, the night was bright enough for the patrol to stand out clearly against the snow and they were spotted by the enemy, who hurriedly retired to their own lines. 'B' Company's patrol returned safely, but emptyhanded in the early hours of 23 March. The day dawned bright with a hard frost, and enemy artillery fell on both front and support lines, wounding two men. That night, the Battalion was relieved by 1/5th South Lancs and returned to Canal Bank. Even though there had been a considerable weight of fire directed against them, casualties in the Cross Roads Farm Sector had been light, with just two men killed and four wounded. This was the only time the Battalion manned these trenches. Between the 25th and the 27th, the usual round of cleaning, inspections, and working parties ensued, but late on 27 March, the Battalion entrained at Ypres for 'A' Camp near Vlamertinghe. They remained at 'A' Camp until the night of 6 April, and despite the weather—frequent heavy rain and snow—they trained hard. Officers and NCOs also attended a number of lectures, including one by Maj. Momber on 2 April about crater consolidation.

While the Battalion were at 'A' Camp, three new subalterns joined the Battalion. William Walker and Eric Sleight were both attached to 'A' Company, Charles Binns to 'D'. Although out of the line, men still ended up in hospital with sickness. One of them, Pte William Barnes from Dalton, had only been with the Battalion for five weeks when he was admitted to hospital with influenza. Sadly, this turned out to be spotted fever and the nineteen-year-old died at St Omer on 7 April. This subsequent diagnosis must have caused some disruption as the MO would need to isolate all those who had been in close contact with him before he reported sick. Just after midnight of 6–7 April, the Battalion were once more at the École readying themselves for a return to Railway Wood on the night of 7 April. 'B' held the left of the line with 'D' in support. 'C' held the right with

'A' in support. This time, the consolidation party in Mud Lane was commanded by Capt. Seward—the other in West Lane, under 2Lt George Honey.

Apart from some harassment by trench mortars, 8 April was fairly quiet. The Stokes batteries immediately retaliated and the exchange of fire subsided. This was repeated on 9 April, around noon and 6 p.m., but once more, the Stokes responded with a dozen rounds for every German one and the enemy batteries fell silent. The weather was still bitterly cold and frequent snow showers blotted out visibility during the day. At 12.50 p.m., a camouflet was blown just to the south of Cotter Crater, but the patrol sent out to investigate after dark found no discernible surface effects. Again, at 9 p.m. on 10 April, another camouflet was detonated in almost the same position, and although this one did break the surface, it was in the middle of the enemy's own belt of wire. The diary describes no other activities that day, but further trench mortar fire was directed against the Battalion's lines, and twenty-four-year-old Lt Sydney Scott suffered a compound fracture of the left femur. He was evacuated to Boulogne, and his parents were telegraphed that their son was dangerously ill and told to apply to the War Office for permission to visit him. His father immediately left for London, but only arrived late on the night of Friday 13th. When he called into the War Office early on Saturday morning, he was given the devastating news that his only son had died at 8.55 p.m. on the 12th.

More snow fell on 11 April, though in between the flurries, visibility remained clear. At 9 p.m., yet another underground explosion occurred when the enemy detonated a small mine in almost the same place as the two camouflets. This caused a small crater so near to the south of Cotter Crater that it almost touched the lip and was immediately occupied by the Germans. A working party went out to increase the Battalion's wire because of this new enemy position. As their covering party deployed close to enemy positions, a grenade landed amidst them, wounding 2Lt Appleyard and at least two men from the Lewis team. Appleyard was only slightly injured, but the others were seriously wounded. Twenty-four-year-old Pte John Hough died that day and twenty-seven-year-old Pte Ernest Jackson died on 12 April. Present at Jackson's funeral were his younger brother, Harold (a gunner with the RFA near Ypres), and his cousin, Pte William Thompson (878), who broke the news to the family.[29]

There was actually another fatality on 11 April, though this happened many miles to the south. Twenty-year-old 2Lt Joseph Goodman, now attached to the Loyals, was killed with them near Arras. Also far away from the Battalion was thirty-two-year-old Pte John Cartmell from Keswick. Wounded some time earlier, he was discharged as medically unfit on 14 April. His wounds continued to cause problems and he died from these on 4 June 1918—his burial in the tranquil surroundings of Crosthwaite Churchyard, amidst the green mountains of the Lake District, contrasting so vividly with the Salient that had been his undoing.

The weather warmed up on 12 April and overnight the Battalion was relieved by 1/5th South Lancs. At least one was seriously wounded by either *Granatenwerfer* or rifle grenades on 12 April, when a considerable number were fired into Railway Wood and Mud Lane in the early hours. Twenty-one-year-old Pte Peter Barnes was hit in the back by splinters, smashing a number of ribs and perforating a lung. He also suffered a broken ankle and was evacuated home. Though very seriously ill, he survived and was medically discharged in December. Nineteen-year-old Pte Sidney Hughes died from wounds at Vlamertinghe on 12 April, and although he may have been one of the wounded from the Lewis team on 11 April, it is more likely he was with Barnes when he was hit. These five days in the line had seen twelve wounded—four subsequently dying. No doubt to their great annoyance, not everyone headed back for a warm drink and clean clothes. Second Lieutenant Honey and forty men from 'A' Company were detailed to remain behind and garrison Half Moon Trench close to Dragoon Farm. However, there was a positive side to this—they missed all the working parties that plagued the remainder of the Battalion over the next few days.

Their period out of the line was casualty free, though they had a close escape on 16 April when two large shells landed very close to the École at 8 a.m. These were probably among the fifty fired at Hellfire Corner that day, a prime target and just 1,000 yards from the École. Ypres also came under an intense bombardment between 7 p.m. and 8.40 p.m. when about 400 shells struck. For newly arrived 2Lt Albert Pickstone, posted to 'B' Company, it must have been like a scene from hell. There were other changes to the Battalion's structure the next day as the men readied themselves for a return to the line. Lt Bennett resumed command of 'A' Company; Capt. Owtram, 'B'; Capt. Briggs, now back with the Battalion, assumed command of 'C'; and Capt. Harriss, 'D'. That night, 'C' and 'D' moved up to relieve two companies of 1/5th Loyals in the Wieltje Sector. Two platoons and three Lewis guns from 'D' occupied the front line and one platoon with a Lewis team occupied Cambridge Trench—the location of Company HQ. The company also established a bombing post at the junction of Haymarket and Cambridge Trench (Road). 'C' Company manned Prowse Trench, apart from two small garrisons in the Garden of Eden and Mill Cotts. The other two companies were in divisional reserve in dugouts on the Potijze Road, while Battalion HQ once again occupied their old dugout at Crump Farm, recently refurbished after a spell of abandonment.

Less than three hours after the relief had been completed, sentries reported smoke and flame from the area of Railway Wood. This had actually been a British camouflet exploded at 2.30 a.m. to disrupt German mining operations and the flames seen by the sentries were rising from Blakeley Crater. The unit in the line, sent out a patrol to check if it had broken the surface, found no new crater—though reported small secondary explosions and amounts of gas from the explosives escaping, making it a very unhealthy place. Although it was a dull and misty day, German artillery knew exactly where British positions lay, and for most of the 18th, Cambridge Trench and Warwick Farm were shelled. On 19 April, it was the turn of Haymarket and Warwick Farm to come under fire. During the night, a patrol erected a number of targets in No Man's Land, and at various times during the day, men in the front line trenches practised firing No. 23 grenades at them—much to the displeasure of the enemy, who called down 77-mm against the front line in retaliation.

The 20th was a much brighter day and a larger than usual number of enemy aircraft flew low over British lines in the early morning, something that reoccurred over several days. The improvement in the weather heralded a period of intense aerial activity, with both sides trying to update their aerial photographs and spot for artillery—opposition fighters equally determined to prevent this. Most of 55 Division's front was quiet on 20 April, apart from the Wieltje Sector—shelled for much of the day by 10.5-cm and 77-mm around Warwick Farm, Mill Cotts, and Cambridge Trench. Division believed enemy artillery was registering the support lines, but, fortunately, the Battalion escaped harm. This pattern of fire continued on 21 April, mostly with 77-mm, though ten Howitzer shells landed around Piccadilly and Cambridge Trench. It was quieter on 22 April and the Battalion rotated its companies, with 'A' relieving 'D' and 'B' Company taking over from 'C'. Between 6 a.m. and 7 a.m., a number of heavy trench mortar rounds were fired at Haymarket and Piccadilly, mostly impacting between these positions. 'B' Company moved their HQ to a dugout in St James Trench, just to the north of Haymarket, and throughout the day, there was light shelling around the Battalion's forward positions. There was also considerable hostile machine-gun fire sweeping No Man's Land during the night—the enemy concerned either about British activity or shielding work of their own.

In the early morning of 24 April, a number of heavy trench mortar rounds hit the front line, damaging the parapet in three places and apart from some intermittent shelling during the day, little out of the ordinary happened. This all changed at 10 p.m. when the Stokes mortars carried out a 'hurricane barrage' against enemy positions where the Ypres–Roulers railway ran through the Railway Wood Sub-sector at I.11.4., firing 511 rounds in just three minutes. The enemy obviously believing that this was the prelude to an attack, sent up a series of distress rockets—repeated every minute from their positions in Railway Wood, to all the way north of Wieltje. In response, their artillery commenced a full-scale bombardment by *Minenwerfers* and trench mortars against British positions along the whole of 55 Division's front and even against the division to their left. Initially, the rounds were directed to 40 yards behind the front line trenches and across the Potijze-Verlorenhoek road, but soon afterwards reduced range to bombard the middle of No Man's Land. At 10.35 p.m., British artillery began a counter-barrage against German artillery positions. Ten minutes later, an uneasy calm settled across the Front.

This enemy retaliation cost the Battalion their first casualties since 12 April. Pte John Butcher from Blackpool and twenty-four-year-old Pte Henry Webster from Askham were both killed outright—another four wounded by the barrage. The most serious of these was thirty-nine-year-old Pte John Cocker from Blackburn, with multiple shrapnel wounds to chest and thigh. He was evacuated home, but his injuries—complicated by pneumonia—led to his death on 29 May. Thirty-seven-year-old Pte James Bell from Bacup was hit in the left arm by shrapnel and treated in England, returning in August. One man in trouble for different reasons was twenty-seven-year-old Pte Albert Parkinson from Manchester, caught smoking on the Potijze Road after dark—an offence that risked both his own life and that of anyone near him, compounded by being late on parade next morning. He was deprived of fourteen days' pay for these offences, but less than two months later, he was in trouble again on a more serious charge. Two subalterns joined the Battalion on 24 April. Second Lieutenant William Metcalfe went to 'C' Company and 2Lt Chapman to 'A' Company. Former schoolmaster Harold Chapman was an ex-sergeant from the Battalion, commissioned that February.

The 25th was much quieter, though there was intermittent shelling across the front, mainly by 77-mm—Railway Wood and Wieltje receiving the lion's share. A patrol sent out after dark reported the enemy firing flares into their own front lines from their support lines—not a normal activity if the line was manned—suggesting that they possibly pulled their men back to the support line overnight. The next day, considerable aerial activity was reported, with seventeen British aircraft returning back over their positions between 7 a.m. and 7.30 a.m. Observers also reported a higher than usual movement of troops to the rear opposite Wieltje and the pattern of artillery fire suggested that there had been a relief of enemy artillery and the new unit was registering its guns.

On 27 April, the Battalion was relieved by 1/5th South Lancs and HQ, 'A', and 'B' Company went by train to 'O' Camp, 'C' and 'D' being billeted in Ypres under the command of Capt. Harriss. Five officers and 200 men from the latter were then attached to the RE as a working party, where they remained until they rotated with the others on 3 May. Those at 'O' Camp spent much of their time training, though after they moved to 'A' Camp on 2 May, 100 men were demanded for road construction the following day. While artillery fire against the front line was much reduced in the last few days of April, considerably more was directed against Ypres—an onslaught that continued into May. The Ramparts, Prison, Menin Gate, and Infantry Barracks all came in for attention from heavy artillery, but on 3 May approximately 3,000 4.2 and 5.9 shells were fired into Ypres, causing casualties at the Infantry Barracks.

The following day, another new subaltern, 2Lt Harold Parker arrived and went to 'D' Company. On 8 May, 2Lt John Mackey returned from convalescence after his wounding the previous August and was posted to 'C'. Second Lieutenant William Pinch, another of the 'Two Hundred' and a former NCO in 'B' Company, joined 'D' Company. There were precious few of the 'Two Hundred' still with the Battalion and they were becoming fewer by the month. The harsh conditions took their toll on one and CQMS James Ewan received a medical discharge for sickness in May. There were other movements in and out during this period. On 9 May a draft of thirty-nine men arrived, though at least one of the returning wounded from this batch supposedly for 1/5th was syphoned off at the IBD, as thirty-four-year-old Pte Arthur Williams from the 'Unlucky Draft', was posted to 8/King's Own and killed with them in December.

Men on working parties did not escape the dangers of war and at least two were wounded. On 7 May, twenty-six-year-old Pte James Bamber from Ulverston was evacuated home with shell shock. He had been wounded with the 1/4th in December 1915 and posted to the 1/5th in January. This time, after his recovery, he was posted to 2/King's Own in Salonika and wounded yet again with them in September 1918. On 10 May, nineteen-year-old Pte Albert Shuttleworth was injured in the arm by shrapnel and transferred to England for treatment. He returned to the Battalion in December, though had not yet escaped fate's unblinking eye. By 8 May, all four companies were reunited at 'Z' Camp near Sint-Jan-ter-Biezen.

Soon after midnight on 16–17 May, the Battalion were back at Ypres, with 'A' Company divided between Half Moon Trench, Hedge Trench and dugouts along the Menin Road, the rest of the Battalion in the École. The next night they moved up to relieve 1/5th King's in Railway Wood. 'B' Company, strengthened by a Lewis team from 'D', held the left front from I.5.3 south to West Lane. The right front was held by 'C', strengthened by two of 'A' Company's Lewis teams. Supports were in Beek Trench, with 'D' on the left and 'A' on the right. 'A' also provided patrols and garrisons for the Grouse Butts and one platoon from 'A' permanently garrisoned the dugouts inside Railway Wood. HQ and attached personnel were once again in dugouts in South Lane. Unlike previous tours of Railway Wood, there was just one crater consolidation party of twenty-seven men, led by Lt Binns, stationed centrally in West Lane closest to the area where most mining occurred. There was every indication they would be needed as mining activity on both sides had escalated—in the first two weeks of May, no less than eight mines or camouflets were fired.

On 8 May, a British mine (Vernon Crater) was blown with the joint objectives of destroying an enemy underground gallery and of gaining control of a small, new crater to the west of Cotter (New Cotter) thus preventing the enemy from mining from that crater. Initially, Maj. Momber was delighted with the result—especially when he was told that three enemy miners had been shot from loopholes in the post established to command New Cotter. Both Momber and Capt. Wilkinson RE had offered to build a short gallery to connect the post to their new crater, but were told by 165 Brigade that it was not needed.

However, on 10 May, Capt. James RE was asked to build this gallery—but by then it was too late. When James visited the bombing post near the junction of the two Cotter Craters at noon on 10 May in order to reconnoitre the site for this gallery, he was astounded to find that there were in fact no loopholes, and through a periscope, he could see a nearly completed breastwork, fashioned from sandbags and stained with wet, blue clay (only found underground). He then watched around six of the enemy knock off work and eat lunch just 40 yards away from him. This breastwork precluded any plans for the gallery. Momber rightly described the situation as 'deplorable' as it was quite clear that the enemy were mining inside New Cotter in broad daylight and this impinged greatly on the chances of success for a British deep mine planned for the end of the month, multiplying the already grievous dangers to his men due to 'absolute neglect in the surface work'.[30] Not only was there the worry that this mining activity was aimed to foil British mining plans, but as this crater was a mere 35 yards from British lines, it could be used to detonate a mine under British positions before counter-mining could be utilised.

A joint raid against Cotter Crater by 1/6th King's and 177 Tunnelling Company on 11 May resulted in two mine shafts being unearthed in New Cotter Crater and four German miners captured. Charges were placed to blow these shafts. This raid gave important new intelligence, as It turned out that Cotter itself was larger than originally believed, but much shallower and New Cotter found to be much deeper than was thought. On 12 May, 177 Tunnelling Company blew another small mine between No. 2a and Cotter, and although the lip was small, it gave a view into the enemy consolidation on the right hand side of Cotter.

Just two hours before the Battalion left the École to relieve the King's, the enemy detonated a small mine on the eastern side of Blakeley Crater, but no action followed from either side. Later that night, the Battalion sent a patrol out to investigate, finding that the mine had merely cut the lip of Blakeley Crater and made some cracks and a small depression in the earth. There are times when the Battalion diary uses the term 'camouflet' when the divisional diary uses 'mine'. A directive was issued by division on 8 May, clarifying that if an explosion breaks the surface it is to be reported as a 'mine' and otherwise as a 'camouflet'. This does not appear to have been properly complied with, so I have used the term appearing in divisional intelligence summaries as the definitive. Shortly after dawn, an enemy aircraft flew up and down the Battalion's sector at low altitude and was engaged unsuccessfully by 166 MGC's Vickers and the Battalion's own Lewis guns on anti-aircraft mountings. During the morning, enemy artillery targeted right along the forward trenches, and although no casualties remain on record for ORs, 2Lt Edmund Simpson was wounded—just three months after returning from his previous wounding. New Cotter Crater was now a priority target for the division's artillery and trench mortars, and between 1 p.m. and 2.30 p.m., they discharged fifty 6-inch Howitzer rounds. Of these, eight fell inside the crater itself; a large number hit the barrier on the south side; and several fell in the sap joining the enemy's front line to the craters—large baulks of timber hurled into the air by the blasts.[31] In the evening, a lone RFC plane made a low pass along the German line, firing a machine gun down into the trenches. That night on the left of their sector, the Battalion sent out a reconnaissance patrol, who reported the sounds of work coming from inside Bliss Crater around 11.20 p.m.

The 19th was another fine and sunny day and German artillery was active against the front line positions and Ypres to the rear. Between 8.20 a.m. and 9.20 a.m., they targeted Railway Wood with a number of medium and heavy trench mortar rounds— an action replied to by division's Stokes mortars, which also kept up an intermittent bombardment against the barrier in New Cotter. At 10.15 a.m., the enemy fired a small mine near Cotter Crater and another between Cotter and James Crater at 11 p.m. Neither brought about any further enemy activity. Soon after the second detonation, the Battalion sent out a patrol to investigate, who discovered the latter to be about 12 to 15 yards in diameter and located on the southern lip of Cotter. No work was heard coming from either location.

The 20th was also another fine day, though it was hazy in the morning. Divisional artillery carried out a shoot against James Crater with 6-inch Howitzers, Stokes, and medium mortars for twenty minutes in the morning—large amounts of timber and other materials being hurled into the air by the explosions. One German was seen to run for cover into James Crater as the first mortar rounds landed nearby—unfortunately for the foe, the first 6-inch Howitzer round followed him in. This activity obviously enraged the enemy, who retaliated against Crater Trench with three heavy mortar rounds and a number of medium mortar rounds, breaching the defences in four places. During the day, a visiting colonel from Divisional Staff found that, despite clear orders following Maj. Momber's earlier report, only one out of four posts to be continually manned was actually occupied and answers were demanded. More questions were asked when it was ascertained that during the relief the King's had not handed over the secret instructions pertaining to this. The most important position was an OP on the lip of Vernon Crater (also known as No. 12 Crater.) The orders stated:

> You are to ensure that this post is kept properly manned, a continuous observation kept on these craters from it and any of the enemy who can be seen, shot or otherwise disabled. You will so place the responsibility that any failure to carry out your orders can be definitely fixed on an individual.[32]

An extremely curt series of correspondence ensued between the GSO1 and 165 Brigade and, judging by the tone, disciplinary action probably ensued. The Staff Colonel ordered its immediate manning, also recording that it had been impossible to man the crater post overlooking No. 12 Crater and Blakeley as the trench connecting them had been destroyed in four places. He left clear orders that the damage was to be repaired, the posts manned as soon as possible, and a report sent to him immediately after this was accomplished. The afternoon of 20 May saw intense aerial activity over the skies of the Salient—though men had to be careful not to expose themselves to enemy snipers as they watched the dogfights. During the afternoon, five British aircraft were seen fighting off nine German fighters, one of the British craft being forced down well behind friendly lines. Around midnight, the Battalion rotated the companies in the line, 21 May seeing a virtual repeat of the previous day's activity, with artillery fire, trench mortar exchanges, and many aircraft duelling overhead.

The weather on 22 May was showery in the morning and early afternoon, but after this had cleared in late afternoon, German observation aircraft were in evidence over Railway Wood, directing artillery fire against the Battalion. Between 5.10 p.m. and 6.40 p.m., approximately 400 77-mm and 10.5-cm shells were fired into Cambridge Trench and the junction between Beek Trench and West Lane. Not all the rounds were on target and two were seen to fall in the enemy's positions—an incident that caused them to promptly fire off a rocket that burst into two red lights—their artillery immediately lengthening their range. Despite the volume of shellfire hitting their positions, the Battalion escaped without any casualties, only two or three wounded suffered by other units also under this onslaught.

On 23 May, British artillery and trench mortars began a fifteen-minute bombardment of the enemy positions either side of the Ypres-Roulers railway and observers from the

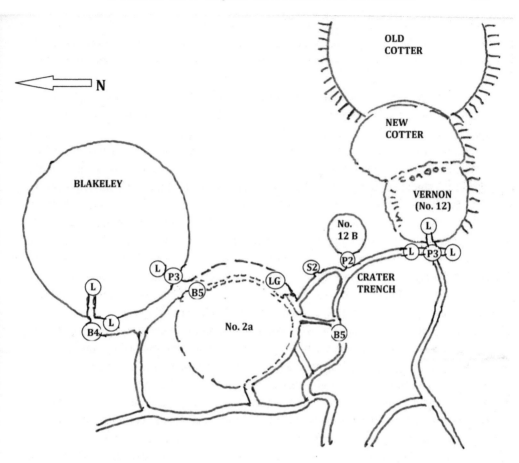

L   loophole

B4   bombing post (and number of bombers)

LG   Lewis Gun 1 NCO and 6 men

P3   post (and number of men)

S2   sniping position (and number of snipers)

CRATER DEFENCES.
Late May 1917

Battalion witnessed much wood and other materials blasted into the air as HE rounds landed inside the enemy's trenches. This time another direct hit against the barricade in Cotter Crater blew it to pieces. The enemy retaliated with their trench mortars against Railway Wood and caused some damage, though no records remain to indicate if any of the men were wounded. Both sides were still battling for air supremacy—very much a gruelling struggle for the RFC, whose fighters were inferior. The men in the trenches witnessed an enemy aircraft forced down behind his own lines and a flight of No. 6 Squadron RFC, RE-8 observation aircraft coming under anti-aircraft fire while flying at 6,000 feet behind German lines. The diary reports two of these being brought down by a single shell; however, the RFC recorded this as a mid-air collision—with Lt C. G. Brodie and Lt A. McKimmie and Capt. W. L. Clark and 2Lt H. S. Diment killed.[33] Whether this was a collision brought about by a sudden avoidance manoeuvre after the explosion of the shell, one aircraft being pushed into the other by the blast (the cause as described in the diary), or just a simple collision from aircraft in close formation to reduce the risks from fighter attack is open to conjecture. Due to divisional boundary changes, which pulled the divisional area further south, the Battalion's left bound was correspondingly moved southwards to the Ypres–Roulers railway.

One of the more unusual entries regarding enemy desertion was recorded in intelligence summaries for the early hours of 24 May, when it notes 'a dog came over into [their] lines in the morning'. Clear weather once more brought the aircraft of both sides out again in large numbers. There were also considerable 77-mm and *Granatenwerfers* directed against the Battalion's positions in West Lane, Beek Trench, and Cambridge Trench and at least one man was wounded. Nineteen-year-old Londoner Pte William Barry was hit in the right shoulder by shrapnel, but returned to the Battalion after his recovery. The division's mortars kept up a constant bombardment of Cotter and the barricade throughout the day—determined to preclude any further attempts by the enemy to recommence mining operations there. One of the men in the observation posts reported that, at 8.15 p.m., a soldier had run out from what appeared to be a shaft at the side of Cotter Crater and run to the enemy side of the Crater before he could be shot—so it was clear that there was still activity going on there. A patrol also reported that once again, there were sounds of work coming from Bliss Crater. The diary chronicles 25 May as a much quieter day, though the divisional diary records that West Lane, Cambridge Trench, and Mud Lane all came under bombardment. Later that night, the Battalion returned to the École to become the support (and 'carrying') battalion for 166 Brigade. There was a new subaltern, twenty-two-year-old Charles Gregg, waiting for them at the École. He had arrived three days earlier, but had been placed with Transport until the Battalion came out of the line and he could be assimilated into 'C' Company. Unlike most new subalterns, he had no previous service in the ranks and was given a platoon with the highly experienced William Lynch DCM as his platoon sergeant. Fate would not be kind to this platoon.

Men were able to rest during daytime on 26 May, but as soon as dark fell, working parties went forward to assist the RE in Beek Trench, while others carried supplies forward for the Loyals. Just after 3 a.m. on 27 May the enemy fired eight or nine shrapnel shells at the École, wounding a man walking down the path leading to the main entrance to the shelters. At times the billeting areas in and around Ypres were possibly more dangerous than the front line! The enemy, well aware of their locations, regularly shelled them during periods they believed that there may be movement outside of shelters. In the early morning of 25 May, the Asylum alone was on the receiving end of over 500 rounds. The following day followed similarly, though there was a 'gas alarm' passed on by the division to 55 Division's right in the early hours of the morning and the Battalion roused its men to 'stand-to'. This was relaxed when it became clear it was a false alarm. At 10.30 p.m. on 29 May, 177 Tunnelling Company detonated a large mine under both Cotter Craters, completely obliterating them—the new crater, 60-yards wide from east to west, by 75-yards north to south, was named Momber Crater. Despite his earlier misgivings due to enemy mining operations in Cotter, Momber got his blow in first. The consolidation of this new crater went extremely well with little German resistance.

Much of the activity in 55 Division's sector was formulated to take German attention away from Messines Ridge. A major attack there, aided by a series of huge mines, was planned for 7 June. It was not possible to disguise the fact that a big push was about to begin, but it was possible to mislead the enemy as to where this attack would transpire. Consequently, 55 Division were party to a number of deceptions to make the enemy believe that the attack would take place in their sector. Much use was made of scaling ladders and helmets on sticks to mislead the Germans into thinking that large numbers of attacking troops were massing and the division's artillery had been engaged in wire cutting for some time. If weather conditions were suitable, it was also planned to discharge 500 gas drums from Livens projectors on 31 May. These preparations required colossal amounts of porterage to put them into practice—most of which was supplied by any infantry not in the front line at the time. On 31 May, the Battalion were relieved at the École, and after completing their working parties, they were moved to L8 and Machine Gun Farm. HQ was established near to L8 at Burgomaster Farm. Despite their distance from Ypres, the distinct smell of lachrymatory gas was detected by men returning from the working parties, the enemy having fired this against nearby artillery positions.

A captured letter, written on 5 June by a soldier from 450 IR (opposite Wieltje) describes the effects of the British gas attack:

One morning at 4 a.m. we noticed the intensity of the bombardment and suddenly we were alarmed. We had to run about 500 metres; we loaded and fixed bayonets as we ran; we were told to throw away our spades and bayonet scabbards. Each man went to his place in the main fire trench; the communication trenches on our right and left had been destroyed by mines (? Trench mortars) [British annotation]. Nothing happened to us, but we found that there had been a gas alarm, as the front line had been bombarded by gas bombs. It was fortunate that we were not there, as one company had 90, another had 60, and a third 40 casualties, mostly gassed; one of the companies lost three Lieutenants. We had three gas alarms and the third time we put our gas masks on before we started, but we could hardly breathe while running.[34]

Throughout their time near Brielen, artillery from both sides worked to a crescendo and battery positions nearby were targeted by hostile fire, while British guns—as part of the general deception—made efforts to draw enemy attention away from the Messines Ridge. On 3 June, divisional artillery carried out a 'demonstration' shoot against German positions central to the division's front and released a smoke screen from Mud Lane right up to C.29.7, again hoping to lead the enemy to presume an attack was underway. The enemy only retaliated lightly, mostly against positions to the south of the divisional boundary and only then after the demonstration finished at 4 p.m. The few rounds fired against 55 Division's line were aimed principally at CTs. The lack of artillery against the front lines was not mirrored at the rear. Around 600 shells were fired at the Asylum; some 100 at the Prison; 500 5.9 at the Battery; and Ypres was beset by gas shells throughout the day. This concentrated shellfire caused transport details moving along the Menin Road considerable difficulties and numbers of mules and horses were killed. Hellfire Corner was not named lightly. Although none were killed during this time, a number of men were wounded. On 2 June, thirty-seven-year-old Pte William Parr was hit in the head by shrapnel and did not rejoin the Battalion until the end of August. In addition, another victim of shrapnel, twenty-eight-year-old Cpl George Ralph was evacuated home with wounds to the head and back. Upon his recovery, he transferred to the Tank Corps and was captured in April 1918. On 4 June, twenty-nine-year-old Pte Thomas Hayhurst was badly affected by a gas shell and evacuated home, later transferring to the Labour Corps.

After dark on 5 June, 'B' Company moved up to occupy billets in the Convent. 'A' remained at L8, 'C' went to billets in Dixmude Street, and HQ and 'D' to billets along the Menin Road. Once again, this was targeted by enemy artillery and Transport lost more horses—though unlike for other battalions no men were hit. The attack against the Messines Ridge began at 3.10 a.m. on 7 June with nineteen huge mines, detonated one after the other and followed up by a massive bombardment. This operation was very successful and all objectives taken. Unsurprisingly, German attention was elsewhere on 7 June and very little activity took place on the division's front.

By 10 June, enemy artillery had regained its former intensity along 55 Division's front and both front and rear areas were targeted throughout the day, leading to casualties among the working parties. One was 2Lt Chapman, wounded by shellfire as he brought a working party forward from L8. Another man badly wounded while on one of the working parties that day was thirty-eight-year-old Pte Fred Edmondson from Blackburn—hit by shrapnel in the left thigh while he was camouflaging the forward lip of a trench and evacuated to England. His injuries took some time to heal properly as a foreign body was left in the wound when it was operated upon at 12 CCS, and it was January 1919 before he eventually left hospital. Even more severely wounded was twenty-two-year-old Pte Joseph Hodson from Bolton. Hit in the arm and head by shrapnel on 11 June, he died from his wounds two days later at Mendinghem. On 12 June, 2Lt Harold White was struck in the back by shrapnel outside the Convent as he left with a working party and twenty-six-year-old Pte Reuben Nicholson (only a month with the Battalion) suffered a minor wound in the right thigh, initiating six days in hospital. Second Lieutenant White never returned, transferring to the RFC. There were changes in command too. On 9 June, Maj. John Johnstone of the Leinster Regiment arrived and took over as 2IC. Four days later, Lt-Col. Adrian Wayte of the Notts and Derby Regiment arrived to become the new CO. Lt-Col. Anderson-Morshead going to command 2/Devonshires. On 27 May 1918 at the Bois de Buttes, he died commanding the remnants of his battalion, holding off repeated attacks by an overwhelming German force—a sacrifice that delayed enemy advance long enough for the British to reorganise and hold a line across the river. The Devonshires fought to the last man.

In the evening of 14 June, some shells fell fairly close to the HQ billets. Lt Hubert Boys-Stones was lightly wounded in the shoulder, but returned to duty once it had been dressed. The chest wounds suffered by nineteen-year-old Pte James Crowther were far more serious and he died from these at Étaples two weeks later. The 15th was much quieter, though artillery fire gradually increased in intensity after noon and between 6 p.m. and 6.30 p.m., fifteen 21-cm shells landed near the Convent. After dark, three companies departed to take over the trenches from 1/9th King's, though the sub-sector bounds had changed due to divisional boundary changes ('A' Company remained at the Convent). HQ was situated in Dragoon Farm and 'C' held the left half of Cambridge Trench and the front from C.29.1 to Haymarket. To their right, 'B' manned the other half of Cambridge Trench and the front line from Haymarket south to I.5.4 opposite Oskar Farm. Second Lieutenant Binns and his platoon from 'C' occupied Mill Cotts. 'D' were in Support in St James Trench.

Relief went awry and was not completed until 3 a.m. on the 16th. One platoon from 'C' Company was caught by a salvo of shells, eliciting thirteen casualties. Platoon Commander 2 Lt Gregg and Sgt Lynch were missing—their bodies discovered next day—the wounded eventually located in the ADS at the Prison. The Battalion diary reports three killed and ten wounded from this salvo, and though most of the names of the wounded are no longer on record, the death toll turned out higher. It is not totally clear who the third fatality was. Twenty-one-year-old Pte Alfred Mitchell died from wounds on 15 June at Mendinghem and was almost certainly wounded at an earlier date. It is probable that twenty-three-year-old Pte John Garnett was the third immediate fatality—though CWGC records his death for 16 June. A local paper reports that he was killed on the night of 15 June and 'received a bullet wound which proved almost immediately fatal' (shrapnel balls were usually described as 'bullets').[35] Wounded in his head and legs, twenty-three-year-old Pte Harold Bramble died at Mendinghem two days later. Also terribly injured with wounds to both legs and an arm, twenty-one-year-old Pte Sam Holden from Accrington had his arm amputated and was evacuated home. He developed gangrene and died on 21 October. Twenty-five-year-old Pte Fred

Ashworth from Manchester was hit in the thigh and head but returned to the Battalion after treatment. Another known to have been wounded was twenty-six-year-old Pte John Davis from Millom. He was treated in Belgium and returned to the Battalion. Another likely casualty from this salvo was father of three Sgt Thomas Sanderson. The forty-three-year-old, veteran of South Africa was an extremely experienced soldier. Less than two weeks previously, he had a close escape when shrapnel knocked his helmet off, but this time a splinter struck him in the thigh. He was treated in Chichester, later returning to the Battalion and was awarded the MM at the war's end. A local paper reports his injury as due to being bombed by an enemy aircraft on 16 June.[36] However, nothing in either battalion or divisional diaries, nor divisional intelligence summaries supports any bombing around this time—though there were ground attacks with machine-gun fire. The likelihood is that he was a casualty of artillery on the night of 15–16 June.

'B' Company put one patrol out on the night of 15–16 June to check an enemy listening post—reported the previous night about half way across No Man's Land at 50°51'38.40"N 2°55'59.30"E. It was searched and found to be unoccupied and the patrol ventured along a disused trench, running from the post back to the German front line, which they then entered—finding no sign of the enemy. This was not unusual, as the foe had taken to pulling his men back to his second line of trenches at night, leaving just a few men behind. Considering 55 Division's penchant for raiding, the nervousness of these sentries—who repeatedly tossed grenades into their own wire—was quite understandable. The Battalion diary remarks that nothing of importance happened on 16 June, though the intelligence summary does paint a broader picture. Most of the division's front was strafed by machine-gun fire from low-flying aircraft and enemy artillery systematically shelled almost every part of the line, Crump Farm, and New Cot (halfway between Mill Cotts and Crump Farm) being particularly heavy shelled by 10.5-cm and 15-cm artillery between 4 a.m. and 9.30 a.m. During the afternoon, the front line and Cambridge Trench were also shelled, with 10.5 cm and lighter 77 mm. Another small reconnaissance patrol went out that night to check upon a sap opposite Crump Farm. This sap was behind the far lip of a crater about twenty-yards in diameter and although the crater itself was not manned, the patrol heard the sound of men talking inside the sap. This same patrol also reported the sound of voices from the Stables, a ruined building in No Man's Land and a frequent destination for German patrols.

The 17th saw yet more shelling of the Battalion's positions throughout the day, and apart from constant aerial activity, the enemy raised four balloons to the Battalion's front, no doubt spotting the fall of shot. What was thought to be an 11-inch gun registered Dragoon Farm, but fortunately no direct hits were scored as a shell this heavy would devastate even the deeper dugouts. The men in Cambridge Trench and Haymarket were less fortunate, hit by 77 mm and 4.2. The diary reports three men wounded from 'D' and one man killed from 'B', with five men and 2Lt Barton also wounded. Records show this report to be optimistic. Nineteen-year-old John Barton was hit in the armpit by shrapnel from a 77 mm and evacuated to a Manchester hospital for treatment.[37] Thirty-five-year-old Pte Samuel Horrocks from Bolton was killed outright, as was thirty-four-year-old Pte Harry Grimshaw from Blackburn. Thirty-two-year-old Pte Ernest Bailey from Bristol was badly hit in the left thigh and died at the Aid Post. Among the wounded was widower Pte James Butterworth from Shaw, who was hit in the neck—though the thirty-year-old professional musician did return. Wounded for the second time was 'B' Company's Pte James Churchouse. Three weeks later, he returned and was promoted to L/Cpl Gravely wounded was 'D' Company Lewis gunner twenty-year-old Pte Cyril Whitehead, another of the talented musicians in the Battalion, though with multiple shrapnel wounds there was little hope and he passed away in No. 3 Canadian CCS at Lijssenthoek on 22 June. Two of his brothers, Reginald and Wilfred, also served in the Battalion, but, sadly, only one would return home. The last known casualty was thirty-six-year-old Pte Benjamin Lamb. He was treated in England for a serious thigh wound and posted to the 1/4th upon his recovery. Despite all this activity, Pte Albert Parkinson was in trouble yet again for risking death and injury to his comrades. When Sgt Kilbride did his rounds of the sentries, he found Parkinson resting on the fire-step when he should have been watching their front and placed him under arrest. He was sentenced to fourteen days' field punishment No. 2 on 22 June—a punishment that considering his record, was remarkably lenient.

Although artillery from both sides were active during the morning of 18 June, this slackened considerable in the afternoon, when a violent thunderstorm rent the skies and torrential rain turned the Salient into a sea of mud. The intelligence summary for the day noted that around 4 p.m. that some German shells began falling short, suggesting that this was due to the change in atmospheric conditions. Although the Battalion diary states that the afternoon was considerably quieter, division recorded that between 2 p.m. and 5 p.m. Cambridge Trench, Half Moon Trench, and St James Trench all came under fire from 77 mm, 4.2, and 5.9. This time, the Battalion escaped without any further casualties. After dark, 'A' Company moved up from the Convent to the Potijze Road, two platoons occupying dugouts and the Potijze strongpoint, another taking over the garrisoning of Mill Cotts from 'C'.

On 19 June, enemy artillery once again shelled the Battalion, with Cambridge Trench and Haymarket receiving most attention. Unluckily for 'C' Company, one 4.2 killed three men in Cambridge Trench. Nineteen-year-old L/Cpl Samuel Hacking and twenty-three-year-old stretcher-bearer Pte Arthur Airey were both killed instantly. Airey's parents had already lost one son to illness in Egypt and another—a lieutenant in the AIF—wounded. Lewis gunner twenty-one-year-old Pte James Lofthouse died on a stretcher on the way to the Aid Post. Though *Soldiers Died* allocates him to 2/5th King's Own, this is incorrect, the letter of condolence written by Lt Bennett.[38] 'D' also lost a man to the shellfire. Twenty-four-year-old Pte Robert Lang from Paisley suffered a compound fracture of the femur and was evacuated to 2 Canadian CCS at Lijssenthoek, where he died on 22 June.

The Battalion began to be relieved by the HLI at 12.45 a.m. on 21 June, completing by 2.45 a.m. (the Battalion diary states 2.45 p.m., but the brigade diary correctly reports this as a.m.). They arrived at Query Camp—a tented facility—at 5.30 a.m. After breakfast, the day was spent resting and cleaning up and by instalments, bathing at Poperinghe. During the night of 22 June, the whole of 'A' Company was detailed to carry ammunition to Barrie Dump. On 23 June, the entire battalion was on working parties, either building gun positions or light railway lines. Some of these men were sent back at midday when no guides turned up to meet them, but the whole of 'A' Company was once more required for a night-time working party. There was no let-up in their labours on 24 June as the diary records. Five parties of eight officers and forty men reported to Goldfish Chateau; another 150 were tasked for clearing ground for a new ammunition dump just to the north of the Poperinghe–Vlamertinghe Road at 50°51'22.70"N 2°46'24.50"E. 'A' Company returned overnight to work on Barrie Dump. Although no information was disseminated to ORs, it must have been obvious that something was in the air. It certainly was to the enemy, who were exhibiting increasing nervousness and carrying out determined efforts to spot troop movements by low-level aerial reconnaissance and artillery strikes against rear areas. Senior officers in the Battalion knew the details as at various times during the week, the CO, 2IC and company commanders all went forward to reconnoitre the Wieltje Sector with, as the diary commented, 'a view to future events'. No record survives to show if the Battalion suffered any casualties during these working parties, but given their location, it is probable that they did not. Working parties continued until the morning of 28 June, when the Battalion left Query Camp at 8 a.m. for the station at Poperinghe, then on for St Omer, arriving at 2.45 p.m., marching to billets in Setques. That evening, the sound of guns was replaced by a tremendous thunderstorm—a prelude of what was to come.

29 June 1917–24 September 1917: The Third Battle of Ypres

Coordinates for Positions Named in this Chapter

Bilge Trench	50°52′10.00″N 2°54′54.60″E	Pommern Castle	50°52′39.70″N 2°57′5.60″E
Bossaert Farm	50°52′40.40″N 2°55′46.10″E	Pond Farm	50°53′6.70″N 2°56′47.20″E
Brigade Forward Station	50°52′13.80″N 2°55′39.60″E	Pond Galleries	50°53′8.00″N 2°56′50.50″E
Cambrai Trench HQ	50°52′17.20″N 2°55′30.20″E	Rat Farm	50°52′39.40″N 2°56′5.00″E
Cambrai Trench/Lane	50°52′21.50″N 2°55′26.00″E	Schuler Farm	50°53′19.50″N 2°57′13.90″E
Cheddar Villa	50°52′51.50″N 2°55′36.10″E	Schuler Galleries	50°53′12.90″N 2°57′10.30″E
Cross Cotts	50°53′11.50″N 2°57′29.60″E	Setques Farm	50°52′33.90″N 2°55′49.30″E
Derby Camp	50°51′27.76″N 2°47′47.28″E	Shrine Camp	50°50′29.10″N 2°40′33.70″E
Estaminet	50°52′30.00″N 2°55′39.30″E	Somme	50°52′56.90″N 2°57′3.50″E
Gallipoli	50°52′53.70″N 2°57′25.00″E	Steenbeek	50°52′53.00″N 2°56′8.50″E
Hindu Cott	50°53′9.40″N 2°56′58.90″E	Strongpoint P1	50°51′12.20″N 2°50′8.10″E
Iberian	50°52′39.80″N 2°57′21.20″E	Sulva	50°52′50.90″N 2°57′28.80″E
Jasper Farm	50°52′17.90″N 2°55′53.40″E	Uhlan Farm	50°52′14.30″N 2°55′55.60″E

Kansas Cross	50°53′9.30″N	Vampir	50°52′14.70″N
	2°57′42.60″E		2°57′41.40″E
Kansas House	50°53′9.40″N	Verlorenhoek Road	50°51′51.60″N
	2°57′33.70″E		2°55′44.50″E
Keir Farm	50°53′1.20″N	Warwick Lane	50°51′59.60″N
	2°57′36.30″E		2°55′35.20″E
Loos	50°53′7.00″N	Well Cottage	50°52′29.10″N
	2°57′13.60″E		2°55′18.60″E
Martha House	50°53′1.60″N	White Sap	50°52′15.70″N
	2°57′47.40″E		2°55′32.00″E
Pickelhaube Farm	50°52′31.30″N	Wurst Farm	50°53′36.20″N
	2°55′31.20″E		2°57′32.80″E

The Battalion remained at Setques until 20 July, training and getting the men as fit as possible. Apart from the usual sporting competitions within the Battalion, both 16 and 36 Division were in the area and numerous inter-regiment competitions were held. However, the main purpose of the training was to familiarise all ranks with the new tactical organisation. No longer were platoons divided into four equal-sized sections—though the introduction of the Lewis had already gone some way towards changing this anyway. The bombers, previously organised separately, now became an integral part of each platoon. Platoons had a Lewis section, usually a junior NCO and four men—though later this would increase when each platoon got two guns instead of one. There was a bombing section (an equal mix of bombers and riflemen, usually of eight men and one NCO); a rifle grenade section; and, finally, a rifle section, which was often as many as sixteen men plus NCOs, though section size varied enormously depending on the stage of the war, Battalion strength, the tasks to be done, and individual company commanders' preferences. On 7 July, the Battalion practised attack with tank support, only their second experience of training with the new weapon.

This reorganisation, made possible by new weaponry, gave infantry a flexibility that was unthinkable in 1914 and infantry tactics from 1917–1918 would not seem out of place to a modern infantryman. Battalions now advanced behind a creeping barrage in 'wave' formation, usually on a two-company-wide front, with two companies forward, two behind. Each company was also divided into 'waves', the first wave comprising half the force, with 70 yards between each wave and 12 yards between each section line (this was later modified to 100 yards between each wave). Platoons advanced in artillery formation until they came under fire from their front, when they quickly moved to extended order. Once in extended order, lead riflemen sometimes used 'walking fire' as they advanced. This method of firing from the hip whist moving can be remarkably accurate after practice and certainly helped to keep the enemy's heads down during the forthcoming attacks—though criticisms about ammunition wastage were aired.[1] Once enemy fire became effective, men advanced in a series of rushes from cover to cover—

half the men moving—the others giving covering fire. The heavier the fire, the shorter the rushes. Once the objective was within range of the grenadiers, the Lewis and rifle grenade section would engage the target to their front from cover, diverting attention from the bombers and riflemen, carrying out a flanking attack against the threat. Sometimes the rifle section was also be used for fire suppression and just the bombers attacked from the flanks. This training had specific purpose and was conducted against a full-scale mock-up of the target they would soon be assaulting.

In the morning of 15 July, all battalion and company runners were taken to the Wieltje dugout to familiarise themselves with the layout. While there, one of the runners, twenty-six-year-old Pte James Atkinson, was wounded by shrapnel to head and left leg. He was evacuated home for treatment and did not return to the Battalion.

On 20 July, the Battalion left for Poperinghe, arriving around 1.30 p.m. From there, 'A' and 'B' marched to Derby Camp near Brandhoek and 'C' and 'D' to Strongpoint P.1 to the east of Vlamertinghe. One new horror, introduced by the enemy while the Battalion was out of the line, was mustard gas—fired in shells known as 'Yellow-X' due to the marking on the projectile. Luckily, the British had what was probably the best gas mask of the war and the box respirator went a considerable distance towards neutralising the effects of this agent. Nasty, frightening, and painful, gas was not a major killer, but it was a major inconvenience—particularly for attackers, who needed to be considerably more active than defenders and had a significant effect on the stamina of respirator-wearing men such gunners, who were active for long periods at a time. Areas shelled with Yellow-X remained toxic for long periods as the liquid pooled on the ground and painful burns resulted from skin contact with it.

In the morning of 21 July, parades were held and then men given passes to visit Poperinghe. Although the Battalion's diary makes no mention of it, P.1 must have been under shellfire for part of the day as at least two men were wounded. Twenty-eight-year-old Pte Robert Berry from Liverpool received a minor shrapnel wound in the leg and was treated at the Field Ambulance, returning briefly four days later (he returned to hospital due to sickness on 2 August). The service record of twenty-nine-year-old Cpl William Bowker from 'C' Company notes him as losing his left thumb as a result of shrapnel. He was transferred to the Labour Corps after leaving hospital. The next day, another man was recorded wounded and gassed. Twenty-year-old Pte Harry Greaves was evacuated home and given a medical discharge and pension due to DAH brought on by 'gas poisoning'.[2] He died from bronchitis in December 1918 and his commemoration by CWGC recognises his service was instrumental in his ensuing death. Intelligence summaries record that the enemy were shelling most areas with all types of gas shell for much of the day.

P.1 was shelled heavily in the morning on 23 July. One shell hit 'D' Company's HQ, killing thirty-two-year-old CQMS Leonard Harrison, a father of four from Caton, whose youngest child was only five months old. Also slain by this shell were Sgt Frederick Eastwood and twenty-two-year-old Pte Robert Martin. The QM reported four other men wounded, but records show another two men were killed, although whether or not these were two of those he reported wounded is not known—both were logged as 'killed in action'. These were Pte Fred Astley from Royton and twenty-one-year-old Pte Joseph Slater from Lindell-in-Furness. Although 'C' remained, it was judged that 'D' Company's billets were unsafe and they were pulled back to Derby Camp. With the start date of the forthcoming attack approaching, officers and NCOs visited the HQ of 19 Corps to view the 1:50 scale model of the ground they would be attacking in just over a week's time.

In the afternoon of 24 July, the Battalion, less 'D' Company who remained at Derby Camp, moved up to relieve 1/7th King's in the front line at Wieltje. 'A' Company went into the front line, their HQ in Monmouth Terrace. 'B' and 'C' occupied Congreve Walk. The division's artillery had been bombarding the enemy since the dawn on 16 July and there was considerable retaliation from German guns of all calibres firing gas, shrapnel and HE. Around 5.30 p.m., just as the Battalion were moving into the line, Lone Street, Garden Street, Congreve Walk, and Bilge Trench all came under bombardment and there were casualties, though no one was killed. Twenty-year-old Pte Arthur Porter was fortunate just to suffer contusions to his left arm from shrapnel and was back with the Battalion two weeks later. He would not be so lucky next time. Twenty-two-year-old Pte Frank Waddington, a former trainee pharmacist from Morecambe, was only 200 yards from the safety of the dugout awaiting him when he was hit. The shrapnel wounds caused a compound fracture of the left fibula leading to evacuation home, transfer to the RAMC and eventual medical discharge. For one man, the cacophony of artillery and violent shockwaves from nearby blasts was unbearable. Still two months short of his nineteenth birthday, this was the first time in the line for Pte Henry Thompson from Belfast. Shaking uncontrollably and dazed, he was led to a nearby dugout by his sympathetic platoon sergeant and a medic summoned. He was treated at 62 CCS and rejoined the Battalion in September.

In the morning of 25 July, Liverpool Trench, Bilge Trench, and Congreve Walk were subjected to intermittent shelling by 15-cm guns and for much of the day, smaller calibres fell on and around battalion positions. Most of the division's artillery was involved in wire cutting, but a patrol sent out after dark reported that in several places to the Battalion's front, the wire was still intact. The activity from the German air force was bordering on frantic, as they sent flight after flight over British lines at various heights, looking for evidence of troop movements prior to an attack—British fighters equally determined to prevent these and artillery spotters correcting the fall of shot. In the afternoon, one German aircraft dropped a bomb near Lone Street, and at 9.30 p.m., a fighter made a number of low passes over the front line at Wieltje, machine-gunning the trenches. Despite all this activity, the only casualty for whom records remain is Pte Frank Scott from Willesden. The twenty-year-old received a shrapnel wound to his left ear and was treated in hospital in Boulogne, only returning in October. In the afternoon of 26 July, 'B' Company moved up from Congreve Walk and relieved 'A', who then went back to L4.

The weather continued fine—so dry that bullets were reported to ricochet off the soil. Intelligence summaries, however, in a report based on the interrogation of German prisoners, warned that some of the positions to be assaulted in the forthcoming attack remained wet and boggy. On 23 July, Division had issued a very detailed summary of German defences on all three 'objective lines' for the 31 July attack and these were constantly updated. To get this information, patrols and small-scale raids were carried out on a nightly basis, checking on the progress of wire cutting and in what strength German positions were occupied.

There was considerable shellfire throughout the 27th, but 'B' in Congreve Walk suffered particularly badly. The diary reported six wounded and three killed, but the actuality was worse. Although documented for 28 July by CWGC, they were casualties from the afternoon of 27 July. Twenty-one-year-old Pte Willie Beard from Glossop; thirty-six-year-old Pte Louis Penrith from Lancaster; twenty-eight-year-old Pte Thomas Shepherd from West Hartlepool; and twenty-eight-year-old Cpl William Roberts from Glossop were all killed outright. Twenty-eight-year-old Pte Charles Bagley, originally from Minehead, though working as a hairdresser in Lancaster when he enlisted, was hit in the leg and evacuated back to a hospital in Guilford. Bagley had originally been rejected when he first tried to enlist, but persisted and was accepted in late 1916. Tragically, he developed a blood clot and died in October. Less seriously injured were twenty-three-year-old L/Cpl Robert Searle and nineteen-year-old Pte Albert Chapman. One shell hitting a front line trench killed thirty-year-old 2Lt William Robertson from Edinburgh and wounded 2Lt Albert Pickstone. On 27 July At 3.10 p.m., 166 Brigade received a signal from 33 Brigade to their left that the RFC had reported the enemy withdrawing from their front line to their second line and consequently, they were sending out daylight patrols to check on this. In view of the absence of Brigadier, Brigade-Major and Lt-Col. Wayte—all at a divisional conference—it was decided to hold off sending patrols out until after dusk, but the Battalion was ordered to put 'A' and 'D' Companies onto 'standby' in case immediate advance was directed. At 6 p.m., a further signal was received from 33 Brigade informing them that the RFC had pronounced the enemy first line clear of defenders and that at 5 p.m. they would advance, and if the enemy line was clear, occupy it.[3]

As soon as it was dusk, four reconnaissance patrols left divisional lines with the dual objectives of checking how successful the bombardment had been in destroying the wire and verifying if the enemy had indeed withdrawn. In this sector, one was from the Battalion, one from 1/5th Loyals to their left and one from 1/7th King's to their right. The Loyals checked Well Cottage, a ruin 450 yards out in No Man's Land, and though this was found to be clear of enemy occupation, when they approached the enemy line, they were bombed from a post at 50°52′30.80″N 2°55′24.00″E and retreated back to friendly lines. Second Lieutenant Pinch's patrol tried to enter the enemy front line at the junction of Cambrai Lane and Cambrai Trench 300 yards to their right. Unfortunately, a German post containing four men—now fully alert following the activities of the other patrols—blocked further progress. Pinch was fired at from here and by another rifle post 40 yards to the right. Bombing posts both sides of this and a machine-gun firing from Kaiser Bill's Nose also joined in. Pinch successfully broke contact without casualties. The King's had more success, their four-man patrol discovering the German sentry sitting on the fire-step instead of keeping a lookout. He was promptly shot when he began to shout and the patrol withdrew safely as more of the enemy rushed to defend their line and opened fire on them. This patrol attained their own line at 9.15 p.m.—though had one close shave just before reaching safety, when two enemy fighters swooped down upon them, machine guns blazing—though none of the patrol was hit. These patrols confirmed that the much of wire was severely damaged, but more still needed cutting and the reception given to the three patrols and the numerous flares fired from the all along the length of the front line, confirmed that a German withdrawal had not taken place.

The 28th was yet another fine day and the contest for air supremacy continued. One British craft, after conducting a low-level reconnaissance, reported that the enemy front line was very lightly held and Cambrai and Camel Trenches and their supports particularly badly damaged (the stretch of enemy line from the Wieltje Road to Kaiser Bill's Nose). With this in mind, a strong raid by 1/5th Loyals was organised for 7 p.m. During the afternoon, 'C' and 'B' Companies rotated. The Loyals left the Battalion's trenches on schedule and covered by a heavy artillery and mortar barrage, raided the enemy line along the 200-yard reach from where Pinch's patrol had visited the previous evening, down to where White Sap left enemy lines. This patrol accounted for twenty of the enemy—who put up a strong resistance—also finding numbers killed by the barrage. Complete with a prisoner from 456 IR, they returned to friendly lines, having lost one man killed and another two and one officer wounded. During that night, four patrols from the division went out to examine the wire and reported that it was now almost non-existent in many places.

The 29th began as another warm and fine day, and it was clear the RFC had finally gained superiority over the actual front as all German attempts to send aircraft over in daylight were beaten off. Enemy artillery was once again less than active, though areas of front line were shelled intermittently during the morning and thirty-two-year-old Pte John Wood from Haslingden killed. After weeks of fine, warm, and, above all, dry weather, torrential rain fell around 10 a.m., flooding shell craters in No Man's Land and making roads and tracks difficult for all users. As darkness fell, 'A' and 'D' moved up through Ypres for the front and 'B' left Congreve Walk. With less than thirty hours to go before the offensive, the Battalion took up its pre-assembly positions. 'A' Company remained in the front line; 'B' was in Warwick Trench; 'C' in Oxford Trench; and 'D' in New Armytage Trench. HQ was in the large dugout in Wieltje.

The attack, scheduled for 3.50 a.m. on 31 July, involved four Corps from Fifth Army, Second Army and the First French Army. The 55th Division was just a small part of Fifth Army's advance. The objectives were titled the 'Blue', 'Black', and 'Green' Lines—each being attacked in that order. Once the Blue Line was captured, the second wave would move through them and attack and consolidate the Black Line, the third wave moving through them to seize and consolidate the Green Line. The 166th Brigade attacked on the left of the divisional front. The 1/5th Loyals, to the left of the brigade line, and 1/5th King's Own, to their right, were both tasked with taking and consolidating the

Blue Line. To their right were 1/6th King's and 1/5th King's from 165 Brigade, similarly tasked. Once the Blue Line was taken, Liverpool Scottish and 1/5th South Lancs would move through to take the Black Line. The 164th Brigade would then advance through them to attack the Green Line. The Battalion's line of advance was bisected by the Wieltje-Gravenstafel Road, 'B' Company ahead of 'D' to the left of the road; 'A' was ahead of 'C' to the right. The Blue Line at 50°52'34.29"N 2°55'53.00"E was just behind the third line of German trenches—1,000 yards in advance of the British front line. The Black Line at 50°52'57.50"N 2°56'38.43"E, a further 1,200 yards ahead and the Green Line at 50°53'8.86"N 2°57'47.74"E, another 1,500 yards forward of that.

Regrettably, no record remains to detail how many men the Battalion actually attacked with that morning. Divisional returns show that they were up to full strength, though a sizeable proportion of the Battalion remained behind with Maj. Johnstone to reconstitute the Battalion should disaster occur.[4] Each company fielded at least two platoons—possibly three. The list detailing the officers for the attack does survive, recording that 'B' was led by Capt. Owtram, with Capt. Roper and 2Lt Pinch; 'A' led by Lt Bennett, with 2Lt Walker and 2Lt Sleight; 'D' was commanded by Capt. Harriss, with 2Lt Parker and 2Lt Lord; and 'C' was led by Capt. Briggs, with Lt Kean and 2Lt Mackey. In view of this, two full-sized platoons plus an HQ platoon of between fifteen and twenty men with a senior NCO and the company commander would seem a reasonable supposition. The latter was combat-capable, though this was not their primary function and evidence from the 1/4th suggests that HQ's platoon comprised of riflemen/bombers, plus company-stretcher-bearers, runners, and signallers (in light of their tougher objective, each company of 1/4th King's Own attacked with three full-sized platoons plus a slightly larger 'HQ platoon' as described above).

In addition to the company forces, Capt. Simpson commanded a group of 'moppers-up', whose task was to clear German dugouts as the main force advanced—preventing any of the enemy from popping up to engage the attackers from behind. With the large number of dugouts in the three lines of trenches, a single standard platoon does not seem adequate and this group was probably made up of an oversized platoon of riflemen and bombers, with two/three sections each side of the road. There was also a Battalion HQ group with the CO, Capt. Milnes as acting 2IC, the Adjutant Lt Macfarlane, and his assistant Lt Boys-Stones. The Intelligence Officer 2Lt Macdonald and the MO Lt Elwood completed the officers from this detachment. With them would have been signallers, runners, and the Battalion stretcher-bearers. Second Lieutenant Binns was assigned to the Brigade Carrying Party—though no mention is made of how many men from the Battalion were assigned with him, if any. With this in mind, it seems likely that the attacking force was made up of no more than 600 men.

Earlier information from prisoners and the RFC about the enemy withdrawing from his front line had not been totally without worth. In the north of Fifth Army's sector, the enemy had pulled back over 500 metres, though this was really just a local withdrawal.[5] In 55 Division's front it was more a redistribution of forces. The German commander was well aware of the damage British artillery had wrought on his front line, with many

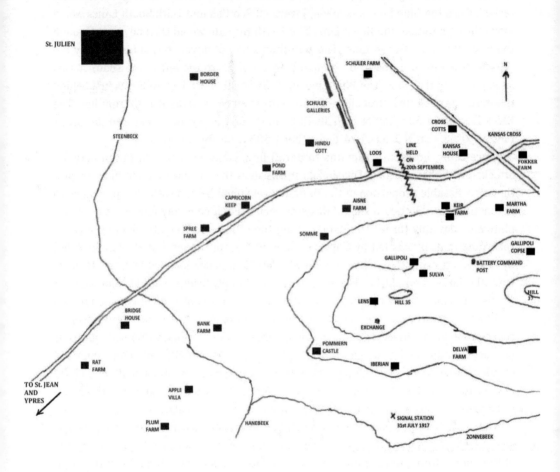

St. JULIEN

BORDER
HOUSE

SCHULER FARM

SCHULER
GALLERIES

N

STEENBECK

CROSS
COTTS

KANSAS CROSS

HINDU
COTT

LINE
HELD
ON
20th SEPTEMBER

KANSAS
HOUSE

FOKKER
FARM

LOOS

POND
FARM

CAPRICORN
KEEP

AISNE
FARM

KEIR
FARM

MARTHA
FARM

SPREE
FARM

SOMME

GALLIPOLI
COPSE

GALLIPOLI

BATTERY COMMAND
POST

SULVA

HILL
37

LENS

HILL 35

BRIDGE
HOUSE

BANK
FARM

EXCHANGE

RAT
FARM

POMMERN
CASTLE

DELVA
FARM

IBERIAN

TO St. JEAN
AND
YPRES

APPLE
VILLA

PLUM
FARM

HANEBEEK

X SIGNAL STATION
31st JULY 1917

ZONNEBEEK

**THIRD BATTLE OF YPRES
JULY AND SEPTEMBER 1917**

trench systems smashed beyond recognition. He had also seen the damage that the larger HE shells did to men inside his concrete dugouts (referred to as 'dugouts'—though 'bunker' is probably a more accurate description as they are mostly above ground). While hardly damaging the structure, the concussion often killed every man inside. Added to these problems was the undoubted superiority of British mining operations and a concern that further massive mines may be the opening gambit of this attack. Consequently, a defence in-depth strategy was invoked, with most of the men from the front lines withdrawn to the 'Black' and 'Green Lines'. These would fight from shell holes in what became known as the 'Stutzpunkt Line'. These holes—garrisoned by just a few men with a machine gun and linked by shallow CTs—were all heavily camouflaged and aerial reconnaissance failed to find most, even though divisional intelligence was specifically searching for them. What did show on the aerial photographs, however, were the ordinary shell holes to the front of these positions, which had been filled with barbed wire to prevent attackers using them for cover. German strategy was to kill or wound as many of the attackers as possible from the Stutzpunkt Line and then to use *'Eingreif'* divisions—specially trained in counterattack—to recapture them before the British could consolidate.

The 30th was another dull day and rain fell at intervals. Enemy artillery was quiet for most of the day, but during the evening, a number of 5.9 fell near Oxford Trench, killing four men from 'B' Company. Unfortunately, it is not possible to say who these were as they were included among the returns for those killed the following morning. At least two men are known to have been wounded. Nineteen-year-old Pte Thomas Wilson from Coniston was hit in the hand and evacuated home for treatment. He was posted to 2/King's Own after his recovery. The second was Pte Richard Lamb from Lancaster. This was the second time the twenty-two-year-old had been wounded and he was treated in Sheffield for serious shrapnel wounds to both arms.

As soon as dark fell, three groups of men from 'A' Company moved silently into No Man's Land, their task to cut gaps in the British wire for the attacking forces to exit by. One party of six, led by thirty-two-year-old L/Cpl Fred Hartley, was cutting the wire when German shells began to fall around them. The other two groups returned to the cover of the front line, but despite his men urging retreat, Hartley insisted on completing the job before bringing everyone back safely. For this and his sterling performance in the attack, he was awarded the MM. Beginning at 10 p.m., the attackers themselves began to move into their jumping-off positions. 'A' Company in particular had difficulty finding their start positions due to the darkness of the night and negotiating shell holes and wire—though all made it before the start time. 'B' and 'A' laid up in No Man's Land on a level with Hopkins Trench, which is described merely as a 'ditch' by Lt Bennett.[6] This trench does not appear on any surviving maps, but as 'D' and 'C' now occupied the front line, it would be reasonable to expect it to be no more than 75 yards further forward in No Man's Land—the determined separation between the two waves.

Considerable intelligence gathered about enemy positions was fed to battalions as and when it arrived. The 1/5th had been warned that in No Man's Land, White Sap, on their right bound, may possibly be occupied in strength by an enemy who moved along it to escape the creeping barrage. It was also suggested that the length of this sap, ending a scant seventy yards from British lines, could be extended to provide a CT to cross No Man's Land should one be later required. Of the three rows of trenches facing them, only the front and reserve had been kept maintained. Support trenches had fallen into disrepair in many places. The gap between front and support was about 100 yards, with a further 150 yards to the reserve line. Connecting these were a number of straight 'tramway' trenches. A number of buildings existed, which could also cause problems in the advance to the Blue Line. The first of these, in 'B' Company's line of advance, was the Estaminet. This had a cellar, which in itself was not very strong, however the French IX Corps had built a strong shelter inside it and it was believed that this had been further strengthened with concrete by the enemy. The next obstacle was also in 'B' Company's line of advance. Bossaert Farm was a strongly built farmhouse, with concrete vaulted cellars and had been used as a terminus for the trench tramway. Recent aerial photographs revealed a new trench, dug eastwards from the cellar and there was evidence that the whole position had been strengthened. To their right and of more concern to 165 brigade were Jasper Farm and Uhlan Farm—though if 165 Brigade did not subdue them quickly, both these positions could enfilade the Battalion as they advanced. To their left and level with the Blue Line, Cheddar Villa could cause similar difficulties—though this was actually on the left flank of 1/5th Loyals. Between the reserve and Stutzpunkt Line, a disused stretch of switch line, consisting of a double trench, ran close to Bossaert Farm and a number of small keeps were in the vicinity. Division cautioned that these buildings and keeps may be used to house numbers of machine guns, yet thought it likelier that these would be sited in shell hole positions.[7]

Preparations had been meticulous and orders for company commanders stretched to twenty pages of type-written foolscap. Each man was issued with 120 rounds of .303—except for the signallers, scouts, runners, Lewis gunners, bombers, and rifle grenadiers, who only carried fifty rounds. In their haversack, worn over the back, men carried towel, soap, oil tin, three days' rations, an extra water bottle containing cold tea without sugar or milk, a groundsheet, and mess tin. Every man carried three empty sandbags and three out of four had either a pick or shovel. Although this may seem an unnecessary burden, without these tools, consolidation could not take place, leaving men extremely vulnerable to counterattack. With the exception of rifle grenadiers, who had the No. 20 grenade, every man carried two No. 23 grenades, complete with cartridges and rods in the top pockets of their jacket.

The No. 23 grenade was an adaptation of the No. 5 Mills, with a longer time fuse and a different base plug into which the rod screwed. The grenade could either be thrown or fired. To fire it, a special blank cartridge was placed in the rifle (this was when the magazine cut-off on the SMLE really came into use as there was no need to remove the live rounds from the magazine); the grenade with rod attached was lowered into the barrel and with the butt on the ground, the grenade was firmly gripped around the lever with one hand and the pin removed by the other. As soon as the spring-loaded lever flew off, a firing pin struck the detonator, activating the time fuse in the grenade, so it was most important to fire as soon as possible and one can imagine that a misfire fairly concentrated the mind. It was possible to arrange the grenade so that the bayonet held the lever in, but this was not fool proof. The cup attachment carried by bombers and rifle grenadiers held the lever in position and allowed unlimited time in which to aim the shot—which could range out to 90 yards. The No. 20 grenade used by rifle grenadiers, who each carried six, was a percussion grenade with a 10-inch long rod attached and like the No. 23 grenade, also propelled by a blank cartridge. The No. 20 grenade had a much longer range than the No. 23 and reliably reached 200 yards, with 250 yards not an unreasonable distance to aspire to with a favourable wind. The higher breech and barrel pressure caused by the rod was pretty hard on the rifles and grenadiers' rifles were bound with wire to strengthen them—though it did not take long before even these weapons lost their accuracy.

The night was dark and damp and the eerie wailing of gas shells, fired by the thousand into German rear and battery areas by divisional artillery added to the strangeness. There was very little reply by German guns, but constant outbreaks of flares and rockets from all along the length of the enemy line was testament to his nervousness. At intervals, this jumpiness would result in a sudden flurry of small explosions as German sentries hurled volleys of grenades into their own wire—often triggering similar outbreaks in neighbouring sectors. There was an 'O' Group at midnight, which all four company commanders attended in the CO's Wieltje dugout. At 3 a.m., the British guns ceased fire and a sudden silence fell on the battle front—broken only by the occasional German shell falling in No Man's Land or to the rear.

It was actually 3.20 a.m. when Bennett, accompanied only by his runner Pte Walter Doyle, finally located the start position for his HQ at the front left of the first wave, just to the right of the road. He had left his platoon in the front line while he attended the 'O' Group, keeping them there until he pinpointed their start position. Satisfied he was in the right place, he hurriedly despatched Doyle to collect them. At 3.48 a.m.—two minutes before zero hour—a sole Vickers began firing over the heads of the attackers, prompting another flurry of flares from enemy positions. Precisely on time, British artillery began a tremendous bombardment of HE and shrapnel against German positions; the synchronisation of this opening blast was so good that Lt-Col. Wayte wrote after the war: 'At 3.45 a.m. ('Z' Day) I went upstairs (from the dugout), and at 3.50 a.m. the mines went up'.[8]

The initial advance was very much a tale of halves. Immediately after the barrage began, the attackers stood up and advanced until they were only about 40 yards to rear of the bursting shells. To their rear the horizon was coloured red by the gun-flashes and forwards of the barrage German SOS rockets lit the sky. Despite the intensity of the bombardment, the rattle of British machine guns could still be heard. The barrage fell on the German front line for six minutes and then lifted 100 yards to allow the attackers to enter their first objective. The darkness and devastation of the ground made navigation difficult for the attackers. For 'A' Company, it was not too bad—they had the remains of the road to guide them—for 1/6 King's there was no such assistance and almost immediately this battalion veered in front of 'A' Company. Bennett was able to sort them out and the advance continued.[9] 'A' Company encountered little resistance in their advance—the few Germans they did meet succumbing quickly to bomb and bayonet. Their only officer hit in that initial advance was 2Lt William Walker, who was wounded. For 'B', it was a very different story. Capt. Owtram was wounded by MG fire in the left knee and groin, effectively ending his days with the Battalion. Twenty-five-year-old Capt. William Roper and twenty-seven-year-old 2Lt Pinch were both killed, leaving 'B' Company without an officer. It was still dark as they battled to overcome the resistance, and Sgt James McDonald took command, steadied the survivors, and reorganised them before continuing their task. So great was the devastation caused by British artillery that it was difficult to discern which line of trenches they were actually attacking. Before advancing further, McDonald made a solo reconnaissance under heavy fire, to establish their exact position, before returning to direct his company in their attack. His cool demeanour settled the men and he continued to lead them until 3 p.m., when Bennett sent 2Lt Sleight over to command the company.[10] McDonald was assisted by Sgt Sidney Taylor, who took over one of the platoons and both men were rewarded for their courage and skill, a DCM for McDonald and MM for Taylor.

Keeping close behind the barrage, the two companies took the support and reserve trenches. By this time, both had become intermingled to some degree and the attack broke up into dozens of small-scale engagements. For one ten-minute period, the only man Bennett could see was Doyle, who stuck to him like a leech for the entire time. There was considerable euphoria from some at capturing three lines of enemy trenches with such relative ease. Bennett describes Signalling-Sergeant Frederick Ball as doing 'a war dance near the German reserve line, throwing his tin hat in the air again and again'.[11] 'D' and 'C' moved through them towards the Blue Line and collecting any men he encountered, Bennett followed on.

These two companies also met with surprisingly little opposition, the main trouble coming from a machine gun in Rat Farm, some 250 yards beyond the Blue Line, which Capt. Briggs engaged and neutralised with two Lewis teams, though Briggs was wounded shortly afterwards—his third time. This occasion, it was a piece of shrapnel, which passed straight through his left wrist. Second Lieutenant Mackey had been wounded in the initial advance to the Blue Line, so this left twenty-two-year-old Lt John Kean the only officer from 'C' Company still on his feet. When Bennett reached the Blue Line, he found that many of his men were already there, having tagged onto the following companies as they passed through. He also discovered that he was also now the only one of the company commanders unwounded. Capt. Harriss had been hit in the right wrist by a bullet. When Bennett found him, he was refusing to be evacuated—insisting he was going to carry on—but in the early evening relented and was evacuated, command of 'D' passing to 2Lt Gilbert Lord.[12] 'D' Company had also lost 2Lt Harold Parker, wounded in the initial advance. Capt. Simpson had been killed just before the German front line as he led his moppers-up forwards. Bennett collected all the men he could find and set them digging a line of defences some 100 yards to the rear of the Blue Line position as marked on the map. His decision was determined by the state of the ground—his chosen position slightly higher and much drier. The line dug by the Battalion ran from 50°52′46.90″N 2°55′33.40″E on the left to 50°52′25.00″N 2°55′50.00″E on the right (the reference C.23.c.3.2. given in the diary for the right-hand bound is clearly incorrect as this places it in the old No Man's Land. C.23.d.3.2. is the correct reference). At 4.45 a.m., Bennett sent a runner back reporting this and another at 5.20 a.m. reporting 'objective gained'.[13]

The divisional signals log illustrates perfectly the problems commanders had getting accurate information about the progress of an attack and goes some way towards explaining why on so many occasions a trusted officer was dispatched from HQ to see for himself.[14] At 5.26 a.m.—six minutes after its despatch from brigade—B.M.160 was received, reporting casualties for the Battalion as 'heavy'. B.M.161, composed a mere four minutes later, reported the Battalion's casualties as 'very slight' and then S.C.139, composed fifteen minutes after B.M.160, gave 'estimated casualties. 1/5 R.Lanc.R. 200 OR'. Luckily, this estimate was grossly pessimistic and greater than the actual total for all six days. Bennett's difficulty in giving an accurate figure was due to the darkness and wide dispersion of the men—most of whom were not from his company. Problems maintaining communications began almost immediately the battle opened, with all telephone wires between the Battalions and the HQs of 165 and 166 Brigade cut by 4.30 a.m. Twenty minutes later, a very heavy barrage along Oxford Trench gave runners extreme difficulties. Visual signals were also unsuccessful due to poor visibility. As the attack pushed further into enemy territory these difficulties were magnified many-fold, especially when the weather deteriorated and the ground became a morass.

Once Bennett was happy that he had a workable trench approximately 3½ feet in depth, he reorganised men into their companies and positioned them along the line, with 'A' on the right—in touch with 1/6th King's—and 'B', 'C', and 'D' on the left. Battalion set up a temporary HQ in a dugout in Cambrai Trench and brigade established a forward station. Once Lt-Col. Wayte had organised his HQ, he left with a small escort to visit the Blue Line and happy that everything was in order and men in good spirits, he returned to his dugout. The battle for the Black Line was still raging in places, though the whole of this was gained by 9 a.m. Worryingly, the right-hand units were not in touch with 15 Division, so a precautionary strongpoint was constructed there. By 10 a.m., 164 Brigade had passed through the Black Line and begun their advance on the Green. There had been very little enemy artillery fire against the Blue Line, but this changed around 8 a.m., when an enemy aircraft flew low over the line, and almost immediately 5.9 began to fall around their trenches. Fortunately, their defensive system—little more than a series of linked shell holes—was very difficult for enemy observers to accurately target and casualties were light. At 10 a.m., it began to rain. In the afternoon, it began to rain harder, and at 8 p.m., a deluge began that did not cease until 5 August—turning the defensive lines and rear areas into one huge swamp. The 164th Brigade had seized most of the Green Line by 2.15 p.m., but their position was precarious, with both flanks in the air and very few men left to defend their line. Ammunition was also running low.

The MO Lt Frederick Elwood had moved his advanced dressing station to a cowshed just behind the Blue Line—a position that attracted very little fire until a tank bogged down in the mud next to it—the subsequent heavy shelling compelling them to move. Conditions were already making work gruelling for stretcher-bearers, and when Elwood and Sgt Richard Clarkson (238) went out with a stretcher to carry in a wounded sergeant, they found it impossible to manage by themselves. Fortunately, Capt. Noel Chavasse VC, the MO of Liverpool Scottish and one of his bearers, noticed their difficulties and came out to help them. Elwood's diary records that Chavasse was hit in the head by shrapnel as he was going down the steps to his dressing station, though after it had been dressed he continued working.[15]

At 3 p.m., Bennett (now officially in command of the Blue Line) sent 2Lt Sleight to take over 'B' Company, concerned that an officer would be needed over there as the enemy was beginning a counter-attack on the left of the Green Line near Schuler Farm. The 164th Brigade held as long as they could, scavenging ammunition from the bodies of the dead and from knocked-out tanks, but once this was expended, they had no option but to carry out a fighting withdrawal with the last of their rounds. British artillery and machine-gun barrages smashed this counterattack, causing severe losses to the enemy and for the rest of the day provided an umbrella for the troops at the front. The appalling conditions became more of an impediment to the enemy as they counter-attacked than they did for the defenders as German weapons soon choked with mud as they struggled to advance. During the night, both Blue and Black Lines were consolidated further, the Battalion now holding the whole of the Blue Line across the brigade's front, the Loyals having been sent forward to strengthen the Black Line.

At 4.10 a.m. on 1 August, Battalion HQ moved up to a dugout at Pickelhaube Farm in Call Reserve trench and Wayte once again toured his line, where the men were concentrating on strengthening the defences. By now, they were standing in 2 feet of water, but so far, morale remained high. The continued rain made all their work that much harder and carrying parties bringing up rations, ammunition and RE supplies were sinking up to their knees in the mud and those struggling to get coils of wire forward to the Black line found it impossible. The main intensity of German artillery fire was against the Black Line, though later in the day, this spread to the Blue Line too. The woes of the MO—whose dressing station was swimming in water—continued as two artillery batteries were placed just behind his position and once again, German counter-battery fire required another move to a safer location—though this security was purely illusory. The captured dugout they moved to at Setques Farm, shared with Chavasse and Fawcett—the MO of 1/5th Loyals had a doorway facing the direction of hostile shellfire.

By 11 a.m., nearly all of 164 Brigade had been withdrawn from the Black Line, the front now held by Liverpool Scottish on the left, 1/5th Loyals in the centre and 1/5th South Lancs on the right. These battalions reported over 200 enemy dead from the last counterattack, lying close to the front of their positions—probably considerably more further back, where the division's artillery had caught them as they assembled. At 4.20 p.m., Lt-Col. Wayte sent an urgent signal back reporting that the troops from the division to their right seemed to be retiring. A further signal sent at 5.30 p.m. informed that the Battalion was in touch with 1/6th King's on their right, who reported that they observed two companies retiring and that there was heavy shelling across the entire front.[16] As soon as he witnessed the withdrawal through his binoculars, Wayte put all his HQ staff on standby and issued more small arms ammunition. He also sent Capt. Milnes and 2Lt Macdonald to investigate personally. Despite mud and heavy shellfire, both officers ran the width of the battlefront, reaching the crisis-point uninjured. The enemy had broken through the Black Line in 15 Division's sector along a 300-yard front and all officers from the unit manning this were casualties—the surviving men retreating. Rallying these, Milnes reorganised them and under the leadership of Macdonald, they counterattacked and sealed the gap. Milnes subsequently received the MC and Macdonald a bar to his MC.[17]

Now under heavy shellfire, casualties increased throughout the divisional frontage, triggering increasing demands from the ADS in Call Reserve for more dressings, stretchers and stretcher-bearers.[18] Manpower was in short supply, but 100 men were garnered from the rear areas and sent forward to help carry the wounded. Working parties also brought forward sandbags containing previously prepared bundles of dressings and other medical supplies from the Aid Post in Wieltje—stored for just such an eventuality. In the early hours of the morning of 2 August, the Blue Line and Battalion HQ were shelled heavily and casualties suffered. At 3 a.m. on 2 August, Elwood was sitting in the medical dugout at Setques Farm, taking a brief rest—having been occupied almost non-stop treating the wounded. When some of this new batch of bearers arrived, he arose to take them to where they were needed, Chavasse taking his place on the seat. Elwood had just rounded the corner of the traverse when a German 4.2 exploded just inside the doorway of the dugout. He and the bearers ran back to find a scene of carnage. Blood was inches deep on the floor of the dugout, seven of the wounded and three men, who had been nearby in the trench, were killed and another six wounded. As Elwood later wrote, 'poor Chavasse, badly hit, hopeless'.[19] Capt. Noel Chavasse VC was wounded in several places, an abdominal wound being the most severe. He died from this at Brandhoek on 4 August and was awarded a posthumous bar to his VC, the only man to be awarded two in the Great War. Elwood's diary ends, 'Finished night dressing! dressing!! dressing!!!'

After breakfast, the adjutant Lt Macfarlane toured the line and was considerably concerned about the condition of the men up to their knees (or deeper) in cold, muddy water for two nights now—with no shelter from either weather or shellfire. Work on the trenches themselves was now impossible, the sides continually subsiding. Unsurprisingly, morale was at a low point, and although an issue of rum boosted spirits for a while, the men were nearing the limit of their endurance. It was not just the Battalion who were suffering as divisional signal logs indicate. The brigade commander of 165 Brigade sent the following signal to Division at 8.30 a.m.:

Men are completely exhausted, but cheerful [I am not sure that 'cheerful' is terribly accurate]. I found men this morning who were unable to stand. If Brigade is not relieved very soon men will be incapable of leaving the trenches at all.[20]

The Blue Line was once again shelled heavily around noon and 'D' Company's stretch blown in, one shell killing five and wounding seven. Second Lieutenant Lord was among them, leaving 'D' without officers. Lord had been wounded in the hand some time earlier, but as all his officers and senior NCOs were already casualties, he had remained with his company. This time, he was wounded in a further two places and evacuated, later being awarded the MC for his courage. Kean immediately came across from his position, bringing men to act as bearers and others to help repair the defences. Despite having been working to save the wounded more or less without rest for nearly three days, the MO also came forward to help, accompanied by Pte Richard Clarkson and Cpl George Mawson—the latter described by Elwood as 'a host in himself' (Mawson and Clarkson were the only two stretcher-bearers from February 1915 still remaining).[21] Elwood and Clarkson carried one man out on a stretcher between them, but after struggling for 300 yards through knee-deep mud, could bear their burden no longer and deposited the casualty in a shell hole for the moment. Elwood returned with 2Lt Macdonald and between them carried the man the rest of the way to the ADS. For the time being, Cpl Henry Large and twenty-eight-year-old Cpl William Fisher commanded 'D' Company. Twenty-seven-year-old Sgt John Butterworth from Rochdale was sent from 'C' Company to take over, but thirty minutes later, he too was killed. From then on, 'D' and 'C' were amalgamated under 2Lt Kean. Large and Fisher were both awarded the MM.

The long-awaited relief began in the afternoon. At 4.20 p.m., a warning order was issued for 107 Brigade to relieve both the Blue and Black Lines, and in the evening, the Battalion was relieved by 15/Royal Irish Rifles. Heavy German artillery fire began to fall shortly before 8 p.m. and relief was far from uneventful. Lt-Col. Cole-Hamilton, CO of 15/Royal Irish, was hit in the shoulder by shrapnel and numbers of his men killed. At 11 p.m., the enemy barrage switched to Battalion HQ and for an hour, 5.9 Howitzers pasted the area around the dugout—blast waves extinguishing the candles almost once every thirty seconds. Once relief was reported, HQ waited for a lull in the shelling and then around midnight, made their escape, the details of which were etched into Lt-Col. Wayte's memory:

We did a bolt through wire and slime past two sections of poor lads wiped out with one shell, along the edge of the craters, in which one man sank up to his neck and prayed to be left there to die, over barbed wire, which cut our clothes into strips; and all the while they shelled and shelled on the front and on the left and in front and behind us.... Throughout the entire operations I cannot say too much in praise of all ranks of the Battalion who took and held their objective through three days of appalling shell and rifle fire, in conjunction with such discomfort that one who has not seen Flanders has any conception of.[22]

Not all of HQ made it back safely. The MO and Lt Macfarlane were together and three times the Doctor sank so far into the mud that Macfarlane had to drag him free. One shell burst 7 yards in front of the pair and Macfarlane was wounded—though luckily Elwood managed to pull him along until they were out of the danger zone. Twenty-seven-year-old Macfarlane never rejoined the Battalion, transferring instead to the RAF. He was killed near Chester in June 1918 when the aircraft he and his instructor were flying collided with another aircraft.

HQ returned to the dugout in Wieltje, 'A' to Oxford Trench, 'B' to New Admiral Trench, 'C' to Warwick Trench, and 'D' to the OBL. Although the night was quiet, the men were not out of danger yet. During the day, search parties went out into the old No Man's Land and old German lines and brought in the bodies of the dead officers and buried any of their comrades they found. Their careful marking of these graves obviously paid dividends as over half the men killed in the attack have a known grave—stark contrast to the 1/4th, most of whose fatalities happened between the Black and Green Lines (80 per cent of whom have no known grave). During this work, nineteen-year-old Pte John Parbery was killed, and in the early hours of 4 August, eighteen-year-old Pte Thomas Dixon was wounded in the right arm and evacuated home. At 9.30 p.m., 14/Royal Irish relieved the Battalion, and at 1.15 a.m. on 4 August, they marched to the Asylum. At 8 a.m., they entrained at Vlamertinghe for Poperinghe. The Battalion marched to Clyde Camp, 2 km south-east of Sint-Jan-ter-Biezen, arriving just after noon. After thanking the men, the CO dismissed them, the rest of the day spent cleaning and resting.

Casualties were high in the division, with 3,550 killed wounded or missing, 90 per cent of these from the three infantry brigades. The 164th Brigade, who made the attack on the Green Line, suffered the worst, with 1,397 killed, wounded, or missing. The 165th and 166th Brigades lost 916 and 908 respectively.[23] The total of 225 and breakdown of figures as reported in the Battalion's diary for 3 August (and repeated by Hodgkinson, who used this to compile his history) are not supported by the returns sent to Brigade and Division—or by the later verified information. The actual figures from 30 July to 4 August inclusive are three officers killed and eight wounded; thirty-seven ORs killed (four of whom died from wounds); 136 ORs wounded; and seven missing (eventually accounted for as 'alive'). One known example of the latter is twenty-six-year-old Pte Thomas Nattrass from Wrekenton. His records show him 'Missing' on 31 July and report him rejoining on 12 August, with no evidence whatsoever in his record to show he was wounded. There were a number of reasons why men were posted missing, apart from the obvious ones of them becoming a casualty or being captured. Men escorting prisoners back were frequently diverted to another unit upon their return to the battlefield; men also got lost and were gathered up by the 'Straggler Posts' and redirected under orders of the Provost Marshall. Whatever the reasons were for his temporary absence—or that of the other six men—they are lost to the annals of history.

In addition to those already mentioned, a number were rewarded for their courage and skills during the attack. Second Lieutenant Gilbert Lord earned the MC. In 'A' Company, Sgt Frederick Ball, Sgt George Campbell, L/Cpl George Carradice, L/Cpl Albert Smallshaw, L/Cpl George Walters, and Pte Isaac Phillipson all got the MM. Those receiving the MM in 'B' Company were Cpl Arthur Parkinson, Pte Joseph Knaggs, and

Pte Thomas Taylor. Thirty-seven-year-old Pte Arthur Murray from 'B' was awarded the MM, but suffered seven shrapnel wounds to his back and was evacuated home. He was posted to 1/King's Own in January 1918 and killed with them in August. From 'C', there was Pte William Buckley, Pte E. Mann (erroneously recorded as C. Murr in divisional orders), and Pte Walter Hunter. Pte William Ayling of 'D' Company was also awarded the MM. Cpl James Dolan received an MM, though his company is not known. Pte James Bettany—now attached to the TMB—expunged his earlier navigational sins by earning the MM. Tragically, he would never be able to wear this to post-war reunions as he was later transferred to the Royal Fusiliers and killed with them in Russia in August 1919.

Killed or Died from Wounds Received between 30 July and 4 August 1917

Pte Thomas Cecil Adams	260013	KIA: 31/7	Pte William Johnson	28037	KIA: 31/7
Pte Arthur Alcock	242516	KIA: 31/7	Pte Edward Jones**	243114	KIA: 31/7
Pte Robert Barker	260039	KIA: 31/7	Pte Albert Lacey	242610	KIA: 31/7
Pte Frederick Percy Barlow	202294	KIA: 31/7	Pte Richard Leaver	201935	KIA: 31/7
Pte George Amos Blake	260023	KIA: 31/7	Pte Joseph Leybourn	28043	WIA: 31/7
Pte Harry Bowers	242534	KIA: 31/7	Pte William Murray	242640	DOW: 12/8
L/Sgt John Shore Butterworth	243087	KIA: 2/8	Pte John Parbery	242650	KIA: 3/8
L/Cpl James Churchouse	240099	KIA: 31/7	Pte William Parker	242415	KIA: 2/8
Cpl William Clapham	242406	KIA: 31/7	2Lt William Pinch		KIA: 31/7
Pte Norman Colston	33914	KIA: 31/7	Pte John James Rawcliffe***	241640	DOW: 11/8
Pte Charles Entwistle	240056	KIA: 31/7	Pte Leonard Hayton Rawnsley	241494	KIA: 2/8
Pte Edward Fisher	242649	KIA: 31/7	Capt. William Edward Roper		KIA: 31/7
Pte Joseph Garside*	201886	KIA: 31/7	Pte Bernard Rosenberg	241630	KIA: 2/8
Pte Matthew Graham	260040	KIA: 31/7	L/Cpl William Rossall	240819	KIA: 1/8
L/Cpl William Frederick Harris	242580	KIA: 31/7	Pte Lambert Ryding****	24608	KIA: 31/7
Cpl Tom Denton Hepworth	240976	KIA: 31/7	L/Cpl John Sandham	243102	KIA: 31/7
Cpl George Hillsley	260011	KIA: 31/7	Capt. Chas. Vernon Martin Simpson		KIA: 31/7
Cpl George Hornby	240452	KIA: 1/8	Pte William Sizer	242656	DOW: 1/8
Pte Edward Victor Humphries	242588	DOW: 3/8	Pte William Walker	201895	KIA: 2/8
Pte Thomas Johnson	242600	KIA: 2/8	Pte John Herbert Walmsley	260043	KIA: 31/7

*CWGC and *Soldiers Died* both record Garside as being killed on 31 January 1917. His service record clearly proves this a typographical error.

**Erroneously recorded as 2/5th King's Own. Medal rolls denote him as 1/5th King's Own.

***Died from wounds as a POW.

****Ryding's service record has contradictory evidence about his battalion, denoting both 1/4th and 1/5th Battalions. Although CWGC, who record him as 1/4th, may be correct, the medal roll only records 8/King's Own followed by 1/5th.

Known to have been Wounded or Missing between 30 July and4 August 1917

Pte Richard Arkwright	26475	WIA: 2/8	2Lt Gilbert Henry Lord		WIA: 2/8
Sgt Frederick William Ball	240562	WIA	Lt William Smith Macfarlane		WIA: 2/8
Pte Robert Barclay	240098	WIA	Sgt James Mackereth	240260	WIA
Sgt John Barnes	240447	WIA	2Lt John Robert Conn Mackey		WIA: 31/7
Pte Herbert Beeley	241349	WIA	Pte Charles Maloney	260035	WIA
CQMS John Blackledge	240206	WIA	Pte George Marsden	28047	WIA: 2/8
Pte Alfred Bramall	33701	WIA: 31/7	Pte Harold Matthews	240163	WIA
Capt. William Noel Briggs		WIA: 31/7	Pte Philip Milburn	28055	WIA: 31/7
Pte Thomas Broxholme	27183	WIA	Pte Frank E. Moncaster	242614	WIA
Pte H. Carder	242549	WIA	Pte Edward Moorhouse	33475	WIA: 1/8
Pte Wilfred Carter	242547	WIA	Pte William Mullin	260055	WIA
Pte William Lamb Carter	240632	WIA	Pte Arthur George Murray	241646	WIA: 31/7
Pte Arthur Clarke	241097	WIA	Pte Thomas Nattrass	28059	MIA
Pte Thomas Cragg	241366	WIA	Pte Simon Nevitskie	242641	WIA
L/Cpl Edward Crane	241017	WIA	Pte Robert William Nickson	243039	WIA: 31/7
Pte Richard William Dean	26874	WIA	Pte Henry F. Noakes	242653	WIA
Pte Thomas Machell Dixon	33954	WIA: 4/8	Capt. Thomas Cary Owtram		WIA: 31/7
L/Cpl Frank Dodgson	241589	WIA	2Lt Harold Parker		WIA: 31/7
Pte Lawrance Stanley Field	260026	WIA: 31/7	Pte John Henry Pickering	26034	WIA
Pte George Fieldhouse	242557	WIA	L/Sgt George Gofton Pinder	20215	WIA
L/Cpl William Henry Freeman	240912	WIA	Pte Bert Rose	27156	WIA
Pte Percy Gething	241252	WIA	Pte William Sidebottom	30748	WIA
Pte James Groves	240922	WIA: 31/7	Pte Richard Simpson	243078	WIA
Pte William Haddow	242976	WIA	L/Sgt Tom Stevens	260004	WIA
Pte William George Harding	260005	WIA	C/Sgt Richard Sumner	5497	WIA
Capt. William Harriss		WIA: 31/7	Pte Thomas Taylor	32595	WIA
Pte George Helm	240243	WIA	Pte James Threlfall	243067	WIA: 31/7
Pte Laurence Hewitt	240858	WIA: 31/7	Pte Charles Tindale	28075	WIA: 1/8
Pte John Hilton	201880	WIA: 31/7	2Lt William Walker		WIA: 31/7
Pte Thomas Hitchen	20839	WIA: 2/8	Pte George A. Walmsley	242440	WIA
L/Cpl Thomas Hodgson	240513	WIA: 31/7	Pte Harry Walton	242484	WIA
Pte Thomas Howard	24294	WIA: 2/8	Pte Robert Wardle Weatherhead	28079	WIA
L/Cpl Robinson Hughes	241508	WIA	Cpl Thomas Wilson	240310	WIA
Pte Richard Lamb	240707	WIA: 30/7	Pte Thomas Victor Wilson	33910	WIA: 30/7
Pte Albert Langtree	240318	WIA: 31/7	Pte James Wintrip	28082	WIA
Pte Samuel Law	242288	WIA	Cpl Ernest Wood	243082	WIA
Pte John Brown Leaver	242604	WIA	Pte George Wood	242479	WIA
L/Cpl Percy Charles Lill	260017	WIA			

On 6 August, the Battalion was on the move again, arriving in La Panne at 6.15 a.m. on 7 August. They were joined there by Lt Henry Hart, now fully recovered from his wound, and a draft of seventy-five replacements. Companies were restructured and Lt Bennett given command of 'A'; Capt. Milnes, 'B'; Lt Kean (soon to be promoted to captain), 'C'; and Capt. Atkinson, returning from his duty as Area Commandant of Bolzeele, took over 'D' on 9 August. The previous day, the entire Battalion paraded for Maj.-Gen. Jeudwine, who thanked them for their magnificent work. During August, 186 replacements arrived, which went a long way towards rebuilding numbers. In the third week of August eleven second-lieutenants joined the Battalion to replace earlier losses. These were Edward Major and Kennedy Toovey on the 16th; Richard Dolby, Arthur Duxbury, John Farrand, Gerald Haywood, Harry Gregson, Edmund Lambert, Albert Livesay, John Parfitt and Alfred Turner all on 18 August. Amazingly, considering the conditions the men had faced over those four days, divisional records only show one officer (Lt Boys-Stones) and ten men in hospital sick during this month. Leave was given to those who had been longest without it and three officers and twenty-nine men benefitted.[24]

The brigade was out of the line until 13 September and during this period of rest and training, considerable effort was put into learning procedures for attacking the new enemy defensive system of isolated pillboxes beefed up by shell-hole positions. The fitness of men and the boosting of their competitive spirit with sporting and military competitions at all levels not neglected either. As always, sickness and accident were present, and a number of men died or were lost to the Battalion as a result. Thirty-seven-year-old Pte George Greenwood from Morecambe was home-posted because of sickness and did not return to active service. Twenty-seven-year-old Pte James Callon from St Helens was also sent home, suffering from trench fever. He too was lost to the Battalion as he was later posted to the 2/5th. One unexpected death was that of twenty-nine-year-old Pte John Jackson, an only son from Skerton. In a seemingly minor accident, he suffered a cut head when he was struck by a box some ten days before his death. The wound had healed, but became re-infected on 31 August. He was admitted to hospital the next day and died on 3 September. His pals were allowed to attend his funeral and laid flowers on his grave.[25] Thirty-one-year-old Pte Henry Titterington had been out with the Battalion since February 1915 and was granted ten days' Home Leave on 9 September. He never returned. Life had become increasingly difficult due to rheumatism and myalgia and he reported sick towards the end of his leave. The doctors were in no doubt as to his fitness to continue and gave him a medical discharge in February. Sadly, he died in August 1918, and a doctor from the Medical Board argued that his death should be seen as due to military service, stating: 'The death Cert is hopeless and one can only conclude that other Dr did not know what was the matter with this man. Death should be regarded as due to service'.[26]

There was no relaxation in discipline when a battalion was out of the line, and in fact, the opposite was the case and expected standards were much higher. One standard maintained whatever the conditions was the cleanliness of rifles. Just four days before he was due to be presented with the ribbon for his MM, Pte William Ayling's rifle did not come up to 2Lt Lambert's expectations and he was 'confined to barracks' for seven days. Another to upset authority was twenty-six-year-old Pte Wilfred Hamblett. The former Darwen weaver swore at his platoon sergeant and was marched in front of the CO and given ten days' field punishment.

One of the more important items of training was a divisional training exercise on 10 September, and a full-scale rehearsal for the attack planned for September. The structure of the Battalion's attacking force was identical (men and organisation) to that to be used in the main attack. As they would be on the day, the Battalion was under the ultimate command of Brig.-Gen. Clifton Stockwell, OC 164 Brigade. Apart from Jeudwine, also present were Field Marshal Sir Douglas Haig, Gen. Gough (Commander of Fifth Army), and two other divisional commanders. The Battalion's diary reports that these luminaries departed well-satisfied with the proceedings; however, Stockwell's private diary was not so glowing, complaining that the Battalion 'had messed it badly'.[27] Although Stockwell did not elaborate at this point, a later entry suggests that Maj. Johnstone had lost touch with his men, who consequently failed to arrive in the right place at the right time.

Lt-Col. Wayte was to remain with the 'B' Team for the attack, so the Battalion was under the command of Maj. Johnstone, with Capt. Milnes as 2IC and Capt. Hart as adjutant. Once again, they used the 'wave' formation, with 'B' front left and 'C' to their right. In the second wave was 'D' to the left and 'A' on the right. 'B' was to be led by the experienced 2Lt Sutherland, with 2Lt Major and 2Lt Duxbury; 'C' had Capt. Kean in command with 2Lt Haywood and 2Lt Dolby; 'D' was led by 2Lt Metcalfe, with 2Lt Lambert and 2Lt Farrand; and Capt. Bennett commanded 'A', but as the senior officer of the four companies, he took three subalterns with him. These were 2Lt Gregson, 2Lt Toovey, and 2Lt Turner. Apart from Sutherland and Metcalfe, the other subalterns were all extremely inexperienced, having only been with the Battalion three weeks—none of that period in the front line.

It was unattainable to replicate the exact conditions of the battlefield while behind the lines and the problems on this exercise ought to have sounded alarm bells within the Battalion's command structure (it is also difficult to believe that Stockwell had not communicated his concerns to Lt-Col. Wayte after the rehearsal—he was a very forthright personality). In the July attack, some platoon commanders from 1/4th King's Own experienced problems staying on track during their long advance across difficult and featureless terrain. The successful ones used a compass bearing to maintain their line of advance, detailing men on each section flank to maintain touch with the neighbouring section. Due to the short nature of their advance in July, the Battalion had not faced this challenge before, but these pitfalls of navigation were disseminated around the division after the July attack in a number of circulations, so should not have come as a surprise on the day. The 'wave' formation was an excellent configuration, but did require the platoon commander to navigate accurately and keep a very tight grip on his sections—something that ideally required a modicum of experience. Difficulties doing this across comparatively unbroken ground did not bode well for success in the actual terrain to be crossed in just ten days' time.

On 13 September, the Battalion left for Goldfish Chateau, arriving there in the evening. It rained heavily overnight, but this ceased in the morning and the CO and company commanders left to reconnoitre the trenches prior to that afternoon's deployment. A draft of twenty-three replacements arrived on 14 September—it should have been twenty-four, but a terrible accident occurred as they left the station. The officer in charge of the various drafts, 2Lt Robinson of 1/7th West Yorks, marched the men off between a railway arch and the track and twenty-year-old Pte Robert Kirby from Burnley was crushed between the arch and a moving train, suffering a ruptured spleen and left kidney. He died from these injuries on 5 November. The Court of Enquiry held Robinson to be responsible.[28] In the afternoon of 14 September, the Battalion moved forward, occupying positions in the OBL. 'A' Company was spread between Wieltje and C.29.9; 'B' took over Bilge Trench from 2/6 Glosters; 'C' held from 'A' Company's bound to where Warwick Lane met the front line; 'D' held from Warwick Lane down to where the trench line met the Potijze–Verlorenhoek Road; and HQ were in the mined dugouts at Warwick Farm. This relief went smoothly and everyone was in position by 7.15 p.m., and apart from the occasional gas shell, a quiet night ensued.

The 15th was a warm day that began quietly enough in the support lines, and apart from a battery adjacent to Warwick Farm being shelled, little happened, most hostile fire being directed against the new front line. In the rear near Goldfish Chateau, Stores was packing to join Transport—who had just left for the Vlamertinghe Brickfields—when a flight of German aircraft bombed their position. Cooks and storemen were in the act of loading their transport when the bombs fell, killing one cook, thirty-year-old Pte Walter Archer. Three other cooks were seriously injured, two of whom died from their wounds, and two storemen were wounded. Records show that twenty-six-year-old Pte John Langstreth was 'killed in action' that day, though his burial at Lijssenthoek suggests that he was actually evacuated as wounded, expiring on his way to the CCS. Twenty-nine-year-old L/Cpl Harry Blair died from his wounds at Mendinghem on 17 September and thirty-four-year-old Pte Albert Steel at Lijssenthoek on the 16th. Wounded was twenty-two-year-old Pte William Thompson (878), who was evacuated home for treatment and presented with the MM awarded to him for 2nd Ypres at the Lancashire Convalescent Camp in Blackpool in February 1918.[29]

The 16th was another warm day and the diary records plenty of aerial activity with a German bombing raid involving fifteen aircraft against the Asylum shortly before 11 a.m. RFC aircraft were also much in evidence and in the late afternoon, one was seen to fall in enemy lines to the south of Iberian. This was probably the 4 Squadron RE 8 of 2Lt L. G. Humphries, who was killed, and 2Lt F. L. Steben who was wounded.[30] Although the diary makes no reference to casualties, records show that twenty-one-year-old Pte Abel Knowles and thirty-three-year-old Pte Edward Maun were both killed. The intelligence summary reports that there was light shelling to the immediate south of Wieltje and it is possible that they died in this. That evening, 2Lt Macdonald packed his kit and went along to Brigade HQ, situated next to the Advanced Divisional HQ at Canal Bank, where he was to become Brigade Intelligence Officer. The previous incumbent, Capt. Robert

Makant had been wounded that morning. At 6.30 a.m., Makant, Capt. Howard, and the Brigade Major had gone forward to reconnoitre the ground for the forthcoming attack and a sniper positioned forward of Pommern Castle shot Makant, pinning the three staff-officers down until dusk. Second Lieutenant Sleight became the new Battalion Intelligence Officer.

Overnight, Lt Henry Forshaw led a working party of 100 men carrying 200 Livens gas projectors forward. With each projectile weighing more than 30 lb and 200 barrels also required, they would have needed to make several journeys. The task was, however, completed successfully and a commendation was forthcoming from division for a job well done. These were successfully discharged against Cross Cotts in the early hours of 18 September. Two casualties are known from 17 September, and it is possible that they were on this working party. Thirty-six-year-old Pte Frederick Proctor was killed and twenty-eight-year-old Cpl George Pinder wounded in the face by shrapnel. He was treated at home for this wound and after leaving hospital served with 3/King's Own in Dovercourt. Carrying munitions was also the downfall of Pte Sam Calvert. The thirty-four-year-old father of three from Blackpool was admitted to hospital the following day, diagnosed with a hernia—he attributed this to 'lifting heavy-weight boxes of S.A.A. at Transport Lines'.[31] He was treated at home and posted to 8/King's Own in July 1918. The Battalion was relieved in the early hours of 18 September and moved to a camp south of Goldfish Chateau. Unfortunately, around noon, a bursting HE shell wounded five men as they rested. The only surviving record is for nineteen-year-old Pte Harold Wearing from Barrow. He was wounded in the thigh and hand by splinters and treated in Lincoln for his injuries. On his return to France in June 1918, he was posted to 1/4th King's Own.

The forthcoming attack was scheduled to begin at 5.40 a.m. on 20 September, with much the same objectives as on 31 July. The 164th Brigade on the left and 165 Brigade on the right, provided the leading waves with the 1/5th King's Own and 1/5th Loyals supporting them. The remaining two battalions from 166 Brigade—Liverpool Scottish and 1/5th South Lancs—were in divisional reserve. The jumping-off line ran along the Stutzpunkt Line from just in front of Hindu Cott on the left, to the front of Somme, then continuing right to 50°52′38.30″N 2°57′13.80″E, roughly midway between Pommern Castle and Iberian. The first objective—known as the Dotted Red Line—ran from a couple of hundred yards to the east of Schuler Galleries on the left, down through Gallipoli, to just forward of Vampir next to the Frezenberg–Zonnebeke Road as the right bound. The second objective, the Yellow Line, ran from the north-eastern edge of Schuler Farm, forward of Keir Farm to 50°52′15.20″N 2°58′12.60″E on the right. The third objective, the Green Line, ran from Wurst Farm on the left, back to Schuler Farm, and along the Langemark–Zonnebeke Road to 500 yards past Kansas Cross, where it turned due south to meet the end of the Yellow Line on the right. It was planned that the Battalion would be thrown into the action with 164 Brigade, at just the right moment to provide the final impetus to take the Green Line under cover of the creeping barrage. The 1/5th Loyals would provide the same function for 165 Brigade.

The Battalion began their move forward to their start positions in Call Reserve at 8.30 p.m. on 19 September, HQ following in the rear. There is no record of how many men the Battalion took into the attack and the Battalion did not complete the 'after-action' reports filled in by others from the division. However, an estimate based upon casualties reported and strength returns from various times of the day, evidence from other units, signal logs, and the Battalion's own report would suggest that two platoons (possibly three 'light' platoons in 'A' Company's case), plus an HQ group of around a dozen men from each company, would be about right—giving a total force of some 450–500 men.

The Battalion were in their assembly positions in Call Reserve by 1.45 a.m. on 20 September and no doubt spent a tense night waiting in the rain for the attack to begin. At 5.40 a.m., shortly after the rain stopped, the barrage began, lighting up the country for miles around with their gun-flashes. The leading waves from the other two brigades left their jumping-off positions and began their assault on the Dotted Red Line. At 7 a.m., 'B' and 'C' began their advance in 'line of section' in artillery formation, the other two companies behind. HQ followed on at 7.17 a.m., the companies ordered to occupy the positions vacated by 164 Brigade. Although it was now daylight, the morning was dull and visibility extremely poor. Still behind the front lines, the Battalion encountered some light shelling from 5.9 and 4.2 along the stretch parallel to Cheddar Villa and Bossaert Farm, and as they reached the Steenbeek, a medium barrage of high (40-foot) bursts of HE was encountered—though this was largely ineffective and very few casualties ensued. The banks of the Steenbeek were quite steep and muddy in places, but despite the night's rain, it was still fordable, and although there were a number of small bridges thrown across the stream, it is possible that some sections ignored these to cross directly along their line of advance. About 150 yards east of the Steenbeek, the enemy laid down an intense barrage of HE with a few shrapnel mixed in. For once, the soft, churned-up ground was advantageous as the effects of these rounds were localised, most of the blast travelling upwards, and although there were casualties, these were few considering the intensity of the fire. This barrage encompassed the ground from there all the way to the Dotted Red Line.

The Battalion's advance certainly did not go to plan, but exactly where it went awry is debateable—possibly even before the leading wave had crossed the Steenbeek. Navigation was extremely difficult due to the condition of the ground. Shell holes were so numerous—many of them filled with water and potential death traps to heavily laden men—that it was impossible to move in a straight line. In artillery formation, it was not too hard to follow the man in front, but it was easy for entire sections to diverge from their track. In open order, sections became split up and it took great coordination by platoon commander and NCOs to keep a platoon together. Later that day, runners had difficulty finding entire companies just a few hundred yards away from them.

By 7.50 a.m., HQ was established in Pond Galleries, a series of four concrete dugouts 150 yards forward of the redoubt at Pond Farm. Maj. Johnstone reported his position back to Advanced Brigade HQ and made contact with 2/5th Lancashire Fusiliers to his left and 1/4th Loyals to his right, but it was not until 8.14 a.m. that a runner from Lt

Bennett reported that his company, with an approximate strength of forty men, was in position 200 yards to the east of Hindu. Casualties are known to have been very light up to this point, so Bennett was missing approximately 60 per cent of his force. Of the other companies there was no sign. At 8.55 a.m., 'C' Company—who set off ahead of Bennett—reported they were now digging in near Hindu to the left of 'A'—'casualties not known'.[32] Ten minutes later, 'D' reported that they were digging in astride the Gravenstafel Road with about seventy men, placing them to the right of the other two companies. During their advance, 'D' Company had been delayed by a machine gun in an enemy strongpoint. Second Lieutenant Metcalfe took one of his platoons and personally led the attack against this obstacle, overwhelming the enemy and capturing the machine gun. He was awarded the MC for his conspicuous gallantry and leadership. Of 'B' Company, there was no sign.

After his men began to dig in, Bennett despatched a patrol to contact the Fusiliers to his left and found that their advance had also not gone to plan. They had come under extremely heavy fire from both their front and left flank and by the time they began their assault against Schuler Galleries, they were down to 50 per cent strength. They captured the Galleries at 6.37 a.m., but one company lost all its officers in the effort and was now commanded by one from Liverpool Irish. This force then began to assault Schuler Farm, their next target. Bennett relayed this information back to HQ and continued to reorganise his force. It was only at 9.55 a.m. that 'B' Company was located on the extreme right boundary of the brigade area and Johnstone was able to report his battalion in position. 'A' Company reported themselves reorganised just two minutes later, with one man killed, eight wounded (including four NCOs) and two men missing. Almost immediately he sent this signal, Sgt Frederick Ball was wounded, but refused to be evacuated, continuing at duty—actions which earned him a bar to his MM.

At 9.48 a.m., the brigade signal log noted the enemy massing for a counterattack from the direction of Passchendaele, forming around Nile, Green House, and Fokker Farm— just 700 yards to the division's front.[33] Divisional artillery brought fire to bear on these positions, and this, combined with devastating enfilading fire from twelve machine guns in Schuler Galleries (nine Vickers and three captured Maxims), backed up by Vickers, Lewis, and more captured Maxims in positions directly in front of the enemy's line of advance, tore the German assault apart.

At 10.43 a.m., Capt. Kean reported that 'C' were now reorganised and that his only casualties were three men missing, though he was unaware of the location of his other platoon. Maj. Johnstone was at an OCs' conference at Advanced Brigade HQ and returned at 11 a.m. with new orders. The conference, chaired by Stockwell, probably had not been the best of times for Johnstone—only able to report a part-battalion of just 130 men, scattered right across the battlefield. Biting comments in Stockwell's diary indicate that the brigadier was obviously far from happy.[34] As the creeping barrage had long-since passed forward, Stockwell was no longer able to deploy the Battalion in a single targeted thrust to take the Green Line—his best chance of securing the final objective now evaporated. Consequently, the Battalion was ordered to advance to the

Dotted Red Line, dig in, and not to commit unless the enemy threatened the Yellow Line. Stockwell was prepared to give up the gains on the Green Line if necessary, but ordered that the Yellow must be held at all costs. When Johnstone returned, he ordered Bennett to take command of the three companies present and lead them forward to the Dotted Red Line. Bennett passed command of 'A' over to one of his subalterns and advanced, siting his HQ—manned by just himself and three runners—in the northern end of Schuler Galleries.

At 11.15 a.m., Capt. John Evans, 2IC of 1/4th King's Own, visited a blockhouse held by his 'D' Company at 50°53′2.40″N 2°57′17.40″E and recounted seeing the Loyals digging in next to the road some 250 yards to the rear of Loos. At the same time, he could see a company from 1/5th King's Own advancing directly to his rear, which was undoubtedly 'B' Company—this position fractionally outside the Brigade's right bound. All went well until they got to within 200 yards of his rear—placing them just to the south of Aisne Farm. At this point, they came under extremely heavy MG fire, which Evans described as originating from Martha House, and sniper fire from Sulva; 'B' Company immediately went to ground. Although the range from Sulva (occasionally 'Suvla' in divisional documents) was over 400 yards, this sniper team proved extremely deadly, and apart from the sixteen men killed by them at the entrance to this blockhouse, Evans's own runner was shot through the head and killed just before they reached it. At 11.30 a.m., the Battalion finally received news from 2Lt Duxbury of 'B'. He reported that 2Lt Sutherland had been wounded and they were now dug in to the east of Aisne Farm, with a strength of forty men. Of 2Lt Major's platoon, there was no news. He also reported that troops to his front were attacking a strongpoint 150 yards away— information that must place him at 50°53′3.60″N 2°57′18.30″E. One of 'B' Company's wounded was thirty-four-year-old Sgt Walter Tedcastle—who had only recently moved from 'A' Company. He made his own way to the rear, though when the Battalion eventually left the line, he was reported as 'missing'. It was only learned on 10 October that he had not survived—his body found by a burial detail, who interred him near to where he was killed. His effects were forwarded to the Battalion, one of which was his pay-book, kept in a breast pocket. This had been pierced by shrapnel and was no doubt the cause of his death.[35] Others had some very close shaves. Twenty-year-old Pte Walter Shuttleworth had a bullet graze his forehead, pass through his ear, and kill the man behind him. Another from 'B' Company who was wounded was twenty-eight-year-old Pte Ernest Porter from Cotherstone. He was hit in the jaw and severely injured—though he survived—requiring over twenty operations, including a graft from a rib bone to repair his jaw, before being discharged.

At 11.53 a.m., the wounded 2Lt Gregson was brought into the Aid Post and shortly afterwards 1/4th Loyals reported they were attacking Kansas House, midway between the Yellow and Green Lines and central to the Battalion's front. At 11.56 a.m., an SOS was launched on the brigade front as the enemy made another counterattack—this time against Cross Cotts—once more stopped in its tracks by effective fire support. Bennett found considerable chaos when he reached Schuler Galleries, with men from just about

A group of four men on 'DROs' at a pre-war camp (1912 or 1913). Standing on the left is 'Jack' Cowell, who died of wounds on 16 May 1915. (*Donna Broadbent*)

The 'Two Hundred' march back after Church Parade on Sunday 6 September 1914. (*King's Own Museum. Ko1203-02*)

A section of 'A' Company guarding the GWR in the Didcot area, September–October 1914. Standing rear left is Pte 'Jack' Cowell. Everyone wore the fifty-round bandoleer as their webbing pouches were not issued until January 1915. (*King's Own Museum. KONeg0173*)

Taken by Capt. Fawcett on 7 March 1915—probably Trench 10a (see Dranoutre map). 'A' Company moved into these trenches after dark on 6 March—their first time in the line. They suffered their first casualty at 1.30 p.m. on 7 March. (*King's Own Museum. ko0784-030*)

Trench 10a Support, taken by Capt. Fawcett in mid- to late March 1915. The left side of this photograph faces towards the enemy. (*King's Own Museum. Ko0784-033*)

Looking back towards British lines in the Dranoutre Sector, from the place where Trench 10a and 9 met at the road. Trench 10a Support was halfway between the photographer and the farm building on the left. (*Author's Collection*)

The battalion's trench line at Polygon Wood ran along just inside the edge of the wood, following the curve of the road. In places, the German line was just to the right of this road.
(*Author's Collection*)

On the right is Pte Matthew Farrell, killed aged sixteen by a sniper at Polygon Wood on 14 April 1915. This photograph was taken at a pre-war camp. When he enlisted in 1912, he added three years to his age and as a 6-footer, got away with the deception.
(*King's Own Museum. Ko1217-04*)

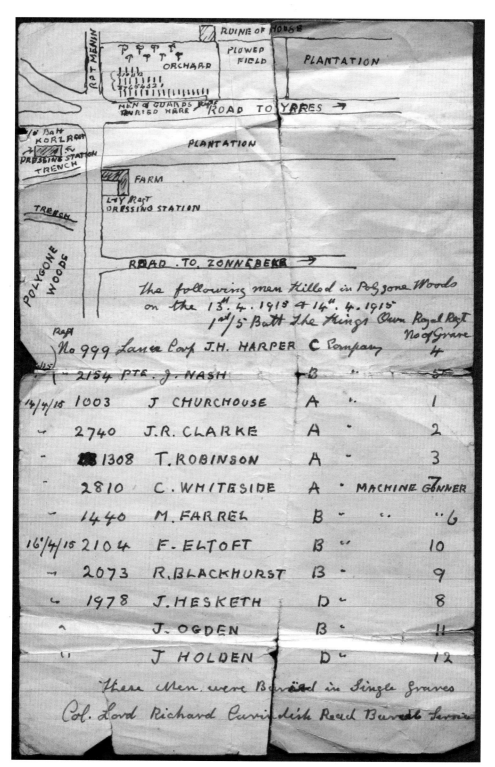

A 1915 sketch map marking the positions of twelve men buried at Polygon Wood, 13–17 April 1915. The last entry for 'J. Holden' is in error and should read 'F. Holding'. This burial ground was never cleared after the war. (*King's Own Museum. Ko2150-02*)

1No evidence remains on the surface to show that the small cemetery used by the battalion at Polygon Wood is directly in front of the camera. (*Author's Collection*)

These fields seem so tranquil now, but on 23 April 1915, the battalion suffered grievous losses when they attacked across them, moving from right to left of the photograph, the left of their line level with the road. (*Author's Collection*)

Stretcher bearer Pte James 'Clifford' Mawson was fatally wounded by shrapnel on 23 April 1915. (*King's Own Museum. Ko2061-39-19*)

The Frezenberg Ridge. Standing on the right of the battalion bound of 4 May 1915 and looking along their trench line. The furthest group of houses are in the same position as the enemy OP used to direct artillery into the battalion's line. The open ground to the rear was referred to as the 'Death Plain'. (*Author's Collection*)

Sanctuary Wood today. The preserved trenches of the museum occupy the central sector of the 1915 GHQ Line. (*Author's Collection*)

Kemmel. Taken from the position of the German front line, overlooking Trench K1, K2, and K2a in the valley (level with the second row of trees). (*Author's Collection*)

Six sons from the Butterworth family served. Four died, the other two were badly wounded. On the left is Pte Hugh Butterworth of the 1/5th, who was killed on 8 August 1915. On the right is Pte William Butterworth of 2/York & Lancs—killed on 18 October 1914, but whose body was only discovered in 2009, eventually identified, and laid to rest in October 2014. Seated is their father, James Butterworth; he died in August 1916, broken-hearted by the loss of so many sons. (*Ian Birnie*)

Relaxing in the sun at Scherpenberg, early September 1915. *From left to right*: 2Lt Reginald Phipp (wearing ORs' boots); Lt-Col. Edward Cadman (killed commanding 10/Cheshires on 27 May 1918); and Capt. William Fawcett. (*King's Own Museum. Ko0784-073*)

1A rifle battery (for three rifles) in the museum at Ocean Villas. (*Author's Collection*)

Company cookhouse in the trenches at Loos, late October to early December 1915. Note the 'crumbly' chalk soil complained about in the Brigade diary.
(*King's Own Museum. Ko0784-118*)

Sgt Herbert Dobson MM was killed on
9 August 1916 when the battalion was
moving forward for an attack. The wooden
cross marking his grave was carved by the
battalion.
(*King's Own Museum. Ko0534-01*)

Herbert Dobson's grave today. Fittingly, the
roses growing at the foot of his headstone
are red. (*Author's Collection*)

Lying near to Herbert Dobson in Quarry Cemetery Montauban is Pte John Hornby, also killed early that morning. (*Author's Collection*)

The MO, Capt. John Deighton RAMC, was fatally wounded as he was moving up to the line on 18 September 1916. The CO and both their orderlies were killed outright by the same shell. (*Kate Mears*)

The battalion carved this oak cross to mark Capt. Deighton's resting place at Heilly Station Cemetery. (*Kate Mears*)

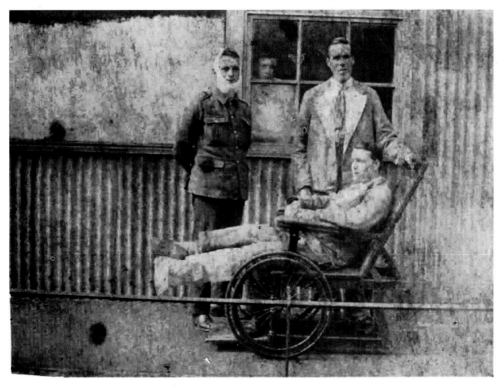

Pte Ernest Porter was seriously wounded in the jaw in the Battle of the Menin Road Ridge on 20–21 September 1917. He is standing on the left, his jaw heavily bandaged. (*Phil Wild*)

The three Whitehead brothers with the battalion—all talented musicians. *From left to right*: Cyril, fatally wounded on 17 June 1917; Reginald; and Wilfred, who died as a POW on 15 November 1918. (*David Fuller*)

L/Cpl Charles Banning, who won the MM at the age of just eighteen. (*John Banning*)

k over the line from the northern end of Schuler Galleries to the divisional boundary
the Hanebeek—which actually left 'A' Company as part of his force. Around 5 p.m.,
5th Lancashire Fusiliers were just initiating an advance against Schuler Farm and
Green Line, when a very heavy enemy barrage fell just to the front of the Galleries,
ectively stopping the first wave in their tracks. By sheer coincidence, the advance
the Fusiliers had coincided with large German counterattacks against 165 Brigade
the right sector and the troops from 174 Brigade on Wurst Farm ridge on the left.
itish artillery and machine-gun fire shattered these counterattacks.

The night was fairly quiet, giving men in the front line a chance to improve their
nsolidation and the medics an opportunity to evacuate more of the wounded. Patrols
re pushed forward across the divisional front, but plans for any appreciable advance
re put on hold due to the difficulty of locating men distributed in deep shell holes
ross the front. Parties of stretcher bearers under George Mawson and Sgt Richard
arkson roamed the battlefield looking for wounded. During his journey to collect 2Lt
therland, Mawson had stumbled upon twenty wounded men sheltering in one shell
le. That night, he returned and brought every single one in, being awarded a long
erdue MM for his courage and selfless actions. For Lt Elwood, the night was one of
-stop treatment of the wounded; when he had run out of patients, he travelled out
o the dark to search for more. During the night, one of the Battalion's stretcher-
arers went forward to what he thought was just behind Schuler Galleries, and finding
o wounded men, began to treat them in a nearby empty dugout. It was not until the
erpool Irish took Schuler Farm at 4.30 p.m. the following day, the bearer realised
at he had missed Schuler Galleries in the dark and was actually in a dugout in the
huler Farm complex. Patrols from 164 Brigade had gone forward to examine Schuler
rm during the night and had found it still to be strongly held—this stretcher-bearer
st have walked straight through the enemy positions with his two casualties.

Between 4 a.m. and 4.30 a.m., some forty gas shells were fired at Pond Galleries,
d at 5.20 a.m., the enemy began a barrage of British lines that lasted until dawn—
doubt as an 'insurance' against further attack. As Elwood was treating a wounded
n from Liverpool Scottish, he asked a padre from one of the neighbouring battalions
help him steady a splint while he attached a bandage. As he did so, a shell burst
arby and a splinter from this wounded the padre in the shoulder. At 6 a.m., another
ll wounded one NCO and 2Lt Eric Sleight. The latter was very badly wounded in the
and Elwood was sure that he would lose his it.[36] Unlike the previous attack, there
re no problems getting ammunition forward and men were plentifully supplied with
s, food, and water. Although no medals were awarded, the QM, Transport Officer
John Gardner, and Sleight were all given a MiD for their role in the attack and their
rformance leading up to it.[37] As soon as flight was possible, German aircraft wer
y active over the front line and some of these bombed forward positions at 6.30 a.
was some two hours after dawn before the RFC arrived and drove off the enemy.

At 2.30 p.m., HQ received orders that the Battalion was going to be withdrawn to
L later in the day. Capt. Milnes was placed in command of an Advance Party, w

An oblique aerial photograph showing the area of line the battalion held on 25 February 1918.
(*Jeudwine Papers, Liverpool Record Office*)

An oblique aerial photograph showing Tuning Fork East, where Pte Edward Kendall was killed
on 26 May 1918. (*Jeudwine Papers, Liverpool Record Office*)

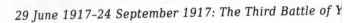

Above: An oblique aerial photograph showing both Cailloux Keeps, Festubert Switch, and Tuning Fork North, positions held be the battalion in June 1918. (*Jeudwine Papers, Liverpool Record Office*)

Below: This section of a panorama looking out into No Man's Land near Silbury Hill in April 1918, demonstrates how 55 Division were able to carry out daylight patrols. In the two lower-central squares, a pair of men can be seen—possibly cooking or washing. Using these for scale, the vegetation is of waist height or higher. (*Jeudwine Papers, Liverpool Record Office*)

every battalion in 164 Brigade and even some from 165 brigade. The ⟨
an RE and there were no NCOs above the rank of corporal. Eventually,
things out, got the men under NCOs from their own units and some sem
emerged. He ordered 'C' Company to dig in to the front of the Galleries,
could find neither 'A' nor 'D' Company. There was considerable hostile
was sticking his head up and making his position obvious if it could be av
out that 'A' had dug in to the left of the Galleries and 'D' to the right, s⟨
Bennett was able to report that he had a defensive line running from the n
boundary down to 200 yards south of Loos along the line of Schuler Galler
164 Brigade held the Yellow Line and some isolated posts as far forward a
200 yards forward of Bennett; although, in reality, this was just a line o
holes—the main defence would be by the troops in Bennett's line. In the n
Yellow and Green Lines merged at Schuler Farm, heavy fighting was stil
Farm itself not falling until 4.30 p.m. on 21 September. Oblivious to the
and machine-gun fire hitting all around him, Bennett behaved with abs
for his own safety, his coolness and courage an inspiration, as he calmly
disparate force to consolidate their position—courage that earned him an

On the right flank, there was mixed success. German defenders in t
fought hard and the attackers lost the cover of the creeping barrage
after 8 a.m., 165 Brigade held Iberian, Kaynorth, Lens, and Gallipoli.
two companies of 1/6th Kings succeeded in taking Hill 37, only to be for
minutes later by a German counterattack. By 2 p.m., all of Hill 35 and it
and Sulva were in British hands. It was not until 3.35 p.m. that a co
1/6th, 1/9th Kings and the South Lancs attacked Hill 37 from the west ⟨
1/5th Kings attacked simultaneously from the south. The joint attack
and despite a number of determined counterattacks by the enemy, Hill

Second Lieutenant Sutherland did not reach the Aid Post until 3.10 ⟨
hours after being shot through a lung—testament of just how difficult mov⟨
ground was. When the news of his wounding reached HQ, Lt Elwood had
party under the command of L/Cpl George Mawson out for Sutherland,
this long to find him and return. Not only was the terrain incredibly diffic
especially with a loaded stretcher—but enemy snipers made no concessi⟨
wounded or those tending them, and anyone exposed for too long became

After 3 p.m., various signals reporting enemy massing for countera
brigade and division and British artillery carried out an intense barra⟨
areas at 4.13 p.m. The enemy replied by shelling the front line betwee
8 p.m., but their observers had difficulty directing their guns onto the a⟨
one shell hole looked pretty much like any other—and the fire was lar⟨
Over on the left, men from various units continually trickled up to Be
were placed to reinforce it. Right across the front, men from the divis⟨
to consolidate their gains and connect the shell-hole positions with
Left Sector, Lt-Col. G. C. Heath, CO of the Liverpool Irish, arrived at B⟨

was despatched to prepare for the Battalion's arrival. The MO visited the men at the front, dodging sniper fire for much of his journey, but returned safely to HQ. During his travels, he found three wounded men from the King's Own and eleven from other battalions—all of whom were brought in. Maj. Johnstone and Capt. Hart toured the defences at the front line at 3 p.m. and returned satisfied that the garrison in Schuler Galleries could hold against counterattack. Less than an hour later, more orders arrived cancelling the move to the OBL—changing it instead to Vlamertinghe. Hurriedly, a runner went to inform Capt. Milnes of the change of plan.

At 6 p.m., a very heavy barrage was directed along the low ridge from Hill 37 to Hill 35 and shortly afterwards SOS rockets went up all along 165 Brigade's front as the enemy advanced in dense waves against Hill 37. Hostile artillery also targeted 164 Brigade's and the Battalion's positions and every approach from the rear. At 7.10 p.m., SOS rockets were also fired from 164 Brigade's positions. The division's artillery replied in kind, shelling the areas the enemy would have to cross to reach the defences. This was an extremely tense time for HQ as all forward contact was lost, though at 7.45 p.m., they were able to establish contact with 'A' Company, who flashed the signal 'OK' by Lucas lamp. By 8 p.m., SOS rockets were being fired all along the line, as many as eight in the air at a time and HQ received orders to 'stand-to'.[38] Mindful that they may be overrun, the Battalion's papers were sent back to Brigade HQ with the orderly clerk and every man at HQ was ordered to prepare to advance. Maj. Johnstone hurriedly departed for Brigade HQ to see if he could gather any more information about the situation, leaving Capt. Hart in command. While this was happening, Sgt Richard Peel (591) was left in charge of 'A' Company, in shell hole positions behind the Liverpool Irish on the left flank. On his own initiative, he gathered the company together and led them forward to the front line, a very creditable action.

Shortly before 8.30 p.m., HQ received a message that the enemy was advancing in strength and the Galleries retaken (erroneously as it turned out). The signal to advance was given and a composite force of stretcher-bearers, mess servants, signallers, and runners—all under the command of RSM Harold Pobgee—advanced in open order against the Galleries. On arrival there, no doubt greatly relieved to find it still in British hands and the German bombardment beginning to subside, the RSM set about reorganising the men and strengthening the defences. Patrols were also sent forward to find out where the enemy actually was. By 9.20 p.m., things had quietened down considerably and the RSM brought HQ's personnel back to Pond Galleries. The enemy had made little progress with his counterattacks. On Hill 37, he had actually reached British defences and penetrated them in few places after some of the 1/5th South Lancs ran short of ammunition—though was soon driven back off the hill. Just north of Gallipoli, near the Keir Farm dugouts, they also broke through in a few places, but again were driven back by the defenders. At 11 p.m., Johnstone was told that the Battalion was to be relieved by 176 Brigade and to withdraw as soon as this was completed, which they did at 1.30 a.m. on 23 September.

Unlike in July, there were very few problems with ammunition resupply to the forward troops. In part, this was due to the leadership of two men. Lt Forshaw was in command of the Brigade Carrying Party, and as this mixed unit struggled forward, heavily laden with boxes of small arms ammunition and bombs, they came under increasingly effective artillery and machine-gun fire. Naturally, as casualties grew, this invoked considerable hesitation from those under fire and confusion among the ranks as NCOs fell. Forshaw strode among them ignoring the fire, calmly urging his men onwards with their vital loads and reorganising them whenever necessary—a performance that resulted in the award of an MC and promotion. On the left, the RSM was equally energetic, working incessantly to get ammunition forward, defying the constant artillery and machine-gun fire as he did so. He too was rewarded with the MC, though unfortunately his excellence resulted in his ultimate loss to the Battalion when he was commissioned into 1/4th King's Own in 1918. One of those awarded the MM never got to see his medal. Thirty-year-old L/Cpl Edward Hedges from Herne Hill remained unwounded during his time at the front, but conditions got the best of him and he was admitted to 55 CCS at Tincourt suffering from pneumonia—ultimately proving fatal on 29 October.

Compared to others in the division, the Battalion had got off very lightly as far as casualties were concerned. There are discrepancies between the numbers in the diary (seventy-three killed, wounded, or missing from all ranks) and those in the later, more accurate divisional casualty statement (101 killed, wounded, or missing from all ranks).[39] In actuality, this turned out to be twenty-eight men killed in action or died from wounds; sixty-four men and officers wounded; and nine missing and later accounted for—such as thirty-six-year-old Pte Herbert Swift. As a whole, the Division suffered 2,730 casualties. One man, not included in the table below, reported missing on 20 September, was twenty-two-year-old Pte James Squire from Liverpool. He had deserted while attached to the divisional RE. Desertion was bad—desertion on the first day of a battle immeasurably worse. He would be in deep trouble if caught, especially going by his disciplinary record, which even the very kindest soul, upon reading it, could best describe him as a 'very naughty soldier indeed'.

Killed or Died from Wounds from the Battle for the Menin Road Ridge

Pte William Armstrong	34517	KIA: 20/9	Pte William Parr	241895	DOW: 22/9
L/Sgt Joseph Ashcroft	242994	KIA: 20/9	Pte Mark Pickthall	242685	KIA: 20/9
Pte Frederick Brimson	260022	DOW: 26/9	Pte Richard Polkinghorn	34781	KIA: 20/9
Pte Henry Johnson Burrows	240370	KIA: 20/9	Pte John William Raffel	28066	KIA: 20/9
Pte William Charnley	243060	DOW: 20/9	CSM Robert Sanderson	240247	KIA: 20/9
Pte William Chorley	27499	KIA: 20/9	Pte John Smith	33252	KIA: 20/9
Pte Edward David Davies	260033	KIA: 21/9	Pte Moses Stables	34784	KIA: 20/9
Pte Harry Faulkner	241509	KIA: 20/9	Pte Jim Steels*	27308	KIA: 20/9

Pte John William Fell	260046	KIA: 20/9	Pte Matthew Sunter Storey	242643	KIA: 20/9
Pte James Jamieson	201152	KIA: 20/9	Sgt Walter Tedcastle	240144	KIA: 20/9
Pte George Kirton	28040	DOW: 26/9	Pte William Henry Timbrell	241781	DOW: 22/9
Pte Thomas McCabe	242684	KIA: 21/9	Pte Albert Arthur Wardle	260027	KIA: 20/9
Pte Philip Milburn	28055	KIA: 20/9	Pte Alexander Watt	240774	KIA: 20/9
L/Cpl Reuben Nicholson	201855	KIA: 20/9	Pte George Myles Wilson	32650	DOW: 20/9

*Recorded by CWGC as being killed in action on 26 September. Not only were the division out of the line then, his service record clearly denotes 20 September as his date of death.

Known to have been Wounded at the Battle for the Menin Road Ridge

Pte James Edward Adamson	242519	WIA	Pte Joseph Knaggs	28041	WIA
Sgt Frederick William Ball	240562	WIA: 20/9	Pte Herbert Kneale**	241249	WIA: 22/9
Pte William Ball	27763	WIA	L/Cpl John Robert Krelle	240190	WIA
Pte Robert Stanley Berry	260036	WIA: 20/9	Pte John Law	200863	WIA: 20/9
Pte William J. Blaylock	33851	WIA	Pte Joseph McBride	25728	WIA
Pte Jacob Morris Boardman**	33926	WIA: 21/9	Pte Terence McGuire	243076	WIA
Pte Thomas Brown	243094	WIA: 20/9	Pte Richard Henry Mottershaw	34756	WIA
Pte Fred Byram	240027	WIA	Pte Edwin Murray	2318	WIA: 20/9
Sgt George Edward Campbell	240845	WIA	Cpl James Ormond	13491	WIA
Pte Albert Herbert Chapman	260016	WIA: 20/9	Pte Richard Pollard	34580	WIA
Pte James Cooper	242968	WIA: 20/9	Pte Ernest Harold Porter	28065	WIA
Pte Henry Richard Cope	34593	WIA	Pte Charles Portnall	34808	WIA
Pte Philip Henry Crow	33848	WIA: 21/9	Pte Harold Radcliffe	34816	WIA: 20/9
Pte John Cunliffe	21521	WIA	Pte Robert Roper	240655	WIA
Pte Eric Dunworth	242490	WIA	Pte Walter Scott Shuttleworth	33042	WIA: 21/9
Pte Fred Elkington	242555	WIA	Pte Cramford Silversides	242487	WIA
Pte Harry Ellams	22752	WIA: 20/9	CSM Claude Simmons	240945	WIA
Pte John Fawcett	34791	WIA	2Lt Eric William Sleight		WIA: 20/9
Pte Thomas Fitzsimmons	201277	WIA	Pte Edward James Smith	241336	WIA
Pte Reginald Rex Fletcher	242455	WIA	Pte Robert Spencer	243079	WIA
Pte Lawrence Gibson	33100	WIA	Pte Alfred George Street	242704	WIA
Cpl Benjamin J. Gillon	240142	WIA	Sgt Joseph Sumner	243096	WIA
L/Cpl Joseph Gornall	240604	WIA	2Lt Frank Sutherland		WIA: 20/9
2Lt Harry Gregson		WIA: 20/9	Pte Herbert Swift*	32504	MIA: 20/9
Cpl Joseph William Guy	241076	WIA	Pte Harry Swindlehurst	33927	WIA
Pte Tom Hagley	242568	WIA	Pte James Taylor	260029	WIA

Pte James Hannon	241283	WIA	Cpl Herbert Teasdale	240540	WIA: 20/9
Sgt Henry Richard Harriott	242661	WIA	L/Cpl George Walters	241557	WIA
Pte Richard Harvey	201909	WIA	Pte James Woodhouse	240962	WIA
2Lt Gerald Haywood		WIA: 20/9	Pte John Roland Woodhouse	27005	WIA
L/Cpl Edward Robert Hingley	33950	WIA: 20/9	L/Cpl Benjamin Woolley	242691	WIA
Pte Thomas Holliday	242574	WIA	Sgt Thomas Wright	240162	WIA
Pte James Johnson	18496	WIA			

*Later accounted for.

**The date appearing in these men's service records is probably incorrect and the actual date of wounding is as reported above.

By 6 p.m. on 22 September, the Battalion were in Derby Camp and next morning began the 8-mile march to Shrine Camp, near Watou east of Poperinghe, arriving about noon. The Battalion paraded on 24 September and were thanked by Brig.-Gen. Lewis. Later that day, an advance party consisting of 2Lt John Parfitt and two men was despatched to Beaulencourt to prepare for the Battalion's arrival there. As they left, sixty-six replacements and six new second lieutenants arrived—Robert Birrell, John Ferguson, James Henderson, Alexander White, James Withey, and William Yare, the latter commissioned from the ranks of the Battalion that June.

25 September 1917
14 December 1917: Épehy

Coordinates for Positions Named in this Chapter

14 Willows Road	50°0'38.00"N 3°8'28.50"E	Leith Walk	50°1'38.80"N 3° 9'1.10"E
Adelphi, the	50°1'8.30"N 3°10'7.30"E	Limerick Post	50°1'3.90"N 3°9'52.00"E
Birdcage, the	50°0'42.40"N 3°11'24.30"E	Little Priel Farm	50°0'32.70"N 3°10'38.20"E
Cannon Gate	50°1'44.20"N 3°11'0.90"E	Mac Trench	50°2'46.80"N 3°10'46.00"E
Crook's Quarry	50°3'9.90"N 3°10'21.00"E	Malassise Farm	50°0'2.90"N 3° 8'50.60"E
Cruciform Post	50°0'32.60"N 3°10'30.80"E	Meath Post	50°1'23.80"N 3°9'38.50"E
Denning Alley	50°2'35.80"N 3°10'33.90"E	Nest, the	50°0'28.60"N 3°10'18.70"E
Falcon Sap	50°0'47.70"N 3°11'29.50"E	Ossus Wood	50°0'51.30"N 3°11'16.20"E
Fallen Tree Road	50°1'1.10"N 3°9'58.80"E	Parr's Bank	50°1'3.40"N 3°9'25.80"E
Gardiner's Bank	50°3'2.50"N 3°10'40.30"E	Pigeon Quarry	50°1'35.80"N 3°10'42.80"E
George Street	50°2'46.30"N 3°10'31.50"E	Pigeon Ravine	50°1'11.70"N 3°9'47.40"E
Gillemont Farm	49°59'25.12"N 3°12'1.98"E	Priel Cutting	50°0'28.30"N 3°10'10.07"E
Heythrop Post	50°0'23.10"N 3°10'36.10"E	Roberts Avenue	50°2'27.60"N 3°10'46.10"E

High Street	50°2′30.10″N	Sherwood lane	50°1′53.80″N
	3°10′34.10″E		3°10′6.10″E
Holt's Bank	50°0′49.10″N	Turner Quarry	50°3′10.80″N
	3°10′28.10″E		3°10′31.80″E
Kildare Lane	50°1′4.20″N	Vaucellette Farm	50°1′35.60″N
	3°10′2.20″E		3°7′53.20″E
Kildare Post	50°0′56.30″N	Vaughan's Bank	50°0′11.50″N
	3°10′15.50″E		3°8′25.50″E
Knoll, the	50°0′2.28″N	Woking Post	50°2′32.30″N
	3°11′49.84″E		3°9′46.90″E
Lark Post	50°0′31.20″N		
	3°11′9.70″E		

The move south was not a rest period as the division was to relieve 35 Division in a sector roughly centred on Épehy, 10 miles to the north-east of Péronne. With another onwards move for the following day, 28 September was designated a general holiday and men were issued with passes to visit Amiens. A number of the officers who had been through the Somme with the Battalion took advantage of the day to ride out to visit their old battlefields, among them the QM:

> ...rode through Le Transloy, Lesboefs, Guinchy, Guillemont' Delville Wood, Longueval, Flers and Guedecourt, back to Beaulencourt by Death Valley—the whole series of villages very like Nineveth [*sic.*]—a mass of bricks showing where a house once stood, or a cradle or chair pointing to someone's habitation. Such a scene of desolation! And the only birds seen were typical—two ravens! Everywhere the little crosses 'To an unknown soldier'.[1]

On 29 September, the CO and a number of other officers reconnoitred the left sector (split into three sub-sectors), to be garrisoned by 166 Brigade. The Battalion was to occupy the right sub-sector of this. The left sub-sector of the left sector ran from 50°2′13.40″N 3°11′1.50″E near Honnecourt Wood in the north, down to Cannon Gate. The centre sub-sector stretched southwards to 50°0′59.00″N 3°10′44.20″E, the right sub-sector running on southwards to Lark Post, where it then headed south-west to join the right sector at 50°0′17.80″N 3°10′35.40″E.

The right sector only needed two battalions, rather than the three necessary for the left. The left sub-sector here stretched from the join with the left sector down to 49°59′35.70″N 3°11′46.30″E; the right-subsector running southwards at 49°58′50.30″N 3°11′27.50″E. This 8,000 yards of frontage stretched the division's manpower to its limit, though when this was extended to 12,000 yards on 28 November, it became critical. The front line was not particularly strong—much of it merely CT linking scattered outposts. Neither was it in good condition, and when the battalions occupied their positions, it was clear to them that much work was needed.

At 2.45 p.m., the Battalion led by Lt-Col. Wayte set off to relieve 16/Cheshires in the front line, each platoon spaced apart by 100 yards as they got within range of German heavy artillery. Despite stopping *en route* for an hour to eat tea, they arrived at Malassise Farm at their expected time, where their guides met them. The night was cold and dry, starlight aiding their silent approach up the line. HQ established themselves in the Nest; 'B' Company were in reserve at Priel Bank (probably Priel Cutting); 'A' Company placed two platoons at Heythrop Post and another two at Cruciform Post; and 'C' and 'D' were in the front line, holding the Birdcage. The relief went smoothly and was completed by 9.30 p.m.

The Birdcage was an unpopular position—being a mini-salient and vulnerable to enfilading fire from north and south. It was very quiet when the Battalion took over, but strong enemy patrols dominated No Man's Land at night—a situation the Battalion determined to remedy. While most men were occupied improving the trenches, a strong fighting patrol crept out of the Birdcage late on 3 October and entered Ossus Wood. Additional care was necessary here as the previous night a patrol from a neighbouring battalion had reported finding a number of booby traps with stick grenades attached to trip wires. The patrol must have been spotted because, as they approached, a twenty-five man German working party hurriedly withdrew into their own lines. The patrol waited in cover for two hours, but the working party did not reappear, so they returned to the Birdcage. Although no booby traps were found, the wood itself was laced with barbed wire at ankle height set to catch the unwary.

The next night, another fighting patrol armed with a Lewis left the Birdcage and penetrated Ossus Wood where the enemy wire began (50°0'54.90"N 3°11'28.80"E) and worked their way west, hoping to cut off the line of retreat for any enemy patrols already in the wood. Once again, this proved fruitless. There was very little hostile artillery so far, and although no one was lost to enemy activity, fifteen were evacuated to hospital sick, one of whom was as nineteen-year-old Pte William Williamson, with ICT of the leg. He was sent back to Blighty and posted to 1/King's Own on his return. In the evening of 6 October, 'A' Company swapped positions with 'D' and 'B' with 'C'. Patrols once more ventured out—again without luck.

To their north, a pair of snipers from Liverpool Scottish had more fortune. Entering No Man's Land at night, they lay up awaiting prey during daylight hours. Two Germans were observed in the open 1,700 yards away. A remarkable single shot dropped one of these—the other immediately jumping into a nearby trench. Five minutes later, they watched a stretcher team recovering the fallen man, but held their fire. German artillery was still light, though a number of registration shots fell around Little Priel Farm. The 7th was a wet and windy day spent improving the trenches, but after dark, two reconnaissance patrols entered No Man's Land. One of these spied a German patrol of about twenty men heading towards the northern side of Birdcage, though they diverted before reaching it and entered Ossus Wood.

The Battalion suffered its first fatality during the morning of 9 October, when twenty-eight-year-old L/Cpl Henry Gardner from 'A' Company was hit by a sniper as he worked on the trenches on the left of the Birdcage. Records also show that, on the same day, twenty-six-year-old Pte Thomas Nattrass was wounded in the right thigh and evacuated home for treatment. However, the probability is that he was a casualty of the previous day's shelling of Little Priel Farm, only appearing on the following day's casualty list. He was transferred to munitions work upon his recovery. On the night of 10 October, a reconnaissance patrol left the Birdcage, and soon afterwards, they watched an enemy fighting patrol of about twenty men close to Falcon Sap. Lewis and trench mortar fire was directed onto these, dispersing them, but provoking enemy retaliation with their own trench mortars. The Birdcage—caught between both fires—was an unhealthy spot while this continued. An enemy MG in Ossus Wood also joined in the retaliation, but was quickly silenced by five rounds from a 3-inch Stokes. The pattern of nightly patrols and work on improving the trenches and wire continued until the evening of 12 October, when the Battalion was relieved by 1/6th King's at 11 p.m., proceeding through the pouring rain to bivouac at Aizecourt-le-Bas.

Here, they found that four replacement second lieutenants were awaiting them. John Henderson went to 'A', Walter Young to 'B', James Hay to 'C', and David Gibson to 'D'. Three days later, another six arrived, one of whom was Thomas Blakeley, now recovered from his wounds. The others were Henry Tringham, Clifford Tucker, David Tweedie, Jack Walker, and Henry Wallis. Conditions at Aizecourt were so unpleasant due to deep mud and pooled water that, on 14 October, the Battalion was allowed to move to the old brigade position. Elsewhere, authority had caught up with Pte Squire, whose time on the run had been brief—just one day. His FGCM in the afternoon of 16 October sentenced him to death—commuted to fifteen years penal servitude by Haig on 27 October. The only time he actually served was between his arrest and then, as he was returned to the Battalion—his sentence under suspension. With the impending departures of Capt. Hart and the MO to England on leave, 2Lt Blakeley became adjutant and Capt. Price RAMC deputised for Lt Elwood.

At 2 p.m. on 22 October, the Battalion moved back up, eating their tea as they marched. They were in the same sub-sector as before, but this time in support to Liverpool Scottish. 'A' Company occupied Kildare Post and Kildare Trench leading northwards to Limerick Post; 'C' Company manned Meath Post; 'D', 14 Willows Road; and 'B' Company and HQ were in Vaughan's Bank. In the evening of 23 October, 'D' Company was relieved by Liverpool Scottish and moved up to Limerick Post. These positions would have huge significance in little over a month. No enemy artillery targeted the Battalion's area, though an MG fired a few rounds over 'A' Company's heads at 8.20 p.m. The usual fatigue parties were tasked for trench improvement and carrying details, and although the 24th was a fine day, 25 October saw high winds and torrential rain, which although making things unpleasant, was not added to by the enemy, whose artillery fire could best be described as desultory. The two new subalterns who joined the Battalion that day must have got entirely the wrong impression. Eric Stainton went to 'B' Company and Reginald Woodward to 'D'. Both had just thirty-six days left with their new platoons. The only casualty on record for this tour is thirty-five-year-old Pte Albert Gartside, wounded in the right forearm and evacuated home.

Late on the night of 29 October, the Battalion moved north to relieve 7/Somerset LI. The division's northern bound now extended right up to the Banteux Ravine, and with a front of 2,600 yards, the Battalion was severely overextended. 'C' Company was in left support, apart from half a platoon in the northernmost front line at Crooks Quarry—facing northwards across 1,500 yards of No Man's Land to enemy positions on the Banteux Spur. One and a half platoons were lined along part of George Street, the other two platoons spaced in between, along nearly 1,000 yards of trenches. In right support was 'D' Company, with three platoons centred where High Street crossed the support line—their fourth platoon with HQ at Woking Post in High Street. The left front line was held by 'B' Company, centred on Gardiner's Bank (now directly under the E17 Motorway). Right front was 'A' Company, their positions running from 'B' Company's southern platoon to 50°2′21.20″N 3°10′31.30″E. These positions were on a forward slope and overlooked Honnecourt Wood and village. Despite their good view of German defences, very little they observed was within range of the 18-pounders—much reducing opportunities to smite careless movement and a lack of capability that would have dire ramifications. The nearest enemy positions to the British line were opposite High Street and these were some 600 yards distant, so considerable manpower was needed maintaining night patrols—this being supplied by the companies in support, who also provided the carrying parties. Any patrol leaving 'A' Company's left at Fife and Mac Trenches, would need to travel 1,500 yards in a north-easterly direction before they reached the enemy wire.

Second Lieutenant Alexander White was slightly wounded on 29 October, but remained at duty after his wound was dressed. Patrols went out that night and although no enemy were encountered, one penetrated the north-west corner of Honnecourt Wood finding an unoccupied enemy post. They also reported that in much of the wood, the ground was waterlogged and heard sounds of movement around Honnecourt village. Casualties remained low, as did sickness, though twenty-four-year-old Pte Tom Haselden was struck down by dysentery and evacuated home. He was posted to 1/King's Own in May 1918, dying from wounds a scant month later. Patrols went out again on the night of 30–31 October to probe enemy defences, though this time the post in Honnecourt Wood was inhabited. The following night also saw patrol activity, and though the Battalion's patrols had nothing new to report, three patrols from the 2/5th Lancashire Fusiliers on the extreme right, placed large notice boards, containing information about recent Zeppelin losses, on the German wire—clearly visible from the enemy front line—and no doubt a source of considerable irritation. These little psychological games all helped raise friendly morale and introduce doubts to the enemy's.

This pattern continued into November, with constant patrolling and little tangible result for their hard work. When a German party of twelve was spotted to the east of Honnecourt Wood in the early hours of 4 November, they disappeared before the Battalion's patrol could move into a position to engage them. Other patrols got right up to the enemy's wire—reporting back on its construction—but found no one to attack, most of the activity on this front happening further south. Thick fog and poor visibility dominated for much of the first week of November, reducing artillery fire and allowing more daylight work on the defences. Casualties across the division were light and the only recorded one from the Battalion in this first week was nineteen-year-old Pte Hugh McGowan, who was lightly wounded and remained at duty after being patched up. A patrol forward of High Street came under heavy small arms fire from a position at 50°2′34.60″N 3°11′15.50″E on the night of 8-9 November and was forced to retire, though without casualties. A riposte was consequently planned for the following night. The weather was fine all day and at 7.10 p.m. a salvo of ten 77-mm rounds crashed around HQ in High Street, though no damage or casualties ensued and a bearing on the location of the battery was obtained and passed to division. Shortly after dark, torrential rain fell, soaking men and dissolving the edges of the trenches, which commenced to collapse in a number of places.

Into this downpour, twelve men under 2Lt Robert Birrell departed the front line, their target an enemy post just 200 yards to the south of the troublesome MG. Any sounds they made were muffled by the pattering of rain, the downpour also shrouding them from enemy observation. Birrell led his men right up to their objective, his bombers to the fore, their grenades ready. On his signal, every man hurled his bomb into the post and retired, covered by their comrades. The detonations were met by neither screams nor gunfire; in fact, nothing happened, apart from a few flares fired off from enemy positions to the rear of what was clearly now an unoccupied position. Cursing their luck, the sodden party returned to friendly lines. During daylight hours on 10 November, watchers through a trench periscope observed movement in another post just 40 yards behind the one attacked the previous night and a sally against this was planned for that night. The rain moderated during the day, but it was still showery when the raiders edged forward. This time, the target protected by wire, was engaged from a longer range by four salvoes of Hales rifle grenades, but once more—enemy reaction was nil.

Artillery from both sides was active on 11 and 12 November, British guns wire busting and the foe retaliating against front and rear. Throughout the 12th, the Battalion's Lewis guns also swept the enemy's parapets. There was much less action by artillery on 13 November, but snipers from both sides plied their trade. One from the Battalion, lurking in Honnecourt Wood, claimed a hit and German snipers made a nuisance of themselves for anyone using the CT near Turner Quarry. They hit no one, but they appeared to be using a new type of round that burst on contact—an example being sent to Brigade for analysis. The only casualty of the day was eighteen-year-old Pte Carey Sager, though his wounds were accidental and he returned next day. Despite a ground mist on 14 November, the Battalion's snipers scored another hit. The 15th was clear and artillery correspondingly more active. Intermittently, the junction between the front line and Roberts Avenue was shelled by 77 mm, though no record remains of any casualties from this. The only man known to have been lost to the Battalion this day was twenty-year-old Pte Walter Wolstenholme, admitted to the Field Ambulance with tonsillitis. He was evacuated home and never returned, the former bookkeeper being posted to the Records Office in Preston as a clerk.

On 17 November, 'C' Company was relieved by a company from 1/5th South Lancs and moved to Mac Trench. The following day, HQ moved forward from Woking Post to a dugout in Denning Alley (Avenue) to make room for 35 Brigade HQ, whose battalions were to assault the German line adjacent to the Battalion, immediately north of the Banteux Ravine on 20 November, the opening day of the Battle of Cambrai. The 55th Division was not directly involved in this offensive, but three battalions from 164 Brigade were to carry out two large diversionary raids against German positions at the Knoll and Gillemont Farm, timed to coincide with the main attack. It was hoped that these would entice German artillery away and prevent the enemy moving any reinforcements northwards. On 19 November, German artillery was very active against the Battalion's line, especially around Mac Trench and Denning Alley—mostly with 77 mm, though some 5.9 were also employed.

At 6.20 a.m. on 20 November, the sky to the rear of the British lines lit up as every gun along the front began to barrage enemy front, support, and rear areas—tracer from the MG barrage arcing over the British front line into German-held areas. Ten minutes later, 400 tanks lumbered slowly across No Man's Land, flattening enemy wire for the following infantry. The front line fell without a fight, though the support line put up more resistance. Unlike on previous occasions, where the route of advance for the tanks had been pulverised into a pitted mess by British artillery, no preliminary bombardment had destroyed the ground, easing considerably the progress for the tanks. In their elevated positions, the men from the Battalion had a grandstand view of the right flank of this attack. Enemy artillery reacted against pre-arranged targets and began to drop rounds onto the Battalion's front line—a guaranteed way to deter onlookers—but hardly effective against the main attack. No casualties were suffered from the front line companies, but Capt. Hart was wounded while watching from HQ. Not surprisingly, the enemy to the Battalion's front were pretty nervous and numerous coloured flares were fired up during the day. Both 'A' and 'B' Company sent out daylight patrols right up to the German wire, but each time these were fired upon by MGs and forced to withdraw smartly. After dark, further patrols probed enemy defences, finding the enemy very alert.

On 21 November, the enemy continued to be watchful and their trench mortars in Honnecourt Wood targeted the front line and Denning Avenue. One 4.2 in the vicinity of Basket Wood fired sixty rounds at the left-hand company and thirty 4.2 were fired into the British wire at High Street, though without fatalities. At least one man, nineteen-year-old Pte Harry Swindlehurst, was wounded. The apprentice boot-maker from Barrow was severely injured, leading to the amputation of his the leg at the thigh. After dark, twenty-two-year-old 2Lt Stainton led a patrol out along Fife Road towards the German post along there. Unobserved by the enemy, he got close enough to see that this position had been strengthened with another two MGs and returned to pass on this information, receiving personal congratulations from Jeudwine. On 22 November, 'A' and 'B' Company rotated, so 'B' now held the left. The following days were very similar, with German artillery—mostly ineffective—interspersed with day and night patrols, all finding an alert enemy. On 24 November, a daylight reconnaissance patrol revisited the position on Fife Road and was met with a fusillade of rifle grenades, fortunately without casualties. Not taking this lightly, the patrol returned and 'loaded for bear', journeyed back to the German position and peppered it with twenty-two Hales grenades—though with indeterminate result.

At 7.45 p.m. on 26 November, the Battalion was relieved by 1/5th South Lancs, though 'B' Company remained as reserve for them in High Street. Two of 'A' Company's platoons went to Sherwood Lane, the other two to 14 Willows Road; 'C' took over Meath Post and 'D' and HQ also moved to 14 Willows Road. The situation seemed calm, the advance successful and Lt-Col. Wayte departed to England on leave, Maj. Anderson from the Loyals taking command in his absence. The next day, one new officer arrived—though 2Lt Walter Harrison was a familiar face, having been a CSM in the Battalion before commissioning. Little did he suspect that this posting would only last three days. On 27 November, 'A' Company took over Limerick Post, and the next day, half of 'B' went to Vaucellette Farm, but were moved south to Vaughan's Bank on the 29th.

Although the front line seemed quiet, there was considerable unease at divisional HQ. All indications were that the enemy was preparing an attack and Jeudwine was doing everything in his power to get ready for this. He was extremely concerned about how thinly his infantry were stretched—taking into account men off duty—this worked out to about one man for every 10 yards of front. Also worrying was the poor condition of his defences—blasted by artillery fire in previous days and discontinuous along most of its length—with insufficient manpower to remedy this. Both Jeudwine and Corps Commander Lt-Gen. Thomas D'Oyly Snow were particularly apprehensive about the Banteux Ravine, where the boundary between VII Corps and III Corps lay and which because of troop dispositions, offered the enemy an open door to the rear (concerns they shared with High Command more than once). On 28 November, Jeudwine issued an urgent divisional warning order:

> Certain indications during today point to the possibility of enemy making an attack against our front. All troops will be warned to be specially on the alert in the trenches and all posts.[2]

Jeudwine had been led to believe that he could rely on a brigade from 12 Division to help defend the Ravine, but when he visited Maj.-Gen. Scott on the 29th, he was told that this would not now be provided. The 55th Division's CRA, Brig.-Gen. A. M. Perreau, had arranged with III Corps for a barrage by their heavy artillery to take place at 6.30 a.m. on the 30th against obvious German assembly positions. However, as reported in the OH, this was cancelled by III Corps on the night of the 29th—a fateful decision (the division's own heavy artillery had earlier been detached to cover the main attack and had not yet been released).[3]

Jeudwine's papers, however, show that there was more to this than appears. In a later letter to Snow, Jeudwine recounted his version of the events:

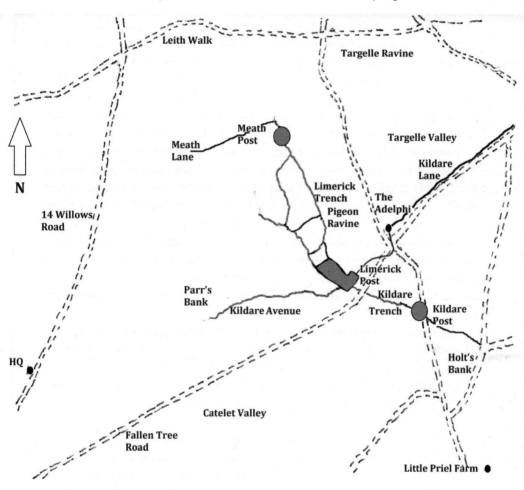

LIMERICK POST

I do not agree with Knapp's [Brig.-Gen. Kempster Kenmure Knapp] account of what passed between himself and me on the night of the 29th. I have a pretty clear recollection of this conversation and this is what I maintain happened. As soon as Perreau, my C.R.A., told me that the assistance of III Corps, Heavy Artillery had been refused. I rang up Burnett-Stuart [Brig.-Gen. Sir John Theodosius Burnett-Stuart B.G.G.S. VII Corps] and made the strongest representations with regard to the necessity for our having the fire of heavy artillery on our front. He said that the III Corps would not agree, and when I still pressed he asked if I would speak to Knapp about it. Knapp, who was apparently in the room, came to the telephone and I renewed my protests to him. He did not however meet them in at all a sympathetic spirit. He pointed out that there was no certainty that we were going to be attacked and that if the heavy artillery fired and there was no attack it would be a great waste of ammunition. I admit that I was infuriated at this way of looking at it, and I put the opposite case to him, *viz.*, that if on the other hand there was an attack and no heavy artillery was brought to bear upon it, there would be a great waste of life and that in my opinion it was better to waste ammunition than to waste lives. I clearly recollect using practically those very words to him.

I have no recollection of Burnett-Stuart saying to me, as Knapp maintains he did, that if I 'considered the matter imperative he would call up the B.G.S., III Corps and reopen the question'. On the contrary, he (Burnett-Stuart) said that he had done everything he could and that if I was not satisfied would I speak to Knapp. The conversation between Knapp and myself then took place which I have given above.[4]

Early each morning special patrols went out along the divisional sector, with orders to check the enemy wire for gaps cut to allow attackers access to No Man's Land. Each day, these returned with nothing to report. The morning of 30 November was no different. A thick fog lay over the sector, filling the ravines with an impenetrable soup. The signal log for 166 Brigade shows an entry for 6.55 a.m.: 'Special patrol report all quiet. Enemy wiring and revetting opposite the right battalion'.[5] Just five minutes later, an intense barrage of HE, shrapnel, and gas shells from artillery and trench mortars fell on the left of the front line, HQs, and battery positions. SOS signals were fired from the left battalion (1/5th South Lancs) and minutes later all telephone communications were cut. What divisional artillery remained, commenced firing on the SOS lines at 7.09 a.m. Troops were already 'stood-to' and the two platoons from B Company in Vaughan's Bank, accompanied by two platoons from Liverpool Scottish, hurried to 14 Willows Road. At 7.32 a.m., 1/5th Loyals, to the immediate south of the 1/5th South Lancs, reported that their line was under heavy bombardment of gas and HE and the wire opposite their left front company had been severed. Three minutes later, they too fired SOS flares. At 7.43 a.m., the South Lancs managed to make contact by visual signal, reporting, 'we know nothing yet. OK'.[6]

In Limerick Post, Capt. Bennett and his men suffered a rude awakening when the barrage began. It was their thirty-ninth day in the trenches and officers not on duty had been allowed to sleep in their pyjamas and men to remove their boots. After hurriedly dressing, Bennett left his dugout and peered towards the front line, now obscured by heavy smoke. The wind was blowing from the south-west and with it came a strong smell of mustard gas, making everyone's eyes water. From the wind direction, Bennett presumed that the attack was to the southern part of the sector and a runner sent forwards to the Liverpool Scottish HQ in the Adelphi returned with a message stating that they knew nothing apart from that their front had been attacked. Bennett also sent a runner to Kildare Post, who were equally uninformed. The creeping barrage had passed over Limerick Post, mostly missing them, though one unlucky shell killed twenty-two-year-old Sgt Louis Dickinson, twenty-two-year-old Sgt Thomas Wilkinson, and three men.

Despite their frontal positions still under heavy bombardment, Liverpool Scottish were able to observe the enemy leaving their trenches and relayed this news to brigade, who immediately forwarded it by telephone to division at 8.15 a.m. At 8.30 a.m., Bennett observed large numbers of men advancing in extended order over the ridge to the north of Pigeon Quarry. As a consequence of heavy smoke and the distance, he was unable to identify them, but presumed they were enemy because of their direction of movement. The attackers were aided by their aircraft, over fifty of which were reported by 1/5th Loyals to be strafing their front-line and the sunken roads. At 8.20 a.m., Bennett watched HQ personnel from Liverpool Scottish line the earth bank in front of the Adelphi, some falling as they were hit. Ten minutes later, a small party of Liverpool Scottish dashed across Fallen Tree Road from the direction of Kildare Post and jumped into Kildare Trench where it led to Limerick Post, a number of Germans in hot pursuit. Second Lieutenant Henderson immediately gathered a few men and bombed these intruders out, the garrison establishing a bombing block in Kildare Trench, about 10 yards from Fallen Tree Road on the south side. A key member of this small party was L/Cpl Percy Barraclough, who led the bombers and was instrumental in constructing this block. Clearly, the enemy had broken through to the south-east of Kildare Post at Holt's Bank.

The situation to the Battalion's north was critical. At 8.30 a.m., a telephone message from the Loyals, advising that the enemy were through on their left, was cut off in mid-report. At the same time, a large party of artillerymen hurried down through Le Petit Sant ravine reporting the enemy had penetrated the British front line and were advancing over the Villers Ridge. To the north of Meath Post, the enemy was also advancing down Gloster Road—it was beginning to look like the whole left flank of the division had been turned. To face this new threat, the two 'B' Company platoons and all available HQ personnel were sent up Thrush Valley to form a defensive line, 'D' Company under 2Lt Metcalfe taking a similar position to the right of 14 Willows Road. An urgent message was also passed to Transport to send along every available man with a rifle. Around 9 a.m., several hundred of the enemy were seen digging in on the slope above Leith Walk and were engaged to good effect with rifle and Lewis fire. One Lewis gunner, twenty-nine-year-old Pte Bert McVittie from Blackpool, was wounded quite early on in this exchange of fire, but remained with his gun, holding off every attempt the enemy made to advance during the day—actions which earned him the MM.[7] He was posted to the 1/4th after he recovered from his wounds and was killed with them in May 1918.

Of the half company with the South Lancs, nothing more was heard. They were either killed, or captured, along with the entire South Lancs Battalion, who were encircled and attacked from behind, fighting on until they were overwhelmed. The 1/5th Loyals and Liverpool Scottish held as long as they could, causing the enemy severe casualties and delaying their advance considerably. Villers Guislain held until 9.30 a.m., but the enemy advance westwards was only brought to a firm stop by a counter-attack at Vaucellette Farm by 1/4th Loyals.

At 9 a.m., Capt. Kean sent two platoons from Meath Post to the Adelphi and these were used to form a line from there to Pigeon Ravine. Not long afterwards, the enemy began to advance from Pigeon Quarry, up the long, gentle slope towards Meath Post. The combined firepower of the Lewis guns in Meath and Limerick Posts cut them down in swathes and the attack lost momentum—though they were able to occupy a small trench (50°1′23.40″N 3°9′43.40″E) just to the front of Meath Post. Bennett noted the somewhat unusual leadership methods employed by the opposition:

> I had watched through my glasses the advance of some Huns, and was interested to notice the methods employed by the officer in command. The men rushed forward and dropped in true 'infantry training' style, but when he wanted them to go on again, he uplifted a whip or cat-o-nine-tails, which he was carrying in his right hand, and laid about his men with great energy. The men, instead of showing resentment, jumped up and dashed forward another 50 yards. They were under fire from Adelphi, hence their reluctance.[8]

By 9.45 a.m., the pressure on Liverpool Scottish and the two platoons from 'C' Company was too great to resist. Pushed from both their right and left and the enemy in front of Meath Post, who were slightly to their rear, they were in danger of encirclement. Abandoning the Adelphi, they fell back to Limerick Trench and Post. Within half an hour, the enemy occupied the Adelphi—a tenure not without risk as Limerick Post enjoyed a very slight height advantage and any of the enemy rash enough to show themselves were shot at. On the other hand, the Adelphi commanded Fallen Tree Road accordingly, making crossing over this between Limerick and Kildare Post impossible during daylight. The fire was not very unidirectional as Bennett was wounded twice before 10.30 a.m. (in a finger and the head), although neither wound was serious. A sniper also killed thirty-three-year-old Pte John Thompson, his best pal Pte George Lupton later writing home to Thompson's father explaining the circumstances. The situation then seemed to calm for a while, so Bennett took advantage to slip to HQ to have his wounds dressed and report on the situation. Normally, a commander would not abandon his post; however, the addition of a couple of dozen men from Liverpool Scottish in

Limerick Post had changed things as one was the 2IC Capt. James Roddick, holding the temporary rank of major and ordered to assume command by Lt-Col. Macdonald, CO of Liverpool Scottish, who was at Kildare Post.[9] While at HQ, Bennett requested a resupply of bombs and small arms ammunition (which presented no problem) and artillery support (which, unfortunately, did). Upon his return to Limerick Post, he found little change, apart from another bombing block, constructed 100 yards down Kildare Lane in the direction of the Adelphi.

The names of trenches and positions named in this narrative are those used by Bennett and Roddick in their reports, which are mostly consistent with the names used in the divisional maps for November 1917. In the trench map of March 1918 (possibly the earliest surviving trench map that actually names any of these trenches), a number of trenches were renamed, the most critical being Kildare Trench, which became Kildare Lane— Kildare Avenue, now extending past Limerick Post, encompassing the original Kildare Lane. The sketch map in this chapter uses the nomenclature from November 1917, but where there is any doubt as to which trench was actually being referred to, it has been commented on.

Bennett had a grandstand view of the enemy advance across the Villers Ridge. Sherwood Lane, the road running from Pigeon Quarry to Villers Guislain, thronged with mounted men, guns and limbers, wagons, and lines of infantry. His men engaged these with their rifles and Lewis guns, but as the range was about 1,500 yards, their shooting had little effect and Bennett ordered cease-fire to preserve ammunition. Around 12.45 p.m., he observed a new brigade of infantry moving across Villers Ridge in extended order, their left flank seemingly threatening Meath Post. As the danger to this position became clearer, twenty men were sent to reinforce 'C' Company, and in case Meath Post was overrun, a bombing block was built in Limerick Lane. Limerick Lane is not labelled on divisional maps; however, it would make tactical sense if the trench named as Limerick Trench in these maps is the one Bennett was actually referring to. The Limerick Lane marked on the March 1918 map did not exist in November 1917 and runs parallel to the newly named Kildare Lane—so does not fit with Bennett's description of the events.

The extra men were of no avail, and at 1.45 p.m., Meath Post fell, with Capt. Kean and just a few of his men managing to escape down Limerick Lane.[10] The enemy followed closely in their footsteps, but were held by the block, despite repeated attempts to force it, valiantly resisted by L/Cpl Barraclough and five men—actions which earned Barraclough the MM.[11] The main force of this latest enemy onslaught swept past to the north of Meath Post and then curled around left to occupy Parr's Bank—an eventuality planned for by the earlier construction of another block in Kildare Avenue. Limerick Post was now all but surrounded, apart from Kildare Trench—the latter held by two platoons of Liverpool Scottish. The garrison of Limerick Post consisted of four officers and ninety men from 1/5th King's Own; three officers and twenty-three men, from Liverpool Scottish HQ; and one officer and twenty-five men from 1/5th Loyals, who had brought the ammunition requested by Bennett. There were three Lewis guns and a plentiful supply of ammunitions and grenades. The garrison, now reorganised, was placed in defensive positions, told they were surrounded, and ordered to resist to the last.

The situation was better further to the west, where the rest of the Battalion were holding. The Loyals at Vaucellette Farm prevented any German advance westwards and the Battalion was just about staying enemy attempts to curve southwards to flank Vaucellette. At noon, 1/4th King's Own arrived from divisional reserve and deployed 300 yards to the rear of the 1/5th, setting up a curved defensive line from 50°0'55.60"N 3°7'44.70"E in the west to a central position 300 yards forward of HQ in 14 Willows Road, then round to a right flank in Fallen Tree Road at 50°0'44.40"N 3°9'10.10"E. As soon as these were in position, they set about consolidating this new line with trenches and wire—work assisted by 422 Field Company RE. Apart from the 1/4th's own Lewis guns, 164 MG Company also brought up four Vickers, which were sited two to each flank. A pair of strongpoints were also constructed on the spurs to the front of Tétard Wood. Just before 3 p.m., Metcalfe sent a 'D' Company patrol forward to establish the actual enemy positions, discovering them dug in strongly along Parr's Bank, confirming that Limerick Post was now entirely cut off from the rest of the Battalion. One of the men in these makeshift positions was wounded as he lay firing at the enemy on the forward slope. Cpl George Carradice, hit by a burst of machine-gun fire, sustained three wounds to the buttocks. The twenty-two-year-old crawled back for half a mile before he got to safety, only reaching the dressing station at 7 p.m.[12]

The afternoon saw a number of attempts to seize Limerick Post. At 2.30 p.m., after a fruitless appeal to the defenders to surrender, the first bid was made from the direction of the Adelphi along Kildare Lane and a fierce struggle developed at the block— Barraclough once again to the fore.[13, 14] Simultaneously, the enemy attacked from the opposite side, along Kildare Avenue from Parr's Bank, and an equally tough scrap developed at the block there. German losses were severe, though the defenders fared better. At 3 p.m., the enemy made yet another attempt to overrun Limerick Post, this time across open ground from the Adelphi, but were cut to pieces by the concentrated fire of the defenders, the attack fizzling out within 5 yards. Bennett recounted that the enemy then proceeded to try to weaken the defences with *Granatenwerfer* fire from Meath Post and an MG sited in Kildare Avenue, where it crossed under Fallen Tree Road. This must be 'Lane' as at no point in its length did Kildare Avenue pass under Fallen Tree Road. Later in his report, Bennett describes this as being just to the south of the Adelphi where Kildare Lane met Fallen Tree Road. This gun was a particular nuisance as it was on slightly higher ground and made any movement inside Limerick Post perilous and totally cut off access to Kildare Trench. Thirty-two-year-old L/Cpl Fred Hartley tried to shoot the men manning this MG, but was caught by a sweeping burst of fire that killed him instantly.[15] At regular intervals, German parties probed the blocks, but they all held. Bennett was not aware when Kildare Post/Trench actually fell, but having seen some men from Liverpool Scottish retreating during the afternoon, presumed (correctly) that they were its garrison. By 5 p.m., the enemy's moves were mostly defensive, with bombs thrown over his own blocks to deter any attempts at counterattack. None of the defenders had eaten all day, so Roddick authorised the issue of one third of the reserve rations and water.

There had been no word from anyone outside the Post since Bennett's return from HQ and Bennett and Roddick decided that the need for information obliged the risk of sending out runners to the last-known position of Battalion HQ. Four men volunteered, but in case of capture, nothing was committed to paper, the volunteers memorising their message. At 6.15 p.m., the two from the King's Own (Privates Wallace Baxendell and William Marland) departed. At 8.15 p.m., the two from Liverpool Scottish also slipped out of Limerick Post into the dark. All four reached HQ in 14 Willows Road.

An hour before the runners arrived, Lt-Col. Macdonald, CO of Liverpool Scottish and around sixty of his men had also reached HQ, having fought their way back from Kildare Post. Recognising that Limerick Post was completely isolated, the runners were asked to return with orders for Roddick to withdraw. All four runners offered to return to help their comrades and another two men from 'D' Company elected to join them (the Battalion's diary states that four men from 'D' accompanied them, but other sources recount that it was just two). The return journey fared badly. The diary states that somewhere along Kildare Lane (Kildare Avenue is more probable), they were ambushed by MG fire and a salvo of grenades, with only Marland and one of the Liverpool Scottish able to break contact and escape. Twenty-year-old Baxendell, a Manchester errand boy prior to the War, did not survive the encounter. Twenty-four-year-old William Marland was awarded the MM for his courage, but was less fortunate next time he risked his life as a runner.[16] Marland's return at 12.15 a.m. prompted an attempt by the Battalion to force a relief party through. This force of fifty from 'D' Company, under 2Lt Metcalfe left at 3.10 a.m., but came under such heavy MG fire from Parr's Bank that they were forced to withdraw.

After dark, efforts to overwhelm Limerick Post had resumed, with desultory moves against the blocks at 8 p.m., more akin to half-hearted reconnaissance to establish if the defenders were still there. At 2.45 a.m., the enemy began to use flare signals to register a *Granatenwerfer* and a couple of small trench mortars in Meath Post and the Adelphi, and at 3 a.m., these began a concentrated bombardment. One round scored a direct hit on one of the Lewis teams, killing L/Cpl William Docherty and killing or wounding the rest of the team, one of whom was blown into the traverse where Bennett and three men were sheltering from the bombardment. Twenty-one-year-old Docherty was a grave loss to the defenders as he was a first class gunner who had accounted for three of the enemy earlier that day.[17]Another killed by this round was twenty-one-year-old Pte Robert Bond from Lancaster. Sgt Arnold Dixon wrote to his parents recounting how their son died. L/Cpl Percy Collier, standing next to Bennett, was also wounded. This bombardment was just the prelude to yet another attack—once again from all sides. At one point, the block to the north in Limerick Trench nearly succumbed, but a frantic counterattack by L/Sgt Isaac Phillipson succeeded in driving the enemy away at bayonet point, sadly leaving the twenty-three-year-old NCO with a serious leg wound.

It was a clear, starry night and the bright full moon helped the defenders considerably as they were able to see and react to attacks before they were overwhelmed, but these onslaughts cost the defenders dearly, their trenches smashed by high explosive and eighteen casualties ensuing.

At 4.30 a.m., Roddick, Bennett, and Kean conferred as to their next steps. Ammunition was running low and it was clear that once dawn broke the trench mortars would be able register accurately enough for the enemy to destroy the defenders without loss to themselves. British artillery was virtually non-existent—just one 18-pounder firing a single round every five or ten minutes. The three officers decided that they had a fair chance of breaking through to their south-west, across Kildare Avenue, then dropping down into the Catelet Valley south of Fallen Tree Road. Roddick divided the men into groups of fifteen, each under one officer, and sent them off into the dark, the lead group of bombers tasked with clearing a passage across Kildare Avenue. Bennett and Capt. Ferguson (Liverpool Scottish) commanded the last two groups to leave, each holding one of the blocks with a Lewis team until signalled by Very light to withdraw. Heartbreakingly, not everyone could leave. There were no stretchers at Limerick Post, and as they expecting to have to fight their way through, it was impossible to bring six of the badly injured. Two stretcher-bearers, thirty-five-year-old Pte William Dawson and Pte James Sharpe, insisted on remaining behind to care for the wounded—an action Bennett considered 'one of the finest deeds of the war'.[18] Those remaining seemingly had their surrender respected by the enemy. Dawson and Sharpe survived the war; L/Sgt Phillipson succumbed from his wounds in a German hospital nine days later, so presumably the other five wounded were also tended. Though Bennett described L/Cpl Collier as 'badly wounded', he must have been able to walk as he transferred to the RE after his recovery.

By 5.05 a.m., evacuation was complete and with a group of scouts 50 yards in advance, the garrison travelled in single file down Lark Spur and along the slope of the Catelet Valley near the edge of Fallen Tree Road for about ¾ mile until they reached friendly lines forty minutes later. The only enemy encountered during the withdrawal was a small group spotted near Kildare Avenue, who fled when they saw Bennett's party. The British line where they crossed had wire to its fore, but no trench, so the men from Limerick Post were immediately spread along it and helped dig in. Bennett then reported to Battalion HQ and was sent to have his wounds properly treated, being evacuated to a London hospital. According to Bennett, approximately ninety men had been withdrawn successfully—seventy from King's Own and twenty from Liverpool Scottish—though the figure given in the Battalion's war diary is 120 men (the difference probably accounted for by the resupply party from 1/5th Loyals).

The Battalion's role was not yet over, as at 12.30 p.m. orders came through for them to carry out an attack half an hour later against Meath, Limerick, and Kildare Posts, then hold these against counterattack. 'A' and 'C' would attack Limerick; 'B' would try to regain Meath Post; 'D' would assault Kildare; and a conglomeration of two squadrons of the Central Indian Horse and men from assorted transport details under Transport

Officer Lt Anthony Hargreaves would attack Parr's Bank and then assist against Kildare Post. Given the lack of time for planning and briefing, the very feeble British barrage from a few 13-pounders belonging to the cavalry, the tired and disparate nature of the attackers, the open nature of the ground, and the quantity of machine guns the enemy had placed on higher ground, it is not surprising this became a complete fiasco.

Concentrated MG fire from Parr's Bank and Kildare Avenue ripped into those attacking on the right (the diary reports Kildare Lane, but this has to be 'Avenue' as it was not possible to direct MG fire onto their line of attack from Kildare Lane). 'B' Company on the left suffered similar grief from MGs in Villers Guislain. Casualties were heavy, but despite this, the diary reported that small parties from 'A' and 'B' penetrated as far as the south side of Kildare Lane (again, Kildare Avenue has to be the correct position), where they then came under rifle fire from Limerick and Kildare Posts. The enemy were in far stronger numbers than the attackers were and immediately counterattacked, driving the remnants of the Battalion back, though when the Germans in Parr's Bank attempted a counterattack, the fire from the Battalion's Lewis guns stopped them dead and in turn, brought about their rapid retreat. Killed while leading 'C' Company was Capt. Kean. This pointless display cost the Battalion 50 per cent casualties among their attacking force. For the stretcher-bearers trying to bring in the wounded, the constant enemy fire made life precarious. Pte George Churchman risked all for the entire day, treating and bringing in the injured, completely oblivious to the bullets kicking up earth all around him. At one point, a bursting shell bowled him head over heels, yet he persisted until all the Battalion's wounded were brought in. After dark, he went out again, bringing back three wounded from the Central Indian Horse. For this fine display of courage, he was awarded the MM, and though his citation states this was 30 November, the involvement of the Indian cavalry must mean it actually occurred on 1 December.[19] Lt Elwood's courage was recognised by an MC. He worked solidly throughout the 30th treating the wounded—his dressing station only 100 yards behind the front line. In the evening of the abortive counterattack on 1 December, he went out into No Man's Land with stretcher-bearers tending and bringing in the wounded. Disappointingly, neither Bennett nor Riddick received the MC for their leadership at Limerick Post—an action that was sufficiently well-regarded by Sir Douglas Haig to be mentioned as a fine example of gallant defence when he gave his speech after being awarded the Freedom of Liverpool post-war.

The Battalion was relieved by the Leinsters at 1 a.m. on 2 December and marched to billets at Longavesnes Aerodrome, arriving at 4 a.m. The exhausted men were allowed to sleep and when the roll was called in the afternoon, the Battalion's strength was around 250 men. Transport and men from the 'B' Team increased this to 412—less than half-strength. Casualties were heavy, with sixteen officers and 247 men killed, wounded, or missing. Of these, sixty-nine would turn out to be have either been killed outright or died from wounds. The 166th Brigade casualties amounted to 1,896 killed, wounded, or missing, 82 per cent of the divisional total.[20] Among these was Brig.-Gen. Lewis, wounded when Brigade HQ was shelled at 3 p.m. on 1 December. His replacement,

Brig.-Gen R. J. Kentish, who arrived on 4 December, was an innovative and strong-minded infantryman, much in the same mould as Brig.-Gen. Stockwell.

At 4 p.m. on 2 December, the Battalion was ordered to move to billets at Hamel near Tincourt as a battalion from 21 Division was taking over the aerodrome billets. On 5 December, the Battalion was on the move again—this time to billets in Flamicourt. This new location was far from satisfactory, the billets limited and in poor condition, either derelict buildings or draughty huts. On 7 December, the Battalion moved on to Avesnes Le Compte and onwards on the 11th, until finally reaching permanent billets at Laires on 14 December, where they remained until 9 February.

The German counterattack of 30 November and losses incurred came as a shock to a British public, regaled with tales of a brilliant victory a mere ten days earlier. Pressed for answers by concerned politicians, Haig requested an immediate report from Gen. Byng; Haig's subsequent criticisms of the performance of the defending troops was based on the contents of Byng's report, which led him to believe that the defences were an unbroken line and in good order. As described earlier, this was far from true. Based on this, Haig expressed doubts about the fighting capacity of the troops who had defended the front in the following statement:

> Risks had to be taken in reducing forces at some points in order to be strong at others, but the risk taken at Cambrai was not an undue risk for the enemy should not have succeeded in penetrating any part of our defence.[21]

Gen. Byng, the commander of Third Army, was quick to blame failure on the poor quality of leadership and fighting ability of soldiers in 55, 12, and 20 Division, particularly junior officers and machine-gunners. He further pronounced that no responsibility was attributable to anyone in High Command, and that he and all his subordinate commanders had been happy that there were sufficient troops available to handle any counterattack.

Byng's insistence that none of his subordinate commanders had been unhappy with the number of troops available to them does not hold up in light of Jeudwine's repeated requests for a brigade to cover the Banteux Ravine. The Court of Enquiry in January 1918 was careful not to criticise High Command and can only be interpreted as a complete and utter whitewash. Maj.-Gen. Jeudwine himself thought the process nothing more than an exercise in self-aggrandisement by Gen. Ivor Maxse, commander of XVIII Corps and member of the Committee of Enquiry. Jeudwine's personal copy of the report was annotated, 'Ivor Maxse again! Personal advertisement'.[22] In summary of his views in a letter to Snow, Jeudwine stated:

> I have read through the report of the Committee of Enquiry. It is of course Maxse pure and simple, and very poisonous Maxse at that. I find a great many points with which I am in total disagreement: for instance, it is stated near the bottom of Page 5 that there appears to have been a lack of vigilance in the outpost lines. This, as I think you know, I deny altogether. It is further stated here that no SOS signals were sent up. This is of

course not the case as you have a copy of a statement from an officer of Artillery in which the reply of the guns to the SOS Signals is referred to. Again, on Page 6, under the heading of 'Warnings from above unheeded', I am as muddled as you are to what is meant by 'Higher Commanders'.

Then at Para. 6 of the note by a member of the Court of Enquiry (same distinguished General again) it is stated that we can 'discover few traces of organised counter-attacks or of methodical resistance'. As you are well aware, the spontaneous counter-attack of the 1/4th Loyal North Lancashires along the Villers Guislain spur stopped for good the enemy's advance in that direction, and pinned him down with the result of making subsequent counter-attacks by the Guards Division possible. But the whole of this memorandum, the anonymity of which is very lightly veiled, is sheer advertisement and hardly worth taking the trouble to contradict.[23]

The mere fact that Haig felt it necessary to order a Court of Enquiry suggests that he was not totally satisfied with Byng's explanation. The OH, originally published around twenty years after the events, rightly attributed the blame to Byng and his COS. They should have been aware of the possible dangers of counterattack through the Banteux Ravine, especially given that Gen. Snow, as one of Byng's corps commanders, had expressed his concerns about this sector to Third Army more than once.[24] Equally, too little artillery had been allocated within the danger area, a problem that could only have been solved at 'Army' level, and yet all requests by Snow for more heavy artillery had been turned down. Much of the criticism aimed at the three divisions was based on the assumption that there must have been a lack of vigilance from the men in the front line because no SOS signals were supposedly sent. Yet officers reported that the men in the forward trenches fired these signals. Timed entries in brigade and divisional signal logs, which the Enquiry would have had access to, unambiguously record SOS signals being fired. Forward artillery observers had been unable to call in a barrage onto the attackers because German artillery fire had cut all telephone lines—not through any lack of vigilance.[25] The dead ground and weather gave the enemy a strategic advantage for they could amass safely out of sight of the defenders and many MGs were put out of action by the barrage. The surviving gunners were either overwhelmed by attackers descending upon them at short range (sometimes from the rear), or remained at their posts until their ammunition was exhausted. Yet the Court of Enquiry found that 'many of the troops had proved unequal to the task ... the training of junior officers, and NCOs demanded immediate attention'.[26]

It is not unreasonable to comment that many troops that day were inexperienced; there had been little time to train the replacements for the Salient casualties. However, this was an Army-wide problem not specific to 55 Division. While frustration that troops were untrained in defensive tactics had some validity, this was also an Army-wide issue, as offence not defence was the overriding mantra. Blame clearly rests with Byng as commander of Third Army, whose focus on the main attack on the 20th was such that despite warnings from his Corps commanders, he failed to take into account events to its flank—an area he had weakened to provide extra impetus to the main push. The most disappointing aspect of this matter is Byng's attempt to deflect culpability away from himself and his staff and onto those too low down the chain of command to be able to defend themselves against this slur. This stain to 55 Division's reputation was later rebuffed by the OH:

> The 55th Division had no reason to reproach itself. Overwhelmed by numbers and by a vastly superior artillery the troops had shown their quality by standing fast amid their broken defences and resisting as long as resistance was possible.[27]

Killed or Died from Wounds in the Defence of Épehy

Pte Manisty Bainbridge	242522	KIA: 30/11	Capt. John Herdman Kean		KIA: 1/12
Pte Allen Bancroft	242523	KIA: 30/11	Pte George Kellett*	23843	KIA: 30/11
L/Cpl William Ernest Barry	260020	KIA: 30/11	Pte Frederick Kendall	33951	KIA: 30/11
Pte Wallace Royle Baxendell	17963	KIA: 30/11	Pte Joseph Leak	34820	DOW: 15/12
Pte George Baynes	240893	DOW: 4/12	Pte Walter Leech	201864	KIA: 30/11
Pte James Harry Bell	243058	KIA: 30/11	Pte Herbert Lewington	25423	KIA: 30/11
Pte Henry Bertlestien	243099	KIA: 30/11	Pte Edward Makinson	240258	KIA: 30/11
Pte Robert Bond	241376	KIA: 30/11	Pte John McDermott	242497	DOW: 1/12
Cpl Thomas Burrow	241624	KIA: 30/11	Pte William McLean	243054	KIA: 30/11
Pte John Gordon Cameron	241659	KIA: 30/11	Pte Richard Ormerod Nuttall **	201915	DOW: 18/12
Pte Peter Cartwright	26069	KIA: 30/11	Pte Edward Henry Ormesher	242642	KIA: 30/11
Pte Richard Casson	241344	KIA: 30/11	Pte Albert Parkinson	242710	KIA: 30/11
Pte Albert Herbert Chapman	260016	KIA: 30/11	Pte David Penny	34038	KIA: 30/11
Pte Charles Cockcroft	201871	KIA: 30/11	L/Sgt Isaac Phillipson**	241213	DOW: 9/12
Pte Joseph Connerton	265562	KIA: 30/11	Pte Frank Pope	34804	KIA: 30/11
Pte James Thomas Curwen*	70365	KIA: 30/11	Pte Arthur Porter	202322	DOW: 5/12
Pte John Daly	242504	KIA: 30/11	Pte Thomas Rose	33597	KIA: 30/11
Sgt Louis Harold Dickinson	241424	KIA: 30/11	L/Cpl George Rostron	201927	KIA: 30/11
L/Cpl William Docherty***	240197	KIA: 30/11	Pte Benjamin Samuel	22819	KIA: 30/11
Pte Thomas Downes	24689	DOW: 2/12	Pte Frank Scott**	260018	DOW: 2/1
Pte Fred Elliott	33235	DOW: 30/11	Pte John Singleton	32637	KIA: 30/11
Pte Frank Emsley	33846	KIA: 30/11	Pte Norman Stead	241513	KIA: 30/11
Sgt William Fisher	240792	KIA: 30/11	Pte Frank Stokes	263015	KIA: 30/11
Pte Thomas Fletcher	242476	KIA: 30/11	Pte John Thompson	241215	KIA: 30/11
Pte Henry Gabbatt*	23837	KIA: 30/11	L/Cpl Percy Thompson	241190	KIA: 30/11
Pte Wilfred Hamblett	243050	KIA: 30/11	Pte Thomas Townson	24516	DOW: 5/12
Pte William Harley	241396	DOW: 24/12	Pte Edward Walmsley	240882	KIA: 30/11
L/Cpl Fred Hartley	243113	KIA: 30/11	Pte George Webb	34584	KIA: 30/11
2Lt James Duncan Hay		DOW: 15/12	Pte George Webster	21518	DOW: 2/12
2Lt James Graeme Henderson**		DOW: 3/12	Sgt Thomas Wilkinson	240316	KIA: 30/11
Pte Richard Holding	24601	KIA: 30/11	Cpl John Wilson	241176	KIA: 30/11

L/Cpl Richard Holmes	242966	KIA: 30/11	Pte John Wilson	260041	KIA: 30/11
Pte William Holt	242631	KIA: 30/11	Pte Moses Wood	243069	DOW: 2/12
Pte Albert George Richd. Houseago	242587	KIA: 30/11	2Lt Reginald Rupert Woodward		KIA: 1/12
Pte John Jackson	242696	KIA: 30/11			

*Attached to 166 MG Company.
**Died as a POW.
***Killed 3 a.m. 1 December.

Known to have been Wounded or Captured at Épehy

Pte Matthew Abbott	242648	WIA	2Lt John Henderson		WIA
Pte Samuel Ackerley	26998	WIA	Pte James Hodgson	201859	WIA
Pte Frank Ainsworth	34803	WIA	Pte Bertie Hollingworth	34749	WIA
Pte John Edward Armstrong	242972	POW	Pte Thomas Houghton	241822	WIA
Pte George Anderson Atkinson*	241159	POW	Pte Bertie Huddleston	30151	POW
Pte Joseph Auty	240235	WIA	Pte George Ingleby	242637	WIA
Pte Joseph Bagshaw	26709	POW	Pte Henry Jamieson	260038	WIA
L/Cpl Albert Bamber	242417	WIA	L/Cpl John Jenkinson	240702	POW
Pte Albert Edward Barber	27625	POW	Pte Matthew Johnson	240864	WIA
Pte Arthur Barnes	242665	WIA	Pte John Jones	25575	WIA
Pte Clifford Baron*	243042	POW	A/Cpl Joseph Kelshaw	10159	WIA
L/Cpl John William Bebbington	24714	WIA	Pte Alfred Ernest Kermode	265131	POW
Pte Joseph Beevours	242537	WIA	Pte John Kirkbride	34787	WIA
Pte Thomas Bell	240274	WIA	Pte Robert Crouch Lamb**	28042	MIA
Capt. Horace Bramwell Bennett		WIA	Pte James Lee	241560	POW
Pte Joseph Christopher Benson	240491	POW	Pte John R. Lee	241547	WIA
Pte Harold Bentley	242536	POW	Pte John William Lloyd	241575	WIA
Pte Frederick Bewes	34813	POW	Pte John James Long	33970	WIA
Pte William Billany	242524	POW	2Lt Edward Major		WIA
Pte William Henry Birch	14569	POW	Pte George Mason	241638	POW
Pte James Birchall	27688	WIA	Pte Archibald McKinlay*	34806	POW
2Lt Robert Reid Birrell		WIA	Pte Alexander McLeod	28053	WIA
Pte William J. Blaylock	33851	WIA	(George) Bertram McVittie	241572	WIA
Pte Robert H. Bloy	27648	WIA	Pte Robert Miller***	28056	POW
Pte Herbert Bolton	242978	WIA	Pte A. Mullen	242512	WIA
Pte Frederick Bonsall	202299	WIA	Pte John Edward Newton	265714	WIA
L/Cpl Henry Boustead	240568	WIA	Pte William Wraith Newton	24287	WIA
Pte Henry Charles Bradford	242533	WIA	Pte James Nolan*	242510	WIA
L/Cpl William Edgar Brumby*	15500	WIA	Pte Joseph Painter	241470	POW

Pte John William Bradshaw	241582	WIA	L/Cpl George Parker	243041	POW
Pte Jack Briers*	25736	WIA	Pte John Parr	34672	POW
Pte Christopher Briscoe	19627	POW	Pte Charles Pattison	24524	WIA
Pte Frederick Brockbank	34814	POW	Pte Frederick Pearson	27490	WIA
Pte Herbert Brown	243043	POW	Pte Thomas Perry	260053	WIA
Pte William Buckley	21921	WIA	Pte William Pollitt	242687	WIA
Pte Harold Burley	27353	WIA	Pte Arthur Punt	242658	WIA
Cpl Harold Eustace Capstick	240592	POW	Pte Ewart Walter Retallick	33504	WIA
Cpl George Carradice	240846	WIA	Pte Thomas Robinson	34782	POW
Pte Percy Childerley*	26797	WIA	Pte John William Rowe	240346	POW
Pte Harold T. Clarke	22619	WIA	Pte Francis Rushton	34823	WIA
Pte Harry Clawson	243123	POW	Pte Tom Russell	242494	WIA
Pte Robert Clitheroe	201902	WIA	Pte Carey Sager	33418	WIA
Pte Edward Colgan	240126	WIA	Pte John William Scott	241070	POW
L/Cpl Percy Collier	241780	WIA	Pte Harry Sedgwick	241478	WIA
Pte Abraham Cooper	242542	WIA	Pte Thomas William Seward	240269	POW
Pte Census George Cornwell	33952	WIA	Pte George Shannon	34834	POW
A/Cpl John William Craig	260051	WIA	Pte Albert Charles Sharp	27028	POW
Pte Henry Cross	34754	WIA	Pte Thomas Shaw	28070	WIA
Pte Richard Crossland	242618	POW	Pte Hugh Shulver	260009	WIA
Pte William Cunningham	243028	POW	Pte Walter Scott Shuttleworth	33042	POW
Pte William Sylvester Dawson	241553	POW	Pte Thomas Edwin Simister	33060	WIA
Pte Thomas Dixon	242673	POW	Pte Robert Edward Singleton	241650	POW
Pte Benjamin Dorcey	15972	POW	Sgt Percy Brown Skeoch	240767	WIA
Pte John Draper	241651	WIA	Pte Thomas William Skidmore	242644	WIA
Pte Charles William Eaton	243072	WIA	Cpl Albert Edward Smallshaw	240191	WIA
Pte Edwin Farmer	242556	POW	Pte Henry Smith	27038	POW
Pte Charles Featherstone	12933	WIA	Pte James Henry Squire	241481	WIA
Pte Harold Felstead	202304	POW	2Lt Eric Stainton		POW
2Lt John McEwan Ferguson		WIA	Pte Herbert Stakes	240719	POW
Pte Lawrance Stanley Field	260026	WIA	Pte Joseph Stalker	241536	POW
L/Cpl Joseph Henry Fielding	241586	WIA	Pte William Henry Stirzaker	240825	POW
2Lt Joseph Edgely Fisher		POW	Pte James Sturzaker	241637	WIA
Pte Walter Fletcher	242561	POW	Cpl Peter Swarbrick	241654	WIA
Pte George Foden	241157	POW	Pte Isaac James Thursfield	242495	WIA
Cpl William John Gathercole	242660	WIA	Pte Thomas William Tomlinson*	33718	WIA
2 Lt David Gibson		WIA	2Lt Kennedy St. Clare H. Toovey***		POW
Pte James Gledhill	243100	POW	Pte Robert Dean Townson	241634	WIA
Pte James Goodwin	34750	POW	Pte Harry Trevallion*	260019	WIA
Pte William Thomas Greaves	18598	WIA	Pte Thomas Tugwell	260010	POW
Pte James Green	34665	WIA	2Lt David Lamont Tweedie		WIA
Pte Walter Greenwood	260028	POW	Pte William George Watts	26847	WIA

L/Cpl Harold Gregory	27247	WIA	Pte Leonard Wells	27321	WIA
Pte Andrew Griffin	260050	WIA	Pte Edward Welsh	260047	WIA
Pte William Guy	243109	WIA	Pte William Whittaker	28080	POW
Pte Joseph Haddow	201852	WIA	Pte Carl Bradshaw Wilson	33578	WIA
Pte William Haddow	242976	WIA	Pte John Winchester	32651	POW
2Lt Walter Harrison		POW	2Lt James David Withey		WIA
Pte Thomas Harwood	243040	POW	Pte John Wilson	241048	POW
Pte Carl Victor Haycock	241558	POW	Pte William Wood	260030	POW
Pte Francis Thomas Hayward	242592	POW	Pte William Thomas Woolley	260025	WIA
Pte Edward Albert Helme	240572	POW			

*WIA and POW.

**MIA and later accounted for.

***Died in captivity of injuries or illness unrelated to wounds.

15 December 1917–8 April 1918: Festubert–Givenchy

Coordinates for Positions Named in this Chapter

Barnton Tee	50°32'30.50"N 2°45'15.20"E	Gorre Chateau	50°32'27.80"N 2°41'50.80"E
Braddell Point HQ	50°30'49.30"N 2°45'12.60"E	Indian Village	50°33'17.00"N 2°45'4.00"E
Brickstacks	50°31'1.90"N 2°46'3.00"E	La Tombe Willot	50°34'59.70"N 2°39'55.30"E
Cailloux Keep North	50°33'3.10"N 2°44'19.70"E	Le Plantin North	50°32'16.60"N 2°44'27.40"E
Cailloux Keep South	50°32'57.60"N 2°44'20.10"E	Le Plantin South	50°31'56.40"N 2°44'45.60"E
Canadian Orchard	50°32'59.40"N 2°46'2.60"E	Pont Fixe South	50°31'17.50"N 2°44'58.40"E
Dead Cow Farm HQ	50°32'46.90"N 2°44'53.40"E	Route-A Keep	50°33'1.30"N 2°43'24.40"E
Ferme du Roi	50°32'51.50"N 2°42'5.50"E	Tuning Fork	50°32'23.90"N 2°42'34.20"E
Festubert Central Keep	50°32'38.90"N 2°44'16.30"E	Windy Corner	50°31'43.55"N 2°44'40.06"E

Their time out of the line was spent training and refitting, with plenty of time put aside for entertainments, sports, and military competitions. Even heavy snowfall did not put a stop to sport—a planned football match had to be postponed, but was replaced by snowball fights and sliding. When leave could be given, men headed home—2Lt Harold Chapman to get married. Former music teacher Pte John Davis returned on time from leave and was promptly hijacked by the Brigade Concert Party, who omitted to tell the Battalion, who consequently reported him AWOL. Reinforcements were for once not a problem due to a particularly unpopular government decision.

At the beginning of 1918, the Army in France and Flanders was short of 75,000 infantrymen and labourers behind the lines. The situation was exacerbated further when Haig was ordered to send five divisions to reinforce the Italian Front. Curbing the supply of reinforcements as a way of preventing Haig from 'wasting' them on offensives was a dangerous policy that put the whole outcome of the war in jeopardy.[1] Changes in Army organisation would soon boost battalion numbers considerably when shortages of infantrymen prompted the Government to intervene once more. On 14 January, 55 Division received notification from I Corps to reduce the number of battalions in the division from twelve to nine. A week later, the Liverpool Irish, 1/9th King's, and 1/5th Loyals all received orders to join 57 (Second West Lancashire) Division.[2] The Germans and the French underwent a similar reshuffle earlier on, but these changes had been gradual and compensated for by an increase in firepower to units affected, by additional MGs and artillery. With no such cushion in place to compensate British divisions, robbed of 25 per cent of their strength, Haig protested, citing the damaging effects on troop morale that such changes would cause at a time when he believed the enemy was planning a major offensive—but to no avail.[3]

This was the second blow to Haig on the subject of manpower. Earlier in 1917, at a conference to which Haig had not been invited, the Government had agreed with the French to extend the length of line held by the BEF. On the 22 December, Haig had written to the War Cabinet warning that he could not undertake the responsibility of defending the Channel ports if such a proposal went ahead. Thus, at a time of chronic shortages of infantrymen due to a deliberate Government policy of withholding replacements, political interference forced Haig to extend a front with defences in a poor state due to a combination of winter, enemy action, and a lack of available labour to repair them. He was also forced to reorganise his divisions, requiring considerable internal restructuring of divisional and brigade staffs whose efforts would have been better employed on strengthening the defences.[4]

One of the battalions disbanded was 7/King's Own and their officers and men were shared between 1/4th and 1/5th King's Own. A number of men were also transferred from the Veterinary Corps, which was of great benefit to Transport as all had horse-management skills, but most were hardly infantry material. While out of the line, the Battalion gained twenty-four new officers and their strength return for 9 February shows a 'trench strength' of 948, with Transport also fully up to establishment.[5] On this day, the Battalion began a series of marches towards their new sector, arriving at Gorre Chateau on 13 February where they relieved 1/5th East Lancs and became brigade reserve battalion. The next day, while men were cleaning billets and equipment, half the officers, senior NCOs, and section commanders reconnoitred the tracks and positions of the Village Line and OBL near Festubert (the other half did their reconnaissance on 18 February). At this time, the division's sector stretched from north-east of Festubert, southwards to just opposite Les Briques, most of it soggy breastwork—the sector split by the La Bassée Canal—a far from ideal situation. Later, divisional boundaries were adjusted to remove this geographical inconvenience.

In late 1917 and early 1918, Haig was paying much more attention to defence than ever before, suspecting that the enemy, aware that large numbers of American troops would overwhelmingly tip the balance in favour of the Allies, may risk all to try to finish the war before the Americans deployed fully. He believed they would endeavour to break through the lines and drive a wedge between the French and British to seize the Channel ports, leaving the Allies with no choice but to sue for peace. However, he was also convinced that in attempting this, the German Army would be so weakened that he would be able to deliver a decisive counterattack on them in Autumn 1918.[6]

Although the campaigns in Verdun, the Somme, and Ypres had seriously weakened the Germans, the situation on the Eastern Front allowed them to pull considerable numbers of men west, adding weight to any offensive—something that would have been unthinkable had Russia still been in the fight. Haig understood that the offensive would breach his front lines, so took a leaf out of the Germans' book.[7] He planned 'defence in depth', leaving the front line relatively weakly manned (not that there were enough men to do much else) and ordered the construction of a series of 'keeps' to form the second and third line. Wire and other natural obstacles would funnel the attackers into 'zones' where they would be engaged from these redoubts. A front line packed with troops was always going to lead to heavy casualties from the initial artillery bombardment, and this strategy would minimise them; moreover, the further the enemy advanced, the less effective his artillery support would be and the more tenuous his logistical lines would become. It was never possible to take this policy to the lengths that the Germans had, for both manpower and preparation time were too little. Technically, the old front line, with its support and reserve positions, would become the 'Forward Zone'. Behind this, another line of defences, the 'Battle Zone', would be constructed on what had been the 'Corps Line', and yet another series of defences further back on the 'Army Line', re-designated the 'Rear Zone' or 'Green Line'.[8] Due to shortages of manpower and time, very little of this work was actually carried out, and whereas the enemy had *Eingreif* divisions, the British could not hold specialised 'counterattack' forces in reserve. In a conversation with the King on his visit to the Front in late March, Haig informed him that his infantry numbered 100,000 less than a year previously, that he was facing a German Army three times the British strength, and that he expected to defend a front a fifth longer.[9]

The Village Line was key to 55 Division's defences and Jeudwine designated this as the 'line of resistance to be denied the enemy at all costs'.[10] It ran through Givenchy and south to Cuinchy—hardly a textbook battle zone—being the rear edge of the Forward Zone, but was the best tactical site for the strongpoints, particularly as both ruined villages contained many intact cellars and fortifiable rubble; this was where 55 Division would make their stand if the enemy attacked. Givenchy itself was also on a slight knoll, providing a useful tactical viewpoint. This was not a continuous line, rather a series of heavily fortified and mutually supportive strongpoints across a battle zone that in many respects resembled Guillemont. Around these strongpoints were thick belts of wire, slanted to funnel attackers into the fields of fire of multiple MGs, which were sited to enfilade these gaps. In case of tank attack, some 18-pounders had been sited near the redoubts—Vickers and Lewis guns positioned nearby with belts and drums of armour-piercing ammunition ready for such an eventuality. Anti-tank mines were laid in belts behind the front line trenches opposite Givenchy. These, fabricated within the division, consisted of a pressure plate on a wooden firing box, connected by instantaneous fuse to a buried medium trench mortar round.[11] In the thick, coarse grass that grew around the strongpoints lurked older, less visible belts of wire to trap attackers.

There seems to be ambiguity as to precisely what is meant by 'Village Line', with most sources defining it as the line from Festubert through Le Plantin and Windy Corner to Pont Fixe, yet units themselves sometimes referred to the defensive positions within Givenchy as part of it.[12] In reality, the Village Line in the Givenchy locality was a wide belt where the Forward Zone and Battle Zone merged into one deep stretch—a characteristic of huge relevance in the weeks to come. About 1 to 2 miles further to the rear, the Green Line was known as the 'Tuning Fork Line' and ran roughly along the line south from Le Touret to the canal just east of its junction with the Canal Beuvry.

Passive defence was only part of 55 Division's strategy. Each infantry platoon in the line was designated as either a 'garrison' platoon or a 'counterattack' platoon, and any loss of territory would be immediately regained before the foe could consolidate. Still smarting from the events at Épehy, Jeudwine was determined that never again would the division face a similar situation. On the receipt of the code word 'Bustle,' units in reserve would rush to pre-prepared defensive positions and all units were expected to have reconnoitred these beforehand. On 15 February, the Battalion practised an immediate move to alternate positions in the eventuality of the chateau coming under artillery fire. On 23 February, 2Lt Richard Dolby's 9 Platoon represented 166 Brigade in the Army Rifle Association competition, which they won—a considerable accolade.

It was not until 9.30 a.m. on 25 February that the Battalion returned to the front line, relieving 1/5th King's in the left sub-sector of the left sector, running from Indian Village in the north, across to Canadian Orchard, then south to 50°32′23.10″N 2°45′27.80″E. HQ was in the OBL, not far from Dead Cow farm; 'A' Company was in the Barnton trenches, centred around Barnton Tee; 'B' Company was near Indian Village; and the other two companies around Canadian Orchard and Cover Trench just to its south. To their right was Liverpool Scottish, but across the divisional boundary to their left, was the Portuguese 2nd Division. Patrols were out in No Man's Land every night and working parties strove to maintain the breastworks and improve wiring. Enemy activity was almost non-existent in the northern stretch of the front, most action-taking place south of the canal—which was probably no bad thing considering the condition of their trenches. The breastworks contained no parados and there was a complete lack of shelter capable of protecting the men from even the smaller artillery rounds or splinters.[13]

One of the difficulties faced by any division after a large battle, was in ensuring that their soldiers carried out their duties properly—mainly due to an influx of inexperienced personnel replacing casualties. On 26 February, Jeudwine sent out a memo to all brigade-commanders ordering that 'all gaps in wire caused by hostile shelling, trench mortaring, or other causes, in front, support, or reserve lines, must be repaired the same night in spite of any difficulties'.[14]

Concern about a German attack or large raid also prompted him to direct that, beginning on 26 February—and continuing until further notice—special patrols went out an hour before daylight, not returning until after dawn. These patrols, consisting of at least six men and an officer, were to examine the defensive wire and any approach routes the enemy may use. Very little progress must have been made improving the wire as Jeudwine sent a very strongly worded letter to all three brigade commanders on 2 March castigating the lack of progress and warning of dire consequences if the situation did not improve.[15]

Despite warnings of a German attack further north at Gheluvelt and a subsidiary attack in the division's sector—both of which failed to materialise, this tour in the trenches remained quiet. Although no documentary evidence remains, there must already have been concern about ability of the Portuguese to hold their line as considerable efforts were being put into building wire defences to protect the extreme left flank of the division—not just the front. The Portuguese had been in the line for over a year—far longer than any British unit would have been expected to sustain and were obviously very tired. At midday on 4 March, 'A' Company was relieved by a company from 1/5th South Lancs and went into support and HQ and two platoons in the OBL, one platoon at Cailloux Keep South, and the other in Festubert Central Keep. In the afternoon of 5 March, the Battalion's position came in for considerable attention from enemy trench mortars, most of the rounds falling around Canadian Orchard and the South Lancs in Barnton, wounding both their company commander and his 2IC—command passing to a very inexperienced twenty-three-year-old subaltern. The mortaring only ceased when the division's artillery carried out a concentration shoot against them at 2.30 p.m. There was more artillery, this time from 10.2 between 3 p.m. and 4 p.m. on 6 March— the enemy appearing to be registering their guns on Barnton and the OBL behind it (behaviour that led division to believe that the enemy may be intending to raid these positions).

These fears were realised in a foggy pre-dawn at 5.05 a.m. on 7 March, when a barrage fell across the whole of the division's front line and the OBL—a box barrage isolating Barnton. Under cover of this, a German raiding party of 120 men and three officers attacked four posts of the 1/5th South Lancs, capturing twenty-three men. The seizure of sixteen out of the nineteen men occupying No. 2 Post, especially when only four of their rifles were later found to have been fired, prompted a Court of Enquiry. The findings did not reflect well and exposed failings at battalion and brigade level. Jeudwine's orders about patrols and the maintenance of wiring had clearly not been carried out as there was a two-day-old, 60-yard gap in the wire in front of Barnton No. 2 Post and the patrol had returned an hour before daylight. Due to their casualties on 30 November, for almost the entire South Lancs Battalion, it was their first time in the front line and the young subaltern, placed in command of the company, was clearly in over his head and should not have been put in that position. Tragically, unable to live with his actions, he shot himself the day after the Enquiry. Jeudwine did consider sacking the CO, but wisely decided that carrying out a witch-hunt would serve no purpose and would merely further damage morale within the inexperienced battalion. The South Lancs would be given an opportunity to redeem themselves by raiding the enemy when they returned to the line; brigade staff procedures were changed and everyone within the division benefitted from the harsh lesson of what happens if proper trench procedures were not followed.

The 1/5th King's Own also suffered in this bombardment when rounds landed around HQ. Twenty-five-year-old Pte Hesketh Cornthwaite was killed and twenty-four-year-old 2Lt Jack Walker severely wounded, dying the next day. Another four men from HQ were wounded and two men in the front line, though their names are no longer on record. Though the rest of the day was quiet, enemy artillery targeted the Battalion's positions again on 8 March, shelling Cover Trench and the OBL. Thirty-two-year-old Pte Frank McAndrew was killed by this and another three wounded. 'B' Company missed all this as, shortly before 8 a.m., they were relieved by a company of Liverpool Scottish and returned to Gorre to train for a raid. During the morning of 9 March, the OBL and Canadian Orchard were shelled again—the latter by 15 cm. Twenty-year-old Pte Frederick Grimsey and twenty-seven-year-old Pte John Reader were both killed and another man wounded. On 11 March, 'D' Company's Cpl Frank Burton died from his wounds, though it is not known if he was a casualty from the 7th, 8th, or 9th. The dates of wounding for twenty-six-year-old Pte John Musgrave who died on 17 March and twenty-year-old Pte William Ayling, who died on 19 March, are also unknown, though both must also be from one of those three dates. Visibility was quite poor on 9 March and the enemy obviously thought they could get away with daylight working parties behind their lines. This proved over-optimistic and a party of eight men in the open next to Eitel Alley South, were sent scuttling back into cover by a fusillade of rifle fire from Canadian Orchard.

On 10 March, HQ moved back to Festubert, though it was a case of 'out of the frying pan' as they were shelled in their new location that very night. The Battalion did, however, win considerable accolades during the afternoon of 11 March when they achieved something no other Battalion in the division had managed to date. In the early afternoon, a low-flying German aircraft passed over Le Plantin South and was engaged with rifle fire, which brought it down. Amazingly, this achievement—vaunted in both brigade and divisional diaries—was not mentioned in the Battalion diary. On 12 March, Liverpool Scottish relieved the Battalion, with 'B', 'C', and HQ going to Gorre Chateau, the remainder to the Ferme du Roi. The 13th was spent cleaning and refitting and the two companies from the Ferme du Roi moved into the chateau, which was shelled overnight eliciting casualties among 166 MG Company. There was considerable shellfire against the whole of the division's front on 13 March and everyone was very much on the alert in case it was the forerunner of another German offensive, orders being issued in case the Portuguese needed rapid reinforcement. The Battalion 'stood-to' in the rain at 5 a.m. on 14 March. At 6 a.m., 'Bustle' was received and the Battalion, minus 'B' Company, moved off to their positions. One platoon from 'A' went to Route-A Keep, the other three to the general area of Festubert; two platoons of 'C' Company went to Le Plantin North, the other two to Le Plantin South; 'D' Company was split between the two Cailloux Keeps; and HQ positioned centrally to the rear at the Tuning Fork. The Battalion was stood down at 9 a.m. on 15 March and returned to billets. Records from 14 March show nineteen-year-old Pte Albert Dent suffered shrapnel wounds to his elbow, which led to his medical discharge.[16] Whether he was wounded during the shelling of the chateau or while in their Bustle positions is unknown.

To make up for their overnight exertions, all working parties were cancelled during the morning of 15 March, though 'B' Company continued their rehearsals, witnessed in the afternoon of 16 March by Jeudwine. Meticulously planned, the raid targeted a 100-yard stretch of Dover Trench and its support line between 50°32′51.10″N 2°46′4.50″E and 50°32′49.20″N 2°46′0.80″E, with three separate entry points through gaps cut in enemy wire by artillery. Capt. Forshaw was to lead the raiders, who were split into three groups, each of six sections. The left and right groups were led by 2Lts Alexander White and Walter Young, with a sergeant commanding the centre party. Accompanying the infantrymen were an NCO and eight sappers from the RE, with explosives to destroy the three dugouts known to be in the target area. A signalling section, with a Lewis team and stretcher-bearers under 2Lt Fred Buckley, occupied a derelict trench in No Man's Land—Buckley also responsible for sending the withdrawal signal.

Everyone had their specific task. The leading sections of the first wave were to immediately head straight up the CT to the enemy support line and turn outwards and form blocks 25 yards further along on the left and right flanks; moppers-up were to turn inwards, clearing dugouts in the enemy support line while the officer and sergeant placed three men, armed with a bucket of bombs apiece at each of the blocks. Hard on their heels, the second wave dealt with the enemy front line, carrying out identical tasks to the first wave. Two men from each of the mopping-up parties were detailed as prisoner escorts and the REs were split into pairs, each with a 'protection party' of an NCO and four men.

At 5 a.m. on 17 March, artillery and trench mortars directed a devastating bombardment against the German line to cover the raiders, who had been in position out in No Man's Land fifteen minutes before the guns commenced. Three minutes later, the fire lifted to form a protective box barrage. The raiders, keeping as close to the artillery as possible, gained entry to Dover Trench without any interference. In fact, the raid went totally without a hitch—partly because there was not one single German to be found. This must have been unbelievably frustrating after all their efforts and following the search and destruction of the dugouts, they returned to friendly lines with an alarm bell and a noticeboard as booty. The enemy trenches were deep and revetted with brushwood, but very badly damaged, particularly on the right where artillery had scored a number of direct hits. Casualties were two men lightly wounded, one of which was probably thirty-four-year-old Pte Charles Dorrell. His pension record notes a flesh wound to the shin for 18 March, though battalion records make no mention casualties for that day.[17] It is possible that the other was twenty-one-year-old Pte Richard Power, who was wounded by shrapnel in the right forearm. His records show that he was evacuated home on 25 March, though the date of his wounding is not given.[18] The most serious casualties as a result of the raid were to 166 TMB when a mortar round exploded prematurely, killing two and wounding one.

The Battalion's billets at Gorre Chateau was taken by 1/5th King's in the afternoon of 17 March and they moved to former Portuguese billets at the Ferme du Roi, which were so filthy that it took two days to clean them. At 5 a.m. on 18 March, the Battalion once more stood-to until 9 a.m., before beginning the routine daily tasks. While men scrubbed away at their billets, the officers and each platoon sergeant reconnoitred the Portuguese area, and on 19 March, 'Bustle' positions. This was a very tense time, with an expectation of a major German offensive and the Battalion remained at one hour's notice to move. When the attack did come on 21 March, it was much further south, though this did not result in the division relaxing its defensive measures—in fact the very opposite—and efforts redoubled, preparing for the worst. The entire battalion was tasked burying telephone cables on 23 March. On 25 March, all leave was stopped for the entire BEF and officers and men away on courses recalled to their units. At 10 p.m. that night, orders arrived to man the Tuning Fork Line by 3 a.m. on 26 March, returning to billets at 8 a.m. A warning order was issued for 27 March that they would be relieving 1/5th South Staffordshires at Guinchy in the Cambrin sector south of the canal, so officers and NCOs hurried south to reconnoitre the sector, an entirely new one for the Battalion. This relief was completed by 3.30 p.m. of 27 March.

This new sector, which stretched from the south bank of the canal down to the Cambrin–La Bassée Road in the south, faced the notorious Brickstacks and was universally detested, though the Battalion would only man it this once. During relief, two companies of 1/5 South Lancs had been attached, but these left as soon as relief was completed. Initially, all four companies occupied the front line, but on 28 March, one went back to the Village line, their place taken by a company from Liverpool Scottish, and on 29 March, 'A' Company was sent up to reinforce the reserve line, their place taken by a company from the South Lancs. The Village Line here ran from Pont Fixe South down to HQ next to Braddell Point.

Most of the hostile artillery fire against this sector had been in the morning before the relief occurred, but two MGs behind the Brickstacks made life difficult for anyone travelling along Harley Street that night (now the D166). On 28 March, German artillery was much quieter, though overnight MG fire was once again directed at Harley Street and Pont Fixe. Little enemy activity was evidenced over the next few days—four light mortar rounds landed at 50°31′0.70″N 2°45′33.20″E, near Grafton Street on 30 March— no casualties ensued. This changed on 31 March when artillery and trench mortars targeted much of the division's line. Two salvoes, each of thirty rounds, fell around HQ and between 12.45 p.m. and 1.45 p.m., twenty light trench mortar rounds dropped around the front line opposite Brickstacks. Twenty-year-old Pte William Woolley was lightly wounded by this, but was back with the Battalion a few days later. He was not so lucky the next time.

On 1 April, Jeudwine called a conference of all battalion and company commanders and briefed them about the German offensive further south. He believed it probable that the division would be attacked and wanted to make sure that everything possible was done to foil it.[19] By 5 p.m. on 3 April, 1/5th South Lancs had relieved the Battalion, who moved to reserve in Cambrin. While the Battalion was in Cambrin, a reorganisation of the British line was undertaken and 1 Division took over the front line as far north as the canal. This would have meant the brigade moving to reserve positions around Le Préol, but a captured German document forced a rethink. This showed plans to prevent the brigade playing any part in the defence of Givenchy by the use of artillery against choke points. As canal crossings were limited, it was prudent to move them north prior to any attack.[20] Consequently, the Battalion moved via an overnight stop in Béthune to La Tombe Willot, arriving at their billets shortly after midday on 8 April. The Portuguese still occupied these billets when the Battalion arrived, so the men sat eating their dinners at the roadside until they were vacated. These billets, scattered over an area of nearly 2 miles, were also in a particularly dirty state. The roads around La Tombe Willot were also in shocking condition, and only light wagons could traverse them, so although Transport moved close to La Tombe Willot, the bulk of the stores were left with a small guard at Le Quesnoy. At 5 p.m., Brigade sent orders for the Battalion to take over the positions of the right Portuguese brigade the following day—though other events would intervene.

8 April 1918–2 May 1918: Backs to the Wall

Coordinates for Positions Named in this Chapter

Le Quesnoy bridge	50°32′10.33″N 2°41′26.80″E	Mesplaux swing bridge	50°33′59.80″N 2°40′33.40″E
L'Ecluse Hamel mill	50°33′12.40″N 2°39′44.20″E	Rue du Bois HQ	50°33′19.70″N 2°41′13.70″E
Les Glatignies farm	50°33′33.50″N 2°40′40.10″E	Vauxhall Bridge	50°31′22.90″N 2°44′22.10″E
Loisne North	50°33′28.50″N 2°42′2.50″E	Westminster Bridge	50°31′33.10″N 2°43′45.50″E
Mesplaux Farm	50°33′54.60″N 2°40′47.20″E		

At 10 p.m. on the night of 8 April, the Battalion was given general instructions that, in the case of an attack, they were to support the two left brigades of the Portuguese division; unfortunately, this was an area the Battalion had no opportunity to reconnoitre. The night was quiet until about 4 a.m. on 9 April, when a very heavy barrage descended upon the rear areas. Although Locon took a battering, La Tombe Willot was ignored for the time being. The Battalion began to assemble, and at 6 a.m., 'Bustle' was given and they made their way through thick fog to the assembly position. Each company had six officers and five Lewis guns. 'A' Company, with just eighty-five riflemen, was well below strength as 2Lt Yare and fifty-six men were on detachment to 251 Tunnelling Company RE; the remaining companies each had 130 men and HQ had fifty. 'Bustle' was cancelled at 7.30 a.m., the Battalion ordered to stand-by, but at 8 a.m., 'Bustle' resumed and the Battalion ordered to support the Portuguese.

At 3.50 a.m., one of the opening rounds hit the officers' billet of 422 Field Company RE at Gorre, killing an RE lieutenant, two civilians in the house, and wounding another four officers and a batman—all of whom were trapped in the collapsed

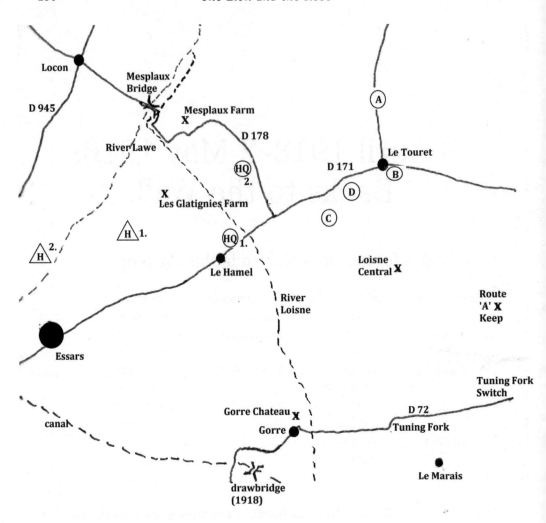

Locon

Mesplaux
Bridge

D 945

Mesplaux Farm
X

D 178

River Lawe

HQ
2.

X
Les Glatignies Farm

/H\ 1.

/H\ 2.

HQ 1.

Le Hamel

River
Loisne

Essars

canal

Gorre Chateau **X**

Gorre

drawbridge
(1918)

Ⓐ

D 171

Le Touret

Ⓑ

Ⓓ

Ⓒ

Loisne
Central **X**

Route
'A' **X**
Keep

Tuning Fork
Switch

D 72

Tuning Fork

Le Marais

Ⓐ company and its position on 9 April

HQ 1. initial Battalion HQ 9 April

HQ 2. Battalion HQ evening of 9 April

/H\ 1. 166 Brigade HQ 6a.m. 11 April

/H\ 2. 166 Brigade HQ 14 April

9 - 14 April 1918
(positions marked on sketch map of modern roads)

structure. One of these was 2Lt Murdoch Paterson, temporarily attached to the RE. Further south, Acting L/Cpl Ernest Bradbury from Blackpool was on detachment with 246 Employment Company ASC, in charge of a traffic control post at the drawbridge over the canal at Le Quesnoy. Few places were more dangerous than known crossing points and the artillery fire was murderous. At 4.30 a.m., one shell landed nearby and two of his four men became casualties, but he remained at his post directing traffic across this vital bridge until 11 April, when he was withdrawn after it became clear that it was suicidal to attempt the crossing during daylight. Bradbury was awarded a well-deserved MM.[1]

The Battalion routed through Locon, which was under heavy bombardment and crossed the River Lawe at Mesplaux Swing Bridge—also being shelled—though they got through without casualties. Respirators were worn as the further east they went, the greater the proportion of gas shells. 'A' Company, under Capt. Oliver Hunt, was ordered to hold a position up Emperor Road (the modern D169) north of Le Touret, until they linked up with a Cyclist battalion who were deploying southwards from La Couture. Immediately south of them, 'B' Company, under Capt. Forshaw, held Le Touret; 'D', under Capt. Metcalfe, garrisoned some trenches to the south-west of Le Touret and a strongpoint at 50°33′35.00″N 2°42′11.50″E: and 'C', under Capt. Briggs, held a strongpoint and trenches at Loisne North.

At 9.10 a.m., HQ was established at the junction between the dyke and the Rue du Bois. As men from HQ platoon began to dig in on the western edge of the dyke and an additional trench protecting their south flank from an attack from the direction of Loisne, two men from the KLR arrived stating that the enemy had overrun Festubert. These were sent on to Brigade HQ and digging-in redoubled in effort. To the Battalion's right, two companies from Liverpool Scottish and their HQ reached the Tuning Fork at 7.15 a.m., their other two companies expected to arrive soon afterwards, though they were being very heavily shelled and casualties were 'uncertain'.[2] The thick fog, restricting visibility to about 20 yards, made navigation difficult and seriously limited the view of anything to their front (most contemporary accounts use 'mist'; however, as visibility was 20–50 yards, this qualifies as 'fog' by modern definition). 'B', 'C', and 'D' Company all reported themselves in position, and although nothing was heard from 'A' Company, 'B' reported that they were in touch with that company's southern posts on their left.

At 10.15 a.m., the signals officer and some of his men moved eastwards along Rue du Bois and reported the sound of heavy small arms fire from all along their front. A patrol went out to Loisne and when it returned, testified that there was no sign of the enemy there, but it was being heavily shelled. All this time, Portuguese soldiers in twos and threes streamed back through HQ's position—most without their weapons—all stating that the Germans were advancing in hundreds. When two full companies came past, these were impounded and pressed into service as a reserve with HQ platoon. The Portuguese were not at all keen to remain, as indicated by Brig.-Gen. Kentish in his later report to Jeudwine:

The urgency of digging in on the line of the Loisne river appeared to me to be obvious and the Portuguese collected by the King's Own, being the only troops available, but at the same time showing a very ardent desire to withdraw to the rear, I sent Capt. Kerr my Staff-Captain and Capt. Abercrombie, my Brigade-Major, to organise them and warn them that any soldier attempting to retire would be instantly shot. This they did, and placing British officers and NCOs with them they were able to get them to carry out my instructions.[3]

It was becoming clear that the entire Portuguese front had collapsed and the enemy was through in large numbers.

The stores left behind at La Tombe Willot (guarded by just one man) were overrun and pillaged by the enemy, with the sentry killed. Fortunately, the poor roads had meant that most equipment had remained behind at Le Quesnoy on 8 April—though the man guarding this was wounded by shellfire. At midday on 9 April, Transport, with as much of the kit as could be obtained and dinner already prepared for the men in the field-cookers, moved from Locon to a field (50°34'29.90"N 2°39'8.70"E) near Le Cornet Malo. Here, they came under very heavy shellfire and were forced to retire across the Lawe to a field near Hingette, and consequently, the men in the firing line did not get any food until later that night.

At 12.30 p.m., two runners from 'A' Company reached HQ, reporting a gap of 1,000 yards between their northern post and the Cyclists and that they had insufficient men to close it. These runners then left to rejoin their company, but returned forty-five minutes later. As soon as they had tried to enter 'A' Company's position, they had come under heavy fire, barely escaping unharmed. 'B' Company sent a patrol under an officer and they too came under heavy small arms fire, as did two subsequent patrols, who reported seeing Germans moving around 'A' Company's positions. One, led by 2Lt James Alexander, pushed on through considerable rifle and MG fire and managed to determine the enemy's positions—information vital for the Battalion's defence—for which he was later awarded the MC. The commander of the other patrol, Sgt Joseph Barnes, was equally fruitful, his success rewarded with the MM.[4] The importance of these patrols cannot be overstated as fog made it impossible for commanders to know what the enemy was up to and early warning of attack was essential. As vital as it was, it was also extremely dangerous; apart from the heavy shellfire, the enemy was sweeping their front with rifle and MG fire and it was very much a case of asking for 'volunteers' for these dangerous exploits. Pte Alexander Roskell volunteered for four patrols, bravery that earned him the MM.[5] It appeared as if 'A' Company had been wiped out.

Shortly after these runners returned, the three remaining companies came under heavy bombardment, followed by a series of onslaughts by waves of infantry. With no artillery support, the companies repelled these with small arms fire. Repeated efforts were made to turn the open left flank of the Battalion, but as the fog lifted, the Lewis gunners and riflemen were able to take a heavy toll of the enemy—though not without cost to themselves. At 5 p.m., 'B' Company reported that the enemy had brought in trench mortars to bombard its positions, and less than an hour later, further attacks were made against all three companies—once more, these were beaten off. Cpl Edward Rimmer had earlier commanded a daylight patrol to establish enemy positions and now, as trench mortar rounds fell on his section's position, a number of his were men buried. Ignoring the explosions and flying shrapnel, he dug them all out—an exploit that earned him the MM. Thirty-four-year-old 2Lt Henry Tringham, a merchant in Ceylon before the war, handled his platoon with great skill, inspiring them with a total disregard for his own safety—preventing his position from being overrun more than once—bravery rewarded by the MC.[6]

Communication between HQ and the forward companies relied upon runners, who braved extreme peril carrying out their tasks. One, Pte George Hazell, was given the MM for his courage on 9 April. The 'lottery' of awards saw others also recommended for the MM fail to get recognition. Pte George Powell—his recommendation, almost identical in wording to George Hazell's—was rejected and he got a MiD instead. Even more unlucky was Pte John Aspray, who repeatedly risked his life delivering messages through shot and shell, was similarly recommended, but ended up with nothing.[7] Communications between battalion and brigade were also difficult to maintain in the heavy fire. Many times telephone wires were cut by shellfire and signallers braved the inferno to find and fix the breaks. Pte Robert Wadsworth repeatedly left cover to do this and was recommended for an MM by the CO, though it was not granted. The next day, Pte James Hall did exactly the same and his MM was endorsed.[8]

By late afternoon, the offensive had been blocked across most of the division's front. In the south, an epic defence by 1/4th King's Own at Givenchy and counterattacks by them and 2/5th Lancashire Fusiliers regained virtually all the territory lost. To their north, 1/4th Loyals retained the original front line up to Le Plantin South. The front line had broken from north of there, but the Village Line up to Cailloux Keep South was held by 1/5th, 1/6th, and 1/7th King's. Route-A Keep had fallen, but Liverpool Scottish were holding the Tuning Fork, with a company of 1/5th South Lancs to their north. These were in touch with 'C' Company's position. On the Battalion's front, the line bent considerably westwards on its left flank where 'B' Company had been pushed, bent, but still clung on. To their left was a composite defensive force of the divisional pioneer company 1/4th South Lancs and two RE Field Companies (419 and 423). The 51st Highland Division had moved in from the north-west, 1/4th Seaforths reaching 55 Division at 2 p.m. and deploying to Mesplaux Farm. At 5 p.m., 'A' Company of the Seaforths was sent to the Battalion, where it was used to strengthen the line at HQ. This line, known as the 'G' Switch Line, curved around to the rear of the Battalion's front line, over the Lawe at Mesplaux, and northwards (where it was named the Gorre–Le Hamel–Lawe River Switch) along its western bank to the front of Locon. To their north, curving eastwards until meeting the original front line, were 1/6th Gordons of 153 Brigade. The inability of 'A' Company 1/5th King's Own to hold Emperor Road had actually worked to the advantage of the defenders; with the men available, it would have been very difficult to link up the new defensive line on the originally planned location.

At 6.30 p.m. on 9 April, Maj. Kidd, OC of 422 Field Company RE, was ordered to take command of the 'G' Switch Line from the right bank of the Lawe down to the Rue du Bois. He had earlier taken over the left of this line with eighty-one of his men and seventy attached infantry. When he arrived on the right flank to inspect the rest of his new command, he discovered one platoon from the 1/5th (HQ platoon) under the command of 2Lt Robert Hamilton and 250 pretty recalcitrant Portuguese. Kidd reported:

> No proper system of trenches had been formed on the right, I therefore instructed a proper system to be made. The Portuguese troop of the garrison appeared rather nervous and their officers requested that as they had had no food they might be relieved. I conveyed to them that events at present could not warrant their moving from the position. Shortly afterwards I received information from 166 Bde. that rations had arrived for these troops [supplied by the Seaforths] and that I was to permit them to proceed to Les Glatignies Farm that they might be issued to them.
>
> With a view to having the line fully manned I interviewed their officer again, who resented my orders to man their position. Under threat of reprisals, my orders were ultimately carried out.
>
> Late in the evening, the G Switch Line was lightly shelled, several of the Portuguese troops vacating their position. Most of these were turned back by our guards who had been posted as a precautionary measure.[9]

German artillery fire slackened from about 7 p.m. and Transport was able to get ammunition and rations up to the three companies in the forward line, although there were outbreaks of heavy, but spasmodic shelling through the hours of darkness. One of the drivers, Pte Harry Walton, was later awarded a MSM for his repeated coolness under fire, delivering rations and ammunition up to the line on 9 April.[10] Battalion HQ moved forward during the night to north of the Rue du Bois, halfway between Le Touret and Le Hamel at 50°33′40.70″N 2°41′20.60″E.

At 5.30 a.m., Capt. Briggs sent back a report about the enemy massing to 'B' Company's east, but as Brigade still lacked artillery assets, they were unable to do anything about it. At 8 a.m., a lance corporal and two men—all that remained of 'A' Company—made it back to friendly lines, explaining that they had been encircled in the fog, rushed from close quarters, and swamped by overwhelming numbers. At this time, men at HQ heard a heavy bombardment of artillery, followed by furious small arms fire from the front as the enemy attacked 'B' Company. The company was hard-pressed, and at one point, it looked as if they were going to be encircled from the left and surrounded. Capt. Forshaw formed up his left platoons and concentrated his Lewis guns on that flank, successfully beating off the repeated attacks. One of his Lewis gunners, Pte Frederick Jones, was almost cut off from the rest of the company, but fought on until he was able to save his gun, for which he was awarded the MM. Another to be similarly rewarded was Pte James Clare, who dug out three of his pals who had been buried by shellfire, then took a heavy toll of the attackers with his cool and accurate rifle fire.[11] While the three fighting companies held off the enemy, the defences to their rear grew in strength by the hour. Shortly after 8 a.m., four Vickers arrived and were placed to the front of Le Hamel—more guns arriving over the course of the day. An artillery officer also arrived in search of an OP and it looked as if the Battalion may get some fire support before too long.

The enemy attacked again around 12.30 p.m., and this time, his left flank in the air, Forshaw was forced to pull his men back 200 yards until he could make contact with a company of the Seaforths. His defence had been epic, with just forty of his 140 men returning unwounded. One of these was L/Sgt Oscar King, whose courage and deadly accuracy with a rifle had been noted by his company commander and resulted in the award of the MM. The courage of L/Cpl Samuel Law was particularly remarkable.[12] On 9 April, he had been partially buried and suffered shellshock, but he had refused to be evacuated. On 10 April, he had remained cool while the enemy advanced directly towards him, cutting them down with his Lewis gun. When artillery fire began to target his position, making it untenable, he picked his gun up and calmly *advanced* before re-engaging the oncoming infantry. He was slightly wounded by shrapnel to his left shoulder on 14 April, but rejoined the Battalion soon afterwards, the ribbon of the MM sewn to his tunic. Law soldiered on until the end of the war, but afterwards the father of two was granted a small pension for the effects of shellshock.[13] L/Cpl Richard Peel also got the MM for the way he commanded his platoon, beating off three attacks. Capt. Forshaw was awarded a bar to his MC for the fine way he had conducted the defence. CSM Joseph Denwood was recommended for the DCM for his courage and devotion to duty. During seven attacks against his company position, he remained utterly cool, his example helping to calm his men and was instrumental in making sure that ammunition was distributed to where it was needed.[14] Although this was not awarded, he did get the CdVM in 1919—very much a consolation prize for this brave and effective SNCO.

When Brig.-Gen. Kentish learned that 'B' Company had been forced back, he ordered Lt-Col. Wayte to gather every spare man, place them under command of 2IC Maj. William Phillips, counterattack, and regain the position. He also ordered Lt-Col. Hopkinson, CO of the Seaforths, to send a company of his men to plug any gap to the left of the Rue du Bois. Lt Macdonald, who had been acting as Kentish's Intelligence Officer, accompanied Phillips in the attack. Moments after they left his HQ, Kentish reported one of the more surreal episodes of the war: 'During this somewhat critical situation 2 shells crashed into my Head Quarters, and a drunken German in a rollicking boisterous state also made his appearance'.[15] Phillips, leading the counterattack force, was hit very early on, lying in a shell hole until after dark. Macdonald took command, succeeded in closing the gap in the line, and though recommended for the DSO by Kentish, was given a second bar to his MC.[16]

Not everyone waited for the cloak of darkness before treating the wounded from the counterattack. Twenty-two-year-old Pte John Baines from Carnforth carried out his duties in full view of the enemy, ignoring shell and small arms fire striking all around him—he was lucky this time. When two of Sgt Percy Roy's men were wounded in the charge, the sergeant twice went back out to bring them back in, even though the enemy were shooting at him as he did so. Both men received the MM. Others too were rewarded for their courage. Twenty-three-year-old L/Cpl William Angus had taken a number of patrols out over the two days and brought back much useful information, which earned him the MM.[17]

German artillery fire was beginning to cause serious damage to the defences in the new lines, partly because the enemy had captured the majority of the Portuguese artillery intact and turned it against the British defenders, in many cases firing over open sights. This new onslaught began at 4 p.m. and was witnessed by Kentish when he visited the Seaforth's HQ at Le Façons Farm (also the Battalion's HQ). Brigade HQ (at Battalion HQ's old position) was also under heavy shellfire and Kentish decided to retire to Les Glatignies Farm, which unsurprisingly was also being shelled. This retrograde movement still left Brigade HQ only 1,000 yards from the front line and very vulnerable. The situation was less critical by 10 p.m. as there was now good artillery support and three effective lines of defence. Kentish was given control of 1/Northumberland Fusiliers from 3 Division and decided to use a company of these fresh troops to relieve 'B' and 'D' Companies of the King's Own, who were pulled back to the 'G' Switch. Only 'C' Company, who had taken part in very little fighting over the two days, remained in position. He also rotated the two companies of Seaforths for two fresh companies from the same battalion. The enemy had been repulsed from La Tombe Willot and the QM took the opportunity to see if they could salvage any of the stores from there. Little remained intact, but these and the bulk of stores from Le Quesnoy were moved by lorry to Transport's new location at Vendin, on the north-western edge of Bethune.

German artillery remained active against the front line overnight, but at 8 a.m., this developed into a full bombardment. Two hours earlier, Kentish had moved his HQ from Les Glatignies to a farm 300 yards to the south-west at 50°33′22.20″N 2°40′21.80″E. Almost immediately, this new location came under heavy fire and he shifted his HQ to behind a haystack on the farm and then to under a culvert of the east bank of the Lawe, in close touch with 51 Division. Brigade HQ was not the only unit constrained to move as 1/4th South Lancs on the left of the front line were also forced to pull back slightly as British 6-inch Howitzer rounds were landing on them and they were unable to contact the artillery to get them to lengthen their fire.

At 8.30 a.m. on 11 April, Kentish was informed that 154 Brigade, to his immediate left, were moving forwards to the north and east of Locon, so he ordered 251 Tunnelling Company and its attached infantry, which included 2Lt Yare and his platoon, forward from their reserve position north of Essars to plug his exposed flank. Soon afterwards, 1/4th South Lancs was heavily assailed and their centre and the left of the Seaforths forced back. At noon, Kentish learned that the South Lancs had retired to just south of Le Casan and that, although they were holding a line from the Pont Tournant on the Lawe, across to Mesplaux, their right flank was still undetermined. This was not good news for the brigade commander, and he immediately ordered a company of South Lancs to counterattack from Mesplaux Farm and a company of the Northumberlands to do likewise from Les Façons. This was very successful, and by 3 p.m., the breach was blocked.

Kentish's actual narrative report to division contains nothing more until 8.30 p.m.[18] However, his draft is slightly more forthcoming about an issue at 4 p.m. that plainly annoyed him considerably:

> The only other matters of interest during this day's operations was the shelling of our Front, Support and Reserve Lines, including Brigade Headquarters, by our own Artillery. I am loath to refer to this, because I do not think that this can be helped when the fighting is of the open nature it was during these 6 days' operations. I think however, that Brigade Headquarters might reasonably expect to be immune, situated as we were 800 yards from the front line, at the nearest point, and 1,500–2,000 yards at the furthest. There was no doubt whatever as to these guns being our own.[19]

Kentish was obviously still feeling umbrage about this when he drafted this report on 15 April, but must have had second thoughts about it eventual inclusion. The impracticalities of siting Brigade HQ in a culvert were beginning to tell, so at 8.30 p.m., Kentish pulled his HQ back 600 yards to the mill at L'Ecluse Hamel.

During the night, the Seaforths were relieved by the Northumberlands, and by 6 a.m. of 12 April, the front line was held by 1/4th South Lancs, 423 Field Company RE, one company of the South Wales Borderers, and the 1/Northumberland Fusiliers. Of the King's Own, only 'C' Company remained in the front line, to the right of the Northumberlands. 'B' and 'D' were in close support, with 'B' deployed behind the South Lancs in a line 150 yards to the rear of Mesplaux Farm and 'D' to the rear of the Northumberlands at 50°33′32.00″N 2°41′30.00″E. HQ moved back to Les Glatignies. Overnight, the hardworking men managed to wire the whole of the front of the 'G' Switch Line. Although the morning passed without incident, at 1.40 p.m., enemy artillery began a furious bombardment of the line on both sides of the Lawe, an infantry attack soon following.

At 2 p.m., Maj. A. Russell, OC of 419 Field Company RE, and commander of the Mesplaux Farm defences, reported that the division to his left—on the opposite side of the Lawe—was falling back and asked if he should conform. Kentish directly ordered him to stand his ground and fight to the finish. He then ordered up a company of 8 Brigade's infantry from reserve. Their timely arrival bolstered the retreat on the western bank of the Lawe. Things quietened down once again until 7 p.m., when another assault was made against Mesplaux Farm—this time the enemy was successful in breaking through Russell's lines between the river and Mesplaux Farm. Russell personally led a counterattack and succeeded in re-establishing their lines. On the west bank, the defenders had slowly been forced back level with the Locon–Le Casan road, and at 8 p.m., Russell asked permission to destroy the two bridges across the river to his rear to prevent him being encircled in the night should the enemy make further progress. Kentish assented and the bridges were blown. Around the same time that Russell was seeking permission to blow the bridges, Transport finally got permission to move to a healthier location. Their position at Vendin was in view of enemy observers and just as the last wagon left the field, enemy artillery rounds began to fall in it. Their new position to the south-west of Béthune at Gosnay, a far safer place.

At 11.30 p.m., enemy artillery once again opened up along the whole of the brigade front and an infantry attack was made against the extreme left of the line at Mesplaux Farm. This attack does not seem to have been pressed very hard and soon fizzled out, leaving a few prisoners in British hands and a number of German dead on and in front of the wire. During the night, 'B' Company King's Own moved forward to form a defensive flank along the eastern side of the Lawe, their numbers enhanced by the addition of 2Lt Yare's platoon.

The morning of 13 April began quietly enough, with some desultory shelling. Maj. Russell, learning that the swing bridge at Mesplaux had not been completely demolished the previous night, visited it at 5 a.m. to complete the job. He was less than amused to discover that the post on the far bank, manned by the KSLI, had withdrawn some 2,300 yards, leaving an unguarded approach behind his defences. Russell went in search of their company commander, ordering him clearly to not leave this post unattended again. It was another very misty morning and when Russell had finished remonstrating with the KSLI captain, he returned towards the bridge. He was only a few yards away from it when he heard the distinctive clatter made when someone drops a rifle; upon investigating the source of the noise, he discovered a Mauser lying on the ground.[20] Fortunately, mist had prevented the enemy seeing that the way behind the Mesplaux Farm defences was wide open. At 3.30 p.m., an intense bombardment from light and heavy artillery descended on British lines. Kentish stated:

> As seen from my HQ, the whole of the Front, Support and Reserve Lines enveloped by the smoke of bursting shells, and with the barrage of shells of a calibre not less than 8″ coming down on the Reserve Line, lengthening as it did to the line of my Brigade Head Quarters at about 4.30 p.m. I felt that he had every intention of launching a big attack. No infantry action however took place, and the shelling died down at about 5 p.m. The troops had a very rough time of it, but stuck it well.[21]

Battalion HQ suffered heavily in this bombardment. L/Sgt Barnett Barrow was killed and a number of men wounded. After dark, HQ retired to a new position 500 yards further back and 'B' and 'D' Companies advanced to relieve the South Lancs and RE at Mesplaux farm around midnight.

Enemy artillery quietened considerably during the night and the morning of 14 April was also without drama. Patrols, one led by Pte John Woodall, went out into the early morning mist to check the wire. However, in the afternoon, 'B' and 'D' were very heavily shelled for a couple of hours. Twenty-two-year-old Pte Harold Burrow, Pte Albert Gover, nineteen-year-old Pte Thomas Hargreaves, thirty-year-old Pte Charles Howe, thirty-seven-year-old Pte William Roper, and thirty-one-year-old Sgt Edward Walker were all killed. John Woodall, in an advanced post, remained with scant cover during this bombardment, reporting the situation regularly to his company commander, receiving the MM for this and his earlier patrol work. Stretcher-bearer Pte Hugh Seacy had put his life on the line many times over the last few days, treating and collecting men from No Man's Land. During this bombardment, he once more braved the shellfire to aid his comrades, though this time his luck ran out. As he was treating one seriously wounded man, he was himself badly wounded in the back, his courage rewarded by the MM.[22] Capt. Metcalfe, directing the two companies at Mesplaux Farm, was a source of strength during the bombardment. His company had held their ground against multiple attacks on 9 April and he was equally determined that no ground would be given up here. His leadership resulted in a bar to his MC. Also recommended for a MC for his coolness under fire—though it was not awarded—was Capt. Hart. More awards were recommended for runners from the Battalion for their courage over the five days of almost constant action. Pte Frederick Bonsall showed total determination to get the messages through, however heavy the shell, rifle, and MG fire; Pte William Cullen delivered no fewer than fifty messages during this period. Pte Thomas Kirkby ignored sniper fire directed at him to get his messages through—all three got the MM. Another runner to be honoured with the MM was Pte Walter Doyle from 'A' Company, though his recommendation no longer survives. Pte Herbert Pearson also ignored sniper fire in his determination to deliver his messages, but his award was not approved.[23]

One of the problems men faced in the 'medal lottery' was the sheer number recommended across the division, for acts of courage that at any other time would almost certainly have been granted. For these five days, 332 MMs were awarded within the division—eighteen to men from the Battalion.[24] The 55th Division's resistance at Festubert-Givenchy was one of the greatest defensive actions of the war and made the division a household name back in Britain. This was to be the Battalion's last day in the line as they were relieved by 1/Northumberlands and 4/Royal Fusiliers by 1 a.m. on 15 April. The exhausted companies marched independently back to Vendin-les-Béthune, where they were taken by lorry to Raimbert, arriving at billets around 5 a.m. Casualties had been very heavy and based upon later returns, rather than the figures given in the diary for the following day, the Battalion lost 280 killed, wounded, or missing, fifty-seven of whom were killed in action or died later from their wounds.[25] The 164th Brigade lost 674 officers and men killed, wounded, or missing; 165 Brigade lost 960; and 166 Brigade lost 659. When support arms are added, this made a divisional total of 3,139.

The enemy received an unexpected setback when they encountered 55 Division, believing erroneously that it would present little opposition—so confident of easy victory—that an entire band complete with their instruments had been sent forward to play their triumphant forces into Béthune.[26] This overconfidence is probably best illustrated by a captured German document that instructed the attacking divisions thus:

In our attack our three regiments will be opposed by at most six companies in front and at most two reserve battalions in Festubert and Givenchy. One battalion in divisional reserve is South of the La Bassée Canal in le Préol. It will be prevented by our powerful artillery fire from taking part in the fight for Festubert and Givenchy. Troops are elements of the 55th Division, which after being engaged on the Somme has suffered heavy losses in Flanders and at Cambrai, and was described by prisoners in March, 1918, as a division fit to hold a quiet sector, that is below the average quality.[27]

Killed or Died from Wounds 9 April to 14 April

Pte Joseph Bannister	33854	KIA: 9/4	Pte Harry Hodgson	27530	KIA: 10/4
L/Sgt Barnett Barrow	200921	KIA: 13/4	Pte Bertie Hollingworth	34749	DOW: 11/4
Pte Joseph Dixon Bell	35693	KIA: 9/4	Pte George Freke Howard	28202	KIA: 11/4
L/Cpl John Frederick Bennett	201160	KIA: 9/4	Pte Charles George Howe	23182	KIA: 14/4
Pte Ernest Dean Bentham	21035	KIA: 9/4	Pte Arthur George Jobbins*	35647	DOW: 9/6
Pte Ernest Boothway	265777	KIA: 10/4	Pte John Leo Kilgallon	22977	KIA: 9/4
Pte Montague Frederick Brame	26413	DOW: 13/4	Pte Joseph Leybourn	28043	KIA: 10/4
Pte Harold Burrow	242987	KIA: 14/4	Sgt William Livesey	240432	DOW: 11/4
Pte James Livesey Butterworth	242358	KIA: 10/4	Pte Albert Percy Lloyd	265138	KIA: 10/4
L/Cpl John Albert Coar	242621	DOW: 27/4	L/Cpl William Marland	200848	KIA: 9/4
Pte Charles Collins	32003	KIA: 11/4	Pte George Marsden	28047	KIA: 9/4
Pte William Leo Crewe*	20510	DOW: 25/4	Pte Samuel John Mayne	27876	KIA: 10/4
Pte James Crook	35788	KIA: 12/4	Pte Frank Millington	26718	KIA: 10/4
Pte John Cummings	213036	KIA: 10/4	Pte Johnson Newton	28060	KIA: 10/4
Pte Joseph Dalton*	242624	DOW: 1/5	Pte Charles Palmer	26724	KIA: 9/4
Pte John Henry Davis	242703	KIA: 9/4	Pte Ernest Reilley	11343	KIA: 10/4
Cpl James Donavan	242965	KIA: 9/4	Pte William Woof Roper	34607	KIA: 14/4
Pte Charles Driscoll	26035	KIA: 9/4	2Lt John Henry Clavell Salter		KIA: 9/4
2Lt Arthur Duxbury		KIA: 9/4	Pte John Clement Scales	35700	KIA: 9/4
Pte Joseph Hugh Ferguson	242707	KIA: 9/4	L/Cpl Edward Silcock**	16908	DOW: 10/4
Pte James Thomas Fielding	22094	DOW: 13/4	Pte William John Sines	30652	DOW: 13/4
Pte Arthur Francom	37627	KIA: 10/4	Sgt Edward Bernard Standen	241486	KIA: 9/4
Cpl William Gifford Garth	241577	KIA: 10/4	Pte Thomas Sidney Thompson	36510	KIA: 9/4
Pte Albert Edward Gover	30699	KIA: 14/4	Pte Isaac James Thursfield	242495	KIA: 13/4
L/Cpl James Cole Grisdale	201853	KIA: 9/4	2Lt Clifford Francis Tucker		KIA: 9/4
Pte Fred Hall	242473	KIA: 9/4	Sgt Edward Walker	12424	KIA: 14/4
Pte Henry Morton Hall	30025	KIA: 11/4	Pte James Walsh	241544	KIA: 9/4
Pte Thomas William Hargreaves	37741	KIA: 14/4	Pte James Wilson	35694	DOW: 13/4
Pte William Arthur Harrington	35988	KIA: 9/4			

*Died while he was a POW.

**Soldiers Died* states that Edward Silcock 'Died'—in other words, accident or natural causes. I believe this to be incorrect and that he 'Died of Wounds'.

Known to have been either Wounded or Taken Prisoner 9 April–14 April

L/Cpl James Ashton	27454	POW	Pte William Jenkinson	33104	WIA: 10/4
Pte Thomas Ashton	20359	POW	Pte Albert Johnson	21222	WIA: 10/4
Pte John Baglin	24283	POW	A/Cpl Frank Knowles Lancaster	30694	WIA
Cpl Stanley Victor Baker	27398	POW	L/Cpl Samuel Law	242288	WIA: 14/4
Pte John Barrow	23904	POW	Pte William Littlefair	30685	WIA/POW
Pte Arthur Frederick Beadle**	202970	POW	Pte John McGowan	21762	POW
Pte Ralph Joseph Black	235055	WIA: 9/4	Pte Fred Newton	241082	POW
Pte Samuel John Brinicombe	24829	WIA: 9/4	Pte Robert Nixon	20946	WIA: 9/4
2Lt Fred Buckley		POW	Pte James Nolan	22672	POW
Pte Josiah Burgess	23031	WIA: 9/4	2Lt Murdoch Fraser Paterson		WIA: 9/4
Pte Walter James Cheetham	30669	WIA: 11/4	2Lt Bernard Percival		POW
2Lt Gerald Conheeny***		POW	Maj. William Mallam Phillips		WIA: 10/4
A/Cpl Nathaniel Constable	30695	POW	A/Cpl Harold Randall	24288	WIA
Pte James Corry	22623	WIA: 9/4	Pte James John Richmond	33257	WIA
Cpl Abraham Crossley	26088	WIA/POW	Pte John Riley	20740	POW
Pte Charles Henry Dorrell	30678	WIA: 11/4	Pte William Edwin Ripley	33472	WIA: 9/4
Pte Thomas Duxbury	21365	POW	Pte Sidney Robinson	30707	POW
Pte William Fisher	33595	POW	Cpl Joseph Ross	14054	WIA/POW
Pte Thomas John Fuller	30260	POW	L/Cpl Samuel Rowe	23065	POW
Pte Wilfred Fullerton	33686	POW	Pte Hugh Seacy	34630	WIA: 14/4
Pte William Gheerbrant	30216	WIA: 13/4	2Lt Arthur Noel Shaw		WIA: 9/4
Pte Archibald Gibbs	30697	POW	2Lt Alfred Henry Smith		WIA: 14/4
Pte Frederick Gilmore	22904	WIA/POW	2Lt Gordon Steel		POW
Pte John James Gray	28198	WIA: 9/4	Pte Reuben Sumner	24320	WIA
Pte Arthur Guile	30702	WIA: 9/4	Pte George William Webster	243056	POW
Cpl Harry Harwood	32600	POW	2Lt Alexander John White		POW
Pte Thomas Houghton	19977	POW	Pte Wilfred Vere Whitehead*	240956	POW
Lt John Roland Humphreys		WIA: 10/4	Pte Ernest Joseph Wilkinson	33916	WIA: 11/4
Capt. Oliver Grahame Hunt		WIA/POW	2Lt Walter Young		POW
Cpl Frank Iniff	240221	WIA: 12/4			

*Died while a POW.

**Wounded while a prisoner.

***Shot dead by a German guard 5 December 1918.

The Battalion was allowed to rest on 15 April, but there was a great deal to do before going back into the line. Much of the kit had been lost and over 250 men and sixteen officers had to be replaced (Capt. Hargreaves was sent home sick). During the five days the Battalion stayed at Raimbert, divisional records show that 252 men arrived to replace the casualties, though only one new officer appeared—Maj. Edward Hoare of KOYLI—replacing the wounded Capt. Phillips as 2IC.[28] Their time at Raimbert was engaged integrating replacements into the company structure and training them in the Battalion's way, 'A' and 'B' Company in particular needing to absorb many of the newcomers.

On 20 April, the Battalion travelled by lorry to Labourse and were in billets by 6.30 p.m. The next day, they received orders to relieve 1/South Wales Borderers in the Festubert–Loisne sector that night, on loan to 1 Division. Travelling north on the light railway, they arrived at Le Quesnoy at 10.20 p.m. and marched to the front, completing the relief by 1.45 a.m. on 22 April. HQ was to the south-west of Loisne Central at 50°32′58.30″N 2°42′14.70″E. The fighting companies holding a line from near Loisne Central on the left to Cailloux North on the right.

Perched rather precariously in the centre of the line as a forward outpost was Route-A Keep, commanded by twenty-four-year-old 2Lt William Yacomeni MM, with 2Lt Alexander and about thirty men from 'C' Company. Ideally, the garrison should have been twice this size. The Battalion had been under fairly constant artillery fire since they occupied these trenches, but the state of Route-A Keep—which had been captured and retaken three times already—horrified Yacomeni, who later stated: 'We had no wire, no SOS, no bombs, no reserve of S.A.A. and no Very lights'.[29]

The garrison had no materials to develop their defences, which in many places had been levelled by the previous fighting and were virtually untenable. Closer to dawn on 22 April, the shelling intensified, with 5.9, *Minenwerfer*, and MGs targeting the Keep. More of the breastworks were blown in, and at 4 a.m., an entire company of German Stormtroopers rushed his position under cover of the bombardment. Thirteen of the men managed to get fight their way out before they were completely surrounded, but the remainder were completely encircled and forced to capitulate.

Yacomeni, Alexander, and ten men were taken prisoner. Twenty-four-year-old Pte Reuben Brown and twenty-year-old Pte David Littler are known to have been among these, the latter with a wound to his left hand. Twenty-six-year-old Pte Fred Ashworth was killed outright and twenty-year-old Pte Albert Shuttleworth died from wounds later that day—the latter probably a victim of the shellfire elsewhere, rather than from Route-A Keep. Two men are also known to have been wounded on 22 April—nineteen-year-old Pte Fred Smith, wounded in the right hip, and thirty-one-year-old Pte Lewis Smith, wounded in the thumb, which was later amputated back in England. Lewis Smith may have been from the Route-A Keep garrison, but it is unlikely that Fred Smith would have reached friendly lines with his wound, so he was probably a casualty from another position.

At midnight of 22–23 April, 'D' Company attempted to retake the Keep, but due to a faulty barrage and several enemy MGs positioned forward of the Keep, the attempt was unsuccessful. Unfortunately, it is not possible in the records to distinguish between the casualties from this abortive attack and those from when Transport lines at Fouquières were shelled that evening. At Fouquières, three men and one officer (Lt Appleyard) were wounded and a storeman killed. The storeman was either Pte Fred Richards or L/Cpl Joseph Fielding—both were buried at Fouquières. Also killed were twenty-year-old L/Cpl Thomas Bell, twenty-nine-year-old Pte William Bryan, and nineteen-year-old Pte William Swallow. Twenty-five-year-old Pte Frank Lawson died from his wounds that day, but was possibly a casualty from the previous day's artillery fire. The only wounded man for whom records survive is nineteen-year-old Pte John Lambert. A warehouseman in civilian life, he may well have been a storeman with the Battalion. He was wounded by shell splinters in the left shoulder and evacuated home.

At 4 a.m. on 24 April, Route-A Keep changed hands yet again. This time the Liverpool Scottish attacked after a much better coordinated artillery and MG barrage. The defenders numbered about seventy-five, thirty of whom were killed and ten captured, along with four machine guns (the enemy retook it on 26 April after Liverpool Scottish had been relieved). The rest of the day was much quieter, with little shellfire. On 25 April, the Battalion's positions were reconnoitred by officers and NCOs from the South Staffordshires, who were to relieve the Battalion around midnight. At various times during the day HQ and company positions were shelled, Loisne Central by 5.9, mortally wounding twenty-year-old Pte William Woolley, who died on 13 May. Records also show that on 26 April, Pte James Johnson was killed, though this probably happened late on 25 April.

After relief, the Battalion went into support just to the south of Le Préol. The entire battalion was detailed for working parties the night of 26 April, and at 7.30 p.m. on 27 April, they were relieved and headed off to billets in Verquigneul. The only exception being 'A' Company, who provided a garrison at Westminster and Vauxhall Bridges—hardly popular places as they attracted so much artillery. Luckily they were not there long as a composite company from 166 Brigade relieved them during the evening of 28 April and they rejoined the others. The time at Verquigneul was spent resting, reorganising, assimilating replacements, and training, though on 30 April, half of 'C' and 'D' Company went to relieve the posts at the two bridges. Finally, officer replacements arrived—Capt. William Hesketh and 2Lts William Deacon, Norman Hill (from the DLOY), Francis Howson, Charles Husband, and John Price—a former corporal from the Battalion.

2 May 1918–19 August 1918: Growing Optimism

Coordinates for Positions Named in this Chapter

2Lt Hill's raid 5 July	50°33′14.70″N 2°44′31.50″E	HQ- 2 May	50°32′10.50″N 2°43′51.40″E
Battersea Bridge	50°31′42.30″N 2°43′15.10″E	HQ- 6 August	50°31′54.20″N 2°42′33.10″E
Blakeley's CP	50°32′59.90″N 2°44′27.80″E	HQ- Addison Road	50°32′3.10″N 2°43′41.20″E
Blakeley Raid- from	50°33′2.30″N 2°44′30.70″E	HQ- Canal House	50°31′50.90″N 2°42′45.40″E
Blakeley Raid- to	50°33′5.60″N 2°44′46.60″E	HQ- Duke Post	50°32′6.70″N 2°43′27.50″E
Capt. Hamilton's raid	50°32′22.00″N 2°44′48.60″E	Kent Lane	50°32′55.80″N 2°44′9.30″E
Chelsea Bridge	50°31′55.90″N 2°42′17.70″E	McMahon Post	50°32′48.20″N 2°44′13.90″E
Estaminet Corner	50°32′20.80″N 2°43′41.40″E	Rigden's hedge	50°33′1.00″N 2°44′33.60″E
Festubert Switch	50°32′41.30″N 2°43′43.60″E	Tuning Fork Switch	50°32′26.90″N 2°43′33.80″E

At 8 p.m. on 2 May, the Battalion left Verquigneul to occupy the right sub-sector of the Festubert sector, Liverpool Scottish to their left and 1/6th King's to their right in the Givenchy sector. HQ was situated in a dugout to the west of Le Plantin; 'C' and 'D' in support; and 'A' on the left and 'B' to the right of the front line stretching from Festubert on the left to just south of Le Plantin on the right. Their route to the front was a precarious one, with heavy shelling along the Annequin–Beuvry road and there were casualties. One shell landed next to one of the Lewis limbers, killing the driver, twenty-two-year-old Pte William Glaister and wounding two others. 'D' Company also lost twenty-one-year-old Pte Henry Marsden.

Much worse followed next morning. A German Howitzer of a very large calibre (the Battalion's diary states 14 inches—the divisional diary, either 11 or 17 inches) was firing armour-piercing shells into 'B' Company's line and its immediate rear. One of these penetrated under one of the dugouts before exploding, causing heavy casualties. Although the Battalion diary reports two killed, four wounded, and ten missing believed killed and the brigade diary states fourteen killed; the CWGC records indicate ten killed and possibly another who died from wounds the following day. The only man known to have been wounded that day was twenty-four-year-old Pte Thomas Titterington, whose wounds to his left shoulder resulted in medical discharge. In consequence of these casualties, two platoons from 'D' Company were brought forward and attached to 'B'. Their place in support was taken by two platoons from 1/5th South Lancs. On 4 May, these were released and replaced by a composite detail of thirty-one new and untrained (by the division) replacements, under 2Lt Robert Park—his first day with the Battalion. Another two officers also arrived on 4 May—2Lt Thomas Curry and 2Lt Frank Dowlen—though both returned home sick within a month. Records also show that thirty-three-year-old Pte Alfred Sullivan returned to England sick and was later discharged suffering from TB. Fortunately, 4 May was a much quieter day, though nineteen-year-old Pte Leonard Powell received a minor wound, returning to duty on 7 May.

Fatalities in 'B' Company's Dugout: 3 May 1918

2Lt Arthur Albert Adie		KIA	Cpl Christopher Quigley	19081	KIA
Pte Arthur Boden	42897	KIA	Pte Nelson Slater	29113	KIA
Pte Albert Herbert Entwistle*	241570	KIA	Pte Thomas Smith	29115	KIA
Pte Owen Gleeson	34825	KIA	L/Cpl Robert Squires**	243066	DOW: 4/5
Pte Sidney Hellens	35989	KIA	Pte Frederick Oliver Whitmore	41007	KIA
Pte David Patterson	28146	KIA			

*Had recently returned to his company after donating blood to a wounded man. He was the brother of John, killed in September 1917.
**Given his burial location at Étaples, he may not be a casualty from 3 May, though he was definitely wounded some time after 22 April.

Apart from five 77-mm shells striking around HQ at 3.30 a.m. on 5 May, most hostile artillery fell in the Givenchy sector. The following day, 'C' Company relieved 'A' in the line and two platoons from 'D' relieved 'B', the composite platoon remaining in support. Intermittent shellfire fell around the Battalion's positions and L/Cpl James Bailiff and Pte Wilfred Firth were both wounded. Early on 7 May, a salvo of 77 mm hit 'B' Company's HQ in the support lines, wounding six men, one of whom—Pte Joseph Shepherd—died later that day. That evening, the composite platoon moved into the right front to relieve the two 'D' Company platoons. The usual shellfire punctuated day and night on 8 May and a decision was made to thin out the front line, making the support line the main line of resistance. This was prompted by information by a prisoner, who stated that an attack was probable for either the 8th or 9th. Brigade HQ retired to Canal House as a precaution. The division had no less than seventeen patrols out in No Man's Land over the night of 8–9 May, though no enemy patrols were encountered and no indication found suggesting the enemy was preparing to attack. The Battalion stood-to all night just in case.

Enemy artillery levels remained routine on 9 May, though the Battalion lost three killed and three wounded—mostly from a couple of heavy bursts around 8 p.m. Nineteen-year-old Pte George Pearson was killed outright and thirty-five-year-old Pte Walter Sharples very badly wounded by shrapnel, dying at the dressing station. Forty-year-old Pte Arthur Green was the victim of a sniper. The father of two and former village postman in Halton continued his trade in the Battalion as a runner and was fatally shot as he brought a message forward. The attack had still not materialised late on 10 May, when Liverpool Scottish relieved the Battalion just before midnight. Moving into support, the remainder of 11 May was deemed a rest day. Another four replacement officers were waiting for them, one of whom was Capt. Bennett, back after his wounding. The other three—all new subalterns—were George Abbott (a former sergeant in the Battalion), James Adams, and James Hollingworth. Abbott was only with them for a week as he went to the South Lancs on 18 May.

The 12th was another misty morning and the Battalion stood-to from 3 a.m. through to 9 a.m. The remainder of the day was spent resting as everyone was required for working parties overnight—a routine repeated until the Battalion moved to billets on 15 May. During the night of 13–14 May, the entire battalion was out at Cailloux Keep, erecting 400 yards of new wire to its west. While thus employed, nineteen-year-old Pte Joel Kavarsky was killed by shellfire. The Battalion also lost Pte Albert Matthews, who died from illness that day at a CCS at Pernes. Around midnight of 14–15 May, the Battalion was relieved by Liverpool Scottish and went straight to their Bustle positions until just before 6 a.m., when they were ordered to stand down and marched to billets in Verquigneul, resting for the remainder of the day.

Although in billets well behind the lines, the Battalion were still within range of German artillery, and at 9.30 p.m. on 17 May, six 4.2 rounds landed near HQ in Verquigneul, wounding nineteen-year-old Pte Hugh McGowan in the thigh. When he left hospital at the end of July, he was posted to 8/King's Own. Another six rounds of HE and gas struck at 4 a.m. on 18 May, this time without result. Later that day, Lt-Col. Wayte arrived back from leave, but departed again almost immediately, Maj. Hoare assuming command (Maj. Claude Marshall was posted in at the beginning of July to become the new 2IC). The 19th saw further shelling of Verquigneul, wounding thirty-year-old Sgt James Dolan. His wound was not acute, but three years in the trenches had taken their toll and he was medically downgraded, transferring to the Labour Corps. Their time in billets at an end, the Battalion departed for the front line at 8.45 p.m. on 20 May, occupying the same positions as last time, though HQ was in the dugout in Addison Road, last used by them on 12 May.

During the morning of 21 May, Addison Road was shelled and the RE Dump next to HQ hit, killing four Sappers and Pte Gilbert Griffin from 1/5th South Lancs. The front line positions were also shelled at various intervals during the day, and although there were no casualties, it was an uncomfortable time. The 22nd began quietly enough with less than the normal amount of shellfire, though HQ and Estaminet Corner were both targeted by 4.2 and 5.9 Howitzers. The CO and brigade-major visited the front line at 6.45 p.m.—rather bad timing on their part—as the enemy chose then to deliver an intense barrage across the whole battalion front for ten minutes, ceasing for ten minutes, before continuing for another fifteen minutes. Pte Thomas Fenn was killed by this. It was much the same on 23 May, with light shelling during the day, but a heavy barrage in the evening—though there were no casualties this time. The 24th and 25th were quieter and most men worked on improving the defences along the Village Line, much to the approval of Brig.-Gen. Kentish who inspected their work. The weather was dull and wet with a low cloud base, cutting down the number of enemy observation aircraft over the lines, the volume of shellfire reducing accordingly.

At 7 a.m. on 26 May, forty-nine-year-old Pte Thomas Neiles from Salford, one of two men in an OP, noticed a German moving from shell hole to shell hole out in No Man's Land near the OBL.[1] Neiles immediately slipped out of the OP and stalked the man across No Man's Land in what was now broad daylight. He eventually nabbed the German, a soldier from the 94th Regiment, and brought him safely back to British lines. The unfortunate prisoner had only gone into the line the previous day, was lost, and judged by his interrogators to be a fairly dense specimen and useless as a source of intelligence, though the unit identification was useful and Neiles was awarded the MM for his courage and initiative.[2] Neiles' actions were particularly impressive for a soldier of his age—a factor couched in terms of what can best be described as 'amazement' in his citation.[3] German artillery once again became active in the evening and Tuning Fork East was heavily shelled killing, Pte Edward Kendall. Further fire was directed against the Battalion's positions the following morning, HQ narrowly missed by a salvo of 4.2.

During the night of 27–28 May, the Battalion provided just one of the eleven patrols across the divisional area. This was led by twenty-one-year-old 2Lt John Price, who despite his youth was a seasoned soldier. They entered the OBL opposite Le Plantin, finding it strongly held by an enemy who put up a fierce resistance, killing Price and badly wounding another soldier, who was captured. Four other men were wounded, but managed to escape back to friendly lines. One of these was twenty-nine-year-old Pte Herbert Mayoh, shot in the left shoulder. Another may have been twenty-seven-year-old Pte George Harman, wounded around this time. The Battalion was relieved by Liverpool Scottish in the early hours of 29 May and moved back to support. This far behind the front, working parties were mostly during daytime and men were thus occupied on 30 May. The following day, however, the requirements were for a large party around

Festubert that night. There was also some shellfire around Le Préol during the morning and the only known casualty, twenty-three-year-old Pte Robert Hare, may have been a casualty from this or the working party. His knee wound was serious enough to bring about his medical discharge.

Late on 1 June, the Battalion was relieved by 1/5th King's and after being released from their Bustle positions next morning, moved to billets at Drouvin, all the brigade now out of the line. Replacements arrived during their time at Drouvin, though the precise numbers are no longer on record as Divisional 'A' & 'Q' returns fail to stipulate the destination of replacements during this period. These and men already with the Battalion, were slotted into appropriate roles. If at all possible, whenever men (as a result of age or fitness) struggled doing their job in the front line, they would be found alternate jobs—such as Pte James Newsham. Out with the Battalion since February 1915, he had had his pipe blown to pieces while he was smoking it in April 1915, was wounded in May 1915, and later suffered trench foot. He had tried his best, but the after-effects of his wound and the trench foot made marching absolute purgatory. A solution was found by making him a company cook. The Battalion remained at Drouvin until 8 June, reorganising, refitting, and training interspersed with morale-boosting activities, such as sports and entertainments. One activity that seems to have qualified as both was an exhibition of bayonet fighting by Brig.-Gen. Kentish. Watching red-tabbed generals wielding a bayonet with gusto was not an everyday event. Kentish, however, was more than capable, as a former company commander with the Royal Irish Fusiliers at Le Cateau in 1914. Drouvin was beyond the range of German guns, but their air force still presented a danger—either from bombs or MG fire, and assistant transport officer Lt John Gardner was badly wounded by machine-gun fire during a ground attack on 7 June. At 8 p.m. on 8 June, the Battalion paraded and moved off to relieve 1/5th King's in the left sub-sector of the left sector in the front line.

The Battalion occupied from Cailloux Keep North on the left, down to Festubert on their right front—though the bulk of their strength was concentrated along the Tuning Fork Switch, Festubert Switch, and Kent Lane. It is clear from these dispositions that the main threat was seen as coming from the north and not the east, with no less than fourteen of the platoons placed to counter this threat—three of them designated 'counterattack' platoons. The night of 8 June and the next day were quiet and they were able to put in some good work on the defences. Cailloux Keep North, projecting out several hundred yards into No Man's Land, was a concern to the CO as it was vulnerable to raids. While the Battalion was at Drouvin, the enemy had carried out two silent daylight raids on consecutive days against posts in Berkeley Street and Orchard Road in the right sector. The latter was driven off without casualties, but the former resulted the capture of seven men from 2/5th Lancashire Fusiliers and left no evidence of how the raiders had accessed the defences (a perfect illustration as to why commanders took such a dim view of sentries sitting on the fire-step instead of keeping a lookout). Aerial photographs of this front from April 1918 appear to show a moonscape of muddy craters, but ground-level panoramas reveal that the terrain was actually covered by scrub vegetation (waist-high in places), and covert activity during daylight was far from impossible.

Around noon on 10 June, a heavy trench mortar fired six rounds at Cailloux Keep North, and although these missed the actual Keep, eighteen-year-old Stephen Kirk and twenty-one-year-old Enoch Hill were killed by the fire. The location of this mortar was not discerned, but it was believed to be somewhere in or near Pioneer Road between the OBL and Rue de Cailloux. Wherever it was, it needed neutralising as soon as possible as the craters it left were 15–20 feet deep and 15 feet across—demonstrating its potential threat. The next day was much quieter and enemy artillery left the Battalion's positions alone and no doubt there some celebrations at Transport, with the award of the MC in the King's Birthday Honours to the transport officer Capt. Harold Bell was announced in divisional orders.

At 12.45 p.m. on 12 June, a British observation aircraft suffered engine failure at low altitude, but managed a forced-landing 350 yards out in No Man's Land forward of McMahon Post. Luckily for the crew, they both made it safely into Cailloux Keep (Cailloux North and South had been merged). The aircraft on the other hand was totally destroyed by a direct hit from a trench mortar. The day also ended badly for thirty-two-year-old signaller Pte Milton Pollard; the previous night, he was on a ration party carrying tins of water up to the line, when the piece of string connecting the two tins he was carrying snapped, causing him to stumble into a shell hole whence his rifle discharged. He failed to mention to Cpl Stanley Hooper that the round had caused a flesh wound to his foot until 4 p.m. the next day. As with all accidental injuries, there was an Enquiry. Apart from the obvious issue of shooting himself in the foot, he had also broken two other rules—that of not having a round in the chamber and safety catch being applied at all times. His platoon commander, 2Lt John Baird, stated:

> I inspected the rifles of the platoon of which Pte Pollard was one before 'stand to' in the evening of 11th inst. I am continually warning the men (and they all know) that live rounds in their rifles should be under the bolt. I am of the opinion that Pte Pollard put a cartridge into the breech of his rifle after stand down.

Capt. Metcalfe also questioned Pollard:

> He could not give me any definite information as to when a live round was inserted into the breech of his rifle or how the discharge was caused. He informed me that he placed it in the breech prior to going to the front line so that he would be ready for any emergency.[4]

The injury was minor—he was only off duty for four days—but there was no doubt as to Pollard's culpability and he was given a FGCM in August, charged with 'negligent Self Injury'. Unfortunately, no record survives of his sentence, though it was probably around fourteen to twenty-eight days' field punishment.

The sector remained quiet until the afternoon of 16 June, when fifteen light and medium trench mortar rounds were fired at Cailloux Keep, killing Pte John Loftus. Twenty-three-year-old Pte Percival Whitmore died from his wounds at Pernes on the same day, though it is not clear whether he was another casualty from the 16th or if he was wounded on the 10th. Another wounded around this time was Boer War veteran, thirty-eight-year-old L/Cpl Walter Couch, a father of two from Haigh near Wigan. He was evacuated home with shrapnel wounds to his right ankle on 22 June. On 17 June, the Battalion was relieved by Liverpool Scottish and moved back to support.

Cailloux Keep once more became the target for trench mortars on 18 June and Liverpool Scottish were fortunate to have no casualties from them. On 19 June, raids by the brigades either side of the Battalion resulted in their own sector being shelled by the enemy, though no casualties resulted as the barrage was fairly light. The retort by Division's artillery, mortars, and machine guns, however, was anything but 'light'; the mortars alone fired 415 rounds, and MGs 38,000—producing a laconic remark in the Battalion's diary: '...we felt sure the Hun did not have a happy time'.[5] The Battalion's relief by 1/7th King's on the night of 20–21 June dragged on and they did not reach their Bustle positions until 3.30 a.m. Upon stand-down, they marched off to billets in Vaudricourt and the next day to Hesdigneul, where they remained until 26 June. This period out of the line was as usual devoted to training, though the Battalion was unable to train as a complete battalion as there was one whole company was detached on working parties each day. Lt Isedore Gillespie left to join the MGC, but was replaced by Lt Arthur Hardy of the Lincolns, seconded to the Battalion.

On 26 June, the Battalion relieved the 1/5th King's in the right subsector at Le Plantin by 3 a.m. of the 27th. Their first day in the front line was very quiet, but on 28 June, there was some artillery fire directed at their trenches in response to British gas shelling. That night, Lt Hardy took out a small patrol to attack an enemy listening post. The three enemy in the post were killed, but Hardy was unable to secure identification of their unit as the enemy responded immediately with a salvo of bombs, driving the attackers off. Fortunately, all the patrol regained friendly lines without casualties. The 29th was another reasonably quiet day and no casualties were suffered. The lack of German activity was probably due to the influenza epidemic, which affected them quite badly over May and June. The last day of June brought scattered shellfire around the Battalion's positions, but no casualties. That night they were relieved by Liverpool Scottish and moved back to support. One of the men actually left the line a day earlier. Pte William Gheerbrant had been wounded soon after joining the Battalion and was finding shellfire difficult to cope with. Thankfully, his platoon commander was sympathetic and sent him to the MO on 29 June. Shell shock was diagnosed, and before the end of July, Gheerbrant was on his way home to be cared for and was still under treatment in 1919.

During the night of 4 July, the Battalion returned to the front line, relieving 1/5th South Lancs in the left sub-sector. Although German artillery was fairly active around the most westerly of their positions on the Tuning Fork during the day of 5 July, no casualties or damage resulted. The most spectacular event of the day being a daring raid by 2Lt Hill's small patrol. At 8 a.m., they crawled out of Cailloux across No Man's Land towards a post located during the night. Unobserved by the enemy, they cut through four belts of wire and slipped into it, finding it empty. The patrol then returned the way they had come. Before dusk, they crept back out into No Man's Land, into the same post and hid there waiting for the night-time garrison to arrive. This time their wait bore fruit, but the enemy did not give up quietly. Hill shot the first as he failed to surrender quietly, but the second fled shouting for help. The struggle brought large numbers of enemy to the scene and a short firefight broke out, killing or wounding several Germans. Faced by overwhelming numbers, the raiders were forced to withdraw. One of the patrol was seriously wounded and Hill wounded in the foot, but despite his own injury, the twenty-three-year-old subaltern carried his wounded man back to friendly lines through a hail of very close range MG fire. For his conspicuous daring and resource, 2Lt Hill was awarded the MC.[6]

Records show that two men died from wounds on 6 July, and though it is not known when they were wounded, it is probable that they were casualties from the 200 4.2 and 77 mm, which bombarded the Village Line, Reserve Line, and Festubert Switch on the night of 5 July. Nineteen-year-old Pte Boris Buckley and thirty-year-old Pte Charles Featherstone both died at the CCS at Pernes. Patrols went out again on the night of 6–7 July, but failed to find any enemy for identification purposes. While these were out others took advantage of a very dark night to improve the defences. Twenty-one-year-old Pte Arthur Durham and twenty-two-year-old Pte James Wedge from 'C' Company were busy adding to the wire in front of their position when the coil of wire Wedge was trying to uncoil tangled. As he struggled to free it silently, he accidentally stepped into a shell hole, the wire in his hands pulling him onto a picket, resulting in lacerations to his groin. He reported this to his platoon officer and Durham wrote a witness statement for the routine Enquiry.[7] Wedge's resulting sojourn in hospital quite possibly saved his life.

It was quiet during the day of 7 July, but at 11 p.m., the neighbouring division carried out a large-scale raid. The patrol already out in No Man's Land took advantage of this covering bombardment to try to get into a German post, but the enemy was fully alert and opened up on the patrol with MG fire when it was 80 yards away. Thwarted, they returned to friendly lines. This activity brought retribution upon the Battalion as all their positions were shelled heavily for about an hour afterwards. One fatality was twenty-one-year-old Post-Corporal James Donohue. Thirty-seven-year-old Pte L/Cpl John Balmforth, who died from wounds the following day at Houchin, may also have been wounded by this bombardment, though there was further shelling of the Battalion's positions by 5.9 and 4.2 during the night of 8 July.

At 9.30 p.m. on 10 July, a force of three officers and eighty-six men under Lt Blakeley, left to raid a number of enemy positions among the ruined houses each side of a 350 yard stretch along the Rue de Cailloux. Their objective was to capture prisoners and upon this being achieved, a whistle was to be blown to signal immediate retirement, hopefully minimising the time fighting in and around the houses. In any eventuality, fifteen minutes after the start of the raid, a rocket bursting into gold and silver rain would be fired for withdrawal and a series of Very lights sent up to guide the raiders home. The force was

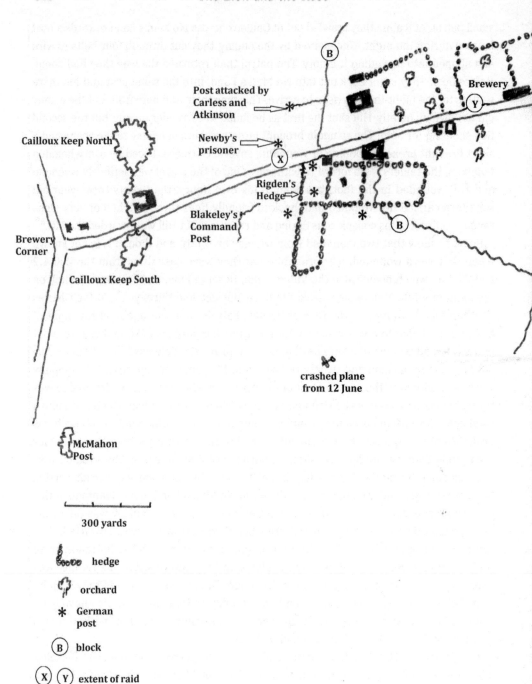

Post attacked by
Carless and
Atkinson

Newby's
prisoner

Cailloux Keep North

Brewery
Corner

Cailloux Keep South

Rigden's
Hedge

Blakeley's
Command
Post

Brewery

crashed plane
from 12 June

McMahon
Post

300 yards

hedge

orchard

* German
  post

B block

X Y extent of raid

Raid 10/11 July 1918

divided into two waves. The first of an officer and thirty men, split into ten groups of men, five to proceed along each side of the road. They were to advance straight through and hold the far side against enemy counterattack from the east. The second wave, divided into eight groups of five men, was to follow behind dealing with buildings, dugouts, and cellars. These were ordered that if one of them became a casualty, the other four were responsible for bringing him back on their return journey. There were also two groups of flankers, each of eight men, whose job was to create a bombing block in the trenches either side, then man this with four men, while the other four kept watch on the nearby hedges. Eight stretcher-bearers went over with the party, with an additional four on standby at Cailloux Keep and another four at Cailloux West.

By 10.50 p.m., the raiding party was in place waiting for the start signal. Exactly twenty-five minutes later, two Very lights were fired simultaneously from Festubert Central and the raiders leapt into action. Blakeley, witnessing this from his command post in a disused trench, heard the first British bombs detonate almost immediately—demonstrating just how close to the enemy the raiders had crawled. German reaction was equally rapid and salvoes of bombs and two MGs south of the road targeted the raiders.

To the north of the road, 2Lt Harry Carless led his men to within 50 yards of the enemy shell-hole line during the bombardment, and when they rose to charge the enemy position—a post in a shell hole—the three occupants fled. Carless and Sgt Thomas Atkinson chased after them, firing as they ran, killing one of the Germans. Unfortunately, Carless tripped over some wire and the other two escaped. While this was happening, the rest of Carless's party were engaged by another cluster of enemy lying out in a post hidden by the grass. These refused to surrender, but when Cpl Joseph Newby charged them, shooting one of the occupants, the other dropped his rifle and put his hands up. Their prisoner secured, Carless blew his whistle and his party began to withdraw, his only casualties a few light wounds from MG bullets and bombs.

On the right flank, south of the road, the raiders were led by 2Lt Harold Woodcock. With him was Sgt William Rigden:

> On the command to rush I made for the hedge with my party. When I reached the hedge I was challenged by a German who levelled his rifle at me. He was immediately shot by one of my party. At that moment a machine gun opened fire from behind the hedge on my left. I threw a bomb at the gun and someone shouted 'Oh.' I threw another and silenced the gun. I tried to get at them through the hedge but the wire was too thick. I moved about 5 yards to my right and made another attempt, but failed. 2Lt Woodcock was just behind me, but after this I lost sight of him. Then I saw the golden rain rocket go up which was the signal for return.[8]

Another to pursue fleeing enemy was Sgt Wilson Prickett. As his section approached their selected target, the garrison fled. Unwilling to give up on his quarry, Prickett led his men deeper into enemy territory in hot pursuit of the two terrified Germans, only withdrawing when his men were met by very heavy MG fire and a fusillade of bombs.

Enemy artillery failed to react to the furious exchanges of small arms fire and bombs, but as soon as British artillery began, a bombardment to cover the escape of the raiders at zero+7, German SOS signals rose and their artillery dropped a very heavy barrage on Cailloux Keep and all the way down Cailloux Road to McMahon Post. This barrage caught the raiders, who up until that moment remained unscathed—apart from a few minor wounds. This barrage killed seven and brought the total number of wounded up to six. Among the dead was Arthur Durham.

In the initial confusion, it was believed that 2Lt Woodcock had returned—several men reported this, though no one had actually seen him themselves. Two men were also astray. When the missing subaltern failed to report to Blakeley, the alternate locations were checked, but no one had seen him. When Blakeley visited these just after 1 a.m., he was told that Woodcock had last been seen bringing in three prisoners and Blakeley presumed that the two missing men were with him and reported the matter to HQ at 1.45 a.m. As the Battalion was due to be relieved, Capt. Briggs volunteered to remain behind in case Woodcock showed up. By 3 a.m., the first signs of dawn were lighting the horizon and it became clear that no one else was going to reappear, so with a heavy heart, Briggs left. That night, a volunteer patrol returned to the front line and searched No Man's Land for their missing comrades—though without success. Woodcock was later reported a POW, the missing men both killed by the artillery barrage.

Prickett and Atkinson had been of great assistance during the bombardment—treating, then organising the evacuation of the wounded and steadying the shaken men. Second Lieutenant Carless was awarded the MC and Newby, Rigden, and Prickett all got the MM. Blakeley also recommended Atkinson for one, but division retorted that 'the Major General ... does not consider the recommendation comes up to the standard of an immediate award, not being the nature of a specific act of gallantry'.[9] The Battalion did not give up and Atkinson received his MM—nine months after the others.

Killed in the Raid on 10–11 July 1918

Pte George Brackenbury	35589	L/Cpl Thomas Lyons	37538
Pte Stanley Chidgey	42902	Pte Fred Pickup	202647
Pte Arthur Durham	28019	Pte Tom Oliver Turner	21282
Pte James Hale	3390		

Newby's prisoner, an NCO from 6 RIR, provided some very useful information when he was later interrogated. Apart from details about dispositions, routines, and information about German aerial reconnaissance (he was a former photographer with the German Air Force), he informed Intelligence that 6 RIR's trench strength was so low that companies were reduced to just two platoons of thirty men each—their losses after Kaiserschlacht never having been made good. He also reported that their sickness rates from influenza were very high, with over 50 per cent of his company having caught it. The Battalion was relieved immediately after the raid by 1/5th King's and taken by lorry to Drouvin Camp.

They returned to the right sub-sector at 1 a.m. on 16 July, HQ having the pleasure of occupying a brand-new dugout at Battersea Bridge—a huge improvement over the sandbagged position they had formerly inhabited. With ten platoons in the reserve line, only four forward, and another two designated counterattack platoons in between, the Battalion's dispositions were intended to minimise casualties during any enemy initial-attack bombardment. There was little activity from enemy artillery, but an overnight thunderstorm rendered the CTs leading to the front nearly impassable and draining these became imperative. The weather remained hot and clammy, threatening further thunderstorms—the humidity making physical effort unpleasant. A number of replacements had arrived since their last tour at the front, including three new officers—2Lt Eric Bunyan, Lt John Heaton, and 2Lt John Holmes (the latter two from the DLOY, like 2Lt Hill).

On 20 July, a company from a Garrison Guard battalion was attached for instruction, and if any of them were out with one of the working parties during the night of 22 July, they would have learned a very valuable lesson indeed. Silence and the dark were good friends to an infantrymen working on wire at night, but these conditions introduced other dangers. Three men were driving in wooden posts. Pte J. Jackson held them, eighteen-year-old Pte John Dale swung the large mallet and twenty-four-year-old Pte Albert Etherington held a folded-up sandbag over the top of the stakes to muffle the noise. Jackson and Dale noticed Etherington fall to the ground in a faint after one blow, and when he was revived, he explained that his forefinger had been between mallet and sandbag when Dale swung. Etherington spent nearly two months in hospital before his crushed finger healed, then a further ten days at IBD—only rejoining on 1 October. Much to everybody's relief, the garrison company departed in the early hours of 23 July when it was realised that a mistake had been made and they should not have been there in the first place.

Shortly after dawn on 23 July, two of the snipers, Pte David McKenna and Pte Stirzaker (probably 454, William), were out in No Man's Land when they spotted a lone German in Post P.24 opposite Le Plantin.[10] They rushed the position, killing the sentry, but were delayed entering the post due to the wire and camouflage around it. Unable to secure any identification before their victim's irate comrades arrived on the scene, the two snipers scarpered back to friendly lines post-haste. Thirty-six-year-old Pte James Pollard's day tuned out particularly badly. With the Battalion for just three weeks, he was escorted back from the front line under close arrest, accused of 'deserting his post when a sentry'. This charge could result in the Death Penalty and he must have been a very nervous soldier indeed.

Late that night, twenty-nine-year-old A/Capt. Norman Hamilton took a small patrol out in the early hours of 24 July, attempting to enter a German post. Unfortunately, an ambush party of about forty enemy was lying in wait for just such an endeavour and Hamilton's men were severely outnumbered. They managed to kill three or four of the enemy, but Hamilton was also killed and the patrol retreated to their own lines. Later that night, the Battalion was relieved by 1/5th South Lancs, and by 8 a.m. of

25 July, they were in support in the woods north of the canal between Battersea and Chelsea Bridges. Records show that two men died from wounds, Pte Richard Brough on 25 July and Pte Harold Watson on 26 July, though the date of their wounding is no longer available. Another man was wounded on 31 July, possibly on a working party, though the Battalion's position was within range of German artillery. Nineteen-year-old Pte Levison Manifold was badly injured in the right forearm and medically discharged. Another wounded around this time—though his records are too badly damaged to read the exact date—was nineteen-year-old L/Cpl Percy Clough, with injuries to right eye and knee acute enough to warrant a 100 per cent pension. Nineteen-year-old Pte Arthur Walker died from his wounds on 1 August and is another who was probably wounded in late July.

The Battalion remained where they were until 3 August, then moved to the support position behind the right sub-sector, relieving 1/7th King's, HQ occupying another new dugout on the canal bank. As the men settled into their tasks on 5 August, James Pollard must have been feeling more than a little anxious as he stood before his FGCM. He was found guilty and sentenced to five years' penal servitude—though he only did thirteen days before the sentence was suspended and he returned to the Battalion.[11] On 6 August, a 77 mm scored a direct hit on a group of men next to HQ on the canal bank, killing five and wounding another five. Thirty-six-year-old Walter Armistead, twenty-two-year-old Joseph Bingham, twenty-two-year-old Joseph Gallagher, Pte Lawrence Shaw, and twenty-two-year-old Arthur Allan were all killed outright. The latter did not even have to be there; he had been wounded at Jutland and invalided out of the RN, but subsequently voluntarily enlisted in the Army. Later that day, forty-year-old Henry Harris succumbed to his wounds and in the following days, another two of the wounded died—twenty-two-year-old Joshua Foster on 8 August and twenty-year-old John Lee on 10 August.

The casualties from the 6th were not the end of the bad news for that week. The Battalion went up to relieve Liverpool Scottish in the left sub-sector late on 7 August. As 'B' Company moved forward, shellfire fell around them, critically wounding twenty-two-year-old Pte John Baines and thirty-four-year-old Pte Noah Bellaby—both of whom died on 8 August. Another four men were also wounded by this salvo. The main change to their dispositions since their last deployment in this sub-sector was that platoons were no longer aligned to defend an attack from the north and only a single platoon designated for 'counterattack'. There was far less unease about a German offensive, reports from prisoners suggesting that morale was poor in the units facing the division due to the length of time they had been in the line and poor food. One prisoner from 96 RIR stated that they had been advised by their NCO to surrender immediately if the British attacked.[12] There was also considerable intelligence suggesting the enemy was withdrawing on the division's left, so a repeat of 9 April was thought most unlikely.

Since establishing themselves in the line, the Battalion received little attention from the enemy. On 9 August, 2Lt Arthur Hart took a daylight patrol out from Cailloux Keep and discovered that the enemy front line was completely unoccupied. Apart from a few small shells that landed near HQ at Duke Post, there was little hostile artillery. Further night reconnaissance patrols established touch with the enemy, who obviously re-manned their outposts during darkness as a precaution against raids. The front line was shelled most mornings, though few casualties ensued. On 13 August, thirty-six-year-old Pte Edgar Loxton was wounded in the right leg, left arm, and thigh—injuries that were treated back in England. On or around the same day, thirty-four-year-old Pte Frederick Southgate was paralysed by shrapnel in the spine. It was not just 2Lt Hart's patrol that found unoccupied trenches, intelligence summaries reported this along the entire divisional front at one time or another and plans were afoot to take advantage of this.

During the night of 15–16 August, the Battalion was relieved by 1/6th King's and went to their 'Bustle' positions, two half-companies to bridgehead defences at Westminster and Vauxhall Bridges. Once 'stood-down', the Battalion moved to No. 2 Camp at Vaudricourt—a facility abhorred by officers and men alike. The 166th Brigade was only going to be in divisional reserve until 20 August, so Kentish decreed that men should be given a good rest on Saturday and Sunday 18 August—though the two half companies still on bridgehead defence did not benefit. The afternoon of Monday 19 August was given over to the semi-finals and finals of the brigade boxing competition, the Battalion represented by Sergeants Thomas Atkinson, Joseph Barnes and John Craig, Cpl Richard Speight, L/Cpl Frank Crabtree, and Pte Robert Batty—the latter two winning cups for the highest number of points scored. The Battalion also received much-needed replacements. Exactly a month earlier, an Arthur John Cole had arrived from the 1st Battalion. Now, an Arthur James Cole, also from the 1st Battalion, turned up; both men were of a similar age, with numbers only three apart—similarities that were to cause infantry records no end of confusion over the coming months. When the Battalion returned to the line, the pace of war was to reach a new dimension.

20 August 1918–11 November 1918: The Road to Victory

Coordinates for Positions Named in this Chapter

Adalbert Alley	50°33′5.10″N 2°46′48.60″E	Moulin des Barges	50°35′12.20″N 3°22′53.50″E
B Coy at Ere	50°34′27.84″N 3°22′35.40″E	Mystery House	50°34′46.20″N 3°23′42.72″E
Basse Rue	50°33′30.90″N 2°54′11.80″E	Petit Hantay post	50°32′28.40″N 2°52′34.33″E
cemetery	50°32′54.40″N 2°46′54.70″E	Piano House	50°33′5.60″N 2°47′34.30″E
Chateau des Barges	50°35′4.90″N 3°23′4.50″E	Pic au Vent	50°35′11.94″N 3°21′2.97″E
Chlle. Morlighem	50°34′43.40″N 3°24′3.40″E	Post 1	50°32′12.40″N 2°45′0.40″E
Ere monastery	50°34′44.10″N 3°22′12.80″E	Post 2	50°32′19.50″N 2°44′44.10″E
German sniper	50°34′47.64″N 3°24′3.60″E	Post 3	2°44′44.10″E 2°44′46.40″E
Grand Ennetières	50°33′9.55″N 3°5′55.74″E	Redoubt Alley North	50°32′41.00″N 2°46′45.40″E
Grand Moisnil post	50°33′10.40″N 2°52′56.84″E	Rue de Marais	50°32′57.00″N 2°46′45.80″E
Hocron Road	50°33′11.50″N 2°53′27.10″E	Seesaw Trench	50°33′29.80″N 2°46′23.50″E
jct. Nora/Serpent Trs.	50°33′30.50″N 2°46′59.30″E	Serpent Tr. Block	50°33′20.90″N 2°46′39.30″E
jct. Serpent/Spook Trs.	50°33′21.90″N 2°46′41.50″E	Tramway House	50°32′25.60″N 2°44′13.70″E

King's Road	50°31′46.80″N	V.7.a houses	50°34′48.10″N
	2°45′26.40″E		3°24′40.20″E
Marie Redoubt	50°31′38.40″N	V.7.c houses	50°34′31.80″N
	2°45′31.00″E		3°24′52.60″E
MGs in houses	50°32′54.70″N		
	2°46′58.60″E		

The Battalion travelled up by light railway late on 20 August and relieved 1/5th King's in the right sub-sector, both relief and the night passing quietly. The usual harassing fire was experienced during the day on 21 August, and at midnight, a patrol attempted to capture an enemy post opposite Festubert Central—an action that was pretty optimistic considering the bright moonlight. The enemy met the patrol with a hail of fire as they approached. After exchanging shots for a period, they retired without loss. The previous day, Division had circulated information from a prisoner, claiming that orders had been issued that no one in the forward areas was to be in a dugout between 8 p.m. and 8 a.m., and that they had been expecting a large-scale British attack for some time. He also conveyed that the companies in his regiment were down to just forty men apiece, though each company had four LMGs. Clearly, this was going to reduce the chances of success for night raids, especially as the enemy also seemed to be placing platoon-sized ambush groups out in No Man's Land, with the specific intention of interdicting raiding parties.

On 22 August, there was more scattered shelling during the day and records show at least one man wounded. Nineteen-year-old Pte George Bailey was hit in the right shoulder and evacuated back to England. In the early hours of 23 August, a 5.9 scored a direct hit on Tramway House—the concrete bunker used as 'B' Company HQ— killing OC 'B' Company, thirty-year-old Lt William Deacon. The 23rd was taken up with planning for an operation due the following morning. Brig.-Gen. Stockwell had devised an audacious plan for 164 Brigade to capture the Craters and Capt. Bennett's 'A' Company was to assist. The main attack, by 2/5th Lancashire Fusiliers on the left and 1/4th King's Own on the right, was scheduled for 7.20 a.m. on 24 August. One platoon from 'A' Company, under 2Lt Yare, was to attack along Cheshire road as far as the OBL. Once there, they were to make contact with the Fusiliers to their right and build three posts: Post 1 at the junction of Yellow Road, Cheshire Road and Fife Road; Post 2 up Lloyd's Avenue; and Post 3 on Cheshire Road.

Unlike for most attacks, there was no preliminary bombardment at all, just the usual harassing fire against the Craters during the night—Stockwell relying on total surprise and advance parties who would cut the wire in the early hours. The RAF were to circle the craters just before zero hour, machine-gunning any defenders they could see and watching for troop concentrations, and if any were observed, drop a message bearing the coordinates onto 164 Brigade HQ—who would pass these directly to the artillery. Snipers had also been placed in vantage points, each sniper team, whose view of the attack would be superior to that of the assaulting force, had a number of runners at their disposal, who could be sent forward to brief commanders. The barrage was not due to begin until zero+10—directed some 200 yards past the objectives to hinder possible counterattack.

Yare was in position by 3.30 a.m., lying in No Man's Land awaiting his allotted time. Red rockets fired from King's Road and Marie Redoubt signalled zero hour, and Yare was to begin his advance thirteen minutes after this. Incredibly, the first shot was not fired until two minutes and thirty seconds had expired—the surprise total and all craters captured with minimal casualties. At a cost of three lightly wounded men, Yare also seized his objective, capturing seven Germans from 86 RIR—six of whom surrendered to company runner Pte Samuel Rowlinson. Shortly afterwards, his platoon came under heavy fire from an MG at fairly close range. Yare immediately ordered his grenadier section to engage it, silencing the gun. By 8.30 a.m., the posts were organised and blocks built in Fife Road and the OBL. Although by now the enemy were fully alert, their artillery was unsure of where the main attackers had reached, so did not shell the Crater positions. However, everywhere to the rear of these came in for significant attention. Yare's platoon sergeant, Matthew Hughes, showed considerable bravery during the consolidation efforts. Despite the constant shellfire, sniping, and MG fire, he stood out in the open, encouraging his men wiring on the new posts. Others from 'A' Company followed behind Yare's platoon, bringing up materials for the consolidation. Eighteen-year-old L/Cpl Charles Banning's section was in the forefront of this supply chain and it was mainly due to the energy of this very young NCO (leading his men back and forth through heavy fire) that consolidation was carried out so effectively. Yare was awarded the MC and Rowlinson, Hughes, and Banning all got the MM.[1] No attempts were made by the enemy to counterattack on 24 August—possibly due to the effectiveness of the division's artillery, who poured heavy fire onto obvious assembly positions. By 6 p.m.—against a frontal area just over 1,000 yards—they had expended an incredible 16,000 rounds of 18-pounders; 3,000 rounds of 4.5-inch Howitzer; 2,000 rounds of heavy artillery; 1,175 rounds of 6-inch trench mortar; and 58,000 rounds of MG fire.[2] It was hardly surprising the enemy stayed low when the 'God of War' was so vociferous.

After dark, German artillery fire intensified with gas, 5.9, and 8-inch making work on consolidating the new positions hazardous and uncomfortable. Unfortunately, one shell dropped amid Yare's men as they wired one of the posts, killing three and wounding another two. Twenty-nine-year-old Pte John Sturzaker left behind a widow and young child (his younger brother, James—who had been wounded three times while with the Battalion—was wounded a fourth time with the Lincs on the same day). Also killed instantly were Privates James Tomlinson and Edward Waite. The wounded fared no better; Pte James Warriner died at the dressing station and Pte John Beauman at a CCS at Houchin the following day. Of the two others known to be wounded on 24 August, twenty-two-year-old Pte George Shaw's wound to his right leg required treatment back in England, but nineteen-year-old Pte John Little was much more seriously injured. With shrapnel wounds to his head, back, right hand, and arm, he was evacuated home and discharged with a 100 per cent pension.[3]

At 5.15 a.m., the men on stand-to watched SOS signals rise from in front of Givenchy, and less than a minute later, British artillery shells whined over their heads as a crushing barrage fell on the enemy to the front of the Craters, pounding assembly positions and No Man's Land for thirty minutes. The half-hearted counterattack melted away in smoke, flame, and red-hot steel. The rest of the day saw some slight shelling of the new positions, but there was no activity from German forward positions. Late that night, the Battalion was relieved by Liverpool Scottish and moved back to support. The attack against the craters signalled a new era. At a cost of twenty lives, the division had secured a significant tactical advantage over the enemy. Prior to 9 April, the division controlled the western lips of the Craters, but the eastern lips had been German-held. Now, the entire Crater field was dominated by the division, giving them positions that overlooked the entire German front line and a stepping-stone for advance.

There were plans for 166 Brigade to carry out an operation to extend their front northwards from the post the Battalion established at the junction of the OBL and Yellow Road, necessitating the Battalion to relieve 1/5th South Lancs on 29 August, but as this was cancelled, relief was delayed for twenty-four hours. German artillery was far more active on 29 August and HQ at Canal House was shelled with gas in the morning; later in the day, Gorre came under fire from 5.9, wounding 2Lt Malcolm Phillips from the DLOY. He and 2Lt Matthews, also DLOY, had joined the Battalion just four weeks earlier. Later the following day, the Battalion returned to the front line, this time in the left sub-sector at Cailloux. There had been changes since their last tour here—the division to their left having advanced and the Battalion established a liaison post about 200 yards north-east of Cailloux North Keep with their new neighbours, the 1/6th Sherwoods.

Years of attrition compounded by losses during the failed Kaiserschlacht had degraded German manpower to the degree that they could no longer man the entire Western Front in sufficient strength. Intelligence believed that the enemy was about to withdraw eastwards to a shorter, more defensible line and Corps were keen to take advantage of this. On 1 September, a conference was held at divisional HQ to discuss actions to be taken when this commenced and on the same day, a directive arrived from Corps, ordering the division to push forward to occupy the OBL in conjunction with any advances made by 46 Division to their left. These orders were distributed around the Battalions before the day's end.

The Battalion carried out a number of uneventful daylight patrols, and late on 2 September, the Battalion was relieved by 1/6th King's and proceeded by bus to Drouvin Camp, arriving in the early hours of 3 September and remaining there until 8 September. The days were spent training or on brigade exercises, though time was put aside for entertainments and sport. On 7 September, official photographer 2Lt David McLellan visited Brigade HQ and every platoon had its photograph taken.

On 8 September, the Battalion relieved 1/6th King's in support in the left sub-sector, everything going smoothly and completed by 11 p.m. Things had moved on apace since the Battalion came out of the line and their new support positions at Cailloux, McMahon, and Festubert Central had been the front line the last time they had been up. Now, the front line, manned by 1/5 South Lancs on the left and Liverpool Scottish on the right, was over 3,000 yards further forward. By now, the hot, sunny weather was beginning to turn and a period of wet and windy weather settled in.

Although the diary reports the days as 'quiet' as far as enemy artillery fire activity, this was really just a comparative description and there was still shelling—though nowhere near as intense as previously. On 11 September, nineteen-year-old Pte Herbert Vaughan was wounded in his head, thigh, and foot by shrapnel—injuries severe enough to bring about his medical discharge. During the night of 12–13 September, the Battalion took over the left sub-sector, with two companies in the forward outpost line. Intelligence summaries had been warning for some days of booby traps discovered by advanced patrols in German positions—information disseminated throughout the division. One of the first to be discovered was a trench mortar round buried in a trench without duckboards, a pressure plate on the nose to detonate it when the unwary trod on this. On 13 September, information was circulated about one with ten shells scattered 10 yards apart along a road, nose caps replaced by a 'potato masher' grenade—all connected by a thin copper wire. Pulling the wire at any place along it would have detonated all ten shells.[4]

That night, the two companies to the rear moved forward until all four shared the outpost line. Division had ordered the two forward battalions (1/5th King's Own on the left and 1/4th Loyals on the right) to attempt to push their positions forward. At 8 a.m. on the 14th, 'C', 'A', and 'B' Company advanced. 'C' Company's objective was the junction between Serpent and Spook Trench. They got to within 30 yards when they were held up by a block in Serpent Trench, bombed, and engaged by two MGs—one to each flank. As they were in such an exposed position, the attackers were forced to withdraw. Things went better for the other companies. 'A' Company met nothing in the way of opposition and succeeded in advancing their position and building a post in Adalbert Alley. 'B' Company were equally successful, and although a small group of the enemy were manning their objective in the Rue de Marais, these just fired off a few rounds and withdrew, enabling 'B' to build their post. Both 'A' and 'B' discovered booby traps in their new positions. The first was two boxes of Ammonal triggered by a trip-wire, which would have caused significant casualties if detonated. The other was much smaller, a bully-beef tin full of explosive, also pull-detonated. With the latter, the men attached a longer wire and pulled it from a safe distance. The former was defused by the RE.

During the morning of 15 September, 'D' Company pushed forward another 150 yards and built a post in Redoubt Alley North and 'C' Company occupied Seesaw Trench, where they were in touch with the brigade to their left. L/Cpl Alfred Dean was killed on 15 September, though the circumstances of his death are unknown.

Although twenty-one-year-old Pte Thomas Blackburn's death is also recorded on this day, he succumbed to illness in England. Throughout the day, the sounds of explosions were heard from enemy lines and it was believed they were destroying dugouts and bunkers—a sure sign of another planned withdrawal—though prisoners from 814 RIR denied any knowledge of this when they were interrogated. When Jeudwine returned from leave that day, he must have been delighted with progress made since his departure on 1 September.

On 16 September, 'C' Company made another attempt to force the junction between Serpent and Spook Trenches, but once again were brought up short by bombing and MG fire. 'A' Company, however, was able to push forward further. One patrol managed to enter a cemetery to the south of the Rue de Marais but had to withdraw when they came under MG fire from some houses 100 yards to their east. Later on in the morning, one of the battalion snipers moved up and shot two Germans manning an MG on a house roof there. Enemy artillery was very vigorous and shelled the Battalion's positions regularly throughout the day, though without result. That night, 1/5th South Lancs relieved them and they returned to reserve.

Reserve was spent on numerous working parties, though there were opportunities for bathing at the baths at Bridge View—a luxury denied those further forward. On 18 September, Lt-Col. Hoare went on leave, leaving Maj. Marshall in charge. Time in reserve was short as they moved to support in the evening of 20 September. That morning, 1/5th South Lancs, in conjunction with 10/R. Warks to the left, pushed the outpost line further forward to the junction of Nora and Serpent Trenches, taking forty-one prisoners in the process, their place in the line then taken by Liverpool Scottish. Progress on the left, however, stalled on 21 September, when a counterattack forced the Glosters to withdraw and the platoon from Liverpool Scottish manning the post, concerned that they were 'in the air', also withdrew—a decision that later led to considerable censure from Kentish. During the night, 'D' Company in the OBL were shelled quite heavily and, though no one was killed, twenty-nine-year-old Pte Frank Haffenden was wounded in the nose. Undoubtedly painful, the injury was not serious and after a spell in hospital and IBD, he returned to the Battalion a week before the Armistice. The 22nd was a quieter day for the Battalion, with little hostile artillery bothering them, though over the night of 22–23 September, the OBL near Festubert Switch, where HQ was situated, was on the receiving end of 100 rounds of Mustard gas in the early hours. As a result of this, nineteen-year-old Pte Ernest Harlow was treated by the West Lancs Field Ambulance, but returned a fortnight later.[5] On the night of 23 September, 1/5th King's relieved the Battalion, who travelled by train to rest billets in Béthune, arriving just after midnight.

Once again, it was the entire brigade that came out of the line and the first day was allocated to rest, but after that the diktat of training ruled the roost—though for one man, his days were considerably longer than those of his comrades. Twenty-one-year-old Pte Harry Hough from Hollinwood celebrated his rest day by going AWOL for three days and was given a fortnight's field punishment for his pains. For others, their rest period ended prematurely when an Advance Party went up to reconnoitre the left sector of the outpost line held by 1/7th King's, remaining with them until the rest of the Battalion joined them on the night of 29–30 September. Records show that twenty-one-year-old Pte William Williams was wounded on 28 September, presumably while part of this Advance party. While at Béthune, the OC wrote up MSM recommendations for a number of NCOs and men whose work had been of great service to the Battalion: transport driver Pte Harry Walton, for his coolness under fire in April; CQMS William Herridge, for his devotion to duty since February 1915; Transport Sergeant Joseph Birtle, whose hard work and coolness in the face of difficulties had ensured that supplies always reached the men at the front; and Cook Sergeant Francis Barnett, whose tireless work ensured that the men got hot food, even during times of great difficulty. All these recommendations were approved by Jeudwine.[6] The relief was made difficult by it being a very wet and dark night and the situation obscure due to an attack made against the King's during the morning and, consequently, was not completed until 2.30 a.m. on 30 September. The outpost line was now even further forward and the Battalion's lead company manned outposts around Piano House, some 700 yards in advance of their previous position. The enemy, not content to let this stand, had made several attempts to regain territory, also subjecting these outposts to considerable artillery.

Late on the night of 30 September to 1 October, a patrol under 2Lt John Barton came up against a strong enemy post and, in the exchange of fire, twenty-seven-year-old Pte Septimus Rigg and thirty-one-year-old Pte Walter Taylor were both killed. By a terrible mistake, Taylor's death notice did not go to his wife, but to the mother of a Pte William Taylor from the Labour Corps. The confusion was eventually sorted out when it was found that both W. Taylors had served in the Labour Corps under each other's number—a mistake that was quickly rectified.[7] Barton and eight of his men were also wounded, but all returned to friendly lines. Only two of these are known—thirty-six-year-old Pte Thomas Taylor (hit in the thigh) and twenty-five-year-old Cpl Robert Bell (wounded in the right hand). There was little enemy artillery directed against the Battalion's positions on 1 October and the Battalion's snipers began to even the score, one of them claiming six hits.

Divisional plans to capitalise on a general German withdrawal, involved sending a telegram containing the code name 'Scurry', followed by the divisional objective and the time an advance was to begin. Each unit would then move to predetermined starting positions. To facilitate advance, each infantry battalion was organised into an advanced guard and a main party. In addition, each of the brigade commanders had at their disposal a number of non-infantry units from 'C' Squadron, King Edward's Horse; one section of RE; an investigation party from the Tunnelling Company; an 18-pounder battery; a section of 4.5-inch Howitzers; a mobile section of medium trench mortars; a company from the MG Battalion; and a contingent of the Field Ambulance. Behind the lines, the RE and working parties feverishly laboured on improving roads for the host of wheeled traffic needed to support advance, and surfaced other tracks for pack animals to follow.[8] No actual 'Scurry' was sent, as the method of German withdrawal did not allow the corps to issue a definite order for an advance at a specific time. Nevertheless, the arrangements for advance worked perfectly. The intention was to maintain pressure on the retreating enemy, but not to force the engagement of the entire division, as the number of divisions available within Fifth Army were inadequate for a full-scale offensive.

On 2 October, the division continued to push eastwards. A daylight patrol sent out by the Battalion located the enemy to the front of the right company and another entered Strasburg Trench (leading from Piano House to Lorgies) and found it empty. Shortly afterwards orders were received to carry out a general advance across a 2,600-yard front and the Battalion moved eastwards, meeting no opposition. Information from prisoners taken the previous day had indicated that the enemy began their withdrawal to a line along the Haute Deûle Canal at 4 a.m. on 1 October, and Jeudwine was keen that his lead battalions should pressure the enemy as hard as possible. By dusk, the Battalion had advanced 1,500 yards and was established to the east of Lorgies. Despite considerable resistance in the division's southern area, advance patrols entered La Bassée itself by late afternoon. The Battalion only lost one man in this advance, twenty-six-year-old Pte Richard Evans, who was critically wounded and died later that night.

Progress continued next day, but both the right and centre companies found that German resistance was much stiffened. Thirty-four-year-old Pte Percy Carter and Pte Clifford Box were both killed and a number of men and Capt. Metcalfe wounded. At dusk, the Battalion had established posts some 1,500 east of Grand Moisnil and 100 yards east of Petit Hantay.

The Battalion actually pushed further east, coming up against stiff opposition on the Hocron road before retiring to where they established these posts. Twenty-three-year-old L/Cpl Robert Nickson is recorded by CWGC as dying on 3 October. His records are severely water damaged, but appear to show that, although he was initially recorded as killed in action, a later entry notes that he died from a wound to the head in a German Field Hospital at Pont á Marcq on what appears to be 5 October. This hospital is some 15 miles from where this firefight happened and it seems unlikely that he would have reached there before 4 October, suggesting that 5 October is probably the correct date of death.[9] It seems likely that his comrades presumed him dead before they were forced to withdraw. That night, Liverpool Scottish took over as lead battalion and the King's Own moved back to support at Marquillies, Transport repositioning to Lorgies. CWGC records the death of nineteen-year-old Pte James Wilkinson on 4 October, and though he may have been a victim of some random shelling that day, he may equally have been a casualty from 3 October. Another from the Battalion is recorded as dying—though his date of death is unknown by CWGC, who attribute it to sometime between 1 and 7 October. Twenty-eight-year-old Pte Henry Kellett was medically discharged for sickness in July. His recent inclusion on the CWGC database indicating that his death must have finally been recognised as related to military service—possibly a pulmonary illness aggravated by past exposure to gas.

It must not be thought that the enemy withdrew without putting up a fight. Although this was a planned withdrawal to a line along the Haute Deûle Canal, the division was pushing hard and faced stubborn resistance from the German rear guard—who were well-equipped with machine guns, often crewed by very determined gunners. Nearly all roads were mined and the bigger ones also blown up; dugouts and houses were booby-trapped and the sappers of 170 Tunnelling Company did marvellous work defusing these. Pioneer detachments followed closely behind the advancing troops, repairing the cratered roads and to the west of Salomé filled in no less than thirty-two craters in 14 miles of road.

While the Battalion rested on 4 October, Liverpool Scottish pushed on forwards, meeting even stiffer resistance from numerous MGs placed along the Haute Deûle Canal—particularly from the railway station in Don, which commanded an uninterrupted view across the flat ground any advance must cross. A night attack fared little better and Liverpool Scottish lost heavily. Their strength return for 5 October shows a decrease (from all causes) of eighty-four officers and men.[10] By the night of 4 October, the divisional line was on the outskirts of Wavrin in the north, running southwards along the western side of the railway to Don and then some 1,000 yards to the east of the Haute Deûle. In the afternoon of 5 October, 'C' Company was ordered to move forward to Hocron as support for Liverpool Scottish in view of their losses—though strength returns show that even with their losses, Liverpool Scottish still had a greater fighting strength than the King's Own—953 against 674.[11] There was no movement on 6 October, and despite occasional shell fire, the Battalion spent this and 7 October resting.

There was scattered shelling across the brigade area on 8 October and 'C' Company returned to the fold, having pulled back to Marquillies when Liverpool Scottish were relieved by 1/5th South Lancs, who then became lead battalion. The 9th saw a similar pattern of shelling, but men still made the most of the sunshine to rest when they could. Lt-Col. Hoare returned from his leave to find his battalion now over 7 miles forward from where he left it—at a cost of seven lives—unthinkable progress not so long before. Intelligence from the corps to the division's right suggested that the enemy was going to carry out another strategic withdrawal on the night of 8–9 October, but when patrols pushed forward, they found the Germans just as determined to resist.

On 10 October, 166 Brigade took over a sector from 74 Division and the Battalion was ordered up as left hand lead battalion to relieve 10/Buffs at Wavrin and Lattre. On the way forward, 'D' Company was caught by a salvo of artillery, probably in Basse Rue, which was hit by 5.9, 4.2, and 77 mm at 7.30 p.m. They suffered fifteen casualties: Pte John Rowland was killed outright, the last man from the Battalion to be so; twenty-three-year-old Pte Simon McStravick had shrapnel penetrate his lungs and died the next day at Cambrin; twenty-four-year-old L/Cpl Alfred Jackson died at Cambrin on 12 October; twenty-eight-year-old Pte William Conchie was wounded in both thighs and the right forearm; twenty-seven-year-old Pte George Davies in the left arm; and Pte Harry Hough in the left buttock. The relief itself was carried out quickly, with these the only casualties. Thirty-one-year-old Pte Harry Pickhover died from wounds on 14

October while a POW, though it is unknown when he was captured and unusually for a prisoner, he has no known grave.

The Battalion's sector was shelled overnight and at daybreak, they pushed patrols forward, making contact with the enemy around Coulin. Further overnight patrols on 11–12 October reported that enemy MGs were constantly active, sweeping likely approaches. HQ in Lattre had a considerably uncomfortable time in the morning and afternoon of 12 October when a number of 8-inch mortar rounds landed nearby and when 1/4th Loyals from 164 Brigade relieved the Battalion late on the night of 12 October, everybody was probably heartily glad to be out of there.[12] Twenty-year-old Pte Frank Webb was lightly wounded in the left thigh by a shell splinter. The 2½-inch long cut went septic and he was evacuated home for treatment, spending ninety-six days in hospital.[13] The Battalion was transported back by lorry to billets near the *jardin public* in Béthune, arriving there at 4 a.m. on 13 October.

While the brigade was at Béthune, there were further developments in the outpost line. The enemy had now been driven from the west bank of the Haute Deûle and on both flanks of the division, the enemy had withdrawn. As a result, on 16 October the brigade was given 'Bustle' and moved up to the line. The King's Own were taken by bus to Gravelin and then marched to Petit Moisnil and Marquillies, on an hour's notice to advance. There was one casualty during this move, but not to enemy action. As Pte James Pollard crossed the embankment of the La Bassée – Don railway line, he slipped and went over on his ankle. Although it wasn't broken, it was so badly twisted that he was returned to England and given a medical discharge—no doubt to his great relief! At noon on 17 October, the Battalion was ordered to march 9 miles to Gondecourt, a journey made more interesting by new countryside—though somewhat tempered by the sight of wanton destruction left by the Germans before their withdrawal from Gondecourt. By now, the front line was well over 6,000 yards to their east, reaching as far forward as Grand Ennetières in the centre of the divisional front.

On 18 October, advance continued, stopping in Seclin for lunch, the Battalion proceeding to billets in Templemars for a night. The locals—long years of occupation at an end, were overjoyed to see British troops—doing everything possible to welcome them. At 4.30 p.m. on 19 October, Brigade received orders to resume the advance and the Battalion marched off to Grand Ennetières, remaining there overnight. Still they advanced, moving to Cysoing, and then Bourghelles on 20 October, the front now as far east as Pic au Vent, less than 2 miles from the city of Tournai and the River Escaut (Scheldt). One man unable to continue was nineteen-year-old Pte William Ward from Tipton. Earlier in the trenches, he would cut his left knee on some barbed wire and, as so often happened, this became septic. His knee so swollen that he was no longer able to march and he was evacuated home. Ward had been in an exempt occupation and when he voluntarily enlisted just under a year earlier, he had been made to sign a disclaimer to this effect.[14]

By now, the Battalion was much closer to the front line, and on 21 October, they moved to Esplechin to relieve 1/5th King's in reserve in the right sub-sector. The

1/5th South Lancs were the outpost battalion, holding the front line at Ere and St Maur. There was no advance on 22 October as the South Lancs met very stiff opposition when they attempted to seize Chateau des Barges and Moulin des Barges at 5.30 a.m.—both positions holding a commanding view of the road to Tournai. Although they took their objectives, casualty numbers forced their withdrawal when the enemy counter-attacked. There was an expectation that the enemy may carry out a large-scale counter-attack at dawn on 24 October, so the previous evening the Battalion was ordered to dig a main line of resistance between Esplechin and Froidmont. Enemy artillery was particularly active throughout the divisional area, lending weight to this belief, though the Battalion's position escaped their attention. When they did not have shovels in their hands, the Battalion spent their time training for this new, more mobile form of warfare—something few of the officers or men had any experience at.

The expected counterattack did not materialise on 24 October and hostile fire slackened, though around 4 p.m., over 100 mustard gas shelled landed in and around the Liverpool Scottish positions in Froidmont, merely an inconvenience for the men with their respirators, but an act of dreadful barbarity upon the civilians in the process of evacuating the town at the time. Although neither divisional nor battalion diaries record any hostile artillery around Esplechin, most transport routes were shelled overnight and it is probable this is how thirty-two-year-old Pte Ernest Rallings was wounded in the head by shrapnel.

During the afternoon of 26 October, the Battalion relieved Liverpool Scottish in support, roughly halfway between Froidmont and Willemeau—Transport occupying an old German motor shed nearby. When the enemy retreated, a shortage of horses had forced them to leave behind a large number of wagons, some of which were 'liberated' by Transport. One allocated to carry the Band's instruments was particularly welcome, as prior to this the bandsmen lugged their instruments in addition to all their normal kit—which was okay for the fifers, but not so grand for the euphonium players. The 27th was a very quiet day for the Battalion and there was very little hostile shellfire, despite divisional artillery expending a great deal of munitions against enemy positions. Although that evening both Ere and Froidmont were shelled, the Battalion positioned halfway between escaped. The weather remained fine while the Battalion was in support and while mornings were set aside for training, afternoons were spent on football, bathing, and even a band concert. The international news was also promising, with Austria seeking terms on 28 October and rumours that Turkey would soon follow suit. These tidings came through on 31 October, boosting morale considerably as the Battalion relieved Liverpool Scottish as lead battalion. 'D' Company held the left in front of the monastery in Ere; centre company was 'B'; on the right was 'A'; and in St Maur, as reserve, was 'C', some 600 yards behind 'D' Company.

The 55th Division's gains were not isolated—the Germans were being forced back across the Western Front. Since 1 August, the British had captured 175,000 prisoners, 2,380 artillery pieces, 2,750 trench mortars, and 17,000 MGs—unsustainable losses for the foe, especially when casualties are added to these totals.[15] The front held by the Battalion was far from level, and from the high ground of their positions, 'D' and 'B' could look down onto the German positions around the Chateau des Barges and the city of Tournai, though today much of this vista is now obscured by the high roadside hedges. There was little daytime enemy activity and small parties of men could move around British positions without drawing fire—night time, however, was a different matter as German MGs swept the open ground in front of their posts, making life difficult for British patrols.

Early on 2 November, 165 Brigade carried out a raid against German positions to the Battalion's left and as part of the diversion, the trench mortars under Lt-Col. Hoare's control carried out a bombardment of the Chateau des Barges. The raid was extremely successful, but there was retribution by the enemy, who shelled St Maur in the afternoon and Willemeau in the evening. At 1 p.m., an 'A' Company patrol under 2Lt Tringham left British lines—their target a house 800 yards to the north of St Maur on the side of the St Maur-Pont au Rieu road. This building, dubbed 'Mystery House', was unmarked on maps and it was impossible to get a good view of it from anywhere along the Battalion's lines—all that could be seen was part of the grey, slate roof and even that was only visible from two positions. Partly hidden by the slope of the ground and obscured by trees, it was only fully visible from the northern slope of the valley, currently held by the enemy.

Tringham led his small patrol from his company positions on the northern edge of St Maur down towards this house. As they approached, they could see that it was a dull grey in colour and shielded by a double apron entanglement of recent wire, easily negotiated. A small trench lay between the house and the road, and upon investigating this, the patrol unearthed a supply of bombs, one of which was appropriated for later examination. Tringham then moved eastwards to the Chlle. Morlighem, a wayside shrine, but found no evidence of any enemy. He then investigated some houses further east, on the Bruyelles-Tournai road, finding these deserted too. So far, not one single shot had been fired at them. Tringham returned towards British lines to the post on 'A' Company's right, held by 16 Division. When Tringham suggested that it appeared that the enemy had withdrawn and they might cooperate, the officer in charge replied that he would not investigate unless he had orders from his commander. Tringham then returned to Company HQ and reported to Lt Hill, acting OC, as Capt. Bennett had gone on leave that morning.

While Hill contacted Lt-Col. Hoare, Tringham took his patrol straight back to the Mystery House. When he was about 30 yards from there, a German sentry fired at him but missed. Tringham, whose aim was considerably better, returned fire and killed the sentry. The exchange of fire roused a hornets' nest and the patrol were forced to hastily withdraw, though no one was hit. Apart from the sentry killed by Tringham, the patrol also managed to neutralise a German sniper firing at them from a stand of trees 100 yards to the north of Chlle. Morlighem. The report, sent to division by Brigade, continues the tale:

2Lt Tringham returned to the village, meeting his Commanding-Officer ... and together they proceeded towards the road in V.7.a and c [the houses along the Bruyelles–Tournai road], where they were met by heavy rifle fire and had great difficulty in returning to St Maur.

In spite of the fact that for some time previously, several officers and men had been wandering about entirely in the open over a radius of 1,000 yards outside the village, no shots had been fired and the enemy seemed to be keeping a very poor lookout.[16]

Jeudwine notated this latter paragraph with the comment, 'a stupid thing to do!' However, the Mystery House seems to have intrigued him and a further note was appended: 'If the enemy ever dare to occupy so near to us as U.11.b.9.2. they might be raided. I should like BGC to consider this'. A later notation added, 'Spoke Kentish'. It would not be long before the wheels turned.

There are no records for any casualties due to enemy action on 2 November, but twenty-six-year-old Pte Thomas Rawlinson died from illness at the CCS at Don. Another, nineteen-year-old Pte Frederick O'Brien, died of illness there on 8 November, possibly both victims of Spanish influenza. On 3 November, nineteen-year-old 2Lt Arthur Card joined the Battalion, but unlike most new subalterns, had no previous experience and would need a very good platoon sergeant (he rose to become a lieutenant colonel in the King's Own during the Second World War). That day, considerable thought was being put into planning a raid by 'B' and 'C' Company against the Chateau des Barges—a very tough target indeed. To be feasible, it was considered necessary to use the full might of the brigade's MG, trench mortars, 18-pounders, and heavy artillery to soften the target and keep its flanking posts quiet. In the event, this raid was cancelled the following day as it was deemed too ambitious under the circumstances, but an alternative plan to raid the Mystery House was agreed upon and set for 2 p.m. on 5 November.

To deceive the enemy, the position was bombarded by the Advance Guard artillery, the TMB, and MG Company for two minutes at 11 a.m. and for a further two minutes at 11.10 a.m., with this pattern repeated at noon and 1 p.m.—the raiders sallying out after the 2 p.m. bombardment. This time was chosen as it was hoped that the sentries, having just eaten, would be less alert and would be well under cover expecting another bombardment at 2.10 p.m. The raiders from 3 Platoon, under Lt Hill, would leave the northernmost position at St Maur, with another platoon in reserve behind them and another on each flank should they be required. The raiders formed up in a farmhouse at St Maur at 1.30 p.m., which unfortunately was promptly shelled by the enemy—though no damage was done.

As soon as the 2 p.m. bombardment ceased, the platoon rushed forward and entered the trench to the south of the Mystery House. They had not been spotted in their dash across the open, the weather favouring them for once, as wind-blown drizzle flew straight into the faces of the enemy. Faced at close range by the fierce countenance and rifle and bayonet of Sgt Albert Swann, the sentry from 360 IR (who turned out later to be Polish) wisely surrendered. While Swann was securing his man, another began to emerge from a shelter and was promptly shot by Lt Hill. Another, who also tried to resist, was killed by Pte Charles Newman. Their aims completed, Hill blew his whistle and the raiders retired at speed under a hail of rifle and MG fire from both flanks—though the fastest man across the open space back to the farmhouse was their prisoner, who led by a long way. Last back was Lt Hill, providing covering fire for his men until the final one reached sanctuary. As German artillery was once more targeting the line, the man returned to Company HQ in twos and threes.

The raid was extremely successful and without a single British casualty. Hill received a bar to his MC for this; Swann and Newman both got the MM. These medals were *Gazetted* around July and August 1919 and another twelve men similarly rewarded at this time—probably for consistent bravery over an extended period, though their citations no longer exist. Some of these had been with the Battalion a very long time: CQMS Richard Kirkby's original number was 375, indicating service with the Battalion since its inception in 1908. Cpl Joseph Mashiter (of cow-milking fame) enlisted in the first week of August 1914 and Pte Omar Steel and CQMS William Newton were also 1914 enlistments. In the evening of 5 November, the Battalion was relieved by 1/5th South Lancs and moved back to Esplechin.

On the 6th, as the Battalion rested, the leading battalions continued raiding German positions, taking nearly sixty prisoners on the 6th and 7th. On 7 November, the Battalion rewarded No. 3 Platoon for their successful raid with a concert and supper in the school in Esplechin. German artillery had been particularly active against the whole of the brigade area on those two days, the reason evident on 8 November, when dawn patrols discovered that the enemy had made another withdrawal—this time across the Escaut. This prompted a battalion advance through steady drizzle to Willemeau at 9.15 a.m. on 8 November. Heavy MG fire from the eastern bank of the Escaut foiled further advance by the leading battalions. During the night of 8–9 November, three companies forced the river crossing and after a pontoon bridge was erected, both Advance Guards crossed, reaching their objectives by 8.25 a.m. These battalions continued their advance—meeting little opposition—and by 2 p.m. had reached their second objective to the north-east of Barry. A battle group, 'Stockwell's Force', then moved through, reaching the western outskirts of Leuze by 8.30 p.m.

The King's Own followed, their band playing as they marched. At 9 a.m. on 9 November, they left for Chercq; passed through Ere—past the Chateau des Barges—crossed the Escaut by pontoon bridge; and through Antoing and Gueronde, where they stopped for dinner, the streets lined with cheering locals, houses bedecked with flags. They billeted for the night in Marais de la Louvière, where the Band's performance, including the Belgian National Anthem, was jubilantly received by the inhabitants. Stockwell's Force was now well to the east and on 10 November, the Battalion continued their march. At 11.30 a.m., they reached Leuze and the massed bands of the brigade, joined by the town band, entertained troops and Belgians alike in the main square. After billeting for the night in Leuze, the Battalion marched off towards Ath at 8 a.m. The enemy were holding at Ath and Jeudwine planned to attack using the entire division. This was not to be as at 10 a.m., the Battalion learned there was to be an Armistice at 11 a.m. When that hour came, every church bell for miles around could be heard to ring. For the first time for more than four years, the guns were finally muted. Men were pleased, though not jubilant—the war had been too long and too hard for that, besides, this was an Armistice, not a surrender. After halting in Moulbaix for dinner, the Battalion marched on to Ath, arriving at 3 p.m., to be billeted in an old chair factory.

Epilogue

The Battalion remained in Ath until 14 November. During this time, numbers of former POWs began to filter back, hungry and exhausted, some of whom were men from the Battalion captured during Kaiserschlacht. The condition of these and tales of their treatment as prisoners caused considerable anger and resentment, and it was perhaps fortunate that the Battalion was no longer anywhere near the enemy. One who never returned home was 2Lt Gerald Conheeny, captured on 9 April 1918. Born in Ashton-in-Makerfield, his family emigrated to the USA and despite being an American citizen, when war began he crossed the Atlantic to help the country of his birth. The story of his death was published in late December:

American Shot Dead in German Prison Camp
Copenhagen Wednesday. Dec. 18 (by the Associated Press). The killing of Lt Conheeny, an American, in the German prison camp at Stralsund on December 5th is reported by three British officers who have arrived here. The American lieutenant, the officers say, went outside the barbed wire for a moment and the German guards fired three times at him. Lt Conheeny was killed by a bullet through the chest. A British officer was seriously wounded by the shots. The guards refused to allow Conheeny's comrades to remove the body.[1]

His death as reported was little short of murder.

Others too met violent deaths at the hands of others. On 10 August 1919, Pte James Bettany was killed in action in Russia with the Royal Fusiliers. For many British soldiers, their war continued when Britain sent troops to aid the White Russians against the Bolsheviks—not the war they had signed up to fight. Another former comrade of Bettany's, thirty-three-year-old Sgt Albert Sweeney, was murdered in Dublin—not by the IRA, but by another British sergeant, who ran amok, killing Sweeney and a sergeant from the Worcesters. Illness—predominantly influenza—also proved fatal. On the day after the Armistice, twenty-seven-year-old Sgt William Cross died; Pte John Lyons on 16 February; and twenty-seven-year-old Pte William Kew on 22 March 1919—all while they were in England. Men still with the Battalion also perished: Pte Martin Scarry on 20 February and Pte William Moloney the day after.

Men were given home leave, some having it extended for personal reasons, such as thirty-four-year-old Pte James Butterworth from Bolton, whose two children were seriously ill with influenza. Others, such as Pte William Hazel, failed to return and were listed as deserters. It is not hard to understand why some men voted with their feet and deserted after the end of the war. Many had enlisted for the duration, or had been conscripted, and once the actual fighting had finished, they did not see why they should remain. It was not the first in that were the first to be demobilised either, as a government policy of prioritising the release of men previously employed in strategic industries, such as coal mining, caused huge resentment, for it was often these men who had spent the shortest time in uniform. For some, demobilisation was actually the last thing they wanted. Many enjoyed the life and comradeship and viewed the Army as the best way to provide for their families and numbers of these signed up as Regulars, considerably more rejoining the TF after the war. Some officers and men served during the Second World War. Lt Hill went on to become an eminent surgeon after the war, but continued his involvement with the Territorials. He was killed in action in Sicily in February 1944 as Lt-Col. Sir Norman Gray Hill RAMC, 2nd Bt. of Green Place.

For some, the war took a terrible toll in years to follow. At least two were confined to insane asylums in the immediate post-war period and the pension records of others paint a picture of men with nervous disorders resulting from their experiences, or men whose bodies were broken by shot, shell, or gas. One ex-officer, twenty-six-year-old William Yacomeni, seemed troubled after his time in captivity and ended his life with his (unlicensed) revolver in a London hotel room on 12 February 1920—a verdict of suicide while temporarily insane given. Most just got on with life after the war and rarely talked about it to their families—something only other soldiers could ever truly understand.

Probably the biggest issue for commanders was maintaining discipline. Bored soldiers cause problems, so everything possible was done to occupy men. Military training had to continue, as an Armistice is merely an interlude in the fighting; soldiers were given education classes as it was felt strongly by command that if possible, men should benefit from their time in the Army—sports and entertainments occupied much of their hours. It was also a time of great flux as many battalions were disbanded and men not eligible for discharge were transferred *en masse* to other battalions. The Battalion received several hundred men in early 1919, not just from the King' Own, but also from other regiments—although these men have not been included in the Roll in Appendix III.

The Battalion remained in Brussels from 17 November until April 1919, when they moved to Germany as part of the Army of Occupation. By now, almost all who actually fought with the Battalion had been demobilised, though a small cadre remained. On 5 September 1919, the Battalion landed at Dover and proceeded, not to Lancaster, but to the Curragh in Dublin, where most of the remaining men were demobilised. On 15 October, the CO, adjutant, QM, and Captain Bennett (plus 2Lt Aldersley, who had joined the Battalion after the Armistice) and a cadre of ten NCOs and men, crossed the Irish Sea to Holyhead, arriving in Lancaster on the 16th. They were met at the station by Capt. Briggs and, along with a party of original men from the Battalion, marched with the Colours held proudly aloft to the town hall. Joining the procession were the two battalion mascots—Johnny, a white pony gifted by 2/King's Own, and Joey, an Indian mule found wandering at Ypres in 1915 and a survivor of so very, very much.

APPENDIX I

Statistics

The analysis below is based on a representative sample of approximately 700 service records from the men of the 1/5th (and approximately 1,000 from 1/4th King's Own).

Perhaps the most shocking statistic to modern readers is that 63 per cent of all men who served in the Battalion became a battle casualty at some time in their service. All units sent in a weekly casualty return, with numbers killed, wounded, or sick in hospital, which were later used to calculate the number of wounded during the war. These statistics are, however, misleading as the returns contained only totals not names, so invariably men wounded on different occasions were counted more than once. A look at Appendix III will show that large numbers of men were wounded one more than one occasion, each occasion counting as a different individual in the official statistics. What is abundantly clear from the analysis is that new men were more than three times as likely as their more experienced comrades to become a casualty within the first three months of arriving at the front. Experience counted.

Hospitalisation: causes other than gas/ penetrating wound	1/5th Battalion	1/4th Battalion
Scabies	4.4% of all men.	7.7% of all men.
Shellshock	3.2% of all men	4% of all men.
Trench foot	2.7% of all men	2.5% of all men.
Trench Fever	6.4% of all men	8% of all men.
Trench nephritis	0.8% of all men	1.1% of all men.
ICT	6.1% of all men	4.8% of all men.
Percentage of men killed	24%	24.6%
Percentage battle casualties (Fatal and wounded)	63%	67%

How Experienced were the Men who became Casualties?

Within first three months of getting to the trenches.	61%	51.3%
Between 4-6 months in the trenches.	19%	16.4%
Between 7-12 months in the trenches.	14%	15.4%
Over 12 months in the trenches.	6%	16.9%

How was the Battalion Employed once Deployed Overseas?

Calculated in 'days' from the war diary 14 February 1915-11 November 1918

Days' Activity	1915	1916	1917	1918	TOTAL	% of TIME
Travelling	12	19	5	3	39	3%
Rest/Intensive Training	87	61	144	91	383	28%
Reserve/Support	112	179	110	101	502	36%
Front Line	127	107	106	121	461	33%

Battalion Roll 1914–1918

Abbott, Francis	Sgt	240230	
Abbott, George Zaccheus	2Lt	240234	WIA (as Sgt). Comm.
Abbott, James Hartley	Pte	33932	
Abbott, Matthew	Pte	242648	Also 1st Bn. WIA.
Abbott, Ninian Jeffrey	Sgt	240229	Comm. 1917
Ackerley, Samuel	Pte	26998	WIA.
Acton, Jonathan Richard	Cpl	3791	KIA 15/8/16
Adams, Cecil (Thomas Cecil)	Pte	260013	KIA 31/7/17
Adams, Edward (John Edw.)	Pte	2069	KIA 23/4/15
Adams, James Thomas	2Lt		
Adamson, James Edward	Pte	242519	WIA.
Addison, William	Pte	241278	
Adie, Arthur Albert	2Lt		DCM. KIA 3/5/18
Ainsworth, Frank	Pte	34803	POW.
Airey, Arthur Richard	Pte	240195	KIA 19/6/17
Airey, Harold	Sgt	240157	WIA
Airey, James Atkinson	Pte	2446	KIA 4/5/15
Airey, Joshua	Pte	3334	KIA with 8th Bn 18/8/16
Airey, Robert	Pte	240280	WIA
Airey, Thomas	Pte	240287	
Akrigg, James Henry	Pte	240671	WIA
Alcock, Arthur	Pte	242516	KIA 31/7/17
Alderson, Edmund Irving	Pte	2066	WIA. & KIA 18/9/16
Alexander, James	2Lt		MC. PoW.
Allan (Allen), Arthur	Pte	33953	KIA 6/8/18
Allen, Fred	Pte	36002	
Allen, Frederick C.	Pte	3022	Trans to Beds
Allen, John	Pte	30700	Ex-RAVC
Allen, Robert	Pte	241617	Also 1/4th.
Allen, William Henry	Pte	240465	MiD

Allred, Fred	Sgt	35256	
Alsbury, Frederick	Sgt	244503	
Alston, (Edward) Douglas	Pte	2028	WIA
Alston, Alfred James	Pte	2444	H
Alston, Richard	Pte	3044	KIA 4/5/15
Ambler, Edmund	Pte	1471	KIA 9/5/15
Anderson, Alban	Pte	1424	WIA. & DOW 10/8/16
Anderson, Burgoyne Frederick	Pte	235537	
Anderson, Charles Alfred W.	Lt-Col.		N. Staffs. KIA 18/9/16
Anderson-Morshead, Rupert Henry	Lt-Col.		KIA 27/5/18- CO 2/Devonshire R.
Anderton, George	Pte	30904	Also 2nd Bn & LC.
Anderton, R.	Pte	877	WIA
Angus, Harry	Pte	2067	KIA 3/5/15
Angus, James	Pte	2725	H
Angus, Thomas	Pte	240413	WIA
Angus, Thomas	Pte	240837	
Angus, William	A/Cpl	240127	WIA x2. MM
Anyon, James Tyson	L/Sgt	494	WIA
Anyon, Richard	Pte	265763	WIA. Trans to LC.
Appleyard, Charles Herbert	Lt		WIA x2
Appleyard, Thomas	Pte	27003	Ex-Lincs, 1st Bn & 1/4th. WIA.
Archer, John	Pte	242520	
Archer, Walter	Pte	242664	Ex 8th Bn. KIA 15/9/17
Arkwright, Ernest	Pte	240839	Trans to LC.
Arkwright, John	Sgt	72	
Arkwright, Richard	Pte	26475	WIA
Armer, Thomas	Pte	241537	ex-8th Bn
Armistead, Alfred H.	Sgt	241494	MSM
Armistead, Walter	Pte	240974	KIA 6/8/18
Armstrong, John Edward	Pte	242972	POW.
Armstrong, William	Pte	34517	KIA 20/9/17
Arnison, James Herring	2Lt		WIA x2
Arnold, William	Cpl	241496	WIA x2
Arscott, George	Pte	37208	
Arthur, Albert	Pte	27439	
Ashcroft, Joseph	L/Sgt	242994	MM. KIA 20/9/17
Ashcroft, Thomas J.	Pte	2554	DOW 2/6/15
Ashdown, Lewis Thomas	Pte	242518	
Ashton, James	L/Cpl	27454	Ex 7th Bn. POW.
Ashton, John	Pte	2555	KIA 9/5/15
Ashton, Stanley	L/Cpl	1986	WIA

Ashton, Thomas	Pte	20359	POW
Ashton, William	Pte	1174	
Ashworth, Frank	Pte	240888	WIA
Ashworth, Fred	Pte	201916	WIA. KIA 22/4/18
Ashworth, Harry	Pte	27403	Ex-LF.
Askew, Albert	Pte	3677	KIA 15/8/16
Askew, John	Pte	1809	Trans to MGC.
Askey, Thomas Proctor	Pte	94	H
Aspden, Albert	Pte	1940	DOW 25/5/15
Aspinall, Charles	Pte	243003	
Aspray, John Thomas	Pte	18434	Ex 1st Bn. MM
Assitt, Jonathon	Pte	1781	DOW 6/5/15
Astle, Thomas	Pte	27690	Ex- 1st Bn & 11th Bn.
Astley, Fred	Pte	13704	Also 9th & 1st Bns. KIA 23/7/17
Atherton, Harry	Pte	24067	Ex-8th Bn.
Atkinson, Anthony William	Pte	240124	WIA
Atkinson, Ernest	Maj.		
Atkinson, George Anderson	Pte	241159	WIA & POW
Atkinson, Harry	Pte	240418	
Atkinson, James	Pte	1668	WIA x4. Trans to MFP.
Atkinson, John Proctor	Pte	240484	Also 1st bn.
Atkinson, Richard	Pte	241129	WIA.
Atkinson, Thomas	Sgt	201114	MM
Atkinson, Thomas	Cpl	240418	Also 8th and 2/5th.
Atkinson, Thomas Andrew	Sgt	241487	
Atkinson, William	Pte	240124	Also 2/5th.
Audley, John	Pte	240299	
Auerback, Wilfred	Pte	24730	Also 7th Bn.
Austin, Charles	Sgt	240339	WIA × 2.
Austin, Frank	Pte	241406	Trans to RE.
Austin, John	Pte	3240	Trans to LC.
Auty, George William	Pte	977	WIA
Auty, Joseph	Pte	240235	WIA
Avison, Frank	2Lt		Trans to RAF
Ayling, William	Pte	242651	MM. DOW 19/3/18
Aylward, David Edward	Pte	26852	Ex 1st & 7th Bns.
Ayres, William	Pte	30683	Ex-RAVC.
Bagley, Charles Sainsbury	Pte	242436	DOW 29/10/17
Baglin, John	Pte	24283	WIA. POW
Bagot, John	Pte	1153	KIA 27/4/15
Bagshaw, Joseph	Pte	26709	Ex LF & 7th Bn. POW.
Bailey, Adam C.	Pte	1999	WIA

Bailey, Albert	Pte	28655	Trans to LC. D. 13/5/21
Bailey, Ernest Wright	Pte	242539	DOW 17/6/17
Bailey, Frank	Pte	241666	Ex 8th Bn.
Bailey, George Henry	Pte	41028	WIA
Bailey, Percy	Pte	241100	Also 7th & 1/4th.
Bailey, Samuel	Pte	1503	KIA 8/5/15
Bailiff, James	L/Cpl	200819	Also 1/4th. WIA.
Bainbridge, Charles	Pte	2064	Trans to LC.
Bainbridge, James	Capt.		WIA
Bainbridge, John	2Lt		Ex ASC.
Bainbridge, Manisty	Pte	242522	KIA 30/11/17
Baines, George	Pte	1755	WIA. Trans to S Lancs
Baines, John	Pte	241416	MM. DOW 8/8/18
Baines, John	L/Cpl	2351	Also 1st & 8th Bns.
Baines, Robert Henry Walker	Cpl	331	WIA. Trans to MFP
Baird, John Harvey	2Lt		MiD
Baird, Robert Samuel	Pte	2072	WIA. Trans to Suff. & N-Hants.
Baker, Frank	Pte	241364	
Baker, Stanley Victor	Cpl	27398	Ex LF & 7th Bn. POW
Baker, Wilfred Ernest	2Lt		MiD
Bakey, John	Cpl	240043	WIA
Balderstone, George Edward	Pte	1386	KIA 23/4/15
Balderstone, J.	Pte	1397	H
Balderstone, William	Pte	2557	Trans to MGC.
Ball, Frederick William	Sgt	240562	WIA X2. MM & Bar.
Ball, Robert	Pte	241122	
Ball, Thomas	Pte	26087	Ex 7th Bn.
Ball, William	Pte	24595	
Ball, William	Pte	27763	WIA. Trans to RWF.
Ballantine, George	Pte	243044	
Balmforth, John William	L/Cpl	14034	Ex 7th Bn. DOW 8/7/18
Bamber, Albert	L/Cpl	242417	WIA x3. To 1st Bn & LC.
Bamber, George William	Pte	1480	WIA. Trans to RE.
Bamber, James Robinson	Pte	242700	WIA x3. To 2nd Bn.
Bamber, Robert W.	Pte	1357	WIA. Trans to RE.
Bamber, Thomas	Pte	3014	DOW 5/5/15
Bamber, William	Cpl	240993	WIA
Bamber, William	Pte	8347	
Bancroft, Allen	Pte	242523	KIA 30/11/17 with 166 TMB
Bancroft, Harry	Pte	13369	Ex 9th & 1st Bns.
Bane, Robert Charles	Pte	28123	Also E. Kents & 7th Bn.

Banham, Ernest Albert	Pte	242526	
Banks, John Blaylock	Pte	241405	
Banning, Charles Richard	L/Cpl	23358	MM.
Bannister, Francis	Pte	14935	Ex 7th Bn.
Bannister, Joseph	Pte	33854	KIA 9/4/18
Barber, Albert Edward	Pte	27625	Ex 1st & 11th Bns. POW.
Barber, Thomas	Pte	242530	
Barclay, Robert	Pte	240098	WIA.
Barclay, Thomas George	Pte	30680	Ex-RAVC.
Barker, Joseph	Pte	41034	
Barker, Robert	Pte	260039	KIA 31/7/17
Barker, William	Pte	266284	Ex Border Regt.
Barlow, Frederick Percy	Pte	202294	KIA 31/7/17
Barlow, John Charles	Pte	3081	
Barnes, Arthur	Pte	242665	WIA.
Barnes, Harry	Pte	38134	
Barnes, John	Sgt	240447	WIA. Trans to 17 KLR.
Barnes, John Robert	Pte	36485	
Barnes, Joseph	Sgt	241625	MM
Barnes, Peter	Pte	241514	WIA × 2.
Barnes, William Taylor	Pte	243057	D. 7/4/17
Barnett, Francis	Sgt	242647	MSM
Baron, Clifford	Pte	243042	WIA & POW.
Barraclough, Percy	L/Cpl	242525	MM
Barrass, Thomas William	Pte	27993	Also 1/4th.
Barratt, William	Pte	37201	
Barrett, Arthur Frederick	Pte	41033	
Barrett, James	Pte	30302	Ex 8th Bn & LC. WIA × 2.
Barrow, Barnett	L/Sgt	200921	MM. KIA 13/4/18
Barrow, Edmund	Pte	27540	Ex 7th Bn.
Barrow, Frederick Harold	Pte	1561	KIA 20/11/15
Barrow, George	Pte	2559	H
Barrow, George Walter	WO1	240011	MiD. WIA. D. 26/1/17
Barrow, Harry	Pte	240490	Trans to ASC.
Barrow, John	Pte	23904	WIA. POW.
Barrow, John Charles	Pte	3081	D. 13/2/19
Barrow, Spencer Ellwood	Lt		DOW 16/11/15
Barrow, William	Pte	38058	
Barry, William Ernest	L/Cpl	260020	WIA. KIA 30/11/17
Bartholomew, Rueben	Pte	240890	WIA
Bartley, Albert	Cpl	242535	

Barton, Frank	Pte	27200	Ex 1st Bn.
Barton, John	2Lt		WIA × 2.
Barton, Peter	Pte	242352	
Barton, Reginald John	Pte	235018	Ex 8th Bn.
Barton, Robert	A/WO2	240034	MiD
Batchelor, Frederick Uglow	Cpl	202967	Ex London Yeo.
Bates, John Henry	Maj.		
Bates, Samuel	A/WO2	1301	WIA. Trans to KLR.
Bates, Stanley Knight	Lt		KIA 9/5/15
Bateson, Benjamin	Pte	1114	Trans to RE.
Bateson, Joseph Terence	Pte	1657	WIA.
Bateson, Thomas Smith	L/Cpl	2683	WIA. Comm. 1/4th-1917. MC.
Battersby, Henry	Pte	3998	
Batty, Robert	Pte	243059	
Bawden, Cecil	Pte	1376	
Baxendell, Wallace Royle	Pte	17963	Also 2nd Bn. KIA 30/11/17
Baxter, Robert George	Pte	202298	
Baynes, George	Pte	240893	DOW 4/12/17
Beadle, Arthur Frederick	Pte	202970	WIA as POW.
Beard, Willie	Pte	243017	KIA 28/7/17
Beatson, John	2Lt		WIA
Beauman, John Henry	Pte	36513	DOW 25/8/18
Beaumont, Theodore	A/Cpl	23720	Ex 7th & 11th Bns.
Beaumont, Thomas	Pte	241161	
Bebbington, John William	L/Cpl	24714	Ex 8th Bn. WIA.
Beck, Ernest	Pte	384	DOW 27/4/15
Beckett, Frank Heseltine	2Lt		
Beckett, George	Pte	1363	KIA 23/4/15
Beckett, Walter	Pte	240024	WIA. Also 2/5th.
Bedford, Harold	Pte	240561	
Bedford, Herbert Alan	2Lt		
Beeley, Herbert	Pte	241349	WIA. Trans to KRRC & DLI.
Beer, Charles	Sgt	25386	Ex 7th Bn.
Beesley, James	Pte	202249	
Beevours, Joseph	Pte	242537	WIA. Trans to LC.
Belcher, Harry	Pte	26794	Ex 7th Bn.
Bell, Colin Allen	Pte	3477	Trans to LNL & RF.
Bell, David	Pte	37468	
Bell, George Hodgson	Sgt	51312	
Bell, Harold	Capt.		MC. MiD (X2)
Bell, Harold	Sgt	240895	
Bell, Harry	Pte	1629	WIA. Trans to LC.

Bell, James Harry	Pte	243058	WIA. KIA 30/11/17
Bell, John William	L/Sgt	241530	
Bell, Joseph Dixon	Pte	35693	KIA 9/4/18
Bell, Joseph Samuel	Pte	33010	
Bell, Robert	Cpl	200707	Ex 1/4th. WIA × 2.
Bell, Robert	Pte	241639	
Bell, Thomas	Pte	240274	WIA.
Bell, Thomas	Pte	242540	Ex 8th Bn.
Bell, Thomas Wilson	L/Cpl	37732	KIA 23/4/18
Bell, William	A/CSGT	242410	WIA. MM.
Bellaby, Noah Vivian	Pte	41675	DOW 8/8/18
Bellamy, John	Pte	242529	
Bennett, Alan	Pte	240204	WIA
Bennett, Albert Hartley	Pte	41021	
Bennett, Charles Benjamin	Sgt	230	
Bennett, Eric Latham	Cpl	2071	WIA. DCM. Comm. 1916.
Bennett, Horace Bramwell	Capt.		WIA. MC.
Bennett, Isaac	L/Cpl	240226	WIA. Trans to RE
Bennett, John Frederick	L/Cpl	201160	KIA 9/4/18 with 1/4th.
Bennett, Thomas Henry	Pte	241407	WIA.
Bennett, William	L/Cpl	19912	Also 2/5th.
Bennett, William	Pte	242315	
Benson, Bert	Pte	2262	Trans to Lancers.
Benson, Joseph Christopher	Pte	240491	WIA. POW.
Benson, Thomas Irwin	Sgt	240489	
Bentham, Ernest Dean	Pte	21035	Ex 9th Bn. KIA 9/4/18
Bentley, Harold	Pte	242536	POW.
Bentley, Herbert	Pte	27667	
Beresford, Joseph	Pte	36149	
Berkins, Charles	A/WO2	330	WIA.
Berrington, E.	Sgt		H
Berry, John Fort	Pte	240896	WIA. DOW 19/12/17 with 7th Bn.
Berry, Robert Stanley	Pte	260036	WIA × 2.
Bertlestien, Henry	Pte	243099	KIA 30/11/17
Berwick, Nelson Thomas	Pte	1117	Trans to MGC.
Bettany, James Albert	Pte	240029	WIA. MM.KIA 10/8/19 with RF
Bettany, William	Pte	24727	Also 1 Bn.
Betton, Walter	Cpl	2235	WIA. Trans to Rifles.
Bewes, Frederick	Pte	34813	POW.
Bewes, Henry James	Cpl	241108	WIA
Bewes, John	Pte	241124	Also 8th Bn.

Bibby, Albert Edward	Pte	33961	Ex1/4th.
Bibby, Charles	Pte	240566	WIA × 2.
Bibby, Harry	L/Cpl	2082	Trans to Lincs.
Bickerton, Robert	Sgt	240459	MM.
Bigland, Thomas	Pte	1887	KIA 24/4/15
Bigland, William	Pte	30736	
Billany, William	Pte	242524	POW.
Billington, Adam	Pte	240173	
Billington, Richard H.	C/Sgt	173	H. Trans to LC.
Bilsborough, James Charles	Pte	2560	KIA 15/8/16
Bilsborough, Thomas	Pte	241328	
Bindloss, John Alfred	Cpl	240199	WIA.
Bingham, Frank Miller	Capt.		KIA 22/5/15
Bingham, Joseph	Pte	27360	Ex Lincs & 1 Bn. WIA × 2. KIA 6/8/18
Binns, Charles Edward Brett	2Lt		
Binns, Frank Thompson	Pte	266104	
Birch, William Henry	Pte	14569	Ex 8th Bn. POW.
Birchall, Albert	Pte	2832	H
Birchall, Harry	Pte	1592	WIA. KIA 20/11/15
Birchall, James	Pte	27688	Also 1st Bn. WIA.
Bird, Frederick Anthony	L/Cpl	1839	KIA 15/8/16
Birkett, Joseph Alfred	Pte	1514	WIA. Trans to MGC.
Birrell, Robert Reid	2Lt		WIA.
Birtle, Joseph	Sgt	240567	MSM.
Black, Charles Dunn	Cpl	240485	
Black, Ralph Joseph	Pte	235055	Ex 7th Bn. WIA.
Blackburn, John James	A/Cpl	241672	
Blackburn, Joshua	Pte	16350	Ex 7th Bn.
Blackburn, Thomas	Pte	241641	D. 15/9/18
Blackhurst, Reginald	Pte	2073	KIA 16/4/15
Blackledge, John	CQMS	240206	WIA.
Blackwell, Alfred Henry	Pte	243006	
Blacow, Norman	Pte	2075	Trans to RAMC.
Blades, Henry Dawson	Pte	240842	WIA. Also 2/5th.
Blair, Harry Thomson	L/Cpl	240079	WIA. DOW 17/9/17
Blake, George Amos	Pte	260023	KIA 31/7/17
Blakeley, Thomas Stapleton	2Lt	2452	WIA × 3. Comm. MC.
Blamire, Cecil	L/Sgt	241670	Also 2/5th.
Blamire, Reginald	Pte	240476	
Bland, William Alfred	Pte	51065	
Blaylock, William J.	Pte	33851	WIA X2. Trans to LC.

Bleasdale, James Edward	Pte	241626	
Bleasdale, John Robert	Pte	240360	WIA. KIA 15/8/16 att. Rifles.
Bleasdale, Richard William	Sgt	240156	WIA × 2.
Bleasdale, Thomas A.	Pte	2264	H.
Bleazard (Blezzard), Arnold	Pte	243105	Ex 6th Bn.
Blissett, Ernest	Pte	2562	H. Trans to LC & Essex.
Blondel, Harold	WO2	240421	WIA.
Bloomfield, Frederick	Pte	240135	
Blout, Percy	Pte	24533	Also Notts & Derby, 9 & 1/4th Bns
Bloy, Robert H.	Pte	27648	Ex 1st Bn. WIA. Trans to MGC.
Boaden, Arthur Frederick	Pte	42896	
Boak, Thomas Fawcett	Pte	241484	
Boardman, Cyril	Pte	27819	Also 11th & 2/5th.
Boardman, Jacob Morris	Pte	33926	WIA.
Boardman, William	Cpl	51	H.
Boden, Arthur	Pte	42897	KIA 3/5/18
Bolan, John	Pte	11452	Also 6th & 7th Bns.
Bolton, Herbert	Pte	242978	WIA × 2. Posted 8th Bn.
Bolton, Tom	Pte	3058	KIA 27/4/15
Bond, Robert	Pte	241376	KIA 30/11/17
Bond, Seth	Pte	2001	DOW 15/3/15
Bonney, William	A/Cpl	241438	
Bonsall, Frederick	Pte	202299	MM. WIA.
Boon, Ernest	Pte	242521	DOW 18/3/17
Booth, Tom Porter	Pte	240785	Att MGC.
Boothway, Ernest	Pte	265777	KIA 10/4/18
Borrowdale, Robert James	Sgt	240487	WIA. Posted 1st Bn.
Bosson, Daniel	Pte	28134	Ex LNL & 7th Bn.
Bostock, Alfred	Pte	2266	KIA 27/4/15
Bostock, Frederick	Pte	3519	H
Bostock, John	Sgt	265756	WIA.
Boswell, Chisinde (Chrisidine)	Pte	240347	
Boswell, Edward	Pte	35967	
Bottomley, William	Pte	266600	
Boulter, Richard	Pte	241636	
Boustead, Henry	L/Cpl	240568	WIA. Decoration Militaire (Belgium)
Bowen, Harry	Cpl	1518	KIA 4/5/15
Bower, Frank	Sgt	240488	WIA. Comm. Indian Army.
Bowers, Harry	Pte	242534	KIA 31/7/17
Bowfield, Albert	Pte	1546	Trans to RE.
Bowker, Alfred	Pte	240161	WIA.

Bowker, Robert	L/Cpl	240677	KIA 18/3/17
Bowker, William	Cpl	1848	WIA × 2. Trans to LC.
Bowman, John	Pte	3046	WIA. DOW 22/7/16
Box, Clifford	Pte	41687	KIA 3/10/18
Box, Ernest	Pte	241432	Also 8th Bn.
Boyd, Benson	L/Cpl	2647	WIA.
Boys, Wilfred	Pte	37231	
Boys-Stones, Hubert	Lt		WIA.
Brackenbury, George	Pte	35589	KIA 10/7/19
Bradbury, Albert	Pte	242528	Also 8th Bn.
Bradbury, Ernest	Pte	241658	MM.
Bradford, Henry Charles	Pte	242533	Also 1st Bn. WIA.
Bradley, Christopher John	Pte	240424	
Bradley, Frank	Pte	1857	WIA. Trans to S Lancs.
Bradley, John Crewdson	2Lt		Att from LNL.
Bradshaw, Anthony	Pte	3818	
Bradshaw, John Thomas	Pte	240179	
Bradshaw, John William	Pte	241582	WIA.
Bradshaw, Thomas	Pte	1980	WIA.
Brady, Thomas Arthur	Pte	22328	Ex 11th Bn.
Braithwaite, Walter	Pte	242967	
Braithwaite, William	Pte	242694	Ex 1/4th.
Bramble, Harold Leslie	Pte	260014	DOW 17/6/17
Brame, Montague Frederick	Pte	26413	Ex 9th Bn. WIA. DOW 13/4/18
Brammall, Alfred	Pte	33701	Ex 11th Bn. WIA.
Brammall, William	Pte	11078	POW.
Brand, Herbert Omar	Pte	26512	Ex 9th Bn.
Bransden, Harold William	Pte	240563	WIA. Also 1/4th.
Brash, Wilfrid	2Lt		KIA 9/3/17
Brash, William Garrett G.	Pte	42898	
Bratherton, William Henry	L/Cpl	1732	KIA 27/4/15
Bray, Henry	Pte	33432	Ex 8th Bn. WIA × 2.
Brayshaw, Arthur	Pte	240042	
Brayshaw, Cecil	Cpl	740	KIA 9/5/15
Brayshaw, Thomas William	A/Cpl	1033	WIA.
Brayshaw, William	Pte	240899	
Brear, Frank	Pte	2062	MM. KIA 18/9/16
Brennan, Thomas	Pte	33293	
Brewer, Henry Hodkinson	Pte	2080	MM. WIA. Trans to LC.
Bridge, Sidney	Pte	263008	Posted 7th Bn. WIA.
Bridgman, John	Pte	38527	

Briers, Jack	Pte	25736	Also 8th & 11th Bns. WIA & POW.
Briggs, Charles	Pte	8409	Ex 2nd & 8th Bns. WIA.
Briggs, William Noel	Capt.		MiD. WIA × 4.
Brimelow, John Henry	Pte	235082	Also 7th Bn.
Brimson, Frederick	Pte	260022	DOW 26/9/17
Brinicombe, Samuel John	Pte	34829	Also 1st Bn. WIA × 3.
Briscoe, Christopher	Pte	19627	POW.
Broadhurst, Frederick Walter	Pte	41678	Also 8th Bn.
Brockbank, Frederick	Pte	34814	POW.
Brockbank, Mark	Pte	240588	
Brockbank, Robert Stanley	Sgt	240464	MSM.
Brockbank, William	Pte	240493	
Brodie, C.	Pte	59	H.
Brodie, Charles	Pte	7	WIA. Trans to LC.
Brodie, Charles	A/Cpl	240010	
Brodie, Joseph	Pte	1205	WIA.
Bromiley, John William	Sgt	242312	
Brooke, Frank	2Lt		WIA.
Brookfield, Lewis Bernard	Pte	265780	Trans to LC.
Brooks, Frank	Pte	2839	WIA. Trans to LC.
Brough, Richard James	Pte	38135	DOW 25/7/18
Brown, Albert E.	Pte	875	WIA. Trans to Tank Corps.
Brown, Cuthbert Benjamin	Pte	240589	
Brown, George William	A/WO1	5144	D. 6/5/17
Brown, Herbert	Pte	243043	POW.
Brown, Herbert Thomas	Pte	242666	
Brown, James William	Pte	24468	Ex 7th Bn.
Brown, John William	Pte	1338	WIA. Trans to LC
Brown, Reuben	Pte	33919	POW.
Brown, Robert	Pte	30747	Ex Cheshires.
Brown, Robert	Pte	243103	Ex 2nd & 7th Bns.
Brown, Roger	Pte	2065	WIA.
Brown, Thomas	Pte	243094	Ex 6th & 8th Bns. WIA × 2.
Browne, John	Pte	37145	
Broxholme, Thomas	L/Cpl	27183	Ex Lincs. WIA. MM.
Bruan, Thomas	Pte	12593	Ex 7th Bn.
Brumby, William Edgar	L/Cpl	15500	Ex 8 7 & 11th Bns WIA × 4. POW.
Bryan, William Philip	Pte	260044	KIA 23/4/18
Bryson, Jonah Taylor	Pte	36628	
Buckley, Boris Bramley	Pte	42899	DOW 6/7/18
Buckley, Fred	2Lt		POW.

Buckley, William	Pte	1375	H.
Buckley, William	Pte	21921	Ex 1st & 8th Bns. WIA × 3. MM.
Bullen, Richard	Pte	1699	DOW 11/5/15
Bunce, Edward	Pte	3577	H.
Bunn, George	Cpl	240787	Also 2/5th.
Bunter, William F.	Pte	2227	WIA. Trans to Leics R.
Bunting, Lawrence William	Pte	3504	Trans to LC.
Bunyan, Eric Edward	2Lt		Att from Lincs.
Burgess, James	Pte	242709	
Burgess, Josiah	Pte	23031	Ex 7th Bn. WIA × 2.
Burke, John	Pte	14766	Ex 6th & 7th Bns.
Burley, Harold	Pte	27353	Ex Lincs & 1 KORL. WIA.
Burns, John	Pte	242696	
Burridge, Henry Charles	Pte	35968	
Burrow, Harold	Pte	242987	KIA 14/4/18
Burrow, Harvey Thwaite	Pte	36157	
Burrow, James	Pte	3146	WIA. Trans to ASC.
Burrow, Richard Wilson	A/Cpl	33941	
Burrow, Robert	Pte	3285	WIA.
Burrow, Thomas	L/Cpl	1512	KIA 23/4/15
Burrow, Thomas	Cpl	241624	KIA 30/11/17
Burrows, Henry Johnson	Pte	240370	WIA. KIA 20/9/17
Burrows, James	Pte	2454	Trans to LF and ASC.
Burton, Alfred	Pte	37159	
Burton, Frank Roland	A/Cpl	30675	DOW 11/3/18
Burton, Noah	RQMS	1830	H.
Burton, William Thomas	Pte	260042	
Bush, Charles	Pte	2457	Trans to MGC.
Bustard, Ralph	Lt		WIA.
Butcher, John	Pte	242390	KIA 24/4/17
Butler, Edward	Pte	2651	KIA 28/4/15
Butler, Reuben	Sgt	240140	WIA.
Butler, Richard Stanley	Pte	2653	POW. DOW 19/5/15
Butler, Robert	Pte	2063	Trans to LC.
Butterworth, Arthur	Sgt	266606	
Butterworth, Hugh	Pte	1304	KIA 1/8/15
Butterworth, James Livesey	Pte	242358	WIA. KIA 10/4/18
Butterworth, James William	Pte	30687	Ex RAVC.
Butterworth, John Shore	L/Sgt	243087	KIA 2/8/17
Buxton, Robert Blowers	Pte	36362	Also 8th Bn.
Byram, Fred	Pte	240027	WIA. Prob trans to ASC.
Byram, Thomas	Pte	383	Trans to LC.

Byrne, Thomas	WO2	240007	MiD.
Cabry, Joseph	Pte	34815	Also 1st Bn.
Cadman, Edward Cadman	Lt-Col.		DSO. MiD. KIA 27/5/18- CO Chesh.
Cairns, William Briscoe	Pte	201851	Also 7th Bn.
Calder, William	Pte	240045	
Calderbank, Frederick	Pte	1415	WIA. Trans to R. Warks.
Callant, George Leslie	Pte	265056	
Callighan, Christopher	Sgt	240160	
Callon, James	Pte	242622	WIA. Posted 2/5th.
Callow, Edward	Pte	1253	KIA 1/7/15
Calvert, Joseph	Pte	241440	Also 2/5th. Trans to LC.
Calvert, Sam	Pte	33918	Posted 8th Bn.
Cambray, Frederick James	Pte	240367	WIA. Posted 2/5th.
Cameron, John	Pte	1761	WIA. Trans to LC.
Cameron, John Gordon	Pte	241659	Ex 8th Bn. WIA. KIA 30/11/17
Camm, George	L/Sgt	240844	
Campbell, George Edward	Sgt	240845	WIA X2. MM.
Campbell, John	Pte	2012	KIA 9/5/15
Cantrill, Frank	Sgt	240903	WIA. Also 2/5th.
Capewell, Arthur	Pte	3286	
Capstick, Francis	Pte	242543	
Capstick, Harold Eustace	Cpl	240592	MiD. POW.
Capstick, James T.	Pte	15147	Ex 7th Bn.
Card, Arthur Trevor T.	2Lt		
Carder, H.	Pte	242549	WIA. Trans to ?
Cardwell, John William	Pte	1559	DOW 11/5/15
Cardwell, William	Pte	1550	WIA. Trans to LC.
Caren, William	Pte	260037	
Carey, Herbert	Pte	240591	WIA.
Cariss, Roland	Pte	2097	KIA 3/5/15
Carless, Harry	2Lt		MC.
Carnell, George	Pte	3327	
Carney, James	Cpl	563	
Carney, John Thomas	Pte	18825	Ex 8th & 7th Bns.
Carney, Michael	Pte	1889	WIA. Trans to S Lancs.
Carney, Michael	Pte	1697	
Carney, Stephen	Pte	241517	
Carr, Edgar Joseph Augustin	Lt		DOW 18/5/15
Carr, Patrick	Pte	2098	WIA.
Carradice, George	Cpl	240846	MM. WIA.
Carradice, Herbert Lewthwaite	Pte	241206	WIA.
Carradus, Michael	Pte	1044	WIA.

Carson, Francis	Pte	265302	
Carswell, John	Pte	265874	
Carter, Charles	L/Cpl	21399	Ex 11th & 2/5th Bns.
Carter, Edward	Pte	1370	POW. DOW 19/5/15
Carter, Henry James	Pte	11144	
Carter, James William	L/Cpl	907	KIA 4/5/15
Carter, John	Pte	242376	Also 7th & 1/4th Bns.
Carter, Percy	Pte	22424	KIA 3/10/18
Carter, Wilfred	Pte	242547	WIA. Also 2/5th.
Carter, William Arthur Rowe	Capt.		KIA 23/4/15
Carter, William Lamb	Pte	240632	WIA.
Cartledge, James Henry	Pte	22878	Also 11th & 8th Bns.
Cartmell, Edward Ernest	Sgt	240497	
Cartmell, Fred	Pte	1998	WIA.
Cartmell, Harold	Pte	1562	WIA. Trans to N Staffs.
Cartmell, John W.	Pte	240496	DOW 4/6/18
Cartmell, Sidney	L/Cpl	240500	WIA × 2.
Cartmell, Joseph	Pte	4402	Also 8th Bn. Trans to KLR.
Cartmell, William	Pte	241609	WIA.
Carton, Edward James	Pte	1949	DOW 10/1/17
Cartwright, Peter	Pte	26069	Ex-LF. 1st Bn. WIA. KIA 30/11/17
Cassells, John James	Pte	242621	Also LC.
Cassidy, James	Pte	37600	
Casson, Harry	Pte	37188	
Casson, Richard	Pte	241344	WIA. KIA 30 /11/17
Casson, William	Pte	240847	
Cathcart, George	Pte	2093	KIA 23/4/15
Cathcart, James	Pte	2091	KIA 4/5/15
Catlow, Samuel	Pte	24820	Ex 7th Bn.
Caton, Albert Pennington	Pte	1511	WIA.
Caton, Joseph	Pte	240064	WIA × 2. KIA 26/10/17 with 2/5th.
Caton, Robert	Pte	54	H.
Caton, Robert P.	Pte	1504	Trans to MGC.
Cattell, Reginald Henry	2Lt		Former N. Staffs.
Cave, Alfred	Pte	1808	DOW 4/8/16
Cavendish, Lord Richard F.	Lt-Col.		CB. CMG. MiD. WIA.
Chadwick, Albert	Pte	27445	Also 7th, 1st & 9th Bns.
Chadwick, John Richard	Pte	201872	
Chamberlain, Frederick Charles	Pte	242550	
Chamberlain, James	Pte	240663	Also RFC.

Chapman, Albert Herbert	Pte	260016	WIA × 2. KIA 30/11/17
Chapman, Frank	Pte	202300	
Chapman, Harold	2Lt	240473	Comm. WIA × 2.
Charlton, Clifford Francis	Pte	33923	Ex 7th Bn.
Charnley, Richard Ogden	Pte	958	WIA.
Charnley, Thomas	Pte	2566	KIA 4/5/15
Charnley, William	Pte	243060	DOW 20/9/17
Cheetham, Walter James	Pte	30669	Ex RAVC. WIA.
Chidgey, Stanley	Pte	42902	KIA 19/7/18
Childerley, Percy	Pte	26797	Ex 7th & 11th Bns. POW.
Chisholme, Harold	L/Cpl	240019	WIA. Trans to LC.
Chisholme, James	Sgt	240104	
Chorley, William	Pte	27499	Ex 8th Bn. WIA. KIA 20/9/17
Christian, Harry	Sgt	242467	Trans to RE.
Christie, Samuel	Pte	3472	
Churchill, Hector	Pte	9970	Ex 2nd & 7th Bns.
Churchman, George R.	Pte	33708	MM.
Churchouse, James	L/Cpl	240099	WIA. KIA 31/7/17
Churchouse, John 'Jack'	Pte	1003	KIA 14/4/15
Clapham, William	Cpl	242406	KIA 31/7/17
Clare, James Thomas	L/Cpl	13974	Ex 7th Bn. MM.
Clark, John	Pte	240848	WIA. KIA 9/4/17 with 1st Bn.
Clark, Robert E.	Pte	4001	Trans to North Staffs & KLR.
Clarke, Arthur	Pte	241097	WIA. Trans to MGC.
Clarke, Frank	Pte	36162	
Clarke, Fred	Pte	21236	Ex 11th Bn.
Clarke, George Allen	Pte	27860	Ex 11th Bn.
Clarke, George Arthur	Pte	27859	Also 11th Bn.
Clarke, Harold T.	Pte	22619	WIA. Trans to LC.
Clarke, Jesse	Pte	28135	Ex LF & 7th Bn.
Clarke, Tom Knight	Pte	2740	KIA 14/4/15
Clarkson, Albert	Pte	242499	
Clarkson, Andrew	Pte	28968	Ex 8th Bn. WIA.
Clarkson, Edward	A/Cpl	681	Trans to RE.
Clarkson, George	Pte	1157	
Clarkson, Richard	Sgt	240185	WIA. Posted 2nd Bn.
Clarkson, Richard William	A/CSGT	240238	MSM
Clarkson, Thomas	Pte	27460	Ex 7th Bn.
Clarkson, William Stephen	L/Cpl	1288	WIA. Trans to MFP.
Clawson, Harry	Pte	243123	Ex 1st Bn. POW.
Clayton, Frederick	Pte	3341	Trans to ASC. Accid. wounded

Clayton, John	Pte	240999	
Clayton, John L.	Pte	4152	WIA. Trans to KLR & RE.
Clegg, Harry	Pte	242291	
Clegg, John	L/Sgt	242620	
Clements, Isaac Routledge	Pte	1362	WIA. KIA 22/9/18 with RF.
Clements, James	L/Cpl	27227	Ex Lincs, 1st & 7th KORL.
Clifford, Percy	Pte	243045	
Clifton, J.	Pte	57	H.
Clitheroe, Robert	Pte	201902	WIA.
Close, Arthur William	Pte	28319	Ex ASC & 11th Bn.
Clough, George	Pte	12896	
Clough, James	Pte	21037	ex 11th Bn.
Clough, Percy	L/Cpl	42904	WIA
Clowes, Alfred	Sgt	1753	WIA. Trans to LC.
Coar, John Albert	L/Cpl	242621	DOW 27/4/18
Coates, Thomas	Sgt	556	
Coburn, Simeon Smith	Pte	241603	WIA.
Cock, Joseph	Pte	240368	Trans to RE.
Cockcroft, Charles	Pte	201871	KIA 30/11/17
Cocker, John	Pte	242623	DOW 29/5/17
Cole, Arthur James	Pte	30424	Ex 1st Bn. WIA.
Cole, Arthur John	Pte	30421	Ex 1st Bn. WIA.
Cole, Edward	Pte	2223	H.
Cole, George William	Pte	22582	Ex 11th Bn. Also 1/4th.
Colgan, Edward	Pte	240126	WIA × 2.
Collier, Percy	L/Cpl	241780	WIA. Trans to RE.
Collins, Charles	Pte	32003	KIA 11/4/18
Collinson, Herbert	L/Cpl	2084	WIA. Trans to LF.
Collinson, Joseph	Pte	241649	
Colston, Norman	Pte	33914	KIA 31/7/17
Conchie, William	Pte	265063	Ex 7th & 1st Bns. WIA.
Conheeny, Gerald	2Lt		MC. POW. Killed 5/12/18
Connerton, Joseph	Pte	265562	KIA 30/11/17
Connolly, Harry	Pte	24788	Ex 8th Bn.
Connolly, John William	Pte	35970	
Constable, Nathaniel	A/Cpl	30695	Ex RAVC. POW.
Conway, William	Pte	1803	KIA 4/5/15
Cook, John William	Pte	241969	Also 2/5th.
Cook, Stephen	Pte	2086	DOW 29/5/15
Cooke, John	Pte	240112	
Cooke, William	Pte	201689	WIA. Also 1/4th.

Cookson, Fred	Pte	1095	WIA.
Cookson, Robert	Pte	240682	
Cookson, William	Pte	242669	Also 9th Bn.
Coombes, Walter Charles	L/Cpl	28187	Ex 7th Bn.
Cooper, Abraham	Pte	242542	WIA. Trans to LNL.
Cooper, (Harold) Gordon	Pte	240097	WIA.
Cooper, Alexander	Cpl	240482	WIA.
Cooper, Christopher Bradshaw	Cpl	2096	WIA.
Cooper, Frederick	Pte	242659	Ex R. Sussex. KIA 9/3/17
Cooper, James	Pte	242968	WIA. DOW 16/5/18 with 1/4th.
Cooper, John	Pte	242545	
Cooper, Samuel	Sgt	240546	WIA.
Cope, Frank	Pte	34824	
Cope, Henry Richard	Pte	34593	Also 1/4th. WIA.
Corless, Albert Edward	Pte	2188	WIA.
Corless, James	Pte	241468	WIA.
Corless, Richard	Pte	2083	WIA.
Corless, Robert	L/Cpl	1249	KIA 15/8/16
Cornall, Rowland	L/Cpl	1163	
Cornthwaite, Hesketh Riley	Pte	201866	KIA 7/3/18
Cornthwaite, Thomas	Pte	240991	WIA × 2. Posted to 1st Bn.
Cornthwaite, William Henry	Pte	240257	WIA.
Cornwall, William Francis	Lt		RAMC. MC.
Cornwell, Census George	Pte	33952	WIA.
Corry, James	Pte	22623	Ex 11th Bn. WIA.
Cottam, Arthur	Pte	19108	Ex 11th & 7th Bns.
Cottam, Frederick	Pte	240545	WIA.
Cottam, Lawrence	Pte	1552	WIA. DOW 25/8/16
Cottam, Nathan	Pte	263006	Also 7th Bn & RE.
Cottam, Thomas	Pte	1975	DOW 6/5/15
Cotton, Cyril	Pte	240550	WIA MiD
Cottrell, John Harry Linton	Pte	23161	Ex 11th & 8th Bns.
Couch, Walter	L/Cpl	24446	Ex 8th Bn-28/12/16. WIA.
Couldick, William	Pte	28095	Ex LF and also 1/4th.
Coulthard, William	Pte	38055	
Coulthurst, George	Pte	2006	WIA.
Coulton, George	Pte	240349	
Coupland, Henry	Lt		DOW 24/4/15
Coupland, Robert	Pte	626	H.
Coupland, W.	Pte	1777	Trans to RFC.
Coward, William	Pte	24473	Ex 7th Bn.

Cowell, Albert Ernest	A/WO2	202423	Also 1/4th.
Cowell, George	Pte	3395	
Cowell, John William	Pte	1401	DOW 16/5/15
Cowell, Robert	L/Cpl	1121	WIA.
Cowell, Sydney	Pte	243986	Also 7th Bn.
Cowell, Thomas Relton	Pte	241623	WIA.
Cowie, Joseph	Pte	24252	
Cowley, Richard Ernest Gordon	Pte	41022	
Cox, Frederick	Pte	4716	Trans to RFC.
Cox, Herbert	Pte	28193	Ex 7th Bn.
Cox, Percy	Pte	2465	Trans to Border R.
Cox, William Charles	Pte	242548	
Coyle, Bernard	Pte	241791	KIA 3/5/17 with 1st Bn.
Crabtree, Frank Holcroft	L/Cpl	241621	
Craddock, Charles Alfred	Pte	22615	Ex 11th.
Cragg, David O.	Pte	265785	H.
Cragg, Harry	Pte	2362	KIA 22/9/16
Cragg, Joseph	Pte	1767	KIA 23/4/15
Cragg, Thomas	Pte	241366	WIA X2.
Crahan, John	Pte	1544	WIA. DOW 15/7/16
Craig, John William	Sgt	260051	WIA.
Crane, Edward	L/Cpl	241017	WIA. Trans to LC.
Crane, James	Pte	242463	Also 8th Bn.
Crarey, William	Pte	3061	WIA × 2. Trans to MGC.
Crawford, John	L/Cpl	9676	Ex 1st Bn.
Crawley, William Rupert	Pte	1045	Trans to MGC.
Crawshaw, Ephraim	Pte	12570	Ex 7th Bn.
Cressey, Robert	Pte	27369	Ex Lincs & 1st Bn.
Crewe, William Leo	Pte	20510	POW. DOW 25/4/18
Critchley, Harold	Lt		
Crofthall	Pte		
Crompton, William	Pte	4952	Ex 7th Bn.
Crompton, William	Pte	243046	
Crook, Fred	Pte	242544	
Crook, James	Pte	35788	KIA 12/4/18
Crook, James	Pte	241472	Also 1st Bn.
Crook, Joseph	Pte	2363	WIA. DOW 15/8/16
Crosbie, John Alex M.	Pte	32835	Trans to KLR.
Cross, Harold	Pte	1613	KIA 14/11/15
Cross, Harry	L/Cpl	2092	WIA. Comm. DLI-1915.
Cross, Henry	Pte	34754	WIA.

Cross, James	Pte	1678	KIA 4/5/15
Cross, John	Pte	240403	Att MGC, also 1/4th.
Cross, William	Sgt	240735	D. 12/11/18
Crossland, Richard	Pte	242618	POW.
Crossley, Abraham	Cpl	26088	Ex 7th Bn. WIA × 2. POW.
Crossley, John Albert	Pte	1805	KIA 1/7/15
Crossley, Thomas	Pte	684	
Crow, Philip Henry	Pte	33848	WIA.
Crowther, James	Pte	242449	DOW 29/6/17
Croxall, Harry	Pte	240849	
Cullen, William	Pte	243091	MM.
Culver, Charles John	L/Cpl	10839	Also 1/4th.
Cumberbatch, Hubert	Pte	241590	WIA.
Cummings, John	Pte	21306	Ex 11th Bn. KIA 10/4/18
Cummings, John Thomas	Pte	240401	
Cumpsty, Alfred	Pte	3137	Trans to LC & RF.
Cumpsty, Robert	Pte	265266	
Cunliffe, John	Pte	21521	WIA. Trans to LC.
Cunliffe, Robert	Pte	2467	KIA 9/5/15
Cunningham, William	Pte	243028	POW.
Currie, Angus	Pte	3343	Trans to RE & LC.
Curry, Thomas Munro	2Lt		
Curtis, Walter	Pte	40858	Ex 8th Bn.
Curwen, James	Pte	240908	
Curwen, James Thomas	Pte	70365	KIA 30/11/17 with 166 MGC.
Curwen, Robert	Pte	2039	H.
Curwood, David	Pte	38542	
Dabbs, Leonard	Pte	4545	KIA 9/8/16 (Unlucky Draft)
Dainty, John	Pte	243449	WIA.
Dainty, Thomas	Pte	241401	WIA. KIA 27/9/18 with 8th Bn.
Dale, John Reginald	Pte	42909	
Dalton, Joseph	Pte	481	KIA 3/6/15
Dalton, Joseph	Pte	242624	POW. DOW 1/5/18
Daly (Daley), John	Pte	242504	KIA 30/11/17
Daniels, William Ernest	2Lt		WIA.
Danson, James	Cpl	240061	
Darbyshire, Peter	Pte	242314	
Darts, William Alfred	Pte	986	H.
Davidson, Alexander	Pte	42908	
Davies, Albert	Pte	23094	Ex 7th Bn. WIA.

Davies, Dennett Howard	Pte	2234	KIA 24/5/15
Davies, Edward David	Pte	260033	KIA 21/9/17
Davies, Frank	Pte	266169	Also 1st Bn & ex KSLI.
Davies, George	Pte	28138	Ex LF & 7th Bn. WIA.
Davies, Harold Charles	Pte	37667	
Davies, Herbert Howell	Pte	42907	
Davies, Howell	Pte	22898	Ex 11th, 8th & 7th Bns.
Davies, Robert Evan	Cpl	240505	
Davies, Thomas	Pte	242671	Ex 1st Bn. Att TMB.
Davies, William Ralph	Pte	25733	
Davis, Alfred	Pte	20387	Ex 11th & 8th Bns.
Davis, Arthur Robert	S/Sgt	A/1365	AOC Armourer-Sgt.
Davis, John Dowbiggin	Pte	3628	KIA 16/10/16
Davis, John Henry	Pte	242703	WIA. KIA 9/4/18
Dawe, Edgar Thomas	Pte	263018	Ex RAVC.
Dawes, Albert Hartley	Sgt	1248	KIA 27/5/15
Dawson, Douglas M.	Pte	242993	DOW 15/8/16
Dawson, John	Pte	265793	MM. Posted 1/4th. WIA.
Dawson, John	Pte	202643	Ex 7th Bn.
Dawson, Joseph	Pte	387	WIA. Trans to LC.
Dawson, Robert	Pte	240594	KIA 9/3/17
Dawson, William Sylvester	Pte	241553	Accid. wounded. POW.
Day, Francis	Pte	23527	Ex 7th Bn.
Day, George Henry	Pte	42910	
Day, John Thomas	Pte	30239	Ex Sherwoods & 7th Bn. Wia X 3.
Day, Joseph	Pte	242672	Ex 7th Bn and also 2nd Bn.
Deacon, William Warren	Lt		MC. KIA 23/8/18
Dean, Albert	Cpl	17082	Ex 7th Bn.
Dean, Alfred	L/Cpl	37746	KIA 15/9/18
Dean, Harry	Pte	23996	Ex 7th Bn.
Dean, Henry	Pte	201952	
Dean, Richard William	Pte	26874	Ex 1st Bn. WIA. Also 2/5th.
Deed, William Robert Wheeler	Maj.		
Deighton, John	Capt.		RAMC. DOW 19/9/16
Dempsey, John	Pte	240443	WIA × 2. Posted 2/5th. Trans to RE.
Dennett, William	Pte	35991	
Denning, Henry Edward	Pte	42911	
Denny, George	L/Cpl	26875	Ex 1st Bn.
Dent, Albert	Pte	26669	WIA.
Denton, John George	Pte	243120	

Denver, William A.	Pte	2445	Trans to RE.
Denwood, Joseph	WO2	240686	CdVM
Denwood, Thomas William	C/Sgt	240297	WIA. Comm. R. Sussex. D. 22/10/18
Derham, Henry	Pte	912	H.
Derham, William	Sgt	38529	Ex MCR Regt.
Dewhirst, Charles Parker	Pte	242404	
D'Hooghe, Charles Samuel	Pte	5486	Trans to KLR.
Diamond, Albert Henry	Pte	28424	Ex 8th Bn.
Dickenson, J. G.	Pte	2098	WIA. Trans to MFP.
Dickinson, Acharia	Cpl	240090	
Dickinson, Charles	Pte	241611	
Dickinson, J. W.	Pte	2657	WIA.
Dickinson, Louis Harold	Sgt	241424	MM. KIA. 30/11/17
Dickson, Alfred Eric	2Lt		
Dickson, Angus	Lt		Killed 14/10/16
Dickson, John	Cpl	2470	Trans to LC.
Didsbury, Thomas	L/Cpl	1960	WIA.
Diggins, George William	Pte	26426	Ex 9th Bn.
Dillon, James	Pte	1799	WIA. Trans to KSLI & R Fus.
Dilworth, Edwin	Sgt	240100	WIA.
Dilworth, Robert	A/Cpl	24732	
Disley, John William	Pte	240426	
Dixon, Albert	Pte	1881	WIA × 2. Trans to LC.
Dixon, Arnold	Sgt	240687	
Dixon, C.	Pte	2102	
Dixon, Charles William	Pte	645	WIA.
Dixon, George Frederick	Sgt	240155	
Dixon, Harry	Pte	240791	WIA × 2. Trans to RE.
Dixon, John	Pte	242485	
Dixon, John Wilson	Pte	1365	WIA.
Dixon, Joseph Livingstone	Pte	3414	KIA 4/5/15
Dixon, Leonard A.	Pte	1730	WIA. Trans to RWF
Dixon, Robert	L/Cpl	1987	
Dixon, Robert	Pte	30679	Ex-RAVC
Dixon, Samuel Derbyshire	Pte	24069	Ex 9th Bn. Deserted 17/6/18
Dixon, Thomas	Pte	3151	WIA. Comm. 1915
Dixon, Thomas	Cpl	241420	Also 1/4th
Dixon, Thomas	Pte	242673	Ex 8th Bn. POW.
Dixon, Thomas Machell	Pte	33954	WIA
Dixon, William	Pte	2469	H
Dixon, William Henry	Pte	1212	

Dobie, John Bullen Pople	Lt		Att from Royal Scots. WIA
Dobson, Henry Richard	Pte	2907	(Prob. 1/4th Bn) KIA 10/9/16
Dobson, Herbert B.	Sgt	2746	MM. KIA 9/8/16
Dobson, John William	Pte	27644	Also 1st Bn
Dobson, Robert Irving	Pte	240188	WIA
Docherty, William	L/Cpl	240197	WIA. KIA 30/11/17
Dodding, John Robert	Pte	241068	
Dodding, Thomas Prince	Pte	1866	H
Dodgson, Frank	L/Cpl	241589	WIA.
Dodgson, John	L/Cpl	1009	DOW 10/5/15
Dodgson, Robert	Pte	3958	DOW 21/6/16
Doherty, David	Pte	37200	
Dolan, Henry	L/Cpl	2100	WIA. Comm. 1915
Dolan, James	Sgt	241298	MM WIA Trans to LC
Dolan, John	Pte	40896	
Dolby, Richard	2Lt		
Dominick, Ernest Horace	Pte	4434	KIA 3/8/16 (Unlucky Draft)
Donavan (Donovan), James	Cpl	242965	KIA 9/4/18
Done, Charles	Pte	2848	Trans to MGC
Donelly, Francis	Pte	16725	Ex 2nd & 7th Bns
Donohue, James	Cpl	240244	KIA 7/7/18
Dooley, Albert	Pte	26753	
Doran, William Henry	Pte	1945	WIA. KIA 9/8/16
Dorcey, Benjamin	Pte	15972	Ex 8th Bn WIA POW
Dorrell, Charles Henry	Pte	30678	Ex RAVC WIA × 2
Double, Rennard	Pte	240740	WIA
Douch, George	Pte	2225	WIA
Dougherty, John William	Pte	240114	
Douglas, George	Sgt	240688	
Douglas, John	Pte	1197	WIA D. 23/7/19
Douthwaite, Harold	Pte	38543	
Dowker, James	Pte	241561	WIA Also 8th Bn
Dowker, William	Pte	240366	
Dowlen, Frank Mark	2Lt		
Downes, Thomas	Pte	24689	DOW 2/12/17
Downey, Thomas	Pte	2184	WIA Trans to E Yorks
Downham, George	Pte	2239	DOW 22/10/18
Downham, James	Pte	41019	
Downham, John W.	L/Cpl	2099	WIA. Trans to S Lancs
Downs, Edward	Pte	243009	Ex 8th Bn

Dowthwaite, Francis	Pte	2474	H
Dowthwaite, Harold Hector	Pte	3002	KIA 22/8/15
Dowthwaite, James	Pte	2475	H
Dowthwaite, Richard	Pte	240990	Trans to LC
Doyle, Walter	Pte	242674	Ex 1st & 7th Bns MM
Draper, Daniel	Pte	27681	Ex 7th Bn
Draper, John	Pte	241651	WIA. Trans to LC.
Drew, William James	Pte	28232	Deserted 26/6/17
Drinkwater, George William	L/Sgt	21470	Ex 8th Bn
Drinkwater, William	Pte	37148	
Driscoll, Charles	Pte	26035	EX 1st Bn KIA 9/4/18
Ducksbury, Orlando Henry	Pte	240674	WIA × 2 Comm. LNL POW
Duckworth, John	Sgt	240174	WIA × 2
Duckworth, John	Pte	42912	
Duckworth, Percy	Pte	37192	
Duerden, William	Pte	201900	
Duggan, James	Pte	1685	WIA. Trans to LF, RF & Seaforths.
Duggan, William Henry	Pte	37191	
Dunkerley, Fred	Pte	26032	Ex 1st Bn.
Dunkley, Albert Francis	Pte	30226	Ex LF & 7th Bn.
Dunn, Joseph	Pte	16454	Ex 9th & 7th Bns.
Dunn, Thomas	Cpl	240256	WIA.
Dunne, John William	Pte	240435	
Dunworth, Eric	Pte	242490	WIA. Trans to Tanks Corps.
Dunville, Sam	Pte	36626	
Durham, Arthur	Pte	28019	Ex 1/4th. WIA. KIA 10/7/18
Dutton, Frank	Pte	241612	DOW 13/3/17
Duxbury, Arthur	2Lt		KIA 9/4/18
Duxbury, Thomas	Pte	21365	Ex 11th Bn. POW.
Eady, Albert Edward	Pte	263017	Ex RAVC.
Eakers, Thomas Charles	Pte	30656	Ex 11th Bn. WIA × 2.
Earnshaw, James	Pte	2476	H.
Eastwood, Frederick	Sgt	240154	WIA. KIA 23/7/17
Eastwood, Frederick Percival	Pte	242554	Att TMB.
Eastwood, Reginald	Pte	4178	
Eastwood, Will	Pte	1332	WIA. D. 9/7/16
Eaton, Arthur Edmund	Sgt	241542	
Eaton, Charles William	Pte	243072	WIA.
Eaton, Herbert	Pte	242553	
Eatough, Frank Eric	Pte	42914	
Eaves, Frederick	Lt-Col.		DSO. MiD (X2).

Eccles, Herbert	Pte	240639	WIA.
Eccles, Thomas	Pte	241351	Ex 8th Bn. KIA 26/6/18 with 1/4th.
Eccles, Thomas Cherry	Pte	3805	KIA 15/8/16
Eccles, William	Pte	240388	Trans to Lincs.
Edgar, William Thompson	Pte	240369	MM.
Edington, Arthur	Pte	38538	
Edmondson, Fred	Pte	201882	WIA.
Edmondson, George	Pte	240143	WIA. Trans to MFP.
Edmondson, Robert	Cpl	240177	WIA × 2.
Edmondson, Sidney	Pte	35690	
Edmondson, Thomas	Pte	2852	DOW 15/8/16
Edwards, Henry	Pte	241109	WIA.
Egan, Joseph	Pte	13804	Also 7th Bn & RE.
Egerton, James	Pte	1982	WIA. Joined RAF.
Elkin, William	Pte	240910	WIA.
Elkington, Fred	Pte	242555	WIA.
Ellams, Harry	Pte	22752	Ex 11th 7th Bns. WIA.
Elliott, Clarence	Sgt	11212	Commissioned 1918.
Elliott, Fred	Pte	33235	DOW 30/11/17
Ellis, William H.	Pte	4145	WIA. Trans to Lincs.
Ellison, Thomas	L/Sgt	432	WIA.
Elliston, Bertie	Pte	34493	
Ellwood, Albert	Cpl	240565	WIA Comm. to 1/4th & KIA 14/4/18
Ellwood, James	Cpl	243061	Also 8th Bn.
Ellwood, John	Pte	574	Trans to RE. D. 7/2/19
Ellwood, John Mount	Pte	241808	Trans to LC.
Eltoft, Fred	Pte	2104	KIA 16/4/15
Elwood, Frederick Barnes	Lt		RAMC. MC.
Emerson, Joseph Herbert	Pte	42913	
Emmerson, George Alexander	Pte	41023	
Emsley, Frank	Pte	33846	KIA 30/11/17
Emsley, Irving	Pte	242498	Also 9th Bn.
England, M.	Cpl	1563	WIA. Trans to RFC.
England, Robert	Cpl	9453	Also 2nd & 1st Bns.
English, Alfred Ernest Clifford	Pte	2105	DOW 21/5/15
Ensor, Frank William	Pte	240095	WIA × 2. Also 2/5th.
Entwistle, Albert Herbert	Pte	241570	Ex-7th Bn. KIA 3/5/18
Entwistle, Charles	Pte	240056	KIA 31/7/17
Entwistle, John	Pte	240084	WIA × 2. KIA 26/9/17 with 8th Bn.
Estill, John	L/Cpl	1151	WIA. Later served with RFA.
Etchells, Joseph	Pte	3972	KIA 9/8/16 (Unlucky Draft)
Etherington, Albert Ernest	Pte	30666	Ex RAVC.

Evans, Charles Henry	Pte	42915	
Evans, George Edward	Pte	5908	DOW 8/1/17
Evans, Reginald George	Sgt	37792	Also 2/5th.
Evans, Richard	Pte	243047	Ex 7th Bn. DOW 2/10/18
Evans, Thomas Alfred	Pte	24242	Ex 11th & 7th Bns.
Eversden, Ralph Arthur	Pte	26881	Ex 1st Bn.
Ewan, James	A/CSgt	240472	
Fairclough, James Pearson	Pte	2190	KIA 3/5/15
Fairclough, John	Pte	1524	Trans to RE.
Fairclough, Tom	Cpl	240503	WIA.
Faith, Ernest Alfred	Pte	243073	
Fallon, John William	Pte	263023	Ex LNL.
Fant, William Ernest	Pte	242297	Ex 8th Bn. Att MGC.
Farmer, Edwin	Pte	242556	POW.
Farmer, Joseph	L/Cpl	23925	Ex 7th Bn.
Farnworth, William Henry	Pte	3488	Trans to MGC. MM.
Farquharson, Francis David	2Lt		DOW 11/4/18 with Royal Scots
Farr, George	Pte	2221	Trans to KLR.
Farrand, John William	2Lt		
Farrar, Robert Henry	Pte	41024	
Farrell, Matthew	Pte	1440	KIA 14/4/15
Faulkner, Harry	Pte	241509	KIA 20/9/17
Fawcett, John	Pte	34791	WIA.
Fawcett, William	Maj.		
Feasey, Arthur Edward	Pte	242560	
Featherstone, Charles	Pte	12933	WIA X2. DOW 6/7/18
Fell, George Edmund	Pte	25608	Also 1/4th.
Fell, Harold	Pte	241384	WIA. Posted 2/5th.
Fell, John William	Pte	260046	KIA 20/9/17
Fellows, John	Pte	1850	WIA. Trans to RFC.
Felstead, Harold	Pte	202304	POW.
Fenn, Thomas Allen	Pte	242493	KIA 22/5/18
Ferguson, Arthur	Pte	243092	
Ferguson, Harry	Pte	240130	WIA × 2.
Ferguson, James	Pte	38133	
Ferguson, John McEwan	2Lt		WIA.
Ferguson, Joseph Hugh	Pte	242707	KIA 9/4/18
Fern, Ernest	Pte	38537	

Fernley, Levi Garth	Pte	1425	KIA 9/8/16
Fetigan, Henry	Pte	19062	Ex 8th Bn.
Field, Lawrance Stanley	Pte	260026	WIA × 2. KIA 30/6/18 with 8th Bn.
Fielder, James Joseph	Pte	22495	Also 11th & 7th Bns.
Fielding, James Thomas	Pte	22094	DOW 13/4/18
Fielding, Joseph Henry	L/Cpl	241586	Ex-7th Bn. WIA. KIA 23/4/18
Fieldhouse, George	Pte	242557	In rolls as 33212. WIA. Trans to LC.
Finley, John	Pte	243983	
Finniganm, Edward	Pte	21787	Ex 7th Bn.
Firman, George Leonard	Pte	40979	
Firth, Wilfred	Pte	241497	WIA.
Fisher, Edward	Pte	242649	KIA 31/7/17
Fisher, Francis Davis	Pte	27640	Ex 1st Bn. WIA.
Fisher, Frederick	Pte	1458	Trans to LC & R. Fus.
Fisher, Joseph Edgely	2Lt		POW.
Fisher, Walter	Pte	3465	
Fisher, William	Sgt	240792	MM. KIA 30/11/17
Fisher, William	Pte	33595	POW.
Fisher, William George	Pte	200820	WIA. Posted to 2/5th.
Fitton, John	Pte	242999	
Fitzgerald, Thomas Frederick	Pte	243126	WIA.
Fitzsimmons, Thomas	Pte	201277	Ex 1/4th. WIA. Posted 2nd Bn.
Fleming, Albert	Cpl	2054	WIA. Trans to LC.
Fleming, George Frederick	Pte	1508	WIA. DOW 15/8/16
Fleming, John	Pte	243106	Ex 8th Bn.
Fleming, William Howard	Sgt	240025	
Fletcher, Francis Statham	Capt.		RAMC. MC.
Fletcher, John Henry	Pte	51434	
Fletcher, Reginald Rex	Pte	242455	Also 2nd Bn. WIA.
Fletcher, Thomas	Pte	242476	KIA 30/11/17
Fletcher, Walter	Pte	242561	POW.
Fletcher, William	Pte	37171	
Flood, James William	Cpl	27686	Ex 1st Bn.
Flood, John	Pte	4028	KIA 3/8/16
Foden, George	Pte	241157	POW.
Forbes, Walter	Pte	15854	Ex 8th Bn. Posted 1/4th. POW.
Forrest, Joseph	Pte	30737	
Forrest, Richard Clarkson	Pte	4124	KIA 15/8/16
Forrester, Robert H.	Pte	1510	WIA. Trans to ASC.

Forshaw, Henry Philip	Capt.		MC and Bar.
Forsythe, John	Pte	36279	
Fosdike, Robert Henry	Pte	11243	
Foster, Douglas	A/Cpl	263020	Ex RAVC.
Foster, Joshua	Pte	24636	Ex 8th & 7th Bns. WIA. DOW 8/8/18
Fox, George	Pte	240601	Att TMB.
Fox, John	Pte	242242	Trans to 13/KLR.
Fox, Thomas	Pte	2102	WIA. Trans to RDC.
Foxall, John	Pte	242558	
Foxon, Sidney William	2Lt		WIA × 2.
Francis, Frank	Pte	26806	Ex 7th Bn.
Francom, Arthur	Pte	37627	KIA 10/4/18
Fraser (Frazer), John James	Pte	240166	WIA. Posted to 1st Bn.
Frear, Thomas Edward	Sgt	240504	Comm. ASC 1918.
Freeman, William Henry	L/Cpl	240912	WIA.
Fricker, George Henry	Pte	242359	
Frisby, Archibald	Pte	33476	Att TMB.
Frost, Horace	Pte	2191	WIA.
Fuller, Thomas John	Pte	30260	Ex RE & 7th Bn. POW.
Fullerton, Wilfred	Pte	33686	POW.
Funk, Henry Alexander	Pte	240569	WIA.
Gabbatt, Henry	Pte	23837	WIA. KIA 30/11/17 with MGC.
Gallagher, James E.	Pte	763	WIA. Trans to MGC & RE.
Gallagher, Joseph	Pte	22970	Ex 11th & 8th Bns. KIA 6/8/18
Gallagher, Robert	Pte	201532	WIA.
Galloway, Charles H.	Pte	2119	Trans to Middx Regt.
Gardiner, John Henry	Maj.		
Gardner, Arthur	Pte	240602	
Gardner, Edward	L/Cpl	1232	WIA.
Gardner, Francis Henry	Pte	240006	WIA.
Gardner, Henry	L/Cpl	240176	WIA. KIA 9/10/17
Gardner, James	Pte	241012	WIA.
Gardner, James	Pte	2241	WIA × 3. Trans to Tank Corps.
Gardner, James	Pte	240603	
Gardner, John	L/Cpl	52013	WIA.
Gardner, John	L/Cpl	240381	
Gardner, John Hinde	Sgt	454	KIA 27/4/15
Gardner, John Walker	Lt		MiD. WIA.
Gardner, John William	Pte	3921	WIA. DOW 18/12/16
Gardner, Richard	Pte	241600	Also 1/4th.

Gardner, Robert	2Lt		KIA 5/5/15
Gardner, Robert L.	Rev		Chaplain.
Gardner, Thomas Briscoe	Pte	241277	WIA × 2. Also 7th Bn.
Gardner, William	Pte	240439	WIA. Posted 1/4th & att to OBLI.
Gardner, William	Pte	240479	WIA. Trans to RE.
Garnett, John Hudson	Pte	240989	KIA 16/6/17
Garside, Joseph	Pte	201886	KIA 31/7/17
Garstang, Rowland	Pte	1551	WIA.
Garth, Matthew	Pte	240836	WIA Trans to LC.
Garth, William Gifford	Cpl	241577	KIA 10/4/18
Gartside, Albert Henry	Pte	242562	WIA.
Gaskell, Arthur	Pte	37230	
Gaskell, John	Pte	15399	Ex 8th Bn.
Gater, Enoch	WO2	36171	Ex Borders. Comm. KORL 1918.
Gathercole, William John	Cpl	242660	WIA.
Gaulter, Cuthbert Vivian	Lt		Trans to RFC.
Gay, Alfred Edward	Pte	241193	WIA. Comm. RFC 1916.
Gaylord, Arthur Reginald	Pte	242566	Att TMB.
Geary, Thomas	Pte	240409	
Geddes, Moses	Pte	240271	WIA × 2.
Gee, Harold	Pte	37219	
Gent, Herbert	Pte	242989	Also 1/4th.
George, William	Lt		RAMC.
Geraghty, John	Sgt	9264	Ex MFP.
Gerrard, Alfred Henry	L/Cpl	3836	KIA 22/9/16
Gerrard, Edward	Pte	374702	Ex 8th Bn.
Gething, Percy	Pte	241252	WIA.
Gething, Walter	Pte	241498	
Gheerbrant, William	Pte	30216	Ex Sussex & 7th Bn. WIA × 2.
Ghorst, Harry	Pte	2479	DOW 2/6/15
Ghorst, John	Pte	240689	WIA.
Gibbs, Archibald	Pte	30697	Ex Sussex. WIA × 2. Trans to RAVC. POW.
Gibson, David	2Lt		Trans to OBLI. WIA.
Gibson, Lawrence	Pte	33100	WIA. Trans to LNL.
Gibson, William	Pte	2577	WIA. DCM.
Gilchrist, John James	2Lt		WIA. MiD. Comm. 1915.
Giles, William	Pte	1878	Trans to LC.
Gill, George H.	Pte	2122	WIA. Trans to RFC & LC.
Gill, Harry	CQMS	423	

Gill, Harry	Pte	38117	
Gill, James Connor	Pte	240511	WIA. Also 2/5th.
Gill, Thomas Foster	Sgt	1778	WIA. Trans to LC.
Gill, William	Pte		H.
Gillam, Percy Albert	Pte	41025	
Gilleran, Patrick Joseph	Pte	19699	Ex 7th Bn.
Gillespie, Isedore	Lt		Trans MGC.
Gillon, Benjamin J.	Sgt	240142	WIA.
Gilmore, Frederick	Pte	22904	Ex 7th Bn. WIA. POW
Glaister, William Alexander	Pte	241422	KIA 2/5/18
Glaskie, Eli	Pte	242334	
Gledhill, James	Pte	243100	Ex 8th Bn. POW.
Gleeson, Owen	Pte	34825	KIA 3/5/18
Glover, Charles	Pte	240323	DOW 11/2/17
Glover, Claude	Pte	37929	Ex 1st Bn & also 2/5th.
Glover, Fred	Pte	1297	KIA 27/4/15
Glover, Walter	Pte	240180	WIA.
Glynn, J.	Pte	1491	
Godbert, Robert	Pte	33930	
Godley, Frank William	Pte	11010	Ex 7th Bn.
Golding, Charles Victor	Pte	33719	Posted 1/4th. WIA × 2.
Golding, George	Pte	26885	Ex 1st Bn.
Goldrick, Edward	Pte	243048	Ex 1st & 8th Bns. MM.
Good, William Knight	2Lt		WIA. KIA 27/2/18 with 5/R. Scots.
Goodall, Edward	Cpl	240469	WIA-8/16-LG8728.
Goodall, Holmes	Cpl	2481	Trans to MGC. MM.
Goode, William	L/Cpl	26743	Ex 7th Bn.
Goodman, Arthur	Pte	2579	WIA.
Goodman, Joseph	2Lt		LNL. KIA 11/4/17
Goodwin, Harry	Pte	201581	WIA. Posted 1/4th.
Goodwin, James	Pte	34750	POW.
Goodwin, John Edward	Pte	240506	WIA. Also 2/5th.
Goodwin, Samuel Thomas	Pte	30726	Ex ASC.
Gordon, Albert	Pte	1817	H. D. 29/8/14
Gordon, Alfred	Pte	21766	Ex 11th & 8th Bns.
Gordon, William Reddy	Pte	37241	
Gornall, Joseph	Pte	240604	WIA X2.
Gorst, Frank	Pte	240917	
Gorst, Henry	Sgt	240918	
Gorst, Robert	Pte	240794	KIA 2/6/18 with 8th Bn.

Gorst, Vernal	Pte	241598	WIA.
Gorton, William Henry	Sgt	265728	Ex E. Lancs.
Goth, Ezekiel	Pte	2121	WIA. Trans to MFP.
Gough, Sydney	Pte	241184	ex 7th Bn.
Goulding, Thomas	Pte	240045	Trans to S. Lancs.
Gover, Albert Edward	Pte	30699	KIA 14/4/18
Gowan, Alexander	Pte	30688	Ex RAVC. Att 166 TMB.
Gradwell, Anthony	Pte	300	DOW 27/4/15
Gradwell, Harold	L/Cpl	240854	WIA. Posted 1/4th.
Grady, John	L/Cpl	299	
Graham, Ernest	A/Cpl	240855	WIA × 2.
Graham, Joseph	Cpl	18591	Ex 7th Bn.
Graham, Matthew	Pte	260040	KIA 31/7/17
Grainger, Enoch Thomas	Pte	34752	Ex 1st Bn.
Graley, John	Pte	12456	Ex 6th & 8th Bns. Also 2/5th.
Gray, Alexander	Sgt	2867	MM. Comm. Northumberland Fus.
Gray, John James	Pte	28198	Carter. Ex 7th Bn. WIA.
Gray, Maurice	Pte	28197	Ex 7th Bn-15/8/17.
Gray, William	Pte	11867	Also 7th, 11th & 8th Bns.
Gray, William	Pte	34676	
Grayson, George Arthur	A/WO2	51119	WIA.
Greaves, Frank	Pte	2667	Trans to Tank Corps.
Greaves, Harry	Pte	241466	D. 5/12/18
Greaves, John	Sgt	1083	MM. CdG. DOW 10/8/18 with MGC.
Greaves, William Thomas	Pte	18598	Also 6th Bn. WIA.
Green, Arthur	Pte	24196	Ex 7th Bn. KIA 9/5/18
Green, James	Pte	34665	WIA.
Green, John	Pte	240460	
Green, John William	Sgt	142	
Green, Richard	Pte	22452	Ex 11th. Also 2/5th.
Green, Rowland	Pte	40980	
Green, William	Cpl	1254	KIA 10/9/16
Greenbank, Harry	Pte	241471	Ex 8th Bn. MM KIA 25/10/18 1st Bn.
Greenbank, Thomas	Pte	42900	
Greenhalgh, Benjamin	Pte	27695	Ex 1st Bn. Also 1/4th.
Greening, Fred	Sgt	13585	Ex 9th & 7th Bns.
Greenwood, Ernest	A/WO1	240016	
Greenwood, George William	Pte	33594	
Greenwood, John Thackeray	Pte	16346	Also 8th Bn.
Greenwood, Mark Utley (Otley)	Pte	2670	KIA 2/12/15

Greenwood, Percy Stobart	Sgt	240920	WIA. Comm. 1918.
Greenwood, Thomas	Pte	32005	Ex 1st Bn. Also 2/5th.
Greenwood, Walter	Pte	260028	POW.
Gregg, Charles Edward	2Lt		KIA 15/6/17
Gregg, George	Pte	1979	
Gregg, Henry	Pte	37167	
Gregg, Joseph	Pte	240799	DOW 19/7/17 with 2/5th.
Gregg, William Henry	Pte	240023	
Gregory, Charles	Pte	3779	DOW 11/8/16
Gregory, Harold	L/Cpl	27247	Ex Lincs, 7th, 1st & 1/4th Bns. WIA.
Gregory, Neil	L/Cpl	1019	KIA 1/8/16
Gregory, Norman Hall	2Lt		WIA.
Gregory, Thomas	Pte	2293	
Gregory, Thomas	Pte	28169	Also 7th & 8th Bns.
Gregory, William Thomas	Pte	240444	
Gregson, Frederick	Pte	34735	Ex 11th & 8th Bns.
Gregson, Harry	2Lt		WIA.
Gregson, Thomas	Pte	241253	WIA.
Gribbin, John Henry	Pte	24131	Ex 7th Bn.
Grice, Harry	Pte	1675	KIA 27/4/15
Griffin, Andrew	Pte	260050	WIA. Trans to RDC.
Griffiths, Alfred	Pte	2869	KIA 2/10/15
Griffiths, John	Pte	18794	Ex 1st & 11th Bns.
Grimsey, Frederick Raymond	Pte	242565	KIA 9/3/18
Grimshaw, George	Pte	3840	
Grimshaw, Harry	Pte	242627	KIA 17/6/17
Grindrod, Edward	WO2	240117	MM. MSM.
Grisdale, James Cole	L/Cpl	201853	KIA 9/4/18
Grove, William	Pte	1016	WIA.
Groves, Albert	Sgt	241585	Also 1/4th.
Groves, James	Pte	240922	Accid. Wounded, WIA. Trans to LC.
Groves, John William	Pte	240132	
Grundy, Herbert Dyson	Pte	4508	KIA 8/9/16 (Unlucky Draft)
Grundy, Richard	Pte	242416	
Gudgeon, George	L/Cpl	1927	WIA. Trans to R Warks.
Gudgeon, John	L/Cpl	240066	WIA. Posted to 2/5th. Trans to LNL.
Gudgeon, Robert	Pte	1361	WIA × 2. Trans to Lincs.

Gudgeon, Thomas	Pte	27451	Also 7th & 1/4th Bns.
Gudgeon, William	L/Cpl	240416	WIA. Trans to RE.
Guest, Edwin David	Pte	41685	
Guile, Arthur	Pte	30702	Ex RAVC. WIA.
Gullen, Frank K. W.	Pte	240078	
Gunn, Albert Alexander	Capt.		RAMC.
Guy, Joseph William	Cpl	241076	WIA.
Guy, Robert Hutchinson	Pte	27452	Ex 7th Bn. Also 2/5th.
Guy, William	Pte	243109	Ex 8th Bn. WIA.
Hacking, Samuel James	L/Cpl	242677	Ex 8th Bn. WIA. KIA 19/6/17
Haddow, Joseph	Pte	201852	WIA.
Haddow, Myles	Pte	3305	
Haddow, William	Pte	242976	WIA X2.
Hadfield, George William	Pte	243018	
Hadwin, Arthur	Pte	240923	
Haffenden, Frank Gordon	Pte	24281	Ex 7th & 1/4th Bns. WIA.
Haffey, Hugh	Pte	240215	Posted to. 2/5th. WIA.
Hagley, Tom	Pte	242568	WIA. SWB.
Hague, Joseph Eugene	Pte	3915	DOW 4/8/16
Haigh, F. A.	CQMS	240057	H
Hailwood, Herbert	Pte	26760	Ex 7th Bn.
Hale, James	Pte	3390	KIA 190/7/18
Halgarth, George	L/Cpl	27248	Ex Lincs. MM.
Hall, Burgoyne	Pte	2192	WIA.
Hall, Ernest Edward	Pte	28203	Ex 7th & 1/4th.
Hall, Fred	Pte	242473	KIA 9/4/18
Hall, Gilbert	Pte	2193	WIA.
Hall, Harold	Pte	1469	Trans to MGC.
Hall, Harry	L/Cpl	240102	KIA 12/5/17 with 8th Bn.
Hall, Henry Morton	Pte	30025	KIA 11/4/18
Hall, James	Pte		D. 5/8/14
Hall, James	Pte	240507	WIA × 3240087. MM.
Hall, James	Pte	24632	Ex 7th Bn. MM.
Hall, John	Pte	3033	H.
Hall, John Newman	Pte	240210	WIA × 2. Trans to LC.
Hall, Joseph William	Sgt	757	WIA. Trans to LC.
Hall, Mark	Pte	40981	
Hall, Robert	Cpl	242663	Ex 1st & 6th Bns.

Hall, Thomas	Pte	240512	
Hall, William Croft	Pte	240089	WIA.
Hall, R.	2Lt		
Hallahan, John	Pte	240343	
Hallam, Richard Cecil	2Lt		
Halleron, James	Pte	19693	Ex 7th Bn.
Halliwell, Jack	Pte	1373	KIA 27/4/15
Hallowes, Abraham	Cpl	18935	Ex 7th Bn.
Halstead, Harry	Pte	12938	Ex 7th Bn.
Halton, Albert	Pte	241475	WIA. Posted 1st Bn & awarded VC.
Halton, Ernest	Pte	1416	H. D. 1/10/14
Hamblett, Wilfred	Pte	243050	KIA 30/11/17
Hambly, Nicholas	Pte	242582	
Hamer, Frederick	Pte	266145	
Hames, Frederick	Cpl	240441	WIA. Trans to RE.
Hamilton, John	Pte	27647	Also 1st Bn.
Hamilton, Lewis	Pte	240233	WIA. KIA 26/10/17 with 2/5th.
Hamilton, Norman Butler	A/Capt.		KIA 24/7/18
Hamilton, Robert Kirkpatrick	2Lt		
Hampson, Henry	Pte	27587	Ex 7th Bn.
Hampson, James Hiram	Pte	5057	KIA 18/9/16
Hand, Henry	Pte	37754	
Hannam, Edmund Talbot	Pte	2126	WIA. Trans to RE. Later comm.
Hannen, James	Sgt	265249	
Hannon, James	Pte	241283	WIA X2. Trans to LC.
Happold, Frederick Crossfield	Pte		H. Comm. in LNL. DSO.
Harbridge, Edward James	Cpl	260006	Att TMB. MM.
Hardie, William Edwin	Pte	241523	
Harding, Joseph	Pte	243062	Also 1st Bn.
Harding, William George	Pte	260005	Also Lincs and East Surrey. WIA.
Hardy, Arthur Bernard	Lt		Att from Lincs.
Hardy, James Edward	2Lt	1432	WIA × 2. Comm- MGC 1917-back to 1/5th.
Hardy, William	Pte	240153	WIA.
Hare, Robert	Pte	22645	Ex 11th & 8th Bns. WIA.
Hargraves, John	Pte	17055	Also 1st & 8th Bns.
Hargreaves, Anthony Newill	Capt.		
Hargreaves, Frederick	C/Sgt	240571	WIA.
Hargreaves, Harry	Pte	3559	WIA.

Hargreaves, John William	Pte	240324	WIA.
Hargreaves, Richard	Pte	1930	WIA. Trans to MGC.
Hargreaves, Thomas	Pte	240745	WIA.
Hargreaves, Thomas William	Pte	37741	KIA 14/4/18
Harland, John Ernest	Pte	242571	
Harley, Herbert	Pte	3954	KIA 14/7/16
Harley, William	Pte	241396	DOW 24/12/17
Harling, Richard	Pte	1795	Trans to LC.
Harlow, Ernest Albert	Pte	41683	WIA.
Harlowe, Ernest	L/Cpl	2198	KIA 27/5/15
Harman, George	Pte	32972	Ex 11th & 8th Bns. WIA.
Harney, John	Pte	240423	WIA. DOW 27/10/17 with 2/5th.
Harper, James Greenhalgh	Pte	201906	
Harper, John Hirst	L/Cpl	999	KIA 13/4/15
Harries, Thomas	Pte	26077	Ex 7th Bn.
Harrington, William Arthur	Pte	35988	KIA 9/4/18
Harriott, Henry Richard	Sgt	242661	WIA.
Harris, Daniel	Sgt	240087	MM. WIA. Comm. LNL att. Tanks.
Harris, Fred	Cpl	242472	
Harris, George Joseph	Pte	4380	Ex 7th Bn.
Harris, Henry	Pte	240692	DOW 6/8/18
Harris, William Frederick	L/Cpl	242580	KIA 31/7/17
Harrison, Albert Edward	Pte	2875	WIA.
Harrison, Ernest	Pte	33717	POW.
Harrison, Harry	A/Cpl	242469	Also 1st Bn.
Harrison, Herbert Michael	Pte	242488	Also 1/4th.
Harrison, John	Pte	3020	WIA. Trans to LC.
Harrison, Leonard Chase	A/CQMS	240002	KIA 23/7/17
Harrison, Thomas	Pte	241041	Also LC.
Harrison, Walter	2Lt	2956	WIA. Comm. 1917. POW.
Harrison, William Schollick	2Lt	200135	Ex SNCO with 1/4th. MiD.
Harrison, William Thomas	Sgt	240510	WIA × 2.
Harriss, William	Capt.		WIA × 2. MC.
Harrold, William	2Lt		
Hart, Arthur George	2Lt		
Hart, Henry Royston	Capt.		WIA × 3. MC.
Hartell, George Arthur	Cpl	241119	Att MGC and KLR. MiD.
Hartley, Albert Edgar	Pte	241533	WIA.

Hartley, Fred	L/Cpl	243113	MM. KIA 30/11/17
Hartley, James	Cpl	22296	Ex 11th Bn.
Hartley, Joseph Lowther	C/Sgt	2133	Trans to MGC.
Hartley, Thomas Edward	L/Cpl	1520	D. 11/3/15
Harvey, Joseph	Pte	240091	WIA. SWB.
Harvey, Richard	Pte	201909	WIA. Trans to RAF.
Harwood, Frank	Pte	263002	Ex 1/4th.
Harwood, Harry	Cpl	32600	Ex 7th Bn. WIA. POW.
Harwood, Thomas	Pte	243040	POW.
Haselden, Tom	Pte	242310	KIA 17/6/18 with 1st Bn.
Haslam, Ralph	L/Cpl	1008	WIA × 2.
Haslam, Reuben Westgarth	Pte	242634	
Haslam, Thurston	Sgt	240448	WIA.
Hatton, George	Pte	35072	Ex KLR.
Hawken, Lewis John	Pte	28205	Ex 7th Bn.
Hawkes, Arthur	Pte	13874	Ex 9th Bn.
Hawley, Frank	Pte	242575	Att TMB. Also 7th & 1/4th Bns.
Haworth, Enoch	Pte	19781	Also 11th & 2/5th Bns.
Hay, James Duncan	2Lt		DOW 15/12/17
Haycock, Carl Victor	Pte	241558	Also 8th Bn. WIA.
Hayes, Geoffrey	Pte	1330	KIA 15/3/15
Hayes, Thomas	Pte	240240	
Hayhurst, Thomas	Pte	242505	WIA × 2. Trans to LC.
Hayton, Edgar	Pte	2877	WIA.
Hayward, Francis Thomas	Pte	242592	POW.
Haywood, George	WO2	240333	MiD (x2). Comm. KLR.
Haywood, Gerald	2Lt		WIA.
Haywood, Harold	Pte		H.
Hazel, William	Pte	12602	Also 7th & 8th Bns.
Hazell, George Edward	Pte	3573	Also 7th Bn. MM
Hea, Thomas Marshall	Cpl	2022	Trans to LC.
Heafield, Francis Thomas	Pte	2582	Trans to MFP.
Healey, Alfred Henry	Pte	242629	
Heap, Benjamin	Pte	202607	
Heath, Francis William	Maj.		London Regt.
Heathcote, Arthur	L/Cpl	14071	Ex 7th Bn.
Heaton, John	Lt		Att from DLOY.

Heaton, Samuel	Pte	38401	Ex LF.
Heaton, Sydney	WO2	240516	MM.
Heaven, William John	Pte	242579	
Hedges, Edward Robert	L/Cpl	26811	Ex 7th Bn. MM. D. 29/10/17
Heginbottom, John	Pte	243027	
Hellens, Sidney	Pte	35989	KIA 3/5/18
Helling, Robert	Pte	35692	
Helm, George	Pte	240243	WIA.
Helm, Thomas	Pte	2131	WIA.
Helme, Edward Albert	Pte	240572	WIA. POW.
Helme, James	Pte	240407	WIA.
Helsby, Joseph Greenwood	A/Cpl	33425	
Henderson, James Graeme	2Lt		DOW 3/12/17
Henderson, John	Pte	241645	WIA.
Henderson, John	2Lt		WIA.
Henderson, Thomas	Pte	241263	
Hendler, Frederick	Pte	40984	
Hepworth, Tom Denton	Cpl	240976	KIA 31/7/17
Herd, Edward	Pte	240694	WIA. Posted 8th Bn.
Herridge, William Charles	A/WO1	240463	MSM.
Hesketh, Joseph	Sgt	1972	Trans to MGC.
Hesketh, Reginald Thomas	Pte	240994	WIA. Comm. 1917.
Hesketh, Thomas	Pte	1978	KIA 17/4/15
Hesketh, William	A/Cpl	240083	KIA 28/9/18 with 2/5th.
Hesketh, William	Capt.		DLOY. To Bn-30/04/18.
Hesmondhalgh, Ernest	Pte	38534	
Hetherington, Robert	Cpl	240125	WIA.
Hewett, George	Pte	35606	
Hewitson, Charles	Pte	240856	WIA. KIA 26/9/17 with 8th Bn.
Hewitt, Edmund	Pte	242635	KIA 9/3/17
Hewitt, Edward Henry	Pte	40982	
Hewitt, Fred	Sgt	30864	Ex KLR. DCM with 15 LNL.
Hewitt, John	Pte	23695	Ex 7th Bn.
Hewitt, Joseph	Pte	243049	
Hewitt, Laurence	Pte	240858	WIA.
Heys, Charles	Cpl	240051	WIA. Trans to RE.
Heywood, James Sargison	Pte	1318	H.

Hibbert, Arthur	Pte	2431	WIA. Also 1st & 8th Bns.
Higgins, Thomas	Pte	240040	WIA. Also 8th Bn.
Higginson, George Albert	Cpl	21619	Also 1/4th.
Higginson, Henry	Pte	3700	KIA 3/8/16
Higginson, James Edmund	Pte	30051	Ex 8th Bn.
Higginson, Robert	2Lt		KIA 15/8/16
Higginson, Samuel	Pte	240193	KIA 8/5/15
Higham, John	Pte	241236	
Hill, Albert	Pte	242573	KIA 9/3/17
Hill, Enoch	Pte	24452	Ex 7th. KIA 9/6/18
Hill, Frederick	Pte	242570	Trans to KLR.
Hill, Herbert	Pte	265772	WIA.
Hill, John Smith	Pte	1167	WIA.
Hill, Joseph Henry	Cpl	242617	Ex 1st & 8th Bns.
Hill, Norman Gray	Lt		DLOY. MC & bar. WIA.
Hill, Thomas	Pte	1617	KIA 9/8/16
Hill, Wallace Arthur	Pte	242583	
Hill, William	Pte	15111	Ex 7th Bn.
Hill, William	Pte	242586	
Hill, William Henry	Pte	27484	Ex 8th & 7th Bns.
Hillman, George	Pte	2380	
Hillsley, George	Cpl	260011	KIA 31/7/17
Hilton, John	Pte	201880	WIA. KIA 30/11/17
Hinchcliffe, Charles William	Pte	242578	
Hinde, John	Pte	240330	A Coy. WIA-23/4/15. Posted 8th Bn.
Hindle, Ernest	Pte	201007	
Hindle, James (Albert James)	Pte	3902	H
Hindle, John James	Pte	242475	
Hindle, Ralph	Pte	32535	Ex 1st Bn. Re-joins 1st Bn. WIA.
Hine, George Stanley	L/Cpl	3886	DOW 9/8/16
Hine, John	Pte	241616	WIA.
Hine, Thomas Herdson	Pte	2034	KIA 27/4/15
Hingley, Thomas	L/Sgt	33950	WIA. Posted 1/4th.
Hinton, Charles Allen	2Lt		
Hirst, George	Pte	241393	DOW 28/6/18 with 1st Bn.
Hitchen, Thomas	Pte	20839	WIA.
Hoare, Edward Godfrey	Lt-Col.		DSO. MiD.
Hockey, Owen	Cpl	241303	WIA.

Hodge, Alfred	Pte	240245	
Hodgkinson, Albert	Capt.		MiD (× 3)
Hodgkinson, Ernest	Pte	266106	
Hodgkinson, John	Pte	1959	WIA. Trans to Cheshires.
Hodgson, Albert	Pte	2882	To 1/5th-4/6/15. Trans to ASC.
Hodgson, Charles Walter	Pte	1228	DOW 2/6/15
Hodgson, Harold	Pte	3031	WIA. Trans to APC.
Hodgson, Harold	Pte	240249	
Hodgson, Harry	Pte	27530	Ex 8th Bn. WIA. KIA 10/4/18
Hodgson, Herbert	Pte	242584	
Hodgson, James	Pte	201859	WIA.
Hodgson, John	Pte	240035	WIA. KIA 26/10/17 with 2/5th.
Hodgson, John	Pte	1162	WIA.
Hodgson, John Robert	Pte	240241	WIA.
Hodgson, Lawrence Gainford	Pte	37196	
Hodgson, Maurice	Cpl	2883	KIA 15/8/16
Hodgson, Robert	Pte	32488	Ex 1/4th. WIA.
Hodgson, Stanley Richard	Pte	242591	
Hodgson, Thomas	A/Cpl	240513	MM. WIA.
Hodgson, William	Pte	1588	WIA.
Hodgson, William	Pte	242590	
Hodgson, William	Pte	242632	
Hodson, Albert	Pte	949	
Hodson, Joseph Merrick	Pte	263005	DOW 13/6/17
Hogarth, William	L/Cpl	1290	WIA. Trans to LC.
Hoggarth, Edward	Pte	2118	KIA 3/5/15
Hoggarth, John	Pte	1093	WIA × 2. Trans to R. Warks.
Hoggarth, John	Pte	202233	Ex 7th Bn.
Holden, George	Pte	240412	WIA × 2. Posted 1st Bn.
Holden, Harry	Pte	242279	
Holden, Harry	Pte	242969	
Holden, James	Cpl	2039	WIA × 2. Trans to KLR. POW.
Holden, Sam Grimshaw	Pte	201925	DOW 21/10/17
Holden, Thomas	Pte	240547	
Holding, Frank	Pte	2117	KIA 17/4/15
Holding, Richard	Pte	24601	Ex 8th Bn. WIA. KIA 30/11/17
Holgate, Ingham	Pte	29068	
Holland, George Thomas	Pte	18687	Ex 6th & 7th Bns.

Holland, John W.	Pte	265798	Trans to LC.
Holland, Thomas C.	Pte	3050	WIA. Trans to LC.
Holland, William	Pte	240747	
Holliday, Thomas	Pte	242574	Also RFA. WIA.
Hollinghurst, William	Pte	2758	WIA × 2. To 2/5th. Trans to Lincs.
Hollingshead, Thomas	Pte	3822	WIA. Trans to LC.
Hollingworth, Bertie	Pte	34749	WIA X2. DOW 11/4/18
Hollingworth, James Leslie	2Lt		
Hollingworth, L.	Cpl	242990	
Hollingworth, Sidney	Pte	25483	Ex 7th Bn.
Hollos, Fred	Pte	35093	Ex MCR.
Holloway, Edgar Augustus	Pte	40983	
Holloway, Louis William Victor	Pte	240573	WIA.
Holme, Harry	Pte	27683	Ex 1st Bn.
Holmes, Charles	Pte	501	WIA. Trans to LC.
Holmes, Charles Nicholas	Pte	240929	WIA.
Holmes, Harold	L/Sgt	753	WIA.
Holmes, Henry	Pte	242633	
Holmes, J.	Pte	2029	
Holmes, James	Pte	240466	WIA. Trans to LC.
Holmes, John	Cpl	240517	
Holmes, John Scott	2Lt		Att from DLOY.
Holmes, Richard	L/Cpl	242966	KIA 30/11/17
Holmes, Richard	Sgt	240077	WIA. Posted 8th Bn.
Holmes, Robert	2Lt		
Holmes, Rowland	Pte	242452	
Holmes, Thomas	Pte	240254	WIA.
Holroyd, Norman	L/Cpl	25742	Also 1st Bn.
Holt, Albert	Sgt	240509	MSM.
Holt, William	Pte	242631	KIA 30/11/17
Holt, William Eccles	Sgt	1963	KIA 10/9/16
Holton, Harry Neville	Pte	37253	
Holyoak, Sidney	Pte	242577	Also 8th Bn.
Honey, George Ronald	2Lt		MC. DOW 25/9/18 with 9th Bn.
Honey, William James	2Lt		
Hook, Robert	Pte	266445	
Hoole, Herbert	Pte	4357	KIA 8/9/16 (Unlucky Draft)
Hooley, James	Pte	22462	Ex 11th & 1st Bns.

Hooley, John	Sgt	219	WIA. Trans to LC.
Hooper, Stanley	Cpl	13261	Also 6th Bn.
Hooper, William John	Pte	242576	
Hopkins, Charles Henry	Pte	36573	
Hopkinson, William	Pte	27652	Also 1st & 6th Bns.
Hopson, George	Pte	240445	
Hopwood, James	Sgt	240250	WIA. Comm. LNL 1917.
Hopwood, Joe	Cpl	241505	WIA. Posted 1st Bn.
Horan, John	Pte	35808	
Horgan, Thomas	Pte	816	
Hornbuckle, James	Pte	4570	DOW 4/8/16 (Unlucky Draft)
Hornby, George	Cpl	240452	KIA 1/8/17
Hornby, John William	Pte	1390	KIA 9/8/16
Hornby, Richard	Pte	240305	WIA.
Hornby, Robert	Pte	1192	
Hornby, William	Pte	33279	WIA.
Horne, Frederick Augustus	Pte	30661	
Horridge, Frank	Pte	24019	Ex 2nd Bn. Also 1/4th.
Horrocks, George Henry	Pte	37802	Also 2/5th.
Horrocks, Samuel	Pte	243125	Ex 8th Bn. WIA × 3. KIA 17/6/17
Hothersall, Richard	Pte	1255	DOW 17/4/15
Hough, Harry	Pte	21103	Ex 1st Bn & 7th Bns. WIA × 2.
Hough, John	Pte	241021	DOW 11/4/17
Houghton, Thomas	Pte	19977	Ex 7th Bn. POW.
Houghton, Thomas	Pte	241822	WIA.
Houghton, William	Cpl	14051	Ex 7th Bn.
Houldsworth, Philip	Pte	34833	
Houseago, Albert George Richd.	Pte	242587	KIA 30/11/17
Houseman, Harry	Pte	1482	H.
Howard, Edward Charles	Pte	28495	Ex 11th Bn.
Howard, George Freke	Pte	28202	Ex 7th Bn. KIA 11/4/18
Howard, John William	Pte	241661	WIA.
Howard, Thomas	Pte	24294	WIA × 2. Posted 2/5th.
Howard, Walter	Pte	2407	Also 1st, 2nd & 8th Bns.
Howard, William	Pte	242267	KIA with 8th Bn 16/8/16
Howarth, James	Pte	3905	Also 7th Bn.
Howarth, John	Pte	242486	
Howe, Charles George	Pte	23182	KIA 14/4/18

Howe, Sydney	Cpl	30667	Ex RAVC.
Howitt, Joseph Gibson	L/Cpl	27415	Ex LF & 7th Bn.
Howse, William	Pte	3701	
Howson, Francis William	2Lt		
Howson, John Robert	Pte	2194	DOW 22/5/15
Howson, Robert	L/Sgt	240158	WIA. Also 2/5th.
Hoyle, William Edwards	Pte	240326	
Huartson, John	Pte	1741	H. D. 30/9/14
Huartson, Richard	Pte	2197	KIA 23/4/15
Huartson, Thomas	Sgt	240365	WIA × 3. DCM.
Hubbard, Reginald	Pte	1484	Trans to RFC.
Huck, William	Pte	24164	Ex 1st & 7th Bns.
Huddleston, Bertie	Pte	30151	Ex 8th Bn. WIA. POW.
Hudson, James	Pte	242567	Trans to LC.
Hudson, John	Pte	28034	Also 1/4th.
Hudson, John William	Pte	242628	
Huggon, Frederick Murdock	Pte	3203	Trans to MGC.
Huggonson, William	Pte	1343	WIA.
Hughes, Frederick	Pte	25932	Ex 9th Bn.
Hughes, Matthew	Sgt	240699	WIA × 2. MM.
Hughes, Robinson	L/Cpl	241508	WIA X2.
Hughes, Sidney Leonard	Pte	242572	DOW 12/4/17
Hughes, William James	Pte	240013	WIA. Trans to RE.
Hull, Harry	Pte	241007	WIA × 2. To 8th Bn. Trans to RE.
Hull, James Henry	Cpl	14252	Ex 7th Bn.
Hull, Richard	Pte	240645	
Hull, Walter	Sgt	240364	WIA.
Hulmston, Thomas Arthur	Pte	29071	
Humpage, Albert	Pte	69	Trans to LC.
Humpage, James	Pte	241499	Also 8th Bn. WIA.
Humphreys, John Roland	Lt		WIA.
Humphries, Edward Victor	Pte	242588	DOW 3/8/17
Hunt, Frank	Pte	28563	Also 11th Bn & LC.
Hunt, John	Pte	242630	
Hunt, John Edward	Pte	27981	Also 1st & 1/4th Bns.
Hunt, Oliver Grahame	Capt.		POW.
Hunter, Herbert	Sgt	240548	Comm. & KIA 26/4/18 with 1/4th.
Hunter, Walter Raymond	Pte	241503	MM.

Hunter, William Ernest	Pte	30671	Ex RAVC.
Huntington, Frank Derwent	2Lt		WIA.
Huntington, William	L/Cpl	2199	Comm. in 1/4th 1915.
Huntriss, William	Pte	240351	MM MiD
Husband, Charles Lawrence	2Lt		
Husband, Peter	Pte	1496	DOW 31/5/15
Hutchinson, T. W.	Pte	1517	H.
Hutton, George Hayward	Pte	2763	WIA.
Huyton, Henry	Pte	2384	KIA 23/4/15
Hyde, Roland	L/Sgt	241810	MSM.
I'Anson, John	Pte	431	WIA. Re-enlisted LC.
Iddeson, Alfred	Pte	33250	Ex 7th Bn.
Iddon, Harold	Cpl	240802	WIA.
Igoe, William	Pte	201899	
Ilott, Leslie	L/Cpl	27938	Ex 1st Bn.
Ingham, James	Sgt	27405	Ex LF & 7th Bn.
Ingham, Ronald	Pte	242421	
Ingleby, George	Pte	242637	WIA.
Iniff, Frank	Cpl	240221	WIA × 2.
Inman, Dick	Pte	2147	H.
Inman, Joseph Edward	Pte	2148	H.
Ireland, John William	L/Cpl	35796	KIA 27/9/18 with 8th Bn.
Irving, Henry	WO2	1221	KIA 8/5/15
Irving, John	Pte	241455	KIA 6/2/17
Irving, John	Pte	241467	
Irving, Richard	2Lt		WIA. KIA 2/8/16
Isherwood, John William	L/Cpl	14333	Ex 7th Bn.
Ismay, John Thomas	Pte	1012	DOW 30 /3/15
Iveson, Richard	Pte	3846	
Jackman, Percy	Pte	26052	Ex 1st Bn.
Jackson, Alfred Oliver	L/Cpl	241255	DOW 12/10/18
Jackson, Andrew	Pte	2959	WIA. Comm. 1916.
Jackson, Eli	Pte	242466	
Jackson, Ernest	Pte	4482	KIA 15/8/16 (Unlucky Draft)
Jackson, Ernest Jonathan	Pte	240610	DOW 12/4/17
Jackson, Frank	Cpl	1280	DOW 10/5/15
Jackson, George	Pte	2136	H.
Jackson, Henry	Pte	19129	

Jackson, Henry	Pte	30741	Also Lincs Regt & 2nd Bn.
Jackson, James Newby	Pte	267	KIA 5/5/15
Jackson, John	Pte	242696	KIA 30/11/17
Jackson, John	Pte	242598	
Jackson, John William	Pte	241627	D. 3/9/17
Jackson, Joseph	Pte	37237	
Jackson, Richard Newby	Sgt	240151	WIA. MM. MiD.
Jackson, Robert	Pte	241548	WIA.
Jackson, Robert	Pte	1525	Trans to Tanks Corps.
Jackson, Solomon	Pte	242356	
Jackson, Sydney	Pte	18676	Also 6th, 7th & 8th Bns.
Jackson, Thomas	Pte	1152	WIA.
Jackson, William	Pte	240518	WIA.
Jackson, William	Pte	240522	
Jackson, William	Pte	241463	
James, Albert Edward	Pte	28209	Also 7th & 2/5th Bns.
James, Ernest	Pte	241038	
James, Frank	Pte	242597	
James, James	Pte	30703	Ex RAVC.
James, John	Pte	41035	
Jameson, Joseph	Pte	1286	H.
Jameson, Richard	L/Cpl	1287	Trans to LC.
Jamieson, Henry	Pte	260038	WIA. Trans to LC.
Jamieson, James	Pte	201152	KIA 20/9/17
Jeffery, Fred	Pte	240520	WIA.
Jefford, William Robert	Pte	242595	
Jeffreys, John William	Pte	240701	
Jenkinson, Albert Cross	Pte	1240	
Jenkinson, Frederick	Pte	1092	WIA.
Jenkinson, Harold	Pte	241550	
Jenkinson, John	L/Cpl	240702	WIA. POW.
Jenkinson, John Abraham	Pte	242599	
Jenkinson, William	Pte	33104	WIA.
Jennians, William John	C/Sgt	26649	Ex 7th Bn.
Jennings, Edward	Pte	1721	
Jesse, Arthur	Pte	29072	
Jobbins, Arthur George	Pte	35647	POW. DOW 9/6/18
Johnson, Albert	Pte	21222	Ex 7th Bn. WIA × 2. Posted 2/5th.

Johnson, Arthur	Pte	2890	Trans to MGC.
Johnson, Frank Herbert	Pte	240521	
Johnson, George Myers	Pte	242593	
Johnson, James	Pte	18496	WIA. Trans to LC.
Johnson, James Henry	Pte	29073	KIA 26/4/18
Johnson, John	Pte	1687	KIA 2/6/15
Johnson, Leonard	Pte	4397	DOW 27/8/16 (Unlucky Draft)
Johnson, Matthew	Pte	240864	WIA.
Johnson, Richard	Pte	1237	
Johnson, Robert	Pte	243984	
Johnson, Thomas	Pte	242600	KIA 2/8/17
Johnson, Thomas	Pte	29074	
Johnson, Thomas Cook	Pte	28036	
Johnson, William	Pte	28037	KIA 31/7/17
Johnson, William	L/Cpl	241602	WIA. Trans to LC.
Johnston, Edward	Pte	18773	Ex 6th & 9th Bns.
Johnston, Ernest	Pte	51907	
Johnston, Frederick Basil	Pte	242460	
Johnston, Gilbert M.	Pte	25339	Also 2/5th.
Johnston, John Septimus	Pte	1505	KIA 23/4/15
Johnston, Joseph	Pte	3553	DOW 3/8/16
Johnstone, John C.	Pte	265532	A Coy. HOS-23/4/15.
Johnstone, John Douglas	Maj.		Leinster Regt.
Jolly, William Henry	Pte	29075	
Jones, Arthur	Pte	1483	DOW 8/9/15
Jones, Edward	Pte	243114	KIA 31/7/17
Jones, Frank	Pte	12980	Ex 7th Bn.
Jones, Frank	Pte	24247	
Jones, Fred	Pte	1785	Trans to MGC.
Jones, Frederick Simpson	L/Cpl	28038	MM.
Jones, George William	Pte	201891	
Jones, Harold	Pte	241545	WIA. Trans to LC.
Jones, Herbert	Sgt	240260	
Jones, John	Pte	25575	WIA. Trans to Lincs.
Jones, Thomas	Pte	1883	DOW 7/4/15
Jones, Watlin John Brimore	2Lt		
Jones, William	Pte	263019	Ex RAVC.
Jones, William Arthur	Pte	24734	Ex 8th Bn.
Jones, William David	Pte	240611	WIA. Posted 2/5th.

Jones, William Henry	Pte	243101	Also 8th & 2nd Bns.
Jordan, Alfred	Pte	34592	
Joyce, John	Pte	32987	Ex RAVC, 11th & 7th Bns.
Karran, John	Pte	19766	Ex 7th Bn.
Kavarsky, Joel	Pte	37750	KIA 13/5/18
Kay, Edward	Pte	28039	Also 1st Bn.
Kean, John Herdman	Capt.		KIA 1/12/17
Keates, Arthur	Pte	27396	Ex 7th Bn and also LF.
Keen, George William	Pte	1950	WIA. KIA 16/8/15
Kehoe, Edward	Pte	1576	KIA 5/5/15
Keighley, Linden Rayner	2Lt		WIA. DOW 3/12/17 with 1/4th.
Kellett, George	Pte	23843	KIA 30/11/17 with MGC.
Kellett, Henry Bernard	Pte	24780	Ex 7th Bn. D. 7/10/18
Kellett, Thomas	Pte	35710	Also 2/5th.
Kelly, Joseph	Pte	202420	Also 8th Bn.
Kelly, Peter	Cpl	241241	
Kelly, Simon	Pte	242601	Trans to 13/KLR.
Kelly, Thomas Edward	L/Cpl	2769	Trans to MGC.
Kelly, William	Pte	11650	Trans to LC.
Kelly, William Norman	Pte	40985	
Kelshaw, Joseph	Cpl	10159	Also 2nd & 7th Bns. WIA.
Kendall, Alfred	Pte	240612	
Kendall, Edward	Pte	242491	KIA 26/5/18
Kendall, Frederick	Pte	33951	KIA 30/11/17
Kendall, Robert William	Sgt	240202	WIA. Posted 2/5th.
Kennedy, John	Pte	242311	
Kenny, John	Sgt	27030	Ex 1st Bn.
Kent, Francis Thomas	Pte	40987	
Kent, Herbert	Pte	40986	
Kenworthy, Albert	Pte	29076	
Kermode, Alfred Ernest	Pte	265131	POW.
Kernick, Wilfred	Pte	3750	WIA. Trans to LC.
Kershaw, Percy	Pte	1315	
Kershaw, Thomas	Pte	32166	Ex 8th Bn.
Kew, Thomas	Pte	1913	KIA 24/4/15
Kew, William	Pte	240930	D. 22/3/19
Kewley, John	Sgt	240803	WIA.
Keyworth, Victor	Pte	1653	KIA 23/4/15
Kidd, Leslie Hurrell	Pte	29077	

Kilbride, John	Sgt	240231	MM.
Kilbride, Joseph	Pte	240865	WIA.
Kilbride, Joseph	C/Sgt	36512	
Kilgallon, John Leo	Pte	22977	Ex 7th Bn. KIA 9/4/18
King, Charles Standley	Pte	28210	Ex 7th Bn.
King, Oscar	Sgt	241402	WIA. MM.
King, Roy	Pte	241390	Also 2/5th.
Kirby, Frederick	Pte	28173	Ex 7th Bn.
Kirby, Richard	L/Cpl	220	WIA.
Kirby, Robert	Pte	21568	Ex 8th BN. WIA. D. 5/11/17
Kirk, Gerald	2Lt		DOW 24/4/15
Kirk, Stephen	Pte	29078	KIA 9/6/18
Kirkbride, John	Pte	34787	Ex 1st Bn. WIA.
Kirkby, James	Pte	241787	Also 8th Bn.
Kirkby, Thomas	Pte	243107	Also 6th Bn. MM.
Kirkby (Kirby), James Sargison	L/Sgt	376	KIA 3/5/15
Kirkby (Kirby), Richard Henry	C/Sgt	240026	WIA. MM.
Kirkman, Thomas	Pte	243052	KIA 11/3/17
Kirton, George	Pte	28040	DOW 26/9/17
Kive, George William	Pte	987	Trans to Scottish Horse.
Knaggs, Joseph	Pte	28041	MM. WIA.
Kneale, Harry	Pte	241534	
Kneale, Herbert	L/Cpl	241249	WIA.
Knight, Charles	Pte	242705	
Knight, Edward	Pte	28231	
Knight, John	Pte	37341	
Knight, William James	Pte	34801	
Knobbs, Ted	Pte	12939	Ex 7th Bn.
Knowles, Abel	Pte	243024	KIA 16/9/17
Knowles, Barton	Pte	241387	
Knowles, Henry Worden	Sgt	23717	Ex 8th Bn. Comm. 1919.
Knowles, John	Pte	3087	KIA 27/4/15
Knowles, Matthew Henry	Pte	41020	
Knox, David Hepburn	2Lt		
Knox, Ernest	Pte	23169	Ex 7th Bn. MiD
Krelle, John Robert	L/Cpl	240190	WIA.
Lacey, Albert	Pte	242610	KIA 31/7/17
Lackey, Michael	Pte	201216	Ex 1/4th.

Laidler, William Charles	Pte	22492	Ex 11th Bn.
Laidman, William Henry	Pte	38116	
Laister, Harry Bryan	Pte	41018	
Laking, Donald	Pte	41026	
Lamb, Benjamin	Pte	263001	WIA. To 1/4th. Trans to LC.
Lamb, Charles	WO2	241167	DOW 13/3/17
Lamb, Jack	Pte	240519	
Lamb, James	Pte	3007	WIA 20/10/16
Lamb, James	Pte	2014	
Lamb, James	Pte	1713	Trans to LC.
Lamb, James Owen	Pte	29079	
Lamb, John Thomas	Sgt	240372	Armourer-Sgt.
Lamb, Richard	Pte	240707	WIA × 2.
Lamb, Robert	Sgt	240523	WIA.
Lamb, Robert Crouch	Pte	28042	Posted 1st Bn. WIA.
Lamb, William	Pte	243458	
Lambert, Albert Edward	Pte	37216	
Lambert, Edmund	2Lt		
Lambert, Frederick	Sgt	240059	WIA.
Lambert, George	Pte	1641	WIA. Trans to LC.
Lambert, John	Pte	29080	WIA. Trans to LC.
Laming, George Alfred	Pte	260059	
Lancaster, Frank Knowles	A/Cpl	30694	Ex RAVC. WIA.
Landing, Daniel	Pte	243053	
Lang, Robert Howard	Pte	243111	DOW 22/6/17
Langford, Frederick William	Pte	241581	
Langhorne, William	Pte	1312	Trans to MGC.
Langstreth, Henry	Pte	2390	
Langstreth, John	Pte	240334	KIA 15/9/17
Langtree, Albert	Pte	240318	WIA. Trans to Lincs. POW.
Large, Henry Jabez	Cpl	240455	MM.
Large, Joseph James	Cpl	51184	
Larkin, Edward	Pte	34757	
Latchford, Arthur Stanley	Pte	40989	
Latham, Frederick David	Pte	22657	Ex 11th Bn.
Latham, Thomas	Pte	12914	
Launchbury, Albert	Pte	242307	
Law, John	Pte	2774	KIA 3/8/16

Law, John	Pte	200863	WIA.
Law, Samuel	Cpl	242288	WIA × 3. MM.
Lawder, Robert John	Pte	265902	
Lawley, Frederick William	Pte	242608	Att TMB.
Lawrence, John	Pte	541	KIA 27/4/15
Lawrence, Thomas William	Pte	243464	WIA X2. Trans to MGC.
Lawson, Frank Albert	Pte	30690	DOW 23/4/18
Lawson, James	Pte	242639	
Layton, Benjamin	Pte	30676	Ex RAMC & RAVC.
Leack, Joseph	Sgt	240175	WIA.
Leaf, Harry	Pte	242605	Also 8th & 2/5th Bns.
Leak, Joseph	Pte	34820	DOW 15/12/17
Leathley, Henry	Pte	28630	Also ASC, 1st Bn & 2/5th.
Leaver, John Brown	Pte	242604	WIA.
Leaver, Richard	Pte	201935	KIA 31/7/17
Lee, Fred	Pte	41029	
Lee, George	Pte	242609	
Lee, Harold	Pte	29081	
Lee, James	Pte	241560	POW.
Lee, James Linsley	Pte	2591	KIA 3/6/15
Lee, John	Pte	26681	Ex 7th Bn. WIA. DOW 10/8/18
Lee, John	Pte	240232	
Lee, John	Pte	29082	
Lee, John R.	Pte	241547	WIA. Trans to LC.
Lee, Stanley	L/Cpl	242511	KIA 9/3/17
Leech, Walter	Pte	201864	KIA 30/11/17
Leeming, John James	Pte	28044	
Leeming, Robert Pearson	Pte	241957	
Lees, Fred	Pte	37731	
Leigh, Harry	Pte	15335	Ex 8th Bn.
Lennon, Vernon	Pte	1908	KIA 23/4/15
Leviston, Alfred	Pte	38535	
Levy, Isaac	Pte	242478	Ex 8th Bn.
Lewes, Reginald	Pte	35793	Ex 7th Bn.
Lewington, Herbert	Pte	25423	Ex 2nd Bn. KIA 30/11/17
Lewis, Ben Marshall	Pte	203060	Also 7th Bn & Northampton Yeo.
Lewis, David Robert Thomas	2Lt		
Lewis, James	Cpl	201860	

Leybourn, Joseph	Pte	28043	WIA. KIA 10/4/18
Leytham, Robert Ronson	Pte	34399	WIA.
Liddle, Edward	Pte	242611	Also 8th Bn.
Liddle, James	L/Sgt	2317	Also 1st & 7th Bns.
Lidford, Edwin John	Cpl	2230	WIA × 2. DCM. Trans to LC.
Light, James Mulvey	Pte	3823	
Lightfoot, Isaiah	Pte	241073	WIA. Also 2/5th.
Lill, Percy Charles	A/Cpl	260017	WIA.
Lilley, Hubert (Herbert)	Pte	2141	WIA.
Limb, William Percy	Pte	41015	
Lincoln, John	Pte	2593	
Lindsay, Jacob	Pte	34930	Also 1/4th.
Lingard, Ernest	Pte	242218	Ex 2/5th. Trans to KOYLI.
Lingard, James	Pte	241569	WIA. Posted 1/4th Bn. POW.
Linney, Frederick	Pte	40991	
Little, John Thomas	Pte	29084	WIA.
Little, William	Pte	41680	
Littlefair, William	Pte	30685	Ex RAVC. WIA. POW.
Littlefield, Edward John	Pte	25948	Also 9th Bn.
Littler, David	Pte	20747	WIA. POW.
Liver, John	Pte	240150	WIA. Posted 2/5th.
Liver, Thomas	Pte	241010	WIA. DOW 29/9/17 with 8th Bn.
Liver, William	Pte	2146	WIA. Trans to R Fus & LC.
Livesay, Albert	2Lt		
Livesey, John	Pte	2308	WIA.
Livesey, John	Pte	29083	
Livesey, William	Sgt	240432	MM. MiD. DOW 11/4/18
Lloyd, Albert	L/Cpl	9811	Ex 2nd & 1st Bns.
Lloyd, Albert Percy	Pte	265138	KIA 10/4/18
Lloyd, George Moss	2Lt		
Lloyd, John William	Pte	241575	WIA.
Lloyd-Evans, Edward Meredydd	Capt.		WIA. KIA 14/3/16
Lockley, Alfred	Pte	1224	KIA 5/5/15
Loe, Sydney James Fuller	Lt		
Lofthouse, James	Pte	240203	KIA 19/6/17
Lofthouse, John	Sgt	240868	WIA × 2.
Lofthouse, Robert Thomas	Pte	2172	Also 1st Bn.
Loftus, Frederick	Sgt	242682	Ex 2nd Bn. Band-Sergeant.

Loftus, John	Pte	40990	KIA 16/6/18
Lomas, William	Pte	242465	
Long, George	Pte	242683	Also 2nd & 1st Bns.
Long, John James	Pte	33970	WIA. Posted 1st Bn.
Long, W.	Pte	2680	WIA. Posted 1st Bn.
Longley, John	Pte	37170	
Longton, Charles	Sgt	240524	
Longworth, Ellis	Pte	26128	Also 7th & 2/5th Bns.
Longworth, Fergus	Pte	34751	KIA 29/5/18 with 1st Bn.
Lord, Gilbert Henry	2Lt		WIA. MC.
Lord, William	A/Cpl	14437	Ex 8th & 7th Bns.
Loughlin, Edmund	Pte	10769	Ex 1st & 2nd Bns.
Love, Benjamin Charles	Pte	2202	WIA.
Lovett, Joseph	L/Cpl	15531	Ex 8th Bn.
Lowe, Frederick Henry	Pte	2134	KIA 3/5/15
Lowe, John	Pte	200967	
Loxton, Edgar	Pte	30686	Ex. RAVC. WIA.
Lucas, Joseph	Pte	682	WIA. Enlisted LC.
Lulham, George Bertram	Pte	241524	
Lumb, John Albert	Pte	201979	
Lumley, Robert	Pte	28045	
Lund, Charles Haley	Sgt	240115	WIA × 2. KIA 18/3/17
Lund, John Edward	Pte	240481	
Lund, Noel Beaconfield	Pte	32790	
Lund, Thomas John	Pte	26194	
Lunn, John William	Pte	242713	KIA 9/3/17
Lunt, Ernest Albert	Pte	29085	
Lupton, Fred	Pte	1353	KIA 5/5/15
Lupton, George	Pte	241289	
Lupton, James William	Pte	202646	Ex 7th Bn.
Lupton, Walter	Pte	4008	KIA 15/8/16
Luttman, Charles Henry	Pte	202612	Ex 7th Bn.
Luxford, John Weymouth	Pte	30654	
Lydiate, Harold	L/Cpl	241488	WIA. KIA 9/3/17
Lynch, William	Sgt	240168	WIA × 2. DCM. KIA 15/6/17
Lynden, William John	A/Cpl	30665	Ex RAVC.
Lyne, Harold	Pte	29086	
Lynes, Sidney George	Pte	2142	DOW 25/4/15

Lyons, John William	Pte	201905	D. 16/2/19
Lyons, Thomas	L/Cpl	37538	KIA 190/7/18
Lyttle, Robert S.	Pte	2682	WIA. Trans to RGA.
Mabbs, James A.	Pte	2245	Trans to RFC & LC.
Macdonald, Ronald	2Lt		WIA. MC (and 2 Bars)
Macfarlane, William Smith	Lt		R. Scots. MC. WIA. K. 20/6/18 (RFC)
Machon, Frederick John	Cpl	203070	Also 2/5th. Comm. London R.1918.
Mack, William	Pte	40992	
Mackenzie, James	L/Sgt	240411	
Mackenzie, William	Sgt	26721	Ex LF & 7th Bn.
Mackereth, James	WO2	240560	WIA X2. MM.
Mackey, John Robert Conn.	2Lt		WIA × 2.
Maclagan, James Graham	Lt		KIA with LNL 1/8/18
Madden, James	Pte	1910	WIA.
Maden, Amos Marshall	Pte	13097	Ex 7th Bn.
Maguire, James	Cpl	240092	WIA.
Maguire, Myles	Pte	30674	Ex RAVC.
Maidman, William Charles	Cpl	28496	Ex 11th Bn.
Mailly, William	Pte	25587	
Major, Edward	2Lt		WIA.
Makinson, Edward	Pte	240258	WIA. KIA 30/11/17
Malkinson, Steele	Pte	20647	
Mallalieu, Joseph	Pte	26770	Ex 1st & 11th Bns.
Mallett, Robert	Pte	30027	Ex 8th Bn. WIA.
Malone, John William	Pte	37240	
Maloney, Charles	Pte	260035	WIA. Trans to LF.
Maloney, John Joseph	Pte	13121	Ex 7th Bn.
Maloney, L.	Pte	1961	WIA.
Mangan, John	Pte	2132	Trans to Borderers & MCR.
Manifold, Levison John	Pte	41674	WIA.
Mann, E.	Pte	242615	MM.
Mansfield, Eversley	Lt		
Mansfield, Richard	Pte	1604	KIA 8/5/15
Mansfield, Richard Eli	A/Cpl	1222	KIA 4/5/15
Manson, Thomas	Pte	28046	
Marchant, John	Pte	30008	Ex 8th Bn.
Marland, William	L/Cpl	200848	MM. KIA 9/4/18
Marriott, James	Pte	200597	Ex 1/4th.

Marsden, George	Pte	28047	WIA. KIA 9/4/18
Marsden, Henry	Pte	36543	KIA 2/5/18
Marsden, Robert	Pte	3710	Trans to LC.
Marsden, William	L/Cpl	1442	WIA. Trans to Welsh Regt.
Marsden, William	Pte	24941	Ex 8th Bn.
Marsh, Herbert	Pte	25950	Ex 9th Bn. Also 2/5th.
Marsh, Victor	Pte	241211	Also 2/5th.
Marshall, Alfred George	Pte	27271	Also Lincs, 1st & 7th Bns.
Marshall, Claude Coltart	Maj.		DSO.
Marshall, John	Pte	240201	
Marshall, John	Pte	2900	Trans to MGC.
Marshall, John William	Pte	2510	Transport. SWB 5/1/17.
Marshall, Thomas Henry	Pte	27656	Also 1st Bn.
Marshall, William	Pte	27411	Ex LF & 7th Bn.
Martin, Edward Henry	Cpl	21686	
Martin, James	Pte	27792	Ex 11th Bn. Deserted 21/8/18.
Martin, John	Pte	1844	Trans Monmouths and RE.
Martin, Robert Leadbetter	Pte	240438	WIA. KIA 23/7/17
Martin, Walter	Pte	579	WIA.
Mashiter, Charles	Pte	2059	Trans to ASC.
Mashiter, Joseph Wren	Cpl	240389	WIA.
Maskell, Joseph	Pte	28048	
Mason, Edward	Pte	1055	WIA.
Mason, George	Pte	241638	WIA. POW.
Mason, James	Pte	240306	WIA.
Mason, Myles	L/Cpl	2393	WIA. Trans to LC.
Massam, Arthur	Pte	27274	Ex Lincs & 1st Bn.
Massey, John	L/Cpl	240419	
Massey, Joseph	Pte	27877	Ex Leics & 11th Bn. Also 1/4th.
Massey, Percy	Pte	38626	Ex 1st Bn.
Masters, Henry	Sgt	240870	WIA.
Masters, Thomas	Pte	2902	WIA. Trans to LC
Mather, John	Pte	1991	Trans to LC.
Mather, Robert	Capt.		
Matthews, Albert Edward	Pte	260049	D. 15/5/18
Matthews, Alfred	Pte	260003	Also 8th Bn.
Matthews, Charles	Pte	33270	
Matthews, Harold	Pte	240163	WIA X2.

Matthews, W.	2Lt		Att from DLOY.
Mattinson, Thomas Rawes	Pte	4052	KIA 9/8/16
Maudsley, Joseph	Pte	202316	
Maun, Edward	Pte	265587	KIA 16/9/17
Mawson, George	Cpl	240616	WIA. MM.
Mawson, Harold	Pte	5921	DOW 6/10/16
Mawson, James Radcliffe	Pte	2152	DOW 24/4/15
Maxwell, John	Pte	241618	
Maxwell, William	Pte	38024	
May, Frederick	Pte	34636	
Mayes, Stanley Herbert	Pte	28238	Ex 11th & 1st Bns.
Mayhew, Thomas	Pte	36517	
Mayne, Samuel John	Pte	27876	Ex 11th Bn. WIA. KIA 10/4/18
Mayoh, Herbert	Pte	30053	Ex 8th Bn. WIA × 2.
Mayor, Edmund	L/Cpl	1648	WIA. KIA 10/9/16
McAndrew, Frank	Pte	24500	Ex 7th & 2/5th Bns WIA. KIA 8/3/18
McBain, John Alexander	Pte	36390	
McBride, Alexander	Pte	13667	Ex 9th Bn.
McBride, Joseph	A/Cpl	25728	WIA.
McBroom, Robert	Pte	2595	H.
McCabe, Michael	Cpl	29087	
McCabe, Thomas	Pte	242684	Ex 1st Bn. WIA. KIA 21/9/17
McConville, Patrick	Sgt	240033	WIA. Posted 2/5th.
McCormack, Thomas	Pte	486	WIA.
McDermott, Frederick	Pte	19105	Ex 11th Bn.
McDermott, John	Pte	242497	WIA. DOW 1/12/17
McDonald, James Francis	Sgt	243086	DCM.
McDonnell, Frank	Pte	1700	Trans to Borderers and MGC.
McGarr, William	Pte	15183	Ex 9th Bn.
McGowan, Hugh	Pte	28050	WIA × 3. Posted 8th Bn.
McGowan, John	Pte	21762	POW.
McGowan, Rowland	L/Cpl	2038	DOW 27/5/15
McGreevy, John	Pte	1958	WIA. KIA.
McGreevy, Peter	Pte	1059	KIA 5/5/15
McGrow, Cecil	Pte	240147	
McGuigan, Nevin	Pte	28051	
McGuire, Terrence	Pte	243076	Trans from ASC. WIA.
McGuire, Thomas	Pte	200240	Ex 4th Bn.

McKenna, David Usher	Pte	35850	Trans to KOYLI
McKeown, Thomas	Pte	28052	
McKinlay, Archibald	Pte	34806	WIA. POW.
McLean, William	Pte	243054	KIA 30/11/17
Mcleod, Alexander	Pte	28053	WIA. Trans to Lincs.
McNeal, John George	Pte	240755	
McNulty, Thomas	Pte	240618	WIA × 2. Posted 7th & 1st Bns.
McStravick, Simon	Pte	242988	DOW 11/10/18
McTigue, James	Pte	1032	KIA 4/5/15
McVittie, (George) Bertram	Pte	241572	WIA × 2. MM. KIA 10/5/18 (1/4th)
Meace, George Henry	Sgt	4204	Also 1st & 2/5th Bns. Trans to WR.
Mead, Arthur	Pte	28344	Ex RAMC. Att R. Scots.
Meadowcroft, Norman	Sgt	240935	
Meadows, Peter	Pte	18613	
Meakin, Arthur	Pte	41682	
Meakins, William	Pte	26637	Ex 9th Bn.
Mealor, Thomas James	Pte	260060	
Melling, William Robert	Pte	240871	Trans to LC.
Mellor, Albert	Pte	29089	
Mellor, Harry	Pte	243013	Posted 8th Bn. WIA × 2.
Mellor, Henry	Pte	240405	
Mellor, Thomas	Pte	34819	
Mellors, Thomas	Pte	242613	
Mercer, George	Pte	241664	KIA with 1/4th.
Mercer, Walter	Pte	265155	
Mercer, William	Pte	242474	
Merrett, Robert Henry	Pte	201131	Ex 1/4th.
Metcalf, William Thomas	Pte	1645	WIA × 2. Trans to KLR & RE
Metcalfe, Herbert	Pte	3490	WIA. Trans MGC.
Metcalfe, John	Pte	4021	KIA 22/9/16
Metcalfe, John	Pte	242450	KIA 9/3/17
Metcalfe, William Henry	Capt.		WIA. MC and Bar
Middleton, James	Pte	13959	Ex 7th Bn.
Middleton, Thomas Harvey	2Lt		Comm. 1/4th 1916. WIA.
Milburn, Charlie	Pte	28054	
Milburn, Philip	Pte	28055	WIA. KIA. 20/9/17
Millard, Arthur Henry	Pte	2597	DOW 6/5/15
Miller, Joseph William	Pte	1871	WIA. Trans to RE & LC.
Miller, Robert	Pte	28056	POW. D. 30/4/18

Miller, Robert	Pte	2598	Trans to MGC.
Millington, Frank	Pte	26718	Ex 7th Bn. KIA 10/4/18
Mills, William Edward	Pte	32013	Ex 1st & 9th Bns. Att R Scots & RIF
Mills, William Godfrey	Pte	28487	Ex 11th Bn.
Milne, Henry	Pte	240062	WIA × 2.
Milner, Samuel	Pte	2507	DOW 6/6/15
Milnes, George Clement	Maj.		MC. MiD (x3).
Minns, Walter	L/Cpl	1433	WIA. Trans to RE.
Minton, George Henry Richard	Pte	29090	
Mitchell, Alfred	Pte	241562	DOW 15/6/17 att 166 TMB.
Mitchell, George Cyril	Pte	1956	WIA. Trans to RAMC.
Mitchell, John	Pte	33278	
Mitchell, John William	Pte	15076	Ex 7th Bn.
Mitchell, Thomas	Pte	241552	WIA. KIA 12/12/17 with 8th Bn.
Mitchell, Thomas A.	Pte	241504	WIA-8/16-LG8728.
Mitchell, Wilson	Pte	240458	
Mogg, Albert	Pte	3316	KIA 12/3/15
Moloney, William Joseph	Pte	241280	D. 21/2/19
Moncaster, Frank E.	Pte	242614	WIA. On roll as 33141. Trans to LC.
Monk, George	Pte	242982	
Monks, Cuthbert Edgar	2Lt		
Monks, Frederick Victor	Cpl	240529	WIA. KIA 15/8/16
Monks, Leonard Miller	Pte	1229	WIA.
Monks, Thomas Miller	Pte	2205	WIA.
Montgomery, John	Pte	2511	
Moody, Harold	Pte	242612	WIA. Deserted 15/8/17.
Moody, John	Pte	1266	KIA 9/4/16 with 6th Bn.
Moore, James Hubert	Pte	242282	
Moore, Thomas	Pte	240428	Also 2/5th.
Moorhouse, Edward	Pte	33475	WIA × 2. Posted 1/4th.
Moorhouse, Ernest	Pte	32634	Ex 7th Bn.
Moreland, Joseph	Pte	240236	Also 1/4th & 8th Bns.
Morgan, Benjamin	Pte	22888	Ex 7th Bn. To 1/5th.
Morgan, George Francis	Cpl	26900	Ex 1st Bn.
Morgan, Robert	Pte	30490	Ex 1st Bn.
Morley, George Henry	Pte	1773	KIA 24/2/18 with RE.
Morley, Harold	Pte	29091	

Morris, Arthur	Pte	263027	Ex LNL.
Morris, Charles Aston	Pte	1475	H.
Morris, Gilbert	Pte	240093	
Morris, John	Pte	26735	Also 7th & 8th Bns.
Morris, William Alfred	L/Cpl	2166	WIA.
Mortin, Robert	Pte	243026	Also 1/4th.
Morton, Christopher G.	Sgt	240937	
Morton, Joseph Dunne	Pte	243014	Att TMB. Also 7th Bn.
Mosey, William	Pte	240872	WIA.
Mosley, Henry	Pte	260052	
Moss, George	Pte	1014	KIA 5/5/15
Moss, George William	Pte	36389	
Mossop, Richard	Pte	241066	
Mottershaw, Richard Henry	Pte	34756	Ex 1st Bn. WIA.
Mount, Matthew	Pte	2056	Trans to MCR and ASC.
Mountain, Thomas	Cpl	1967	DOW 17/10/16
Mountcastle, Leonard	Pte	26949	Also 1st & 2/5th Bns.
Muckalt, James	Pte	1733	WIA. DOW 12/4/18 with R. Warks.
Muckalt, James	Pte	2317	H.
Mullaney, Lawrence	Pte	240440	KIA 20/4/17 with 8th Bn
Mullen, A.	Pte	242512	WIA. Trans to RS.
Mullen, Joseph Jesse	Pte	243016	Also 8th Bn.
Mullin, William	Cpl	260055	WIA.
Munro, Andrew	Pte	241549	
Murday, John Henry	Pte	29092	
Murphy, Charles	Pte	28057	
Murray, Andrew	Pte	241614	
Murray, Arthur George	Pte	241646	WIA. MM. KIA 8/8/18 with 1st Bn.
Murray, Edwin	Pte	240619	WIA × 2. Trans to ASC.
Murray, James	Pte	243115	
Murray, William	Pte	242640	DOW 12/8/17
Musgrave, John William	Pte	28058	DOW 17/3/18
Myers, George	Pte	1477	H.
Myerscough, Samuel	Pte	3745	KIA 15/8/16
Nash, Edward	Pte	240551	WIA.
Nash, Joseph	Pte	2154	KIA 13/4/15
Nattrass, Thomas	Pte	28059	WIA × 2.
Naylon, Patrick	Pte	240376	WIA.

Needham, Frank	Sgt	820	WIA × 2. Trans to LC.
Needham, Joseph	Pte	240121	WIA. Trans to LC.
Neil, James	Pte	38631	Ex 1st Bn.
Neiles, Thomas John	Pte	11990	Ex-1st Bn. MM. Trans to LC.
Nelson, David	Pte	2395	DOW 9/5/15
Nelson, George Edward	CQMS	240012	WIA. D. 14/6/18
Nelson, Robert	Sgt	244502	
Nelson, Robert	Pte	240313	
Nelson, Robert	Pte	34835	Also 8th Bn.
Nelson, Thomas	Pte	30743	
Nevitskie, Simon	Pte	242641	WIA. Trans to LC.
Newboult, Jack	L/Sgt	240528	WIA. Comm. 1917.
Newby, James Walter	Pte	34211	WIA.
Newby, Joseph	Cpl	24179	Ex 7th Bn. MM.
Newby, Nicholas	Pte	241515	WIA. To 2/5th. DOW 24/5/19
Newman, Charles L.	Pte	41030	MM.
Newsham, James	Pte	240712	WIA.
Newsham, John	Pte	2782	H.
Newsham, Thomas	Pte	2020	WIA. Trans to LC.
Newsholme, Herbert	Pte	3984	Trans to KLR.
Newton, Ernest	Pte	41032	
Newton, Fred	Pte	241082	POW.
Newton, John Edward	Pte	265714	Also 8th & 1/4th Bns. WIA.
Newton, Johnson	Pte	28060	KIA 10/4/18
Newton, Joseph	L/Cpl	1771	DOW 7/5/15
Newton, Leonard	Pte	26775	Also 7th & 1st Bns.
Newton, Myles	Pte	242502	MSM.
Newton, Samuel	Pte	37759	
Newton, William	C/Sgt	240936	WIA. MM.
Newton, William Wraith	Pte	24287	WIA.
Nichol, Ernest Hedley	Pte	28061	
Nicholls, Edward Cliff	L/Cpl	240713	WIA × 3. MM.
Nicholson, James	L/Cpl	1143	WIA.
Nicholson, Leonard	Pte	3445	Trans to MGC.
Nicholson, Reuben	L/Cpl	201855	WIA. KIA 20/9/17
Nicholson, Richard	Pte	1763	WIA. Trans to S Lancs.
Nickson, Robert William	L/Cpl	243039	WIA. POW. DOW 3/10/18
Nield, John	Pte	27657	Also 1/4th & 9th Bns.

Nightingale, Robert	Pte	240071	WIA.
Nisbett, Thomas	Pte	1041	WIA. MM.
Nixon, John	Pte	1211	
Nixon, Robert	Pte	20946	Ex 11th & 7th Bns. WIA × 2.
Nixon, Thomas	Cpl	240609	
Noakes, Henry F.	Pte	242653	WIA. Trans to Tank Corps.
Noble, Samuel	Pte	26	H.
Nolan, Andrew	Pte	1574	Trans to LC. SWB.
Nolan, J.	Pte	2689	WIA.
Nolan, James	Pte	22672	Ex 11th Bn. POW.
Nolan, James	Pte	242510	WIA & POW.
Nolan, John	Pte	27532	Ex 8th Bn.
Norbury, Tom	Pte	240341	WIA.
Norledge, John Robert	Pte	28145	Ex LF & 7th Bn.
Nut, James Waldermar	Pte	38037	
Nuttall, Richard Ormerod	Pte	201915	POW. DOW 18/12/17
Nuttall, William	L/Cpl	19377	Ex 11th Bn.
Oak, Herbert	Pte	243077	
Oakley, George Samuel	Pte	25353	Also 7th & 8th Bns.
O'Brien, Frederick	Pte	37250	D. 8/11/18
O'Brien, John	Pte	2911	Trans to MGC.
Oddy, Harry	Pte	243118	
O'Donnell, John Porter	Pte	2605	Trans to LC.
Ogden, Cecil	Pte	37193	
Ogden, Christopher Henry	L/Cpl	22600	Ex 11th Bn.
Ogden, Frederick	Pte	22512	Also 11th & 2/5th Bns.
Ogden, John	Pte	1921	KIA 16/4/15
Ogle, Kenneth William Swan	Lt		
Oglesby, Arthur	Pte	202236	
Oglethorpe, John	Pte	240183	WIA.
Oldham, Adam	Pte	2328	Also 7th & 8th Bns.
Oldham, Charles Arthur	Pte	1393	WIA.
Onyett, Albert	Pte	1195	WIA.
Opie, Thomas Richard	Pte	201232	
Ormandy, John	Pte	33700	Also 1/4th. WIA.
Ormesher, Edward Henry	Pte	242642	KIA 30/11/17 with 166 MGC.
Ormond, James	Cpl	13491	WIA. Trans to LC.
Orrell, Robert	Pte	15382	Also 8th & 1/4th Bns.

Osborn, Harold Arthur	Pte	40993	Att TMB.
Osborne, William Henry	Pte	1379	WIA. KIA 9/5/15
Osman, Edward	Pte	240304	MiD.
Oswald, James Alexander	Pte		WIA.
Oswald, Ronald	Pte	1642	Trans to RWF.
Ousalice, George	Pte	29093	
Owen, Alec	C/Sgt	66	H.
Owen, David	Pte	934	KIA 5/5/15
Owen, Ernest Harold	Pte	30706	Ex RAVC.
Owen, Joseph Albert	Pte	2095	Ex-Army Cyclist Corps. Trans to ASC.
Owen, William	Pte	240270	WIA.
Owens, Harold James	Pte	28213	Ex 7th Bn.
Owsnett, John	Pte	28062	
Owtram, Thomas Cary	Capt.		WIA × 3. MC.
Painter, Joseph	Pte	241470	POW.
Painter, Walter	Pte	2320	WIA. Trans to Tank Corps.
Palin, Samuel Edward	Pte	966	WIA. DCM. Trans to LC.
Palmer, Charles	Pte	26724	KIA 9/4/18
Parbery, John	Pte	242650	KIA 3/8/17
Parfitt, Albert Sidney	A/Cpl	28491	Ex 8th Bn.
Parfitt, John Herbert	2Lt		
Park, Dewhurst	Pte	38132	
Park, Henry	Pte	24136	Ex 11th & 1st Bns.
Park, Norman Morley	Pte	3093	Trans to MGC.
Park, Robert	2Lt		
Park, Robert	Pte	22085	Ex 7th Bn.
Parker, Alan	Capt.		H. D. 1/4/17
Parker, Bruce	A/Cpl	2246	WIA. Trans to RE.
Parker, George	L/Cpl	243041	POW.
Parker, George William	Pte	240650	
Parker, Harold	2Lt		WIA.
Parker, Henry	Pte	242444	
Parker, John	Pte	33948	Also 11th & 9th Bns.
Parker, Robert William	Pte	240357	
Parker, Thomas	Pte	240200	WIA X2. SWB.
Parker, William	Pte	242415	KIA 2/8/17
Parker, William	Cpl	241145	MM.

Parkinson, Albert	Pte	242710	KIA 30/11/17
Parkinson, Arthur	Pte	2321	KIA 23/4/15
Parkinson, Arthur	Cpl	240356	MM.
Parkinson, Arthur	Pte	241635	
Parkinson, Fred	Pte	34802	
Parkinson, Harry	Pte	265822	WIA. D. 27/12/20
Parkinson, Herbert	Pte	1837	WIA. Re-enlisted LC.
Parkinson, James	Pte	34670	Also 1/4th.
Parkinson, John	Pte	1976	WIA. Re-enlisted in MGC.
Parkinson, John L.	Pte	2322	Trans to Tank Corps.
Parkinson, Joseph Allan	2Lt		Trans to RFC
Parkinson, Percy	Pte	29095	
Parkinson, Thompson	L/Cpl	27642	Also 1st Bn.
Parkinson, William Edgar	Pte	241085	WIA. Also 2/5th.
Parkinson, William James	Pte	240065	
Parr, Albert	Pte	241226	
Parr, John	Pte	34672	Ex 8th Bn. POW.
Parr, William	Pte	241895	WIA. DOW 22/9/17
Parr, William	Pte	1213	WIA. Re-enlisted in AOC.
Parratt, David Walter	Pte	51933	Also Northumberland Fus.
Parratt, John	Pte	37115	
Parratt, Walter	Pte	35855	
Parrington, William Alexander	Pte	13755	Also 9th & 7th Bns.
Parry, Thomas Frederick	Pte	29096	WIA.
Parsonage, George	L/Sgt	47	
Parsons, Walter	Pte	29097	
Parsons, William Josiah	Capt.		D. 27/10/18
Partridge, George	Pte	38541	
Partridge, Richard	Pte	265821	
Pashley, George Francis	Pte	40996	
Paterson, Murdoch Fraser	2Lt		WIA.
Patten, William	Pte	241511	
Patterson, David	Pte	28146	Ex 7th Bn. KIA 3/5/18
Patterson, John	Pte	1993	WIA.
Patterson, John	Pte	241325	
Pattinson, John Sport	Pte	1625	Trans to LC.
Pattison, Charles	Pte	24524	Ex 1st Bn. WIA × 2.
Pearce, Harry	L/Cpl	11746	Also 6th & 7th Bns.

Pearcy, George	Pte	240575	WIA × 2.
Pearson, Frederick	Pte	27490	Also 1/4th & 8th Bns. WIA.
Pearson, George Henry	Pte	40994	KIA 9/5/18
Pearson, George Victor	Pte	241594	WIA × 2.
Pearson, Herbert	Pte	241243	WIA. MiD.
Pearson, Thomas	Pte	27914	Also 11th & 7th Bns.
Peaston, Alfred Edwin	Pte	36000	
Pedder, Harold	Pte	34890	
Pedder, Thomas	Pte	241526	
Pedder, William Birbeck	Pte	2786	DOW 4/8/16
Peel, James Edward	Pte	1790	WIA.
Peel, Joseph	Cpl	2185	WIA × 2. Trans to MGC.
Peel, Richard	Sgt	241591	
Peel, Richard	Sgt	240379	MM.
Pendlebury, William	Pte	21067	Ex 11th & 9th Bns.
Penny, David	Pte	34038	KIA 30/11/17
Penrith, Herbert	Pte	2403	KIA 9/8/16
Penrith, Louis	Pte	241510	D. 28/7/17
Pepper, George Alfred	L/Cpl	203002	Ex London Yeo and 8th Bn. WIA.
Percival, Bernard	2Lt		POW.
Perry, Arthur John	Pte	28405	
Perry, Francis Charles	Pte	1694	H.
Perry, Thomas	Pte	260053	WIA.
Pettey, Henry William	Pte	35768	Ex Devonshires.
Petty, William	Pte	3124	
Pew, Robert	Pte	4268	Ex 9th Bn. Trans to KOYLI.
Philips, Walter	Sgt	240814	WIA X2.
Phillips, Malcolm McGregor	2Lt		Att from DLOY. WIA.
Phillips, William Mallam	Maj.		From 4/Lincolns. WIA.
Phillipson, Isaac	L/Sgt	241213	MM. POW & DOW 9/12/17
Phipp, Reginald Arthur H.	2Lt		
Phythian, Richard	Pte	263026	Also LNL.
Pickering, John Henry	Pte	26034	Ex 1st Bn. WIA.
Pickhover, Harry	Pte	32530	DOW 14/10/18
Pickstone, Albert	2Lt		WIA.
Pickthall, Edward	Pte	241489	
Pickthall, Mark	Pte	242685	Ex 8th Bn. WIA. KIA 20/9/17
Pickthall, William	A/Cpl	241036	WIA. SWB.

Pickup, Fred	Pte	202647	KIA 190/7/18
Pilkington, Arthur	Pte	35907	
Pilkington, Walter	Pte	33007	Ex 1/4th. WIA.
Pilkington, William	L/Sgt	23186	Ex 8th Bn.
Pilling, John	Pte	26025	Ex 1st Bn.
Pinch, William	2Lt	240471	WIA. KIA 31/7/17
Pinchen, Norman	Pte	241113	Att MGC.
Pinder, George Gofton	L/Sgt	20215	WIA X2.
Platt, Charles Fred	Pte	4018	DOW 1/8/16 (Unlucky Draft)
Plumbley, J.	Pte	2100	Trans to Mil Ft Pol.
Plummer, Walter	Pte	243093	Ex 7th & 8th Bns.
Pluse, John William	Pte	28064	
Pobgee, Harold Amos	WO1	30273	Ex 5DG. MC. Comm. 1/4th 1918.
Polkinghorn (erroneously spelled Polkingham), Richard	Pte	34781	KIA 20/9/17
Pollard, Charles Ernest	Pte	2608	WIA. D. 15/4/20
Pollard, James Henry	Pte	32560	Ex 7th Bn.
Pollard, Milton	Pte	241942	Ex 2/5th.
Pollard, Richard	Pte	34580	WIA.
Pollitt, William	Pte	242687	Also 8th Bn. WIA.
Pope, Frank	Pte	34804	KIA 30/11/17
Porter, Albert E.	Pte	240982	WIA. Trans to Cheshires.
Porter, Arthur	Pte	202322	WIA. DOW 5/12/17
Porter, Charles	L/Cpl	1193	KIA 8/5/15
Porter, Ernest Harold	Pte	28065	
Porter, James	Cpl	1067	
Porter, Richard	Pte	1545	WIA. Trans to MGC.
Porter, Thomas	Pte	240561	WIA.
Porter, Thomas	Pte	240653	Also 8th Bn.
Porter, William	Pte	11285	Also 2nd, 7th, 8th & 1/4th Bns.
Portnall, Charles	Pte	34808	Also 1st Bn. WIA.
Pothicary, William	Cpl	240431	MiD.
Potter, Joseph Lindsay	Pte	40995	
Poulton, Frank	Pte	994	H.
Povell, Charles William	Cpl	1078	WIA. Trans to LC.
Powell, George	Pte	243029	MiD.
Powell, Leonard Stanley	Pte	29098	WIA.
Power, Richard Francis	Pte	32557	Ex 7th Bn. WIA.

Pownall, Harry	Pte	243021	WIA. KIA 20/9/17 with 1/4th.
Powrie, Thomas Hall	Pte	203118	
Praed, William Lee	2Lt		
Preston, Christopher Thomas	Sgt	19325	Ex 11th Bn.
Preston, John Harold	Pte	3780	
Preston, R. J. H.	Lt		
Preston, William Wadsworth	Cpl	1168	
Price, Alfred	Sgt	32	WIA × 2. DCM.
Price, John Turner	2Lt	241126	KIA 27/5/18- CO 2/Devonshire R.
Price, Percival Allen	Pte	29099	
Prickett, Wilson	Sgt	241348	MM.
Priest, Walter	Pte	37164	
Prince, Edward	Pte	240263	KIA 26/4/17 with 8th Bn.
Prince, John Thomas	Pte	1674	KIA 27/4/15
Procter, James H.	Pte	2916	Trans to MGC.
Procter, Oliver	Pte	240967	Comm. to DCLI 1917.
Proctor, Frederick	Pte	34606	KIA 17/9/17
Pryce, Ernest	Pte	243117	Also 1/4th.
Pullen, Frank Knowle	Pte	240078	WIA × 2.
Pullen, John Arthur	Cpl	24267	Ex 7th Bn. WIA.
Punchard, James Septimus	Lt		D. 2/4/19
Punt, Arthur	Pte	242658	WIA. Trans to LC.
Purdon, Bartholomew Hamilton	Maj.		MC.
Purvis (Purves), Joseph Slater	L/Cpl	27346	Ex 1st & 1/4th Bns. WIA × 3. KIA 3/5/18
Pye, John	Pte	785	KIA 27/4/15
Pye, John Richard	Pte	1296	KIA 8/5/15
Pye, Richard	Pte	241333	Also 11th & 2/5th Bns.
Pye, William Thompson	Pte	2788	
Quayle, George	L/Sgt	2251	WIA. Also 1st, 8th & 7th Bns.
Quigley, Christopher	Cpl	19081	KIA 3/5/18
Quinn, Joseph	Pte	1490	Trans to Tank Corps.
Quinn, William Patrick	Pte	10909	Also 1st, 2nd & 7th Bns.
Radcliffe, Francis Wilfred	Pte	241665	
Radcliffe, Harold	Pte	34816	WIA.
Radcliffe, Rupert Francis	Pte	1828	WIA. Trans to Cheshires.
Raffel, John William	Pte	28066	KIA 20/9/17
Rafferty, Thomas	Pte	34832	

Raine, William	L/Cpl	1279	WIA × 2. Trans to E. Yorks.
Rainford, Harry	Pte	1241	Re-enlisted RFA.
Rallings, Ernest	Pte	30691	Ex RAVC. WIA.
Ralph, George Edward	Cpl	1813	WIA × 2. Trans to Tank Corps. POW.
Ralph, Robert	Pte	241075	WIA × 2. Trans to LC.
Ralph, William	WO2	240001	WIA.
Ralph, William A.	Pte	2958	Trans to Cheshires.
Ramsbottom, Norman	A/Cpl	30528	Ex 8th Bn.
Ramsden, Arthur	Pte	242509	
Ramsey, William	Pte	28067	
Randall, Harold	A/Cpl	24288	Ex 1st Bn. WIA. D. 28/8/19
Randolph, William Edgar	Pte	30500	Also 1st Bn.
Raske, Maurice James	Pte	41027	
Ratcliffe, George	Pte	1246	WIA.
Ratcliffe, John	Pte	1836	H.
Rawcliffe, Albert Edward	A/Cpl	266120	
Rawcliffe, John	Sgt	240408	WIA.
Rawcliffe, John James	Pte	241640	WIA X2. POW & DOW 11/8/17
Rawes, Harry	A/L/Cpl	2918	WIA. Trans to RDC.
Rawes, John	L/Sgt	50661	
Rawes, John	L/Sgt	241538	
Rawlinson, Herbert Barton	Pte	201868	
Rawlinson, Thomas	Pte	240874	D. 2/11/18
Rawnsley, Leonard Hayton	Pte	241494	KIA 2/8/17
Rawson, Thomas (?)	Pte	2966	Trans to ?
Ray, Arthur	Cpl	240470	Also 8th Bn.
Ray, William J. F.	L/Sgt	134	DOW 5/11/15
Raymond, Joseph	Pte	35833	Att TMB. Ex RAMC.
Read, Harry	Pte	2048	WIA.
Read, John Miles	Sgt	242320	
Reader, John Henry	Pte	22362	Ex 7th & 11th Bns. WIA. KIA 9/3/18
Reast, Fred	Pte	41031	
Redfearn, Robert	Pte	1665	WIA. Trans to MGC.
Redfern, Soloman	Pte	3012	Trans to Monmouths & LNL.
Redhead, James	Pte	1214	WIA. Trans to MGC.
Redhead, Percy	A/Cpl	240531	
Redhead, Walter	Cpl	240533	Also 8th Bn.

Redhead, William	Pte	34702	
Redman, Elimelech	Pte	202237	Also 7th Bn. Trans to KLR
Redman, Thomas	Pte	1968	
Redman, William	Pte	1688	WIA.
Reid, William	L/Cpl	26102	Ex 7th Bn.
Reilley (Reilly), Ernest	Pte	11343	Ex 2nd Bn. KIA 10/4/18
Relph, Robert	Pte	240301	WIA.
Relph, Roland Alfred	Pte	240532	
Remington, Edward	Sgt	2209	Pioneer-Sgt. Trans to LC.
Renshall, Peter	Pte	240129	WIA. KIA 12/3/17
Renshaw, Thomas Arthur	Pte	29102	
Retallick, Ewart Walter	Pte	33504	WIA.
Reynolds, Thomas	Pte	27432	Ex LF & 7th Bn.
Rhodes, Everitt	Pte	40998	
Richards, Fred	Pte	14923	KIA 23/4/18
Richardson, Albert	Pte	240086	
Richardson, David	Pte	241541	
Richardson, John	Sgt	844	
Richardson, John	Pte	1607	Trans to LC.
Richardson, P.	Pte	1660	WIA. Trans to RFC.
Richardson, Richard	Pte	241267	Accid. burned.
Richardson, Thomas	Pte	2023	Trans to Herefords.
Richardson, Walter	Pte	243035	
Richardson, William Ernest	2Lt		Trans to MGC.
Richardson, William Henry	Pte	240762	
Richmond, James John	Pte	33257	WIA. Also 7th Bn-15/9/17.
Rickerby, Herbert	Pte	265831	WIA.
Rickett, Joseph	Pte	235320	Also 1st Bn.
Ridding, John	Sgt	1235	KIA 2/8/17 with 20 KLR.
Riding, Edison	Pte	240352	WIA × 2. Also 2/5th & 1/4th.
Riding, Harold	Cpl	1217	
Rigby, Charles	Sgt	240303	
Rigby, Edwin	Pte	240763	
Rigby, Harold	Pte	243011	
Rigby, Richard	L/Cpl	2009	WIA.
Rigby, Richard	L/Cpl	27406	Ex LF, 7th & 1st Bns.
Rigden, William Thomas	L/Sgt	260015	MM.
Rigg, Edward	Pte	240625	WIA.

Rigg, Frank	Pte	25361	Ex 7th Bn.
Rigg, Septimus	Pte	38540	KIA 1/10/18
Riley, Alfred	Pte	34148	
Riley, Henry	Cpl	1165	WIA.
Riley, John	Pte	20740	Ex 7th Bn. POW.
Riley, Robert	Cpl	243461	Ex Warks. Trans to RWF 1920.
Riley, Stanley	Pte	242357	Att TMB.
Riley, William	Cpl	1236	
Riley, William Henry	Sgt	241227	
Rimmer, Edward Richardson	Cpl	242508	WIA. MM.
Rimmer, Jesse	Pte	13908	Ex 7th Bn.
Rimmer, Peter	Pte	2248	KIA 23/4/15
Rimmer, Richard	Pte	1307	H. Trans to LC and RE.
Ripley, George	Pte	27289	Ex Lincs, 1st, 8th & 11th Bns.
Ripley, Robert	Pte	1278	H
Ripley, William	Pte	27546	Ex 7th Bn.
Ripley, William Edwin	Pte	33472	Ex 8th Bn. WIA.
Ripper, Allan Gilbert	L/Cpl	2159	KIA 8/5/15
Ritchie, William	Pte	4146	KIA 25/6/16
Roberts, Alfred	Cpl	1845	Trans to LC.
Roberts, Edward	Pte	37718	
Roberts, Edward	Pte	51829	Ex MCR.
Roberts, Norman	Pte	37233	
Roberts, Richard Henry	Pte	28578	Also 2/5th & LC.
Roberts, William	Cpl	241461	KIA 28/7/17
Robertson, John	Pte	29103	
Robertson, William Dickson	2Lt		KIA 28/7/17
Robinson, Alfred	Pte	30501	Also 1st Bn.
Robinson, Ambrose	Pte	240817	WIA.
Robinson, Charles	Pte	242996	
Robinson, Christopher	Pte	240943	WIA.
Robinson, Frank	Pte	709	Trans to Lincs.
Robinson, Frank	L/Sgt	21563	
Robinson, Hilton	Pte	240264	Trans to LC.
Robinson, J.	Pte		WIA.
Robinson, James Milner	Pte	2791	H.
Robinson, John	Pte	243451	KIA 20/11/17 with 1/4th.
Robinson, John	A/WO1	240018	MiD. Comm. Northumb. Fus 1917.

Robinson, John Edward	Pte	3018	Comm. N. Som. Yeo 1917.
Robinson, John Roper	Pte	3008	Accid. wounded.
Robinson, Maurice James	Pte	1707	WIA. Trans to Scottish Rifles.
Robinson, Nathaniel	Pte	201936	
Robinson, Reginald Humphreys	Pte	32992	Comm. & KIA 4/10/18 with 1/4th.
Robinson, Richard Townson	Sgt	4330	Also 9th Bn.
Robinson, Robert	Sgt	242411	WIA.
Robinson, Sidney	Pte	30707	Ex RFA & RAVC. POW.
Robinson, Thomas	Pte	1308	KIA 14/4/15
Robinson, Thomas	Pte	1239	WIA.
Robinson, Thomas	Pte	34782	WIA. POW.
Robinson, Walter	Pte	4193	DOW 4/8/16
Robinson, William	Pte	1806	Trans to MGC, KSLI, Essex & RE.
Rodgerson, John	Pte	200789	Ex 1/4th. WIA × 3.
Roebuck, Frank	Pte	21150	Ex 11th Bn. WIA × 2.
Rogers, William	Pte	243121	
Rogerson, Richard	Pte	1423	WIA. Trans to LC.
Rogerson, Samuel	Cpl	271	Trans to LC.
Rogerson, William	Pte	29104	
Rollason, John Harold	Pte	25963	Ex 2nd Bn.
Rollinson, William	Cpl	242981	
Rome, Andrew	2Lt		WIA. Trans to MGC.
Ronson, William	Pte	240765	
Roocroft, Thomas	Pte	1749	WIA. KIA 3/8/16
Rooke, George	Pte	29105	
Root, Harry	Pte	30704	Ex RAVC.
Roper, Robert	Pte	240655	WIA X2. Trans to Lincs.
Roper, William Edward	Capt.		WIA. KIA 31/7/17
Roper, William Woof	Pte	34607	KIA 14/4/18
Roscoe, Clifford	Pte	2162	WIA × 2. Comm. LNL 1915.
Roscow, John	Pte	241250	Accid. wounded.
Rose, Bert	Pte	27156	Ex Lincs. Also 1/4th Bn. WIA.
Rose, Fred	Pte	37155	
Rose, James	Pte	4141	KIA 10/9/16
Rose, Thomas	Pte	33597	KIA 30/11/17
Rosenberg, Bernard	Pte	241630	KIA 2/8/17
Roskell, Alexander	Pte	241613	MM.
Roskell, Henry	Pte	14120	Also 7th Bn.

Roskell, Richard	Pte	2616	DOW 7/5/15
Ross, Joseph	Cpl	14054	Ex 7th Bn & ASC. WIA. POW.
Ross, William	Pte	265367	Att OBLI
Rossall, William	Pte	3420	WIA. KIA 15/6/17 with MGC.
Rossall, William	L/Cpl	240819	KIA 1/8/17
Rostron, George	L/Cpl	201927	KIA 30/11/17
Rothwell, Harry	Pte	242708	
Round, Edwin	Pte	36403	
Rourke, Hugh	Pte	1818	KIA 13/3/15
Rowe, John William	Pte	240346	WIA. POW.
Rowe, Samuel	L/Cpl	23065	Ex 7th & 1/4th Bns. WIA. POW.
Rowland, John William	Pte	40997	Ex-Leics Regt. KIA 10/10/18
Rowland, Thomas	Pte	1341	WIA. Trans to Middx.
Rowley, Arthur	Pte	29106	
Rowlinson, Samuel	Pte	241473	MM.
Roy, Percy Harold	WO2	241610	Ex 7th Bn. MM.
Roy, Thomas William	Pte	241403	
Roy, Victor John	C/Sgt	14066	Also 8th Bn. MiD.
Royle, George	Pte	5951	WIA. KIA 13/12/16 (Unlucky Draft)
Ruddock, Reginald Llewellyn	Pte	1821	WIA.
Rumley, James Boyd	Pte	917	WIA.
Rundle, Watkin	Sgt	240536	WIA. Also 2/5th. MM.
Rushton, Francis	Pte	34823	Also 1st Bn. WIA.
Rushton, William	Pte	200277	Ex 1/4th & 1st Bns. WIA × 2.
Rushworth, Benjamin Thomas (James)	Pte	240308	
Rushworth, John	Pte	29107	
Russell, Arthur	Pte	41017	
Russell, Tom	Pte	242494	WIA.
Rutlidge, Alfred	CSM	2413	H.
Rutter, William	Cpl	1489	WIA. Trans to Tank Corps.
Rydeard, John	Sgt	607	Trans to LC.
Rydeard, Stephen	Sgt	1964	KIA 21/3/18 with MGC
Ryder, Harry Clifford	Pte	15146	Also 7th & 1st Bns.
Ryding, Lambert	Pte	24608	Ex 8th & 1/4th Bns. KIA 31/7/17
Saer, Charles	2Lt		WIA.
Sager, Carey	Pte	33418	Accid. wounded; WIA × 2. To 8th Bn.

Salmon, Stanley	Pte	36651	
Salter, John Henry Clavell	2Lt		KIA 9/4/18
Salthouse, Hall Sheard	Pte	1995	KIA 4/5/15
Salthouse, Harold	Pte	3946	D. 15 /9/16
Salthouse, Sheard	Pte	1990	KIA 5/5/15
Samuel, Benjamin	Pte	22819	Also 11th Bn. KIA 30/11/17
Sandall, Arthur C.	Pte	2415	H.
Sandall, George Stanley	Pte	868	WIA. DOW 15/8/16
Sanderson, Alexander	Pte	240537	
Sanderson, Alfred Shaw	Pte	4130	KIA 1/8/16
Sanderson, Edward	Pte	1572	KIA 9/8/16
Sanderson, Robert	CSM	240247	WIA. KIA 20/9/17
Sanderson, Thomas	Cpl	1260	WIA.
Sanderson, Thomas	Sgt	240030	WIA. MM.
Sandford, Charles	Pte	240172	
Sandham, Albert Edward	Cpl	901	KIA 27/5/15
Sandham, Edward	Pte	265382	
Sandham, John	L/Cpl	243102	Ex 2nd Bn. WIA × 2. KIA 31/7/17
Sandham, Richard	Pte	241566	Also 8th Bn.
Saunders, Percy John	Pte	30692	Ex RAVC. WIA.
Saunders, Robert	Pte	1797	
Saunders, Thomas	Pte	1796	Trans to MCR.
Scales, John Clement	Pte	35700	KIA 9/4/18
Scarborough, Edward Owen	Cpl	240417	
Scarry, Martin J.	Pte	34434	D. 20/2/19
Schofield, Joseph	Pte	26780	Ex 7th & 11th Bns.
Scholes, Cecil	Sgt	51178	Also 7th Bn.
Scholes, John Hodkin	Pte	29108	
Scott, Edwin John	Pte	28221	Also 7th Bn.
Scott, Frank	Pte	260018	WIA × 2. POW. D. 2/1/18
Scott, John David	Pte	28069	Also 9th Bn.
Scott, John William	Pte	241070	
Scott, Sydney Towers	Lt		DOW 12/4/17
Scriven, Ernest	Pte	1509	WIA. Trans to LC.
Seacy, Hugh	Pte	34630	WIA. MM.
Searle, Robert	Sgt	241419	WIA × 2.
Seddon, Arthur	Pte	5053	DOW 22/9/16
Seddon, Robert	Pte	5044	KIA 11/11/16

Sedgwick, Harry	Pte	241478	WIA.
Seed, John Edward	L/Sgt	240145	
Sempers, Frank	L/Cpl	27302	Ex Lincs, 1st & 7th BNs.
Senneck, Samuel	Pte	38115	
Seward, Alfred Schrigley	Capt.		WIA × 2.
Seward, Thomas William	Pte	240269	POW.
Seward, Walker	Pte	24742	
Seymour, Arthur	Pte	29110	
Shannon, George	Pte	34834	POW.
Sharp, Albert Charles	Pte	27028	POW.
Sharpe, Gerald Whittaker	Capt.		
Sharpe, James Edward	Pte	12923	
Sharples, Walter	Pte	24957	Ex 1st Bn. WIA × 2. DOW 9/5/18.
Shaw, Albert	Pte	1166	
Shaw, Allan	Pte	240577	
Shaw, Arthur Noel	2Lt		WIA.
Shaw, Charles Edward	L/Sgt	887	WIA.
Shaw, Francis Henry	Pte	1769	WIA.
Shaw, George	Pte	22706	Ex 7th Bn. WIA × 3.
Shaw, George	Lt		WIA
Shaw, Gilbert	Pte	2520	WIA. Trans to LC.
Shaw, Harry	2Lt		
Shaw, Jack	Pte	23019	Ex 8th Bn. WIA × 2.
Shaw, John	Pte	1204	
Shaw, John	Pte	243015	
Shaw, John James	Pte	240068	WIA.
Shaw, Joseph	Pte	241482	Also 8th Bn.
Shaw, Lawrence	Pte	37151	KIA 6/8/18.
Shaw, Richard	Cpl	20935	Ex 11th Bn. WIA.
Shaw, Robert	Pte	16462	Also 9th, 1/4th Bns & Northum.
Shaw, Thomas	Pte	28070	Fus.
			WIA. Trans to LC.
Shaw, Walter Thomas	Pte	27887	Also 11th & 2/5th Bns.
Shelley, Albert	Pte	28071	
Shepherd, David	Pte	34657	Also 2nd Bn.
Shepherd, Harold Ewart	Pte	28222	Also 7th Bn.
Shepherd, Joseph	Pte	14566	DOW 7/5/18
Shepherd, Leonard	A/WO2	240178	WIA.
Shepherd, Thomas William Andrew	Pte	28072	KIA 28/7/17

Shepherd, William	Pte	4380	DOW 16/8/16
Shepherd, William Leo	Pte	1485	DOW 18/9/16
Shore, James	Pte	241120	WIA. Also 1/4th.
Shore, Joseph Charles	Pte	30272	Ex Sherwoods.
Shorrock, James	Pte	24888	Also 11th Bn.
Shulver, Hugh	Pte	260009	Also 1/4th. WIA.
Shuttleworth, Albert	Pte	26680	DOW 22/4/18
Shuttleworth, Charles	Pte	260034	
Shuttleworth, George	Pte	3078	KIA 4/5/15
Shuttleworth, Harry	Sgt	2057	WIA. Trans to ASC.
Shuttleworth, Joseph	Pte	240052	WIA. Posted 8th & 1st Bns.
Shuttleworth, Walter Scott	Pte	33042	WIA. POW.
Siddall, Harold	Pte	29112	Also 1/4th.
Siddle, Thomas	Sgt	240015	
Sidebottom, William	Pte	30748	Ex Cheshires. WIA.
Sighe, Edward	Pte	243055	Ex 8th Bn. WIA. DOW 10/3/17
Silcock, Edward	L/Cpl	16908	D. 10/4/18
Silk, Thomas	Pte	26983	Also 11th & 2/5th Bns.
Silversides, Crawford	Pte	242487	WIA.
Silverwood, Robert	Pte	240336	WIA × 2.
Simister, Thomas Edwin	Pte	33060	WIA.
Simmons, Claude	CSM	240945	Also 8th Bn. WIA.
Simmons, Richard	Pte	1261	DOW 24/5/15
Simpson, Arthur Weaver	Pte	2792	WIA.
Simpson, Charles Vernon Martin	Capt.		WIA. KIA 31/7/17
Simpson, Edmund Richard	Lt	2157	WIA × 2. Comm. KORL.
Simpson, Edwin	Pte	242413	
Simpson, Frank	Pte	240393	Att MGC.
Simpson, George	Pte	3791	KIA 3/8/16
Simpson, Granville	Pte	19793	Also 11th Bn.
Simpson, Harry	Pte	1899	WIA.
Simpson, Herbert	Cpl	240538	
Simpson, James	Pte	1515	KIA 23/4/15
Simpson, John	Pte	2210	KIA 4/5/15
Simpson, John	Sgt	1556	WIA. Trans to LC.
Simpson, Reginald	Cpl	240534	WIA.
Simpson, Richard	Pte	243078	Ex-ASC. WIA. Trans to Tanks.
Simpson, William	Pte	135	H.

Simpson, William	Pte	1601	Trans to MGC.
Simpson, William Edward	A/WO1	265238	WIA.
Sinclair, William	Pte	22895	Ex 8th & 7th Bns. WIA.
Sines, William John	Pte	30652	DOW 13/4/18
Singleton, Arthur	Pte	240821	WIA.
Singleton, Fred	Sgt	1108	WIA. Trans to RFC.
Singleton, John	Pte	32637	KIA 30/11/17
Singleton, Robert	Pte	241246	
Singleton, Robert Edward	Pte	241650	POW.
Singleton, William	Pte	2049	WIA.
Sizer, William	Pte	242656	DOW 1/8/17
Skate, Harry	Pte	27309	Ex Lincs, 1st, 8th & 11th Bns.
Skeats, Charles	Pte	240656	WIA.
Skeoch, Charles David	Pte	2622	Trans to MGC & RE.
Skeoch, Percy Brown	Sgt	240767	WIA X 2.
Skidmore, Thomas William	Pte	242644	WIA.
Skinner, George Lewis	L/Cpl	1478	WIA.
Slater, Fred	Pte	243030	
Slater, Gilbert Ferrace	Pte	34828	
Slater, Joseph	Pte	243065	KIA 23/7/17
Slater, Nelson	Pte	29113	KIA 3/5/18
Slater, Richard	Pte	241114	
Slater, Thomas	Pte	568	KIA 23/4/15
Sleight, Eric William	2Lt		WIA. MiD.
Slinger, George James	Pte	240530	Posted-7th & 1/4th Bns.
Slinger, Harry	Pte	241356	
Slinger, Thomas Edward	Pte	34785	Att TMB.
Smalley, Charles	Sgt	240657	WIA.
Smallshaw, Albert Edward	Sgt	240191	WIA × 2. MM.
Smallshaw, George Edward	A/Cpl	240876	WIA.
Smiley, Herbert	Pte	37753	
Smith, Alfred Henry	2Lt		WIA.
Smith, Andrew	Pte	242997	
Smith, Cecil	Sgt	243085	WIA. KIA 9/3/17
Smith, Edgar Landless	Pte	37206	
Smith, Edward James	Pte	241336	WIA. Also 2/5th.
Smith, Ellis	Pte	26136	Also 7th & 1st Bns.
Smith, Ernest	Pte	241574	WIA.

Smith, Fred	Pte	37764	WIA.
Smith, George	Pte	241880	Trans to RDC.
Smith, Harry	Pte	263034	Ex S. Lancs.
Smith, Henry	Pte	27038	Ex Lincs & 1st Bn. POW.
Smith, J. W.	Pte	3000	WIA.
Smith, James	Pte	1454	Trans to MGC. MM.
Smith, James	Pte	37254	Trans to KLR.
Smith, James Colin	Pte	1148	
Smith, James Robert	Pte	1783	WIA.
Smith, John	Pte	33252	KIA 20/9/17
Smith, John	Sgt	240036	
Smith, John	Pte	34626	
Smith, John	Cpl	243088	Also 2nd Bn.
Smith, John Hartley	Pte	32609	Also 7th Bn.
Smith, John Wilfred	Pte	2058	WIA.
Smith, Joseph	L/Cpl	1155	WIA.
Smith, Lewis	Pte	24327	Ex 1st & 8th Bns. WIA × 2.
Smith, Matthew	WO2	240047	Accid. burned.
Smith, Percy	Pte	1762	
Smith, Percy W.	Pte	1789	WIA.
Smith, Richard	Pte	241668	
Smith, Robert William	Pte	28073	
Smith, Sydney Oliver	2Lt		
Smith, Thomas	Pte	242446	DOW 10/3/17
Smith, Thomas	Pte	29115	KIA 3/5/18
Smith, Thomas Henry Birkett	L/Cpl	241071	MiD.
Smith, Tom	Pte	1946	WIA.
Smith, William	L/Sgt	1560	KIA 1/8/15
Smith, William	Pte	3077	WIA. Trans to West Lancs RFA.
Smith, William	Pte	265376	Also 1st & 1/4th Bns. WIA.
Smith, William	Cpl	1292	Trans to Tank Corp.
Smith, William Godman	Pte	24277	Ex 7th Bn.
Smith, William Henry	Pte	2524	DOW 16/4/15
Snape, Richard Rawlinson	Pte	1026	DOW 11/5/15
Snape, Thomas Higginson	Pte	243002	
Snedker, Walter	Pte	9399	Also 2nd & 1st Bns.
Snelson, Richard	RSM	3310	Comm. as Capt. in Reserve Bn.
Snow, Charles Godfrey	Pte	17962	Also 1st & 7th Bns.

Snowden, George R.	Sgt	185	WIA. Trans to LC.
Snowden, Harold	Pte	1718	H. D. 19/10/14
South, James	Pte	3893	KIA 3/8/16
Southgate, Frederick Charles	Pte	30705	Ex RAVC. WIA.
Sparks, Joseph	Pte	2016	KIA 8/5/15
Spedding, Percy Pearson	Pte	29117	
Spedding, Thomas James (Jesse)	Pte	240328	
Speight, John	Pte	1814	WIA. Trans to LC.
Speight, Richard	Cpl	241156	
Spencer, Frederick Walter	Pte	35860	
Spencer, George	Pte	240451	WIA. Att MGC.
Spencer, John	Pte	26956	Also 11th & 2/5th Bns.
Spencer, Robert	Pte	243079	Also 1st Bn & ASC. WIA.
Squire, James Henry	Pte	241481	Trans to Beds and LC.
Squires, Robert	L/Cpl	243066	DOW 4/5/18
Squirrell, George	Pte	1342	WIA. Trans to LC.
Squirrell, John	Pte	1639	WIA. Trans to KOYLI.
Stables, Moses	Pte	34784	KIA 20/9/17
Stafford, Walter	Pte	26778	
Stainrod, George Arthur	Pte	32035	Also 7th & 1/4th.
Stainton, Eric	2Lt		POW.
Stakes, Herbert	Pte	240719	POW.
Stalker, Joseph	Pte	241536	POW.
Stamp, Frank	Pte	1729	WIA.
Stamper, Reginald	Pte	240628	DOW 23/4/15
Standen, Edward Bernard	Sgt	241486	KIA 9/4/18
Standen, Walter W.	Sgt	1144	KIA 23/4/15
Stanley, Thomas	Pte	3953	KIA 15/8/16
Stanton, A.	Pte	3021	Trans to MFP.
Stark, Thomas	Pte	240433	
Stead, Norman	Pte	241513	KIA 30/11/17
Steel, Albert Bernard	Pte	242701	DOW 16/9/17
Steel, Gordon	2Lt		POW.
Steel, Omar	Pte	240406	MM.
Steel, William	Pte	265771	H. To BEF with 1/4th.
Steel, William Henry	Pte	18908	Also 1st Bn.
Steele, Thomas Arthur	Pte	41677	
Steels, Jim	Pte	27308	Ex 1st Bn. WIA. KIA 20/9/17

Stephenson, Bernard	Pte	240453	WIA × 2. Also 2/5th.
Stephenson, George	Pte	1829	WIA. Trans to RWF & RE.
Stephenson, James	Pte	4107	KIA 3/8/16
Sterland, Arthur	Pte	2040	WIA. Trans to LC. SWB.
Stevens, Tom	L/Sgt	260004	WIA.
Stevenson, Harry	Pte	202125	Ex1/4th. WIA.
Stevenson, John Charles	2Lt		WIA.
Stevenson, Richard	Pte	581	WIA.
Stevenson, Theophilus	Pte	260048	
Stewart, William	Pte	2794	DOW 4/8/16
Stirzaker, Charles	Pte	2251	KIA 29/3/15
Stirzaker, Richard Remington	Pte	1535	Trans to MGC.
Stirzaker, William	Pte	240454	WIA.
Stirzaker, William Henry	Pte	240825	POW.
Stirzaker, William Spencer	Pte	240456	WIA. Also 2.5th. Trans to Lincs.
Stobbart, James	Pte	2800	Trans to Middx. WIA. POW.
Stockdale, Herbert	Pte	240009	
Stoddart, William	Pte	1429	KIA 8/5/15
Stokes, Frank	Pte	263015	KIA 30/11/17
Stokes, Harold	Sgt	2526	Trans to MGC.
Stonall, John William	Pte	15434	Also 8th Bn.
Stone, Horatio Nelson	Pte	13819	Also 9th Bn.
Stones, James	Pte	2021	KIA 4/5/15
Storer, Joseph	Cpl	1538	WIA. Trans to LC.
Storey, Matthew Sunter	Pte	242643	KIA 20/9/17
Storey	L/Cpl		
Street, Alfred George	Pte	242704	WIA.
Street, Charles	Pte	30682	D. 16/10/20
Streeter, Robert	Pte	28074	
Strickland, Bert	Pte	35154	Also 2nd Bn. Att MCR. WIA.
Strickland, Thomas	Pte	240661	
Strickland, William	Pte	2709	KIA 8/5/15
Strutt, Harry	Pte	26844	Also 7th Bn.
Stubbings, Francis	Pte	260021	Posted 8th Bn.
Sturzaker, James	Pte	241637	WIA × 3. Trans to Lincs.
Sturzaker, John Robert	Pte	38109	KIA 24/8/18
Styran, Walter	Pte	36414	
Suart, John Robert	Pte	2155	

Sugden, George	Pte	241196	
Sugden, Joseph	Pte	29121	
Sullivan, Alfred	L/Cpl	2612	Ex 1st Bn.
Sullivan, Herbert	Pte	27458	
Sumner, Edward	Pte	241034	
Sumner, Francis	Pte	34680	
Sumner, James Robert	Pte	1906	Trans to RE.
Sumner, John	Pte	241146	
Sumner, John R.	Pte	240770	Trans to R. Fus.
Sumner, Joseph	Sgt	243096	Also 1st & 8th Bns. WIA.
Sumner, Reuben	Pte	290	WIA. KIA 17/10/16
Sumner, Reuben	Pte	24320	Ex 7th Bn. WIA × 2.
Sumner, Richard	WO2	5497	Ex 1st Bn. WIA.
Sunnucks, Stanley Lloyd	Capt.		
Sutcliffe, Robert	Pte	2207	H.
Sutherland, Frank	2Lt		WIA × 2.
Swain, James	Pte	240946	
Swain, Thomas	Pte	240948	
Swallow, William Henry	Pte	40999	KIA 23/4/18
Swann, Albert John	Sgt	240559	MM.
Swarbrick, Peter	Cpl	241654	WIA.
Sweeney, Albert	Sgt	240477	Also 1/4th. WIA. Murdered 20/9/20
Sweetman, John Thomas	Pte	244504	
Swift, Herbert	Pte	32504	Ex 7th Bn.
Swindlehurst, Harry	Pte	33927	WIA X2. SWB.
Sykes, Elvery Verdon	Sgt	240384	WIA.
Tattersall, Harold	L/Cpl	32610	MM. Trans to E Lancs.
Tattersall, James	Pte	3979	KIA 10/9/16
Taylor, A.	Sgt	240827	
Taylor, Clifford	Cpl	241580	
Taylor, Edward	Pte	241026	
Taylor, George	Pte	241647	
Taylor, Isaac	Pte	33401	Ex 7th Bn.
Taylor, James	Pte	1740	WIA.
Taylor, James	Pte	260029	WIA.
Taylor, James Parker	Pte	242492	
Taylor, John	Pte	27054	Ex Lincs & 1st Bn. Also 1/4th.
Taylor, John	Pte	38662	Also 2/5th.

Taylor, John George	Pte	34466	
Taylor, Jonathan	Pte	33570	
Taylor, Joseph	Pte	2927	Also 2nd & 11th Bns & LC.
Taylor, Richard	L/Sgt	240325	WIA.
Taylor, Robert	Pte	3197	
Taylor, Sidney	Sgt	240721	MM.
Taylor, Thomas	Pte	32595	WIA. MM. Trans to Notts & Derby.
Taylor, Thomas William	Pte	30698	Ex RAVC. WIA.
Taylor, Walter	Pte	28534	Ex LC. KIA 1/10/18
Teale, Arthur	Pte	265393	
Teasdale, Herbert	Cpl	240540	WIA × 2.
Teasdale, Matthew	Pte	266133	
Tedcastle, Walter	Sgt	240144	WIA × 2. KIA 20/9/17
Tennant, Henry	L/Sgt	464	WIA.
Terry, James	Pte	241778	
Tester, Alfred	Pte	240302	
Tester, Thomas	L/Cpl	1966	KIA 5/5/15
Tetley, Lawrence	Pte	1682	KIA 5/5/15
Thacker, Herbert Norman	Pte	240578	WIA. POW.
Theobald, William Henry	Pte	1324	KIA 23/4/15
Thomas, Mortimer	L/Cpl	2217	DOW 9/6/15
Thomas, Mortimer Cecil	Pte	3518	WIA.
Thomas, William	L/Cpl	23162	Also 11th & 8th Bns.
Thompson, Albert Edward	Pte	22795	Also 11th & 1st Bns.
Thompson, Arthur James	Pte	243116	Also 1st Bn.
Thompson, Charles	Pte	241045	
Thompson, Charles	Pte	36421	
Thompson, F.	Pte	200616	
Thompson, Fred	Pte	242483	
Thompson, G.	Pte	1870	Trans to MFP.
Thompson, George	Pte	201834	
Thompson, George Albert	Pte	240321	
Thompson, George William	Pte	41676	
Thompson, Henry	Pte	32515	WIA.
Thompson, James	Pte	36569	
Thompson, James William	Pte	2171	DOW 14/1/18 with Yorks R.
Thompson, John	Pte	241215	KIA 30/11/17
Thompson, Leonard	Pte	2056	DOW 29/4/15

Thompson, Percy	L/Cpl	241190	KIA 30/11/17
Thompson, Peter	Pte	1912	WIA. D. 3/1/17
Thompson, Peter	Pte	241518	WIA.
Thompson, Peter William	Pte	11	
Thompson, Richard	Pte	242418	Also 1/4th.
Thompson, Thomas Brockbank	Cpl	242457	Att TMB.
Thompson, Thomas Sidney	Pte	36510	KIA 9/4/18 (May be with 1/4th.)
Thompson, William	Pte	1326	WIA. Trans to KLR.
Thompson, William	Pte	240878	WIA. MM.
Thompson, William	Pte	34807	
Thornton, Fred	Pte	242697	
Thornton, George	Pte	2714	WIA.
Thornton, Harry	Pte	241555	
Thornton, James Marsh	Pte	2426	KIA 8/5/15
Thornton, John	Cpl	240949	Also 1st Bn.
Thornton, Nathaniel	Pte	2531	WIA. Trans to Hussars.
Thornton, William	Pte	242095	Also 2/5th.
Thorpe, Thomas	Pte	244	WIA.
Threlfall, Herbert	Pte	240950	
Threlfall, James	Pte	243067	WIA. KIA 20/11/17 with 1/4th.
Threlfall, James Henry	Pte	2933	DOW 19/8/16
Threlfall, Robert	Sgt	2176	KIA 27/5/15
Threlfall, Robert Batty	Pte	33118	Att US Army III Corps 1919.
Thursfield, Isaac James	Pte	242495	WIA. KIA 13/4/18 with 8th Bn
Thurston, Percy William	Pte	1352	Trans to LC.
Thwaite, William	Pte	242974	
Thwaites, John Henderson	Cpl	2181	KIA 11/5/17 with MCR.
Thwaites, Joseph	Pte	2803	DOW 12/5/15
Till, Daniel Clayton	Sgt	3792	Trans to MGC.
Till, George Singleton	Pte	35583	
Timberlake, John	Pte	242272	Also 8th Bn.
Timbrell, William Henry	Pte	241781	DOW 22/9/17
Timms, John	Pte	2050	Trans to Northum Fus. Comm into KORL
Timperley, Thomas	Pte	201580	KIA 20/11/17 with 1/4th.
Timperly, James	Pte	1840	Rejoined in LC.
Tims, John	Cpl	241789	
Tindale, Charles	Pte	28075	WIA.

Titchener, Leonard Raymond	L/Sgt	1474	WIA. K. 3/12/17 with RFC.
Titterington, Henry	Pte	240579	D. 31/8/18
Titterington, Thomas	Pte	22263	Ex 11th 7th Bns. WIA.
Todd, John George	Pte	28076	
Todd, John Hardman	2Lt		WIA. Att to Indian Army.
Toft, Arthur	Pte	35272	Also 1st Bn.
Tomlinson, James	Pte	18416	KIA 24/8/18
Tomlinson, James	Pte	37729	
Tomlinson, John Richard	Pte	5919	KIA 16/10/16
Tomlinson, Robert Croft	Pte	241837	Also 2/5th.
Tomlinson, Thomas William	Pte	33718	WIA & POW.
Tomlinson, Thomas William	Pte	241837	
Tonge, Fred	Cpl	22803	Ex 7th Bn. WIA × 2.
Toon, Charles Edward	L/Cpl	1138	Trans to MGC.
Toovey, Kennedy St Clair Hamilton	2Lt		POW. D. 15/10/18
Topham, John	Sgt	240322	WIA. Also 2/5th.
Topping, Thomas	Pte	3992	WIA. Trans to Tank Corps.
Toulmin, John	Pte	1654	DOW 22/5/16
Towers, Alfred	Pte	265271	
Towers, Harry Gilbert	Pte	240543	WIA. Comm. with LNL 1918.
Towers, Joseph Edward	Sgt	348	WIA. KIA 15/8/16
Towers, Oswald	Pte	1244	DOW 15/4/15
Towers, Thomas	Pte	2215	DOW 26/4/15
Townley, Joseph	Pte	240951	WIA.
Townley, William	Pte	202837	Also 2/5th.
Townson, Albert	Pte	3428	WIA. Trans to Monmouths.
Townson, Alfred	Pte	487	SWB.
Townson, Christopher	Pte	2340	
Townson, John George	Pte	240070	WIA.
Townson, Robert Dean	Pte	241634	WIA.
Townson, Thomas	Pte	24516	Ex 11th Bn. DOW 5/12/17
Tranter, William Henry	Pte	33162	Ex 8th Bn.
Trevallion, Harry	Pte	260019	WIA & POW.
Trigg, Walter George	Pte	27319	Ex Lincs & 1st Bn.
Trim, Arthur	Pte	114	
Tringham, Henry Vincent	2Lt		MC. MiD.
Tripp, Herbert	Pte	240329	
Troughton, Richard	Pte	240880	WIA.

Tubb, Sidney Herbert	Pte	30672	Ex RAVC.
Tuck, Arthur	Pte	28404	
Tuck, Walter Vernon	Sgt	30730	Ex LC.
Tucker, Clifford Francis	2Lt		KIA 9/4/18
Tuckwood, Charles Frederick	Pte	27976	Also 1st & 11th Bns.
Tugwell, Thomas	Pte	260010	POW.
Turner, Alfred Ernest	Pte	242654	Also 2nd Bn.
Turner, Alfred Henry	Capt.		MiD.
Turner, Harry	Pte	242319	
Turner, James Vincent	Cpl	2013	WIA.
Turner, John	Pte	1667	KIA 19/5/15
Turner, Llewellyn	Pte	1516	Trans to LC.
Turner, Robert Smith	Sgt	27729	Also 8th & 11th Bns. Comm. 1918.
Turner, Tom Oliver	Pte	21282	Ex 2nd & 2/5th Bns. KIA 10/7/18
Turner, Walter Harry	Pte	26930	Also 1st & 1/4th Bns. POW.
Turner, William	Pte	229	
Turner, William Thomas	Pte	26931	Also 1st Bn.
Turton, Robert Spruce	Pte	33503	Ex 8th Bn.
Tweedie, David Lamont	2Lt		WIA.
Twigg, John Leonard	Pte	1620	WIA. Posted 1/4th.
Twist, Albert	Pte	1710	Trans to MCR & E.Lancs.
Tyrell, William Lyness	Pte	1591	KIA 3/8/16
Tyson, Charles Edward	Pte	3187	DOW 26/7/15
Tyson, Frank	Pte	242979	
Tyson, Robert	Pte	22	WIA. Trans to LC.
Tyson, Sampson	Sgt	794	Trans to LC.
Vanbiene, Bernard	L/Sgt	3438	Also 2nd Bn.
Vanstone, Leonard	L/Cpl	27984	Also 1st Bn.
Varty, Frederick	Pte	38056	
Vaughan, Herbert Raymond	Pte	29128	WIA.
Veevers, Richard William	Pte	2805	DCM.
Verden, Harry	Pte	1587	WIA. Also 1/4th.Trans to KLR.
Vickers, William	Pte	241588	WIA. Also 8th Bn.
Vince, Bertrand James	A/Cpl	2177	WIA. Trans to KLR & Beds.
Vincent, Sidney	Pte	27894	Also 11th & 8th Bns.
Vooght, Harry	Pte	260024	
Waddington, Craven	Pte	34826	Also 2/5th.
Waddington, Frank	Pte	240554	WIA. Trans to RAMC.

Waddington, Herbert	Pte	30330	Ex 1st Bn. WIA.
Waddington, Robert	Pte	243068	DOW 14/3/17
Wade, Amos	Pte	13548	Also 9th & 7th Bns.
Wadeson, Arthur	Pte	240881	WIA. DOW 2/9/18 with 1st Bn.
Wadsworth, Robert	Pte	240468	WIA. MM.
Waite, Edward	Pte	30693	KIA 24/8/18
Waite, Henry Ernest	Pte	1381	KIA 23/4/15
Walker, Albert	Pte	4282	KIA 3/8/16 (Unlucky Draft)
Walker, Arthur	Pte	41003	DOW 1/8/18
Walker, Charles Wyatt	Pte	2233	Trans to MGC.
Walker, Edward	Sgt	12424	KIA 14/4/18
Walker, George William	Pte	241516	WIA. Trans to RE.
Walker, Granville Charles	Pte	26846	Also 8th Bn.
Walker, Henry	Pte	3731	
Walker, Jack Bertram	2Lt		DOW 8/3/18
Walker, John	Pte	263024	Also LNL.
Walker, Robert	Pte	2051	WIA. Trans to LC.
Walker, Sydney	Pte	1523	WIA.
Walker, Thomas	Pte	1534	Trans to S Lancs.
Walker, Thomas	Sgt	1787	Trans to LC.
Walker, William	Pte	201895	KIA 2/8/17
Walker, William	2Lt		WIA.
Walker, William	Pte	41681	
Wallbank, Richard	Sgt	93	KIA 4/5/15
Walling, Thomas	Pte	241776	DOW 22/3/17
Wallis, Henry	2Lt		
Walls, William	Pte	1655	KIA 8/3/15
Walmsley, Edward	Pte	240882	KIA 30/11/17
Walmsley, George A.	Pte	242440	WIA. Trans to LF.
Walmsley, John	L/Cpl	1486	KIA 26/4/15
Walmsley, John	Pte	241338	
Walmsley, John Herbert	Pte	260043	KIA 31/7/17
Walmsley, Richard	Pte	241501	Also 8th & 1/4th Bns.
Walmsley, Thomas	Pte	243070	Also 1/4th. WIA.
Walsh, James	Pte	241544	KIA 9/4/18
Walsh, Michael	Pte	28157	Ex LF & 7th Bn.
Walters, George	L/Cpl	241557	WIA. MM. Trans to RDC.
Walton, Edward	Pte	240094	WIA.

Walton, Harry	Pte	240109	MSM. MiD.
Walton, Harry	Pte	242484	Also 8th Bn. MiD with 8th Bn. WIA.
Walton, James	Pte	1091	H. D. 1/10/14
Walton, Thomas	A/Cpl	1102	WIA.
Warbrick, Frederick	Pte	2125	Trans to RE.
Ward, James	Pte	2342	KIA 27/4/15
Ward, John Coward	Pte	34478	
Ward, William	Pte	41684	
Wardle, Albert Arthur	Pte	260027	KIA 20/9/17
Wareing, Albert	Pte	51360	
Wareing, William	Pte	241576	WIA.
Wareing, William H.	Pte	938	WIA. Trans to RE & LC.
Warner, Thomas H.	Pte	1522	Trans to RE.
Warren, Bertie	Pte	20889	Ex RDC.
Warren, Eric Norman	Pte	41006	
Warriner, James William	Pte	29130	DOW 24/8/18
Warwick, Herbert	Pte	2630	WIA. Trans to R High & RE.
Warwick, Louis	Pte	1621	KIA 8/5/15
Warwick, Stanley	Pte	1693	WIA x2. KIA 12/4/18 Monmouths
Waterhouse, John	Pte	24	WIA.
Waterhouse, Robert	Pte	241540	
Waterhouse, William Thornley	Pte	5953	KIA 22/9/16 (Unlucky Draft)
Waters, Edward J.	L/Cpl	2537	WIA. Trans to Monmouths & APC.
Watson, Edward	Pte	241421	KIA 26/4/17 with 8th Bn.
Watson, George William	Pte	41002	
Watson, Harold	Pte	28077	DOW 26/7/18
Watson, John	Pte	243083	Trans to ASC.
Watson, John Cochrane	Pte	240291	WIA × 2. KIA 12/5/17 with 8th Bn.
Watson, John Edward	Pte	30898	Ex LNL. Also 1/4th.
Watson, Richard	Pte	23724	Also 1st Bn.
Watson, William	A/WO1	202003	Also Royal Munsters & 1st Bn.
Watt, Alexander	Pte	240774	KIA 20/9/17
Watt, Harold	Pte	28078	
Wattleworth, John	Pte	38118	
Watts, William George	Pte	26847	WIA. Also 11th & 1/4th Bns.
Wayte, Adrian Barclay	Lt-Col.		Notts & Derby. DSO. MiD.
Weall, Joseph	Pte	34609	
Wearing, Harold	Pte	33956	WIA. Posted 1/4th.

Wearing, Robert	Pte	241559	KIA 1/9/18 with 8th Bn.
Weatherhead, Robert Wardle	Pte	28079	WIA.
Weaver, Robert	Pte	30223	WIA. Also 7th Bn.
Webb, Ernest Frederick	Pte	242711	
Webb, Frank Rowland	Pte	41009	WIA.
Webb, George	Pte	34584	KIA 30/11/17
Webb, William	Pte	22567	Also 11th & 9th Bns.
Webber, Richard	Pte	28305	Also 11th, 2/5th Bns & ASC.
Webster, Alfred Newby	Pte	41012	
Webster, George	Pte	21518	Ex 8th Bn. WIA. DOW 2/12/17
Webster, George William	Pte	243056	POW.
Webster, Henry	Pte	242690	Ex 1st Bn. KIA 24/4/17
Webster, John	L/Cpl	16872	Also 2nd, 8th, 1/4th and 1st Bns.
Webster, Paul	Pte	240385	B Coy. HOS-8/5/15. Also 2/5th.
Wedge, James Arthur	Pte	33947	WIA.
Weedon, Thomas H.	Pte	2632	DOW 15/5/15
Wells, Leonard	Pte	27321	Ex Lincs & 1st Bn. WIA.
Welsh, Edward	Pte	260047	WIA.
West, Herbert Spencer	Pte	240883	WIA. Trans to RE.
West, John Cooper	Pte	2174	WIA × 2. Trans to LC.
Westby, Gordon	L/Sgt	22182	Ex 1st & 7th Bns.
Western, Joseph	L/Cpl	240404	WIA. KIA with 2/5th 19/2/17
Westhead, William Henry	Pte	240300	Trans to MGC.
Westwater, Lindsay A.	2Lt		Att from Royal Scots. WIA.
Westwood, Philemon	Cpl	10079	Also 1st & 7th Bns.
Whalley, Anthony	Pte	1351	WIA × 2. Trans to RFC & LC.
Whalley, George	Sgt	20332	MM. Trans to RE.
Whalley, Robert	Pte	241158	
Whalley, William	Pte	240021	WIA. Also 2/5th.
Wharton, Leslie	Pte	263025	Ex LNL.
Wheeler, Ernest	Pte	243084	
Wheelwright, Edgar	Pte	241465	
Whinray, Robert	Pte	240953	WIA. Trans to Lincs.
White, Alexander John	2Lt		POW. D. 20/2/20
White, Charles	Pte	242692	Also 1st Bn as A/WO2 and 2nd Bn.
White, Harold Damant	2Lt		WIA. Trans to RAF.
White, James	Cpl	1784	Trans to KLR.

White, John Wesley	Pte	26165	Also 9th Bn.
White, Percy Charles	Pte	41014	
White, Robert Beesley	Sgt	204705	Ex Lancs Hussars Yeo.
Whitehead, Cyril Vere	Pte	240955	DOW 22/6/17
Whitehead, Harry Howarth	Pte	235075	Also 7th Bn.
Whitehead, Norman	Pte	37190	
Whitehead, Reginald Vere	Pte	240216	
Whitehead, Walter Hudson	Pte	202251	
Whitehead, Wilfred Vere	Pte	240956	POW. D. 15/11/18
Whiteside, Ambrose	Pte	1704	H.
Whiteside, Christopher	Pte	2810	KIA 14/4/15
Whiteside, Clarence	Pte	1392	WIA.
Whiteside, Cyril	Pte	240542	
Whiteside, George	Pte	240831	
Whiteside, Joseph Faint	A/Cpl	240119	Trans to RE.
Whiteside, Richard	Pte	240553	WIA.
Whiteside, Robert	Pte	2436	WIA. Trans to LNL.
Whiteside, Robert	L/Cpl	12998	Also 7th Bn.
Whiteside, Walter	Pte	11536	Also 6th, 7th, & 1/4th.
Whiteside, Walter	Pte	243098	Also 7th & 1/4th.
Whitley, Jonathan Wilfred	Pte	241535	
Whitmore, Frederick Oliver	Pte	41007	KIA 3/5/18
Whitmore, Percival Charles	Pte	26940	Ex 1st Bn. DOW 16/6/18
Whittaker, Edward	Pte	201932	
Whittaker, William	Pte	28080	POW.
Whittam, John James	Pte	3702	DOW 4/8/16
Whittle, Thomas	Pte	243124	Also 8th Bn.
Widdows, William	Pte	241399	
Widger, Donald James	Pte	30716	Ex LNL. WIA.
Wignall, Thomas	Pte	3390	WIA. Trans to MGC.
Wilcock, John	Pte	1298	KIA 8/5/15
Wilcock, John	A/C/Sgt	240474	WIA.
Wilcock, Percy Edward	Pte	240958	
Wild, Harold	Pte	242995	Ex Cheshires and Also 8th Bn.
Wild, Robert	Pte	19518	Also 11th & 7th Bns.
Wilding, John	Cpl	595	WIA.
Wilkins, Frank George	Pte	29132	
Wilkinson, Ernest Joseph	Pte	33916	WIA.

Wilkinson, Frederick William	Sgt	51179	WIA.
Wilkinson, George	Pte	2635	KIA 27/4/15
Wilkinson, George Nicholas	L/Cpl	784	
Wilkinson, Henry	Pte	240085	
Wilkinson, Howard	Pte	241143	
Wilkinson, James Henry	Pte	41008	KIA 4/10/18
Wilkinson, Joseph	Pte	1146	WIA.
Wilkinson, Thomas	Sgt	240316	WIA. KIA 30/11/17
Wilkinson, William James	Pte	243459	Also 2/5th. WIA × 2.
Willacy, Thomas	Pte	1606	DOW 3/4/16
Williams, A. O.	Pte	1775	Trans to RGA.
Williams, Arthur	Pte	243025	KIA 12/12/17 with 8th Bn.
Williams, Charles H.	Pte	2344	Trans to MGC & RE.
Williams, Edmund	L/Sgt	1147	WIA.
Williams, George	Sgt	27801	Also 11th & 2/5th Bns.
Williams, James	Pte	1957	
Williams, John	Pte	37211	
Williams, Robert	Pte	15696	Also 8th, 7th & 1/4th Bns. MM.
Williams, Thomas	Pte	29133	
Williams, Thomas John 'JT'	Sgt	240041	WIA.
Williams, William	L/Cpl	20582	Ex 7th Bn. WIA × 4.
Williamson, John William	Sgt	1408	Trans to LC.
Williamson, William	Pte	33684	Posted 1st Bn. WIA × 2.
Wilson, Albert	Pte	1636	WIA. Trans to MGC.
Wilson, Albert	C/Sgt	240063	MM.
Wilson, Carl Bradshaw	Pte	33578	WIA. Trans to MGC.
Wilson, David	Pte	41013	
Wilson, Edward	Pte	240113	
Wilson, Ernest	Pte	3820	WIA × 2. Rejoined 2nd Bn.
Wilson, George E.	Pte	2636	Trans to RE.
Wilson, George Edward	Pte	241531	Also 7th & 1/4th Bns.
Wilson, George Myles	Pte	32650	DOW 20/9/17
Wilson, George W.	Pte	2214	Trans to LNL.
Wilson, Harry	Pte	241573	
Wilson, James	Pte	635	Trans to LC. D. 8/1/18
Wilson, James	Pte	35694	DOW 13/4/18
Wilson, James	Pte	1420	WIA.
Wilson, James	WO2	23596	Also 7th Bn.

Wilson, John	Pte	2182	KIA 3/5/15
Wilson, John	Cpl	241176	WIA. MiD. KIA 30/11/17
Wilson, John	Pte	260041	KIA 30/11/17
Wilson, John	Pte	241048	POW.
Wilson, John Thomas	Pte	2348	H. KIA 2/12/17 with Borderers.
Wilson, Joseph Mann	Pte	22070	Also 7th, 8th, 11th & 1st Bns.
Wilson, Matthew	Pte	38526	
Wilson, Ralph Croom	Pte	203117	
Wilson, Richard	Pte	1247	WIA.
Wilson, Richard	Pte	240088	Also 8th Bn.
Wilson, Samuel Hadwen	Cpl	240395	KIA 9/3/17
Wilson, Samuel Leith	Pte	3639	D. 12/7/16
Wilson, Thomas	Cpl	240310	WIA.
Wilson, Thomas Ernest	Pte	41037	
Wilson, Thomas James	Pte	3575	KIA 3/8/16
Wilson, Thomas Victor	Pte	33910	WIA. Posted to 2nd Bn.
Wilson, William	Pte	68	WIA.
Wilson, William	Pte	37157	
Wilson, William Thomas	Pte	240884	
Winchester, John	Pte	32651	POW.
Winder, Daniel	Cpl	1111	Trans to Lincs.
Winder, Edward	Pte	2213	KIA 3/5/15
Winder, Ernest	Pte	2216	WIA. Trans to S Lancs.
Winder, Henry	Pte	2546	KIA 27/4/15
Winder, Isaac	L/Cpl	1179	WIA.
Winder, John	Pte	1447	WIA × 2. Trans to MGC.
Winder, John	Pte	240357	WIA. Trans to Tank Corps.
Winder, Robert	Pte	979	WIA. Trans to LC.
Winder, Thomas	Pte	437	WIA.
Winder, William	L/Cpl	24168	Ex 1st Bn. MM.
Winder, William Henry	Pte	2175	H.
Winskill, Christopher	Pte	27791	Also 11th Bn.
Winterburn, Ernest William	Pte	22531	Also 11th & 8th Bns.
Wintrip, James	Pte	28082	WIA. Trans to Lincs.
Witham, Albert	Sgt	1479	WIA.
Withey, James David	2Lt		WIA.
Wolfendale, George	Pte	1766	WIA × 2. Trans to ASC.
Wolfendale, William Atkinson	Lt		WIA. MC.

Wolfenden, Harry	Pte	27466	Also 7th Bn.
Wolfenden, Tom	C/Sgt	240054	MSM. MiD.
Wolstenholme, Walter Wrigley	Pte	34786	
Wood, Ernest	Cpl	243082	Also ASC. WIA.
Wood, George	Pte	242479	WIA.
Wood, James	Pte	240731	
Wood, James	Pte	243112	Also 1st Bn.
Wood, John	Pte	201948	KIA 29/7/17
Wood, Moses	Pte	243069	DOW 2/12/17
Wood, W.	L/Cpl	2548	WIA. Trans to RFC.
Wood, William	Pte	1869	WIA. Trans to LC.
Wood, William	Pte	260030	POW.
Woodall, John William	Pte	235076	Also 7th Bn. MM.
Woodburn, Albert Edward	Pte	2347	WIA.
Woodcock, Harold Frank	2Lt		POW.
Woodcock, Joseph	WO2	92	
Woodford, Charles Ernest	Pte	26991	Also 11th Bn.
Woodhouse, Allen	Pte	4009	KIA 1/8/16
Woodhouse, Jack	Pte	1622	WIA × 2. Re-enlisted Yorks and Lancs.
Woodhouse, James	Pte	240962	WIA. SWB.
Woodhouse, John Roland	Pte	27005	Also 1st & 11th Bns. WIA.
Woodhouse, Lawrence Wilfred	Pte	2949	Trans to MGC.
Woodhouse, Ronald Bertram	2Lt		Dismissed the service.
Woodhouse, Thomas	Pte	2950	WIA. Trans to S Lancs.
Woodhouse, Thomas William	Pte	37149	
Woodhouse, William	L/Cpl	241593	Trans to LC.
Woods, Ernest	Cpl	243082	Ex ASC.
Woods, Fred	Cpl	265419	Also 7th Bn.
Woods, John	Pte	2173	KIA 26/4/15
Woods, Thomas	L/Cpl	28304	Ex ASC, 11th & 8th Bns. WIA.
Woods, William	Pte	36542	Att TMB.
Woods, William	Sgt	241495	
Woodward, Albert Hercy	Pte	41004	
Woodward, Reginald Rupert	2Lt		KIA 1/12/17
Woof, Charles Mason	Pte	240732	Ex 1st Bn. WIA.
Wooff, Joseph Edward	Pte	24751	
Wooff, Lancelot Burton	Pte	1435	WIA.

Woolcock, William	Pte	1812	WIA. Trans to LC.
Woolley, Benjamin	L/Cpl	242691	Also 7th Bn. WIA. SWB.
Woolley, William Thomas	Pte	260025	WIA × 2. DOW 13/5/18
Worby, Wilfred	A/Cpl	240327	WIA.
Worden, John Edgar	Pte	240580	POW.
Wren, Herbert	Pte	242377	
Wren, James Henry	Pte	2592	Trans to LC.
Wrench, George Edward	Pte	243019	Also 1st & 8th Bns.
Wright, Douglas Campbell	Pte	2037	KIA 23/4/15
Wright, Ernest	Pte	1637	WIA.
Wright, Harold John	Pte	18866	Also 7th & 1/4th Bns.
Wright, Harry	Pte	37165	
Wright, Harry Harold	Pte	240467	WIA.
Wright, John	L/Cpl	2637	MM.
Wright, John	Pte	35155	Also 2nd Bn.
Wright, John	Cpl	241633	Att TMB.
Wright, John Richard	Sgt	590	WIA x2. MM. MiD. KIA 20/9/17 with MGC
Wright, John Robert	Cpl	37734	Ex-RAVC.
Wright, John William	Pte	242693	Also 8th Bn.
Wright, Thomas	Cpl	240214	WIA. Also 2/5th.
Wright, Thomas	Sgt	240162	WIA X2.
Wright, Thomas	Pte	41679	
Wright, William	Pte	4113	KIA 3/8/16
Wright, William	Sgt	160	
Wright, William Thomas	Pte	1928	KIA 3/5/15
Wrightson, William	Pte	41010	Trans to KLR.
Wrigley, Samuel	Pte	243090	
Wylie, John	2Lt		Att from LNL.
Yacomeni, William McEwen	2Lt		MM. POW. D. 17/2/20
Yare, Richard	Pte	240335	WIA.
Yare, William Thomas	2Lt	240539	Comm. 1917. MC.
Yates, George	Pte	2178	WIA x2. KIA 15/8/16
Yates, John	Pte	37745	
Young, James McLaren	Capt.		
Young, Walter	Pte	240422	WIA. Trans to LC.
Young, Walter	2Lt		POW.

Endnotes

Chapter 1

1. *Regulations for the Territorial Force and for County Associations* (London: HMSO, 1908), para. 274.
2. War diary of the 1/5th King's Own (Royal Lancaster) Regiment. WO 95 2274-3 (National Archives).
3. *The Lancaster Guardian*, 8 August 1914.
4. *Ibid.*
5. *Ibid.*
6. *Ibid.*
7. *The Lancaster Observer and Morecambe Chronicle*, 7 August 1914.
8. *Ibid.*, 14 August 1914.
9. *The Lancaster Guardian*, 28 August 1914.
10. *Ibid.*, 3 October 1914.
11. *The Lancaster Observer and Morecambe Chronicle*, 11 September 1914.
12. *The Lancaster Guardian*, 5 September 1914.
13. *The Lancaster Observer and Morecambe Chronicle*, 27 November 1914.
14. *Ibid.*, 24 December 1914.
15. *The Lancaster Guardian*, 2 January 1915.
16. *Ibid.*

Chapter 2

1. *The Lancaster Observer and Morecambe Chronicle*, 12 March 1915.
2. *The Lancaster Guardian*, 6 March 1915.
3. *The Lancaster Observer and Morecambe Chronicle*, 26 February 1915.
4. *The Lancaster Guardian*, 6 March 1915.
5. *Ibid.*
6. *The Lancaster Guardian*, 20 March 1915.
7. *Ibid.*
8. *Ibid.*
9. *The Lancaster Observer and Morecambe Chronicle*, 19 March 1915.
10. *The Lancaster Guardian*, 20 March 1915.
11. *Ibid.*
12. *The Lancaster Observer and Morecambe Chronicle*, 12 March 1915.
13. *Ibid.*, 5 March 1915.
14. *Ibid.*, 1 April 1915.
15. *The Lancaster Guardian*, 20 March 1915.
16. *Ibid.*

17. *The Lancaster Guardian*, 1 May 1915.
18. *Ibid.*, 20 March 1915.
19. *Ibid.*, 27 March 1915.
20. *The Lancaster Observer and Morecambe Chronicle*, 26 March 1915.
21. *Ibid.*
22. *The Lancaster Observer and Morecambe Chronicle*, 1 April 1915.
23. *The Lancaster Guardian*, 17 April 1915.
24. *Ibid.*, 10 April 1915.
25. *Ibid.*, 3 April 1915.
26. *The Lancaster Observer and Morecambe Chronicle*, 9 April 1915.
27. *Ibid.*
28. *Ibid.*
29. James Madden, WO 363 (National Archives).

Chapter 3

1. *The Lancaster Guardian*, 1 May 1915.
2. *The Lancaster Observer and Morecambe Chronicle*, 30 April 1915.
3. Hodgkinson, A., *The King's Own 1/5th Battalion, TF in the European War 1914-1918* (Lancaster: The King's Own Royal Regimental Museum, 2009), p. 11.
4. Edmonds, J. E., *Official History of the Great War, Military Operations France and Belgium, 1915. Volume 1* (Uckfield: Naval & Military Press, 2009), p. 160.
5. *The Lancaster Guardian*, 24 April 1915.
6. *Ibid.*
7. *The Lancaster Guardian*, 1 May 1915.
8. *The Lancaster Observer and Morecambe Chronicle*, 23 April 1915.
9. *The Lancaster Guardian*, 1 May 1915.
10. *Ibid.*, 24 April 1915.
11. *Ibid.*
12. *Ibid.*
13. *The Lancaster Observer and Morecambe Chronicle*, 7 May 1915.
14. *The Lancaster Guardian*, 24 April 1915.
15. *Ibid.*
16. *Ibid.*
17. *Ibid.*
18. John Livesey, WO 364 (National Archives).
19. *The Lancaster Observer and Morecambe Chronicle*, 23 April 1915.
20. *Ibid.*
21. Hodgkinson, *op. cit.*, p. 11.
22. *The Lancaster Guardian*, 24 April 1915.
23. *The Lancaster Observer and Morecambe Chronicle*, 7 May 1915.
24. *Ibid.*, 14 May 1915.
25. *The Lancaster Guardian*, 8 May 1915.
26. Edmonds, *op. cit.*, pp. 176-180.
27. War diary of the 1/5th King's Own (Royal Lancaster) Regiment, WO 95 2274-3.
28. Edmonds, *op. cit.*, p. 205.
29. *The Lancaster Guardian*, 8 May 1915.
30. *Ibid.*, 1 May 1915.
31. *The Lancaster Observer and Morecambe Chronicle*, 11 June 1915.
32. *The Lancaster Guardian*, 1 May 1915.
33. *Ibid.*, 8 May 1915.
34. *The Lancaster Observer and Morecambe Chronicle*, 7 May 1915.
35. *Ibid.*, 11 June 1915.
36. *The Lancaster Guardian*, 8 May 1915.
37. *The Lancaster Observer and Morecambe Chronicle*, 7 May 1915.
38. *The Lancaster Guardian*, 8 May 1915.
39. *The Lancaster Observer and Morecambe Chronicle*, 11 June 1915.

40. *Ibid.*, 7 May 1915.
41. *Ibid.*, 14 May 1915.
42. *Ibid.*
43. *The Lancaster Observer and Morecambe Chronicle*, 7 May 1915.
44. *Ibid.*
45. *The Lancaster Guardian*, 1 May 1915.
46. *The Lancaster Observer and Morecambe Chronicle*, 7 May 1915.
47. Supplement to *The London Gazette*. 15 April 1916.
48. *The Lancaster Guardian*, 8 May 1915.
49. War diary of the 1/5th King's Own (Royal Lancaster) Regiment, WO 95 2274-3.
50. Hodgkinson, *op. cit.*, pp. 15-17.
51. War diary of 83 Infantry Brigade, WO 95 2273-3 (National Archives).
52. *The Lancaster Guardian*, 8 May 1915.
53. *The Lancaster Observer and Morecambe Chronicle*, 7 May 1915.
54. *Ibid.*
55. *Ibid.*
56. *The Lancaster Guardian*, 8 May 1915.
57. Edmonds, *op. cit.*, p. 276.
58. War diary of 83 Infantry Brigade, WO 95 2273-3.
59. *The Lancaster Guardian*, 1 May 1915.
60. War diary of 83 Infantry Brigade, WO 95 2273-3.

Chapter 4

1. *The Lancaster Observer and Morecambe Chronicle*, 21 May 1915.
2. Edmonds, J. E., *Official History of the Great War, Military Operations France and Belgium, 1915. Volume 1* (Uckfield: Naval & Military Press, 2009), pp. 277-288.
3. Hodgkinson, A., *The King's Own 1/5th Battalion, TF in the European War 1914-1918* (Lancaster: The King's Own Royal Regimental Museum, 2009), p. 18.
4. War diary of the 2/ King's Own (Royal Lancaster) Regiment, WO 95 2274-2 (National Archives).
5. Hodgkinson, *op. cit.*, pp. 18-19.
6. *The Lancaster Observer and Morecambe Chronicle*, 14 May 1915.
7. *The Lancaster Guardian*, 15 May 1915.
8. *The Lancaster Observer and Morecambe Chronicle*, 14 May 1915.
9. *The Lancaster Guardian*, 12 June 1915.
10. *The Lancaster Observer and Morecambe Chronicle*, 29 September 1916.
11. *Ibid.*, 14 May 1915.
12. *Ibid.*
13. *The Lancaster Guardian*, 8 May 1915.
14. *Ibid.*, 10 July 1915.
15. *The Lancaster Observer and Morecambe Chronicle*, 21 May 1915.
16. *Ibid.*
17. *The Lancaster Observer and Morecambe Chronicle*, 14 May 1915.
18. *The Lancaster Guardian*, 22 January 1916.
19. *The Lancaster Observer and Morecambe Chronicle*, 4 June 1915.
20. *The Lancaster Guardian*, 12 June 1915.
21. *The Lancaster Observer and Morecambe Chronicle*, 11 June 1915.
22. *Ibid.*, 14 May 1915.
23. *The Lancaster Guardian*, 15 May 1915.
24. *The Lancaster Observer and Morecambe Chronicle*, 14 May 1915.
25. *Jeudwine Papers.* 356/FIF/6/3/17. (Liverpool Record Office).
26. Stanley Butler, WO 363 (National Archives).
27. *The Lancaster Observer and Morecambe Chronicle*, 2 July 1915.
28. *The Lancaster Guardian*, 15 May 1915.
29. *The Lancaster Observer and Morecambe Chronicle*, 14 May 1915.
30. *The Lancaster Guardian*, 15 May 1915.

31. *Jeudwine Papers*. 356 FIF/6/1/19. (Liverpool Record Office).
32. *The Lancaster Observer and Morecambe Chronicle*, 14 May 1915.
33. Hodgkinson, *op. cit.*, p. 19.
34. War diary of 83 Infantry Brigade, WO 95 2273-3.
35. *The Lancaster Observer and Morecambe Chronicle*, 21 May 1915.
36. *Ibid.*, 14 May 1915.
37. *Ibid.*
38. *The Lancaster Observer and Morecambe Chronicle*, 21 May 1915.
39. *The Lancaster Guardian*, 15 May 1915.
40. *The Lancaster Observer and Morecambe Chronicle*, 21 May 1915.
41. *The Lancaster Guardian*, 22 May 1915.
42. *The Lancaster Observer and Morecambe Chronicle*, 28 May 1915.
43. *Ibid.*, 14 April 1916.
44. *The Lancaster Guardian*, 22 January 1916.
45. *Ibid.*, 22 May 1915.
46. Class P (T) Reserve was for men whose fitness level was not below 3iii, and who, if discharged, would be eligible for a pension for either time-expired or illness/injury; and whose service in a civilian role was deemed of more value to their country than their remaining in the military.
47. *The Lancaster Observer and Morecambe Chronicle*, 26 November 1915.
48. *Ibid.*, 21 May 1915.
49. *The Lancaster Guardian*, 15 May 1915.
50. *Ibid.*, 21 May 1915.
51. War diary of 83 Infantry Brigade, WO 95 2273-3.

Chapter 5

1. War diary of the 2/ King's Own (Royal Lancaster) Regiment, WO 95 2274-2.
2. War diary of 83 Infantry Brigade, WO 95 2273-3.
3. War diary of the 1/5th King's Own (Royal Lancaster) Regiment, WO 95 2274-3.
4. *The Lancaster Guardian*, 12 June 1915.
5. *The Lancaster Observer and Morecambe Chronicle*, 11 June 1915.
6. *Ibid.*, 4 June 1915.
7. *The Lancaster Observer and Morecambe Chronicle*, 11 June 1915.
8. Benson Boyd. WO 364. The National Archives.
9. *The Lancaster Observer and Morecambe Chronicle*, 11 June 1915.
10. War diary of 83 Infantry Brigade, WO 95 2273-3.
11. *The Lancaster Guardian*, 24 July 1915.
12. War diary of 83 Infantry Brigade, WO 95 2273-4 (National Archives).
13. *The Lancaster Guardian*, 6 August 1915.
14. *The Lancaster Observer and Morecambe Chronicle*, 14 August 1915.
15. *Ibid.*, 20 August 1915.
16. *Ibid.*, 27 August 1915.
17. *The Lancaster Guardian*, 14 August 1915.
18. War diary of 83 Infantry Brigade, WO 95 2273-4.
19. *The Lancaster Observer and Morecambe Chronicle*, 27 August 1915.
20. War diary of the 2/ King's Own (Royal Lancaster) Regiment, WO 95 2274-2.
21. War diary of 83 Infantry Brigade, WO 95 2273-4.
22. *Ibid.*, WO 95 2273-3.
23. War diary of the 1/5th King's Own (Royal Lancaster) Regiment, WO 95 2274-3.
24. War diary of 83 Infantry Brigade, WO 95 2273-5 (National Archives).
25. *The Lancaster Observer and Morecambe Chronicle*, 15 October 1915.
26. War diary of the 1/5th King's Own (Royal Lancaster) Regiment, WO 95 2274-3.
27. War diary of 83 Infantry Brigade, WO 95 2273-5.
28. The Brigade war diary states 85 Brigade, but this is clearly in error as this sector was held by 84 Brigade. The Battalion's own diary correctly attributes 84 Brigade.

Chapter 6

1. George William Brown, WO 363 (National Archives).
2. War diary of 2 Infantry Brigade, WO 95 1267-2 (National Archives).
3. The Battalion war diary attributes these to the 15th. Letters of sympathy, the CWGC and the Brigade diary all show that the correct date for the casualties was 14 November.
4. *The Lancaster Guardian*, 20 November 1915.
5. War diary of Headquarters 1 Division. General Staff, WO 95 1230-2 (National Archives).
6. Frank Needham WO 363 (National Archives).
7. *Jeudwine Papers*. 356/FIF/6/1/19 (Liverpool Record Office).
8. War diary of 2 Infantry Brigade, WO 95 1267-2.
9. War diary of Headquarters 1 Division. General Staff, WO 95 1230-3 (National Archives).
10. *The Lancaster Observer and Morecambe Chronicle*, 24 December 1915.
11. War diary of Headquarters 1 Division. General Staff, WO 95 1230-3.
12. *Jeudwine Papers*. 356 FIF/6/1/19.
13. Hodgkinson, A., *The King's Own 1/5th Battalion, TF in the European War 1914-1918* (Lancaster: The King's Own Royal Regimental Museum, 2009), p. 29.
14. Stanley Warwick. WO 363. (National Archives).
15. *Jeudwine Papers*. 356 FIF/6/1/19.
16. War diary of Headquarters 1 Division. General Staff, WO 95 1230-3.
17. War diary of 2 Infantry Brigade, WO 95 1267-2.
18. *The Lancaster Guardian*, 14 January 1916.
19. *The Lancaster Observer and Morecambe Chronicle*, 4 February 1916.

Chapter 7

1. Henry Langstreth WO 364 (National Archives).
2. Henry Alexander Funk WO 363 (National Archives).
3. War diary of Headquarters 55 Division. General Staff, WO 95 2899-1 (National Archives).
4. The Battalion war diary states Bellacourt, but the 'Dispositions Map' in the divisional war diary clearly shows the location as Bretencourt, 1/5 South Lancs garrisoning the Grosville position.
5. *The Lancaster Observer and Morecambe Chronicle*, 24 March 1916.
6. Intelligence summary noon 7 March 1916–noon 8 March 1916. War diary of Headquarters 55 Division. General Staff, WO 95 2899-2-1 (National Archives).
7. War diary of Headquarters 55 Division. General Staff, WO 95 2899-1.
8. *Ibid.*, WO 95 2899-2-1.
9. *Ibid.*
10. He initially believed his brother had been badly wounded and *The Lancaster Guardian* of 17 June 1916 reports this as such. However, his pension record shows that he was actually admitted for epilepsy.
11. *The Lancaster Guardian*, 10 June 1916.
12. *Ibid.*, 24 June 1916.
13. *Ibid.*, 24 June 1916.
14. *Ibid.*, 22 July 1916.
15. War diary of Headquarters 55 Division. General Staff, WO 95 2899-4-1 (National Archives).
16. *Ibid.*

Chapter 8

1. War diary of Headquarters 55 Division. General Staff, WO 95 2900-2-1 (National Archives).
2. The Battalion war diary reports these working parties on two separate days, though it is

actually the same party out overnight and the figures should be combined.

3. *The Lancaster Guardian*, 12 August 1916.
4. War diary of 166 Infantry Brigade, WO 95 2928-1 (National Archives).
5. *The Lancaster Guardian*, 12 August 1916.
6. *Ibid.*, 12 August 1916.
7. An entry for 7 August in the Battalion war diary attributes this to the night of the 4th, though it is clear from other sources that it is regarding the night of 3-4 August.
8. Burial return. Serial: VR/874/1005/R (Commonwealth War Graves Commission, 1930).
9. *Jeudwine Papers.* 356/FIF/6/2/24. (Liverpool Record Office).
10. *The Lancaster Guardian*, 12 August 1916.
11. War diary of 166 Infantry Brigade, WO 95 2928-1.
12. *The Lancaster Guardian*, 19 August 1916.
13. *Ibid.*, 19 August 1916.
14. Coop, J. O., *The Story of the 55th (West Lancashire) Division* (Liverpool: Liverpool Daily Post, 1919), p. 35.
15. War diary of the 1/5th King's Own (Royal Lancaster) Regiment, WO 95 2930-1_1 (The National Archives).
16. *The Lancaster Guardian*, 9 September 1916.
17. *Ibid.*, 19 August 1916.
18. Supplement to *The London Gazette*. 20 October 1916.
19. *The Lancaster Observer and Morecambe Chronicle*, 25 August 1916.
20. *Jeudwine Papers.* 356/FIF/6/2/24.
21. Supplement to the London Gazette. 20 October 1916.
22. *Jeudwine Papers.* 356/FIF/6/2/24.
23. *The Lancaster Guardian*, 26 August 1916.
24. *The Lancaster Observer and Morecambe Chronicle*, 8 September 1916.
25. *The Lancaster Guardian*, 26 August 1916.
26. *Ibid.*, 26 August 1916.
27. *The Lancaster Observer and Morecambe Chronicle*, 8 September 1916.
28. Burial return. Serial: 122, Guillemont British Cemetery, (Commonwealth War Graves Commission, 1919).
29. Burial return. Serial: VR/874/1255/R, (Commonwealth War Graves Commission, 1931).
30. *The Lancaster Guardian*, 2 September 1916.
31. *The Lancaster Observer and Morecambe Chronicle*, 1 September 1916.
32. War diary of Headquarters 55 Division. A & Q Branch, WO 95 2909-1 (National Archives).
33. *Jeudwine Papers.* 356/FIF/6/2/24. (Liverpool Record Office).
34. War diary of the 1/5th King's Own (Royal Lancaster) Regiment, WO 95 2930-1_2 (National Archives).
35. Hartley, J., *More than a Name*—www.stockport1914-1918.co.uk/index.php
36. Arthur Seddon WO363 (National Archives).
37. *Jeudwine Papers.* 356/FIF/6/3/17. (Liverpool Record Office).
38. Hodgkinson, A., *The King's Own 1/5th Battalion, TF in the European War 1914-1918* (Lancaster: The King's Own Royal Regimental Museum, 2009), p. 41.
39. Wadham W. F. A., & Crossley J., *The Fourth Battalion The King's Own (Royal Lancaster) Regiment and the Great War* (1935), Appendix E. VI.
40. War diary of Headquarters 55 Division. A & Q Branch, WO 95 2909-1.
41. *The Lancaster Observer and Morecambe Chronicle*, 29 September 1916.
42. *The Lancaster Guardian*, 4 November 1916.
43. *Ibid.*, 30 September 1916.
44. Most likely the night of 19-20 September and not that of 20-21 September
45. *The Lancaster Observer and Morecambe Chronicle*, 6 October 1916.
46. *Ibid.*, 6 October 1916.
47. War diary of Headquarters 55 Division. A & Q Branch, WO 95 2909-1.
48. *Jeudwine Papers.* 356/FIF/6/2/24.
49. Hodgkinson, *op. cit.*, p. 42.
50. *Ibid.*

Chapter 9

1. War diary of Headquarters 55 Division. A & Q Branch, WO 95 2909-3_1 (National Archives).
2. *Ibid.*, WO 95 2909-5 (National Archives).
3. *Ibid.*, WO 95 2909-3_1.
4. *Ibid.*, WO 95 2909-2 (National Archives).
5. *Ibid.*, WO 95 2909-5.
6. War diary of Headquarters 55 Division. General Staff, WO 95 2901-2_1 (National Archives).
7. War diary of the 1/5th King's Own (Royal Lancaster) Regiment, WO 95 2930-1_2.
8. War diary of Headquarters 55 Division. A & Q Branch, WO 95 2909-2.
9. *Ibid.*, WO 95 2909-5.
10. War diary of Headquarters 55 Division. General Staff, WO 95 2901-4 (National Archives).
11. War diary of Headquarters 55 Division. A & Q Branch, WO 95 2909-2.
12. War diary of Headquarters 55 Division. General Staff, WO 95 2902-1_1 (National Archives).
13. *The Lancaster Guardian*, 21 January 1917.
14. War diary of the 1/5th King's Own (Royal Lancaster) Regiment, WO 95 2930-1_2.
15. *The Lancaster Guardian*, 10 March 1917.
16. *Jeudwine Papers*. 356/FIF/6/3/17.
17. Hodgkinson, A., *The King's Own 1/5th Battalion, TF in the European War 1914-1918* (Lancaster: The King's Own Royal Regimental Museum, 2009), p. 51.
18. Information courtesy of Colin W. Taylor.
19. *The Lancaster Guardian*, 24 March 1917.
20. *Jeudwine Papers*. 356/FIF/6/6/80. (Liverpool Record Office).
21. *Ibid.*
22. *Ibid.*
23. *Ibid.*
24. War diary of Headquarters 55 Division. General Staff, WO 95 2902-2_1.
25. *Ibid.*, WO 95 2902-2_1.
26. Henshaw, T., *The Sky Their Battlefield II* (High Barnet: Fetubi Books, 2014), p. 72.
27. War diary of Headquarters 55 Division. General Staff, WO 95 2902-2_1.
28. *The Lancaster Guardian*, 24 March 1917.
29. *Ibid.*, 21 April 1917.
30. War diary of Headquarters 55 Division. General Staff, WO 95 2902-4_2 (National Archives).
31. *Ibid.*
32. *Ibid.*
33. Henshaw, *op. cit.*, p. 362.
34. War diary of Headquarters 55 Division. General Staff, WO 95 2903-1_1 (National Archives).
35. *The Lancaster Observer and Morecambe Chronicle*, 29 June 1917.
36. *The Lancaster Guardian*, 30 June 1917.
37. *The Lancaster Observer and Morecambe Chronicle*, 29 June 1917.
38. *Ibid.*, 29 June 1917.

Chapter 10

1. *Jeudwine Papers*, Report on Operations of 164th Infantry Brigade. 356/FIF/2/2/39. ((Liverpool Record Office))
2. Harry Greaves WO 364 (National Archives).
3. War diary of 166 Infantry Brigade, WO 95 2928-3 (National Archives).
4. War diary of Headquarters 55 Division. A & Q Branch, WO 95 2909-4-1 (National Archives).
5. Edmonds, J. E., *Official History of the Great War, Military Operations France and Belgium, 1917. Volume 2* (Uckfield: Naval & Military Press, 2009), pp. 141-142.

6. Hodgkinson, A., *The King's Own 1/5th Battalion, TF in the European War 1914-1918* (Lancaster: The King's Own Royal Regimental Museum, 2009), p. 57.
7. War diary of Headquarters 55 Division. General Staff, WO 95 2903-2_2 (National Archives).
8. Hodgkinson, *op. cit.*, p. 55.
9. War diary of Headquarters 55 Division. General Staff, WO 95 2903-2_1 (National Archives).
10. McDonald's DCM Citation (26.1.18) states that he led for four hours. In fact, Bennett reports that Sleight was not sent to take over the Company until 3 p.m.
11. Hodgkinson, *op. cit.*, pp. 57-8.
12. *The Lancaster Guardian*, 11 August 1917.
13. Divisional signal log, WO 95 2903-2_1 (National Archives).
14. *Ibid.*
15. Hodgkinson, *op. cit.*, pp. 58-9.
16. Divisional signal log, WO 95 2903-2_1 (National Archives).
17. Supplement to *The London Gazette*. 16 August 1917.
18. Signal logs of 166 Brigade war diary of 166 Infantry Brigade, WO 95 2928-3.
19. Hodgkinson, *op. cit.*, p. 59.
20. Divisional signal log, WO 95 2903-2_1 (The National Archives).
21. Hodgkinson, *op. cit.*, p. 59.
22. *Ibid*, p. 56.
23. War diary of Headquarters 55 Division. A & Q Branch, WO 95 2909-4_1 (National Archives).
24. *Ibid.*, The National Archives. (WO 95 2909-4_2).
25. *The Lancaster Guardian*, 22 September 1917.
26. Henry Titterington WO 364 (National Archives).
27. Diary of Clifton Inglis Stockwell. 10 September 1917.
28. Robert Kirby WO 363 (National Archives).
29. *The Lancaster Guardian*, 9 February 1918.
30. Henshaw, T., *The Sky Their Battlefield II* (High Barnet: Fetubi Books, 2014), p. 117.
31. Sam Calvert WO 364 (National Archives).
32. War diary of the 1/5th King's Own (Royal Lancaster) Regiment, WO 95 2930 1-4 (National Archives).
33. Signal logs of 166 Brigade war diary of 166 Infantry Brigade, WO 95 2928-3.
34. Diary of Clifton Inglis Stockwell. 20 September 1917.
35. *The Lancaster Guardian*, 20 October 1917.
36. Hodgkinson, *op. cit.*, p. 64.
37. *Jeudwine Papers*. 356/FIF/6/4/32. (Liverpool Record Office).
38. Action of 165 Infantry Brigade, WO 95 2903-4_1 (National Archives).
39. War diary of Headquarters 55 Division. A & Q Branch, WO 95 2909-5.
40. Harry Mellor WO 364 (National Archives).

Chapter 11

1. Hodgkinson, A., *The King's Own 1/5th Battalion, TF in the European War 1914-1918* (Lancaster: The King's Own Royal Regimental Museum, 2009), p. 65.
2. Miles, W., *Official History of the Great War, Military Operations France and Belgium, 1917. Volume 3* (Uckfield: Naval & Military Press, 2009), p. 373.
3. *Ibid.*, p. 172.
4. Letter to General Snow. 356 FIF/8/2. (Liverpool Record Office).
5. Diary of 166 Infantry Brigade, WO 95 2928-4 (National Archives).
6. War diary of Headquarters 55 Division. General Staff, WO 95 2904-3 (National Archives).
7. *Jeudwine Papers*. 356/FIF/6/6/80.
8. Hodgkinson, *op. cit.*, p. 71.
9. Supplement to *The London Gazette*. 25 January 1918.
10. Bennett named this as 'Limerick Lane', though he was obviously referring to Limerick Trench—the north-south trench connecting the two posts—Limerick Lane actually ran along the edge of Pigeon Ravine next to Parr's Bank.

11. *Jeudwine Papers*. 356/FIF/6/6/80.
12. *The Lancaster Guardian*, 15 December 1917.
13. In Roddick's report, which can be found in the divisional war diary, he states 3.15 p.m. as the time these attacks began. The timings reported in this narrative are those given to Hodgkinson by Bennett when the former was compiling the Battalion history.
14. Although later renamed 'Avenue', the nomenclature 'Lane' used by Bennett in his report was correct at the time of this action.
15. *The Lancaster Guardian*, 22 December 1917.
16. *Jeudwine Papers*. 356/FIF/6/6/80.
17. *The Lancaster Guardian*, 27 December 1917.
18. Hodgkinson, *op. cit.*, p. 72.
19. *Jeudwine Papers*. 356/FIF/6/6/80.
20. War diary of Headquarters 55 Division. A & Q Branch, WO 95 2910-1 (National Archives).
21. Miles, *op. cit.*, p. 295.
22. *Jeudwine Papers*, Annotations to Report of Court of Enquiry. 356/FIF/8/2/2. (Liverpool Record Office).
23. *Jeudwine Papers*, Letter from General Jeudwine to General Snow. 356/FIF/8/3. (Liverpool Record Office).
24. Miles, *op. cit.*, pp. 298-9.
25. *Ibid.*, pp. 300-301.
26. *Ibid.*
27. *Ibid.*, pp. 184-5.

Chapter 12

1. Edmonds, J. E., *Official History of the Great War, Military Operations France and Belgium, 1917. Volume 2* (Uckfield: Naval & Military Press, 2009) p. 470.
2. Coop, J. O., *The Story of the 55th (West Lancashire) Division* (Liverpool: Liverpool Daily Post, 1919), pp. 85-86.
3. Edmonds, *OH France and Belgium, 1917, Volume 2*, pp. 470-471.
4. *Ibid.*, pp. 472-473.
5. War diary of Headquarters 55 Division. A & Q Branch, WO 95 2910-2_1 (National Archives).
6. Reid, W., *Architect of Victory—Douglas Haig* (Edinburgh: Birlinn, 2006), p. 409.
7. *Ibid.*, p. 424.
8. Edmonds, *op. cit.*, p. 477.
9. Reid, *op. cit.*, p. 428.
10. Edmonds, *op. cit.*, p. 161.
11. War diary of Headquarters 55 Division. General Staff, WO 95 2905_4 (National Archives).
12. Coop, *op. cit.*, p. 91.
13. War diary of Headquarters 55 Division. General Staff, WO 95 2905_1 (National Archives).
14. *Ibid.*
15. *Ibid.*
16. Albert Dent WO 363 (National Archives).
17. Charles Henry Dorrell WO 364 (National Archives).
18. Richard Francis Power WO 363 (National Archives).
19. War diary of 166 Infantry Brigade, WO 95 2928-5_1 (National Archives).
20. Coop, *op. cit.*, pp. 89-90.

Chapter 13

1. *Jeudwine Papers*. 356/FIF/6/6/80.
2. War diary of Headquarters 55 Division. General Staff, WO 95 2905_3 (National Archives).
3. *Ibid.*
4. *Jeudwine Papers*. 356/FIF/6/6/80.
5. *Ibid.*
6. *Ibid.*

7. Aspray is given the wrong number in his recommendation—that belonging to CSM Denwood. The Medal Rolls only record service with 1/King's Own, but this recommendation MM clearly proves otherwise.
8. *Jeudwine Papers*. 356/FIF/6/6/80.
9. War diary of 166 Infantry Brigade, WO 95 2928-5_1.
10. *Jeudwine Papers*. 356/FIF/6/5/21. (Liverpool Record Office).
11. *Jeudwine Papers*. 356/FIF/6/6/80.
12. *Jeudwine Papers*. 356/FIF/6/6/80.
13. Samuel Law WO 364 (National Archives).
14. *Jeudwine Papers*. 356/FIF/6/6/80.
15. War diary of Headquarters 55 Division. General Staff, WO 95 2905_3.
16. *Jeudwine Papers*. 356/FIF/6/6/80.
17. *Ibid.*
18. War diary of Headquarters 55 Division. General Staff, WO 95 2905_5 (National Archives).
19. War diary of 166 Infantry Brigade, WO 95 2928-5_1.
20. *Ibid.*
21. War diary of Headquarters 55 Division. General Staff, WO 95 2905_5.
22. *Jeudwine Papers*. 356/FIF/6/6/80.
23. *Ibid.*
24. War diary of Headquarters 55 Division. A & Q Branch, WO 95 2910-3_1 (National Archives).
25. War diary of Headquarters 55 Division. General Staff, WO 95 2905_2 (National Archives).
26. Edmonds, J. E., *Official History of the Great War, Military Operations France and Belgium, 1918 Volume 2* (Uckfield: Naval & Military Press, 2009), p. 174.
27. Coop, J. O., *The Story of the 55th (West Lancashire) Division* (Liverpool: Liverpool Daily Post, 1919), p. 108.
28. War diary of Headquarters 55 Division. A & Q Branch, WO 95 2910-2_1 (National Archives).
29. William McEwen Yacomeni WO 339/91370 (National Archives).

Chapter 14

1. Neile's Citation and the divisional diary give 25 May as the date for this, but Brigade and Battalion diaries both state 26 May.
2. Hodgkinson, A., *The King's Own 1/5th Battalion, TF in the European War 1914-1918* (Lancaster: The King's Own Royal Regimental Museum, 2009), p. 83.
3. *Jeudwine Papers*. 356/FIF/6/6/80.
4. Milton Pollard WO 364 (National Archives).
5. War diary of the 1/5th King's Own (Royal Lancaster) Regiment, WO 95 2930 1_4.
6. *Jeudwine Papers*. 356/FIF/6/6/80.
7. James Arthur Wedge WO 363 (National Archives).
8. War diary of the 1/5th King's Own (Royal Lancaster) Regiment, WO 95 2930 1_4.
9. *Jeudwine Papers*. 356/FIF/6/6/80.
10. The Battalion war diary gives the 24th. The divisional intelligence summary records this for 23 July. A similar discrepancy is found with other events and the death of A/Capt. Hamilton—a discrepancy that was noted at the time and pencilled into the margin of the Brigade diary. The dates given in this narrative have been checked against movement orders, CWGC records, intelligence summaries, and both brigade and divisional diaries and should be taken as correct.
11. James Henry Pollard WO 364 (National Archives).
12. War diary of Headquarters 55 Division. General Staff, WO 95 2906-3_1 (National Archives).

Chapter 15

1. *Jeudwine Papers*. 356/FIF/6/6/80.
2. War diary of Headquarters 55 Division. General Staff, WO 95 2906-3_1.
3. John Thomas Little WO 364 (National Archives).

4. War diary of Headquarters 55 Division. General Staff, WO 95 2906-4_2 (National Archives).
5. Frustratingly, the date in his records when he was injured by the gas shell has been burnt and only the date the records were written up remains legible. However, the date given in the narrative is the most plausible one.
6. *Jeudwine Papers*. 356/FIF/6/6/80.
7. Walter Taylor WO 363 (National Archives).
8. 55 Division Narrative of Operations. 24 August-11 November 1918. *Jeudwine Papers* 356/FIF/3/3/1. Liverpool Record Office.
9. Robert William Nickson WO 363 (National Archives).
10. War diary of Headquarters 55 Division. A & Q Branch, WO 95 2910-4_1 (National Archives).
11. *Ibid.*
12. Once again, the dates given in the Battalion's war diary are at odds with both brigade and divisional war diaries for most of this period and at times, Hodgkinson's memoirs. The dates given in the narrative are those supported by more than one source.
13. Frank Rowland Webb WO 364 (National Archives).
14. William Ward WO 364 (National Archives).
15. War diary of Headquarters 55 Division. General Staff, WO 95 2907-2_1 (National Archives).
16. War diary of 166 Infantry Brigade, WO 95 2928-6 (National Archives).

Epilogue

1. *Poughkeepsie Eagle News*. 20 December 1918.

Bibliography

Published Sources

1914-15 Star Medal Roll (Lancaster: King's Own Royal Regiment Museum, 2005)
55th (West Lancashire) Division Trench Orders (Lancaster: King's Own Museum, 2013)
Ainslie G. M., *Hand Grenades, A Handbook on Rifle and Hand Grenades* (London: Chapman & Hall, 1917)
British War and Allied Victory Medal Roll, Vol. 1 (Lancaster: King's Own Royal Regiment Museum, 2006); *British War and Allied Victory Medal Roll*, Vol. 2 (Lancaster: King's Own Royal Regiment Museum, 2006)
Coop, J. O., *The Story of the 55th (West Lancashire) Division* (Liverpool: Liverpool Daily Post, 1919)
Edmonds, J. E., *Official History of the Great War, Military Operations France and Belgium, 1915*, Vol. 1 (Uckfield: Naval & Military Press, 2009); *Official History of the Great War, Military Operations France and Belgium, 1915*, Vol. 2 (Uckfield: Naval & Military Press, 2009); *Official History of the Great War, Military Operations France and Belgium, 1917*, Vol. 2 (Uckfield: Naval & Military Press, 2009); *Official History of the Great War, Military Operations France and Belgium, 1918*, Vol. 2 (Uckfield: Naval & Military Press, 2009)
Henshaw T., *The Sky Their Battlefield II* (High Barnet: Fetubi Books, 2014)
Hodgkinson A., *The King's Own 1/5th Battalion, TF in the European War 1914-1918* (Lancaster: The King's Own Royal Regimental Museum, 2009)
Miles W., *Official History of the Great War, Military Operations France and Belgium, 1916*, Vol. 2 (Uckfield: Naval & Military Press, 2009); *Official History of the Great War, Military Operations France and Belgium, 1917. Volume 3* (Uckfield: Naval & Military Press, 2009)
Notes for Infantry Officers on Trench Warfare (Uckfield: Naval & Military Press, 2008)
Philpott W., *Bloody Victory* (London: Little, Brown and Co., 2009)
Regulations for the Territorial Force and for County Associations (London: HMSO, 1908)
Reid W., *Architect of Victory-Douglas Haig* (Edinburgh: Berlinn Ltd, 2006)
Soldiers Died in the Great War: The King's Own Royal Lancaster Regiment (Polstead. J. B., Hayward/IWM, 1989)
Wadham W. F. A., & Crossley J., *The Fourth Battalion The King's Own (Royal Lancaster) Regiment and the Great War* (London: Crowther & Goodman, 1935)
War Office, *General Staff. Infantry Training (4-Company Organisation)* (London: HMSO, 1914)

Newspapers, Web Pages, and Periodicals

Baker, C., The Long, Long Trail. www.1914-1918.net/
Barrow Guardian 1914-1919
Barrow News 1914-1919
Hartley, J. *More than a Name.* www.stockport1914-1918.co.uk/

Millom Gazette 1915-1917
The King's Own Museum. www.kingsownmuseum.plus.com
The Lancaster Guardian 1914-1919
The Lancaster Observer and Morecambe Chronicle 1914-1919
The Times 1915-1918 (London)
War Office Weekly Casualty Lists (London: HMSO, 1917-1918)

Unpublished Sources

Archives of the King's Own Museum, Lancaster
Burial returns. Commonwealth War Graves Commission
Medal Index Cards WO 372 (National Archives)
Officers' service records, (WO 339). The National Archives
Officers' service records, WO 374 (National Archives)
Pension records, WO 364 National Archives)
Private diary of Clifton Inglis Stockwell (Stockwell Family)
Service records, WO 363 (National Archives)
The Jeudwine Papers, 356/FIF (Liverpool Record Office)
War diary of 1/4 King's Own (Royal Lancaster) Regiment, KO 1017/64 (King's Own Museum,
    Lancaster)
War diary of 166 Infantry Brigade, WO 95 2928 1-6 (National Archives)
War diary of 2 Infantry Brigade, WO 95 1267-2 (National Archives)
War diary of 83 Infantry Brigade, WO 95 2273 1-5 (National Archives)
War diary of 84 Infantry Brigade, WO 95 2276 1-4 (National Archives)
War diary of Headquarters 1 Division. General Staff, WO 95 1230 (National Archives)
War diary of Headquarters 28 Division. General Staff, WO 95 2268 (National Archives)
War diary of Headquarters 55 Division. A & Q Branch, WO 95 2909-2910 (National Archives)
War diary of Headquarters 55 Division. General Staff, WO 95 2899-2904 (National Archives)
War diary of the 1/5th King's Own (Royal Lancaster) Regiment, WO 95 2274-3 (National
    Archives)
War diary of the 1/5th King's Own (Royal Lancaster) Regiment, WO 95 2930 1-4 (National
    Archives)
War diary of the 2/ King's Own (Royal Lancaster) Regiment, WO 95 2274-2 (National Archives)

Index